Caribbean New Orleans

Caribbean New Orleans

Empire, Race, and the Making of a Slave Society

CÉCILE VIDAL

Published by the
Omohundro Institute of Early American History and Culture,
Williamsburg, Virginia, and the
University of North Carolina Press, Chapel Hill

*The Omohundro Institute of Early American History and Culture
is sponsored by the College of William and Mary. On November 15, 1996,
the Institute adopted the present name in honor of a bequest from
Malvern H. Omohundro, Jr.*

Cover illustrations:
[Jean-Pierre Lassus]. *Veüe et perspective de la Nouvelle Orléans.* 1726.
ANOM France 04 DFC 71 A. Courtesy of Les archives nationales d'outre-mer.
Aix-en-Provence, France
[Simon Dusault de la Grave]. *Veüe et perspective du Cap-Français ....* 1717.
Département cartes et plans. GE B-1197 (RES). Courtesy of
Bibliothèque nationale de France. Paris

Library of Congress Cataloging-in-Publication Data
Names: Vidal, Cécile, author.
Title: Caribbean New Orleans : empire, race, and the
making of a slave society / Cécile Vidal.
Description: Williamsburg, Virginia : Omohundro Institute of Early American
History and Culture ; Chapel Hill : University of North Carolina Press, [2019] |
Includes bibliographical references and index.
Identifiers: LCCN 2018058605 | ISBN 9781469645186 (cloth : alk. paper) |
ISBN 9781469645193 (ebook)
Subjects: LCSH: Slavery—West Indies, French—History. | Slavery—Louisiana—
New Orleans—History. | New Orleans (La.)—Social conditions—18th century. |
New Orleans (La.)—Race relations—History. | France—Colonies—America—
History. | New Orleans (La.)—History—Social conditions.
Classification: LCC HT1107 .V53 2019 | DDC 306.3/620976335—dc23
LC record available at https://lccn.loc.gov/2018058605

The University of North Carolina Press has been a
member of the Green Press Initiative since 2003.

In memory of my father, Jacques Vidal,
and for Sylvia R. Frey

Acknowledgments

Caribbean New Orleans has been a long but fascinating endeavor in the making. I started to collect the primary sources in New Orleans in 2000. Thus, I had already been working on this social history of the Louisiana capital during the French regime for a few years when Hurricane Katrina struck the city in 2005. It has been incredibly moving to study the early eighteenth-century genesis of this urban center when the present-day residents of what had become a metropolis were not sure that it would survive. Thankfully, New Orleans was able to celebrate the tercentenary of its founding in 2018. The death of the city no longer threatens, even though global warming, combined with the fragile state of the levees, still makes the future uncertain.

The book began as the original manuscript for my *habilitation à diriger des recherches (HDR)*—the diploma that an academic has to obtain to become a full professor and be authorized to supervise Ph.D. students in the French system. I am deeply grateful to two colleagues and friends who supported me throughout this process. Sylvia R. Frey, to whom the book is dedicated, encouraged me from the outset, welcomed me in her home during my annual trips to New Orleans, discussed my research with me more times than I can remember, and read several versions of the manuscript. With her sharp mind, intellectual curiosity, moral rectitude, warm generosity toward students and younger colleagues, and political engagement against racial and gender discriminations, she represents for me the perfect role model of an academic. François-Joseph Ruggiu agreed to be my *garant,* or advisor, for the HDR. In the last two decades, no other historian has been more instrumental in developing the history of the early French Empire in France at a time when colonial and imperial history had long been marginalized. Sharing this struggle, we have developed over the years an intellectual friendship that I value dearly. His talent as a social historian and his vast historiographical knowledge have been inspiring. In addition to my mentor and my advisor, I would like to warmly thank the other colleagues who were members of the jury before which I publicly defended my HDR at the University Paris-Sorbonne in December 2014: Laurent Dubois,

Antoine Lilti, Brigitte Marin, Marie-Jeanne Rossignol, and François Weil. Their thoughtful comments have enriched the manuscript as I revised it for publication.

Many other people helped me with this project. Colleagues—and friends—who have read the whole manuscript or parts of it include Trevor Burnard, Emily Clark, Catherine Desbarats, Philip Morgan, and Thomas Wien as well as Nicolas Barreyre, Rafe Blaufarb, Alexandre Dubé, Gilles Havard, Maud Mandel, Sara Le Ménestrel, Jean-Frédéric Schaub, Silvia Sebastiani, and Ibrahima Thioub. The book has greatly benefited from their precious insights. A sincere appreciation is also due to the students of my research seminar at the École des Hautes Études en Sciences Sociales (EHESS)—or School of Advanced Studies in Social Sciences, Paris—with whom I discussed all the chapters while I was writing and rewriting them. My gratitude goes as well to the readers of the Omohundro Institute of Early American History and Culture and to my editor, Paul Mapp, who has been an invaluable guide and critic.

Over the years, I have profited from the helpful feedback of many participants at several conferences and seminars where I presented my arguments. They comprise two annual meetings of the French Colonial Historical Society (La Rochelle 2007 and Saint-Denis 2010); the fourth workshop of the French Atlantic History Group at McGill University; an annual meeting of the American Historical Association (New Orleans 2013); the American History Research Seminar at the Rothermere American Institute, Oxford University; the Transitions to Modernity Colloquium at Yale University; the workshop on "Familles en situation coloniale, XVIe–XXe siècles" at the University Paris-Sorbonne; the international conferences "New World Orders: Violence, Sanction, and Authority in the Colonial Americas" at the McNeil Center for Early American Studies, "Louisiana and the Atlantic World in the Eighteenth and Nineteenth Centuries" at the EHESS and at Tulane University, "Être et se penser français: Nation, sentiment national, et identités dans l'Atlantique français, XVIIe–XIXe siècle" at the EHESS, and "Saint-Louis, Senegal, and New Orleans: Two Mirror Cities, 17th–21st centuries" at the University Gaston Berger, Saint-Louis, Senegal, and at Tulane University. Several of these meetings were attended by all or some members of a group of Louisiana historians who have been greatly influential and who share my attachment to the Big Easy: Guillaume Aubert, Alexandre Dubé, Jean Hébrard, Jean-Pierre Le Glaunec, Martha Jones, Rebecca Scott, and Sophie White. Among all the friends New Orleans brought me, Emily Clark, a native of the city, deserves special thanks for having shared so much with me, in work and life, on both sides of the Atlantic.

This book required a great deal of archival research in both the United States and France. This would not have been possible without the generous assistance of the Centre d'études nord-américaines (EHESS), the Deep South Regional Humanities Center of Tulane University, and the Franco-American Fulbright Commission. An Andrew W. Mellon Senior Fellowship at the John Carter Brown Library also gave me some time away from teaching to write the manuscript. While I was researching this book, I benefited from the help of many archivists at the Archives Nationales, the Bibliothèque Nationale de France, and the Bibliothèque de l'Institut de France in Paris; the Archives Nationales d'Outre-Mer in Aix-en-Provence; the Archives of the Archdiocese of New Orleans; the Louisiana Research Collection in the Howard-Tilton Memorial Library of Tulane University; the Louisiana State Museum; the New Orleans Notarial Archives; and the New Orleans Historical Collection. Many thanks to them.

I am indebted to Elizabeth Rowley-Jolivet who revised my English for the HDR and to Kaylan Stevenson, the Omohundro Institute of Early American History and Culture's copyeditor. They made the perilous adventure of writing a book in another language than my own mother tongue a pleasant and instructive journey. Thanks also to Gildas Zalio, who helped me with the index.

My final thoughts go to my family and friends from outside the academic world who have accompanied me in this project as they understood that this book meant more to me than an academic accomplishment. My mother, Tuula, my siblings, Mathilde and Jérôme, as well as Maud and Camille, whom I met as an historian but who have become like family, have all my love for their unshakeable support. The book is also dedicated to my deceased father, Jacques Vidal. I owe my being a historian to him.

Contents

Acknowledgments / vii

List of Illustrations / xiii

Abbreviations / xv

INTRODUCTION.
When the Levees Rose / 1

CHAPTER 1. A Port City of the French Empire
and the Greater Caribbean / 43

CHAPTER 2. The City with Imaginary Walls:
The Natchez Wars, Slave Unrest, and the Construction of
a White Urban Community / 94

CHAPTER 3. The Hustle and Bustle of City Life:
The Politics of Public Space and Racial Formation / 143

CHAPTER 4. "The Mulatto of the House": The Racial Line within
Domestic Households and Residential Institutions / 183

CHAPTER 5. "A Scandalous Commerce": The Disorder of Families / 244

CHAPTER 6. "American Politics": Slavery, Labor, and Race / 285

CHAPTER 7. "Everybody Wants to Be a Merchant":
Trade, Credit, and Honor / 329

CHAPTER 8. Lash of the Tongue, Lash of the Whip:
The Formation and Transformation of Racial Categories
and Practices / 369

CHAPTER 9. From "Louisians" to "Louisianais":
The Emergence of a Sense of Place and the Racial Divide / 444

CONCLUSION. From Louisiana to Saint-Domingue and
from Saint-Domingue to Louisiana / 498

Index / 515

List of Illustrations

FIGURES

1. [Adrien de Pauger], *Plan de la ville de la Nouvelle Orléans*, May 29, 1724 / 3

2. "French Louisiana in the Eighteenth Century" / 16

3. [Claude Bernou], *Carte de l'Amérique septentrionale et partie de la méridionale depuis l'embouchure de la rivière St Laurens jusqu'à l'isle de Cayenne*, circa 1681 / 48

4. [François Chéreau], *Le Mississipi ou la Louisiane dans l'Amérique septentrionale*, circa 1720 / 96

5. [Jean-Pierre Lassus], *Veüe et perspective de la Nouvelle Orléans*, 1726 / 100

6. [François Saucier], *Carte particuli[è]re du cours du fleuve St. Louis depuis le village sauvage jusqu'au dessous du détour aux anglois*, circa 1749 / 126

7. *Plan de la Nouvelle Orl[é]ans telle qu'elle estoit au mois de dexembre 1731 levé par Gonichon* / 145

8. [François Ignace] Broutin, *Partie du plan de la Nouvelle Orléans … et les projets pour le gouvernement et l'intendance …*, July, 25, 1734 / 151

9. [François Ignace] Broutin, *Plan du premier Étage [et] du rez-de-chaussée du grand bâtiment projetté à faire … pour loger les Religieuses Ursulines hospitalières de La Nouvelle Orléans*, Nov. 10, 1745 / 228

10. [Bernard] Devergès, *Carte du cours du fleuve St. Louis au détour des anglois avec les plans et les profils des fortifications projettées à y faire*, May 9, 1747 / 427

TABLES

1. Population of New Orleans and the Lower Mississippi Valley, 1721–1766 / 121

{ xiii }

2. Census Categories, 1721–1763 / 190

3. Family and Household for White Settlers and Company of the Indies Indentured Servants, 1721 / 195

4. Family and Household for Whites Categorized and Counted as "Masters," 1726 / 196

5. Ethnic and Racial Labels of Enslaved Children Recorded in New Orleans Baptism Certificates, 1729–1733 and 1744–1769 / 380

6. Ethnic and Racial Labels of the Illegitimate Children Born to Free Women of Color Recorded in New Orleans Baptism Certificates, 1744–1769 / 382

7. Judicial Punishments, 1736–1737 / 396

Illustrations

Abbreviations

AANO	Archives of the Archdiocese of New Orleans
AGI	Archivo General de Indias, Seville, Spain
AN	Archives Nationales, Paris
ANOM	Archives Nationales d'Outre-Mer, Aix-en-Provence, France
BNF	Bibliothèque Nationale de France, Paris
COL	Fonds des colonies
DFC	Dépôt des Fortifications des Colonies
Favrot Papers	Favrot Papers, Howard-Tilton Memorial Library, Louisiana Research Collection, Tulane University, New Orleans, Louisiana
FRLG	French Royal Land Grants, 1753–1769, Louisiana Research Collection, Howard-Tilton Memorial Library, Tulane University, New Orleans, Louisiana
HNOC	The Historic New Orleans Collection, New Orleans, Louisiana
LHQ	*Louisiana Historical Quarterly*
NONA	New Orleans Notarial Archives, Notarial Archives Research Center, New Orleans, Louisiana
RSCL	Records of the Superior Council of Louisiana, Louisiana State Museum, New Orleans, Louisiana

Caribbean New Orleans

INTRODUCTION
When the Levees Rose

When the levees broke after Hurricane Katrina passed over New Orleans in 2005, its inhabitants feared that their city might die. The reactions of federal and local authorities to the catastrophe and its aftermath, as well as the opposition of some Americans to the reconstruction of the Big Easy, revealed the persistence of racial prejudice and discrimination. For years, it was not clear whether the city would be able to recover from this sociopolitical disaster. The social disintegration along racial lines that New Orleans experienced at the dawn of the twenty-first century has a long history. The construction of the levees and the construction of racial categories—that is, those things that protect and divide the city—were born together at the very moment of New Orleans's creation. The system of earthen ridges erected against the risk of flooding soon after the city's founding in 1718 and racial formation intersected from the start to lend the urban center its distinctive character.[1]

To explain this congenital development of a system of racial domination, *Caribbean New Orleans* locates the genesis of the city, created ex nihilo under French rule, within a greater Caribbean world marked by the interplay of slavery and race. The Louisiana capital may be viewed as a test case to analyze the expansion of racial slavery from the Antilles to the surrounding mainland throughout the seventeenth and eighteenth centuries, to examine the historical formation of a slave society within a port city located in the midst of a plantation region, and to reconsider what it meant for a society to become racialized by showing how race was woven into the fabric

---

1. *When the Levees Broke: A Requiem in Four Acts* is the title of the documentary Spike Lee shot after Katrina. It was produced by 40 Acres and a Mule Filmworks, Inc., based out of Brooklyn, N.Y., and released in 2006. For an analysis of the sociopolitical disaster associated with Hurricane Katrina and its aftermath, see Romain Huret and Randy J. Sparks, eds., *Hurricane Katrina in Transatlantic Perspective* (Baton Rouge, La., 2014).

of everyday life. As people internalized the notion of race, a racial order co-alesced that could perpetuate itself in the *longue durée*. By probing such a case study, this book proposes to better take into account the variety of slave societies that developed in the Americas, including those in urban settings, and offers a fresh perspective on racial formation. It also contends that his-torians need to move away from a comparative history of racial slavery in the western hemisphere that contrasts the Caribbean and North America as two distinctive models. Instead, they should consider all American colo-nial and slave societies as parts of a continuum. Last, but not least, *Carib-bean New Orleans* situates early North American history on the periphery of Caribbean history and, as a result, contributes to a broader historiographi-cal trend aimed at decentering North America.[2]

THE LATE FOUNDING OF A NEW PORT CITY
ON THE FRINGE OF THE FRENCH EMPIRE

Nowadays, the levees are built along the Mississippi River and Lake Pont-chartrain, the two bodies of water that virtually surround New Orleans, as well as the three canals connecting the river with the lake. Nearly three hundred years ago, the engineers who designed the first plan for the urban center only envisioned a grid of eighty-eight hectares located on one outside curve of the river. They oriented the city toward the Mississippi, with a first row of blocks facing the quay and a main square in the center opening onto the water. After experiencing several spring floods and a hurricane in 1722, which destroyed most of the original shacks, the engineers decided to re-inforce the natural levee along the river. New Orleans's participation in the transatlantic slave trade had begun almost from the moment of the urban center's inception, and it was African slaves who built the "embankment which was tightly packed, in order to prevent the river from overflowing into the City." The earthen ridges extended beyond the capital, bordering the plantations that spread over time on both sides of the river, upstream and downstream.[3]

2. For an historian arguing for the need to analyze all colonial and slave societies as part of a continuum very early on, see George M. Fredrickson, "From Exceptionalism to Variability: Recent Developments in Cross-National Comparative History," *Journal of American History*, LXXXII (1995), 587–604. For a work seeking to decenter North American history, see Eliga H. Gould, "Entangled Histories, Entangled Worlds: The English-Speaking Atlantic as a Spanish Periphery," *American Historical Review*, CXII (2007), 764–786.

3. On the construction of the levee, see "Lettre à la Nouvelle Orléans," Apr. 24, 1728, in [Marie Madeleine] Hachard, *Relation du voyage des dames religieuses Ursulines de*

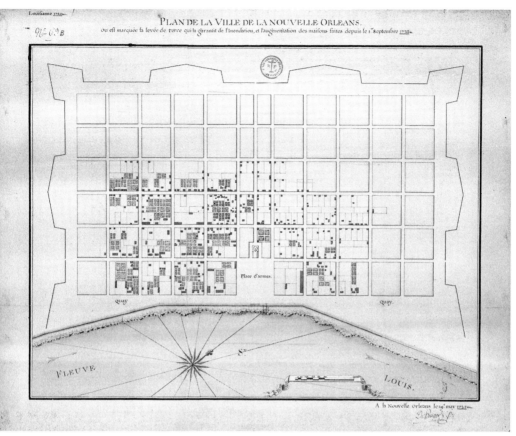

Figure 1: [Adrien de Pauger]. *Plan de la ville de la Nouvelle Orléans où est marquée la levée de terre qui la garantit de l'inondation et l'augmentation des maisons faites depuis le 1er septembre 1723.* May 29, 1724. ANOM France 04 DFC 69 B. Courtesy of Les archives nationales d'outre-mer. Aix-en-Provence, France

Although the levee was first and foremost raised for protection and security, it quickly became more than a technical feat of engineering. It was the economic and social core of New Orleans. Since no overland road was constructed until well into the nineteenth century, it served as the unique

Rouen à La Nouvelle-Orléans (1728) (Paris, 1872), 88 (quotation); Dumont de Montigny, *Regards sur le monde atlantique, 1715–1747,* transcribed by Carla Zecher (Sillery, Quebec, 2008), 169–170; [Antoine-Simon] Le Page du Pratz, *Histoire de la Louisiane . . . ,* 3 vols. (Paris, 1758), II, 265–266; Marcel Giraud, *Histoire de la Louisiane française,* 4 vols. (Paris, 1953–1974), IV, 404–405, 412–413; and Giraud, *A History of French Louisiana,* V, *The Company of the Indies, 1723–1731,* trans. Brian Pearce (Baton Rouge, La., 1991), 206–210.

gateway through which to enter the city. Functioning as a port—which welcomed all sorts of traffic, ranging from ocean vessels going up the Mississippi River from the Gulf of Mexico to barges bringing pelts and foodstuffs down from the Illinois Country to pirogues coming from the surrounding outposts and plantations—the levee was New Orleans's principal link to the broader Atlantic world. Despite plans to locate one or two marketplaces within the grid, it also became the site of the first marketplace, since it was there that merchandise arrived in the city. Apart from trading, the levee was used as a promenade where urban dwellers of all backgrounds came to take a breath of fresh air, go for a walk, have a chat, and gossip. White elites and people of lower means participated in the new sociability of showing off that had developed in European cities from the late seventeenth century onward, but the embankment was also appropriated by slaves.[4]

On the levee, contradictory social forces, which both drew together and pulled apart the various components of New Orleans's population, were at work. It is for this very reason that the levee as an urban place embodies so perfectly the city itself, with all its tensions, instabilities, and fragilities. It symbolizes the invention, in a short period of time, by all social actors of a way of living together and forming an urban society, regardless of the ex-

4. On the new sociability of showing off, see Peter Borsay, *The English Urban Renaissance: Culture and Society in the Provincial Town, 1600-1770* (Oxford, 1989); and Laurent Turcot, *Le promeneur à Paris au XVIIIe siècle* (Paris, 2007). On the use of the levee as a promenade by white settlers of all social ranks, see [Marc-Antoine Caillot], "Relation du voyage de la Louisianne ou Nouvlle. France; fait par le Sr. CAILLOT en l'année 1730," HNOC, MSS596, fol. 102; Criminal Hearings of the Superior Council of This Province of Louisiana, May 28, 1738, ANOM COL F3 242, fols. 265–290; Honoré-Gabriel Michel to the minister of the navy, Jan. 15, 1752, ANOM COL C13A 36, fol. 224r; Michel to the minister of the navy, Sept. 20, 1752, ANOM COL C13A 36, fol. 267; Vincent-Gaspard-Pierre de Rochemore to the minister of the navy, Aug. 24, 1760, ANOM COL C13A 42, fols. 131–133, 140–142; and RSCL 1745/05/05/02; 1767/11/06/02; 1768/05/13/01. On slaves' appropriation of the levee, see RSCL 1744/02/26/01; 1764/01/31/01; 1764/07/17/01; 1766/07/29/04; 1766/07/23/03; 1766/11/13/02, 1766/11/14/01. On the use of the levees for ceremonies and festivities, see Louis Billouart de Kerlérec to minister of the navy, May 5, 1753, ANOM COL C13A 37, fols. 52–53. On the levee as a marketplace, see Marc de Villiers, ed., "L'établissement de la province de la Louisiane: Poème composé de 1728 à 1742 par Dumont de Montigny," *Journal de la société des américanistes,* New Ser., XXIII (1931), 307, 390. On the levee in the nineteenth century, see Dell Upton, "The New Orleans Levee: Street of the World," in Samuel C. Shepherd, Jr., ed., *The Louisiana Purchase Bicentennial Series in Louisiana History,* XIV, *New Orleans and Urban Louisiana,* Pt. A, *Settlement to 1860* (Lafayette, La., 2005), 377–386; and Lake Douglas, *Public Spaces, Private Gardens: A History of Designed Landscapes in New Orleans* (Baton Rouge, La., 2011), 36–38.

acerbated power struggles and the greater tendency toward segmentation inherent to any colonial and slave society. On the levee, both physical proximity and social distance could coincide.

At the heart of this book lie the conflicting social dynamics intrinsic to a new port city born out of imperialism and colonialism in the eighteenth-century Atlantic world. New Orleans was originally conceived as a city whose function was to serve as a bridgehead for the French colonizing project in the Mississippi Valley while connecting the colony to the metropole. The various components of the urban population were caught from the start in a colonial situation—on the basis of their alleged cultural and religious superiority, the French claimed that they could legitimately settle Native American territories and exploit those lands with a workforce of free and enslaved laborers brought from Europe and Africa.[5] How did people of such varied origins and opposing interests manage to coalesce as an urban society? And what kind of social order emerged from this colonial situation over the first two generations, between 1718 and 1769, when French sovereignty was replaced by Spanish rule?[6]

5. The French sociologist Georges Balandier, who worked on western Africa, proposed this concept of "colonial situation" in a seminal article published in 1951. See Balandier, "La situation coloniale: Approche théorique," *Cahiers internationaux de sociologie,* XI (1951), 44–79. Since the 1990s, Balandier's reflection on how colonialism operated has deeply influenced colonial studies and the new imperial history in both Francophone and Anglophone historiographies, whereas early American historiography has ignored the concept of "colonial situation." For Balandier's original article, translated into English, see Balandier, "The Colonial Situation: A Theoretical Approach," in Stephen Howe, ed., *The New Imperial Histories Reader* (New York, 2010), 23–40. See also Frederick Cooper, *Colonialism in Question: Theory, Knowledge, History* (Berkeley, Calif., 2005), 33–55. For French works on Balandier's concept of "colonial situation," see Jean Copans, "La 'situation coloniale' de Georges Balandier: Notion conjoncturelle ou modèle sociologique et historique?" *Cahiers internationaux de sociologie,* New Ser., CX (Janvier–Juin 2001), 31–52; Isabelle Merle, "'La situation coloniale' chez Georges Balandier: Relecture historienne," *Monde(s),* II, no. 4 (2013), 211–232; and Natacha Gagné and Marie Salaün, "L'effacement du 'colonial' ou 'seulement de ses formes les plus apparentes'? Penser le contemporain grâce à la notion de situation coloniale chez Georges Balandier," *Cargo: Revue internationale d'anthropologie culturelle et sociale,* [nos. 6–7] (2017), 219–237.

6. At the end of the Seven Years' War, New Orleans and the western bank of the Mississippi River were given to Spain by the Treaty of Fontainebleau in 1762. Britain obtained the eastern part of the colony, the capital excepted, by the Treaty of Paris in 1763. Whereas the English quickly settled in their new colony, it was only in March 1766 that the first Spanish governor, Antonio de Ulloa, arrived. Lacking sufficient military forces, he did not immediately take official possession of the colony. Thus, for two years, Louisiana was governed by a French officer in the name of the king of Spain. For political and

Such questions could be raised for any urban center established by Europeans in the Americas. By the time the French started to build New Orleans, most of the colonial port cities that would become major nodes of connection in the eighteenth-century greater Caribbean had already been founded. The wave of Spanish settlements in the sixteenth century—Havana (1515), Veracruz (1519), Cartagena de Indias (1533), and Portobelo (1597)—had been followed by a new spate in the seventeenth century under the control of the English, Dutch, and French—Bridgetown, Barbados (1628), Willemstad, Curaçao (1634), Saint-Pierre, Martinique (1635), Charleston (1670), Cap-Français (1670), and Kingston, Jamaica (1692). Throughout the French period, New Orleans could hardly compare, particularly with those cities located on plantation islands. When the Spanish took over the Louisiana capital in the late 1760s, its population did not exceed 3,000 inhabitants, and its economy was still struggling. Only a few dozen ships visited its port annually. In contrast, by the early 1770s, Kingston was made up of 14,200 inhabitants, Bridgetown, 14,000, Saint-Pierre, 13,400, and Cap-Français, 4,500. These Caribbean port cities and their plantation regions played a crucial role in the colonial trade that enriched their metropoles. They formed the core of the plantation complex of the English and French Empires that dominated the eighteenth-century Atlantic world economically and socioculturally. Why study, then, a tiny colonial outpost perched on the Mississippi River instead of one of the era's great Caribbean hubs?[7]

---

economic reasons, the French inhabitants of Lower Louisiana rose up in revolt against Ulloa, who was expelled in October 1768. However, in August 1769, the new Spanish governor, Alejandro O'Reilly, effectively imposed the order and sovereignty of the Spanish crown. In 1800, the Treaty of San Ildefonso gave Spanish Louisiana back to France, but the French took possession of the colony only three weeks before the United States assumed control of the territory in the Louisiana Purchase of 1803.

7. For works on port cities that became major hubs in the eighteenth century, see Franklin W. Knight and Peggy K. Liss, eds., *Atlantic Port Cities: Economy, Culture, and Society in the Atlantic World, 1650–1850* (Knoxville, Tenn., 1991); Gary B. Nash, "A Worm's Eye View," in "Early Cities of the Americas," special issue, *Common-Place: The Interactive Journal of Early American Life*, III, no. 4 (July 2003), http://www.common-place.org /vol-03/no-04/talk/; Alejandro de la Fuente, with the collaboration of César García del Pino and Bernardo Iglesias Delgado, *Havana and the Atlantic in the Sixteenth Century* (Chapel Hill, N.C., 2008); and Emma Hart, *Building Charleston: Town and Society in the Eighteenth-Century British Atlantic World* (Charlottesville, Va., 2010). For the port cities' population numbers in the early 1770s, see Trevor Burnard, "Kingston, Jamaica: Crucible of Modernity," in Jorge Cañizares-Esguerra, Matt D. Childs, and James Sidbury, eds., *The Black Urban Atlantic in the Age of the Slave Trade* (Philadelphia, 2013), 127–130, David P. Geggus, "The Slaves and Free People of Color of Cap Français," 101–102; Geggus, "The

Paradoxically, what gives heuristic value to New Orleans as a case study is its late founding and location at the western edge of the French Empire. Since the Louisiana capital was created decades after what became the most prominent British and French urban centers in the Caribbean, the circumstances of its birth were necessarily different. The city emerged within an Atlantic world that was marked by advanced integration, the consolidation of several European Atlantic empires, the rise of the transatlantic slave trade, the multiplication of slave societies within the tropical and subtropical zones, and a general but differentiated racialization. New Orleans thus constitutes an ideal place to evaluate the impact of ongoing Atlantic trends on new colonial societies. The specific way these Atlantic dynamics played out in the city depended on its connections with the rest of the French Empire and, more globally, the Atlantic world. Among all these relationships, the links with the Antilles and with Saint-Domingue, in particular, were of crucial importance. Hence the book's title: *Caribbean New Orleans*. But what does it mean to characterize New Orleans as a Caribbean port city? How does such a stance contribute to new understandings of both the Louisiana capital and the expansion and differentiation of racial slavery in the Atlantic world?[8]

A CARIBBEAN PORT CITY DEFINED BY RACIAL SLAVERY

Located on the mainland, New Orleans might appear, at first glance, to be more closely connected to the North American continent than to the Carib-

---

Major Port Towns of Saint Domingue in the Later Eighteenth Century," in Knight and Liss, eds., *Atlantic Port Cities*, 105; Abel A. Louis, *Les libres de couleur en Martinique*, I, *Des origines à la veille de la Révolution française, 1635–1788* (Paris, 2012), 296; and Pedro L. V. Welch, *Slave Society in the City: Bridgetown, Barbados, 1680–1834* (Kingston, Jamaica, 2003), 53. For a history of the plantation complex, see Philip D. Curtin, *The Rise and Fall of the Plantation Complex: Essays in Atlantic History* (Cambridge, 1990).

8. For global histories of the Atlantic world, see Nicholas Canny and Philip Morgan, eds., *The Oxford Handbook of the Atlantic World, c.1450–c.1850* (Oxford, 2011); and Douglas R. Egerton et al., *The Atlantic World: A History, 1400–1888* (Wheeling, Ill., 2007). On the Atlantic paradigm that posits that the evolution of societies on both sides of the Atlantic Ocean was greatly affected by the relationships that linked Europe, Africa, and the Americas between the fifteenth and the nineteenth centuries, see Bernard Bailyn, *Atlantic History: Concept and Contours* (Cambridge, Mass., 2005); Alison Games, "Atlantic History: Definitions, Challenges, and Opportunities," *American Historical Review*, CXI (2006), 741–757; Jack P. Greene and Philip D. Morgan, eds., *Atlantic History: A Critical Appraisal* (Oxford, 2009); and Cécile Vidal, "For a Comprehensive History of the Atlantic Word or Histories Connected in and Beyond the Atlantic World?" *Annales: Histoire, Sciences Sociales*, LXVII (2012), 279–300.

bean. The Mississippi Valley was first explored from the north by French adventurers, traders, and missionaries who came from Canada. After Louisiana's founding, the colony officially belonged to New France and depended on the general governorship of Quebec, although in practice it was administered directly by Versailles. Canada also gave Louisiana several of its governors, and some Canadian settlers of more modest means were among the first migrants to the colony. Furthermore, the French crown claimed sovereignty over a huge territory extending from the Great Lakes to the Gulf of Mexico and from the Allegheny to the Rocky Mountains. To control such a vast expanse, the French depended on their Native American allies, as in the Saint Lawrence Valley and in the Great Lakes region. For all these reasons, Louisiana has often been depicted as the younger sister colony of Canada. Not surprisingly, in both Francophone and Anglophone historiographies, New Orleans often figures in treatments of Louisiana or New France instead of those of the Antilles.[9]

Yet it is more accurate to view eighteenth-century New Orleans as a Caribbean port city rather than a North American one: its late founding, its position within the French Empire, and its connections with Saint-Domingue explain why the interplay of slavery and race profoundly informed its society from the outset. The Louisiana capital quickly found its place within a greater Caribbean decisively shaped by racial slavery. With the expansion of the transatlantic slave trade in the eighteenth century, the greater Caribbean was a region of connected slave societies. Although plantations commanded significant demographic and economic resources, port cities also housed sizable populations (the majority of whom were slaves) and played crucial commercial roles. In a world of maritime transportation and export-driven economies, they connected scattered territories affected by racial slavery. The greater Caribbean was not confined to the West Indian islands but also extended to mainland areas surrounding the Gulf of Mexico and the Caribbean Sea.[10] Located at the northern margin of this

9. For New Orleans as a North American port city, see Jerah Johnson, "Colonial New Orleans: A Fragment of the Eighteenth-Century French Ethos," in Arnold R. Hirsch and Joseph Logsdon, eds., *Creole New Orleans: Race and Americanization* (Baton Rouge, La., 1992), 12–57.

10. For a conception of the Caribbean region as defined by its shared history of racial slavery, see Sidney W. Mintz, "The Caribbean Region," *Daedalus*, CIII, no. 2 (Spring 1974), 45–71; and Mintz, "Enduring Substances, Trying Theories: The Caribbean Region as Oikumenê," *Journal of the Royal Anthropological Institute*, II (1996), 289–311. For studies on racial slavery in the Caribbean islands, see Verene A. Shepherd and Hilary McD. Beckles, eds., *Caribbean Slavery in the Atlantic World: A Student Reader* (Kings-

greater Caribbean region, French New Orleans looked to the south and, especially, Saint-Domingue. The West Indian territory was well on the way to becoming France's richest colony and the colonial center that drove the French Empire. As Louisiana authorities and settlers sought to emulate the fast-emerging pearl of the Antilles, the French section of the big island and its system of racial slavery exerted a profound influence on New Orleans's society.[11]

In situating the Louisiana capital within the greater Caribbean, this ar-

---

ton, Jamaica, 2000); Franklin W. Knight, ed., *General History of the Caribbean*, III, *The Slave Societies of the Caribbean* (London, 1997); and Stephan Palmié and Francisco A. Scarano, eds., *The Caribbean: A History of the Region and Its Peoples* (Chicago, 2011). For the importance of port cities in plantation colonies, see Trevor Burnard, "Towns in Plantation Societies in Eighteenth-Century British America," *Early American Studies*, XV (20017), 835–859; Burnard and Emma Hart, "Kingston, Jamaica, and Charleston, South Carolina: A New Look at Comparative Urbanization in Plantation Colonial British America," *Journal of Urban History*, XXXIX (2013), 214–234; and Philip D. Morgan, "The Caribbean Islands in Atlantic Context, circa 1500–1800," in Felicity A. Nussbaum, ed., *The Global Eighteenth Century* (Baltimore, 2003), 59. For other works using the concept of the greater Caribbean, see David Barry Gaspar and David Patrick Geggus, eds., *A Turbulent Time: The French Revolution and the Greater Caribbean* (Bloomington, Ind., 1997); John W. Catron, "Evangelical Networks in the Greater Caribbean and the Origins of the Black Church," *Church History*, LXXIX, no. 1 (2010), 77–114; Wim Klooster, "The Rising Expectations of Free and Enslaved Blacks in the Greater Caribbean," in Klooster and Gert Oostindie, eds., *Curaçao in the Age of Revolutions, 1795–1800* (Leiden, Netherlands, 2011), 57–74; J. R. McNeill, *Mosquito Empires: Ecology and War in the Greater Caribbean, 1620–1914* (Cambridge, 2010); Matthew Mulcahy, *Hurricanes and Society in the British Greater Caribbean, 1624–1783* (Baltimore, 2008); and Edward B. Rugemer, "The Development of Mastery and Race in the Comprehensive Slave Codes of the Greater Caribbean during the Seventeenth Century," *William and Mary Quarterly*, 3d Ser., LXX (2013), 429–458.

11. For general studies on Saint-Domingue, see John Garrigus, "History of St. Domingue, 1697–1791," in [Priscilla Lawrence], ed., *Common Routes: St. Domingue-Louisiana; The Historic New Orleans Collection, March 14–June 30, 2006* (New Orleans, 2006), 31–53; and Trevor Burnard and John Garrigus, *The Plantation Machine: Atlantic Capitalism in French Saint-Domingue and British Jamaica* (Philadelphia, 2016). For general studies on slavery in the French Antilles, see Gabriel Debien, *Les esclaves aux Antilles françaises (XVIIe–XVIIIe siècles)* (Basse-Terre, Guadeloupe, 1974); Frédéric Régent, *La France et ses esclaves: De la colonisation aux abolitions (1620–1848)* (Paris, 2007); Laurent Dubois, "Slavery in the French Caribbean, 1635–1804," in David Eltis and Stanley L. Engerman, eds., *The Cambridge World History of Slavery*, III, *AD 1420–AD 1804* (Cambridge, 2011), 431–449; and Garrigus, "French Slavery," in Robert L. Paquette and Mark M. Smith, eds., *The Oxford Handbook of Slavery in the Americas* (Oxford, 2010), 173–200.

gument draws on scholarship that has refined our understanding of the rise and fall of the plantation complex, the transformation of plantation societies into slave societies, and the interplay of African slavery and race in the Atlantic world. The first European colonizing powers in the Americas, the Spanish and the Portuguese, immediately resorted to two institutions, slavery and the plantation, that both already existed on the Iberian Peninsula as well as the islands they started to occupy and exploit off the African coast from the fifteenth century onward. Over the early modern period, colonization fostered the spread of the plantation system through a large part of the western hemisphere, while all American colonial societies developed some forms of chattel slavery, even though not all became slave societies—that is societies in which slavery was "pivotal to the entire institutional structure and value complex."[12]

A complex historical relationship ties plantation societies to slave societies. Although all plantation societies became slave societies over time, the advent of slave societies followed different chronologies throughout the New World. Though a dependence on slave labor came to be tightly linked to the development of plantation agriculture and export economies, the plantation system did not initially rely on African enslaved laborers. In sixteenth-century Brazil, settlers first exploited Native Americans under various statuses alongside African slaves, whereas the English and the French in the West Indies and North America mainly resorted to European indentured servants during the early seventeenth century and continued to employ them in the eighteenth century. Moreover, these societies did not develop full-fledged plantation economies and transform themselves into slave societies all at once; for most, the two stages did not coincide.[13]

12. For new interpretations of the expansion of the plantation system and of slavery in the English Atlantic, see Trevor Burnard, "Plantation Societies," in Jerry H. Bentley, Sanjay Subrahmanyam, and Merry Wiesner-Hanks, eds., *The Cambridge World History*, VI, *The Construction of a Global World, 1400–1800 CE*, Part 2, *Patterns of Change* (Cambridge, 2015), 263–282; Burnard, *Planters, Merchants, and Slaves: Plantation Societies in British America, 1650–1820* (Chicago, 2015); Simon P. Newman, *A New World of Labor: The Development of Plantation Slavery in the British Atlantic* (Philadelphia, 2013); Paul M. Pressly, *On the Rim of the Caribbean: Colonial Georgia and the British Atlantic World* (Athens, Ga., 2013); and Michael Guasco, *Slaves and Englishmen: Human Bondage in the Early Modern Atlantic World* (Philadelphia, 2014). For the definition of a slave society, see Arnold A. Sio, review of Orlando Patterson, *The Sociology of Slavery: An Analysis of the Origins, Development, and Structure of Negro Slave Society in Jamaica*, in *Social and Economic Studies*, XVII (1968), 96–99 (quotation, 96).

13. For works on sixteenth-century Brazil and the seventeenth-century English West Indies and French Antilles, see Philip P. Boucher, *France and the American Tropics to*

It was in the English colony of Barbados that the plantation system and African slavery intersected most rapidly, even though it was a gradual transformation and not a revolution. Between the 1640s and the 1660s, the island experienced a triple shift from the cultivation of tobacco and cotton to sugarcane, from the exploitation of small to large plantations, and from a labor force of predominately European indentured servants or convicts to African slaves. The relationships among these three changes were complex, as slaves did not start to arrive en masse until after the island was successfully exporting tobacco, cotton, and indigo. Sugar did not bring slavery; it only accelerated an evolution that was already underway. Likewise, while race-thinking was present from Barbados's founding, the rise of large integrated sugar plantations and the advent of a slave society precipitated and strengthened racialization. For sugar planters, imposing the terrible conditions of work that they required on laborers of European descent was inconceivable. The system also relied on white solidarity between slaveholders and the indentured servants who came to take up managerial and skilled positions. Although custom distinguished slaves by their status from the beginning, two major comprehensive laws regarding indentured servants and slaves enacted in 1661 enshrined the overlapping of slavery and race in law. As the titles of the legal texts demonstrate—Act for the Good Governing of Servants, and Ordaining the Rights between Masters and Servants and Act for the Better Ordering and Governing of Negroes—only servants had rights. Following the passage of this legislation, slavery and race remained closely entangled in Barbados and in other English colonies.[14]

1700: Tropics of Discontent? (Baltimore, 2008); Richard S. Dunn, *Sugar and Slaves: The Rise of the Planter Class in the English West Indies, 1624–1713* (Chapel Hill, N.C., 1972); and Stuart B. Schwartz, *Sugar Plantations in the Formation of Brazilian Society: Bahia, 1550–1835* (Cambridge, 1985).

14. For a renewed interpretation of the "sugar revolution" in Barbados, see John J. McCusker and Russell R. Menard, "The Sugar Industry in the Seventeenth Century: A New Perspective on the Barbadian 'Sugar Revolution,'" in Stuart Schwartz, ed., *Tropical Babylons: Sugar and the Making of the Atlantic World, 1450–1680* (Chapel Hill, N.C., 2004), 289–330. For the effect of the implementation of the system of the large integrated sugar plantation on racial formation, see Burnard, *Planters, Merchants, and Slaves*, 53–97; and Jerome S. Handler, "Custom and Law: The Status of Enslaved Africans in Seventeenth-Century Barbados," *Slavery and Abolition*, XXXVII, no. 2 (2016), 233–255. Some historians have argued that race was irrelevant to understanding social dynamics in Barbados during most of the seventeenth century, as both European indentured servants and African slaves were badly treated; they even describe indentured servants as "white slaves." This interpretation, however, has been contested. For historians defending the idea of "white slavery," see Hilary McD. Beckles, *White Servitude and Black Slavery in*

The economic success of Barbados gave ideas to other colonial entrepreneurs. Although English colonies founded in the first half of the seventeenth century were not originally intended as slave societies, those created during the second wave of English colonization after the Stuart Restoration looked to slavery as their preferred system of labor. Hence, while Virginia, founded in 1607, witnessed the development of a successful plantation economy and the rise of a slave society at roughly the same time, one century after the settlement of Jamestown, South Carolina quickly evolved into a slave society only two generations after the colony's creation in 1663 and decades before its plantation economy really took off. Relations with Barbados played a major role. Not only was one of the aristocratic founders of the Carolinas a member of an eminent Barbadian family, but many poor planters also moved from the island to South Carolina. They brought with them their slaves and their laws. The diffusion of the 1661 Barbados slave code in South Carolina and in the rest of the English Empire fueled the racialization of people of African descent outside the sugar colonies, where racial slavery had already started to become institutionalized in its harshest form. Even Georgia, founded in the early eighteenth century, came to share many of the characteristics of West Indian plantation economies and societies, although its proprietors were initially opposed to the development of slavery in their colony.[15]

_____

Barbados, 1627–1715 (Knoxville, Tenn., 1989); Beckles, "The Concept of 'White Slavery' in the English Caribbean during the Early Seventeenth Century," in John Brewer and Susan Staves, eds., *Early Modern Conceptions of Property* (London, 1996), 572–584; and Newman, *New World of Labor*, 71–107. For a refutation of this thesis, see Handler and Matthew C. Reilly, "Contesting 'White Slavery' in the Caribbean: Enslaved Africans and European Indentured Servants in Seventeenth-Century Barbados," *New West Indian Guide*, XCI (2017), 30–55.

15. On the desire to develop slave societies during the second wave of English colonization, see Christopher Tomlins, "Transplants and Timing: Passages in the Creation of an Anglo-American Law of Slavery," *Berkeley Law Scholarship Repository*, X (2009), 389–421, esp. 389–209, available at: http://scholarship.law.berkeley.edu/facpubs/2311. On the timing of the expansion of a plantation economy and the formation of a slave society, see Burnard, *Planters, Merchants, and Slaves*, 1–21. The growth of African slavery in Virginia in the second half of the seventeenth century was also influenced by the relations the Chesapeake colony maintained with Barbados. See April Lee Hatfield, *Atlantic Virginia: Intercolonial Relations in the Seventeenth Century* (Philadelphia, 2004), 137–168. For the diffusion of the 1661 Barbadian slave code within the English Empire, see Richard Dunn, "The English Sugar Islands and the Founding of South Carolina," *South Carolina Historical Magazine*, LXXII (1971), 81–93; David Barry Gaspar, "With a Rod of Iron: Barbados Slave Laws as a Model for Jamaica, South Carolina, and Antigua, 1661–1697,"

Caribbean New Orleans demonstrates that the expansion of racial slavery from the Caribbean to North America that occurred in the English Empire also took place in the French Empire. This process deeply shaped Louisiana and its capital. The colony was founded in 1699, but its settlement progressed slowly during the first two decades because of the War of the Spanish Succession. When the French crown granted the monopoly on Louisiana trade to the Company of the Indies in 1717, the company's directors' initial plan, besides exploiting the fabled silver and gold mines of the Illinois Country and expanding trade with Spanish colonies, was to develop a plantation society and economy, growing tobacco and indigo with a mixed workforce composed of black slaves and white indentured servants and convicts. New Orleans was intended to serve as the trading entrepôt of this new colony that fostered such great expectations. The importance given to tobacco and the decision to rely on a mixed labor force suggest that the company's directors sought to emulate the English colonies in the Chesapeake. Louisiana should have followed Virginia's path. Its actual trajectory, however, was ultimately more similar to that of South Carolina's.[16]

For various reasons, this experiment quickly turned into a disaster. Many indentured servants died or left, and the arrival of slave ships from Africa dropped off at the end of 1721. After the reorganization of the company in

in Darlene Clark Hine and Jacqueline McLeod, eds., *Crossing Boundaries: Comparative History of Black People in Diaspora* (Bloomington, Ind., 1999), 343–366; Gaspar, "'Rigid and Inclement': Origins of the Jamaica Slave Laws of the Seventeenth Century," in Tomlins and Bruce H. Mann, eds., *The Many Legalities of Early America* (Chapel Hill, N.C., 2001), 78–96; Newman, *New World of Labor*, 250–255; Bradley J. Nicholson, "Legal Borrowing and the Origins of Slave Law in the British Colonies," *American Journal of Legal History*, XXXVIII (1994), 38–54; Justin Roberts and Ian Beamish, "Venturing Out: The Barbadian Diaspora and the Carolina Colony, 1650–1685," in Michelle LeMaster and Bradford J. Wood, eds., *Creating and Contesting Carolina: Proprietary Era Histories* (Columbia, S.C., 2013), 49–72; Rugemer, "Development of Mastery and Race," *William and Mary Quarterly*, LXX (2013), 429–458; Tomlins, "Transplants and Timing," *Berkeley Law Scholarship Repository*, X (2009), 389–421; and Peter H. Wood, *Black Majority: Negroes in Colonial South Carolina; From 1670 through the Stono Rebellion* (1974; rpt. New York, 1996), 13–34. For the development of a slave society in Georgia, see Pressly, *On the Rim of the Caribbean.*

16. The company was first called Compagnie d'Occident (Company of the West). It was only in 1719 that it was renamed Compagnie des Indes (Company of the Indies) as it united a great number of previously separate companies that traded in Asia, Africa, and the Americas. For the early choice of developing a tobacco plantation colony in Louisiana, see Erin M. Greenwald, *Marc-Antoine Caillot and the Company of the Indies in Louisiana: Trade in the French Atlantic World* (Baton Rouge, La., 2016), 2–3.

1723, the transatlantic slave trade resumed. Local authorities and settlers had become convinced that they could not make the colony prosper without relying on a Caribbean-style slave labor force. They could have made another choice, but, out of both economic and sociocultural motivations, they decided to expand slavery. Their goal was to create a "second Saint-Domingue" in the Mississippi Valley. During the second half of the seventeenth century, the system of the large integrated sugar plantation had spread first to the French Lesser Antilles and then to Saint-Domingue. That colony's rise in the 1720s to a major producer of sugar as well as indigo, when no sugar plantation or mill had existed there before 1690, made it an appealing model.[17]

Saint-Domingue not only provided Louisiana authorities and settlers with the impetus to establish a slave society and economy but also offered them a set of means and practices to do so. Poor planters from the French Lesser Antilles did not move to the mainland, as Barbadians did, especially to South Carolina, bringing their system of racial slavery with them. In the Mississippi colony, the transference of ideas and practices occurred because the French crown played a crucial role in the circulation of slave laws between colonies. The racial conceptions of West Indian officials and settlers were disseminated through the Code Noir and mediums such as books and correspondence. Since ships navigating between Europe or Africa and New Orleans necessarily had to make a stop at Saint-Domingue, all migrants from France also experienced the intricacies of a slave society firsthand before their arrival in the Mississippi Valley. Over time, these intercolonial movements intensified and came to exercise great influence on local social dynamics. In such a transatlantic and imperial context, the commitment of local authorities and colonists to the slave system never wavered despite the vicissitudes their settlements underwent. Although Louisiana struggled to develop a full-fledged plantation economy, the colony succeeded in establishing a slave society very early on that was profoundly shaped by race.[18]

17. For the desire to develop a "second Saint-Domingue" in Louisiana, see [Caillot], "Relation du voyage de la Louisianne ou Nouvlle. France," HNOC, MSS596, fol. 108. For the rapid transformation of Saint-Domingue into a sugar plantation colony, see Charles Frostin, *Les révoltes blanches à Saint-Domingue aux XVIIe et XVIIIe siècles (Haïti avant 1789)*, [rev. ed.] (Rennes, France, 2008), 23–26, 79, 81–83.

18. A few historians have already underlined that Saint-Domingue and Louisiana shared a common history from early on. See Thomas Marc Fiehrer, "The African Presence in Colonial Louisiana: An Essay on the Continuity of Caribbean Culture," in Robert R. MacDonald, John R. Kemp, and Edward F. Haas, eds., *Louisiana's Black Heritage* (New Orleans, 1979), 3–31; D. W. Meinig, *The Shaping of America: A Geographical Perspec-*

Even as a slave society quickly took shape in the capital, it did not do so uniformly across the colony's vast territory. The center of Louisiana's slave society was located in New Orleans and the plantation region that extended along the Mississippi River above and below the city. But slavery also became a crucial institution in other scattered and distant outposts on the river, notably the German Coast, Pointe Coupée, and the Natchez and Natchitoches settlements. The attraction of the slave system was even felt as far north as the Illinois Country—although settlers of Kaskaskia and other French villages produced wheat flour and hams for the Lower Louisiana markets, they sought to purchase as many African slaves as possible. From the English Turn up to Cahokia, however, these colonial and slave territorial pockets formed nothing but an archipelago in the midst of Indian Country. French Louisiana only looked like a contiguous continental colony on maps. Located above the Mississippi Delta, New Orleans was supposed to control this imperial infrastructure of outposts, forts, and missions scattered along the Mississippi and its tributaries.[19]

Outside these colonial settlements, the French were dependent on the system of alliances they concluded and maintained with most of the First Nations that they encountered. At different times, war broke out variously between the French and the Foxes, the Chickasaws, and the Natchez. In the early 1730s, the French went as far as conquering and destroying the Natchez. They also employed indigenous slaves following what they had

tive on 500 Years of History, I, Atlantic America, 1492–1800 (New Haven, Conn., 1986), 200; Alfred E. Lemmon and John H. Lawrence, "Common Routes: St. Domingue and Louisiana," in [Lawrence], ed., Common Routes St. Domingue—Louisiana, 85–91; and "The Common Routes of Louisiana and Haiti: A Creative Power," special issue, Southern Quarterly, XLIV, no. 3 (Spring 2007), 6–129. For the opposite idea that Louisiana society did not manage to become a genuine slave society before the nineteenth century, see Ira Berlin, Many Thousands Gone: The First Two Centuries of Slavery in North America (Cambridge, Mass., 1998), 77–92, 325–357; and Jennifer M. Spear, Race, Sex, and Social Order in Early New Orleans (Baltimore, 2009), 12–13.

19. For works on the slave system in the Mississippi Valley outside the New Orleans region, see H. Sophie Burton and F. Todd Smith, Colonial Natchitoches: A Creole Community on the Louisiana-Texas Frontier (College Station, Tex., 2008); Ronald L. F. Davis, The Black Experience in Natchez, 1720–1880: Special History Study (Natchez, Miss., 1993); Gwendolyn Midlo Hall, Africans in Colonial Louisiana: The Development of Afro-Creole Culture in the Eighteenth Century (Baton Rouge, La., 1992); David J. Libby, Slavery and Frontier Mississippi, 1720–1835 (Jackson, Miss., 2004); Reinhart Kondert, The Germans of Colonial Louisiana, 1720–1803 (Stuttgart, Germany, 1990); and Cécile Vidal, "Les implantations françaises au Pays des Illinois au XVIIIe siècle (1699–1765)," 2 vols. (Ph.D. diss., École des Hautes Études en Sciences Sociales, 1995), 534–557.

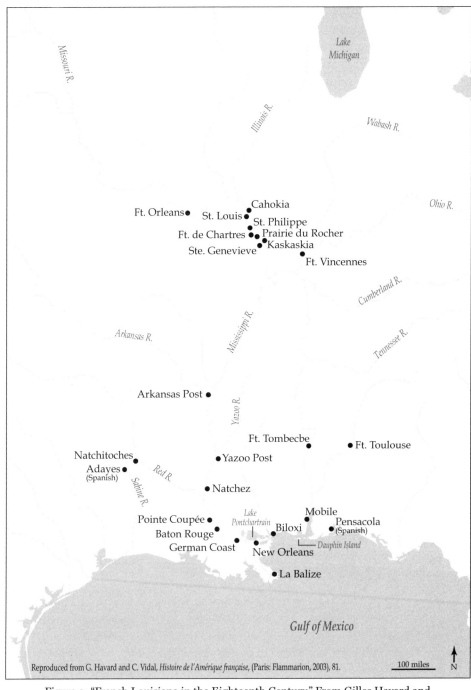

Figure 2: "French Louisiana in the Eighteenth Century." From Gilles Havard and
Cécile Vidal, *Histoire de l'Amérique française* ([Paris], 2003), 81.

started to do in the Saint Lawrence Valley and the Upper Country. Even though Canadian authorities and settlers were inspired by the Caribbean islands in their desire to rely on an enslaved workforce, the rise of Native American slavery in New France was the result of French alliances with indigenous peoples. Enslaved enemies were exchanged in diplomatic rituals, and "slave raids helped to maintain alliances by enforcing their boundaries, defining who was included or excluded." All in all, the whole Mississippi Valley can be likened to a borderland in which no single party was able to impose its domination. Despite dramatic episodes of extreme violence, the interactions of the French and First Nations stood in sharp contrast to the uniformly harsh exploitation of slaves of African descent within colonial centers. While New Orleans was a Caribbean port city, the whole of greater Louisiana was not a Caribbean colony with its system of racial slavery.[20]

Furthermore, the early prevalence of racial prejudice in the port city under the influence of Saint-Domingue does not mean that the way race informed the social order arrived fully formed and remained static throughout the French regime. There are multiple ways for a society to be racialized. Although Louisiana initially derived many of its social and symbolic mechanisms from Saint-Domingue, the techniques by which race was embodied in the colony's laws, institutions, and practices of slavery never ceased to be readjusted. To a large extent, these readjustments represented responses to the changing political, economic, demographic, and social situation of the colony after 1731. A Natchez attack in November 1729 prompted a war that, coinciding with an attempted slave revolt, hardened the colonial situation between settlers of European descent, Native Americans, and slaves of African descent in a way similar to King Philip's War (1675–1678) in New England, Bacon's Rebellion (1676) in Virginia, and the Pueblo Revolt (1680)

20. For the causes of the expansion of Native American slavery in New France, see Brett Rushforth, *Bonds of Alliance: Indigenous and Atlantic Slaveries in New France* (Chapel Hill, N.C., 2012), 12. On French-native American relations in greater Louisiana, see among many studies Kathleen DuVal, *The Native Ground: Indians and Colonists in the Heart of the Continent* (Philadelphia, 2006); Gilles Havard, *Empire et métissages: Indiens et Français dans le Pays d'en haut, 1660–1715* (Sillery, Quebec, 2003); Daniel H. Usner, Jr., *Indians, Settlers, and Slaves in a Frontier Exchange Economy: The Lower Mississippi Valley before 1783* (Chapel Hill, N.C., 1992); and Richard White, *The Middle Ground: Indians, Empires, and Republics in the Great Lakes Region, 1650–1815* (Cambridge, 1991). For a different characterization of New Orleans as a frontier city, see Usner, "Colonial Projects and Frontier Practices: The First Century of New Orleans History," in Jay Gitlin, Barbara Berglund, and Adam Arenson, eds., *Frontier Cities: Encounters at the Crossroads of Empire* (Philadelphia, 2013), 27–45.

in present-day New Mexico. These events also persuaded the Company of the Indies to abandon its trade monopoly two years later.

Before 1731, Louisiana was not a royal colony but was governed by a trade company. The significance of the transfer of power from company to crown, however, should not be exaggerated. Royal authorities closely supervised and controlled the company and the colony. Sovereignty ultimately belonged to the king not only in theory but also very much in practice, as the monarch appointed the company's directors. In Louisiana, the Company of the Indies did not constitute in any way a "Company-State" that functioned as a political authority and community in its own right on the model of England's East India Company. Political continuity was also maintained by Jean-Baptiste Le Moyne de Bienville, who served as commandant general or governor of the colony three times, before, during, and after the company's monopoly (1702–1713, 1716–1724, and 1733–1743). It was Bienville who chose the site of New Orleans and who is celebrated as the city's founder. Still, the company's economic motivations influenced the way it ruled the colony. After Louisiana came back under the king's direct rule, all social actors took advantage of the opening of trade to French merchants, which fostered economic growth.[21]

The year 1731 is also a significant date for demographic and social reasons. Following its creation in 1717, the company organized the only migratory wave from Europe and Africa from which the colony benefited. After 1731, only scattered migrants of European descent arrived from France and the Antilles, and the slave trade from Africa practically ceased. This lack of mass migration hampered the colony's demographic and economic growth. But it gave New Orleans and Louisiana greater social stability, since the colonial society did not have to integrate and acculturate to the slave system numerous free or coerced migrants who were all arriving at the same time. It also forced slaveholders to treat their enslaved laborers less harshly than was the case in the Antilles. For slaves, however, it meant that their

21. For the best analysis of the Company of the Indies in Louisiana, see Giraud, *Histoire de la Louisiane française,* I–IV; and Giraud, *A History of French Louisiana,* V, trans. Pearce. See also Greenwald, *Marc-Antoine Caillot and the Company of the Indies in Louisiana.* On the English East India Company, see Philip J. Stern, *The Company-State: Corporate Sovereignty and the Early Modern Foundations of the British Empire in India* (Oxford, 2011). On Jean-Baptiste Le Moyne de Bienville, see Giraud, *Histoire de la Louisiane française,* I–IV; Giraud, *History of French Louisiana,* V, trans. Pearce; Khalil Saadani, *La Louisiane française dans l'impasse, 1731–1743* (Paris, 2008); and Lawrence N. Powell, *The Accidental City: Improvising New Orleans* (Cambridge, Mass., 2012).

connections with Africa were quickly severed. With the early creolization of the slave population in the 1740s and 1750s and the replacement of the first generation of metropolitan migrants with children born in the colony in the late 1750s and early 1760s, the slave system should have reached a phase of stabilization and maturation, as this was the system that the majority of both slaveholders and slaves had always known.[22]

Yet the departure of the Company of the Indies in 1731 also impacted New Orleans's integration within the greater Caribbean, and the multiplication of links with the Antilles contributed to the creation of social disturbances. Throughout the French period, metropolitan migration to the colony remained limited, and transatlantic relationships were increasingly supplemented by exchanges with the Antilles. Although connections with Saint-Domingue existed from the beginning of Louisiana's colonization, they intensified in the last decades of the French regime. The sporadic arrival of slaves from the Antilles and the embroilment of the Mississippi colony in the great turmoil that affected the Caribbean region during and after the Seven Years' War combined with the growth of New Orleans's population and the emergence of a small elite group of free people of color made social control more difficult. Even before the arrival of the Spanish in Louisiana in 1766, the biracial order that local authorities and settlers had to a large extent succeeded in enforcing thanks to favorable local circumstances had already begun to disintegrate. By the late 1760s, when the French handed over control to Spain, a more unstable but no less racialized three-tiered society had slowly started to emerge.

NEW ORLEANS: A CREOLE CITY?

Caribbean New Orleans seeks to change the terms of the debate that has developed about race in Louisiana history by approaching the French port city from the perspective of its own epoch and by offering a new chronology and interpretation to the expansion of racial slavery in the Mississippi colony's capital. Since the renewal of the historiography on colonial, territorial, and antebellum Louisiana in the early 1990s, one of the main topics of debate has been the absence or prevalence of racial ideas and practices during the French regime. This argument has been driven, not so much by the desire to understand French Louisiana or the early French Empire for its own

22. In 1731, the Company of the Indies gave up its trade monopoly on Louisiana, except for the introduction of slaves from Africa. However, it did not send any slave ships to the colony, since the slave trade with Louisiana was much less profitable than that with the Antilles.

sake, but by a preoccupation with what happened after the United States acquired the colony with the Louisiana Purchase in 1803. It is biased by a teleological perspective. Unlike other cities and regions first settled by the Spanish, such as Los Angeles and California, which have come to embody a vibrant component of American culture, New Orleans is still perceived as different. It remains marginalized in America's history and imagination, as if the place cannot escape its non-English origins and be fully American-ized. This essentialized alterity is expressed through its characterization as a Creole city no matter the period and despite its transformations through time.[23]

New Orleans's distinctive character allegedly comes from a different re-lation to race at the time it was incorporated within the United States. That the Louisiana capital was home to the largest proportion of free people of color in any United States city by 1810 is interpreted as a sign of a less divi-sive and less exclusive racial regime or even of a blindness to racial identi-ties. New Orleans's three-tiered socioracial structure, composed of whites, free people of color, and slaves, formed a contrast with the biracial order opposing whites and blacks that prevailed in the rest of the United States. This situation was the result of the growth of the population of free blacks throughout the Spanish period, thanks to the system of *coartacion* (a legal mechanism enabling slaves to enter into an agreement with their mas-ters to acquire their freedom for a fixed price with installments paid over a set period of time), as well as the arrival in 1809 of nine thousand Saint-Dominguan refugees from Cuba, one-third of whom were categorized as free people of color. Historians of Louisiana, however, disagree about the role of the French period in the growth of the city's population of free blacks and the impact of race on these circumstances. Some have described "French New Orleans as a brutal, violent place. But it cannot be understood by projecting contemporary attitudes toward race backward in time. There is no evidence of the racial exclusiveness and contempt that characterizes

23. For the characterization of New Orleans as a Creole city, see Virginia R. Domín-guez, *White by Definition: Social Classification in Creole Louisiana* (New Brunswick, N.J., 1986); Hirsch and Logsdon, eds., *Creole New Orleans;* Nathalie Dessens, *Creole City: A Chronicle of Early American New Orleans* (Gainesville, Fla., 2015); and Dianne Guenin-Lelle, *The Story of French New Orleans: History of a Creole City* (Jackson, Miss., 2016). Dessens denounces the long marginalization of New Orleans within United States history and historiography while continuing to describe New Orleans as a Creole city. See Dessens, "Du Sud à la Caraïbe: La Nouvelle-Orléans, ville créole," *E-rea: Revue élec-tronique d'études anglophones sur le monde anglophone,* XIV, no. 1 (2016), https://erea .revues.org/5216.

Introduction

more recent times." Others have claimed that "the most important factor in molding this society was color: in a slave society, all relations are determined by a legally defined 'race' of slaves." As a consequence, it has been concluded that French New Orleans "was indisputably North American in character, not Caribbean."[24]

The debate on race is not the sole problem raised by the way Louisiana historiography has developed. Historians of the Mississippi colony do not share the same understanding of racial formation, but they agree to describe French New Orleans as a "large urban-rural community." They rank it as a "town" and consider that it did not become a "city" before the end of

24. Gwendolyn Midlo Hall and Thomas N. Ingersoll have formulated the two most conflicting points of view on racial formation in French Louisiana. See Hall, *Africans in Colonial Louisiana*, 155; and Thomas N. Ingersoll, *Mammon and Manon in Early New Orleans: The First Slave Society in the Deep South, 1718–1819* (Knoxville, Tenn., 1999), xv–xix. Since the publication of these two provocative studies, more nuanced perspectives have started to appear, although they do not all share the same assumptions. See Guillaume Aubert, "'Français, nègres, et sauvages': Constructing Race in Colonial Louisiana" (Ph.D. diss., Tulane University, 2002); Emily Clark, *Masterless Mistresses: The New Orleans Ursulines and the Development of a New World Society, 1727–1834* (Chapel Hill, N.C., 2007); Shannon Lee Dawdy, *Building the Devil's Empire: French Colonial New Orleans* (Chicago, 2008); Spear, *Race, Sex, and Social Order in Early New Orleans;* Sophie White, *Wild Frenchmen and Frenchified Indians: Material Culture and Race in Colonial Louisiana* (Philadelphia, 2012); and George Edward Milne, *Natchez Country: Indians, Colonists, and the Landscapes of Race in French Louisiana* (Athens, Ga., 2015). For a summary of the debate on race in French Louisiana, see Paul Lachance, "Existe-t-il un seul modèle colonial français en Amérique du Nord? Recherches récentes sur les relations raciales en Louisiane," in Thomas Wien, Cécile Vidal, and Yves Frénette, eds., *De Québec à l'Amérique française: Histoire et mémoire; Textes choisis du deuxième colloque de la Commission franco-québécoise sur les lieux de mémoire communs* ([Sainte-Foy, Quebec], 2006), 139–153; and Joseph Zitomersky, "Culture, classe, ou État? Comment interpréter les relations raciales dans la grande Louisiane française avant et après 1803?" in Marcel Dorigny and Marie-Jeanne Rossignol, eds., *La France et les Amériques au temps de Jefferson et de Miranda* (Paris, 2001), 63–89. On the rise of the free population of color over the Spanish period, see Kimberly S. Hanger, *Bounded Lives, Bounded Places: Free Black Society in Colonial New Orleans, 1769–1803* (Durham, N.C., 1997). On the arrival of Saint-Dominguan refugees, see Emily Clark, *The Strange History of the American Quadroon: Free Women of Color in the Revolutionary Atlantic World* (Chapel Hill, N.C., 2013); Nathalie Dessens, *From Saint-Domingue to New Orleans: Migration and Influences* (Gainesville, Fla., 2007); Rashauna Johnson, *Slavery's Metropolis: Unfree Labor in New Orleans during the Age of Revolutions* (Cambridge, 2016); and Rebecca J. Scott and Jean M. Hébrard, *Freedom Papers: An Atlantic Odyssey in the Age of Emancipation* (Cambridge, Mass., 2012).

the eighteenth century. When they refer to "New Orleans," they mean both the urban center and its plantation region and neglect what separated and distinguished the urban milieu from its rural environment.[25]

In opposition to the perspective shared by most monographs published on French New Orleans since the 1990s, this book posits that it is necessary to better take into account the colonial capital's specificity as an urban center. "City" is used here to translate the French term *ville* and to differentiate a kind of territory characterized by its urbanity. In early modern French language and culture, there was no distinction such as the one that exists in English between "city" and "town," which is based on both demographic and legal parameters. Urban social scientists have deplored the elusive and loose definition of their object; they have shown that the city is hardly a universal category of analysis but refers to a myriad of distinct historical experiences. Instead of asking when New Orleans acquired an urban character based on objective criteria, it thus seems more interesting to take seriously that New Orleans was conceived of as a *ville* from the start by both public authorities and settlers. Undoubtedly, the place was still a small urban center at the end of the French regime. For a long time, it resembled a rural town and had no municipal institutions before the Spanish period. It also lived in symbiosis with the surrounding plantation region. Nevertheless, New Orleans was planned as a city, carried out some urban functions, and housed specific social groups. Half of the migrants to Louisiana probably came from cities, as did their counterparts in Canada, and they brought with them an urban culture and a particular representation of the urban milieu. A distinct urban society existed early on, both spatially and in the conception city dwellers had of themselves.[26]

Caribbean New Orleans takes a different stance from that predominating in French Louisiana historiography on two questions: on the one hand,

25. Ingersoll, *Mammon and Manon in Early New Orleans*, xv, xx, 27–33; Hall, *Africans in Colonial Louisiana*, 119–155.

26. There was originally a distinction between *ville* and *cité* in French, *cité* designating an urban center with a cathedral (a bishopric), but this distinction became less significant in the early modern period. See the first edition of the *Le dictionnaire de l'Académie françoise* ..., 2 vols. (1694), http://artfl-project.uchicago.edu/node/45. On the evolution of the vocabulary used to designate urban phenomena in various languages, see Christian Topalov et al., eds., *L'aventure des mots de la ville* (Paris, 2010). For the polysemy of the concept of the "city" in urban studies, see Marcel Roncayolo, *La ville et ses territoires* (Paris, 1997), 28. For the urban origins on many migrants to Canada, see Leslie Choquette, *Frenchmen into Peasants: Modernity and Tradition in the Peopling of French Canada* (Cambridge, Mass., 1997), 21.

this monograph focuses on the city and analyzes what defined racial slavery within the urban center in comparison with its surrounding plantations; on the other, it contradicts both antagonist views of racial formation that have been previously advocated by historians of the Mississippi colony, arguing that New Orleans was deeply shaped by racial ideas and practices from the outset and that this early implementation of a system of racial domination made it a Caribbean port city. Such a thesis goes against the tension frequently highlighted by American scholars between North American and West Indian racial regimes, the former being allegedly marked by rigidity and the latter by fluidity. New Orleans was not a Caribbean port city because its system of racial slavery was less oppressive and exclusive and offered more loopholes than in English North American colonies—a leniency that would have been epitomized by a group of free men and women of color. The Louisiana capital was a Caribbean port city for the way racial prejudice quickly came to inform all its social institutions and relations, despite the lack of a large population of free blacks during most of the French regime. Even though race did not operate in the same manner in West Indian and in North American slave societies, it mattered as much in both places. Moreover, the mainland surroundings of the greater Caribbean constituted places of intersection between the North American and West Indian worlds.

To be sure, the North American and Caribbean plantation systems did differ. The relatively small size of its plantations, the moderate disproportion of slaves in comparison with white settlers, the presence of masters on estates, and the natural growth of the slave population after the 1740s brought the French Louisiana plantation system closer to the one prevailing in the southern colonies of British North America than to the one thriving in the British or French Caribbean islands. The proximity between some North American and West Indian colonies, nevertheless, is more obvious when their port cities are considered, rather than their plantation regions. To the comparison drawn by Emma Hart and Trevor Burnard between the main urban centers of South Carolina and Jamaica one can add the Louisiana capital and argue with them that New Orleans, "Charleston[,] and Kingston shared much more with each other than they did with their hinterlands." The three cities developed "a surprisingly diverse economy, only partially connected to the plantation world that lay outside their borders."[27]

Even more importantly, the existence of differences between North

27. Burnard and Hart, "Kingston, Jamaica, and Charleston, South Carolina," *Journal of Urban History*, XXXIX (2013), 216, 220, 221–222.

American and Caribbean slave systems, whether on plantations or within cities, does not mean that the various ways slavery and race intersected in both places should be considered as two antithetical models. Many American historians still consider the American racial regime as exceptional. Because they tend to reduce racialization to the issue of the status of free people of color, they contrast the biracial society that emerged in English North America and flourished in the United States with the three-tiered societies of the British West Indies or French Antilles instead of viewing all of them as variations of slave societies that were equally shaped by a racial vision of the social order. In their conception, the presence of large groups of free people of color in the British and French islands should be read as a sign of a weaker significance of race. Yet these Caribbean societies posited the same superiority of white people as in North America and increasingly discriminated against free people of color. Moreover, race manifested itself in many other ways than in the status of free blacks.[28]

SLAVERY, URBANITY, AND RACE

By focusing on the urban slave society and challenging the traditional historiographical boundaries between North America and the Antilles on the issue of racial slavery, *Caribbean New Orleans* aims to do more than participate in the debate that has developed about race in Louisiana history. First, the book calls for the development of a more complex understanding of the concepts of slavery and slave society. Although chattel slavery is frequently reduced to a form of bound labor in American historiography, this view cannot explain why Europeans always perceived the slave institution as different from other types of bound labor and only enslaved non-Europeans. Likewise, an economically successful plantation society is often posited as

28. For studies on people of color in the French Antilles, see Yvan Debbasch, *Couleur et liberté: Le jeu du critère ethnique dans un ordre juridique esclavagiste*, I, *L'affranchi dans les possessions françaises de la Caraïbe (1635–1833)* (Paris, 1967); John D. Garrigus, *Before Haiti: Race and Citizenship in French Saint-Domingue* (New York, 2006); Stewart R. King, *Blue Coat or Powdered Wig: Free People of Color in Pre-Revolutionary Saint Domingue* (Athens, Ga., 2001); Auguste Lebeau, *De la condition des gens de couleur libres sous l'Ancien Régime; D'après des documents des archives coloniales* (Paris, 1903); Louis, *Les libres de couleur en Martinique*, I; Jessica Pierre-Louis, "Les libres de couleur face au préjugé: Franchir la barrière à la Martinique aux XVIIe–XVIIIe siècles" (Ph.D. diss., Université des Antilles et de la Guyane, 2015); and Dominique Rogers, "Les libres de couleur dans les capitales de Saint-Domingue: Fortune, mentalités, et intégration à la fin de l'Ancien Régime (1776–1789)" (Ph.D. diss., Université Michel de Montaigne, 1999).

Introduction

the only true model of a slave society instead of considering the concepts of a society with slaves and a slave society as two extreme archetypes with many variations in between, which could allow for the existence of several kinds of slave societies.[29]

What characterized a slave society was the way slavery came to shape all social institutions and relationships. The importance of the enslaved in the overall population and system of production was a necessary but not a sufficient condition. Labor was central in defining slavery in the New World, as slaves there spent most of their time toiling under harsh conditions, but American chattel slavery was more than a labor regime—it was first of all a form of ownership. Enslaved people could be exploited in dreadful ways because they were legally considered chattel property. In fact, they had a dual legal character, being defined by law as both a thing and a person. Because slavery meant holding human beings as possessions, enslaved people found themselves under the permanent personal domination of owners who could control every aspect of their lives—not only their work—and could even take their lives with impunity (in practice, if not in law) and dispose of their children. Hence, the reliance on chattel slavery everywhere in the western hemisphere stemmed not only from the economic benefits such a system provided but also from the social preeminence conferred by the exercise of proprietary power over other human beings. Slavery participated in a moral economy of dignity and honor typical of ancien régime societies. For slaves, it meant that the dishonor associated with slavery and the slave stain were thought to remain with them after manumission. When this violent and abusive system was applied to a large section or even to a vast majority of the overall population, who had to be forcibly brought from abroad, the

29. On the distinctive character of slavery, see David Eltis, "Labour and Coercion in the English Atlantic World from the Seventeenth to the Early Twentieth Century," *Slavery and Abolition*, XIV, no. 1 (1993), 207–226; and Eltis, "Europeans and the Rise and Fall of African Slavery in the Americas: An Interpretation," *American Historical Review*, XCVIII (1993), 1399–1423. For the most influential conceptions of societies with slaves and slave societies in American historiography, see Berlin, *Many Thousands Gone*, 8–9; and Philip D. Morgan, "British Encounters with Africans and African-Americans, circa 1600–1780," in Bernard Bailyn and Morgan, eds., *Strangers within the Realm: Cultural Margins of the First British Empire* (Chapel Hill, N.C., 1991), 157–219. For works criticizing Moses Finley's definition of a slave society, which has been a source of inspiration for Berlin and Morgan, see Paulin Ismard, "Écrire l'histoire de l'esclavage: Entre approche globale et perspective comparatiste," *Annales: Histoire, Sciences Sociales*, LXXII (2017), 9–43; and Noel Lenski and Catherine M. Cameron, eds., *What Is a Slave Society? The Practice of Slavery in Global Perspective* (Cambridge, 2018).

whole free society, both slaveowners and free nonslaveholders, had to be committed to its perpetuation, since this highly unequal and exploitative social order could never become self-evident and remained contested and resisted. Slavery thus necessarily operated as a regime of collective governance that involved all free people while reflecting the preeminent political and social position of slaveowners.[30]

With such a definition of a slave society, it becomes possible to view urban slavery differently from many of the studies that have started to multiply on the subject. Urban societies with slavery are often depicted as "frontier societies" because urban slaves were generally less harshly exploited and were offered more opportunities for autonomy and even freedom via manumission (always more frequent in urban settings) than on plantations. But such characterizations fail to explain how urban slavery managed to reproduce itself despite the subversive forces that tended to mitigate the slave system in the urban milieu. Admittedly, New Orleans became a different kind of slave society from that of its surrounding plantation region; as in any other city, slaves there did enjoy certain distinct advantages. Yet what defined urban slavery was, not its supposed openness and fluidity, but rather the continual tensions between slaves' unrest and struggle for greater autonomy and dignity, on the one hand, and an adaptive collective policy of surveillance, discipline, and containment, on the other. These tensions were further enhanced by the connections that existed between the urban and plantation worlds, even though the city formed a distinct sociopolitical space. New Orleans played a crucial role in the monitoring and

30. On the centrality of work in defining the various slave systems and shaping slave life, see Ira Berlin and Philip D. Morgan, eds., *Cultivation and Culture: Labor and the Shaping of Slave Life in the Americas* (Charlottesville, Va., 1993). Although I include the concept of property in my definition of slavery, I draw on Orlando Patterson's conception of slavery as one of the most extreme relationships of domination, which could be motivated by the search for economic benefit or social prestige or even by both. See Patterson, *Slavery and Social Death: A Comparative Study* (Cambridge, Mass., 1982). For slaves' legal duality as being defined as both property and personhood, see Malick W. Ghachem, "The Slave's Two Bodies: The Life of an American Legal Fiction," *William and Mary Quarterly*, LX (2003), 809–842; and Jean-François Niort, "L'esclave dans le Code Noir de 1685," in Olivier Grenouilleau, ed., *Esclaves: Une humanité en sursis* (Rennes, France, 2012), 221–240. My definition of a slave society is inspired by Elsa V. Goveia's pioneering book on the Leeward Islands. See Goveia, *Slave Society in the British Leeward Islands at the End of the Eighteenth Century* (New Haven, Conn., 1965). For the role of Goveia alongside Moses Finley in promoting the concept of a slave society, see B. W. Higman, "The Invention of Slave Society," in Brian L. Moore et al., eds., *Slavery, Freedom, and Gender: The Dynamics of Caribbean Society* (Kingston, Jamaica, 2001), 57–75.

Introduction

discipline of the surrounding plantation slave population while the way en-slaved laborers were treated on plantations nearby affected the relations urban slaveholders maintained with their slaves. Moreover, in some ways, the relative demographic balance between free and enslaved people, the greater social and ethnic diversity, the presence of a large transient popu-lation of sailors and soldiers, the spatial proximity that facilitated all kinds of exchanges, and the size and density of the population that complicated efforts of surveillance and control made race even more important in cities than on plantations.[31]

Secondly, *Caribbean New Orleans* seeks to propose a renewed perspec-tive on race. Rather than studying race relations, it focuses on racial forma-tion, or racialization. The former tends to reify and essentialize racial iden-tities and confuses racial categories with social groups. Even when race is a crucial category of identification, it always intersects in complex ways with other categories of difference, such as status, class, religion, and gender, all those categories reinforcing or contradicting each other. The concept of racial formation conveys the idea that race is an unstable and contested social construct that needs to be constantly re-instantiated and re-enacted. Racialization is viewed as a dynamic and protean process.[32]

31. For the characterization of urban societies with slavery as "frontier societies," see Morgan, "British Encounters with Africans and African-Americans," in Bailyn and Mor-gan, eds., *Strangers within the Realm*, 190–193. For studies of urban slavery outside New Orleans, see among other books Ira Berlin and Leslie M. Harris, eds., *Slavery in New York* (New York, 2005); Herman L. Bennett, *Africans in Colonial Mexico: Absolutism, Chris-tianity, and Afro-Creole Consciousness, 1570–1640* (Bloomington, Ind., 2003); Cañizares-Esguerra, Childs, and Sidbury, eds., *Black Urban Atlantic in the Age of the Slave Trade*; Mariana L. R. Dantas, *Black Townsmen: Urban Slavery and Freedom in the Eighteenth-Century Americas* (New York, 2008); Thelma Wills Foote, *Black and White Manhattan: The History of Racial Formation in Colonial New York City* (Oxford, 2004); Jared Ross Hardesty, *Unfreedom: Slavery and Dependence in Eighteenth-Century Boston* (New York, 2016); Mary C. Karasch, *Slave Life in Rio de Janeiro, 1808–1850* (Princeton, N.J., 1987); Jill Lepore, *New York Burning: Liberty, Slavery, and Conspiracy in Eighteenth-Century Manhattan* (New York, 2005); Morgan, "Black Life in Eighteenth-Century Charleston," *Perspectives in American History*, New Ser., I (1984), 187–232; Anne Pérotin-Dumon, *La ville aux îles: La ville dans l'île: Basse-Terre et Pointe-à-Pitre, Guadeloupe, 1650–1820* (Paris, 2000); Tamara J. Walker, *Exquisite Slaves: Race, Clothing, and Status in Colonial Lima* (Cambridge, 2017); and Welch, *Slave Society in the City*. For a similar understand-ing of urban slavery in early nineteenth-century New Orleans than the one advocated in this book, see Johnson, *Slavery's Metropolis*.

32. For Michael Omi and Howard Winant, racial formation is "the sociohistorical process by which racial categories are created, inhabited, transformed, and destroyed."

With an emphasis on the circulation of racial ideas and practices within the French Empire and the Atlantic world, this monograph contributes not only to the debate about racial formation in Louisiana history but also, more broadly, Atlantic studies. A racial dimension is often presented as what distinguished the chattel slavery developed by Europeans in the Americas from other slave systems in world history. Nonetheless, a long-standing debate has been waged in Anglophone historiography about the origins of African slavery and the relationship between African slavery and racism—within the English Atlantic world—racism being considered alternatively as a cause or a consequence of African slavery. Most historians now agree that racial prejudice against Africans existed long before northwestern Europeans joined the Iberians in colonizing the New World but that the growth of the Atlantic slave trade and the expansion of the slave system in the Americas reinforced this original racism. Although scholars admit that all American slave societies became more racialized over time, they disagree on chronology.[33]

See Omi and Winant, *Racial Formation in the United States: From the 1960s to the 1990s*, 2d ed. (New York, 1994), 55. For theoretical work distinguishing categories and groups, see Pierre Bourdieu, "The Social Space and the Genesis of Groups," *Theory and Society*, XIV (1985), 723–744; Rogers Brubaker, "Ethnicity without Group," *European Journal of Sociology*, XLIII (2002), 163–189; and Brubaker, Mara Loveman, and Peter Stamatov, "Ethnicity as Cognition," *Theory and Society*, XXXIII (2004), 31–64. On the interplay between race, culture, and religion in the early modern period, see Silvia Sebastiani, *The Scottish Enlightenment: Race, Gender, and the Limits of Progress*, trans. Jeremy Carden (New York, 2013), 13–14. For a call to better take into account both race and class and to analyze their complex relationships in American history, see Barbara J. Fields, "Ideology and Race in American History," in J. Morgan Kousser and James M. McPherson, eds., *Religion, Race, and Reconstruction: Essays in Honor of C. Vann Woodward* (New York, 1982), 143–178.

33. For summaries of the debate on the relationship between slavery and racism in the case of Virginia, see Alden T. Vaughan, "The Origins Debate: Slavery and Racism in Seventeenth-Century Virginia," in "'A Sense of Their Own Power': Black Virginians, 1619–1989," special issue, *Virginia Magazine of History and Biography*, XCVII (1989), 311–354; John C. Coombs, "Beyond the 'Origins Debate': Rethinking the Rise of Virginia Slavery," in Douglas Bradburn and Coombs, eds., *Early Modern Virginia: Reconsidering the Old Dominion* (Charlottesville, Va., 2011), 239–278; and Rebecca Anne Goetz, "Rethinking the 'Unthinking Decision': Old Questions and New Problems in the History of Slavery and Race in the Colonial South," *Journal of Southern History*, LXXV (2009), 599–612. Among many works on the origins of African slavery in Atlantic perspective, see David Eltis, *The Rise of African Slavery in the Americas* (Cambridge, 2000); David Brion Davis, *Inhuman Bondage: The Rise and Fall of Slavery in the New World* (Oxford,

The debate on the chronology of racial formation mobilizes two kinds of arguments. The first one concerns the intellectual history of race. Many historians—like most people—commonly think of race as a set of ideas and discourses; practices of racial discrimination and violence are the fruit of these racist ideas. Ideas always precede and propel actions. Hence, an intellectual history of race is the necessary foundation of a sociopolitical history of race. Racial prejudice cannot be mobilized to explain discriminative and violent treatment of people deemed as inferior before the development of an intellectual and scientific debate on race in the second half of the eighteenth century or the formulation of coherent theories of race in the nineteenth century. In contrast, *Caribbean New Orleans* conceives of race as a political resource that was used not only to justify but also to operate the slave system. Race and racism are always intertwined. The intellectual and practical manifestations of race invariably develop in tandem and stimulate each other, even though they maintain complex relationships. Consequently, the book contends that racialization in the Atlantic world started well before the second half of the eighteenth century.[34]

The reluctance of many historians to use the concept of race to characterize relations of domination between people of European, African, and Native American descent in the Atlantic world before the second half of the eighteenth century and, for some, before the nineteenth century, is based on a series of problematic assumptions. During the early modern period, historical actors did not often use the word "race" to designate the transmission of physical or moral and social characters through bodily fluids, such as blood or sperm, from one generation to the next. Yet it does not mean that the notion behind the word did not already belong to their conception of the social order and inform social dynamics. Furthermore, the documentation on slave societies reveals multiple forms of discrimination, exploitation, and violence against the enslaved, but historical actors in positions of domination rarely justified such behavior. Thus, opponents to an early chronology of racial formation maintain that other categories of difference such as religion and culture explain slaves' harsh treatment. In the case of French New Orleans, little evidence remains of the way local authorities and colonists

---

2006); and Robin Blackburn, *The Making of New World Slavery: From the Baroque to the Modern, 1492–1800* (London, 1997).

34. On the complex relationships between the intellectual and practical manifestations of race, see Sebastiani, *Scottish Enlightenment*, trans. Carden; and Claude-Olivier Doron, *L'homme altéré: Races et dégénérescence (XVIIe–XIXe siècles)* (Ceyzérieu, France, 2016), 36–37.

defined and conceived of race. What there is, however, shows that race-thinking, not only color prejudice, informed the attitude and policy of officials and colonists toward African slaves and their descendants. Elite men are the only historical actors who left writings on the subject, but the differences they emphasized and the hierarchy they established between whites, blacks, and people of mixed descent were related to the idea of race in association with genealogy and heredity.[35]

Another reason for the skepticism against an early chronology of racial formation is the association commonly made between "biological racism" and scientific racism. Nevertheless, some scholars have shown that the notion of race was already available when New Orleans was founded. It existed well before the naturalists and philosophers of the Enlightenment started to discuss the subject in the second half of the eighteenth century. Race does not necessarily need science to transform itself into an ideology. The early prevalence of racial prejudice in French New Orleans demonstrates that slave societies only needed rudimentary notions of race to become racialized, not fully formalized and systematized scientific racist theories. The way slaves were exploited and abused further fueled racial

35. It is essential to pay attention to the vernacular categories used by historical actors as they reveal much about their sociocultural conceptions. At the same time, scholars should not let historical actors define their analytical categories, as Paul A. Kramer has argued for the concept of empire or imperial formation. Similar to "race," the word "empire" was rarely used by historical actors to designate the early modern French Empire before the revolutionary period. Yet global France did operate as an imperial formation. See Kramer, "Power and Connection: Imperial Histories of the United States in the World," *American Historical Review*, CXVI (2011), 1348–1391; and François-Joseph Ruggiu, "Des nouvelles France aux colonies—Une approche comparée de l'histoire impériale de la France de l'époque moderne," *Nuevo Mundo Mundos Nuevos*, 2018, https://journals.openedition.org/nuevomundo/72123#. For the idea that most works on race do not really study race but trace the impact of other categories of difference, see Joyce Chaplin, "Race," in David Armitage and Michael J. Braddick, eds., *The British Atlantic World, 1500–1800* (New York, 2002), 155. In opposition to *Caribbean New Orleans*'s early chronology of racial formation, Francophone historians of the early modern Antilles, often refuse to use the concept of race and prefer to write about color prejudice (*"préjugé de couleur"*), which they view as distinct from "biological racism." See Florence Gauthier, *L'aristocratie de l'épiderme: Le combat de la Société des Citoyens de Couleur, 1789–1791* (Paris, 2007), 9; Mélanie Lamotte, "Colour Prejudice in the French Atlantic World," in D'Maris Coffman, Adrian Leonard, and William O'Reilly, eds., *The Atlantic World* (London, 2014), 151–171; Frédéric Régent, *Esclavage, métissage, liberté: La Révolution française en Guadeloupe, 1789–1802* (Paris, 2004); and Rogers, "Les libres de couleur dans les capitales de Saint-Domingue."

Introduction

conceptions. Discriminative and violent practices against racialized people are as important as intellectual and scientific theories, for they sustain and reinforce racist assumptions as they help internalize them. Because racialized people are treated differently, the thinking goes, they must therefore be different and inferior. The intellectual and scientific debate about race that intensified from the 1760s onward was not the cause but an expression of the general process of racialization that had started to expand within the Atlantic world alongside imperialism and colonialism and that took its harshest forms in the slave societies of the Americas starting in the late seventeenth century. This debate arose as the slave system flourished and began to require further justification in the face of emerging criticism in the mid-eighteenth century; even so, the system of racial domination was already well advanced by that time in American slave societies.[36]

36. For the availability of the notion of race in the early modern period as early as the fifteenth century, see James H. Sweet, "The Iberian Roots of American Racist Thought," *William and Mary Quarterly*, LIV (1997), 143–166; Jean-Frédéric Schaub, *Pour une histoire politique de la race* ([Paris], 2015); and Schaub and Silvia Sebastiani, "Savoirs de l'autre? L'émergence des questions de race," in Dominique Pestre, ed., *Histoire des sciences et des savoirs*, I, *De la Renaissance aux Lumières*, ed. Stéphane Van Damme (Paris, 2015), 283–304. For the opposite view that the idea of race only took hold in the second half of the eighteenth and early nineteenth centuries, see Ivan Hannaford, *Race: The History of an Idea in the West* (Baltimore, 1996). For works on the eighteenth-century intellectual and scientific debate on race in the French Empire, see Andrew S. Curran, *The Anatomy of Blackness: Science and Slavery in an Age of Enlightenment* (Baltimore, 2011); and Doron, *L'homme altéré*. Some historians oppose biological and cultural racism. However, historical actors always conceive of race as a mixture of biology and culture. They consider that racial difference can manifest itself through phenotype or other physical characters but also through the way people speak and behave. For studies demonstrating such a phenomenon even at the peak of scientific racism in the second half of the nineteenth century and in the first half of the twentieth century, see Ariela J. Gross, *What Blood Won't Tell: A History of Race on Trial* (Cambridge, 2008); and Ann Laura Stoler, *Carnal Knowledge and Imperial Power: Race and the Intimate in Colonial Rule* (Berkeley, Calif., 2002). Still a biological dimension has to be involved in order to differentiate the concept of race from that of ethnicity and to distinguish racism from xenophobia. See Schaub, *Pour une histoire politique de la race*, 97–166. The concept of race-thinking expresses the idea that racialization started to expand before the development of philosophical and scientific theories of race in the second half of the eighteenth century. It was first borrowed from Hannah Arendt by Irene Silverblatt to demonstrate how "the dance of bureaucracy and race" originated in early modern imperialism. See Arendt, "Race-Thinking before Racism," *Review of Politics*, VI (1944), 36–73; and Silverblatt, *Modern Inquisitions: Peru and the Colonial Origins of the Civilized World* (Durham, N.C., 2004), 3–4, 16–19. For the view that a partial and incoherent idea of race in

Social scientists who argue that racism characterizes modernity also claim that race was not needed before the expansion of abolitionism or even before the abolition of slavery. Yet defending an early chronology of racial formation is compatible with the recognition that the racialization of the Atlantic world, albeit in no way a linear and inescapable process, experienced several inflexions from the fifteenth century onward. Before the development of an intellectual and scientific debate on race in the mid-eighteenth century, the last decades of the seventeenth century constituted one such critical moment. The early questioning of the religious foundations of government and knowledge in Europe coincided with the rise of the transatlantic slave trade and the multiplication of slave societies in the Americas. The new significance of race in English and French slave societies was linked to the tensions between slavery and religion. Institutional and social actors disagreed on both the need to Christianize the enslaved and the consequences of slaves' evangelization. As it became more difficult, in the context of this debate, to use religion to justify slavery, they increasingly turned to race to legitimize the enslavement and the discriminative and violent treatment of Africans as slaves. In the English Empire, the growing emphasis on race over religion in defining black slaves' alterity led settlers in the 1680s to stop referring to themselves primarily as Christians and, instead, to collectively self-identify as English or whites.[37]

------

the absence of full-blown racial theory was enough to sustain an exploitive and violent system of domination, see Sweet, "Iberian Roots of American Racist Thought," *William and Mary Quarterly*, LIV (1997), 165; and Chaplin, "Race," in Armitage and Braddick, eds., *British Atlantic World*, 166–167. For the idea that a discriminative and violent treatment of racialized people further fuels racism, see Barbara Jeanne Fields, "Slavery, Race, and Ideology in the United States of America," *New Left Review*, CLXXXI (May–June 1990), 95–118, esp. 106–108.

37. For the debate on the religious foundations of systems of government and knowledge beginning in the late seventeenth century, see Paul Hazard, *La crise de la conscience européenne, (1680–1715)*, 2 vols. (Paris, 1935); and David A. Bell, *The Cult of the Nation in France: Inventing Nationalism, 1680–1800* (Cambridge, Mass., 2001), 22–49. On the relationships between slavery, religion, and race, see Winthrop D. Jordan, *White over Black: American Attitudes toward the Negro, 1550–1812* (Chapel Hill, N.C., 1968), 20–24, 91–98, 179–215; Colin Kidd, *The Forging of Races: Race and Scripture in the Protestant Atlantic World, 1600–2000* (Cambridge, 2006); Guillaume Aubert, "'To Establish One Law and Definite Rules': Race, Religion, and the Transatlantic Origins of the Louisiana Code Noir," in Cécile Vidal, ed., *Louisiana: Crossroads of the Atlantic World* (Philadelphia, 2014), 21–43; Rebecca Anne Goetz, *The Baptism of Early Virginia: How Christianity Created Race* (Baltimore, 2012); and Katharine Gerbner, *Christian Slavery: Protestant Missions and Slave Conversion in the Atlantic World, 1660–1760* (Philadelphia, 2018).

As the issue of slaves' religious integration shows, historians also discuss the chronology of racial formation on the basis of the material and social manifestations of race—the practices of discrimination, exploitation, and violence justified by a belief in the allegedly natural inferiority of a subordinated people. In the case of the French Empire, many consider that racial prejudice became prevalent only after the Seven Years' War. They point out that, after the conflict, it became increasingly difficult for elite planters of mixed descent in Saint-Domingue to pass as whites and that discrimination against free people of color started to spread. For all that, does this shift in the system of racial domination necessarily imply that race did not already decisively shape social dynamics before that period? Does it mean that a society cannot be considered racialized if class seems to take precedence over race, even if this holds true for only a small minority of men and women? The willingness of some free men and women of color to pass as white is evidence that their socioracial status was unbearable. The existence of racial crossing does not mean that a society that allowed such a change of condition was flexible. In Saint-Domingue, as everywhere in the Americas, whitening sanctioned the idea of white supremacy.[38]

Such a discussion raises the question of how to measure, circumscribe, and comprehend racialization in all its dimensions. The book's answer is that, besides the legal and social treatment of *métissage* (interracial unions) and the status of free people of color, on which most social historians of early American societies focus, one also needs to take into account the multiple mechanisms by which race insinuated itself in every domain of social life, not only in the intimate sphere of sexuality and the family. *Caribbean New Orleans* demonstrates that the Louisiana capital's society became racialized even though free people of color remained a small minority in comparison with slaves who quickly became the city's majority. The enslaved—not free people of color—were the first targets of racial politics. As a result, the book also questions the idea that the opposition between biracial societies and three-tiered societies, where free people of color occupy a space in-between whites and black slaves, can subsume the diversity of racial regimes. This divide highlights major differences existing between systems of racial slavery in the Americas, but it also obscures many other expressions of racial domination that they in fact shared.[39]

38. Garrigus, *Before Haiti*.

39. I use the modern French expression *métissage*, which was not in use in the early modern period, since the word "miscegenation" has such a racist connotation in present-day American society. However, the idea of métissage in the eighteenth century was no

Treating the biracial and three-tiered slave societies of North America and the Caribbean as two distinct models also gives the impression that racial regimes linked to the slave system were immobile, whereas they always adapted themselves in reaction to changing circumstances. Such an approach goes along with the idea that fixity characterizes racialized societies. Admittedly, the very idea of race implies fixity since it is based on biological determinism. As Jean-Frédéric Shaub has observed, "Racial thinking immobilizes populations in a time without history." However, following the work of Kathryn Burn and other historians, we need to unfix and historicize race. Even when race becomes embedded in a society, racial ideas and practices, or, the meanings and uses of racial categories, are never fixed and stable. French New Orleans provides an ideal case study to demonstrate that, although race played a significant role from the start, the way racial prejudice materialized never ceased to evolve with changing local and extralocal circumstances. It also shows that racial crossings are inherent to racialized societies; yet these societies are not less racialized because the racial order can never be absolute and monolithic. Social dynamics always contradict the immobilization in time that race-thinking seeks to achieve, making racial formation a contingent and pliable process, one that adapts to constant and multiple tensions and perturbations.[40]

------

less related to race-thinking than that of miscegenation. When the expression "métissage" appeared in the nineteenth century to designate hybridity or crossbreeds between first animals and then human beings, it was linked to the development of a scientific theory of race. See Laurier Turgeon and Anne-Hélène Kerbiriou, "Métissages, de glissements en transferts de sens," in Turgeon, ed., *Regards croisés sur le métissage* (Sainte-Foy, Quebec, 2002), 1–20.

40. The idea that racialized societies are characterized by their fixity is commonly shared by historians of slavery and race. Simon Newman, for instance, seems to imply such a view when he writes that "other scholars have suggested that such fixed ideas and practices of race were unusual in the seventeenth and even the eighteenth centuries. [Some historians] have all demonstrated that multiple understanding of race existed in Britain and its Atlantic world, with a binary understanding of black and white emerging only in the eighteenth century, and not achieving primacy until the nineteenth century." See Newman, *New World of Labor*, 248. For the idea of immobilization in time at the heart of race-thinking, see Schaub, *Pour une histoire politique de la race*, 124–125; and Maurice Olender, *Race sans histoire* (Paris, 2009). On the necessity to better historicize racial ideas, categories, and practices, see Kathryn Burns, "Unfixing Race," in Margaret R. Greer, Walter D. Mignolo, and Maureen Quilligan, eds., *Rereading the Black Legend: The Discourses of Religious and Racial Difference in the Renaissance Empires* (Chicago, 2007), 188–202.

Caribbean New Orleans draws on two methodological approaches in order to analyze how racial formation unfolded under the influence of global, regional, and local circumstances: it practices a situated Atlantic history and develops a microhistory of race within the urban center. First, this monograph offers a comprehensive social history of New Orleans as a port city in imperial and Atlantic perspectives, but it does not intend to provide an explicit comparative history of the Louisiana capital with other urban hubs of the West Indies. Instead, the focal point is the social dynamics of the city over half a century within a broader geographical framework that helps to explain how local circumstances changed over time. It is a kind of cisatlantic history (studying the impact of Atlantic dynamics on a specific location and highlighting that, among all the connections New Orleans maintained with the rest of the Atlantic world, those with Saint-Domingue were crucial) rather than a transatlantic history (a comparative history of two or more locations within the Atlantic world), to use David Armitage's terminology. Still, to understand what made New Orleans a Caribbean port city, it is necessary to refer at points to what happened in Cap-Français, Port-au-Prince, Fort-Royal, or Saint-Pierre. The difficulty is that the historiography on the early Caribbean is much sparser than that on early North America. This is especially true for the French Antilles in comparison with the British West Indies. Prior work has also concentrated on the plantation world instead of cities; at present, there is still no modern monograph on early Cap Français, Saint-Pierre, Kingston, or Bridgetown. In the same way, whites have been the subject of less research than the enslaved and free people of color.[41]

41. For David Armitage's three ways of practicing Atlantic history, see Armitage, "Three Concepts of Atlantic History," in Armitage and Braddick, eds., *British Atlantic World*, 11–27. For previous studies of French New Orleans and Louisiana in Atlantic perspective, see Bradley G. Bond, ed., *French Colonial Louisiana and the Atlantic World* (Baton Rouge, La., 2005); William Boelhower, ed., *New Orleans in the Atlantic World: Between Land and Sea* (New York, 2013); and Vidal, ed., *Louisiana: Crossroads of the Atlantic World*. For historiographical works on the Caribbean, see Danielle Bégot, ed., *Guide de la recherche en histoire antillaise et guyanaise: Guadeloupe, Martinique, Saint-Domingue, Guyane, XVIIe–XXIe siècle*, 2 vols. (Paris, 2011); Juanita De Barros, Audra Diptee, and David V. Trotman, eds., *Beyond Fragmentation: Perspectives on Caribbean History* (Princeton, N.J., 2006); B. W. Higman, ed., *General History of the Caribbean*, VI, *Methodology and Historiography of the Caribbean* (London, 1999); Pérotin-Dumon, *La ville aux îles*, 48–86; Pérotin-Dumon, "Les ancêtres d'Aimé Césaire et Alexis Léger:

While locating New Orleans within a greater Caribbean world, it is also essential to consider the metropole and the colony in the same framework of analysis. The French Antilles had a huge impact on the way French New Orleans society developed, but this influence concerned mainly slavery and race. The Louisiana capital was never isolated from the metropole; ships carrying merchandise and people did not cease to circulate between New Orleans and France throughout the French regime. That Saint-Domingue increasingly mediated some of the connections with the Old World from the 1730s does not mean that New Orleans society was not also informed by the metropole.

Although Louisiana authorities and settlers could not reproduce the metropolitan social order, New Orleans was still an ancien régime society. The king was more distant than in metropolitan France. With only a handful of missionaries belonging to the regular orders, the Catholic Church could not exercise the same degree of control as it did in the kingdom. There were fewer nobles, and the significance of noble status was different, especially, since the central noble privilege of tax exemption was meaningless in the Mississippi colony where no direct taxes were imposed. Unlike in metropolitan France, public offices and military charges were not sold, which transformed the relationship between lineage, property, and power. The social composition of the population of European settlers was also much less complex and diversified in Louisiana. Above all, the development of racial slavery distinguished the colony from the metropole. Racial slavery, however, did not contradict the fundamental logic of the metropolitan ancien régime society but carried it to its logical extreme. France was a hierarchical, corporative society that was based on the acceptance of the principle of natural inequality. The main divide was between noblemen and commoners, and this divide was naturalized. This vision of the social world facilitated the racialization of multiethnic colonial and slave societies, both in the Antilles and in Louisiana. The ancien régime culture that people of European descent shared in both places helps to explain the way they behaved toward the enslaved.[42]

L'historiographie des Antilles françaises, 1970–1990," *Anuario des Estudios Americanos,* LII, no. 2 (1995), 289–316; and Dominique Rogers, "Les Antilles à l'époque moderne: Tendances et perspectives d'un demi-siècle de recherches francophones et anglophones en histoire sociale," in Cécile Vidal and François-Joseph Ruggiu, eds., *Sociétés, colonisations, et esclavages dans le monde atlantique: Historiographie des sociétés américaines des XVIe–XIXe siècles* (Bécherel, France, 2009), 243–281.

42. For the transformation of nobility in French colonies, see François-Joseph Ruggiu, "Une noblesse atlantique? Le second ordre français de l'Ancien au Nouveau Monde," in

Even as *Caribbean New Orleans* demonstrates that racial slavery did not develop in the Mississippi colony in isolation from both the metropole and the Antilles, it also argues that, although "law was one of [European] colonizing's most potent technologies—a means by which colonizers' designs, structures and institutions might be imagined, created, implemented and distributed," one needs to go beyond law to take the full measure of what it meant for an urban slave society to become racialized. The Code Noir was instrumental, but it should not be the sole or main object of investigation if one wants to track down the pervasive character of race in all its facets. Indeed, the enslaved were sometimes treated in the same way in different colonies even though the laws varied. In addition, the legal approach often tends to view racial formation as a top-down process. The Company of the Indies, and then the French crown, undeniably influenced the development of racial slavery through not only the elaboration and promulgation of slave laws but also the administration of justice, the production of censuses, the enrollment of slaves for the corvée, and the military enlistment of enslaved and free people of African descent. Public authorities were also directly involved as slaveholders, since they owned and managed a large group of slaves, and as slave traders for the Company of the Indies. Still, all historical actors, at every level of the social hierarchy, took part, consciously or unconsciously, willingly or reluctantly, in racialization.[43]

Caribbean New Orleans combines a legal and institutional perspective with the complementary approach of studying race in the individual interactions of daily life within the city. To put this methodological imperative into practice, every kind of primary source relevant for social history kept in French and American archives has been collected and analyzed: administrative correspondence and files, passenger lists, censuses, military rolls, land grants, lists of plantations, sacramental records, notarial deeds, court records, travel accounts, private correspondence, maps, engravings, and drawings.[44]

"L'Atlantique Français," special issue, *Outre-mers: Revue d'histoire*, XCVII, nos. 362–363 (2009), 39–63. For works showing how conceptions of nobility and race had much in common in the French Empire, see Guillaume Aubert, "'The Blood of France': Race and Purity of Blood in the French Atlantic World," *William and Mary Quarterly*, LXI (2004), 439–478; and Aubert, "Kinship, Blood, and the Emergence of the Racial Nation in the French Atlantic World, 1600–1789," in Christopher H. Johnson et al., eds., *Blood and Kinship: Matter for Metaphor from Ancient Rome to the Present* (New York, 2013), 175–195.

43. For the role of the law as a powerful tool in the service of colonization, see Tomlins, "Transplants and Timing," *Berkeley Law Scholarship Repository*, X (2009), 419.

44. This book adopts an anthropological and microsociological approach. For major

Among all the primary sources, the court records are certainly the most valuable. The Records of the Superior Council of Louisiana are located in the Louisiana State Museum in New Orleans. The Superior Council was established temporarily in 1712 and permanently in 1716. It functioned as high court of first instance for the colonial capital and its region and as high court of final appeal for the entire colony; it also prosecuted people of all statuses, free and enslaved. Separate slave courts were never created in French colonies, as in Spanish and Portuguese ones, while a dual system of criminal justice was established in British slave colonies. Soldiers, however, were tried before a military court. The collection is incomplete, but, besides many other documents, it comprises around two hundred civil or criminal suits over insults, assault, murder, theft, runaways, and desertion that have survived the ravages of time. Half of them concerned slaves and slavery. Yet the enslaved were not the only ones among the lowest rungs of the social ladder who were brought to court; free people of color and poor whites were also tried or appeared as witnesses. Still, plantation slaves quickly became the prime target of royal justice; urban slaves, in contrast, were rarely prosecuted. Enslaved men were also tried much more frequently than women. Although legal ordinances and judicial practice deprived many categories of people of the ability to testify in criminal trials, the social identities of witnesses were more diverse and partially compensate for the race, gender, and class imbalances among defendants.[45]

---

studies in microsociology, see Erving Goffman, *The Presentation of Self in Everyday Life* (1959; rpt. Harmondsworth, U.K., 1971); and Goffman, *Relations in Public: Microstudies of the Public Order* (New York, 1971).

45. This monograph draws on Arlette Farge's pioneering use of judicial archives. Among her many inspiring works, see Farge, *Vivre dans la rue à Paris au XVIIIe siècle* ([Paris], 1979); and Farge, *La vie fragile: Violence, pouvoirs, et solidarités à Paris au XVIIIe siècle* (Paris, 1986). For the creation of the Superior Council in Louisiana, see "Copie des lettres patentes pour l'établissement d'un Conseil Supérieur à la Louisiane pendant trois ans," Dec. 23, 1712, ANOM COL A 22, fols. 10v–12v; and "Édit pour l'établissement définitif d'un Conseil Supérieur de la Louisiane," September 1716, ANOM COL A 22, fols. 19–20. For slave courts in English colonies, see Diana Paton, "Punishment, Crime, and the Bodies of Slaves in Eighteenth-Century Jamaica," *Journal of Social History*, XXXIV (2001), 927; and Betty Wood, "'Until He Shall Be Dead, Dead, Dead': The Judicial Treatment of Slaves in Eighteenth-Century Georgia," *Georgia Historical Society*, LXXI (1987), 380. A few trials of soldiers are kept in the records of the Superior Council of Louisiana. The administrative correspondence mentions or includes other criminal trials. For the evolution in the choice of witnesses in the French judicial system throughout the eighteenth century, see Benoît Garnot, "La justice pénale et les témoins

The voices of destitute people, slaves in particular, have been recorded. Defendants and witnesses were questioned in private by the magistrate in charge of the case. The judicial procedure was inquisitorial and secretive, and hearings were not public. At the beginning of the French period, judges sometimes needed to rely on an African or French interpreter of African languages to translate statements into French. In interrogatory after interrogatory, testimony after testimony, one can sense variations in the way the clerk transcribed the words of the defendants and witnesses, but most of the time it is impossible to identify the nature and to quantify the level of distortion and translation except for the use of indirect discourse. What is certain is that, although not everyone shared the same ability to tell stories and to adapt their level of language to the judicial circumstances, especially when French was not their native language, most recorded statements were made intelligible. The clerk only occasionally transcribed incorrect grammatical sentences in direct speech.[46]

Although the content of the interrogatories was oriented by the questions that were asked and that were prepared in advance, the judge let the defendants reply freely and at great length, and they provided much more information than what strictly concerned the offense or crime itself. Their responses were nevertheless shaped by the issues at stake. Slaves risked terrible corporal punishment and even the death penalty. They were sometimes subjected to preparatory questioning (torture imposed before the final sentence in order to elicit the defendant's confession) or preliminary questioning (torture applied before the execution of the sentence to obtain the confession of other crimes or the denunciation of accomplices). Fear and the need to defend oneself could trigger omissions, distortions, or lies, but it could also lead defendants to say much more than they needed to. Moreover, explanations had to appear plausible. What men and women summoned in court thought could convince a judge is as much of interest for the historian as what really happened. The interrogatories and testimonies reflect norms public authorities wanted to impose, but they also reveal, through the stories the defendants and witnesses told and the manners

---

en France au 18e siècle: De la théorie à la pratique," *Dix-huitième siècle*, no. 39 (2007), 99–108.

46. For the use of interpreters of African languages, see RSCL 1723/12/02/01, 1723/12/02/02, 1723/12/02/03; 1729/09/05/05, 1729/09/05/06; 1729/11/06/01; 1765/02/16/01. In 1767, exceptionally, the judge had to ask for an English translator for several slaves belonging to an English merchant residing in New Orleans. See RSCL 1767/04/25/01, 1767/04/29/01.

they used to express themselves, the representations, beliefs, and values of the speakers.[47]

The court records offer an extraordinary window into the daily lives and social worlds of New Orleans's dwellers. Without them, it would have been impossible to focus so closely on individuals of all conditions and backgrounds. The judicial proceedings, when contextualized with other kinds of primary sources, present a chorus of voices and a collection of snapshots of social encounters, a polyphonic and relational history of urban slavery. It is in the fabric of everyday life that the manifestations and expressions of racialization are analyzed. Thanks to the myriad anecdotes told by defendants and witnesses, the doings of all historical actors have been captured in the city's streets, at church and in taverns, in workshops, stores, and domestic interiors, in the marketplace, and at court as they talked, socialized, exchanged, and dealt with one another.

This microhistory of the Louisiana capital reveals that race shaped the slave system and expressed itself in multiple ways. It drove the language that all historical actors used to express their vision of the social order. It informed the way people presented themselves, socialized, and solved their conflicts in public. It directed the organization of both public and domestic spaces. It changed the conception of and relation to labor among whites while modeling trading exchanges. It structured the family and friendship networks on which people relied for assistance. It transformed the way justice was rendered, shaped the system of charity, and informed the military defense of the colony. Since New Orleans became a place of refuge for white people and a place of repression for the enslaved, it even influenced the relationships all social actors maintained with the Louisiana capital. The "process of calling blackness into being," to borrow an expression from Jennifer Morgan, was matched by a similar progressive construction of whiteness, as

47. For reflections about the problems raised by the use of judicial archives, see Joanne Bailey, *Unquiet Lives: Marriage and Marriage Breakdown in England, 1660–1800* (Cambridge, 2003), 22–27; Bailey, "Voices in Court: Lawyers' or Litigants'?" *Historical Research*, LXIV (2001), 392–408; Natalie Zemon Davis, *Pour sauver sa vie: Les récits de pardon au XVIe siècle*, trans. Christian Cler (Paris, 1988); Arlette Farge, *Le goût de l'archive* (Paris, 1989); Michel Heichette, *Société, sociabilité, justice: Sablé et son pays au XVIIIe siècle* (Rennes, France, 2005), 19–41; Robert Muchembled, *La violence au village (XVe–XVIIe siècle): Sociabilité et comportements populaires en Artois du XVe au XVIIe siècle* (Turnhout, Belgium, 1989); Natalie Zacek, "Voices and Silences: The Problem of Slave Testimony in the English West Indian Law Court," *Slavery and Abolition*, XXIV, no. 3 (December 2003), 24–39; and Gunvor Simonsen, *Slave Stories: Law, Representation, and Gender in the Danish West Indies* (Aarhus, Denmark, [2017]).

settlers not only racialized, discriminated, and abused people of African or mixed descent but internalized and performed their own contrasting racial identity. The development of this totalizing system of racial slavery made New Orleans a Caribbean port city.[48]

RACIAL FORMATION UNDER VARIOUS LENSES

To demonstrate how the system of racial domination in New Orleans was shaped both by relationships with Saint-Domingue and by local circumstances and to make sense of the ways race informed every aspect of social life from the most public to the most private, this book keeps to a spatial logic while paying attention to the evolution of racialization. It follows a double movement of zoom in and out, moving from outside the city to the intimate heart of New Orleans and the other way round. The first chapters analyze how urban social dynamics were fashioned by connections between New Orleans and the rest of the Atlantic world (Chapter 1) and the Louisiana capital and its hinterland (Chapter 2) as well as by interactions in the public space of the port city (Chapter 3) and within urban households (Chapter 4). Over time, New Orleans emerged as a distinct sociopolitical community whose elite vainly tried to stand aloof from Native Americans and to control the movements of the surrounding slave populations, even as a racialization of space and spatialization of race developed within the city. In domestic households and residential institutions, where physical proximity was inescapable, social mechanisms were implemented to create and perpetuate social distance and racial domination. As for the most intimate relationships (explored in Chapter 5), the modalities of sexuality and family were, to a great extent, determined by status, race, and gender.

The focus then broadens once more as the remaining chapters examine how social institutions such as labor (Chapter 6), trade and credit (Chapter 7), and justice and militia service (Chapter 8) were transformed in this

48. For the "process of calling blackness into being," see Jennifer L. Morgan, *Laboring Women: Reproduction and Gender in New World Slavery* (Philadelphia, 2004), 12. On the rise of whiteness studies since the 1990s, see the essays by Peter Kolchin, "Whiteness Studies: The New History of Race in America," *Journal of American History*, LXXXIX (2002), 154–173; and "Whiteness Studies: II: An Update on the New History of Race in America," *Journal de la Société des Américanistes*, XCV, no. 1 (2009), 144–163. For studies on the early modern period, see, for example, Kathleen M. Brown, *Good Wives, Nasty Wenches, and Anxious patriarchs: Gender, Race, and Power in Colonial Virginia* (Chapel Hill, N.C., 1996); David Lambert, *White Creole Culture, Politics, and Identity during the Age of Abolition* (Cambridge, 2005); and John Wood Sweet, *Bodies Politic: Negotiating Race in the American North, 1730–1830* (Baltimore, 2003).

urban slave society in the making. Chapter 6 on labor, which primarily took place within domestic households, mirrors Chapter 4 on households; Chapter 7 on commerce, which was conducted in shops and on the levee, extends the analysis of Chapter 3 on the politics of public space; and Chapter 8 on justice and military service, which were instrumental in enforcing the city's domination of its hinterland, continues Chapter 2, which deals with the relations between the capital and the colony. These social institutions—labor, commerce, justice, and military service—defined various contexts in which relationships of domination and subordination were enforced, negotiated, and contested. While labor, justice, and military service all contributed in their own ways to the construction of race, the market consolidated the socioeconomic power of the elite and democratized slaveownership but also allowed some slaves to redeem themselves. Finally, Chapter 9, which is the counterpart of Chapter 1, resituates New Orleans within the Atlantic world, analyzing how its inhabitants forged a sense of place over time. Racial formation prevented the development of a shared relationship to the city between settlers, slaves, and free people of color. Even so, after the succession of two generations by the end of the 1760s, as the elite fought to keep the colony within the French Empire, New Orleans emerged as a distinctive place in relation to both the metropole and Saint-Domingue.

CHAPTER ONE

A Port City of the French Empire and the Greater Caribbean

In 1765, at sundown, while walking down Bourbon Street, a white resident of New Orleans, Sieur Xavier Duverger de Saint-Sauveur, met a black man wearing a sword. Since a local regulation based on the Code Noir forbade slaves to bear arms and required whites to intervene in the event of a violation, he questioned the man, whom he took for a local slave. It is also possible that this prohibition had been extended to free men of color, as had been the case in Saint-Domingue since at least 1758. When the black man, whose name was Antoine, refused to be led to his master, Duverger threatened to take him to jail. Resenting this act of dishonor, Antoine objected to being treated like a "dog," insulted his opponent, and tried to engage him in a fight. The white man then beat him with his cane and, with the assistance of a passerby, took him to prison. According to Duverger, when the guard arrested the lawbreaker, the latter protested "that he [Antoine] had a certain social standing, that he came from Paris and had influence and that he [Duverger] would pay for it." After the Superior Council had investigated the case, Antoine was discharged, maybe because of his origins. He told the judge that he was a twenty-eight-year-old Catholic "free negro" from the "Senegal nation" and that he had come to Louisiana as a sailor on the ship *L'espérance,* which sailed between Lorient, Cap-Français, Havana, and New Orleans. He complained that "it was unfortunate that he was brought to jail in such a manner, being of negro condition, and since his father supplied the French with negroes." He was probably related to a *habitant* (permanent resident) of Gorée or Saint-Louis in Senegambia who sold captives to the Company of the Indies.[1]

1. For Antoine's trial, see RSCL 1765/10/15/01, 1765/10/16/01, 1765/10/16/02. For the local regulation, based on the Code Noir, forbidding slaves to bear arms and requiring

In this conflict over race and honor, the two protagonists had antagonistic visions of the social order: one that was locally rooted and an alternative that was the fruit of a life spent traveling between West Africa, metropolitan France, and the French and Spanish Caribbean. Paradoxically, Antoine's life history and job as a sailor took him to all the places in Europe, Africa, and the Americas with which New Orleans maintained, at various times, close connections. His social background and mobility, nevertheless, gave him a degree of self-respect and dignity that was denied to most blacks in the Louisiana port city. Although Antoine and Duverger did not share the same experience and worldview, their encounter probably left an imprint on both men. It would be presumptuous to assume that they were transformed by their clash, but one can postulate that it was the multiplication of similar interactions between local actors and outsiders that made New Orleans the singular place it became during the French regime. Their conflict illuminates the problematic relationship that the local and the extra-local maintained in the Atlantic world: people's lives were shaped and places constructed by a complex and dynamic combination of mobility and sedentariness, of openness to the outside world and rootedness.

Racial formation in New Orleans did not take place in isolation from the rest of the Atlantic world. The Louisiana capital and its colony were no different from other new societies established by Europeans in the Americas. All of them were migratory communities that were being made and remade by the continuous arrivals and departures of migrants, but their links with Europe, Africa, and other regions in the Western hemisphere were maintained by circulation of all kinds. The combined mobility of people, goods, capital, and information, not transatlantic migrations alone, constantly transformed these new societies. A series of technical, political, geopolitical, economic, and sociocultural factors, however, constrained these various movements, posing two multilayered questions. How did the location and history of New Orleans determine the nature, direction, and intensity of the connections the port city was able to maintain with the rest of the Atlantic world throughout the French period? And were imperial or trans-

ne in the event of violation, see "Règlement sur la police pour la province Feb. 28–Mar. 1, 1751, Article 23, ANOM COL C13A 35, fols. 47r–48v. n prohibiting free people of color to bear arms in Saint-Domingue, see "Arrêt en règlement du Conseil du Cap, touchant la police des esclaves," Apr. 7, 1758, Article XVIII, in M[édéric Louis-Élie Moreau] de Saint-Méry, *Loix et constitutions des colonies françoises de l'Amérique sous le vent*, 6 vols. (Paris, 1784–1790), IV, 228, and "Ordonnance du gouverneur général, touchant le port d'armes des gens de couleur," May 29, 1762, 466–467.

imperial relationships most influential in shaping the way New Orleans's society developed?[2]

From the seventeenth century onward, the greater Caribbean came to constitute an Atlantic crossroads. The Spanish, English, French, and Dutch Empires all intersected in the region as various maritime circuits linked the islands and their mainland surroundings in transimperial networks. Caribbean geography made it difficult for imperial states to enforce their trade monopolies. Smuggling thrived, both the illicit trade by northwestern Europeans with Spanish colonies and that between English, French, and Dutch settlements. One of the primary motivations behind the Dutch, English, and French presence in the region was to compete with the Spanish for New World resources and to acquire some of Spain's colonial riches for themselves. As a result, some historians consider contraband to be the main force that shaped the Caribbean. Yet New Orleans did not become a Caribbean port city because of its participation in smuggling. Its commerce with nearby Spanish colonies did grow over time, but it remained secondary. Located on the fringe of the main trading circuits of the greater Caribbean and deprived of a group of powerful merchants, the Louisiana capital failed to oust English and Dutch hubs as a leader in Spanish trade.[3]

What gave New Orleans its Caribbean character was racial slavery. In the early eighteenth century, local authorities and settlers on Saint-Domingue, acting against the wishes of the French minister of the navy, Jérôme de Pontchartrain, determined to pursue an economy based on sugar, rather

2. Atlantic studies are based on the assumption of the importance of transimperial relationships. See Alison Games, "Atlantic History: Definitions, Challenges, and Opportunities," *American Historical Review,* CXI (2006), 741–757.

3. For general studies on smuggling, see Alan L. Karras, *Smuggling: Contraband and Corruption in World History* (New York, 2010); and Wim Klooster, "Inter-Imperial Smuggling in the Americas, 1600–1800," in Bernard Bailyn and Patricia L. Denault, eds., *Soundings in Atlantic History: Latent Structures and Intellectual Currents, 1550–1830* (Cambridge, Mass., 2009), 141–180. For studies insisting on the political and sociocultural impact of contraband, see Charles Frostin, *Les révoltes blanches à Saint-Domingue aux XVIIe et XVIIIe siècles (Haïti avant 1789),* [rev. ed.] (Rennes, France, 2008); Christian J. Koot, *Empire at the Periphery: British Colonists, Anglo-Dutch Trade, and the Development of the British Atlantic, 1621–1713* (New York, 2011); and Linda M. Rupert, *Creolization and Contraband: Curaçao in the Early Modern Atlantic World* (Athens, Ga., 2012). For an opposite view arguing for the importance of smuggling in New Orleans's development, see Shannon Lee Dawdy, "La Nouvelle-Orléans au XVIIIe siècle: Courants d'échange dans le monde caraïbe," *Annales: Histoire, Sciences Sociales,* LXII (2007), 663–685; and Dawdy, *Building the Devil's Empire: French Colonial New Orleans* (Chicago, 2008), 99–137.

than continue to chase the elusive "Spanish mirage" and attempt to make a fortune off illicit trade with the wealthy Spanish Empire. This decision would profoundly impact Louisiana. Already familiar with the big island, a necessary stop on the sea road from Europe or Africa to New Orleans, the Mississippi colony sought to develop an export economy based on plantation slavery, directed toward the metropole, and modeled on that of Saint-Domingue's. This social and economic choice, combined with New Orleans's relative isolation, explains why French imperial relationships remained the most important for the port city throughout the French period.[4]

Within this French imperial framework, connections between the colony and its metropole were increasingly replaced by intercolonial exchanges. Before 1731, the Company of the Indies made a real effort to populate the territory with both free and forced migrants from metropolitan France and from its slave-trading outposts in Senegambia. Once the company released its trade monopoly and ceased to transport African slaves to the Mississippi colony after 1731, interactions between New Orleans and the Antilles grew in importance. These ever-closer ties between the port city and the Caribbean continued and reinforced the direct influence that the islands had already exerted on Louisiana with the promulgation of a modified version of the Antillean Code Noir in 1724. The horizons of all New Orleans's urban dwellers quickly came to include the French islands as well as Europe and Africa. For them, Saint-Domingue became the most important imperial center after the metropole.

THE MISSISSIPPI COLONY: A LATECOMER ON THE PERIPHERY OF SAINT-DOMINGUE

In 1681, Abbé Claude Bernou, a contributor to the *Gazette*, allegedly supervised the production of a beautiful map depicting North America and part of South America. Employed by the offices of the ministry of the navy, he corresponded with René-Robert Cavelier de La Salle and wrote many reports to support La Salle's expeditions in the Mississippi Valley. The map is remarkable for several reasons. First, it represented all the territories explored and settled by the French since the start of the seventeenth century

---

4. New Orleans was not completely isolated, but, by the end of the French regime in Louisiana, only dozens of ships docked there every year, not hundreds, as was the case in Kingston and Cap-Français. On the choice made by local authorities and settlers in Saint-Domingue to privilege sugar over the "Spanish mirage," see Charles Frostin, "Les Pontchartrain et la pénétration commerciale française en Amérique espagnole (1690–1715)," *Revue historique*, CCXLV (1971), 330.

in relation to nearby English and Spanish colonies. Second, the map was painted while La Salle was on his way to the Gulf of Mexico during his second expedition through the Mississippi Valley. In the painting, the Mississippi River stops at the latitude of the Ohio River, with a blank space instead of its southern half. The map suggests the promise of a future Louisiana and highlights that the exploration of the Mississippi Valley was initially undertaken as part of the western expansion of New France toward the Great Lakes and beyond. Yet, lastly, the map, which is centered on the Caribbean Sea and the Gulf of Mexico, also serves as a reminder that, after the Mississippi Delta had been reached in 1682, La Salle's third and final expedition three years later came from the sea. Thereafter, most of the connections that Lower Louisiana maintained with the rest of the Atlantic world took the seaway. This maritime route was long and perilous and necessarily involved stops in the Antilles, which fostered the development of intercolonial relations between New Orleans and the islands. Founded at the very end of the seventeenth century and located on the western edge of the French Empire, Louisiana might have managed to overcome the competition with older and better located colonies in Canada and in the Caribbean if the grandiose plans imagined by John Law, a Scottish financier and adviser to the French regent, had succeeded, but they failed. As a result, the Mississippi colony remained in a peripheral position vis-à-vis Saint-Domingue.[5]

In the sixteenth century, all French attempts to establish colonies in the New World came to unsuccessful conclusions. The wealth, pomp, and brilliance of Italy exercised a much greater pull on the French crown during the first half of the century. Afterward, the Wars of Religion deterred all ambitious overseas policy. It was not until peace was restored that Henri IV and then Richelieu, under Louis XIII, supported a program of commercial and maritime expansion driven by mercantilist theories. France then joined England and the Netherlands in their efforts to challenge the Iberians' colonial monopoly. The French first started to settle Nova Scotia and the Saint Lawrence Valley in the early years of the seventeenth century, founding Quebec City in 1608 and Montreal in 1642. They also began to take hold in the Caribbean in the mid-1620s. From their original base in Saint-Christophe (1625), the French moved to Guadeloupe (1635), Martinique (1638), and

5. On the western expansion of New France toward the Great Lakes and beyond, see Francis Parkman, *The Discovery of the Great West: An Historical Narrative* (London, 1869); and Gilles Havard, *Empire et métissages: Indiens et français dans le Pays d'en Haut, 1660-1715* (Sillery, Quebec, 2003).

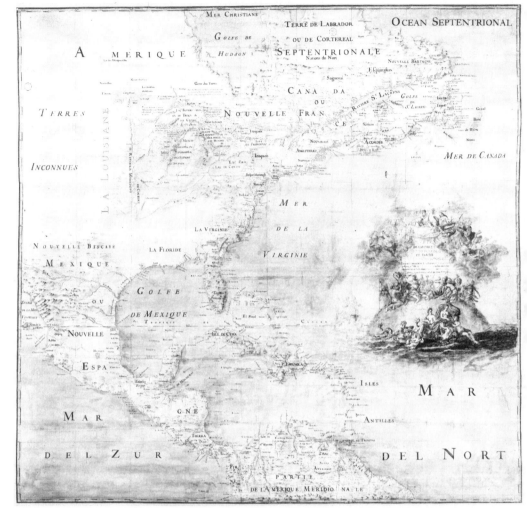

Figure 3: [Claude Bernou]. *Carte de l'Amérique septentrionale et partie de la méridionale depuis l'embouchure de la rivière St Laurens jusqu'à l'isle de Cayenne avec les nouvelles découvertes de la rivière de Mississipi ou Colbert.* Circa 1681. Département cartes et plans. CPL SH 18E PF 122 DIV 2 P 0 RES. Courtesy of Bibliothèque nationale de France. Paris

then several smaller islands. Saint-Domingue did not formally become a French colony until later. Although buccaneers and freebooters, including many French, lived on Tortuga and the northern coast of the big island from the 1620s onward, French officials only succeeded in imposing their authority in 1655. The Spanish finally recognized the sovereignty of the French on the western side of the island by the Treaty of Ryswick in 1697. In addi-

Port City of the French Empire and the Greater Caribbean

tion to pursuing trade with the Spanish, the French islands in the Caribbean quickly sought to develop plantation economies growing tobacco, cotton, and other plants with a workforce of European indentured servants
and increasingly African slaves, whereas the main economic motivation in
Canada was the fur trade.[6]

France's two separate colonial domains in Canada and the Caribbean
were brought together for the first time by La Salle's third and final expedition in 1685–1687. Until the destruction of Huronia by the Iroquois in
the late 1640s, Native Americans came to Quebec City or Trois-Rivières
to exchange furs and pelts for European merchandise. Afterward, French
traders traveled beyond the falls of Lachine to collect furs and pelts within
indigenous villages in the Great Lakes region. La Salle was one of the adventurers and entrepreneurs who participated in the development of new
trading circuits in the Upper Country. Following the success of his first two
expeditions, he obtained the support of the king to establish a colony in the
lower Mississippi Valley and decided to reach the Mississippi Delta by sea.
La Salle's expedition, however, ended as a disaster, and it was only in 1699
that the first settlement was established by Pierre Le Moyne d'Iberville.
Despite the participation of some freebooters, sailors, and soldiers from
Saint-Domingue in d'Iberville's expeditions and the shipment of food to the
colony during its early years, the French section of the island did not play
a direct role in Louisiana's founding. Still, geography and technology immediately tied the Mississippi colony's fate to Saint-Domingue.[7]

With the construction of Fort Maurepas (now Biloxi), Louisiana became
the French Empire's most remote American colony, as the Gulf route from
the Antilles added 1,000 kilometers to the 6,600 already separating the
islands from the metropole. After the founding of New Orleans in 1718,
further inland, and its promotion to the status of colonial capital in 1722,
the distance between France and the nascent colony included another 160
kilometers. La Balise, a small outpost, was built in 1723 at the mouth of
the Mississippi, but it was used not so much as an outer harbor for New
Orleans as a last stop before sailing upriver. Because navigation in the
Gulf of Mexico and on the Mississippi River was particularly hazardous,
a pilot in charge of guiding sea ships through the delta resided there per-

6. Gilles Havard and Cécile Vidal, *Histoire de l'Amérique française* ([Paris], 2008);
Philip P. Boucher, *France and the American Tropics to 1700: Tropics of Discontent?* (Baltimore, 2008).

7. Marc de Villiers [du Terrage], *L'expédition de Cavelier de La Salle dans le golfe du
Mexique (1684–1687)* (Paris, 1931); Guy Frégault, *Pierre Le Moyne d'Iberville* (Montreal,
1968); Marcel Giraud, *Histoire de la Louisiane française*, 4 vols. (Paris, 1953–1974), esp. I.

manently. In his travel account, Company of the Indies employee Marc-Antoine Caillot compared his experience accompanying a flotilla of small boats loaded with slaves from La Balise to New Orleans to an encounter with three of the four Horsemen of the Apocalypse. Once in the city, he expressed his relief at having left the "war, plague, and famine we faced during this little trip. War, because it had been necessary for us to have a stick in hand to keep the Negroes under control; plague, for the stench that the scurvy-ridden people had given to us; and famine, because as a rule we had nothing to eat." Caillot landed in New Orleans after eight days of hardship, but, according to Antoine-Simon Le Page du Pratz, the journey between La Balise and the colonial capital could take as long as one month. Although in theory it should have been possible to sail from France to New Orleans in about twelve weeks, in practice, the average crossing amounted to seventeen weeks, one-third to double the usual seven to nine weeks necessary to reach the Antilles.[8]

Given the difficulties navigating the Gulf of Mexico and the Mississippi, all ships coming to New Orleans from Europe or Africa had to stop in a Caribbean port before heading to the Louisiana capital to repair damage and to stock up on water, wood, and food supplies. The former officer and planter Jean-François-Benjamin Dumont de Montigny underscored this necessity in bad verse at the beginning of the fourth canto of his poem entitled "L'établissement de la province de la Louisiane" ("The Settlement of the Province of Louisiana"): "When, from some port city, one sees some ships / Travelling by sea sailing with the current / Wanting to reach New France [Louisiana] / Braving winds and perils, one therefore comes / To look for Cap-Français, where taking water / And fresh supplies, that is

8. On La Balise, see Jean M. Farnsworth and Ann M. Masson, eds., *The Architecture of Colonial Louisiana: Collected Essays of Samuel Wilson, Jr., F.A.I.A.* (Lafayette, La., 1987), 24–40. On the difficulties of sailing up the Mississippi River, see Erin M. Greenwald, ed., *A Company Man: The Remarkable French-Atlantic Voyage of a Clerk for the Company of the Indies; A Memoir by Marc-Antoine Caillot*, trans. Teri F. Chalmers (New Orleans, 2013), 74; N[ancy] M. Miller Surrey, *The Commerce of Louisiana during the French Régime, 1699–1763* (New York, 1916), 42–54; and Gilles-Antoine Langlois, *Des villes pour la Louisiane française: Théorie et pratique de l'urbanistique coloniale au 18e siècle* (Paris, 2003), 51–57. On the duration of the journey from France to Louisiana, see [Antoine-Simon] Le Page du Pratz, *Histoire de la Louisiane*, 3 vols. (Paris, 1758), II, 259–260; Kenneth J. Banks, *Chasing Empire across the Sea: Communications and the State in the French Atlantic, 1713–1763* (Montreal, 2002), 65–87; and Jean de Maupassant, "Les armateurs bordelais au XVIIIe siècle: L'expédition de François Lavaud à la Louisiane (1761–1763)," *Revue philomathique de Bordeaux et du Sud-Ouest*, XII (1909), 166.

everything that is needed / to at least complete the rest of the journey ....". Most often these stops took place in a port on Saint-Domingue, either at Cap-Français on the northern coast of the island or sometimes Les Cayes in the southern province. During the return trip, vessels could also stop in Léogane, and, beginning in 1749, Port-au-Prince. Stays on the island lasted several days or even weeks.[9]

In addition to the close ties between Louisiana and Saint-Domingue formed by sea-lanes, the two colonies were originally founded with the same goal. At the turn of the century, the development of trade with Spanish territories was one of the primary objectives of French colonial expansion in the greater Caribbean. This impetus explains both the creation of the Company of Saint-Domingue in 1698 and the establishment of Louisiana in 1699. Spain did not provide its American colonies with enough manufactured goods, especially fabrics, to meet their needs while the latter produced the silver that was highly sought after by rival European powers. Curaçao and Jamaica dominated this contraband trade. In the second half of the seventeenth century, Port Royal, in particular, used its strategic location in the heart of the Spanish West Indies to develop a dual economy based on the export of agricultural products and trade with Spanish colonies. But the Jamaican port city was destroyed by an earthquake in 1692. Founded a few years later and ideally located to trade with Pensacola, Havana, Veracruz, and Campeche, Mobile and, later, New Biloxi, Louisiana's first and second capitals before New Orleans, could have taken the place of Port Royal, leaving the commerce of Cartagena to the southern province of Saint-Domingue and that of the South Sea to merchants from Saint-Malo. Yet, by the time New Orleans emerged, the situation had changed. The Treaty of Utrecht (1713) gave the asiento (the agreement to furnish Spanish colonies with slaves) to the British, which facilitated smuggling with Spanish territories.[10]

9. On the need to stop in a Caribbean port before heading to New Orleans, see Marc de Villiers, ed., "L'établissement de la province de la Louisiane: Poème composé de 1728 à 1742, par Dumont de Montigny," *Journal de la société des américanistes*, New Ser., XXIII (1931), 383. For the various ports used in Saint-Domingue, see Le Page du Pratz, *Histoire de la Louisiane*, III, 388; and Dumont de Montigny, *Regards sur le monde atlantique, 1715–1747*, transcribed by Carla Zecher (Sillery, Quebec, 2008), 203, 352. In his travel account, Marc-Antoine Caillot drew a beautiful sketch of Cayes Bay. See [Caillot], "Relation du voyage de la Louisianne ou Nouvlle. France; fait par le Sr. CAILLOT en l'année 1730," HNOC, MSS596.

10. On Spanish trade as the main motivation for French expansion in the greater Caribbean in the late seventeenth century, see Frostin, "Les Pontchartrain et la pénétra-

Although Louisiana could not compete with Jamaica, the monarchy still hoped it could benefit from the colony's exploitation. A few years after the end of the War of the Spanish Succession, an ambitious and grandiose imperial project was assigned to the Mississippi colony by the Company of the West, which was granted its trade monopoly in 1717. Louisiana was intended to play a crucial role in the global sociopolitical, financial, and economic schemes of John Law. To conceive and implement his plan of turning France into a commercial nation, the Scottish financier drew on a debate on the need to reform state and society that had been developing in the kingdom since the late seventeenth century and relied on various political and intellectual networks. In the wake of Louis XIV's expensive wars, Law convinced France's regent, Philippe d'Orléans, that he could pay off the national debt, which had skyrocketed, by combining all the public finances, the issuance of currency, and the mass of the country's private capital into a single mechanism. In May 1716, he founded the Banque générale, a private bank that became the Banque royale in December 1718. The bank recalled some of the metallic currencies in circulation in exchange for newly issued paper money that was guaranteed by the state through the right to collect taxes on its behalf. But the bank could not immediately reimburse the holders of paper money seeking conversion to metallic currency because that amount had been lent to the crown.[11]

While the Banque générale was envisioned as the crown's financial arm, the Company of the West was intended to become its instrument of commercial glory. The purpose of the company, created fifteen months after the bank's founding, was to remedy the financial institution's vulnerability. Its capital was formed of shares that could only be purchased with paper money and hereditary annuities granted by the state. The idea was to turn the state's creditors into company shareholders who would make a fortune thanks to Louisiana. Although trade with neighboring Spanish colonies remained a definite impetus, more was expected from the fabulous riches to

———
tion commerciale française en Amérique espagnole," *Revue historique*, CCXLV (1971), 307–336. On the dominant role played by Jamaica and Curaçao in Spanish trade, see Nuala Zahedieh, "The Merchants of Port Royal, Jamaica, and the Spanish Contraband Trade, 1655–1692," *William and Mary Quarterly*, 3d Ser., XLIII (1986), 570–593; Wim Klooster, *Illicit Riches: Dutch Trade in the Caribbean, 1648–1795* (Leiden, Netherlands, 1998); and Rupert, *Creolization and Contraband*.

11. Nicolas Buat, *John Law: La dette, ou comment s'en débarrasser* (Paris, 2015); Edgar Faure, *La banqueroute de Law, 17 juillet 1720* (Paris, 1977); Antoin E. Murphy, *John Law: Economic Theorist and Policy-Maker* (New York, 1997); Arnaud Orain, *La politique du merveilleux: Une autre histoire du Système de Law (1695–1795)* ([Paris], 2018).

be found in the gold and silver mines of the Illinois Country and the development of tobacco and indigo plantations in the lower Mississippi Valley. The location of New Orleans, far from the coast, testified to these new priorities. But Law had even more global ambitions. From August 1718 to September 1720, the company expanded its operations within and beyond the Atlantic world: it acquired the tobacco farm (the monopoly over the importation, processing, and sale of tobacco in France), annexed several companies in charge of commerce with various African and Asian territories, and obtained exclusive rights to engage in the slave trade. These mandates concentrated all maritime and colonial trade under the sole authority of the company. In May 1719, the resulting conglomerate was renamed the Company of the Indies. In January 1720, Law was appointed controller general of finances of France. The following month, the Banque royale and the company were united within the same financial and commercial institution.

What became known as the System collapsed at the end of 1720. Because Law issued too much paper money and guaranteed too high dividends on the company's shares, the public speculated wildly. As the settlement of Louisiana drove up expenses, the colony's trade brought in meager profits. Dividends on the company's shares dropped, trust disappeared, and people rushed to convert paper money into coin: the Mississippi bubble burst. The dreams of a new El Dorado dissipated—mines in the Illinois Country did not yield any gold or silver, tobacco and indigo production was slow to meet the company's expectations, and trade with the Spanish did not thrive—but, without these ambitions, the company would never have asked for the monopoly on Louisiana trade and would never have made the initial heavy investments necessary to develop a new colony.

THE ADVENT OF A SLAVE SOCIETY DISCONNECTED FROM AFRICA

The Company of the Indies's peopling and labor strategy had a great impact on the connections that Louisiana was able to develop with the rest of the Atlantic world. It experienced three major phases. Initially expecting high profits, the company was eager to develop a genuine settler colony. To that end, it organized the single migratory wave that the colony experienced during the French regime. This wave in fact comprised two interlinked movements from Europe and Africa. By the early eighteenth century, colonization in the subtropical and tropical regions of the French Empire could no longer be conceived of without slavery. Even before the company's involvement in Louisiana, local officials had repeatedly and vainly asked the crown for permission to exchange North American Native captives for black slaves from the Caribbean. Once the company was granted control of the colony, its directors favored a mixed approach, intending to develop the lower Mississippi Valley as quickly and cheaply as possible by using the combined labor of African slaves and European indentured servants and convicts. But this project did not go as planned, and the company decided to focus on the slave trade after 1723. In turn, the new policy privileging African captives came to an end after the company released its trade monopoly in 1731 and opted not to send any more slave ships from Africa to Louisiana. The company's inconsistent efforts to provide the colony with free and forced migrants gave birth to a slave society that would be deprived of any massive influx of enslaved workers from that point forward.[12]

In the early 1720s, the Company of the Indies spared no trouble or money to people the colony. It supported migration to Louisiana in many different ways. Since the commercial enterprise had a monopoly on the slave trade, it took responsibility for supplying New Orleans with African slaves. It also saw to the transportation of French soldiers, convicts, and vagrants sent by the crown as well as launched an advertising campaign in French and Dutch newspapers to attract both investors and candidates for emigration. The company was able to recruit indentured servants from France, Germany, and Switzerland to work in its service and to settle specific outposts that it managed directly. It also granted land concessions in the Mississippi Valley to French speculators and entrepreneurs, including members of the highest nobility. These metropolitan concession holders were responsible for the recruitment of their own indentured servants, who were nevertheless transported to Louisiana on company vessels. Finally, company officers on their way to the Mississippi colony tried to recruit free migrants and to buy slaves in Saint-Domingue, targeting, in particular, skilled settlers and workers who knew how to grow and produce tobacco and indigo.[13]

12. For local authorities seeking permission to exchange North American Native captives for black slaves from the Caribbean, see Annotated summary of Jean-Baptiste Le Moyne de Bienville's letters, 1706, ANOM COL C13A 1, fols. 514–544; minister of the navy to Bienville, June 30, 1707, ANOM COL B 29, fols. 9–19; Bienville to the minister of the navy, Oct. 12, 1708, ANOM COL C13A 2, fols. 165–176; Summary of a letter from Robert, Nov. 26, 1708, ANOM COL C13A 2, fols. 359–362; minister of the navy to Bienville, May 10, 1710, ANOM COL B 32, fols. 41–47; and Jean-Baptiste Duclos to the minister of the navy, May 2, 1713, ANOM COL C13A 3, fols. 109–112.

13. For the advertising campaign in French and Dutch newspapers, see Mary Rush Gwin Waggoner, ed., *Le plus beau Païs du Monde: Completing the Picture of Proprietary Louisiana, 1699–1722* (Lafayette, La., 2005); and Giraud, *Histoire de la Louisiane française*, III, 129–153. On the concession system, see ibid., 154–220. On efforts by com-

With regard to European migrants, the company did not limit itself to French national borders but also looked for laborers in Germany and other places. Although resorting to nonnationals might have been seen as a potential danger, the difficulties of recruiting candidates willing to take their chances overseas forced the company to resort to the increasingly integrated transnational labor market of the Atlantic world. But, unlike the Germans who moved to British North America in the eighteenth century, those recruited by Law in the Rhine Valley had to travel overland to reach a French port (most often Lorient or Port-Louis). Their transatlantic migrations, therefore, remained within a French imperial framework. While waiting in ports where departures were sometimes delayed for weeks and months, causing heavy mortality, indentured servants from German and Swiss states were joined by convicts taken from jails in Paris, Orléans, Rochefort, Rennes, Lyon, and Bayonne and by other indentured servants recruited in Paris, La Rochelle, Lorient, and Port-Louis. Most of those who signed a contract in Lorient and Port-Louis came from Brittany whereas those wishing to emigrate in Paris and La Rochelle came from all over France and even other European countries such as England, Ireland, and Spain. Some were also servants of African or mixed descent, which testifies to the slow growth of a free population of color in Paris, La Rochelle, and Bordeaux.[14]

In four years, from 1717 to 1721, instead of the twenty-five years fixed by its letters patent, the Company of the Indies succeeded in fulfilling its obligations in the matter of European immigration, transporting around 6,000 civilian migrants to Louisiana. In addition to a few free passengers, they included around 120 *filles du roi,* or king's daughters—young single

---

pany officers to recruit free migrants and to buy slaves in Saint-Domingue, see Étienne Périer to the minister of the navy, Apr. 30, 1727, ANOM COL C13A 10, fol. 217v.

14. On initial French suspicion against foreign migrants, see Bertrand Van Ruymbeke, "'A Dominion of True Believers Not a Republic for Heretics': French Colonial Religious Policy and the Settlement of Early Louisiana, 1699–1730," in Bradley G. Bond, ed., *French Colonial Louisiana and the Atlantic World* (Baton Rouge, La., 2005), 90–91. On German migrants, see Giraud, *Histoire de la Louisiane française,* III, 277–283, IV, 154–167; Reinhart Kondert, *The Germans of Colonial Louisiana, 1720–1803* (Stuttgart, Germany, 1990); and René Le Conte, "The Germans in Louisiana in the Eighteenth Century," trans. and ed. Glenn R. Conrad, *Louisiana History,* VIII (1967), 67–84. On the geographic origins of other migrants of European descent, see Giraud, *Histoire de la Louisiane française,* III, 221–276. For free people of color migrating to Louisiana, see Glenn R. Conrad, trans. and comp., *The First Families of Louisiana,* I (Baton Rouge, La., 1970), 25, 71, 117; and RSCL 1724/07/27/01.

women whose migration was sponsored by the king—1,300 convicts and exiles (among whom were 150 women of low repute), 2,400 French indentured servants recruited by the concession holders, 250 workers hired by the company, and 1,300 German migrants. Nevertheless, few of these 6,000 migrants were able to contribute to the colony's development: 60 percent of them died during the transatlantic crossing or shortly after their disembarkation. The migrants traveled on as many as forty ships in only five years—three in 1717, four in 1718, ten in 1719, seventeen in 1720, and six in 1721. Failing to take into consideration the arrival of such a large number of people in such a short period, the company did not make adequate provisions for food to sustain them or for boats to quickly transport them from New Biloxi to their land grants in the Mississippi Valley. Because the company also confiscated their personal foodstuffs to feed its employees and the garrison, the new migrants lay dying for months on the sandy shores of what is now the state of Mississippi. These apocalyptic visions would haunt the colony's memory for decades to come.[15]

In the space of a few years, high mortality but also departures heavily reduced the European part of the colonial population. As some employees of the concession belonging to Eugène-Marie de Béthizy, marquis de Mézières, wrote in a letter in 1721, survivors begged to leave "this Mississippian hell." Many indentured servants initially moved to Louisiana with the intention of going back to the metropole. Their desire to return was further enhanced not only by the high death rate and the transportation of convicts to the colony but also by several other important factors: the collapse of the System and Law's flight from France in December 1720; the subsequent reorganization of the Company of the Indies, which no longer expected much profit from Louisiana and consequently restricted its investments; and the failure of the concession system and its replacement by plantations under local private initiative. Most migrants attempted to go back to the metro-

15. Of the four thousand German and Swiss migrants recruited by John Law, only three hundred reached the colony. If they did not run away before embarking in Lorient or another French port, they died at one of the various stages of their long journey. For documentation on ships bound to Louisiana, see Conrad, trans. and comp., *First Families of Louisiana*, I. For a comprehensive study of migrations from France, see Giraud, *Histoire de la Louisiane française*, IV, 120–153, 168–195. On the colony's lingering memory of the early mortality crisis, see Pierre de Rigaud de Vaudreuil de Cavagnal and Honoré-Gabriel Michel to the minister of the navy, May 20, 1751, ANOM COL C13A 35, fol. 15r; and Guillaume-Thomas Raynal, *Histoire philosophique et politique; Des établissemens et du commerce des Européens dans les deux Indes*, VI (Amsterdam, 1770), 106–107.

pole though a few also tried their luck in Saint-Domingue. As for the indentured servants who remained, they refused to continue to work for absentee proprietors. The disintegration of a concession system that relied on metropolitan owners reduced the speculative and exploitative character of the colonial project and allowed for the development of a more locally rooted society. In that respect, Lower Louisiana started to resemble the British colonies in North America rather than the French Antilles or the British West Indies.[16]

After undergoing a reorganization in 1721–1722, the company decided to abandon its efforts to populate and develop the colony with a mixed labor force and to rely more heavily on slave labor instead, a decision that ultimately led to the Africanization of Louisiana's colonial population. The slave trade, which had been interrupted after the arrival of the first set of slave ships between 1719 and 1721, resumed in 1723. The rationale behind this choice was that the company held the trade monopoly on both Senegambia and Louisiana. As the exclusive buyer and seller, the commercial enterprise was in a position to more easily and cheaply acquire slaves in Saint-Louis and Gorée and to sell them at a profit in New Orleans. All in all, from 1719 to 1731, the company transported between fifty-seven hundred and six thousand slaves on twenty-two slave-trading ships. At least two men landed for each woman. Between 50 and 70 percent of the slaves sent to Louisiana came from Senegambia; the rest were brought from Congo-Angola and the Bight of Benin.[17]

16. For complaints about life in Louisiana, see Moret [de la Brosse?] and [Jean Baptiste] Delaye to Jean Gravé de La Mancelière, circa August 1721, E. and Emile Kuntz Collection, French Colonial Period, 1655–1768, Manuscripts Collection 600, Louisiana Research Collection, Howard-Tilton Memorial Library, Tulane University, New Orleans. It is impossible to calculate the exact rate at which Louisiana migrants of European descent returned to France, but it was probably even higher than that in Canada (which was between 46 and 70 percent). For Canada, see Gervais Carpin, *Le réseau du Canada: Étude du mode migratoire de France vers la Nouvelle-France (1628–1662)* (Sillery, Quebec, 2001), 39–40; and Leslie Choquette, *De Français à paysans: Modernité et tradition dans le peuplement du Canada français*, trans. Carpin (Sillery, Quebec, 2001), 19. For Louisiana settlers who tried their luck in Saint-Domingue, see Giraud, *Histoire de la Louisiane française*, IV, 230; and Marcel Giraud, *A History of French Louisiana*, V, *The Company of the Indies, 1723–1731*, trans. Brian Pearce (Baton Rouge, La., 1991), 164.

17. Gwendolyn Midlo Hall, *Africans in Colonial Louisiana: The Development of Afro-Creole Culture in the Eighteenth Century* (Baton Rouge, La., 1992), 56–95, 171–172. See also Daniel H. Usner, Jr., "From African Captivity to American Slavery: The Introduction of Black Laborers to Colonial Louisiana," *Louisiana History*, XX (1979), 25–48;

More slaves might have arrived, but, in addition to accidents and revolts, deaths on board the company's ships took a heavy toll, especially after 1726. Furthermore, vessels bound for Louisiana had to stop in the Antilles (Saint-Domingue, Martinique, and Grenada), and local authorities and colonists sometimes forced captains to sell part or all of their cargoes in the islands. Occasionally, the company also decided to supply Saint-Domingue instead of Louisiana because the journey was shorter, the planters had less difficulty paying their debts, and the ships' return cargoes were less uncertain and more profitable. Still, the massive death and departure rates experienced by European migrants and the rapid arrival of slaves from Africa soon resulted in Africans becoming the majority in the colonial settlements of the Mississippi Valley. By 1731, "The racial composition of the Louisiana population," as Paul Lachance has pointed out, "was [then] more Caribbean than Canadian."[18]

The slave trade tore Africans from their homelands, stripped them of all material possessions, and shattered social relationships and kinship networks for which even the shared experience of bonding on board slave ships could not completely compensate. It was impossible for Africans to maintain the kinds of direct links with Africa that European migrants had with Europe—enslaved people could not go home. Moreover, the flow of newcomers from Africa quickly ceased in Louisiana after the crown retook possession of the colony in 1731, following the Natchez Wars. African-born slaves still arrived in New Orleans, but, from then on, except for one ship in 1743, they were brought from the Antilles. Lower Louisiana had become a plantation society that no longer participated in the transatlantic slave trade.

THE ELITE'S METROPOLITAN HORIZON

Whereas Africans forcibly taken to Louisiana could not preserve connections to Africa without the arrival of new captives, European migrants found themselves in a different situation. The circulation of people, capital,

---

and Thomas N. Ingersoll, "The Slave Trade and the Ethnic Diversity of Louisiana's Slave Community," *Louisiana History*, XXXVII (1996), 133–161.

18. For examples of ships bound to Louisiana that stopped in Martinique, see Copy of a request sent to Jacques-Charles Bochart, marquis de Champigny de Noroy, and Jacques Pannier, seigneur d'Orgeville, by René de Rhuais, Sept. 9, 1729, ANOM COL C8A 55, fol. 128; and Champigny de Noroy and Pannier d'Orgeville to the minister of the navy, Dec. 7, 1730, ANOM COL C8A 41, fols. 94–98. On the Caribbeanization of Louisiana's population, see Paul Lachance, "The Growth of the Free and Slave Populations of French Colonial Louisiana," in Bond, ed., *French Colonial Louisiana and the Atlantic World*, 207, 222.

goods, books, newspapers, and correspondence from Europe helped them to maintain close links with their native countries. Yet, even among European migrants, not all could sustain ties as easily as members of the upper class. Literacy affected the possibility of correspondence and the propensity to write while the cost of transatlantic travel made it difficult if not impossible for most settlers to travel back and forth between the colony and the metropole. The elite were the only ones whose lives were not trapped in Louisiana. Even when they decided to settle in the colony, their families, social strategies, and careers often had an imperial dimension. Although the collapse of the concession system reduced the number of absentee concession holders, the elite who resided in the colony looked toward the metropole.

The correspondence of Jean-Charles de Pradel (1692–1764), the only collection of private letters left from the French period, reveals the diversity of links that attached a member of the colonial elite to metropolitan France. The very existence of his prolific, lifelong correspondence with different family members (his mother and his brothers) whom he left behind in Uzerche testifies to the attachment and nostalgia he felt for both his family and his native country and his province, Limousin. Exchanging letters helped family on both sides of the Atlantic stay connected despite the distance that separated them. Forty years after Pradel moved to Louisiana, he wrote:

> I have received, my dear brothers, through the King's vessel which should travel back to France shortly, your letters dated last December 30, that I read again and again, always with great pleasure; the long interval that goes by until the reception of your letters greatly lessens this pleasure; isn't it sad and painful for us, my dear friends, to spend our lives so far away from each other when our mutual friendship brings us together so tenderly? Nearly every day I have this kind of thoughts, and each time that my body walks around in my garden, my mind is all with you.

Through his marriage and children in the colony, Pradel constituted for himself a new family that he referred to as "my Louisiana family," an expression that throws light on the distress this man felt on leaving the metropole. His connections with France, however, were not only sentimental. He maintained "a quadruple relationship to the home country" to advance his career, increase his fortune, perpetuate his noble way of life, and promote his family's interests. Even when he decided to put down roots in the colony, which was a long and complex process, he did not cease to view himself and his children as belonging to the metropolitan world.[19]

As one of the youngest among his brothers, Pradel moved to Louisiana to make a career and a fortune. He first obtained a commission as a military officer in the navy, came as an ensign to the Mississippi colony in 1714, served the king for more than twenty years in various outposts, and climbed the military ranks, becoming a captain in 1720, before retiring to New Orleans in 1735. His military career linked him closely to the metropole, since his success depended on the patron-client relationships he was able to maintain with the minister of the navy and his circle. Early on, impecunious, he started to trade, which he could not have done without the financial and material assistance of his metropolitan family. His brothers lent or gave him money (to buy goods and later slaves), helped him hire skilled workers from Limousin, and provided him with influential connections. On his retirement, Pradel purchased a plantation in the vicinity of New Orleans in 1736. His involvement in commerce with the metropole and Saint-Domingue then took on a new dimension, as he sold indigo, tobacco, wax, planks, and bricks in exchange for metropolitan merchandise, wine, and tafia that he then resold in the colony. His fortune depended on his trading connections in La Rochelle and Cap-Français. Until his acquisition of a plantation, Pradel kept hoping to "exit" the colony. Only in the last years of his life did he give up this dream and cease to mention the possibility in his letters.[20]

19. For Pradel's Louisiana family, see A. Baillardel and A. Prioult, eds., *Le chevalier de Pradel: Vie d'un colon français en Louisiane au XVIIIe siècle d'après sa correspondance et celle de sa famille* (Paris, 1928), 191, 237. For an analysis of the relationships Pradel maintained with France, see François-Joseph Ruggiu, "Une noblesse atlantique? Le second ordre français de l'Ancien au Nouveau Monde," in "L'Atlantique Français," special issue, *Outre-mers: Revue d'histoire*, XCVII, nos. 362–363 (2009), 54–55.

20. On Pradel's military career, see "Pradel de Lamase (Jean, chevalier de), capitaine en Louisiane, † 1764," ANOM COL E; and Carl A. Brasseaux, *France's Forgotten Legion: A CD-Rom Publication: Service Records of French Military and Administrative Personnel Stationed in the Mississippi Valley and Gulf Coast Region, 1699–1769* (Baton Rouge, La., 2000). On Pradel's commercial activities, see Baillardel and Prioult, eds., *Le chevalier de Pradel*, 36–37, 51–53, 65, 80–90, 92–93, 97, 100, 109, 119–120, 126–127, 175–178, 184, 193, 204, 210, 221–222, 226, 236, 249, 259, 261–262, 310–311. On Pradel's acquisition of a plantation near New Orleans, see "Procuration," Oct. 6, 1736, in Heloise H. Cruzat, ed., "RSCL XXVII: Supplement Index, no. 4," *LHQ*, VIII (1925), 500; and "Act of Occupation as Owners," June 19, 1737, in "RSCL XVI," *LHQ*, V (1922), 400. On Pradel's desire to return to France, see Baillardel and Prioult, eds., *Le chevalier de Pradel*, 48, 58, 75, 95, 121, 123.

Nevertheless, during his lifetime, Pradel returned to France on several occasions to manage his family, professional, and trading affairs. As an officer, he was entitled to take leave and was given free passage on the king's vessels, which regularly transported passengers from Louisiana. Except for soldiers, most of the travelers belonged to the upper classes, as their titles of civility (*"Monsieur," "Sieur," "Dame," and "Demoiselle"* ["Mr.," "Sire," "Mrs.," and "Miss"]) on the passenger lists reveal, but a few settlers of more modest means were also allowed on board. Although Pradel and his family do not appear to have traveled with servants or slaves, elite voyagers were often accompanied by a few white but most often black domestics. Such transatlantic journeys enabled these individuals to bring back a glimpse of the metropolitan world to other people of African or mixed descent, the majority of whom were stuck in the colony.[21]

The family's material culture also linked Pradel and his closest relatives to France. The officer married Alexandrine, the daughter of Jacques de La Chaise, the king's commissioner, in May 1730. Thanks to stays in the metropole and to personal correspondence, his French-born wife followed Parisian fashions, and she did not hesitate to order luxurious clothes from the French capital. More generally, Pradel and his family sought to reproduce the metropolitan elite's way of life. He carefully undertook to build and decorate a large house on his plantation, called *Monplaisir* (My pleasure), ordering furniture, hinges, overmantels, window glass, mirrors, and tapestries from France. After he had spent a fortune on his house, he wrote to his brothers about "the extravagance of my *Castel Novo* [New Castle]: I wish it could be transferred to Brive-la-Gaillarde, with its surrounding lands and the revenue it produces, and I would have no regret at all at having built it." Following in the steps of the provincial nobility in imitating the aristocracy, the colonial elite conformed to the metropolitan cultural model as a strategy of distinction.[22]

21. On Pradel's journeys to the metropole, see Baillardel and Prioult, eds., *Le chevalier de Pradel*, 33–46, 82–115, 139–140, 145, 175; and "Passenger list on *Le Parham*," Sept. 30, 1749, Colonies: Passagers embarqués pour France, Louisiana, 1732–1765, ANOM COL F5B 34. For wills mentioning that slaves had accompanied their masters to France, see RSCL 1738/08/26/03; 1758/11/16/01. For examples of slaves returning from Bordeaux to Louisiana following their masters, see Certificats d'identité et de catholicité, soumissions, et passeports concernant les passagers embarqués à Bordeaux, Passeports et soumission, Attributions administratives, Fonds de l'amirauté de Guyenne, Archives départementales de Gironde, Feb. 26, 1752, 6B 51 102, Mar. 14, 1752, 6B 51 105v, Feb. 20, 1762, 6B 52 150v, Mar. 31, 1762, 6B 52 153, Apr. 3, 1762, 6B 52 153, and Mar. 21, 1765, 6B 53 71.

22. For Pradel's marriage, see Earl C. Woods and Charles E. Nolan, eds., *Sacramental*

Two of Pradel's children were born during various visits to the home country. His oldest daughter died there in 1761, when she was thirty, without ever having seen New Orleans. As was the custom among the colonial elite, Pradel's children, including those born in the colony, were educated in France. In 1752, four young women and men, daughters and sons of military or militia officers, embarked on board *Le Rhinocéros*. According to the passengers' list, Mademoiselle Pradel, Mademoiselle Demorand, Sieur Le Bretton *fils* (son), and Sieur Villars fils "crossed over to France for their education." Pradel's daughters studied at the Ursulines' convent in Quimperlé. All of them were married in France.[23]

Pradel's son, Charles, followed in his father's footsteps and joined the navy because he lacked the financial means to be accepted in the *Mousquetaires* (Musketeers). Inheriting his father's estate and increasing his fortune through the management of a plantation was not considered sufficient to sustain his social rank as a nobleman; he needed to serve the king. Charles started his military career in France and served successively in Rochefort, Toulon, and, after a one-year leave in Louisiana, Brest. At the end of the Seven Years' War, he was sent to the Mississippi colony to take part in the transfer of troops to Saint-Domingue. He died there soon after his arrival in January 1764. His early death foiled his father's plans. After Charles' marriage in Saintonge in 1762, Pradel had begun to accumulate property for his son in the colony in the hope that, after a career in the home country, Charles would be able to obtain a commission as a lieutenant and settle in Louisiana. Putting down roots in the colony was a long and complicated process for elite families, and, even those who decided to settle for good did not break off their relationships with France but instead developed differ-

---

Records of the Roman Catholic Church of the Archdiocese of New Orleans, 19 vols. (New Orleans, 1987–2003), I, 213. On Madame Pradel following the metropolitan fashion, see Sophie White, "'This Gown . . . Was Much Admired and Made Many Ladies Jealous': Fashion and the Forging of Elite Identities in French Colonial New Orleans," in Tamara Harvey and Greg O'Brien, eds., *George Washington's South* (Gainesville, Fla., 2004), 86–118. On Pradel's large house on his plantation, see Baillardel and Prioult, eds., *Le chevalier de Pradel*, 181, 183, 194, 196, 198, 204–205, 207–208, 219–221, 244, 261; and NONA Mar. 30, 1764.

23. For the metropolitan birth and death of some of Pradel's children, see Baillardel and Prioult, eds., *Le chevalier de Pradel*, 82, 119, 141, 145–180, 191–193, 199–200, 287–293. For an early example of elite Louisiana children being educated in France, see "Family Affair in Desfontaines Estate," May 8, 1726, in "RSCL X," *LHQ*, III (1920), 405. For the journey of one of Pradel's daughters to France to be educated, see "Passenger list on *Le Rhinocéros*," Oct. 4, 1752, Colonies: Passagers embarqués pour France, Louisiane, 1732–1765, ANOM COL F5B 34.

ent strategies for all their children, depending on their gender. Their professional, social, and cultural interests necessarily gave an imperial dimension to their lives and family histories. In that regard, the navy had been instrumental in the Pradel family's evolution and connections with the Empire.[24]

IMPERIAL MOBILITY IN THE KING'S SERVICE

The French Empire was unique among European powers in that there was a single institution, the navy, that managed not only ships, sailors, arsenals, and commercial ports in the metropole but also all the colonies and trading outposts. Once the Company of the Indies released its trade monopoly, sword officers, pen officers, and civil employees came under the navy's direct administration. The management of their careers and the requirements of the service led to great mobility both between France and Louisiana and between Louisiana and other colonies. The multidirectional movements of the king's servants were of tremendous significance. In many ways, these professional peregrinations and the subsequent circulation of knowledge made the Empire, strengthening in particular the connections between the Mississippi colony and the Antilles. In contrast, soldiers from the *compagnies franches de la Marine* (companies of regulars under the navy's supervision) always came from France and completed their time in Louisiana. Their recurring renewal maintained a strong metropolitan presence in the colony.[25]

All Louisiana's governors, who headed the local military hierarchy, were chosen from among Canadians or metropolitans. Because of the movements of sword officers over the course of their military careers, however, many of them had family connections with Saint-Domingue or some experience in the Antilles. Étienne Périer had a nephew who served as a sword officer in Saint-Domingue in 1730. Pierre de Rigaud de Vaudreuil de Cavagnal's brother, Joseph Hyacinthe, spent his whole military career in Saint-Domingue and even governed the colony between 1753 and 1757. Finally, before serving as governor of Louisiana, Louis Billouart de Kerlérec participated in several naval campaigns in the Caribbean and escorted a convoy of merchant vessels to Saint-Domingue during the War of the Austrian

24. On the life, career, and inheritance of Pradel's son, see Baillardel and Prioult, eds., *Le chevalier de Pradel*, 146, 169, 178–179, 188, 217–219, 227–228, 233, 241–242, 245–247, 269, 281, 300, 312–313, 317–319; and NONA Jean-Baptiste Garic Feb. 18, 1764.

25. On the French navy, see Alexandre Dubé, "Making a Career out of the Atlantic: Louisiana's Plume," in Cécile Vidal, ed., *Louisiana: Crossroads of the Atlantic World* (Philadelphia, 2014), 44–67.

Succession; he also served in a naval campaign against interlopers off the coast of the island in 1750–1751.[26]

Apart from Louisiana's governors, the mobility of military officers who served in the colony was particularly great. The compagnies franches de la Marine were created in the 1680s and early 1690s to defend overseas territories. Contrary to the norm in most eighteenth-century armies, navy officers' commissions were not available for purchase but were open to anyone in a position to benefit from royal favor. The king frequently granted them to the sons of colonial elite to attach them to royal and metropolitan power. The first officers of the companies garrisoned in Louisiana came not only from France but also from Canada and the Antilles. After some years in the Mississippi Valley, they often sought new appointments in Saint-Domingue because they had relatives and property in that colony or wanted to take advantage of the greater opportunities for making a fortune there. This is what Dumont de Montigny implied when he wrote about the campaign against the Chickasaws in 1736 during which the commandant of the Illinois Country, Pierre Dartaguiette, died. Pierre was the brother of Bernard Diron Dartaguiette, who was sent to Saint-Domingue in 1739 after having served as general inspector for the Company of the Indies and commandant in Mobile:

> Finally, from this place, during the first war
> Diron, esquire, after he had lost his brother
> who, as I said, was burnt with his people
> At the Chickasaw fort, as he could not save himself
> From the barbarous fury and from the hands of the Native
> Who, laughing at us, threw the tempest,
> The King sent him to be Lieutenant
> To the Cap in Saint-Domingue, where at present,
> He enjoys with pleasure the great advantage of living away from this
>   savage country
> Which is reduced to war and to a large forest.

Although Saint-Domingue was the most coveted posting, officers were also assigned to Martinique, Grenada, and Cayenne. Antoine Lemoyne de

26. Périer to the minister of the navy, Aug. 1, 1730, ANOM COL C13A 12, fol. 310v; Guy Frégault, *Le grand Marquis: Pierre Rigaud de Vaudreuil et la Louisiane* (Montreal, 1952), 50; Hervé Gourmelon, *Le chevalier de Kerlérec, 1704–1770: L'affaire de la Louisiane* ... (Spézet, France, 2003); Pierre-Georges Roy, *La famille de Rigaud de Vaudreuil* (Lévis, Quebec, 1938), 162–166.

Chateauguay, for instance, moved from Louisiana to Martinique where he served as *lieutenant de roi* at Fort Saint-Pierre in 1727. With the passing of generations, vacant or new commissions in the Mississippi colony were granted to the sons of military officers and prominent planters and merchants, who were often Creole-born. Yet, as was the case with Charles Pradel, they sometimes had to start their military careers outside Louisiana, in the metropole or in another colony, before they could come back.[27]

In contrast with sword officers, there were far fewer positions available for pen officers, and civil servants were generally recruited among metropolitans. The most important office was that of the *commissaire-ordonnateur*, for the king never appointed an *intendant* in Louisiana. As the state's second representative after the governor, the commissaire-ordonnateur was in charge of administrative, judicial, financial, and commercial matters. All the men who successively held this position in New Orleans were born in France, but two of them were posted in another colony when they received their nomination: Honoré-Gabriel Michel had been serving in Canada, and Sébastien François Ange Le Normant de Mezy had been in Saint-Domingue, where he owned a large plantation. A few employees of lesser rank also moved between Louisiana and the Antilles.

In comparison with the imperial movements of military and civil officers, troops who were sent to Louisiana always came from the metropole and were never recruited locally. Although the Company of the Indies chose to maintain a low-level military presence after the collapse of Law's System, reducing the number of companies from sixteen in 1721 to eight by 1728,

27. Except when otherwise specified, all information on the careers of sword or pen officers comes from "List of Officers Who Served in Louisiana," 1728–1777, ANOM COL D2C 59, fols. 1–81; Brasseaux, *France's Forgotten Legion;* Giraud, *Histoire de la Louisiane française;* and Gabriel Debien and René Le Gardeur, "Les colons de Saint-Domingue réfugiés à la Louisiane (1792–1804)," *Revue de Louisiane/Louisiana Review*, IX, no. 2 (1980), 101–140, X, no. 1 (1981), 11–49, X, no. 2 (1981), 97–141. For lists of names of sword and pen officers circulating between Louisiana and the Antilles, see Cécile Vidal, "Caribbean New Orleans: Urban Genesis, Empire, and Race in the Eighteenth-Century French Atlantic" (Habilitation à diriger des recherches original manuscript, Université Paris-Sorbonne, 2014), 62–68. On the mobility of Canadian military officers, see Lorraine Gadoury, *La noblesse de Nouvelle-France: Familles et alliances* (Ville La Salle, Quebec, 1991). For Saint-Domingue as the most coveted posting for sword officers, see Villiers, ed., "L'établissement de la province de la Louisiane: Poème composé de 1728 à 1742," *Journal de la société des américanistes,* XXIII (1931), 424 (quotation). For an example of a nomination of a Louisiana officer to Martinique, see François de Pas de Mazencourt, marquis de Feuquières, to the minister of the navy, Mar. 27, 1727, ANOM COL C8A 37, fol. 301rv.

the colony's geopolitical value meant that the crown immediately began to rebuild its military strength after retaking possession of the territory in 1731. By 1732, the king had increased the number of companies again to thirteen. He also transferred the Karrer Swiss Regiment along with 150 Swiss and German soldiers of Catholic or Protestant faith. Although the Mississippi colony was not a priority during the War of the Austrian Succession, the number of companies stationed there rose again in 1750 to thirty-seven, with a theoretical growth of 50 men in the Karrer Swiss Regiment, in preparation for the next conflict. With the capture of Havana by the British in 1762 at the end of the Seven Years' War, the monarch sent the Angoumois Regiment with ten companies, expecting New Orleans to be the British navy's next target. But the regiment was ordered to move to Saint-Domingue with some compagnies franches de la Marine on the announcement of the cession of the colony to Great Britain and Spain in 1763. Only six of the navy's companies were left in New Orleans and the western part of Louisiana to wait for the Spanish.[28]

When the French Empire was not at war, the need to replenish companies depleted by death, discharge, or desertion meant that there was a continual flow of soldiers between the metropole and New Orleans. Those who were discharged and refused to stay in Louisiana had to be sent back to France while new recruits had to be brought to fill those places left vacant. Because of this strong military presence, a large percentage of the colonial population, including that of the capital, always remained metropolitan. Some of these French-born regulars, greatly encouraged by the authorities, chose to settle in Louisiana at the end of their enlistments. Consequently, New Orleans's city dwellers included many former servicemen. Soldiers formed a large proportion of the new settlers. Thanks to the extension and diversification of the colony's trading circuits after 1731, civil migration also played a role in the slow growth of the colonial population.[29]

28. René Chartrand, "The Troops of French Louisiana, 1699–1769," *Military Collector and Historian*, XXV, no. 2 (Summer 1973), 58–65; David Hardcastle, "Swiss Mercenary Soldiers in the Service of France in Louisiana," in Alf A. Heggoy and James J. Cooke, eds., *Proceedings of the Fourth Meeting of the French Colonial Historical Society, April 6–8, 1978*, [IV] (Washington, D.C., 1979), 82–91; Susan Gibbs Lemann, "The Problems of Founding a Viable Colony: The Military in Early French Louisiana," in J. J. Cooke, ed., *Proceedings of the Sixth and Seventh Annual Meetings of the French Colonial Historical Society, 1980–1981*, [VI/VII] (Washington, D.C, 1982), 27–35; Bernard Lugan, *La Louisiane française, 1682–1804* (Paris, 1994), 165–181, 244–249; Brasseaux, *France's Forgotten Legion*.

29. On this policy of peopling the colony with former soldiers, see Cécile Vidal, "Les

On January 1731 and September 1732, following the crown's resumption of direct rule over the Mississippi colony, Louis XV issued two decrees opening Louisiana's trade "to all the ports privileged to deal with the French colonies, except for the beaver trade and the commerce in Negroes which remained in the hands of the Company of the Indies." The minister of the navy then took a series of measures to facilitate the inclusion of New Orleans within the transatlantic and Caribbean circuits developed by French private merchants. After a few years during which the king's vessels played a crucial role in supplying the colony, merchants from La Rochelle and other French ports started to integrate New Orleans in their transatlantic and Caribbean trading expeditions because it was a convenient port from which to participate in Spanish trade. Yet the communications that the Louisiana capital maintained with the rest of the Atlantic world were increasingly mediated by Saint-Domingue. Whether they came from a French or a Caribbean port, the ships that docked at New Orleans employed transnational crews, including black sailors. Although Louisiana's export trade remained to a large extent contained by the French imperial framework, despite trade with the Spanish and wartime smuggling, this transient population of sailors helped bring news and rumors to the Mississippi colony from throughout the Atlantic and Caribbean world.[30]

The start of free trade—at least for the privileged ports—within the Empire was difficult, and Louisiana would not have endured during the first few years without the arrival of the king's vessels. After 1731, the minister of the navy usually sent one to four ships a year to the colony to transmit orders, written in dozens of letters accumulated over the previous months; bring new officers, employees, and soldiers; carry pay in cash or goods for all the king's personnel; supply flour (and other food products) for all those

---

implantations françaises au Pays des Illinois au XVIIIe siècle," 2 vols. (Ph.D. diss., École des Hautes Études en Sciences Sociales, 1995), 173–177; and Brasseaux, "Introduction: The French and Canadian Precursors of Louisiana's Administrative and Military Institutions," in Brasseaux, *France's Forgotten Legion*, 70–73.

30. The king's two decrees opening the Louisiana trade to all ports privileged to deal with French colonies were later renewed in 1741 and 1751. See Émile Garnault, *Le commerce rochelais au XVIIIe siècle; d'après les documents composant les anciennes archives de la Chambre de Commerce de la Rochelle*, III, *Marine et colonies: De 1718 à la paix d'Aix-la-Chapelle (1748)* (La Rochelle, France, 1891), 45–52; and John G. Clark, *New Orleans, 1718–1812: An Economic History* (Baton Rouge, La., 1970), 64 (quotation).

entitled to receive the king's ration; and convey equipment such as uniforms, arms, and gunpowder for the garrisons as well as boxes of medicine and presents for indigenous allies. Most of the time, ships arrived in La Balise and New Orleans in the spring (March, April, May) or fall (September, October, November) and left a few weeks later, taking with them replies from local authorities to the minister of the navy, private correspondence, and the products of the fur trade along with officers on leave, discharged or sick soldiers, passengers having family business in the metropole, or settlers leaving the Mississippi Valley for good. The arrivals and departures of these ships punctuated life in Louisiana; delays caused anxiety because the colony's finances, its geopolitical situation with the Natives, and the well-being of its employees and soldiers depended on them.[31]

During the 1730s, the minister of the navy, Jean-Frédéric Phélypeaux, comte de Maurepas, used government freight to interest private merchants in the Louisiana trade and to regulate their number and arrival in New Orleans. He signed treaties with private merchants to transport the king's personnel and cargoes. The plan was to progressively reduce the volume of wares the crown had to send to the colony. Even so, this goal was not reached until the end of the French regime. A permanent lack of cash and the subsequent overdrawing of bills of exchange, first to encourage the development of trade with France and then to meet its expenses, forced the king to become a major stakeholder in the fur trade. Throughout the eighteenth century, the monarch imported huge amounts of European merchandise that were subsequently distributed through his trading stores to his officers, employees, and soldiers, instead of wages and pay, and then exchanged for pelts and furs.[32]

From the mid-1730s onward, ships outfitted on behalf of private owners from La Rochelle, Bordeaux, Saint-Malo, Lorient, Nantes, Marseille, and Bayonne started to reach La Balise and New Orleans. La Rochelle became the leading port trading with Louisiana, ahead of Bordeaux, sending four ships from 1720 to 1729, thirty-three from 1730 to 1739, forty-nine from 1740 to 1749, fifty-four from 1750 to 1759, and thirty-three from 1760 to 1769, many being from two to three hundred tons. Over time, the number

31. It was not exactly a "free trade" within the French Empire, since the letters patent of 1717 and 1727 limited the number of metropolitan port cities authorized to trade with the colonies.

32. On the action of the state to develop "free trade" in Louisiana, see Clark, *New Orleans, 1718–1812*, 71–72. On the role of the state in the fur trade, see Alexandre Dubé, "Les biens publics: Culture politique de la Louisiane française, 1730–1770" (Ph.D. diss., McGill University, 2009).

of merchants from La Rochelle involved in the Louisiana trade grew, although commerce with the Mississippi colony generally remained secondary to their other trading endeavors.[33]

The arrival of private ships from the metropole in New Orleans fluctuated according to the volume of Louisiana's exports (mostly deerskins, tobacco, and indigo but also lumber, planks, shingles, and pitch and tar), opportunities for commerce with the nearby Spanish colonies, and cycles of peace and war. The Seven Years' War, in particular, was a period of isolation and deprivation in the Mississippi Valley. Even though the minister of the navy and commercial interests did not neglect the colony during the conflict, many of the ships sent to New Orleans were intercepted by the English, who controlled the seas. Still, given that most of the time goods from France were not paid down but were bought on credit and the payment of bills and letters of exchange was long and difficult, metropolitan merchants retained incentive to maintain trade with Louisiana even during periods of war. At the time of the colony's transfer to Spain, the amounts owed to La Rochelle's merchants were so huge that Spanish authorities allowed French commerce to continue until 1772 in order for merchants to collect their debts.[34]

During the War of the Austrian Succession and the Seven Years' War, Louisiana's isolation was reduced somewhat by rising competition from foreign interlopers. In times of peace, a few British or Dutch ships from Jamaica and Curaçao had already begun to sell their cargoes there, but the colony's slow demographic and economic development did not make it attractive as a site of economic opportunity. The few contraband vessels that visited the Louisiana coast apparently preferred to unload clandestinely in Mobile. In wartime, these foreign ships arrived at La Balise and

33. On La Rochelle's preeminent role in Louisiana commerce, see Henri Robert, *Les trafics coloniaux du port de La Rochelle au XVIIIe siècle*, in *Mémoires de la société des antiquaires de l'Ouest*, 4th Ser., IV (Poitiers, France, 1960), 19–20; and John G. Clark, *La Rochelle and the Atlantic Economy during the Eighteenth Century* (Baltimore, 1981), 29. For a table of all annual arrivals in New Orleans by port of origin in France and the French West Indies, see Clark, *New Orleans, 1718–1812*, 83. For a year-by-year narrative of the trade between metropolitan France and Louisiana from the point of view of New Orleans, see Surrey, *Commerce of Louisiana during the French Régime*, 169–225.

34. Banks, *Chasing Empire across the Sea*, 208–216; Dubé, "Les biens publics," 224–227; Robert, *Les trafics coloniaux du port de La Rochelle au XVIIIe siècle*, 85; Jean Tarrade, "La France et la Louisiane espagnole à la fin de l'Ancien Régime (1763–1789)," in *L'Europe, l'Alsace, et la France: Problèmes intérieurs et relations internationales à l'époque moderne* (Colmar, France, 1986), 337–344, esp. 338–339.

were sometimes allowed by local authorities to trade in the colony in an effort to procure necessary food supplies, presents for Native Americans, or merchandise for the fur and pelt trade. Such authorizations were granted, for instance, during Vaudreuil's governorship. Hence, Governor Kerlérec's decision to permit the British ship *Le Texel*, called *parlementaire* by the French because it served to exchange prisoners of war and was used for smuggling, to do business in the colony during the Seven Years' War should have gone unnoticed. In 1759, however, the governor's action turned into a political scandal that came to be known as the Louisiana Affair when Vincent-Gaspard-Pierre de Rochemore accused Kerlérec of prevarication.[35]

Whenever Louisiana's top officials wrote about the "foreign trade," they were always referring to illegal commerce with British and Dutch ships, never to business with Spanish vessels and settlements. From the outset, the minister of the navy never ceased to promote the Spanish trade, and local authorities, eager to please their superior and to make a profit, implemented measures to develop it. From the Spanish perspective, commercial exchanges between the French, British, or Dutch with Spanish ships and outposts were usually considered smuggling. Because Madrid's policy constantly fluctuated, Spanish colonial governments opened or closed trade depending on the circumstances. Even though it was a risky and uncertain business, commerce with the Spanish remained the main impetus for French merchants to include Louisiana in their trading circuits.[36]

35. On trade with the English, see Surrey, *Commerce of Louisiana during the French Régime*, 443–463. For illegal trading vessels unloading in Mobile in times of peace, see Bienville and Edmé Gatien Salmon to the minister of the navy, Apr. 5, 1734, ANOM COL C13A 18, fols. 58–61; Charles François Cullo de Crémont to the minister of the navy, Oct. 27, 1734, ANOM COL C13A 19, fols. 171–179; Bienville to the minister of the navy, Sept. 4, 1736, ANOM COL C13A 21, fols. 213–217; and Bienville to the minister of the navy, Dec. 12, 1737, ANOM C13A 22, fols. 107–110. For foreign ships arriving in La Balise in times of war, see Vaudreuil to the minister of the navy, Nov. 24, 1746, ANOM COL C13A 30, fols. 104–105; Charles Philippe Aubry to the minister of the navy, Aug. 8, 1755, ANOM COL C13A 39, fols. 118–120; and Louis Billouart de Kerlérec and Guillaume Le Sénéchal d'Auberville to the minister of the navy, July 3, 1754, ANOM COL C13A 38, fol. 7. On the Louisiana Affair, see Dubé, "Les biens publics."

36. For examples of references to "foreign trade," see Bienville and Salmon to the minister of the navy, Sept. 4, 1736, ANOM COL C13A 21, fols. 94–100; and Report by Vincent-Gaspard-Pierre de Rochemore on the Administration of Louisiana, 1749, ANOM COL C13A 33, fols. 150–162. For Spanish trade as one of the main motivations for the colonization of Louisiana, see Surrey, *Commerce of Louisiana during the French Régime*, 388–406, 431–442. On French merchants' interweaving of trade between Louisi-

French metropolitan merchants dominated the maritime trade with the Spanish colonies of the Gulf of Mexico, Havana, and Veracruz, leaving New Orleans traders largely dependent on the arrival of Spanish ships in Louisiana or on the circulation of French metropolitan vessels that stopped in a Spanish port. Vessels coming from a metropolitan port followed complex circuits between France and various French and Spanish colonies in the Caribbean. Antoine's ship, *L'espérance,* circulated between Lorient, Cap-Français, Havana, and New Orleans. These ships primarily sold French textiles and apparel that had been specifically chosen to suit Spanish tastes. In return, French merchants obtained piastres, which became the principal currency in the Mississippi colony. Piastres compensated for the lack of Louisiana products stowed as return cargo from New Orleans. Consequently, apart from exotic goods from the Antilles (coffee, sugar, molasses, and tafia), most of the food supplies (wheat flour, bacon, salted beef, apples, wine, and alcohol, for example) and manufactured wares (clothes and fabric, especially, but also paper, wax, soap, tools, ornaments, and so on and so forth) exported to Louisiana came, directly or indirectly, from metropolitan France, although they might have been produced in another country. As a result of both supply circuits and taste, Louisiana's material culture was heavily shaped by French fashion, even when products were only re-exported to the colony from other places.[37]

After 1731, various sea-lanes followed by ships coming from French ports to New Orleans connected Louisiana's capital with the Antilles and the

---

ana and the Spanish colonies, see, for instance, Report by Gradis on Louisiana, May 21, 1748, ANOM COL C13A 32, fols. 248–251.

37. Pensacola was not considered as important as Havana and Veracruz and was mostly supplied by Mobile. See Bienville and Salmon to the minister of the navy, June 1, 1737, ANOM COL C13A 22, fols. 37–41; and Vaudreuil to the minister of the navy, July 26, 1743, ANOM COL C13A 28, fols. 61–64. On trade with Pensacola, see Surrey, *Commerce of Louisiana during the French Régime,* 418–430. On the failure of some Louisiana expeditions to Havana and Veracruz organized by the New Orleans merchant Gérard Péry and the arrival in Louisiana of French ships having traded in Spanish colonies, see Vaudreuil to the minister of the navy, July 26, 1743, ANOM COL C13A 28, fols. 61–64. For the circuit followed by *L'Espérance,* see RSCL 1765/10/16/02. For the choice of merchandise to fit Spanish taste, see Sophie White, "Geographies of Slave Consumption: French Colonial Louisiana and a World of Goods," *Winterthur Portfolio,* XLV (2011), 237. For the role of piastres in Louisiana commerce, see Robert, *Les trafics coloniaux du port de La Rochelle au XVIIIe siècle,* 85; and Jean-Marie Loncol, "La Louisiane et les colonies espagnoles d'Amérique, 1731–1748," *Revue d'histoire de l'Amérique française,* XVIII (1964), 196–201.

greater Caribbean. In the late 1730s, an independent intercolonial trade also began to rapidly expand between the Mississippi colony and Saint-Domingue and, to a lesser extent, between Louisiana and Martinique. To prevent contraband and to sustain the economic development of France's overseas territories, the minister of the navy adopted a series of dispositions favoring intercolonial trade. In 1737, he exempted Louisiana settlers from harbor fees on direct trade with the islands for a span of ten years. This exemption was later renewed. Thereafter, with the exception of the king's vessels, which got under way every year in times of peace, many ships coming from the home country ceased to continue on to New Orleans but stopped in ports on Saint-Domingue. They escaped the long and dangerous navigation in the Gulf of Mexico and up the Mississippi River and secured a more interesting return cargo. A particular trade then developed between Saint-Domingue and Louisiana: the latter furnished the former with lumber, planks, shingles, bricks, pitch and tar, rice, corn, peas, and beans, while Saint-Domingue supplied New Orleans with slaves, tafia, sugar, molasses, coffee, and European goods. European wares imported from the islands were sold at a much higher price than if they had been brought directly from France, an inflation that was denounced by Louisiana authorities, merchants, and settlers.[38]

The intercolonial trade between Louisiana and the French Caribbean, which expanded from the early 1740s onward, impacted the ways information circulated within the Empire. Because Saint-Domingue was more closely connected to the metropole than the Mississippi colony, Louisiana officials and settlers often had to send their letters to the home country

38. Most of the commerce between Martinique and the northern French colonies was with Canada via Louisbourg or Quebec City. See Movements and Cargoes of Ships between Martinique and Canada or Louisiana in 1737, 1743, 1744, 1750, 1751, ANOM COL C8B 17, nos. 10, 11, 20, 21, 31, 32, 50, 55, 58. For an attempt to develop trade between Louisiana and Guadeloupe, see Charles de Brunier, marquis de Larnage, to the minister of the navy, June 28, 1735, ANOM COL F3 17, fol. 484. The minister of the navy started to give orders to develop trade between Louisiana and Saint-Domingue in 1731. See Salmon to the minister of the navy, June 1, 1731, ANOM COL C13A 13, fol. 101. On Louisiana settlers' exemption from harbor fees on direct trade with the islands, see the minister of the navy to de Champigny de Noroy and Pannier d'Orgeville, Mar. 25, 1737, ANOM COL F3 24, fol. 298; and Bienville and Salmon to the minister of the navy, Dec. 12, 1737, ANOM COL C13A 24, fol. 33. On the products exchanged between Louisiana and the Caribbean islands, see Le Page du Pratz, *Histoire de la Louisiane*, III, 386–388. On inflation and European merchandise brought from the Antilles to Louisiana, see Report of Dubreuil on the Trade between Louisiana and France, 1752, ANOM COL C13A 36, fols. 327–329.

by way of the island. Pradel sometimes noted in his correspondence that he had sent or received letters via Saint-Domingue. These exchanges also formed common interests and interdependence between the authorities of the two colonies. Although there is little extant evidence left, a specific correspondence probably developed between them as well.[39]

All the ships coming from France via the Antilles or directly from the islands also brought a transient population of sailors of European and African descent to Louisiana who often disturbed the socioracial order that local authorities and settlers sought to implement. Some of these seamen were enslaved or free blacks born in Africa, as was the case with Antoine. These maritime workers represented the only loose connections maintained with Africa after 1731. A few of them emerged from the archives because they caused trouble and generated an inquiry or even a trial. In 1767, for instance, George, a twenty-eight-year-old slave, "speaking good English," who belonged to a merchant of Port-au-Prince and served as a sailor on a ship from Nantes, took advantage of his boat being moored alongside the quay at New Orleans to escape, and the captain was unable to find him. These mariners might have helped to propagate news among people of African descent within the Atlantic world.[40]

In the same way, as another trial reveals, rumors circulated from one side of the Atlantic to the other among white sailors. Seamen of European descent were no less unruly than their black counterparts, although they were prosecuted for different reasons. In 1767, "Baude de Marseille" (his full name was Jacques Toussaint Baude) was sentenced to death for the murder of a fellow countryman from Provence. He had killed the man while intoxicated in a fight outside a New Orleans tavern where he had drank and played pool with friends from Provence and Spain. The criminal's wanderings had taken him from Marseille to Cádiz, then Nice, Port-au-Prince, Havana, Campeche, Pensacola, Mobile, and New Orleans. In fact, he first fled Provence because he had already killed two men after two different tav-

---

39. On the role of Saint-Domingue in the circulation of letters between France and Louisiana, see Baillardel and Prioult, eds., *Le chevalier de Pradel*, 87, 238, 270, 303. For instances of independent correspondence between Louisiana and Saint-Domingue, see Michel to the minister of the navy, May 18, 1751, ANOM COL C13A 35, fols. 205–210r; Copy of the Letter of Mr. Bart, governor of Saint-Domingue, to Mr. de Kerlérec, governor of Louisiana, July 6, 1750, ANOM COL C13A 46, fol. 122r; Aubry to the minister of the navy, May 23, 1769, ANOM COL C13A 49, fol. 28; Saint-Léger to the Superior Council of Louisiana, Feb. 9, 1769, ANOM COL C13A 49, fol. 208, and Grenier to the Superior Council of Louisiana, Feb. 9, 1769, fol. 209.

40. For the trial of the slave named George, see RSCL 1767/02/04/02.

ern fights and refused to marry a girl who was pregnant by him. His story and travels were revealed in his own examination as well as through the testimonies of several of his fellow countrymen from Provence, ship's officers, sailors, and merchants who had known him or heard of him in France, Spain, or the Caribbean. Together, the ships, products, and communities of sailors that operated between France, the Antilles, and Louisiana connected the far-flung pieces of the French Empire.[41]

NEW COLONISTS AND SLAVES FROM THE ANTILLES

The very same maritime activity that made Louisiana's developing trade connections with the rest of the French Empire possible also facilitated the settlement of new migrants. Contrary to the Company of the Indies, the crown did not organize another migratory wave from Europe or from Africa. Having decided to keep Louisiana mainly for geopolitical reasons, the king wished to maintain the colony as cheaply as possible. Apart from sending troops, the minister of the navy only transported a few salt smugglers there on occasion. He also sentenced one hundred or so men and women from Alsace to exile to the Mississippi colony in the 1750s, after they had abjured Protestantism. Immigrants of both European and African descent, however, continued to come on private initiative. One cannot speak of mass migration as the successive arrivals of isolated individuals or small groups scattered over time. Yet their numbers added up. Since mortality became higher than fertility, the population would not have continued to grow except for this sustained influx of new people. Although a greater equilibrium was reached, the failure of the sex ratio to decline below 127 males for every 100 females for whites and 129 males for every 100 females for blacks in 1763, combined with low child-to-woman ratios, confirms that the colony continued to receive a fair number of male migrants. Free migrants came from both France and the Antilles, but slaves were brought from Saint-Domingue and Martinique. Enslaved workers played a crucial role in the Caribbeanization of New Orleans and Louisiana society.[42]

41. For the prosecution of sailors of European descent, see Extracts from the Registers of the Criminal Hearings of the Superior Council of Louisiana during the year 1736, ANOM COL F3 242, fols. 234–237v; Salmon to the minister of the navy, Feb. 10, 1737, ANOM COL C13A 22, fols. 124–125v; and Michel to the minister of the navy, Sept. 29, 1749, ANOM COL C13A 34, fol. 215. For Jacques Toussaint Baude's trial, see RSCL 1767/11/06/01, 1767/11/06/02, 1767/11/08/01, 1767/11/09/01, 1767/11/09/02, 1767/11/10/01, 1767/11/10/02, 1767/11/11/01, 1767/11/12/01, 1767/11/12/02.

42. For an example of the arrival of smugglers, see Bienville and Salmon to the minister of the navy, Mar. 25, 1742, ANOM COL C13A 27, fols. 21–22r. For the forced mi-

Migrants of European descent appeared individually or in small groups throughout the closing decades of the French regime. The difficult transition from the Company of the Indies's trade monopoly to a system of free trade within the Empire and the quasi ending of the slave trade from Africa in 1731 no doubt discouraged migrants of European descent from moving to Louisiana. During these harsh years, local authorities also tried to impede settlers from leaving New Orleans by refusing them passage on the king's vessels. Yet, from the late 1730s through the 1740s and early 1750s, the colony benefited from a degree of economic expansion, since Louisiana planters were then able to acquire slaves in the islands. The number of indigo and tobacco plantations grew, and commerce with both France and the Antilles developed. Consequently, the colony attracted some migrants of various backgrounds and means from both France and the Caribbean, although departures never stopped completely. In 1733, for instance, on his way back to New Orleans from the metropole to begin his third term as governor, Jean-Baptiste Le Moyne de Bienville met some former Louisiana colonists in Cap-Français who expressed a wish to return to the Mississippi colony.[43]

The merchants, settlers, and indentured servants of European descent and the few free blacks who migrated from French ports emerge randomly through the archives. The same is true for migrants from the Antilles, even though there were some unsuccessful attempts to generate a more massive influx. In 1741, two brothers-in-law from Martinique, Mercier and Tatin,

gration of Protestants from Alsace, see Glenn R. Conrad, "L'immigration alsacienne en Louisiane, 1753–1759," *Revue d'histoire de l'Amérique française*, XXVIII (1975), 565–577. For the evaluation of the number of migrants from France after 1731, see Lachance, "Growth of the Free and Slave Populations of French Colonial Louisiana," in Bond, ed., *French Colonial Louisiana and the Atlantic World*, 207.

43. For the impact of the retrocession of Louisiana to the crown on migrations from France, see Lachance, "Growth of the Free and Slave Populations of French Colonial Louisiana," in Bond, ed., *French Colonial Louisiana and the Atlantic World*, 221. On attempts by local authorities to impede settlers from leaving New Orleans, see Périer and Salmon to the minister of the navy, Dec. 5, 1731, ANOM COL C13A 13, fol. 10v; and Bienville to the minister of the navy, July 25, 1733, ANOM COL C13A 16, fols. 269v–270v. For migrants coming from France and the Antilles, see Salmon to the minister of the navy, Sept. 13, 1733, ANOM COL C13A 17, fol. 202v; César-Marie de La Croix to the minister of the navy, May 17, 1739, ANOM COL C8A 50, fol. 266; Bienville to the minister of the navy, Feb. 4, 1743, ANOM COL C13A 28, fol. 38; RSCL 1747/04/13/01; and NONA Sept. 11, 1764, Nov. 7, 1764. On the meeting between Bienville and former Louisiana settlers in Saint-Domingue, see Bienville to the minister of the navy, Jan. 28, 1733, ANOM COL C13A 16, fol. 223v.

landed in New Orleans with nine or ten slaves. Together, they bought a house with a big garden in the city and a plantation on the Mississippi River. Mercier then returned to Martinique to bring back their families and the rest of their slaves. The two men assured the Louisiana authorities that around fifteen hundred small planters from the island were in search of land and were ready to follow them if only they received confirmation that "this country was as good as they had been told." Governor Bienville and Commissaire-ordonnateur Edmé Gatien Salmon asked the minister of the navy to allow these migrations, but the latter refused because of opposition from the island's top officials, who argued that the development of one colony should not be pursued to the detriment of another. From 1742, Martinique's population actually began to decline. Ten years later, Commissaire-ordonnateur Michel told the minister that some Martinique planters had expressed a wish to migrate with their slaves to the Mississippi Valley because new lands were no longer available on the island. In the following years, some migrants from Martinique did settle in Louisiana, especially after the English occupation of the territory in 1762, taking advantage of Article 28 of the act of capitulation authorizing settlers and merchants to move with their slaves to Saint-Domingue or Louisiana.[44]

Not all migrants from the Antilles, however, were as financially secure as

44. On the attempt to expand migrations from Martinique to Louisiana in the early 1740s, see Bienville and Salmon to the minister of the navy, Sept. 27, 1741, ANOM COL C13A 26, fols. 29–30; Bienville to the minister of the navy, Sept. 30, 1741, ANOM COL C13A 26, fols. 108–109; Salmon to the minister of the navy, Sept. 29, 1741, ANOM COL C13A 26, fol. 169; Vaudreuil and Salmon to the minister of the navy, Aug. 24, 1743, ANOM COL C13A 28, fol. 28; and Vaudreuil and Sébastien-François-Ange Le Normant de Mézy to the minister of the navy, Jan. 4, 1745, ANOM COL C13A 29, fols. 9v–10. On the decline of Martinique's population starting in the early 1740s, see Léo Élisabeth, *La société martiniquaise aux XVIIe et XVIIIe siècles, 1664–1789* (Paris, 2003), 81–149. On a new attempt to develop migrations from Martinique to Louisiana in the early 1750s, see Michel to the minister of the navy, Sept. 23, 1752, ANOM COL C13A 36, fols. 274v–275. On the arrival of migrants from Martinique in the early 1760s, see Alice Daly Forsyth and Ghislaine Pleasonton, eds., *Louisiana Marriage Contracts,* [I], *A Compilation of Abstracts from Records of the Superior Council of Louisiana during the French Regime, 1725–1758* (New Orleans, 1980), 7, 230; RSCL 1745/02/08/02; Woods and Nolan, eds., *Sacramental Records of the Roman Catholic Church of the Archdiocese of New Orleans,* II, 6, 126, 263; and NONA Jan. 16, 1762, Jan. 27, 1762, Feb. 12, 1762. For the 1762 act of capitulation authorizing settlers and merchants in Martinique to move with their slaves to Saint-Domingue or Louisiana, see P. F. R. Dessalles, *Les annales du conseil souverain de la Martinique,* Tome II, Vol. II, *Notes et index,* ed. Bernard Vonglis (1786; rpt. Paris, 1995), 153–154.

these merchants, ship's captains, and planters from Martinique. Some free people of color and whites of the lower sort also migrated from the British, Dutch, Spanish, and French West Indies. Moreover, the colony received criminals banished from Saint-Domingue while Louisiana authorities exiled their own criminals to the island in return. In 1766, one couple was sentenced to perpetual banishment from New Orleans and the payment of a fine of twenty livres to the king because they had sold tafia to slaves and had taken some turkeys stolen from the commissaire-ordonnateur in exchange. During their trial, the husband denied everything, but the woman, Marie Langlois, wife of Bousquet, born in Fatière in Beauvaisis, told the judge "that she had come after the death of her first husband in Saint-Domingue, that she had been in the môle Saint-Nicolas, but that she came to this country because her health did not allow her to stay there" and that her brother-in-law had also died on the island. She then explained "that she had brought [with her] a barrel of wine and a barrel of tafia which she sold to earn a living, with her husband who was a fisherman, but did not make a lot of money with this profession." Poverty turned some men and women into maritime vagrants, wandering from one colony of the greater Caribbean to another.[45]

Apart from these free and forced migrants of European descent, Louisiana received some slaves from the French West Indies. The volume of this trade was certainly greater than has been previously assumed. Pradel ranked "Negroes" second on his "list of merchandise brought by ships which navigat[ed] from the islands of Saint-Domingue, Martinique," after "the products from France of which they have a surplus." In April 1755, he wrote to his brother that "during the last two years a lot [of slaves] came." He succeeded in purchasing several of them between 1755 and 1764, not only because he had the means to do so but also because he benefited from Kerlérec's favors. Like every governor, Kerlérec had the right to keep some slaves from each

45. For free people of color voluntarily immigrating from the Caribbean (from Saint-Domingue and Martinique but also Saint Eustache and Jamaica), see AANO, Saint-Louis Cathedral Baptisms, 1731–1733 and 1744–1753, 11/11/1731, 03/26/1751, 02/14/1752; AANO, Saint-Louis Cathedral Marriages, 1720–1730 and 1764–1774, 06/30/1725, 06/05/1730, 09/10/1764; NONA Aug. 05, 1766; and RSCL 1767/05/25/01. For examples of criminals sent from Saint-Domingue to Louisiana, see RSCL 1765/10/10/03, 1765/10/21/01, 1765/11/06/01, 1765/11/07/01, 1765/11/09/04, 1765/11/09/05, 1765/11/09/06, 1766/01/02/01, 1766/01/02/02, 1766/01/20/01, 1766/01/31/01, 1766/02/01/02, 1766/02/01/04. For examples of criminals sent from Louisiana to Saint-Domingue, see RSCL 1763/09/21/04. For the 1766 trial of the Bousquet couple, see RSCL 1766/11/14/01, 1766/11/14/02, 1766/11/20/04.

slave ship that entered the colony's port, and he allowed his friend to take advantage of this privilege. In turn, Pradel stood security for the governor with two merchants from Nantes, who lived in Saint-Domingue. When Louisiana settlers did not want to wait for a ship from Saint-Domingue or Martinique to bring a few slaves to New Orleans, they could also come to an agreement in advance with merchants from the islands. Although it is impossible to evaluate their overall number precisely, the judicial archives attest to the growing presence of slaves sold from the Antilles to Louisiana in the 1750s and 1760s.[46]

This influx of Caribbean slaves could not but be limited, irregular, and contingent since the islands' officials were opposed to larger exports. This was particularly true for Martinique, which received fewer slave ships than Saint-Domingue. Despite many requests from merchants in 1752, the island's intendant, Charles-Martin Hurson, prohibited the sale in Louisiana of the "remnants of shiploads" or "shares of negroes," that is "the thirty heads they [the slaveship captains] could not get rid of if they retailed them and which they could dispose of more easily by wholesaling them." On the other hand, he was in favor of exporting one or two slaves on each boat going to New Orleans in order to empty the jails of "bad subjects, poisoners, maroons, unruly," claiming that "in the Mississippi the Negroes are much more restrained by their masters, and even more by fear of the Natives, and they often mend their ways when they are given a change of scenery." This policy was well known in Louisiana and aroused suspicion and anxiety. At the end of the Seven Years' War, the Superior Council issued a ruling prohibiting the introduction into the colony of "negroes having resided or having been creolized in Saint-Domingue." Three years later, it extended this prohibition to the Lesser Antilles. The fear that creolized slaves from Saint-Domingue aroused was the negative counterpart of the attraction that the pearl of the

46. On previous attempts to evaluate the slave trade from the Antilles to Louisiana, see Hall, *Africans in Colonial Louisiana,* 56–95, 179–183; Ingersoll, "Slave Trade and the Ethnic Diversity of Louisiana's Slave Community," *Louisiana History,* XXXVII (1996), 133–161; and Gregory E. O'Malley, "Beyond the Middle Passage: Slave Migration from the Caribbean to North America, 1619–1807," *William and Mary Quarterly,* LXVI (2009), 152–154. For the importance of the slave trade from the Antilles to Louisiana according to Pradel, see Baillardel and Prioult, eds., *Le chevalier de Pradel,* 212, 224–225, 230–231, 235, 239–240, 254–255, 259, 319. For evidence of slaves brought from the Antilles in the judicial archives, see RSCL 1752/02/17/02, 1764/02/17/01, 1764/07/31/02 (from Saint-Domingue); and 1752/03/27/02, 1752/10/06/01, 1765/02/26/01, 1766/07/23/03 (from the Lesser Antilles).

Antilles exercised over New Orleans's authorities, elites, and colonists of European descent.[47]

Louisiana settlers and officials' fascination with Saint-Domingue as both a model and a source of competition becomes apparent in travel accounts and histories of the colony. Several travel narratives or histories were written by military officers, planters, Ursulines, Company of the Indies employees, and ship's officers. Except for the latter, most of these authors spent years in the colony before returning to the home country. Not all of these manuscripts were published at the time, although most were written for a metropolitan audience with the obvious ambition of paving the way for their male authors to enter the Republic of Letters. They sought to be both informative and entertaining and to participate in Enlightenment debates about degeneracy in the New World, human diversity, and slavery. They fueled the eighteenth-century thirst for scientific curiosity and exoticism while trying to promote or restore the image of the Mississippi colony, and they testified to the power of the metropolitan cultural model for the colonial elite. Above all, their content reveals that Saint-Domingue occupied a central position in their imagination.[48]

All these travel accounts mentioned Saint-Domingue, if only on the occasion of the requisite stopover on the island during the transatlantic journey. Stays lasted several days, enabling some European travelers to explore the port city and the countryside. They became "agents of cultural cross-pollination." These stops were nevertheless depicted in a superficial and conventional way. Authors started by emphasizing the warm welcome they

47. For the severe limitations imposed on the slave trade from Martinique to Louisiana, see Charles-Martin Hurson to the minister of the navy, September 1752, ANOM COL F3 90, fols. 70–71. For the 1760s ordinances prohibiting the introduction of Creolized slaves from Saint-Domingue and the Lesser Antilles, see "Arrêt du Conseil Supérieur de La Nouvelle-Orléans interdisant l'importation en Louisiane, sous peine d'amendes, de nègres venant de Saint-Domingue," July 9, 1763, ANOM COL C13A 43, fols. 302–303, 308–309; and "Arrêt du Conseil Supérieur de la Louisiane autorisant la vente à la barre de la Cour de 21 nègres arrivés de la Martinique en Louisiane," Nov. 16, 1765, ANOM COL C13A 45, fols. 100–101.

48. Daniel Roche, *Les Républicains des lettres: Gens de culture et Lumières au XVIIIe siècle* (Paris, 1988); Roche, *Humeurs vagabondes: De la circulation des hommes et de l'utilité des voyages* (Paris, 2003), 18–241.

received from the local officials and elite, and they stressed the pleasures offered to them by Cap-Français. As Dumont de Montigny noted, "Among them, there was no end of meals, dances, amusements, rendezvous, liquor, gaming; nothing was lacking in this place for those who had money." Then, writers briefly described the city where they stayed, the surrounding landscapes, and the paradisiacal vegetation, particularly the exotic fruits they tasted, while expounding on the climate. They also sometimes told the history of the island and included some anecdotes about Saint-Dominguan society, insisting on the wealth and Creoleness of its settlers. But, as Dumont de Montigny acknowledged, it was "not necessary to provide a description of Cap François, since so many others have written of it." He concluded his accounting by stating, "So I shall say only that it is a land of cockaigne, especially for the newly arrived."[49]

Even if travelers did not devote long sections to Saint-Domingue in their books, they did pay attention to local phenomena and realities during their stay there. For many Frenchmen and women from the home country, the Caribbean colony was probably where they first encountered black people and certainly where they first came into contact with a slave society. In his unpublished travel account, Caillot, a company employee, noted: "This is the first place [Caye Saint Louis] where I saw male and female Negroes going about naked. At first view, this seemed to me the most ridiculous

49. For mentions of Saint-Domingue in travel accounts to Louisiana, see [Jean-Bernard] Bossu, *Nouveaux voyages aux Indes occidentales* ... (Paris, 1768), 5–19; Bossu, *Nouveaux voyages dans l'Amérique septentrionale* ... (Amsterdam, 1777), 350–380; Dumont de Montigny, *Regards sur le monde atlantique*, 91–92, 134–135; [Valette de Laudun], *Journal d'un voyage à la Louisiane fait en 1720* (The Hague and Paris, 1768), 157–181; Le Page du Pratz, *Histoire de la Louisiane*, I, 30–33; M. G. Musset, ed., "Le voyage en Louisiane de Franquet de Chaville (1720–1724)," *Journal de la société des américanistes*, IV (1902), 111–112; [Caillot], "Relation du voyage de la Louisianne ou Nouvlle. France," HNOC, MSS596, fols. 68–92; [Marie Madeleine] Hachard, *Relation du voyage des dames religieuses Ursulines de Rouen à La Nouvelle-Orléans* (1728) (Paris, 1872), 55–60; and Rev. Mère St. Augustin de Tranchepain, *Relation du voyage des premières Ursulines à la Nouvelle Orléans et de leur établissement en cette ville* ... (New York, 1859), 21–23. For the idea of European travelers as "agents of cultural cross-pollination," see Alfred E. Lemmon and John H. Lawrence, "Common Routes: St. Domingue and Louisiana," in [Priscilla Lawrence], ed., *Common Routes: St. Domingue–Louisiana; The Historic New Orleans Collection, March 14–June 30, 2006* (New Orleans, 2006), 85–86. For an example of a short description of Saint-Domingue, see Gordon M. Sayre and Carla Zecher, eds., *The Memoir of Lieutenant Dumont, 1715–1747: A Sojourner in the French Atlantic; Jean-François-Benjamin Dumont de Montigny*, trans. Sayre (Chapel Hill, N.C., 2012), 101.

thing I had ever seen, but I was not there but eight days when I became accustomed to seeing them like that, and even to going about almost like them because of how terribly hot it is in that place." Nor did Dumont de Montigny fail to mention the presence and use of African slaves to fan him during his afternoon naps in a hammock or to carry his provisions on a picnic in the mountains surrounding Cap-Français. In so doing, he highlighted how the newcomers became accustomed to being surrounded and served by black slaves and how they experienced relationships of racial domination in daily life.[50]

Saint-Domingue's system of racial slavery offered a framework for Louisiana planters to establish a slave society of their own in the Mississippi Valley. Considerations on the topic in both places intermingled in travel accounts and histories of the colony. Jean-Bernard Bossu only dealt with slavery when he described stops in Saint-Domingue during transatlantic crossings, but he included some anecdotes about master-slave relationships in Louisiana in the section of his account in which he spoke of slavery on the island. Other authors such as Le Page du Pratz and Dumont de Montigny described the slave system in the Mississippi colony in detail while making some comparisons with Saint-Domingue. On the punishment of slaves in the Caribbean, Dumont de Montigny explained:

> When a Negro goes maroon, that is, when he runs away from his master's house, after he has been recaptured, he is whipped; and to do that he is ordered to lie on the ground on his stomach, with his two legs close together and his arms stretched out and tied to two stakes placed wide apart, so that in this position he forms the figure of a Y. In that state, he is given one hundred and sometimes two hundred lashes with a carter's whip; .... After their skins have been torn to shreds, they are rubbed with a sponge soaked with pepper and vinegar; in Cap-Français, Saint-Domingue, lemon juice, and hot or long pepper are used for that purpose. The sauce is piquant; but it is a sovereign balm, which heals wounds in twenty-four hours.

Louisiana planters borrowed some Saint-Domingue practices, even if they adapted them to local conditions.[51]

50. Greenwald, ed., *Company Man*, trans. Chalmers, 53; Dumont de Montigny, *Regards sur le monde atlantique*, 92.

51. On the mention of slavery in Louisiana in the sections of Bossu's travel accounts devoted to Saint-Domingue, see Bossu, *Nouveaux voyages aux Indes occidentales*, 18; and Bossu, *Nouveaux voyages dans l'Amérique septentrionale*, 369–392. On the transfer of slave punishment practices from Saint-Domingue to Louisiana, see Dumont [de Mon-

Given that ships sometimes needed to stop in Havana, Louisiana travel accounts also included sections on Cuba. Although these stays familiarized French travelers and migrants with the Spanish Empire, authors still viewed Spanish colonial societies with a critical eye. Bossu, in particular, wrote extensively on the subject in his two books. In the vein of the Black Legend, he recounted horrific stories about the early colonization of the New World by the Spanish. In his description of Havana, he denounced the propensity of the Spanish to engage in all sorts of *métissage:* "As you can well imagine, my dear friend, all these felonies were committed by the vile rabble, which here is only composed of races of *mulâtres, métis, quarterons, jambos* [mulattoes, metis, quadroons, sambos] (1), shaped by all the vices of the various nations from which they came; because the genuine Castilians, of pure, unmixed blood, are very honest with strangers, as loyal and as faithful to their monarch as the French are to theirs." For this officer, imbued by race-thinking, the Spanish island, unlike Saint-Domingue, offered a repulsive model of a racial regime.[52]

Travel accounts and histories also frequently mentioned Saint-Domingue in sections other than those devoted to their authors' stays on the island. They invariably noted the agricultural imports from the Caribbean to Louisiana, such as tobacco, indigo, sugarcane, orange trees, cotton seeds, or bedding plants. They also described the importance of trade between the two colonies. In his chapter about La Salle's expeditions, Le Page du Pratz emphasized that trade was the main motivation in establishing the first French settlements on the coast:

> The report of the pleasantness of Louisiana spreading through Canada, many Frenchmen of that country repaired to settle there, dispersing themselves at pleasure along the river St. Louis [the Mississippi River], especially towards its mouth, and even in some islands on the coast, and on the river Mobile, which lies nearer Canada. The

---

tigny], *Mémoires historiques sur la Louisiane* …, ed. [Jean-Baptiste Le Mascrier], 2 vols. (Paris, 1753), II, 243–244 (quotation).

52. For Bossu's negative view on Spanish colonization, see Bossu, *Nouveaux voyages aux Indes occidentales*, 6–16; and Bossu, *Nouveaux voyages dans l'Amérique septentrionale*, 49–50, 358. After the list of racial categories—"mulâtres, métis, quarterons, jambos"—Bossu included the following footnote: "Name that is given in the West Indies to the children born to a Negro and an Indian woman, or an Indian man and a Negress. Those who are born to an Indian man and a Spanish woman are named métis, and those to a savage and a métis woman are named jambos; they all vary in color, which makes a rather singular variegation of white, black, red, yellow, swarthy or copper-skinned men and women." See ibid., 8, 344–345, esp. 344n.

facility of the commerce with St. Domingo was, undoubtedly, what invited them to the neighborhood of the sea, though the interior parts of the country be in all respects far preferable.

Writers were keenly aware of Saint-Domingue's significance for Louisiana, not only as a model but as a source of trade and economic opportunity.[53]

The principle reason authors continually mentioned Saint-Domingue was to draw a comparison with Louisiana, because, for most, it was the only other colony that they knew, and they felt compelled to defend their new place of residence against the competition posed by the French section of the island. Few were ready to admit the superiority of Saint-Domingue's crops, especially indigo. They weighed the quality of each colony's tobacco, indigo, and oranges, with most concluding that Louisiana's products were as good as or even better than those from Saint-Domingue.[54]

To highlight the assets of the Mississippi Valley, travel writers, who were well aware of its weak power of attraction, also compared the climate and sanitary conditions of the two colonies. In the pages devoted to Le Page du Pratz's stop in Saint-Domingue, he took the occasion of a yellow fever epidemic in Cap-Français "to reflect on the behavior of those who seek their fortune in this country (in the Islands), while we have other beautiful Colonies; I decided that taking such great risks to purchase such great goods, however immense they may be, is always paying too high a price for them." Caillot also made a case for Louisiana in 1731, arguing that "it is quite certain that if the Company of the Indies would send only two thousand Negroes with the same number of whites, you would see a second Saint-

53. For agricultural imports from the Antilles to Louisiana, see [Jean-Baptiste Bénard de La Harpe], *Journal historique de l'établissement des Français à la Louisiane* (New Orleans, 1831), Oct. 29–Nov. 12, 1722, 139, 345, 369–370; Bossu, *Nouveaux voyages aux Indes occidentales*, 157, 179; Le Page du Pratz, *Histoire de la Louisiane*, II, 21, 39, 355, 379–380, 386–388; and [Montigny], *Mémoires historiques sur la Louisiane*, ed. [Mascrier], 57. For descriptions of trade between the islands and the Mississippi colony, see *Journal de Vaugine de Nuisement (ca 1765); Un témoignage sur la Louisiane du XVIIIe siècle*, ed. Steve Canac-Marquis and Pierre Rézeau ([Sainte-Foy, Quebec], 2005), 19–20. For commerce with Saint-Domingue as the main motivation to colonize Louisiana, see *The History of Louisiana, or of the Western Parts of Virginia and Carolina ... Translated from the French of M. Le Page Du Pratz ...*, new ed. (London, 1774), 4 (quotation).

54. For comparisons of the two colony's products and their quality, see Bossu, *Nouveaux voyages aux Indes occidentales*, 181; Le Page du Pratz, *Histoire de la Louisiane*, II, 359–361; [Montigny], *Mémoires historiques sur la Louisiane*, ed. [Mascrier], I, 34; P. Laval, *Voyage de la Louisiane, fait par ordre du roy; en l'année mil sept cent vingt ...* (Paris, 1728), 125; and [Hachard], *Relation du voyage des dames religieuses Ursulines*, 95.

Domingue reborn in this country, and better in terms of health, the air being more temperate. You would load ships with rice as beautiful as that which comes from the Levant; maize, or Turkish wheat, grows marvelously well here, the indigo found here is admirably beautiful, and the millet too. French wheat grows here, too, in the Illinois country, which is five hundred leagues from this city." Despite these promoters' efforts, however, French Louisiana would remain in Saint-Domingue's shadow.[55]

SLAVE LAW, EMPIRE, AND RACE

One of the instrumental ways the French islands decisively shaped New Orleans's society was through the influence of slave laws. Besides the movement of personnel, soldiers, migrants, and merchandise, ideas of law and legal texts also circulated within the Empire. They contributed to the development of an imperial system of racial domination, although differences existed between the racial regimes of the various colonies. The French Empire was not an integrated legal space: no law, including slave law, was ever published for all the overseas territories under French sovereignty. The Code Noir, the first comprehensive and systematic French slave law regulating the status of enslaved and freed persons as well as the relationships between masters and slaves, was not promulgated for the whole Empire but successively enacted in the various colonies: the Lesser Antilles in 1685, Saint-Domingue in 1687, Guyana in 1704, the Mascarene Islands in 1723, and Louisiana in 1724. Although there were some minor differences between the first versions, those for the Mascarene Islands and Louisiana introduced important changes that embodied race more thoroughly. Still, the French Empire differed from all other empires before the second half of the eighteenth century because the Code Noir originated in the metropole. Even so, central authorities were not the sole producers of slave law, and they did not ignore legislation written locally by the governors, intendants, or superior or sovereign councils in the various colonies. The elaboration of slave law within the Empire followed complex channels of communication, negotiation, and influence between the metropole and colonies as well as between colonies. Yet the French crown was increasingly eager to have a

55. For comparison of the two colony's climates and sanitary conditions, see Le Page du Pratz, *Histoire de la Louisiane*, I, 33 (quotation). On the climate, see also [Bénard de La Harpe], "Mémoire destiné à faire connaître l'importance de la colonie de la Louisiane," in *Journal historique de l'établissement des Français à la Louisiane*, 355–356. For Caillot's wish to transform Louisiana into a second Saint-Domingue, see Greenwald, ed., *Company Man*, trans. Chalmers, 85 (quotation).

comprehensive view of the whole body of legislation related to its colonial territories and to maintain the ascendency of royal over local law. For all these reasons, the legal apparatus participated in the creation of a genuine imperial formation. It also played a crucial role in the process of racialization within every colony.[56]

As a consequence of these imperial legal dynamics, Louisiana distinguished itself from all the other French colonies of the greater Caribbean because it did not experience a long legal vacuum regarding slavery. The Code Noir was published in the Antilles, which were first settled in the seventeenth century, half a century after the introduction of the first African slaves to the islands in the mid-1630s. By contrast, the Mississippi colony inherited a code from the Lesser Antilles only a few years after the arrival of the first slave ships from Africa in 1719. This early transference of laws testifies to the shared desire of the monarch, the Company of the Indies, and local officials to develop a slave society and economy modeled on that of the French West Indies. The crown fought hard to impose the preeminence of the Code Noir even though local legislation did not contradict but sought to enforce the royal edict's spirit, if not its actual provisions. Both central and local authorities shared similar ideas about the interplay of slavery and race.[57]

From the outset, slave law in the French Caribbean had to do with race. The establishment of the first Code Noir in the Lesser Antilles in 1685 followed on the heels of François Bernier's publication of a text entitled "Nouvelle division de la terre, par les différentes espèces ou races d'hommes qui l'ha-

56. Guillaume Aubert, "'To Establish One Law and Definite Rules': Race, Religion, and the Transatlantic Origins of the Louisiana Code Noir," in Vidal, ed., *Louisiana: Crossroads of the Atlantic World*, 21–43; Yvan Debbasch, *Couleur et liberté: Le jeu du critère ethnique dans un ordre juridique esclavagiste* ... (Paris, 1967); Vernon Valentine Palmer, "The Origins and Authors of the Code Noir," *Louisiana Law Review*, LVI (1995), 363–390; Palmer, *Through the Codes Darkly: Slave Law and Civil Law in Louisiana* (Clark, N.J., 2012), 3–41; Bernard Vonglis, "La double origine du Code Noir," in Liliane Chauleau, ed., *Les abolitions dans les Amériques: Actes du colloque organisé par les Archives départementales de la Martinique, 8–9 décembre 1998* (Fort-de-France, Martinique, 2001), 101–107; Malick W. Ghachem, *The Old Regime and the Haitian Revolution* (Cambridge, 2012), 29–76.

57. Most of the time, historians of French Louisiana read metropolitan and locally authored laws in opposition, as if they were not all integrated within a hierarchized legal apparatus supervised by the monarch. See, for instance, Jennifer M. Spear, *Race, Sex, and Social Order in Early New Orleans* (Baltimore, 2009), 52–78.

bitent" ("A new division of the earth according to the different species or races of men who inhabit it") in the *Journal des Sçavans* the year before. His essay testifies to the availability of the idea of race in French culture by the 1680s. This traveler, physician, and Gassendist philosopher was the first to replace the old definition of race as lineage by a new one that could be extended to the whole of humanity. He divided all populations on the globe into "species" or "races" distinguished by physical characteristics such as skin color, facial type, and body shape that were transmitted endogenously by sperm or blood and were thus immutable. His description of Africans was informed not so much by the expanding transatlantic slave trade as by the slave markets that he had observed in the Islamic world. Yet, given that the philosopher posited that not all human beings had the same intellectual capacities and accepted the legitimacy of natural slavery, Siep Stuurman believes that "it is hard to avoid the conclusion that black Africans [were] considered 'natural slaves' by Bernier." It is not mere coincidence that the first Code Noir was enacted one year later in the Lesser Antilles. The concomitance of the two events reflected the imperial debate about race that was developing in various places, both in the metropole and in the colonies, in the context of French colonial expansion. The discussions in Martinique and Guadeloupe were closely linked to the transformation of the two islands into slave societies.[58]

Far from being a product of the French central government alone, the 1685 Code Noir was conceived in dialogue between metropolitan and local authorities—including not only the Lesser Antilles' general governor and Martinique's intendant but also Martinique's Superior Council, which was consulted by local officials—in reaction to the expansion of slavery. The code was also a response to the rise of métissage and to the debate that had developed on the status of individuals born from mixed unions between free whites and black slaves. As Guillaume Aubert has pointed out, the arguments exchanged in the discussions "revealed an entrenched belief in inherent and transmissible differences between French and African." Those who wrote the edict drew on both Roman law and local regulations published earlier in the islands. The code's vocabulary (the text used "slaves" and "negroes" in an interchangeable way) and provisions (compatibility be-

58. François Bernier, "A New Division of the Earth," trans. T. Bendyshe, in Robert Bernasconi and Tommy L. Lott, eds., *The Idea of Race* (Indianapolis, Ind., 2000), 1–4; Pierre H. Boulle, *Race et esclavage dans la France de l'Ancien Régime* (Paris, 2007), 47–58; Siep Stuurman, "François Bernier and the Invention of Racial Classification," *History Workshop Journal*, L (Autumn 2000), 1–21, esp. 10.

tween Christianity and slavery, matrilineal heritability, harsh punishments against slaves' criminality, involvement of all free settlers in the control of slaves' mobility, the special deference owed by freed people to their former masters, the punishment of freed people like slaves in cases of theft, and the greater penalties meted out to free blacks over whites who provided assistance to runaways) can be read as evidence of the early racialization of Caribbean slavery. This racial component, however, had not yet been pushed to its logical extreme. The ordinance created sanctions against free men who had children with enslaved women, but it automatically granted freedom to enslaved women who married free men; it also authorized and regulated the manumission of slaves and conceded French citizenship as well as the rights of freeborn people to freedmen and women. The legislation was more concerned with regulating enslaved persons than free people of color because the main issue at the time was the justification and implementation of a slave society based on African slavery. What was at stake first and foremost was the control and discipline of a rising number of uncooperative and rebellious slaves brought from Africa.[59]

The publication of the Code Noir in various Caribbean islands and in Guyana between 1685 and 1704 did not put an end to the debate about the status of freed blacks, whose numbers in the Antilles continued to rise. Several local regulations and royal ordinances policing their behavior were enacted in the Caribbean between 1685 and 1724. These new royal ordinances prevailed over the related provisions in the 1685 code. The content of the new local and royal laws was integrated in the Louisiana edict of 1724. Those provisions further reinforced the legal distinctions between whites and free persons of African or mixed descent: slaves could not be manumitted without the authorization of local authorities; marriages between whites and blacks were prohibited; donations from whites to free people of color were also outlawed; and, finally, free blacks convicted of assistance to runaway slaves could be reenslaved. Although the centrality of race in the 1685 code for the Lesser Antilles is subject to discussion, the same cannot be said of the code adopted in Louisiana in 1724.[60]

Early Louisiana legislation on slavery was not intended to contradict the content of the Code Noir. One of the first local regulations ever written by

59. Aubert, "'To Establish One Law and Definite Rules,'" in Vidal, ed., *Louisiana: Crossroads of the Atlantic World*, 37.

60. "Code Noir ou édit du roi servant de règlement pour le gouvernement et l'administration de la justice, police, discipline, et commerce des esclaves nègres de la province et colonie de la Louisiane," March 1724, ANOM COL B 43, fols. 388–407.

the colony's Superior Council dealt precisely with slavery. The "Statutes and Rulings ... concerning Slaves" issued in 1714, two years after the temporary creation of the court, were inspired by the 1685 royal edict. Years before the beginning of the slave trade from Africa, local authorities had already envisioned the development of a slave system. In 1721, they began asking for the adoption of the Code Noir in Louisiana. The same year, the Superior Council also started to issue several regulations on slaves and slavery that aimed to impose the company's monopoly on the slave trade and to enforce provisions similar to those existing in West Indian legislation. After the local implementation of the code in 1724, they produced more ordinances to recall and enforce some of its provisions. Following the company's cession of the colony back to the crown, the code was published once more. Similar rulings were also promulgated by the governor and the commissaire-ordonnateur in the late 1730s, but these publications were fewer in number than those in the 1720s, maybe because the 1724 edict was then better known. On the one hand, the repetition of these regulations demonstrates that authorities did not succeed in enforcing them; on the other, it reveals their belief in the importance of law to define the interests of the community as a whole.[61]

61. For early local legislation on slavery in Louisiana before the Company of the Indies's trade monopoly, see "Statuts et règlements faits par le conseil supérieur de la Louisiane concernant les esclaves du 12 novembre 1714," ANOM COL A 23, fols. 5–6; and "Ordonnance de Ms. de La Motte Cadillac gouverneur et Duclos commissaire-ordonnateur qui défend de rien acheter des esclaves," May 20, 1714, ANOM COL A 23, fol. 4v. For Louisiana authorities asking for the local promulgation of the Code Noir, see "Mémoire de Charles LeGac cy devant directeur pour la Compagnie des Indes à la Louisiane," Recueil A, MS 487, Mélanges historiques, Manuscrits de la Bibliothèque de l'Institut de France, fol. 549. For various rulings and ordinances about slaves and slavery promulgated by the Superior Council during the Company of the Indies's monopoly before the 1724 Code Noir, see Sept. 2, 1721, ANOM COL A 23, fols. 31v–33v, Mar. 12, 1722, fols. 36–36v, Apr. 29, 1723, fols. 38v–39, Nov. 13, 1723, fols. 43–43v, and Nov. 13, 1723, fols. 43v–44. For various rulings and ordinances about slaves and slavery promulgated by the Superior Council or by the governor and commissaire-ordonnateur, together or separately, at the time of the Company of the Indies's monopoly and after the promulgation of the 1724 Code Noir, see Apr. 22, 1725, ANOM COL A 23, fol. 59, Oct. 17, 1725, fols. 63v–64r, Dec. 11, 1725, fol. 67, Jan. 31, 1726, fols. 67v–68, July 7, 1726, fol. 68, July 20, 1726, fol. 68v, Aug. 31, 1726, fol. 75, and Mar. 2, 1727, fol. 84. For the republication of the Code Noir after the retrocession of the colony, see the minister of the navy to Salmon, Oct. 14, 1732, ANOM COL B 57, fols. 854–855. For ordinances on slaves and slavery promulgated after 1731, see "Ordonnance de Ms. Bienville et Salmon pour la déclaration des

Moreover, local legislation was closely observed by the central government. In 1744, the minister of the navy ordered every colonial intendant to collate in a single volume all the ordinances and rulings serving as laws in his colony. In New Orleans, Commissaire-ordonnateur Le Normant asked the attorney general, François Fleuriau, to complete the task, which he did by September 1746. This legal anthology has been kept in the colonial archives. In the margins of the document, there are many comments about both local and royal legislation. For the local regulations on slavery published just before or after 1724, the anonymous commentator noted that they had been invalidated and replaced by the Code Noir or that they were useless since the royal edict had already dealt with those issues, clearly establishing its preeminence. In the margins of the copy of the code and of the local regulations enacted after 1731, the comments aimed at evaluating whether the various stipulations were enforced. Only local authorities could have known or made such remarks. Since governors and commissaire-ordonnateurs had to deal with slave unrest and were in charge of the protection and security of the crown's subjects, they shared the ministry of the navy's preoccupation with the weak enforcement of some of the code's articles. The state's main goal when the edict was originally conceived and circulated, both in its humanitarian and repressive stipulations, was to provide safety to settlers, curb slave criminality, and prevent slave revolts as well as assert the king's monopoly on legal violence, which could be weakened by the domination masters exercised over their slaves.[62]

Another example of how local legislation was monitored by Versailles and how the crown imposed the preeminence of the Code Noir is the "Ruling on the Administration for the Province of Louisiana" issued by Governor Vau-

nègres marrons du 1er septembre 1736," ANOM COL A 23, fol. 121v; "Ordonnance de M. Salmon du 7 décembre 1736 qui défend de donner à boire aux esclaves sans permission de leurs maîtres," ANOM COL A 23, fol. 122r; and "Ordonnance de Ms. Bienville et Salmon du 5 janvier 1743 portant amnistie en faveur des nègres marrons," ANOM COL A 23, fol. 130.

62. "Circulaire aux intendants ordonnateurs des colonies," Nov. 20, 1744, ANOM COL F3 81, fol. 217; Extracts from letters by Le Normant to the minister of the navy, Nov. 8, 1745, ANOM COL F3 81, fol. 222, Sept. 1, 1746, fol. 223; [Rochemore], "Mémoire sur l'administration de la Louisiane," 1749, ANOM COL C13A 33, fol. 151v; "Édits, lettres patentes, déclarations, arrêts, ordonnances, et règlements concernant la colonie de la Louisiane depuis le 24 septembre 1712 jusqu'au 27 août 1746," ANOM COL A 23. On the state's goals with the promulgation of the 1685 Code Noir, see Ghachem, *Old Regime and the Haitian Revolution*, 55–67.

dreuil and Commissaire-ordonnateur Michel in 1751. The Superior Council and the local elites had nothing to do with the regulation. The bylaw originated in an attempt to reestablish the authority of the state's representatives and to escape the monarch's criticism after a huge scandal involving the *major* (the military officer in charge of the New Orleans garrison) and the sale of alcohol, which was supposed to be strictly controlled (the major had tried to monopolize this trade). The ruling not only regulated the sale of alcohol but also addressed all matters related to public order. Slaves were held accountable for the general state of disorder that allegedly prevailed in the port city and the surrounding plantation region while both masters and nonslaveholders were reminded of their responsibilities in the discipline of slaves and threatened with severe punishments for failure to comply.[63]

Because Vaudreuil and Michel wanted to regain Louis XV's favor, the text of the 1751 ruling was sent to the minister of the navy for approval, and an anonymous author, likely an employee of the Bureau des colonies, was given the task of evaluating it. Both the bylaw and the metropolitan commentator referenced the Code Noir, but the commentator used the 1685 version as his ultimate source of legality. The reviewer also compared Articles 24 and 25 of the 1751 ruling, which dealt with the illicit mobility of slaves by foot or on horse, to local regulations promulgated on the subject in Saint-Domingue. Most of the criticisms of Louisiana's 1751 ruling that emerged were related to the harshness of the punishments outlined by Vaudreuil and Michel against whites and free people of color. The analyst ruled that these provisions overstepped the Code Noir as well as infringed on kingly prerogatives. He obviously believed that Louisiana ought to conform to the legal model offered by the sugar island.[64]

During the first half of the eighteenth century, Saint-Domingue dominated the Mississippi colony in the imperial legal hierarchy. Yet twenty years after the loss of Louisiana to Spain and Great Britain, when the West Indian lawyer Médéric Louis-Élie Moreau de Saint-Méry published his collection of laws promulgated in the Caribbean colony in the mid-1780s, he included the 1724 Louisiana Code Noir and explained that the execution of

63. "Règlement sur la police des cabarets, des esclaves, des marchés en Louisiane," Feb. 28–Mar. 1, 1751, ANOM COL C13A 35, fols. 39–52r. For a different point of view on the origins of the 1751 bylaw, see Thomas N. Ingersoll, "Slave Codes and Judicial Practice in New Orleans, 1718–1807," *Law and History Review*, XIII (1995), 41; and Spear, *Race, Sex, and Social Order in Early New Orleans*, 68–69.

64. Anonymous Comments on the 1751 Ruling, May 27, 1751, ANOM COL C13A 35, fols. 53–55.

the edict on the French section of the island was ordered by several courts as well as by the king himself. Slave laws circulated both ways between the Antilles and Louisiana.[65]

The financier Law had imagined a glorious destiny for France and Louisiana on a global stage. After the Mississippi bubble burst, local authorities and settlers narrowed their ambition to the greater Caribbean and dreamed of emulating Saint-Domingue. The Antilles offered them a model for developing a genuine slave society, while also providing them with a set of means and practices to accomplish this goal. Louisiana landowners acquired the plants they needed to start plantations in the Mississippi Valley from Saint-Domingue as well as the knowledge of how to produce indigo and tobacco from settlers and slaves who migrated from the Caribbean colony. They also quickly inherited a Code Noir from the islands. Furthermore, Saint-Domingue continued to inspire Louisiana throughout the French period. From the 1740s and 1750s, the Jesuits and a few other eminent planters started to conduct trials with the cultivation of cane and the production of sugar. Although they went no further than experimentation, local authorities were hopeful. In 1760, Commissaire-ordonnateur Rochemore reported to the minister of the navy that several settlers who had relocated to Louisiana from Saint-Domingue and Martinique had praised the quality of the sugar that had been produced locally. The Mississippi colony did not transform itself into a sugar producer and even failed to develop a successful plantation economy based on the cultivation of tobacco and indigo, but it rapidly succeeded in becoming a slave society deeply shaped by race, both in New Orleans and its plantation region.[66]

The Company of the Indies's initial investments secured the colony's foundations and gave it the demographic impetus it needed to take root. As many migrants of European descent who had come with the only migratory wave to the colony ever organized died or left Louisiana, a black majority quickly formed in the colonial settlements of the lower Mississippi Valley. The company's subsequent departure and its decision to limit its slave trade to the Antilles after 1731 were responsible for the development of a singular slave society whose links with Africa were quickly severed. The

65. [Moreau de] Saint-Méry, *Loix et constitutions des colonies françoises de l'Amérique sous le vent*, III, 88–95.

66. Rochemore to the minister of the navy, Dec. 17, 1760, ANOM COL C13A 42, fols. 163–166r. See also "Mémoire concernant la population et le commerce à la Louisiane et Cayenne par H.P.," 1761, ANOM COL C13A 42, fol. 300r.

families, lineages, and villages that the enslaved had been forced to leave behind when captured in Africa likely continued to haunt their thoughts, but they would no longer have the opportunity to rekindle memories with newcomers brought directly from their homelands. By contrast, the slaves, born in Africa or the Antilles, who were transported in greater numbers from the islands and made up the majority of arrivals in Louisiana after 1731, were better able to preserve the recollections of oppression and resistance borne out of their Caribbean experiences since the colony's connections with Saint-Domingue and Martinique were never interrupted up to the end of the French regime.

Nor did migrants of European descent forget the metropolitan society from which they came. The world of the elite, in particular—their field of social interaction and the scale on which they could search for resources of all kinds—was not limited to the colony but extended to the whole Empire. They considered themselves part of an imperial formation whose center was located first in the metropole and, secondarily, in Saint-Domingue. Louisiana's elite could not conceive of the local without the extra-local, which they mainly conflated with the Empire. They looked toward the metropole as the main source of their prestige and distinctiveness as well as drew on Saint-Domingue's longer history and experience as a colony to make sense of and to adapt to their new social situation. The ancien régime complex of values imported from the metropole fit the development of slave societies overseas well. Colonists in Louisiana could rely on and combine the sociocultural models of both metropolitan France and the Antilles.

Empires mattered within the Atlantic world, a fact especially true for the French Empire. French officials might have been reluctant to describe the kingdom and its overseas territories as an empire and to develop an imperial ideology. Nevertheless, global France did operate as an imperial formation. The absolutist project of the crown made the state a crucial imperial actor and increased the centralization of the Empire. The king supervised the movements of sword and pen officers through the navy and controlled the elaboration and circulation of slave law between the metropole and the colonies as well as among colonies. In Louisiana, the state's direct intervention was made all the more necessary as the colony was young and remote and could not have developed without its support. After 1731, the monarch was heavily involved not only in the colony's political and legal operations but also in its financial, commercial, and economic life. The political, economic, and financial dimensions of the Empire were intrinsically linked in the Mississippi colony. Likewise, the sociocultural domain, noticeably the way authorities and colonists conceived of race and used it as a political resource, did not escape the Empire's impact. Even though New Orleans existed in close connection with Spanish Florida, Cuba, and New Mexico and even though many officers, merchants, and settlers had some knowledge of Spanish colonial societies, the sociocultural model of reference for local authorities and residents of European descent living in the port city remained the French imperial one.[67]

Within the French Empire, Saint-Domingue exerted a crucial influence on New Orleans, having elevated itself to the rank of "the best and most considerable of all the colonies that [France] owns in the New World." Racial formation within the Louisiana capital was nonetheless enhanced by local circumstances as well, including relationships with Native Americans living close to the port city. Besides transatlantic and Caribbean mobility and communication, French New Orleans was also constructed out of connections and networks with its hinterland.[68]

67. Cross-cultural influence might have been stronger in places like Mobile and Natchitoches than in New Orleans because of these locales' proximity respective to Pensacola and Los Adaes. On the importance of empires, see Trevor Burnard, "Review: Empire Matters? The Historiography of Imperialism in Early America, 1492–1830," *History of European Ideas*, XXXIII (2007), 87–107; Christopher Grasso and Karin Wulf, "Nothing Says 'Democracy' Like a Visit from the Queen: Reflections on Empire and Nation in Early American Histories," *Journal of American History*, XCV (2008), 764–781; and Cécile Vidal, "Introduction: Le(s) monde(s) atlantique(s), l'Atlantique français, l'empire atlantique français," *Outre-mers: Revue d'histoire*, XCVII, nos. 362–363 (2009), 7–37. On the debate that has developed about the existence of a genuine French Empire during the early modern period, see Banks, *Chasing Empire across the Sea;* James Pritchard, *In Search of Empire: The French in the Americas, 1670–1730* (Cambridge, 2004); Alexandre Dubé, "S'approprier l'Atlantique: Quelques réflexions autour de *Chasing Empire across the Sea*, de Kenneth Banks," *French Colonial History*, VI (2005), 33–44; and Christopher Hodson and Brett Rushforth, "Absolutely Atlantic: Colonialism and the Early Modern French State in Recent Historiography," *History Compass*, VIII (2010), 101–117.

68. Bossu, *Nouveaux voyages dans l'Amérique septentrionale*, 359 (quotation).

CHAPTER TWO

The City with Imaginary Walls

The Natchez Wars, Slave Unrest, and the
Construction of a White Urban Community

In the late 1720s, Ursuline Marie Madeleine Hachard, newly arrived in New Orleans, exchanged letters with her father in the metropole, who missed her and was worried about her. He purchased several maps to locate and visualize the remote colonial port city where his daughter now lived. Yet the first two maps he acquired were too old and did not include New Orleans. He then found a more recent one, but the colonial capital was wrongly located on the shores of Lake Pontchartrain, instead of on the left bank of the Mississippi River. This map might have been the splendid engraving attributed to François Chéreau and dated circa 1720. Such images were used for propaganda purposes. Although only a few shacks had been erected at the time of Chéreau's engraving, the artist represented New Orleans as an imposing fortified city, with a majestic church, several monuments, and stone houses. The multiple ships cruising in the Gulf of Mexico and the Native American forts and villages scattered in the background recalled that "the Mississippi" had been integrated within the French Empire through colonial expansion. The contrast between the indigenous wooden stockades and the stone walls surrounding the city, built in the manner of Sébastien Le Prestre de Vauban, materialized the colonial situation, that is the asymmetrical relationships in which the newcomers and First Nations were caught, and highlighted the difference that colonists thought existed between Europeans and Native Americans, civilization and savagery. For all the complexity that governed Franco-Native interactions in practice, the colonial project still relied on French claims to ethnic and religious superiority over indigenous peoples and implied constructing a divide between the colonizers and the First Nations whose lands were colonized.[1]

Most Europeans of the era saw the lack of monumental cities built in stone on North America's indigenous lands as a sign of the cultural backwardness of First Nations. In opposition to this common view, Antoine-Simon Le Page du Pratz, one of the most careful observers of Native American cultures, believed that indigenous "bunch[es] of cabins" qualified as genuine *"ville[s] ou village[s]"* ("cit[ies] or village[s]"). In the ethnographic section of his *History of Louisiana*, he argued that the French were wrong when they considered that a city ought to be built of stone and include magnificent temples, palaces, and bridges within its walls. "But those who have taken the pains to learn about what a City is," he observed, "have learnt that it was nothing less than a large number of lodgings gathered in the same place, and that any differences among the buildings depended only on the wealth of the nation forming the City." Le Page du Pratz also stressed that "our Americans thought of building Cities according to the means and materials they could procure the most easily, in order to resist the blows of enemies." Whether the settlements on Chéreau's engraving, either French or Native American, were identified as "villes" or not, their first function was to provide protection and security. Le Page du Pratz was isolated in his relativistic opinion over the qualification of indigenous settlements as towns, but his comparison raises the crucial question of what made a city in the eyes of eighteenth-century social actors. His answer points to density of population and the presence of defensive works.[2]

On all subsequent maps of New Orleans drawn by the Company of the Indies's or the king's engineers, the city was always depicted surrounded by stone walls. None, however, were ever built during the French regime. Imbued with traditional representations of urban centers, metropolitan cartographers could not conceive of a new colonial capital without fortifications. The image of a city as an enclosed place remained powerful throughout the eighteenth century, despite the demolition or absorption of

1. "Lettre à la Nouvelle Orléans, ce vingt septième octobre 1727," in [Marie Madeleine] Hachard, *Relation du voyage des dames religieuses Ursulines de Rouen à La Nouvelle-Orléans* (1728) (Paris, 1872), 34, "Lettre à la Nouvelle Orléans ce vingt-quatrième avril 1728," 88. For the concept of "colonial situation," see George[s] Balandier, "The Colonial Situation: A Theoretical Approach," in Stephen Howe, ed., *The New Imperial Histories Reader* (New York, 2010), 23–40.

2. [Antoine-Simon] Le Page du Pratz, *Histoire de la Louisiane ...*, 3 vols. (Paris, 1758), II, 171–172.

Figure 4:
[François Chéreau].
Le Missisipi
ou la Louisiane
dans l'Amérique
septentrionale. Circa
1720. Département
estampes et
photographie. EST
VD-21 (2). Courtesy
of Bibliothèque
Nationale de France.
Paris

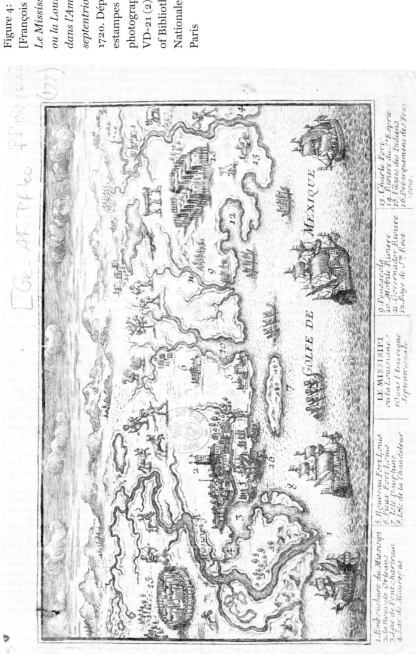

urban walls within expanding cities throughout the metropole. Additionally, fortifications continued to be a defensive necessity in many colonies. For Jean-François-Benjamin Dumont de Montigny, New Orleans's lack of stone walls was thus its defining characteristic. Still, the persistence of nonexistent fortifications on maps reflected the company's and later the king's project of constructing a city. New Orleans was conceived of as a central place that ought to be differentiated from the countryside by its urbanity. What made New Orleans a genuine city, if it was not its walls? What distinguished the urban center from its immediate surroundings and the rest of the colony? What did the Louisiana capital represent for the various people living in or outside the city?[3]

Racial tensions shaped the understanding urban dwellers came to have of New Orleans as an urban place as well as their relationship to the city. Despite the many connections that linked the Louisiana capital with nearby Native American villages and the surrounding plantation region, the material building of the city over swamps and cypress forests was matched over time by a symbolic construction of New Orleans as a white civic community united by a common goal to perpetuate the colonial situation as well as the system of racial slavery. Stone walls were never raised, but urbanites of European descent came to develop a sense of collective belonging that was defined in confrontation with the world outside the imagined fortifications. Their civic and racial identities became tightly linked.[4]

New Orleans quickly came to be recognized as a place offering shelter and assistance to white colonists, where they could survive and even prosper thanks to commerce. Despite the alliances forged with some Native groups

3. For metropolitan representations of cities and fortifications in France, see Claude Petitfrère, "Regards sur les villes dans la France au XVIIIe siècle," in *Traditions et innovations dans la société française du XVIIIe siècle: Actes du Colloque de 1993*, Association des historiens modernistes des universités, bulletin no. 18 (Paris, 1995), 57–95; Roger Chartier et al., *Histoire de la France urbaine*, III, *La ville classique de la Renaissance aux Révolutions*, ed. Georges Duby (Paris, 1981), 16–20, 121–122, 454; and Bernard Lepetit, *Les villes dans la France moderne (1740–1840)* (Paris, 1988), 52–81. For fortifications in colonial cities, see André Charbonneau, Yvon Desloges, and Marc Lafrance, *Québec, the Fortified City: From the 17th to the 19th Century* (Ottawa, Canada, 1982); and Laurent Vidal and Émilie d'Orgeix, eds., *Les villes françaises du Nouveau Monde: Des premiers fondateurs aux ingénieurs du roi (XVIe–XVIIIe siècles)* (Paris, 1999). For New Orleans's lack of fortifications, see Dumont de Montigny, *Regards sur le monde atlantique, 1715–1747*, transcribed by Carla Zecher (Sillery, Québec, 2008), 170, 355.

4. For a study of the way Spanish colonialism and urban governance intersected in Havana, a walled city whose fortifications were not imaginary, see Guadalupe García, *Beyond the Walled City: Colonial Exclusion in Havana* (Oakland, Calif., 2016).

to counteract white Louisianans' demographic minority in comparison with indigenous peoples and increasingly black slaves, major conflicts still broke out. Insecurity in the wake of the Natchez Wars between 1729 and 1731 and expeditions against the Chickasaw in the 1730s led many settlers to live in the colonial capital. During this time of war, local authorities proposed to build a wooden stockade around the city in 1730, although the structure was never completed. From the late 1740s, the rise in the number of slaves because of natural growth and transportation from the Antilles made the control of slave mobility between New Orleans and the surrounding plantations more difficult as well. When slave revolts multiplied in the greater Caribbean during the Seven Years' War, local authorities became increasingly sensitive to slave unrest. In such a context, the need for fortifications resurfaced once again. A stone wall was out of the question, given the lack of quarries nearby and a want of funds to import materials, but a wooden stockade was finally erected in 1760. Born of anxieties regarding the protection of the capital against a Native American attack and the maintenance of public order within the city, the completion of the defensive perimeter around New Orleans gave a physical reality to the invisible boundaries that already existed in the colonists' minds. In a poem written during his stay in the colony, Dumont de Montigny celebrated the function the Louisiana capital fulfilled as a haven, proclaiming that "the city is all the good, and the source of everything, and support for everyone." But slaves were not included in the substantive "everyone." For those living on plantations nearby, New Orleans increasingly symbolized both a space of greater autonomy and a place of repression.[5]

NEW ORLEANS OR "BALABANJER"

Native Americans played a crucial role in New Orleans's founding and development. Under French rule, the city formed part of an environment that remained to a large extent Indian Country. The Choctaw were one of the most numerous and powerful First Nations with which the French interacted in the lower Mississippi Valley. The name they gave to New Orleans, "Balabanjer," or the "town of strangers," expressed their acceptance of the presence of the French, even though they considered them to be outsiders. When the city was established in 1718 on the site of a Native American portage, the French had already spent two decades developing alliances with all

5. Marc de Villiers, ed., "L'établissement de la province de la Louisiane: Poème composé de 1728 à 1742 par Dumont de Montigny," *Journal de la société des américanistes*, New Ser., XXIII (1931), 307.

the indigenous nations, including the Choctaw, within a certain radius of what would become the Louisiana capital. They chose the site because of the possibilities for communication facilitated by its geography. They also opted for a place with Native American villages nearby that could supply food and be of assistance in case of attack. This dependency was reversed over time, but First Nations from the whole Mississippi and Mobile Valleys continued to visit the city frequently for trade and diplomacy. Louisiana was a shared French-Native world, as demonstrated by the daily presence of Native Americans within New Orleans. All in all, the alliance worked to the benefit of both sides.[6]

Jean-Baptiste Le Moyne de Bienville selected the location for the future city on the Mississippi River with the help of indigenous informants. Given that the ground was covered by a field of cane, the officials dispensed with the usual ceremony of laying a foundation stone to mark the beginning of construction. According to a lost manuscript written by a settler of English origins:

> In 1718, Mr. de Bienville, Commandant General of Louisiana, arrived with six ships loaded with men and supplies. There were thirty workers, all convicts, six carpenters and four Canadians. There was also Mr. Pradel who had been appointed Commandant of the future city, Mister Chassin, *intendant du commerce*, and Mister Dreaux.... Mr. de Bienville cut the first cane, Messrs. Pradel and Dreaux the second one, and they tried to open a passage through the thick screen of canes from the river to the place where the barracks ought to be erected.... The whole area was a compact cane field, with only a small path leading from the Mississippi to the bayou connecting with Lake Pontchartrain.[7]

6. For the origins of the Choctaw name "Balabanjer," see Journal and Field Notes of Levin Wailes, 1809, Box 2, Folder 16, fol. 26, John F. H. Claiborne Papers, Southern Historical Collection, Manuscript Division, Wilson Library, University of North Carolina at Chapel Hill, quoted in James Taylor Carson, "Sacred Circles and Dangerous People: Native American Cosmology and the French Settlement of Louisiana," in Bradley G. Bond, ed., *French Colonial Louisiana and the Atlantic World* (Baton Rouge, La., 2005), 65–82.

7. The name of the last official listed was probably Dreux, not Dreaux. See Samuel Wilson, Jr., *Le vieux Carré New Orleans, Its Plans, Its Growth, Its Architecture* (New Orleans, 1968), 3–4, quoted in Gilles-Antoine Langlois, *Des villes pour la Louisiane française: Théorie et pratique de l'urbanistique coloniale au 18e siècle* (Paris, 2003), 324. Wilson, in turn, originally quoted Conrad M. Widman, ed., "Some Southern Cities (in the

Figure 5: [Jean-Pierre Lassus]. *Veüe et perspective de la Nouvelle Orléans.*
1726. ANOM France 04 DFC 71 A. Courtesy of Les archives nationales d'outre-mer.
Aix-en-Provence, France

The area had not been previously occupied by Native Americans, even though some villages of *petites nations* (Acolapissa, Houma, and Quinipissa) were located near the mouth of Bayou Saint John at the time of the city's founding. Some Canadian settlers also attempted to form settlements there in 1708. The draw for Bienville was the two points of access the site offered to the sea, through the Mississippi River and through Lake Pontchartrain and Lake Borgne. Unlike First Nations who used overland routes as well as the Mississippi River and its tributaries to move about for belligerent, economic, and sociocultural purposes, the French, by contrast, were much more dependent on waterways. Dumont de Montigny complained that one had "always ... to travel on water by boat to go from one post to another."[8]

U.S.), about 1750," *Records of the American Catholic Historical Society of Philadelphia,* X, no. 2 (June 1899).

    8. On the choice of the site for New Orleans, see Marcel Giraud, *Histoire de la Louisiane*

        The City with Imaginary Walls

As Jean-Pierre Lassus's painting of early New Orleans reveals, the city was oriented toward the river. The Mississippi River formed the backbone of colonization in French Louisiana, which is why the name of the river was frequently used to designate the colony, as in the title of Chéreau's map.

française, 4 vols. (Paris, 1953–1974), IV, 254; Tristram R. Kidder, "Making the City In-evitable: Native Americans and the Geography of New Orleans," in Craig E. Colten, ed., *Transforming New Orleans and Its Environment: Centuries of Change* ([Pittsburgh, Pa.], 2000), 9–21; and Shannon Lee Dawdy, *Building the Devil's Empire: French Colonial New Orleans* (Chicago, 2008), 78–79. On river transportation, see Helen Hornbeck Tanner, "The Land and Water Communication Systems of the Southeastern Indians," in Peter Wood, Gregory Waselkov, and M. Thomas Hatley, eds., *Powhatan's Mantle: Indians in the Colonial Southeast* (Lincoln, Neb., 1989), 6–20; Gilles Havard, *Empire et métissages: Indiens et Français dans le Pays d'en Haut, 1660–1715* (Sillery, Quebec, 2003), 124–126; and Gordon M. Sayre and Carla Zecher, eds., *The Memoir of Lieutenant Dumont, 1715–1747: A Sojourner in the French Atlantic: Jean-François-Benjamin Dumont de Montigny*, trans. Sayre (Chapel Hill, N.C., 2012), 378 (quotation).

The territory over which the French crown claimed to extend its sovereignty covered the entire Mississippi Basin. Located above the Mississippi Delta, New Orleans could control the whole imperial infrastructure along the river. Even the second hydrographic system on the Mobile River was also ultimately headed by the city through Lake Pontchartrain. Moreover, Mobile did not play the role of Montreal in relation to Quebec. This lack of urban diarchy made the colonial capital "the only quasi-primordial city."[9]

Given French demographic imbalances with Native peoples, most of this vast territory, in practice, remained under indigenous control, despite French imperial designs. Although all the First Nations of greater Louisiana suffered some population losses, many stayed large, and the number of French settlers and slaves, for instance, never even exceeded that of the Choctaw. Under these demographic circumstances, the French had no choice but to conclude alliances with Native peoples to maintain peace. They were nonetheless driven by an imperialist project. They purposely built an imperial infrastructure consisting of missions, forts, and stores that was ultimately centered on New Orleans and that brought the colonial presence to the heart of Native American lands. These forts and stores were crucial both to assert French sovereignty against English and Spanish encroachments and to develop the fur trade on which alliances were based. Native Americans perfectly understood that these forts and stores were instruments of colonial domination. When the Natchez launched a war against the French in 1729, they not only killed most of the colonists and soldiers; they also took possession of the company's store and mimicked the storekeeper and his employees in distributing the goods.[10]

New Orleans adopted a model of dual settlements, with a French outpost and Native villages living in proximity, that was replicated everywhere the

9. On the name of the Mississippi River, see Marc de Villers, "La Louisiane: Histoire de son nom et de ses frontières successives (1681–1819)," *Journal de la société des américanistes*, XXI (1929), 1–20. On Louisiana as a river empire, see Joseph Zitomersky, "Ville, État, implantation, et société en Louisiane française: La variante 'mississippienne' du modèle colonial français en Amérique du Nord," in Alain Saussol and Zitomersky, eds., *Colonies, territoires, sociétés: L'enjeu français* (Paris, 1996), 23–48 (quotation, 27).

10. On Native American demography, see Peter H. Wood, "The Changing Population of the Colonial South: An Overview by Race and Region, 1685–1790," in Wood, Waselkov, and Hatley, eds., *Powhatan's Mantle,* 35–103; and Gilles Havard and Cécile Vidal, *Histoire de l'Amérique française* ([Paris], 2008), 194–203. On the French imperial project, see Havard, *Empire et métissages,* 255–324. For the Natchez attack, see [Marc-Antoine Caillot], "Relation du voyage de la Louisianne ou Nouvlle. France; fait par le Sr. CAILLOT en l'année 1730," HNOC, MSS596, fol. 145.

French established themselves in the Mississippi Valley. Since the Company of the Indies had originally intended to build a trade entrepôt, it made no effort to people the city or to ensure its food supply. The company's directors had a town planning and architectural project but not a sustainable economic one. The first inhabitants would not have survived without the assistance of the petites nations nearby. From the outset, more remote Native American villages also became involved in the city's food supply. Located within a hundred-mile radius, the Acolapissa, Bayogoula, Biloxi, Chaoucha, Chitimacha, Houma, Pascagoula, and Tonica villages, which moved around several times during the French period, all came to play a crucial role in furnishing the colonial capital with food and other products. Native American women provided the city dwellers with corn, squash, beans, and poultry that they raised for that purpose. They also made clay pots and reed baskets for sale. Men brought pelts, game, and bear oil. According to Marc-Antoine Caillot, in the late 1720s, up to two or three hundred Biloxi came to New Orleans every winter to go hunting for its inhabitants in exchange for a few pieces of merchandise. Indigenous warriors also helped to track down runaway slaves around the city or accompanied convoys to the Illinois Country.[11]

Although French reliance on Native American allies never ceased, the relationship of economic dependence between the two groups was quickly reversed. As settlers and slaves developed their own food supply networks, Native peoples came to look to them for trade goods and alcohol, which

11. On the system of dual settlements, see Joseph Zitomersky, "The Form and Function of French-Native American Relations in Early Eighteenth-Century French Colonial Louisiana," in Patricia Galloway and Philip P. Boucher, eds., *Proceedings of the Fifteenth Meeting of the French Colonial Historical Society: Martinique and Guadeloupe, May 1989* (Lanham, Md., 1992), 154–177; and Zitomersky, "Espace et société en Amérique coloniale française dans le contexte comparatif du Nouveau Monde: Essai interprétatif," in Ronald Creagh, ed., with John P. Clark, *Les Français des États-Unis d'hier à aujourd'hui: Actes du premier colloque international sur les Français des États-Unis–Montpellier* (Montpellier, France, 1994), 43–74. On the role of Native Americans in supplying New Orleans with food and other products, see Daniel H. Usner, Jr., "American Indians in Colonial New Orleans," in Wood, Waselkov, and Hatley, eds., *Powhatan's Mantle*, 115; Usner, *Indians, Settlers, and Slaves in a Frontier Exchange Economy: The Lower Mississippi Valley before 1783* (Chapel Hill, N.C., 1992), 63, 145–275; and [Caillot], "Relation du voyage de la Louisianne ou Nouvlle. France," HNOC, MSS596, fol. 117. For Native Americans hunting down runaway slaves, see RSCL 1738/04/11/01; 1741/01/10/01; 1748/05/18/02. For indigenous involvement in convoys to the Illinois Country, see Pierre de Rigaud de Vaudreuil de Cavagnal to the minister of the navy, Sept. 22, 1749, ANOM COL C13A 33, fols. 79–88.

many began to rely on to cope with all the transformations they faced. Alcoholism came to wreak terrible devastation among the petites nations. It accelerated their demographic decline and weakened the system of dual settlements, which gradually disappeared around New Orleans in the closing years of the French regime. As Dumont de Montigny realized, the expression that was used to qualify Native groups who lived in the vicinity of New Orleans, the petites nations, could refer not only to their demographic size but also to their subordinated status. Their position contrasted with that of the more powerful, larger nations of the interior, such as the Choctaw, who managed to maintain their sovereignty, economic independence, and cultural integrity much more successfully.[12]

Despite the demographic decline of the petites nations, many urban dwellers maintained personal relationships with the Native Americans who frequently visited the city. A soldier interrogated about his participation in an assault against a sergeant recounted how, at the time of the incident, "he was with Indians for the meat, that he had known these Tonica for a long time since he went hunting with them." What is unknown is in what language they communicated, since most Native Americans were reluctant to learn French. This soldier, who had been in the colony for ten years, might have learned Mobilian, the lingua franca used by some of the First Nations of the Southeast to communicate and trade. Most city dwellers must have been dependent on interpreters, however, and they probably could only interact with Native Americans in a superficial way.[13]

12. On French colonists' development of their own food supply system, see Ariane Jacques-Côté, "L'empire du riz en Louisiane française, 1717-1724," *Études canadiennes/Canadian Studies*, LXXXII (2017), 139–162. On the demographic evolution of the petites nations, see "État des nations sauvages de la Louisiane et des Illinois," in Louis Billouart de Kerlérec to the minister of the navy, Dec. 12, 1758, ANOM COL C13A 40, fols. 135–156; and Dumont de Montigny, *Regards sur le monde atlantique*, 390. On the disappearance of the system of dual settlements, see Zitomersky, "Ville, État, implantation, et société en Louisiane française," in Saussol and Zitomersky, eds., *Colonies, territoires, sociétés*, 37. On the evolution of the situation of the Choctaw, see Richard White, *The Roots of Dependency: Subsistence, Environment, and Social Change among the Choctaws, Pawnees, and Navajos* (Lincoln, Neb., 1983).

13. For the soldier's trial, see RSCL 1747/04/20/02. On the reluctance of Natives to learn French, see Havard and Vidal, *Histoire de l'Amérique française*, 321–324. On the use of Mobilian, see Le Page du Pratz, *Histoire de la Louisiane*, II, 219; Kennith H. York, "Mobilian: The Indian *Lingua Franca* of Colonial Louisiana," in Patricia K. Galloway, ed., *La Salle and His Legacy: Frenchmen and Indians in the Lower Mississippi Valley* (Jackson, Miss., 1982), 139–145; Galloway, *Practicing Ethnohistory: Mining Archives, Hearing Testimony, Constructing Narrative* (Lincoln, Neb., 2006), 225–243; and Gilles

The indigenous presence in New Orleans was not restricted to the petites nations. As the networks of forts, garrisons, and stores served to bring the French Empire into the heart of Indian Country, all allied groups regularly visited the city. They came "to give the calumet" to the governor and thereby renew their alliances with the French. For the nations of the lower Mississippi Valley, the annual distributions of presents, which were essential to sustain these privileged relationships, took place either in New Orleans or in Mobile. Caillot recounted one of these ceremonies, which could draw hundreds of Native Americans, in the Louisiana capital. Before arriving in the city, Native peoples announced their coming with screams and dances. Lasting at least two days, the ritual included a calumet ceremony, harangues, dances, banquets, and an exchange of presents. Besides these annual festivities, parties of indigenous warriors came throughout the year to obtain arms and powder, sell pelts, and buy goods at the company's or king's store. They also frequently brought letters from Mobile or other outposts.[14]

All the nations adhering to the system of Gallic alliances came to New Orleans, yet they did not recognize the political preeminence of the French over their peoples or their lands. As Dumont de Montigny insisted, it was "for the French" that New Orleans was the capital. From the perspective of Native American cosmology, these visits and exchanges of presents were rituals of hospitality that governed relations between insiders and outsiders. The powerful First Nations kept their own conception of space and territory. Balanbajer was located outside the sacred circles that symbolically delimited their own societies from the rest of the world. Even so, most of the time the Natives allied to the French maintained peaceful relations, with one exception—the Natchez.[15]

Havard, *Histoire des coureurs de bois: Amérique du Nord, 1600–1840* (Paris, 2016), 477–492. For an anecdote pointing to the dependence of most city dwellers on interpreters, see RSCL 1744/03/03/01, 1744/03/05/01.

14. Dumont de Montigny gives the example of an Illinois party arriving in New Orleans in January 1729. See Dumont de Montigny, *Regards sur le monde atlantique*, 229. For the annual distribution of presents, see [Caillot], "Relation du voyage de la Louisianne ou Nouvlle. France," HNOC, MSS596, fols. 129–131. For an example of Tonica who came to the city to get some wares from the royal store, see RSCL 1746/10/18/01, 1746/10/18/02. For the use of Native Americans as couriers, see Honoré-Gabriel Michel to the minister of the navy, Sept. 15, 1749, ANOM COL C13A 34, fol. 175.

15. On New Orleans as Louisiana's capital in French eyes only, see Dumont de Montigny, *Regards sur le monde atlantique*, 355. On Native American cosmology, see Carson, "Sacred Circles and Dangerous People," in Bond, ed., *French Colonial Louisiana*, 65–82; Gregory A. Waselkov, "Indian Maps of the Colonial Southeast," in Wood, Waselkov, and Hatley, eds., *Powhatan's Mantle*, 292–343; and Havard, *Empire et métissages*, 118–124.

Drawing on previous experience with indigenous diplomacy, Louisiana's first commandants or governors, who were all born in Canada, did not initially view the neighboring First Nations as a threat to the Mississippi colony's capital. Because of this apparent lack of danger, stone walls were never built around New Orleans, and its garrison was kept relatively small in comparison with those of other colonial outposts. Yet this perception of the city's situation changed dramatically in 1729. In an unpublished travel account, Company of the Indies employee Caillot recounted how in late November he saw a pirogue coming from upriver while he was strolling on the levee with a group of friends around 5:00 P.M. He first hoped that the boat was bringing merchandise from a partnership he had formed with an associate, but he quickly realized that the boat was full of naked or half-naked people. Its unfortunate passengers told the passersby that the Natchez outpost "was on fire and covered in blood." Their arrival broke the news of the Natchez attack in New Orleans.[16]

Tension between the Natchez and the French had started to grow as early as 1715, one year before the establishment of Fort Rosalie near the main settlements of the Natchez. On November 28, 1729, after a dispute with the French commandant over the occupation of Native lands to develop tobacco plantations, the Natchez started a war by killing around 250 settlers. The conflict, which could have led to a complete inversion of the colonial order, left an indelible mark on the colony's history and memory. In 1744, a slave named Margo presented herself to a magistrate as being "born in the year of the Natchez War." This dramatic set of events played a crucial role in the militarization of Louisiana society. Although the return of peace to the lower Mississippi Valley halted the construction of a wooden stockade around the city before the structure's completion in the early 1730s, local authorities and colonists would never entirely trust allied Natives again.[17]

16. Erin M. Greenwald, ed., *A Company Man: The Remarkable French-Atlantic Voyage of a Clerk for the Company of the Indies: A Memoir by Marc-Antoine Caillot*, trans. Teri F. Chalmers (New Orleans, 2013), 124.

17. On the Natchez, see Patricia Galloway and Jason Baird Jackson, "Natchez and Neighboring Groups," in Raymond D. Fogelson, ed., *Handbook of North American Indians*, XIV, *Southeast* (Washington, D.C., 2004), 598–615. On French-Natchez relationships and the Natchez Wars, see Arnaud Balvay, *La révolte des Natchez* (Paris, 2008); Giraud, *Histoire de la Louisiane française*, IV, 289–298; Marcel Giraud, *A History of French Louisiana*, V, *The Company of the Indies, 1723–1731* (Baton Rouge, La., 1991), 388–439; George Edward Milne, *Natchez Country: Indians, Colonists, and the Land-*

After the assault on the Natchez outpost, New Orleans's settlers mourned and trembled for months, as grief competed with panic. Carried away by imaginations fueled by fear, urban dwellers found visual and sonorous signs of fantastic dangers all around them. The appearance of "a kind of comet" in the night sky in the weeks between December 1, 1729, and February 15, 1730, heightened the feeling of apocalypse. In the evenings around mid-March 1730, New Orleans's residents also heard voices lamenting in the air just outside the city that nobody, neither the colonists, the Biloxi, nor the slaves, could explain. In such an anxious atmosphere, white urbanites began to be suspicious of all Native Americans, including those allied with the French, and lived in expectation of attacks on the colonial capital itself. As Governor Étienne Périer wrote to the minister of the navy in October 1730, the Natchez "are starting to get very close to New Orleans." The climate of terror had pushed him to take excessive measures a few months earlier, such as ordering some African slaves to attack and kill all the warriors belonging to the Chaoucha, one of the petites nations living nearby.[18]

For most white residents of New Orleans, the feeling of being besieged was aggravated by the weakness of the city's system of defense. "In a brief space of time," Caillot observed, "we found ourselves surrounded by misfortunes without hope of any rescue, since there were only three to four hundred men to hold off so many enemies." "To reassure the settlers of this city who had become extremely alarmed by the bold venture of the Natchez," local authorities took a series of measures aimed at reinforcing the capital's protection. Making use of a slave corvée, they ordered ditches to be dug around New Orleans. They also organized four urban militia compa-

<hr />

scapes of Race in French Louisiana (Athens, Ga., 2015); and Usner, *Indians, Settlers, and Slaves in a Frontier Exchange Economy*, 65–76. On Natchez and Bambara relationships and slave conspiracies during the Natchez Wars, see Gwendolyn Midlo Hall, *Africans in Colonial Louisiana: The Development of Afro-Creole Culture in the Eighteenth Century* (Baton Rouge, La., 1992), 96–118. For Margo's trial, see RSCL 1744/03/11/02. Another slave, like Margo, also referenced the conflict to date an important moment in his life, explaining that de Bellisle had been his master since the Natchez Wars. See RSCL 1748/01/12/01.

18. For the feeling of panic, see Dumont de Montigny, *Regards sur le monde atlantique*, 258; Giraud, *History of French Louisiana*, V, trans. Pearce, 401; and [Caillot], "Relation du voyage de la Louisianne ou Nouvlle. France," HNOC, MSS596, fols. 147, 167. For the suspicion of all allied nations and the imminency of a Natchez attack on the city, see ibid., fols. 146, 150, 167–169; and "Mouvements des sauvages de la Louisiane depuis la prise du fort des Natchez par M. de Périer sur la fin de janvier 1731," ANOM COL C13A 13, fols. 90–91. For the attack on the Chaoucha, see Giraud, *History of French Louisiana*, V, trans. Pearce, 401; and Hall, *Africans in Colonial Louisiana*, 102.

nies. Before the conflict with the Natchez, the militia system, as it existed in New France, had not yet been implemented. Like the Iroquois Wars in Canada, the campaigns of 1729–1730 provided impetus for the militarization of Louisiana society. All white men of arms-bearing age were required to participate in the exercise of colonial power in New Orleans and other French settlements. The organization of militia units specific to the city contributed to the development of a white civic identity. Even so, these measures did not succeed in completely dispelling the fears of urban dwellers of European descent.[19]

The settlers needed some kind of diversion in order to relieve the tension. Caillot's extraordinary narrative of the Natchez Wars broke off between February 25 and March 6, 1730. The end of the first Natchez expedition corresponded to the last Fat days, interrupting the forty days of Lent before Easter. The state of alarm in which New Orleans's inhabitants had lived since the end of November was implicitly compared to the penance associated with this religious period. On Fat Sunday, after a day of hunting, Caillot spent the whole night dancing and singing with some friends in the city. On Fat Monday, he persuaded his colleagues to organize a masquerade near Bayou Saint John. The location of the festivities outside New Orleans represented Caillot and his friends' desire to take their fear out of their hometown.[20]

To express a temporary inversion of the sociopolitical order, as was common practice on Mardi Gras, many of these men disguised themselves as women. Caillot was attired all in white as a shepherdess. A typi-

19. For city dwellers' complaints about a lack of security, see Greenwald, ed., *Company Man*, trans. Chalmers, 127. For the digging of ditches around the city, see Jean-Baptiste Le Moyne de Bienville and Edmé Gatien Salmon to the minister of the navy, May 12, 1733, ANOM COL C13A 16, fols. 64–65; and "Plan de l'enceinte projetée suivi des observations de Brison sur La Nouvelle-Orléans," Apr. 10, 1730, ANOM 04 DFC 85B. For the creation of urban militia companies, see Étienne Périer and Salmon to the minister of the navy, Dec. 5, 1731, ANOM COL C13A 13, fol. 8; and [Caillot], "Relation du voyage de la Louisianne ou Nouvlle. France," HNOC, MSS596, fols. 150–151. For the militarization of Canada at the time of the Iroquois Wars, see Louise Dechêne, *Le peuple, l'État, et la guerre au Canada sous le Régime français*, ed. Hélène Paré et al. (Montreal, 2008).

20. Masquerades were common enough for a Natchez chief to have been able to purchase a new Harlequin suit. Le Page du Pratz mocked how he wore it, as if he were a prominent character. See Le Page du Pratz, *Histoire de la Louisiane*, I, 86–87. The tradition of masked balls near Bayou Saint John was perpetuated in the nineteenth century. See R. Randall Couch, "The Public Masked Balls of Antebellum New Orleans: A Custom of Masque Outside the Mardis Gras Tradition," *Louisiana History*, XXXV (1994), 403–431.

The City with Imaginary Walls

cal eighteenth-century female figure of the theater and opera, especially of Italian comedy, the shepherdess was usually associated with romance in the countryside. Since the shepherdess was a keeper of flocks, Caillot could also appear as a leader taking responsibility for guiding his colleagues and friends. The party formed a small procession led by eight black slaves carrying torches and accompanied by musicians. On their way, they allegedly met four big bears and forced them to flee by using a whip. The maskers then joined a wedding party on the Rivard plantation, where they spent the night drinking, dancing, and courting. They came back the following night to dance once again near Bayou Saint John. A visit by Governor Périer gave tacit approval to these parties.[21]

The role reversals enacted by Caillot and his friends during the Mardi Gras festivities reflected anxieties about gender and racial hierarchies upset by the conflict. Caillot's licentious tone throughout his narrative, especially with regard to his boasts of having won the heart of Mademoiselle Carrière, a young woman who was a boarder at the Ursuline convent, during these Carnival balls, suggests that what was at stake in his semifictional tale was the sexual hegemony of white men over white women. During the war, many female colonists were believed to have been raped by their Native American captors, and Caillot included such rumors in his account. Although the writer might have distorted and exaggerated what happened, such a scenario is not entirely implausible. What is certainly more accurate is that French women had been used as slaves. As Dumont de Montigny noted, referring to the role played by some African slaves who took sides with the Natchez, "The negro slaves became free, you might say, and the Frenchwomen, slaves." Such treatment constituted an overturning of the colonial order.[22]

The bears the young men encountered while they were dressed as women might have been seen as the embodiment of Native American warriors who wanted to impose their sovereignty over the colony and sexually enslave

21. [Caillot], "Relation de voyage de la Louisianne ou Nouvlle. France," HNOC, MSS596, fols. 154–163.

22. Ibid., 145. Native Americans were not known for committing rape, even if there are some traces in the documentation of war captives being raped. For an article insisting on the lack of evidence, see Thomas S. Abler, "Scalping, Torture, Cannibalism, and Rape: An Ethnohistorical Analysis of Conflicting Cultural Values in War," *Anthropologica*, XXXIV (1992), 3–20. For evidence in support of the rape of captives by Native American warriors, see Gilles Havard, *Histoire des coureurs de bois*, 630n. On the treatment of white women by the Natchez as an inversion of the colonial order, see Sayre and Zecher, eds., *Memoir of Lieutenant Dumont*, trans. Sayre, 240.

French women. Although the bear had been dethroned by the lion as the king of animals in Europe since the early thirteenth century, fascination with the bear might have been revived in North America, where the animal was plentiful. In early medieval Europe, it was believed that drinking a bear's blood, eating its meat, wearing its fur, imitating its howls, and killing it were ways to acquire its strength. Another common belief, which was still widespread during the early modern period, was that male bears were sexually attracted to young women, whom they kidnapped and raped. Their unions gave birth to creatures who were half men and half bear. They were considered as invincible warriors, founders of dynasties, or totemic ancestors. In that sense, the bears in Caillot's narrative reflected white men's fear that they stood to lose both their colonial and sexual power if the Natchez won the war.[23]

The whip the maskers used to scare the bears, in the presence of African slaves lighting up the scene, symbolized the restoration of colonial domination and the slave order through violence. The black enslaved domestics were the only ones in the party who were not masked, as if they could be nothing else than slaves. The tradition of donning masks and costumes does not seem to have been adopted by slaves in New Orleans as it was by their enslaved fellows in Cap-Français, at least in the 1760s. Their lack of costumes could be read as a reminder of the servile stain that allegedly marked them forever. By continuing to perform their role as slaves throughout the masked festivities, they were taught the futility of trying to revolt against the French.[24]

As war against the Natchez resumed after Easter, another ritual took place in New Orleans that also aimed at restoring the colonial order. To symbolically repel danger from the city and take revenge for atrocities perpetrated by the Natchez against French women, Governor Périer asked the Tonica, one of the nearby petites nations, to burn a Natchez woman whom they had captured and brought to the Louisiana capital. In the Upper Coun-

23. In his travel account, the officer Jean-Bernard Bossu told an interesting story that illustrates how medieval beliefs about bears were revived in the New World. See Bossu, *Nouveaux voyages aux Indes occidentales . . .*, 2 vols. (Paris, 1768), I, 234–236. For the symbolic power of the bear in European culture, see Michel Pastoureau, *L'ours: Histoire d'un roi déchu* (Paris, 2007), 87–119, 285–290.

24. For slaves' use of carnival masks in Saint-Domingue, see "Ordonnance du juge de police du Cap, qui défend aux esclaves de courir les rues en masque, notamment en Carnaval," Feb. 15, 1768, in [Médéric Louis-Élie Moreau] de Saint-Méry, *Loix et constitutions des colonies françoises de l'Amérique sous le vent*, 6 vols. (Paris, 1784–1790), V, 157.

The City with Imaginary Walls

try, French officers and soldiers often watched and sometimes participated in and even initiated the torture of war captives according to indigenous customs. During the wars against the Iroquois in Canada at the end of the seventeenth century, captives were burned alive in Quebec City and Montreal. These executions conformed to the French culture of violence that expressed itself in war brutalities and in the judicial use of torture and corporal punishment. Despite the many anthropological similarities between the French culture of violence and that of the Natives, however, the former often condemned the latter for their war rituals. This condemnation fueled the construction of First Nations as uncivilized "others." When Périer asked the Tonica to burn the Natchez woman, the governor might have sought to associate savagery with Native Americans, notwithstanding the Tonicas' close alliance with the French.[25]

The Tonica, for their part, probably agreed to torture the Natchez woman to renew their alliance with the French at a time when the latter were suspicious of all First Nations. A few days before the torture ceremony, Cahura-Joligo, the Tonica's main chief, and one of the Tonica war chiefs presented two infants for baptism at the New Orleans church, an exceptional event given that usually only enslaved Natives were baptized in the colonial capital. The Tonica understood that the French looked favorably on Native groups that embraced French culture and viewed evangelization as a requirement of the alliance, even though leaders and their families were the only ones baptized. As Caillot noted in 1730, Cahura-Joligo himself "[had] been baptized and [was] almost *francisé* [Frenchified]," while, decades later, Vaugine de Nuisement asserted that the Tonica were "the most civilized of all the small nations," likely an allusion to their adoption of the Christian faith. Yet maintaining their alliance with the French was not the Tonica's only motivation when they agreed to torture the Natchez woman. They also sought to perpetuate their own traditional antagonism toward the Natchez. At the same time, they subverted the meaning of their participation, since they let a Natchez refugee who lived among them carry out most of the ritual. Cahura-Joligo only scalped the woman's long hair. In return for their

25. For a more detailed and slightly different interpretation of Caillot's manuscript on the Mardi Gras festivities and this scene of execution, see Sophie White, "Massacre, Mardi Gras, and Torture in Early New Orleans," *William and Mary Quarterly*, 3d Ser., LXX (2013), 497–538. For the burning of Native captives in Quebec and Montreal during the Iroquois Wars, see Havard, *Empire et métissages*, 741–747. For French judgments of Native American war rituals, see, for instance, Instructions Given by the Commandant Macarty to the Officer Favrot, Apr. 14, 1758, Favrot Papers, 550-R48.

compliance, the Tonica succeeded in keeping the trust of the French, but, a few months later, they suffered a deadly retaliatory attack by the Natchez. Cahura-Joligo, the other chiefs, and eighty-two people were killed.[26]

Before the Tonica experienced this dramatic outcome at the hands of their enemies, they conducted the torture ceremony in New Orleans. All the circumstances—the time, the location, the choice of victim, the forms and perpetrators of violence—were chosen to give an exceptional character to the event and to convey a message to the audience. The unprecedented brutality of the scene was supposed to reflect the acts of wanton cruelty committed by the Natchez. The ritual took place in front of the house of the company's storekeeper, the day after Easter, on April 10, 1730. The location reaffirmed the company's right to impose its own economic agenda and highlighted the role of trade in the colonial situation; the date gave a meaning of expiation to the performance. In a continuation of the imagery of atonement, the victim was attached to a wooden frame. The instrument struck Caillot's imagination so powerfully that he even drew a picture of

26. On the Tonica as the French colonists' closest ally, see Bossu, *Nouveaux voyages aux Indes occidentales,* I, 40; Le Page du Pratz, *Histoire de la Louisiane,* I, 137n; and Dumont de Montigny, *Regards sur le monde atlantique,* 188. On the Frenchification of the Tonica, see [Caillot], "Relation du voyage de la Louisianne ou Nouvlle. France," HNOC, MSS596, fol. 167; and Steve Canac-Marquis and Pierre Rézeau, eds., *Journal de Vaugine de Nuisement: Un témoignage sur la Louisiane du XVIIIe siècle* ([Sainte-Foy, Quebec], 2005), 23–24. Cahura-Joligo might have also adopted some French practices related to food and clothes. See Dumont de Montigny, *Regards sur le monde atlantique,* 214, 360, 382; and [Jean-Bernard] Bossu, *Nouveaux voyages dans l'Amérique septentrionale . . .* (Amsterdam, 1777), 261–262n. For the 1730 baptisms, see Baptisms of François Antoine and Rose Angélique, AANO, Saint-Louis Cathedral Baptisms, 1731–1733, 04/04/1730. In 1733, however, there was another exceptional baptism of an eight-year-old Tonica, whose godfather was Henry de Louboey, *lieutenant de roi* in the colony, the second highest ranking military officer after the governor. The child was given the Christian name Henry. See Baptism of Henry, AANO, Saint-Louis Cathedral Baptisms, 1731–1733, 09/08/1730. After the war, the king awarded Cahura-Joligo a *"brevet de Brigadier des armées des hommes Rouges* [a royal commission as brigadier of the Red men's armies]," a blue sash with a medal representing the "wedding" of the king with the city of Paris, and a gold-headed cane. The choice of the medal symbolized the special relationship between the Tonica chief and New Orleans. See Bossu, *Nouveaux voyages aux Indes occidentales,* I, 41; and Le Page du Pratz, *Histoire de la Louisiane,* II, 220. For the long-standing antagonism between the Tonica and the Natchez and the killing of the Tonica by the Natchez, see Dumont de Montigny, *Regards sur le monde atlantique,* 259, 363; Jeffrey P. Brain, George Roth, and Willem J. de Reuse, "Tunica, Biloxi, and Ofo," in Fogelson, ed., *Handbook of North American Indians,* XIV, 586–597, and Galloway and Jackson, "Natchez and Neighboring Groups," 610.

the scene that resembled a Native American adaptation of Christ's Passion, although the fact that the woman's body was burned made all possibility of salvation impossible according to Christian beliefs. That a woman was offered up as a sacrifice was also a departure from European practices. The victim was the spouse of a chief called La Farine, who was held responsible for the death of three Frenchmen. Usually women were spared the most extreme forms of violence. The authorities and settlers, however, had been horrified by the alleged rape and torture inflicted on the fifty or so white women (and children) taken prisoner by the Natchez. Violence against women, particularly pregnant women, and children was considered a flagrant sign of the utmost barbarity. In retaliation, some white women who had escaped from the Natchez and found refuge in New Orleans took part in the execution, just before the Native woman died after five or six hours of painful torture. To repair their honor and dignity, they stepped out of the role that was traditionally expected of them.[27]

Apart from being a display of revenge and expiation for the sufferings of white women, the spectacle could also have been intended to undermine the Natchez's war ethic by feminizing them, since only male warriors captured in war were supposed to be executed this way. According to an anonymous French author who witnessed the event, the ceremony was

completely new for the continent, as no example of a woman having been burnt at the stake has ever been found, as is the practice for native men who are captured at war; and this contradicts what they usually say, namely that the fate of a warrior is to perish by fire.

When they capture women and children that they want to get rid of, they like to break their skulls or throw them behind the fire.

When natives want to talk about a weak man they say that he is a woman, they have too much contempt for a woman to inflict on her the same torments as on a warrior, on whom the highest praise they can bestow is to say that he is a man.

27. All the information on the ceremony is based on [Caillot], "Relation du voyage de la Louisianne ou Nouvlle. France," HNOC, MSS596, fols. 169–171; and "Femme brulée au poteau à La Nouvelle Orléans," 1730, ANOM COL F3 24, fol. 187. Other travel accounts mentioned this way of torturing and killing war captives, and Dumont de Montigny also made a drawing. See Dumont de Montigny, *Regards sur le monde atlantique*, 372–373; and Le Page du Pratz, *Histoire de la Louisiane*, II, 420–437. On the meaning of burning bodies, see Pascal Bastien, "Usage politique des corps et rituel de l'exécution publique à Paris, XVIIe–XVIIIe siècles," *Crime, Histoire, et Sociétés / Crime, History, and Societies*, VI, no. 1 (2002), 31–56.

War was seen by Native Americans as an activity that was related to reproduction and that had a feminine dimension. Women from the victorious
village decided whether male captives were to be adopted or tortured and
killed. Although women captured in war were usually adopted and married,
contrary to what this anonymous author claimed, they were also sometimes
executed. In New Orleans, the Natchez woman endured hours of suffering
with the stoicism her culture usually required from male warriors. She was
not a passive victim but an active participant whose courage enhanced the
ritual. Several commentators, including Caillot, acknowledged the fact, implicitly recognizing that, paradoxically, the performance also paid tribute to
their enemies' bravery and greatness.[28]

The execution of the Natchez woman was influenced by both Native
American and French culture, but, afterward, the French went back to
their own way of dealing with enemies taken in battle, which was in complete contradiction with indigenous war customs. Whereas First Nations
generally sought to assimilate captives physically through torture and even
cannibalism or socially through adoption, French authorities made the remarkable decision to transport five hundred Natchez captives to Saint-
Domingue, after the second military expedition in January 1731. Le Page
du Pratz recounted how the Natchez prisoners were so numerous when
they arrived in New Orleans that they were sent to the company's plantation in front of the city on the other side of the river. They were first removed
from their territories, excluded from the colonial capital, and then expelled
from the colony. This practice of expulsion within the Empire was not without precedent. Even before the decision to transport the Natchez, repression against criminal disorder in Louisiana had had an imperial dimension.
White convicted criminals were sometimes banished to Saint-Domingue or
sent to the galleys in the metropole, while, conversely, some criminals tried
on the island were exiled to the Mississippi colony. Similarly, in Canada in
the 1680s, dozens of Iroquois had been sent to the Mediterranean galleys,
where they were treated as black slaves, although the French government
had been forced to abandon this policy after the resumption of even more

28. "Femme brulée au poteau à La Nouvelle Orléans," 1730, ANOM COL F3 24, fol.
187. Dumont de Montigny recounted that he had witnessed Native women, including a
teenage one, being burned on the frame with great courage. See Dumont de Montigny,
Regards sur le monde atlantique, 372–373; and Villiers, ed., "L'établissement de la province de la Louisiane," *Journal de la société des américanistes*, XXIII (1931), 402–404.
On the meaning of Native treatment of war captives, see Havard, *Empire et métissages*,
145–166; and Daniel K. Richter, "War and Culture: The Iroquois Experience," *William
and Mary Quarterly*, XL (1983), 528–559.

The City with Imaginary Walls

acrimonious hostilities. The deportation of the Natchez in 1731 was distinguished only by its scale. The action also deprived them of their status as an autonomous allied nation and reduced them to that of colonial subjects and enemies of the imperial state. The choice of Saint-Domingue as a destination was highly symbolic since it further debased them to the condition of slaves of African descent in a colony where the slave system was one of the harshest. As Le Page du Pratz observed, the goal was in fact to "extinguish this nation in the colony."[29]

Even after the removal of the Natchez prisoners, tensions in the lower Mississippi Valley did not immediately recede. Conflict with the Chickasaw, who had supported the Natchez, continued to simmer, and, to complicate matters, in late June 1731 some slaves of African descent took advantage of the troubled situation to plot a revolt. They were probably spurred on by some of their number who had been taken prisoner by the Natchez and then released. The conspiracy, led by several drivers from the company's plantation, is believed to have mainly concerned the Bambara and to have extended up to the Illinois Country, where the leaders had friends and family members. It is thought that their goal was, not to escape and form their own society away from the French, but to take over the colonial capital and govern their former masters. The enslaved domestic who leaked the plot in a dispute with a soldier claimed that she was going to become Madame Périer, the governor's wife, stating that "each of the leading negroes was to have ... a position as councilor, major, captain, officer, and storekeeper, they were even to take on their names." Because of this revelation, the revolt was stopped before it could be realized, but local authorities did not know at first who had participated in its preparation. Le Page du Pratz, who was the

29. On the deportation of 500 Natchez to Saint-Domingue (for various reasons, only 160 actually arrived in Saint-Domingue), see Le Page du Pratz, *Histoire de la Louisiane*, III, 326–327; and Havard and Vidal, *Histoire de l'Amérique française*, 305. For Iroquois sent to the galleys in France, see Brett Rushforth, *Bonds of Alliance: Indigenous and Atlantic Slaveries in New France* (Chapel Hill, N.C., 2012), 145–152, 217–218. At the time of the Natchez deportation to Saint-Domingue, some Fox captives were also sent to France, where they had to perform forced labor. See Gilles Havard, "Un *Américain* à Rochefort (1731–1732): Le destin de Coulipa, Indien renard," in Mickaël Augeron and Pascal Even, eds., with Burghart Schmidt, *Les étrangers dans les ports atlantiques: Expériences françaises et allemandes, XVe–XIXe siècle* (Paris, 2010), 143–155. On the integration of Native Americans within the French Empire, see Havard, "'Les forcer à devenir Cytoyens': État, sauvages, et citoyenneté en Nouvelle-France (XVIIe–XVIIIe siècle)," *Annales: Histoire, Sciences Sociales*, LXIV (2009), 985–1017. For the meaning of enslavement for the Natchez prisoners, see Dumont de Montigny, *Regards sur le monde atlantique*, 261; and Le Page du Pratz, *Histoire de la Louisiane*, III, 327.

manager of the company's plantation at the time, discovered and exposed some of the company's slaves who had played a decisive role in the plot's organization. The leaders were tortured several times before their execution to force them to denounce their accomplices.[30]

Despite this expeditious and cruel response, Périer had doubts about the reality of the conspiracy. Racial prejudice might have inhibited the governor's ability to imagine a slave rebellion, but it is also possible that Le Page du Pratz considerably exaggerated the plot to magnify his own role in identifying the culprits. Although some slaves very likely planned an uprising, the way the settlers understood it probably reflected their fear of a complete overthrow of the colonial order. The same feeling of anxiety might explain the rumor that broke out in December 1731 about a plan by slaves to massacre all the colony's white inhabitants during Christmas Mass. The reality of this conspiracy was even more dubious, and *Commissaire-ordonnateur* Edmé Gatien Salmon mocked "all the modest settlers [who] were on their guard and those who went to mass as heavily armed as Don Quixote." Nevertheless, suspicion was high enough for the authorities to abandon the idea of establishing a permanent free colored militia company, even though they had occasionally used and would continue to use slaves and free people of color in expeditions against the Natchez and later the Chickasaw.[31]

The Natchez Wars marked a major turning point in the way the French apprehended and managed their relationships with both Native Americans and slaves of African descent. After the organization of several military expeditions against the Natchez in 1730 and 1731 and later against the Chickasaw (who had sheltered some Natchez refugees) in 1736 and 1739, tensions with First Nations declined, and slaves did not attempt to revolt again before the late eighteenth century. Yet Louisiana's settlers never completely lost their fear of violence at the hands of indigenous people and black slaves. A desire to maintain distance from Native peoples competed with colonists' realization that they could not remain in the Mississippi Valley without indigenous assistance, a point particularly true of New Orleans's residents.

30. For the revelation of the conspiracy by an enslaved woman, see "Mémoire ..., joint à la lettre de Mr Amyault du 20 janvier 1732," ANOM COL C13A 14, fols. 273–274. For Le Page du Pratz's role in confounding the plot's organizers, see Le Page du Pratz, *Histoire de la Louisiane*, III, 304–317.

31. "Mouvements des sauvages de la Louisiane depuis la prise du fort des Natchez par M. de Périer sur la fin de janvier 1731," ANOM COL C13A 13, fol. 87; Périer to the minister of the navy, Dec. 10, 1731, ANOM COL C13A 13, fols. 63–64; Jean Jadard de Beauchamp to the minister of the navy, Nov. 5, 1731, ANOM COL C13A 13, fol. 200; Salmon to the minister of the navy, Jan. 18, 1732, ANOM COL C13A 15, fols. 25–26.

As Le Page du Pratz acknowledged after the war: "I wished we could have been done with them forever, if we did not need them; but we did not have a butcher or a fishmonger; without their assistance we had to rely only on the farmyards and the gardens to obtain food; hence we could not do without them." Given their economic and military dependency, the French renewed their alliances with Native peoples, but they remained on their guard.[32]

Once hostilities ceased, Louis XV started to look for culprits. Held responsible for the disaster of the Natchez Wars, Governor Périer was removed from his post. He was especially criticized by the commandant of Mobile for allowing the Choctaw chiefs to come to Biloxi and New Orleans to collect their annual presents, a measure his predecessor, Bienville, had avoided in an effort to prevent them from forming "an idea of the colonial forces and troops." Believing Bienville to have more experience with Native Americans, the king reappointed him as governor. On his way from France, the Canadian officer met and talked with some Natchez chiefs who had been deported to Saint-Domingue, renewing a policy of dealing with indigenous groups that combined a show of force and negotiation. Bienville's arrival in the colony in 1733 coincided with a return to normal for Louisiana's colonists, and he stopped the digging of ditches around the city.[33]

Despite the peace that followed, both the imperial center and local authorities supported the maintenance of large numbers of troops in New Orleans throughout the last decades of the French regime, especially during the imperial wars of the midcentury, when tensions with Native Americans resurfaced. They hoped that a show of force would impress First Nations.

32. On French-Native relationships after 1731, see Havard and Vidal, *Histoire de l'Amérique française*, 293–307. For the continuation of French dependency on Natives, see Le Page du Pratz, *Histoire de la Louisiane*, I, 200.

33. For criticisms of Périer, see Beauchamp to the minister of the navy, Nov. 5, 1731, ANOM COL C13A 13, fol. 199. For the meeting of Bienville with enslaved Natchez in Saint-Domingue, see Bienville to the minister of the navy, Jan. 28, 1733, ANOM COL C13A 16, fol. 223. For Bienville's arrival in the colony, see Khalil Saadani, *La Louisiane française dans l'impasse, 1731–1743* (Paris, 2008), 39–40. For the end to the construction of the wooden stockade, see Bienville and Salmon to the minister of the navy, May 12, 1733, ANOM COL C13A 16, fols. 64–65; the minister of the navy to Salmon, Sept. 8, 1733, ANOM COL B 59, fol. 584; and the minister of the navy to Bienville and Salmon, Sept. 15, 1733, ANOM COL B 59, fols. 590–594. In 1749, at the end of the War of the Austrian Succession, which induced a lot of tensions with allied Native Americans, Commissaire-ordonnateur Vincent-Gaspard-Pierre de Rochemore proposed once again to dig a ditch and build a stockade around New Orleans "to protect the city from an expected attack by the natives." See [Rochemore], "Mémoire sur l'administration de la Louisiane," 1749, ANOM COL C13A 33, fol. 158v.

The governor also started to organize the annual exchanges of presents in Mobile, rather than New Orleans, because it was "not advisable for some people who could one day rebel against us to get used to the main city and its surroundings." These measures helped to reduce the anxiety urban dwellers felt over the Native American danger. New Orleans was able to maintain the demographic prominence it achieved during the war when white colonists moved to the capital in search of safety.[34]

A PLACE OF REFUGE IN THE MIDST
OF A PLANTATION DISTRICT

After the mid-1730s, New Orleans always represented a sizable part of the colonial population. This process of urban attraction and concentration started to accelerate with the arrival of the women who escaped from the Natchez attack. Many of these widows remarried settlers from the capital or the surrounding countryside. In 1730, twenty-four of the fifty-one marriages celebrated in the Saint-Louis church concerned such widows. The Ursulines also took thirty orphans into their convent at this time.[35] Louisiana's checkered history with the Natchez Wars, the retrocession of the colony to the king, and the quasi ending of access to the slave trade from Africa resulted in weak economic growth that slowed the city's expansion, but these events also paradoxically explain a high degree of urbanization. This level of urban growth was uncommon among other plantation societies, although it was more typical of the Caribbean than of New France or most of British North America.[36]

34. For the policy of maintaining the size of the New Orleans garrison, see "Mémoire du roi pour servir d'instruction au Sr. chevalier de Jumilhac colonel d'infanterie commandant des troupes de milice de la Louisiane," Jan. 18,1762, ANOM COL B 114, fol. 155 (6r); and Kerlérec to the minister of the navy, Mar. 8, 1753, ANOM COL C13A 37, fol. 36. For a description of a distribution of presents in Mobile, see Canac-Marquis and Rézeau, eds., *Journal de Vaugine de Nuisement*, 69–70. In 1760, Rochemore complained about Kerlérec because he no longer respected the custom of organizing these ceremonies in Mobile and continued to summon the Choctaw and Alibamon to the city. See Rochemore to the minister of the navy, June 22, 1760, ANOM COL C13A 42, fols. 109v–110r.

35. Emily Clark, *Masterless Mistresses: The New Orleans Ursulines and the Development of a New World Society, 1727–1834* (Chapel Hill, N.C., 2007), 98–99.

36. The degree of urbanization among colonial populations usually varied between 5 and 20 percent. It was higher in plantation colonies, except in the Chesapeake. See Anne Pérotin-Dumon, *La ville aux îles, la ville dans l'île: Basse-Terre et Pointe-à-Pitre, Guadeloupe, 1650–1820* (Paris, 2000), 302–303 (20 percent for Guadeloupean cities); Trevor Burnard, "Towns in Plantation Societies in Eighteenth-Century British America," *Early American Studies*, XV (2017), 835–859, esp. 864 (8 percent for Jamaica in 1784

Moreover, despite socioeconomic integration between the city and the surrounding plantation district, New Orleans was perceived as a unique place characterized by its urban way of life. After moving to New Orleans, Dumont de Montigny wrote: "I thus changed from a country dweller to a *bourgeois* [resident] of the city" or "We lived the life of bourgeois." Likewise, planters such as Jean-Charles de Pradel, who chose to live on their plantations, rarely named the city but instead wrote about "la ville" (the city). Pradel also implicitly compared New Orleans to Paris, a commonplace among residents of French descent who sought to highlight the colonial capital's urbanity, which was the privileged site of elite sociability.[37]

Initially, the Company of the Indies did not take any steps to populate the city. The plan was to use New Orleans as a trade entrepôt while focusing on the peopling and exploitation of the countryside. Those who were supposed to live permanently in the urban center were the company's employees and a few soldiers and workers. Both the company and concession holders, however, felt that the latter needed residences where they could stay when business brought them to New Orleans. In 1721, the port city housed only 472 civilian inhabitants, but they represented 22 percent of the colonial population in the lower Mississippi Valley.[38]

———

and 12 percent in 1788); and Emma Hart, *Building Charleston: Town and Society in the Eighteenth-Century British Atlantic World* (Charlottesville, Va., 2010), 2 (10 percent for Charleston through the entire colonial period). In the Caribbean, "urban places were also impressive–the proportion of the population living in towns was at least 20 percent in most Spanish and Dutch islands, and 10 percent in most French and British territories. Higher percentages of island populations lived in urban places than did people in North America." See Philip D. Morgan, "The Caribbean Islands in Atlantic Context, circa 1500–1800," in Felicity A. Nussbaum, ed., *The Global Eighteenth Century* (Baltimore, 2003), 59.

37. Sayre and Zecher, eds., *Memoir of Lieutenant Dumont, 1715–1747*, trans. Sayre, 257, 275; "Lettre à la Nouvelle Orleans," Apr. 24, 1728, in Hachard, *Relation du voyage des dames religieuses Ursulines*, 89–90; [Caillot], "Relation du voyage de la Louisianne ou Nouvlle. France," HNOC, MSS596, fol. 105; A. Baillardel and A. Prioult, eds., *Le chevalier de Pradel: Vie d'un colon français en Louisiane au XVIIIe siècle d'après sa correspondance et celle de sa famille* (Paris, 1928), 50, 56, 87, 182, 187, 198, 211, 221, 228, 235, 248, 252–254, 260, 264, 282–283, 319.

38. For the Company of the Indies's lack of planning with regard to peopling the city, see Giraud, *Histoire de la Louisiane française*, III, 320, 332, IV, 205–206, 214, 217. The 1726 census still bore the mark of this initial attitude: it mentioned 9 houses out of 262 that belonged to concession holders yet were rented or left empty. See "Recensement général des habitations et des habitants de la colonie ainsi qu'ils se sont nommés au premier janvier 1726," ANOM COL G1 464. The analysis of the evolution of the urban popu-

After 1722, the failure of the concession system, the replacement of concessions by plantations, and the focus on African slavery nearly doubled the size of New Orleans's population. Former indentured servants moved out of the countryside and settled in town. By contrast, the number of black slaves declined in the city between 1721 and 1726, from 36.6 to 10.7 percent of the city's population, because most of the slave labor force was concentrated on plantations. In 1726, 755 persons resided in New Orleans, which accounted for around 26.3 percent of the colonial population on the Mississippi from the Arkansas River to the sea.

Between 1726 and 1731, according to Paul Lachance, the colonial capital benefited from some additional growth (2.6 percent) but at a much slower rate than the Illinois Country (4.2 percent) or the banks of the lower Mississippi (18.6 percent). Some former indentured servants who had taken refuge in the city died, resettled elsewhere in Louisiana, or left the colony. This decline of the white population was partially offset by the purchase of black slaves. As New Orleans took advantage of a second wave in the slave trade from Africa, the number of enslaved men and women in the city rose in 1731 to 258, representing 28.9 percent of the city's total 893 inhabitants.[39]

In the next five years, New Orleans's population more than doubled, reaching 1,748 individuals, which constituted more than one-third of the colonial population of the lower Mississippi Valley (35.7 percent). This dramatic growth was related to the climate of insecurity fostered by the Natchez Wars and the Chickasaw expeditions during the 1730s. The tensions between the French and these Native Americans forced the crown to divert financial and human resources to pay for defensive measures rather than the colony's development. They also made traveling on the Mississippi and life in the continental interior dangerous. Dumont de Montigny claimed: "Thus it is that our Frenchmen in this colony work and are reduced to misery, being obliged or forced to take refuge in the capital, unable to continue to develop the farms …." With the use of "Frenchmen," Dumont de Montigny was also distinguishing between colonists born in metropolitan France and Canada and accusing Governor Bienville of favoring Canadians. Whatever their origins, many settlers chose to relocate to the colonial

---

lation draws heavily on Paul Lachance, "The Growth of the Free and Slave Population of French Colonial Louisiana," in Bond, ed., *French Colonial Louisiana and the Atlantic World*, 204–243.

39. Lachance, "Growth of the Free and Slave Population of French Colonial Louisiana," in Bond, ed., *French Colonial Louisiana and the Atlantic World*, 217.

The City with Imaginary Walls

TABLE 1. Population of New Orleans and the
Lower Mississippi Valley, 1721–1766

| | New Orleans | | | | | | Lower Mississippi Valley (including New Orleans) | |
| | Whites | | Slaves of African descent | | Native slaves | | | | |
Date	N	%	N	%	N	%	Total	Total	% urban
1721–1723	278	58.9	173	36.6	21	4.4	472	2148	22.0
1726	649	86.0	81	10.7	25	3.3	755	2871	26.3
1731–1732	626	70.1	258	28.9	9	1.0	893	5264	17.0
1737	759	43.4	963	55.1	26	1.5	1748	4899	35.7
1763	1284	53.1	1098	45.4	37	1.5	2419	8231	29.4
May 1766	1626	55.8	1286	44.2	—	—	2912	10680	27.3

Sources: "Recensement des habitants et concessionnaires de La Nouvelle-Orléans ...," 1721, ANOM COL G1 464, "Recensement des habitants du fort St. Jean-Baptiste des Natchitoches ...," May 1, 1722, "Recensement ou dénombrement des habitants et concessionnaires qui sont établis sur le fleuve du Mississippi à prendre depuis les Cannes brûlées ... jusqu'au village sauvage des Tonica," May 13, 1722, "Recensement fait aux Natchez," Jan. 19, 1723, "Recensement ... Arkansas," Feb. 18, 1723, "Recensement général des habitations et habitants de la colonie de la Louisiane ainsi qu'ils se sont nommés au 1er janvier 1726," "Recensement des habitations le long du fleuve," 1731, "Recensement général de la ville de la Nvelle Orléans ... fait au mois de janvier 1732"; "Récapitulatif du recensement général de la Louisiane en 1737," ANOM COL C13C 4, fol. 197; "Recensement général 1763," AGI, Audiencia de Sto Domingo, Luisiana y Florida, Años 1766 a 1770, 2595–588 and 589, "Estado General de Todos los Habitantes de la Colonia de la Luisiana Segun los Padrones Que Se Han Hecho el Año de 1766"; Paul Lachance, "The Growth of the Free and Slave Population of French Colonial Louisiana," in Bradley G. Bond, ed., *French Colonial Louisiana and the Atlantic World* (Baton Rouge, La., 2005), 204–243.

Note: The figures for the lower Mississippi Valley are made up of all the colonial settlements in the Mississippi Valley on the Arkansas River and south of the junction between the Arkansas and Mississippi Rivers, including the city of New Orleans. The villages of the Illinois Country in Upper Louisiana and the settlements on the Gulf Coast (including Mobile) have not been taken into account because censuses are not available for all the years for which a census was taken in New Orleans and the lower Mississippi Valley. The 1763 census also listed nineteen freed men or women. There are small differences between this table and Paul Lachance's figures for various reasons. Given the mistakes in those censuses and their lack of standardization, these figures should be taken only as indicators of trends.

capital for security and economic reasons and tried to take advantage of the lifting of the company's trade monopoly to make a living from commerce.[40]

A rise in trade with the Antilles in the 1740s and early 1750s brought about a period of economic expansion that led to some resettlement in the plantation district around New Orleans as well as more distant outposts including the Natchez settlement. From the mid-1750s, the crisis the colony suffered during the Seven Years' War might have also induced new departures for different reasons. In 1762, Jean-Baptiste Fourgueux requested land in the countryside, arguing that he had a large family to support and that he had decided to leave the city because of the high cost of basic food and consumer goods.[41] Despite these internal migrations, by 1763, New Orleans numbered 2,419 inhabitants, having increased another 38.4 percent since 1737, even as the percentage of the lower Mississippi Valley's urban population dropped to 29.4 percent. The cession of the left bank to Great Britain precipitated one last rapid increase in the urban population between 1763 and 1766. Yet the city only accounted for 22.8 percent of all slaves of the lower Mississippi Valley in 1766, who numbered 5,637. The large majority of the enslaved lived on plantations.[42]

The mobility of the soldiers and officers of the *compagnies franches de la Marine* also contributed to fluctuation in the city's population. Although all soldiers arrived in New Orleans, most did not stay there long. Local authorities developed a system of military transfers to prevent the breakdown of discipline that a prolonged stay in the same outpost could generate, choosing which garrison they would assign the various companies to at random. This policy impacted soldiers' lives but also constrained military officers' social and economic integration. Most officers would rather have resided in the colonial capital for reasons of political necessity, economic opportunity, and cultural preference. They needed to court the governor to plead for advancement, many chose to open a plantation in the vicinity of New Orleans, and the urban way of life better suited their social rank. Some did not respect their obligations of service at distant outposts. Others did leave

40. Sayre and Zecher, eds., *Memoir of Lieutenant Dumont, 1715–1747*, trans. Sayre, 378.

41. "Requête de Jean-Baptiste Fourgueux," Aug. 2, 1762, FRLG. See also RSCL 1769/06/12/02.

42. From 1712 to 1834, the average percentage of Barbados's slave population living in Bridgetown was 16.5 percent. This number was lower than was the case in New Orleans at the end of the French regime, but not by very much. See Pedro L. V. Welch, *Slave Society in the City: Bridgetown, Barbados, 1680–1834* (Kingston, Jamaica, 2003), 95.

The City with Imaginary Walls

but chose to keep a town house or a plantation, or sometimes both, near New Orleans. While they were away on duty, their town houses were taken care of by enslaved domestics or their wives. The officer Antoine Valentin de Gruy Verloins, for instance, was garrisoned in Fort de Chartres from 1739 until his death in 1759, but his post did not prevent him from marrying Marie-Thérèse Aufrère, the daughter of a member of the Superior Council, or from having at least two children who were born in the capital.[43]

The colonial elite were instrumental in the economic integration of New Orleans with its immediate surroundings. Most of them, particularly the military officers, administrative officials, missionaries, and merchants who were compelled to live in the city to fulfill their professional obligations felt the need to purchase plantations nearby out of economic motivation. Both the Capuchins and the Ursulines, for example, bought an estate because it was a source of food, was profitable, and constituted an investment. But, the acquisition of a plantation was also a matter of social status. To own both land and a large number of slaves was a sign of class identity and was consonant with European culture. Although the nobility tended to become more urbanized over the eighteenth century, the possession in the country-side of a seigniory and a castle associated with the name and history of one's lineage remained a distinctive feature of the aristocracy. Conversely, some prominent planters residing in the countryside, who had no offices except commissions as militia officers, chose to obtain a town house because they needed to maintain connections with the colonial authorities and elite and because they enjoyed the amenities and pleasures of urban life.[44]

43. For the circulation of navy companies between outposts, see Cécile Vidal, "Les implantations françaises au Pays des Illinois au XVIIIe siècle (1699–1765)," 2 vols. (Ph.D. diss., École des Hautes Études en Sciences Sociales, 1995), 169–173. At least three houses belonging to military officers were only occupied by a slave in 1727. See "Recensement général des habitants, nègres, esclaves, sauvages, et bestiaux au département de La Nouvelle-Orléans qui se sont trouvés au 1er juillet 1727," ANOM COL G1 464. On Valentin de Gruy Verloins, see Earl C. Wood and Charles E. Nolan, eds., *Sacramental Records of the Roman Catholic Church of the Archdiocese of New Orleans*, II, *1751-1771* (New Orleans, 1988), 73; Vidal, "Les implantations françaises au Pays des Illinois au XVIIIe siècle," 197–199; and Carl J. Ekberg, "Antoine Valentin de Gruy, Early Missouri Explorer," *Missouri Historical Review*, LXXVI (1982), 136–150.

44. On the Ursuline plantation see Clark, *Masterless Mistresses*, 195–219; and Emily Clark, "Patrimony without Pater: The New Orleans Ursuline Community and the Creation of a Material Culture," in Bond, ed., *French Colonial Louisiana and the Atlantic World*, 95–110. On the metropolitan elites' relationships with the urban world, see Gauthier Aubert, "La noblesse et la ville au XVIIIe siècle: Réflexions à partir du cas rennais,"

As a result, many of New Orleans's officials and other prominent inhabitants divided their time between the city and their plantations. Some settled permanently in New Orleans and employed a white overseer to manage their rural property. Other masters chose to spend most of their time in the countryside while maintaining a town house. They only visited the city to take care of business, run errands, attend Mass, cultivate relationships of patronage, and socialize. Health reasons but also the pleasure of managing their rural domain and other entrepreneurial activities might have taken them away from New Orleans. Yet their stays in town do not seem to have been as seasonal as those of the South Carolina merchant-planters in Charleston because of the generally healthier environment in Louisiana compared with that of the Lowcountry.[45]

The choice to live in the city or in the countryside also differed according to gender among the planter elites. In his letters, Pradel recounted with patriarchal leniency that his wife often stayed in New Orleans to purchase clothes, fabric, and other baubles and to spend time with other women of her rank, including the governor's wife. The former officer turned planter identified New Orleans as the most important place to practice an elite sociability that was founded on the art of showing off. This strategy of distinction was expensive, but competition in spending and liberality were part of the elite ethos. Wives of prominent plantation holders and residents who made their home in the city played a crucial role in this elite sociability, which fueled relationships of patronage organized around the governor. Given that women were apparently not expected to take any part in the management of their families' plantations, their urbanity was part of their gender and class identity.[46]

Histoire urbaine, IV, no. 2 (2001), 127–149; and François-Joseph Ruggiu, *Les élites et les villes moyennes en France et en Angleterre (XVIIe–XVIIIe siècle)* (Paris, 1997), 93–95, 158–174.

45. RSCL 1723/07/13/01; 1730/04/06/01, 1730/04/29/01; 1741/02/04/02; 1764/02/17/01; NONA, Feb. 26, 1765, Jan. 31, 1766; Michel to the minister of the navy, July 15, 1751, ANOM COL C13A 35, fols. 291r–292v; Jean-Charles de Pradel to his brother, Apr. 10, 1755, HNOC, MSS 589, Chevalier de Pradel Papers 62; Baillardel and Prioult, eds., *Le chevalier de Pradel,* 50, 182, 187, 228, 235, 252–254, 264, 283. On the circulation of planters between Charleston and the Lowcountry, see Hart, *Building Charleston,* 4, 113–121.

46. According to the 1732 census, at least four elite men lived alone on their plantation while their spouse occupied their town house. This was the case with a couple named Dubreuil. See "Recensement général de la ville de la Nouvelle-Orléans ... fait au mois de janvier 1732," ANOM COL G1 464. On Pradel's wife, see Pradel to his brother, Apr. 10, 1755, HNOC, MSS 589, Chevalier de Pradel Papers 62.

Despite the attraction of New Orleans, elite sociability occasionally included some outings in the countryside to visit a plantation for a banquet or to organize a picnic or drinking party, near Bayou Saint John in particular. These rural gatherings allowed for less formal etiquette than in the city. The immediate surroundings of New Orleans were also used by other social categories than the upper class to relax and have fun. A *guinguette* (open-air drinking house) located downriver was a favorite spot to drink beer brewed with roasted corn. White settlers, however, were not the only colonial actors who circulated between the countryside and the capital. Slaves also did.[47]

SLAVE MOBILITY AND "RIVAL GEOGRAPHY"

The frontiers between the city and the nearby plantation region were also porous for the enslaved, although their opportunities for movement were more limited and constrained. Slaves from the surrounding plantations came to New Orleans because their masters required them to do so for various reasons, but they also circulated between the city and the countryside on their own initiative. Their uncontrolled mobility shaped a "rival geography" to the "geography of containment" that authorities and masters tried to impose. Yet not all slaves had the means to participate in this *petit marronnage* (temporary desertion). In the lower Mississippi Valley, below the German Coast, two slave worlds seem to have coexisted: one in which enslaved laborers were more strictly confined to their plantations and had only occasional experiences of the colonial capital and a relatively small slave "neighborhood" straddling the city and the nearby plantations. Trade exchanges, a common sociability, courting, and family ties linked those slaves who lived just beyond and within New Orleans, even if they did not form an exclusive community. Over time, a growing number of runaways also sought to hide and survive in the city. Their success in merging with the urban population depended on their ability to appropriate the material culture of New Orleans's enslaved and free people of color, who increasingly distinguished themselves from plantation slaves.[48]

47. For elite sociability in the countryside, see Michel to the minister of the navy, Jan. 15, 1752, ANOM COL C13A 36, fol. 221v; RSCL 1748/06/09/01; 1768/05/19/04, 1768/05/30/01; and Pradel to his brother, Apr. 10, 1755, HNOC, MSS 589, Chevalier de Pradel Papers 62. For the "guinguette," see [Caillot], "Relation du voyage de la Louisianne ou Nouvlle. France," HNOC, MSS596, fol. 105.

48. For the idea of a "rival geography," see Stephanie M. H. Camp, *Closer to Freedom: Enslaved Women and Everyday Resistance in the Plantation South* (Chapel Hill, N.C., 2004), 6–7. I use the expression "neighborhood," but, unlike Anthony E. Kaye, not in the

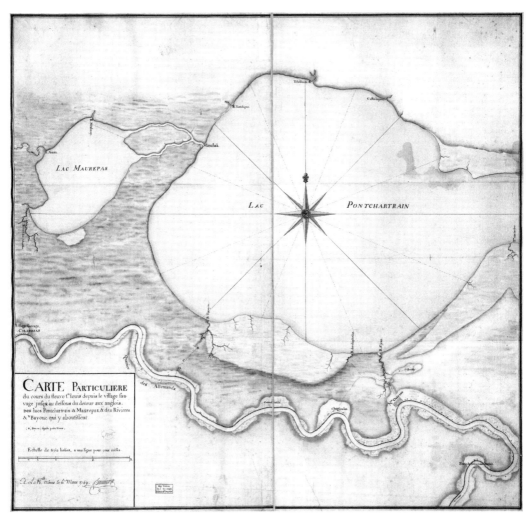

Figure 6: [François Saucier]. *Carte particuli[è]re du cours du fleuve St. Louis depuis le village sauvage jusqu'au dessous du détour aux anglois des lacs Pontchartrain et Maurepas, et des Rivi[è]res et bayouc qui y aboutissent.* Circa 1749. Geography and Map Division. G4042.M5 1749 .S3. Courtesy of Library of Congress, Washington, D.C.

The judicial archives are an extraordinary source of documentation on the movement of the enslaved between New Orleans and the surrounding plantation region. Nevertheless, most court records relate to rural slaves coming to the city. Only one legal procedure against an overseer named Michel

---

sense of an exclusive community extending over several plantations. See Kaye *Joining Places: Slave Neighborhoods in the Old South* (Chapel Hill, N.C., 2007).

The City with Imaginary Walls

Lamoureux alias Mégret alludes to urban slaves going to the countryside. Lamoureux had been thrown in jail because he had shot "negroes from the city." He complained that they had come to his garden and smashed the fences with an axe to steal some goose eggs. Some hints in the administrative correspondence, however, reveal that slave mobility went in both directions and that New Orleans's enslaved domestics also frequently visited nearby plantations. Since this circulation seldom surfaces in the trial proceedings, the capital, which was the site of the state apparatus, must have been a more dangerous place for plantation slaves than the countryside was for urban ones.[49]

Plantation slaves' reasons for going to New Orleans were diverse. Serving their owners as domestics gave some women the opportunity to switch from one milieu to the other. Some accompanied their masters in their movements back and forth. Margot, who belonged to Joseph Carrière, explained that she had "six daughters and a son, including two girls as tall as she is, another one younger who always accompanies her mistress to the city." These moves could also be more permanent. One of Jean-Baptiste Prévost's slaves, Marianne, told the judge that she had no idea what was going on in the city because she had only just arrived from her master's rural estate, where she used to work, to start a new job as a domestic in his town house.[50]

The necessities of plantation management allowed other slaves to come to New Orleans with no supervision. While giving his testimony as a witness in a murder trial, Joseph, a slave who usually worked on one of Jean-Baptiste Raguet's plantations as a gardener, had to report his schedule. He recounted that he had arrived in the city at noon to look for some peas to sow and that he did not return until 1:30 P.M., after having lunch at his master's town house. Some enslaved laborers were also sent by their owners to sell products from plantations at the urban market or to perform work needed for urban dwellings, such as chopping wood. They could take advantage of being in the city to do many other things besides what they were supposed to do.[51]

49. For Michel Lamoureux's trial, see RSCL 1742/03/13/01, 1742/03/15/01. On slave mobility from the city to the countryside, see "Mémoire pour servir à l'établissement de la Louisiane," [after 1750], ANOM COL C13C 1, fol. 110; and Kerlérec to the minister of the navy, Mar. 30, 1760, ANOM COL C13A 42, fols. 22–25.

50. For Margot's testimony, see RSCL 1744/03/11/01. For another example, see RSCL 1764/07/14/04. For Marianne's interrogatory, see RSCL 1744/02/26/01.

51. For Joseph's trial, see RSCL 1748/01/06/02. For slaves sent to the city to work or sell goods, see RSCL 1741/01/16/01; 1743/11/04/02; 1744/03/02/01, 1744/02/29/01, 1744/03/03/01, 1744/03/05/01, 1744/03/11/02, 1744/03/12/01; 1747/06/26/02; 1748/01/

Plantation slaves were occasionally sent to the capital by their masters for reasons other than trade or work. Some sick slaves were brought to the military hospital or to a surgeon for medical treatment. Since the city housed the only church in the New Orleans region, Christianized slaves from the surrounding areas also came to attend Mass, although there are few clues left in the archives about the frequency and regularity of their worship. They probably went to church to marry or to baptize their infants, and then only once or twice a year for the most important holidays of the Catholic calendar, Easter and Whit Sunday. The Capuchins organized collective baptisms of enslaved adults on these occasions.[52]

Slaves were also taken to New Orleans by their owners to be punished. Most slave discipline took place on plantations, but, in Louisiana, as in Jamaica, some masters relied on public authorities in a nearby city to help them control their enslaved workforce. Janot, a slave who had been arrested for running away, told the judge that he had left "because his mistress wanted to take him to the city to have him whipped for the insults and criticism that she said he voiced about her husband." The state apparatus located in the Louisiana capital often served planters' interests.[53]

Conversely, some slaves came to New Orleans on their own initiative to obtain protection from state officials. Arrested for running away, Scipion told the judge that the first time he had escaped was to come to the city with some companions to complain to Governor Pierre de Rigaud de Vaudreuil de Cavagnal about the mistreatment they suffered from their master, Mr. Lange. These slaves seemed aware of the power the king's representatives held to grant pardons. Governor Bienville and Commissaire-ordonnateur Salmon had promulgated amnesty for runaway slaves a few years earlier.

05/04; and Pradel to his brother, Apr. 10, 1755, HNOC, MSS 589, Chevalier de Pradel Papers 62. For slaves taking advantage of time in the city for their own benefit, see ibid.; and RSCL 1764/02/17/01.

52. For slaves sent to the city to be cured, see RSCL 1729/11/16/01; 1739/04/10/01; 1745/03/15/02; 1746/08/23/02. For slaves attending Mass, see "Observations sur le règlement de police de Ms. de Vaudreuil et Michel du 6 mars 1751, publié et affiché à la Louisiane les 28 février et 1er mars," Article 29, ANOM COL F3 243, fols. 84–89; and RSCL 1748/06/10/04, 1748/06/10/05; 1764/08/04/01.

53. In Jamaica, some slaveholders asked the common whipman (someone employed by the parish whose services could be purchased by masters) to punish their slaves on their behalf. Such a practice was probably especially common within cities and on small plantations in the immediate vicinity. See Diana Paton, "Punishment, Crime, and the Bodies of Slaves in Eighteenth-Century Jamaica," *Journal of Social History*, XXXIV (2001), 927. For Janot's trial, see RSCL 1743/09/10/02.

Vaudreuil, however, did not follow their example, and he very likely sent the slaves back to their owner.[54]

The uncontrolled mobility of the enslaved challenged the sociospatial order that authorities and planters sought to implement. In their free time, many slaves earned money by carrying water as well as selling wood, eggs, poultry, pigs, or vegetables in the city that they produced on their own individual plots of land. They could then buy fabric, clothes, jewelry, or alcohol. Pierre, who had been arrested for running away, refuted the allegations that he had come to New Orleans, but he admitted that on previous trips he had gone to Madame Carpentras and two other places to buy alcohol and that he had paid with the poultry and eggs he had brought to the city. It is nonetheless impossible to know when or how often, whether on weekends or only on special occasions, enslaved people came to New Orleans for recreation. Most slaves denied that they went to the city at night because it was an aggravating circumstance. Joseph, who was a young and restless man, told the judge that "he does not go at night to taverns to buy alcohol, goes there during day time to buy some shots, yesterday morning went to the Swiss canteen, but on Sunday during the night François negro belonging to his master went to La Languedoc's to get a small bottle of *guildive* [high-grade rum] that they immediately drank." The most privileged slaves probably went on Sundays, the only day that most of them did not have to toil for their masters.[55]

Women were also a powerful magnet drawing male slaves into the city, since the sex ratio between men and women was more balanced there than on plantations. During an interrogation, a judge asked Jupiter if he kept a mistress in New Orleans. Likewise, in 1741, Sans Soucy, who belonged to Pradel and Lange, confessed to a magistrate that he had run away "because Mr. Lange always wanted him to be whipped as he accused him of coming every day to this side [to New Orleans] to see the female negro belonging to Mr. Pradel, who is his wife and because Mr. Lange wanted to give him

54. For Scipion's trial, see RSCL 1751/06/21/01. For an ordinance granting pardon to runaways, see "Ordonnance de Bienville et de Salmon portant amnistie en faveur des nègres marrons," Jan. 5, 1743, ANOM COL A 23 264, fol. 130.

55. For slaves coming to the city to earn money, see RSCL 1738/04/24/02; 1744/03/03/01; 1764/08/02/01; 1767/08/12/01. For slaves as urban consumers, see RSCL 1738/04/24/02; 1744/02/22/02; 1764/07/14/04; 1764/07/31/01; 1764/08/02/01; 1764/09/04/01, 1764/09/04/02; 1766/07/23/03; 1767/08/12/01, 1767/08/13/01. For Pierre's trials, see RSCL 1764/08/02/01. For Joseph's trial, see RSCL 1753/04/24/01. For Sundays in the city, see RSCL 1738/04/24/02.

another wife." Conjugal and family relationships extended for some slaves across the boundaries between the city and the countryside.[56]

Despite the capital's association with judicial repression, New Orleans represented a space where rural slaves could enjoy a more autonomous life. They could meet people, buy goods and alcohol, multiply their experiences, and enlarge their horizons in ways that were more difficult than when confined to their plantations. Although the allure of the city was strong, not all enslaved men and women of the countryside had the same access to urban amenities. Because plantations extended on both sides of the river, rural slaves living on the west bank had to find a way to cross the river. To that end, they stole or borrowed pirogues. When Le Page du Pratz became the director of the Company of the Indies's and then the king's plantation, he realized that the slaves under his supervision owned several small pirogues "that they used to cross the River, to steal from the settlers on the other side, where the City was." He seized and destroyed the pirogues and forbade the slaves to possess any; he also built a slave camp surrounded by a wooden stockade with only one entrance. Another constraint on the coming of the enslaved to the capital was the distance that they had to walk. The easiest route was to follow the levee built along the line of plantations, but the meanders of the Mississippi River lengthened the distance. Otherwise, slaves had to cut through cypress woods and swamps. Those who only wished to visit the urban center before returning to their plantations needed to be able to go back and forth overnight, which greatly reduced the number who were able to do so. Moreover, the degree of slaves' familiarity with New Orleans varied with each individual's occupation, as evidenced by the accounts two men who lived on the German coast gave of their respective situations to magistrates in 1764. Pierrot hardly ever left the German coast and visited the city only occasionally whereas Jassemin regularly spent one week on the German coast and one week in town with his mistress when she went there to sell the rice that she had bought from the German farmers.[57]

56. For Jupiter's trial, see RSCL 1744/03/03/01, 1744/03/12/01. For Sans Soucy's trial, see RSCL 1741/01/16/02.

57. For slaves stealing, borrowing, or keeping pirogues, see RSCL 1739/11/07/02; 1739/12/21/02; 1744/02/26/01; 1748/05/18/03; 1765/09/09/02; and Le Page du Pratz, *Histoire de la Louisiane*, III, 226–227. Only two trials mention slaves borrowing horses to move between plantations, and these instances occurred at night. See RSCL 1753/04/24/01; 1764/11/14/01. There are few mentions of itineraries taken by runaways in the judicial archives. For an example of a slave recounting how he followed the road on the levee, see RSCL 1765/02/26/01. For Pierrot's and Jassemin's trials, see RSCL 1764/01/31/01; 1764/07/14/04.

Some of the slaves who left their plantations to reach New Orleans tried to flee for good. They came from nearby estates and from more remote settlements, including the villages of the Illinois Country in the Upper Mississippi Valley. In 1748, two slaves from Fort de Chartres were arrested at Pointe Coupée on their way to the capital; they explained that their master, Mr. de Gruy, overworked and mistreated them, that nobody paid attention to their complaints upriver, and that they wanted to reach Mrs. Aufrère, de Gruy's mother-in-law, to persuade her to sell them to another planter. In the last decades of the French regime, however, most runaways came to New Orleans to remain unseen. In the early days of the colony, more slaves might have attempted to reach a Spanish settlement or to take refuge among Native Americans, when they did not roam from one plantation to another. Throughout the Americas, African and Creole slaves followed different patterns of escape: the former usually ran away in groups to form their own maroon communities outside colonial territories while the latter tended to flee individually but stayed within colonial settlements. With the quasi ending of Louisiana's access to the French slave trade from Africa, the creolization of the local slave population, and the arrival of creolized slaves from the Antilles, New Orleans might have better suited the expectations of runaways. At that time, the city began to be demographically and economically important enough to offer some measure of anonymity and to provide work for fugitives. But disappearing was not easy.[58]

Different strategies were employed by runaways within and beyond New Orleans to hide and support themselves. Some remained in the countryside and only occasionally sneaked into the city, whereas others settled there. They subsisted by selling cane or wood or by hiring themselves out to white urban dwellers to do various kinds of work. Some chose to supplement their income by stealing or to completely live off theft and the clandestine trade in stolen goods. Survival was always difficult. After having been sheltered for three months by another slave in the countryside, the runaway Janot came to New Orleans to "beg for his bread" and was caught by his master. Apart from finding food and work, fugitives also had to look for a place to

---

58. There are only a few declarations of runaway slaves to the clerk of the Superior Council that document desertion among urban slaves, and it is not always certain that the slaves lived in the city. See RSCL 1745/03/08/03; 1745/03/15/01; 1746/06/23/01; 1746/08/03/02; 1746/09/28/01; 1747/10/10/01. For slaves coming from upriver, see RSCL 1748/06/09/03, 1748/06/11/01, 1748/06/11/02, 1748/06/24/02; 1764/01/31/01; 1764/09/04/02. For differentiated patterns of desertion among African and Creole slaves, see Philip D. Morgan, "Colonial South Carolina Runaways: Their Significance for Slave Culture," *Slavery and Abolition*, VI, no. 3 (December 1985), 57–78.

sleep. Some left the city at twilight to rest in the woods or on the levee in the countryside. Others benefited from urban slaves' solidarity. César and Louis, two runaways, spent months together in the capital, occasionally finding shelter in the cabins of female slaves working at the Charity Hospital before finally being caught and tried separately for desertion and theft.[59]

Although some slaves were able to survive for months in New Orleans without getting caught, it is likely that the urban center was not yet big enough to allow them to permanently escape from their masters and royal justice. The Louisiana capital's slow demographic growth meant that it remained a small society for a long time, and most people knew each other, at least by sight. The 1760s were a critical point in that respect, since the rise of the urban population with the arrival of colonists and slaves from the east bank ceded to the British made it possible for runaway slaves to live anonymously, at least for a time. After César's trial in July 1764, it took the authorities a few more weeks before they succeeded in arresting Louis in early September. Although Louis, according to a witness named Louison, "went fearlessly about the city," the attorney general and the Superior Council's other members were obsessed with gathering information to identify him. César's trial, like the suits of other fugitive slaves before Louis's arrest, included many questions about the latter's appearance and clothing. The city's growth and Louis's dauntlessness—but also racial prejudice toward people of African descent—might explain the difficulty that officials had in catching him quickly, as they might have been unable to easily recognize him.[60]

59. For fugitive slaves hiding on plantations and only occasionally visiting the city, see RSCL 1764/01/31/01. For runaways staying in the countryside but sending other slaves to the city to buy food, see RSCL 1765/09/09/02; 1766/07/25/02. Staying in the countryside without assistance required having lead and powder to hunt and to make a fire. For runaways supporting themselves through trade or labor, see RSCL 1764/07/31/01; 1764/09/03/01, 1764/09/04/02; 1766/07/01/01; 1767/08/21/01. For runaways stealing, see RSCL 1764/07/08/01, 1764/07/10/03, 1764/07/14/01, 1764/07/14/04, 1764/07/21/01, 1764/07/24/03; 1764/07/31/01, 1764/07/31/02, 1764/08/04/01; 1764/09/03/01, 1764/09/04/01, 1764/09/04/02, 1764/09/08/01. For Janot's trial, see RSCL 1764/04/12/01. For runaways' sleeping arrangements, see RSCL 1764/04/12/01; 1764/07/08/01, 1764/07/10/03, 1764/07/14/01, 1764/07/14/04, 1764/07/21/01, 1764/07/24/03; 1764/09/03/01, 1764/09/04/01, 1764/09/04/02, 1764/09/05/01, 1764/09/05/02, 1764/09/08/01; 1765/10/29/02; 1766/07/01/01. For another example of a plantation slave named Louis helped by an urban slave named Marguerite, see RSCL 1765/09/09/02.

60. Some slaves succeeded in getting lost. In 1746, a master reported to the Superior Council's clerk that he had seen two of his slaves who had run away opposite the church. See "Declaration," Jan. 15, 1746, in Heloise H. Cruzat, ed., "RSCL LIII: January–February, 1746," *LHQ*, XV (1932), 125. For Louis's trial, see RSCL 1764/07/14/01.

The City with Imaginary Walls

For his part, Louis had carefully fashioned his sartorial appearance to reinvent himself and look like an urban free man of color. Since he claimed he first came "naked" to New Orleans, he must have stolen most of his clothes. He used his garments to assert his masculine power over his enslaved fellows, and his apparel played an important role in the impression he left on them. He was described as being "well dressed," wearing a soldier's jacket, large cotton breeches, a ginga shirt (under which he concealed a large mark on his chest), and a large hat; he also had his ears pierced to wear pendant earrings. He probably succeeded in hiding because he did not look like a plantation slave. In contrast, another Louis, who was an urban slave who belonged to the king, told the magistrate that, when he came to Bousquet's to have a drink, "he found there other negroes drinking, mostly negroes from the plantations." Rural slaves might have been identified as such by their language, manners, or clothes. A cultural divide probably widened over time between plantation and urban slaves, as the latter had greater access to European goods and increasingly assimilated themselves to urban culture. Connections among the enslaved and free people of color from the city and the countryside did not completely prevent markers of difference from emerging between the two groups.[61]

"DISORDER IS IN THE CITY"

Slaves' rival geography fostered a feeling of disarray among officials and colonists. After 1731, measures to better oversee and control New Orleans multiplied as slave unrest seemed to grow with the rise of the slave population. These policies targeted both slaves and whites of the lower sort who were accused of facilitating slave criminality. Police deployments and judicial executions sought to regulate mobility from the countryside and to build a line of containment around the city. By the end of the Seven Years' War, authorities and settlers felt particularly vulnerable as military operations and an epidemic of slave rebellions raged through the Caribbean. The governor and commissaire-ordonnateur decided to build the wooden stockades that had been planned since New Orleans's founding while the Superior Council launched a highly repressive campaign against slaves accused of running away and stealing. The local elite aimed to increase their

61. For Louis's apparel, see 1764/07/08/01, 1764/07/10/03; 1764/07/31/01; 1764/09/04/02; and Sophie White, "'Wearing Three or Four Handkerchiefs around His Collar, and Elsewhere About Him': Slaves' Constructions of Masculinity and Ethnicity in French Colonial New Orleans," *Gender and History*, XV (2003), 528–549. For the distinctive characteristics of plantation slaves, see RSCL 1766/11/05/05.

sociopolitical autonomy and to be recognized as the head of the white civic community. Although some slaves paid a heavy price, the colonial administration largely failed to stop slaves' vexatious behavior.

Soon after the last military expeditions against the Natchez in 1731, local government came to view slave agitation as the main threat to New Orleans. In 1733, Governor Bienville cited fear of slave rebellion as the principal cause for concern in his efforts to persuade the minister of the navy to increase the number of troops in the city: "However, I have the honor to observe to My Lord, that, although this capital is not very much exposed to Native attacks, it may have more dangerous enemies such as negroes, and even the unhappy French who cannot leave this country where they have much to suffer. It would therefore be preferable if the Swiss company were complete, and an increase of fifty men in such a good troop would fortify this garrison." The governor asked for a larger contingent of men from the Swiss company, and not French troops, because he distrusted soldiers. Since New Orleans lacked a regular police force, the servicemen who were supposed to police the city and maintain social order were also one of the groups, besides slaves, sailors, and other poor whites, who were considered the most troublesome. Maintaining both Swiss and French servicemen who were commanded and garrisoned separately could prevent a joint revolt of all the military forces in the Louisiana capital.[62]

Colonial authorities often complained about the disorder generated by the incessant movement of slaves and other destitute social categories between the countryside and the city. Denunciations of solidarity among the "rabble" of both European and African descent was a common trope of administrative correspondence. The anonymous author of a report about Louisiana to the minister of the navy, probably written in the 1750s, bemoaned "the freedom to roam both by night and by day that the settlers, sailors, natives and slaves from both the inside and the outside enjoy, in addition to the numerous taverns for negroes, run by settlers who had to leave their farms out of indolence and misery and who survive thanks to fencing stolen goods, the thick woods and the bushes that border the City keep the humidity and facilitate many acts of banditry." The disorder that threatened the urban center was facilitated by the wild nature surrounding New Orleans.[63]

62. Bienville to the minister of the navy, July 25, 1733, ANOM COL C13A 16, fol. 275.
63. "Mémoire pour servir à l'établissement de la Louisiane," [after 1750], ANOM COL

Throughout the period, the governor and commissaire-ordonnateur repeatedly sought to enforce new measures to restrict unwanted movements among slaves. In the early 1730s, they complained that the troops stationed in the capital were not numerous enough and that they had to ask civilians to guard the city. They organized three guard units, each composed of forty soldiers and inhabitants chosen from among laborers. These guards patrolled at night while servicemen were placed on sentry duty at the ends of streets. This military surveillance started once retreat was sounded at dusk, that is 7:00 P.M. during winter. Over time, local authorities also multiplied the number of guard houses in New Orleans. Although for decades there had been only two, one situated near the royal jail on the main square and another one near Bayou Saint John, their number was increased to four and eleven sentry boxes were added in 1760. Before that, a *juge de police* (police judge) was appointed in 1751, after the promulgation of Vaudreuil and Honoré-Gabriel Michel's general ruling. He was replaced by a *lieutenant de police* (police lieutenant) along with four *huissiers de police* (police bailiffs) in the early 1760s. In contrast, the position of police inspector was created in 1739 in Cap-Français, and their number was raised to two in 1762.[64]

To more efficiently hunt down runaways, who tended to gather in the woods surrounding New Orleans, insulting passersby and pillaging plantations at night, officials ordered masters to declare escaped slaves at the office of the Superior Council's clerk. They also planned to create a *maré-*

C13C 1, fol. 110 (quotation); Michel to the minister of the navy, Aug. 18, 1750, ANOM COL C13A 34, fols. 329–330.

64. There is no specific documentation on the police system in Louisiana. Evidence is scattered throughout the administrative correspondence and judicial archives. For administrative correspondence, see Périer and Salmon to the minister of the navy, Dec. 5, 1731, ANOM COL C13A 13, fols. 8–25; Vaudreuil and Michel to the minister of the navy, May 21, 1750, ANOM COL C13A 35, fol. 22; Michel to the minister of the navy, May 18, 1751, ANOM COL C13A 35, fols. 206v–207v; Michel to the minister of the navy, Jan. 8, 1752, ANOM COL C13A 36, fol. 193r; Vaudreuil and Michel to the minister of the navy, Sept. 28, 1752, ANOM COL C13A 36, fols. 17–18v; "État des dépenses à faire à la Louisiane pour le service du roi pendant l'année 1764," ANOM COL C13A 44, fols. 39–46; and "Inventaire général et estimation de toute l'artillerie, armes, munitions, effets, magasins, hôpitaux, bâtiments de mer appartenant à sa majesté très chrétienne dans la colonie de la Louisiane," 1766, ANOM COL C13A 46, fols. 131–278. For judicial archives, see RSCL 1764/02/22/01; 1764/07/08/01; 1764/07/13/01; 1767/04/25/01; 1767/04/25/01. On the creation and role of police inspectors in Cap-Français, see [Moreau] de Saint-Méry, *Loix et constitutions des colonies françoises de l'Amérique sous le vent*, III, 574–578, IV, 478–483, 495–503.

chaussée (a rural police force), such as the one existing in the French Antilles, to stop brigandage within and around the city. In keeping with a suggestion made four years earlier by Commisssaire-ordonnateur Michel in
1751, Governor Louis Billouart de Kerlérec proposed to recruit West Indian
slaves, who would be freed on the condition that they come to Louisiana to
settle and serve in the police force. The creation of this maréchaussée would
have institutionalized the previous occasional use of free blacks against runaways.[65]

Apart from these police measures, which sought to compensate for the
lack of stone walls around the city, local authorities also published ordinances to expel poor whites from the capital. Such individuals were held
responsible, along with slaves, for urban disorder. Officials targeted "disreputable people" without a trade or profession and a residence, who were often
grouped, especially in the early 1720s, with the convicts and vagrants deported to the colony. It is difficult to verify whether these rulings were ever
enforced, but the efforts of the governor and the commissaire-ordonnateur
to establish a new outpost downriver suggest that they were apparently in
use in the late 1740s and early 1750s. They tried to persuade poor whites
and free people of color to move to the English Turn or to other established
settlements, such as the German Coast and Pointe Coupée. However, according to Michel:

> Too many ne'er-do-wells who are good for nothing have stayed in the
> city against my advice and thanks to the great leniency of Mr. de Vau-
> dreuil, most do not have a trade, those who do are lazy, and all find
> it very easy to secretly sell brandy or guildive to soldiers, negroes and
> natives whom they seduce and incite to steal: it is entirely against
> the bylaw that we have promulgated, and in addition to the canteens
> where alcohol is delivered without any limit, their behavior is such

65. On the behavior of runaways in the vicinity of New Orleans, see RSCL 1741/01/10/01;
Michel to the minister of the navy, May 18, 1751, ANOM COL C13A 35, fols. 207–209; and
Vaudreuil to the minister of the navy, Jan. 28, 1752, ANOM COL C13A 36, fols. 49–52v.
For the obligation to declare runaways, see "Ordonnance de Ms. Bienville et Salmon pour
la déclaration des nègres marrons du 1er septembre 1736," ANOM COL A 23, fol. 121v;
and "Arrêt du conseil supérieur de La Nouvelle-Orléans sur les esclaves marrons," Apr. 6,
1763, ANOM COL C13A 43, fols. 304–307. On the proposal to create a maréchaussée on
the model of that in Saint-Domingue, see Kerlérec to the minister of the navy, June 26,
1755, ANOM COL C13A 39, fols. 12v–13; and Stewart R. King, "The Maréchaussée of
Saint-Domingue: Balancing the Ancien Régime and Modernity," *Journal of Colonialism
and Colonial History*, V, no. 2 (Fall 2004). On the use of free blacks to hunt runaways,
see RSCL 1730/04/21/01; 1741/01/10/01.

that disorder is in the city, and that it is not possible to have any kind of order and police.

The anonymous author of the circa 1750s report proposed, as others had before him, to evacuate "the useless and wicked people to the Illinois country." He also advocated the erection of stone walls.[66]

It was only in 1760, after the capitulation of Canada, that local authorities finally ordered the digging of a ditch and the building of a wooden stockade. To justify the decision and the subsequent expense, Kerlérec told the king that they had heard that the English boasted they would take the Louisiana capital from upriver. Since the governor and commissaire-ordonnateur wanted urban dwellers to pay for half of the expense, "despite the general opinion that it is the king's responsibility to finance fortifications," they convened a general meeting where they outlined for settlers the advantages to be gained from the construction of a wall. In so doing, they gave a sociopolitical identity to the white civic community that was tightly connected to the establishment of a physical boundary between the city and the outside world:

1) This city of New Orleans, the capital of the province, which has been without any walls since it was first established, has always been a place of abomination without any governance. Two-thirds of the buildings are taverns serving guildive and places of debauchery, which constantly make the negroes and the natives drunk; the former pay thanks to the thefts they repeatedly commit against their masters and others, and the latter in exchange for the game they hunt or their harvest; consequently, apart from the frequent incidents their drunkenness creates, they keep misbehaving towards the settlers who do not cease to heap reproaches on us about the low profits they draw from their labor.

2) The domestic negroes of the city roam all over the countryside at night, and those from the plantations do the same in the city; it is easy to understand how little use they are when one has to set them to work, due to their state of exhaustion and debauchery.

66. For the idea that poor whites as well as slaves were responsible for urban disorder, see [Caillot], "Relation du voyage de la Louisianne ou Nouvlle. France," HNOC, MSS596, fol. 105. For the failure to remove poor whites to the English Turn, see Michel to the minister of the navy, Jan. 18, 1752, ANOM COL C13A 36, fols. 226–228 (quotation). For a proposal to both expel poor whites from New Orleans and build stone walls, see "Mémoire pour servir à l'établissement de la Louisiane," [after 1750], ANOM COL C13C 1, fol. 110 (quotation).

3) New Orleans is surrounded by native nations, some of them not very large it is true, but the Choctaw comprises around 3,000 warriors, who from day to day are becoming more and more insolent because of our growing need of them and because the English urge them to abandon us, all these nations together require for the tranquility of the settlers who are always frightened when they see a native, that this city of New Orleans should become for them, the old people, their wives and their children, a safe refuge against the incursions of those Indians, as they have only too often experienced their success.

By enclosing this city and thanks to the police that will be housed in well-located guard houses when we have troops, complete tranquility and perfect order, which are so essential in a civil society, will be ensured.

This discourse dwelled on the trope of urban disorder, typical of the ancien régime's political culture on both sides of the Atlantic. While acknowledging that some trouble came from inside the city, where numerous taverns and inns sold alcohol to nonwhites, the document mainly espoused a rhetoric associating insecurity with mobility by outsiders who needed to be expelled from the city.[67]

Despite the various police measures taken from the 1730s to the late 1750s and the construction of the wooden stockade in late 1760s, officials were helpless to stop slave unrest. In the mid-1760s, they felt particularly vulnerable: the colony's west bank had just been granted to the English, after years of war and isolation from the metropole, and a series of slave revolts ravaged the Caribbean. In this context, Nicolas La Frénière, the first Creole attorney general, launched a repressive campaign against enslaved runaways and thieves who survived in New Orleans by passing as free blacks. Apart from disciplining slaves, this outburst involved a political agenda. Local authorities believed they had to escalate the level of legal violence inflicted on the enslaved if they wanted to impose the primacy of royal justice and to give the white civic community a sense of empowerment and identity. In the absence of municipal institutions, the Superior Council,

67. Kerlérec to the minister of the navy, Mar. 30, 1760, ANOM COL C13A 42, fols. 22–25 (quotation). It was finally decided that the urban dwellers did not have the means to finance half the expense of the construction but that they would take care of the maintenance of the stockade and the ditches. See "Relevé des dépenses faites par le roi en 1760–1761 pour enceinte et fortification de la ville de La Nouvelle-Orléans," ANOM C13A 42, fols. 189–192; and "Résultat du conseil tenu à l'hôtel de gouvernement le 2 janvier 1760, sur les fortifications de La Nouvelle-Orléans," ANOM C13A 42, fol. 193.

which combined the interests of the state representatives and the colonial elite, used public executions to impose its political authority.

In the eighteenth century, corporal punishment and the death penalty were enforced in public to act as a deterrent and as a lesson in both the metropole and the colonies. Such sentences punished culprits, who were marginalized by the infamy that came with chastisement; terrified spectators; and purified the social body. The settings of these judicial performances were highly symbolic. In slave societies such as French Louisiana, this policy especially targeted the enslaved. Those sentenced to flogging and mutilations were attached to the back of a cart and pulled to each of the crossroads in New Orleans, where they were whipped, before being taken to the main public square at the heart of the capital. At the church door, they were whipped once again, branded with the letter "V" or the fleur-de-lis, and had their ears, hand, or hamstring cut. The slaves condemned to honorable amends and the death penalty had to stand half naked in a plain white shirt with a rope around their neck and ask to be forgiven by God and the king while holding a heavy candle. They were then executed by hanging or were broken on a wheel. The dead bodies of criminals were displayed outside the city on the road to Bayou Saint John. They were hung on a scaffold until they were completely rotten or thrown to the dogs and were not buried in sanctified ground. These rituals sought to repossess the urban space from slaves' invisible spatial appropriation and to symbolically cleanse New Orleans of disorder and crime.[68]

The climax of the repressive campaign of 1764–1765 might have also been a response to the uselessness of the wooden stockades, whose construction was finally completed in December 1760. They did not impede what local authorities considered as unwanted mobility and crime. In 1764, César told

68. On the meaning of capital execution and corporal punishment in eighteenth-century France, see Michel Foucault, *Surveiller et punir: Naissance de la prison* (Paris, 1975); Arlette Lebigre, *La justice du roi: La vie judiciaire dans l'ancienne France* (Paris, 1988), 131–143; Robert Muchembled, *Le temps des supplices: De l'obéissance sous les rois absolus, XVe–XVIIIe siècle* (Paris, 1992), 115–122; and Pascal Bastien, *L'exécution publique à Paris au XVIIIe siècle: Une histoire des rituels judiciaires* (Seyssel, France, 2006), 10–13, 93–97, 143–203. One exception where the body of a slave criminal in New Orleans was buried rather than left to rot was the case of Baraca, a slave belonging to the king, who had killed his wife. The Superior Council rejected the attorney general's request that he be left to rot on the bayou road and ordered him interred. See RSCL 1748/05/03/02, 1748/05/04/09. Likewise, in 1764, a slave who was hanged was probably buried in the cemetery afterward as he had confessed to a priest before his execution. See RSCL 1764/06/23/09.

the judge that, when he came to the capital after he had run away, he nearly got caught the first time, but he had escaped by jumping over the stockade and taking refuge under a bridge. Bringing order to the city and forming a protective line around New Orleans was a difficult and endless task.[69]

The life of another slave, a "negro named among them Foÿ and Louis by the French," illustrates the complex nature of enforcing social control on an individual level. This Bambara slave, who had been deported from Cap-Français to New Orleans, had been overworked in the lead and salt mines of the Illinois Country before running away and living freely in the city for eight months. Helped by some slaves, he was nevertheless captured by another from whom he had stolen a shirt. Sentenced to the wheel, he was finally strangled by a black executioner. Louis's life testifies to the extreme social instability of colonial and slave societies. These tensions, common to all, were particularly exacerbated in a young city that was both the location of colonial power and a milieu facilitating the erosion of the system of racial slavery.[70]

Over time, Chéreau's engraving of New Orleans and Louisiana acquired some measure of accuracy. It anticipated the demographic, political, and sociocultural importance acquired by the city. In contrast, Le Page du Pratz's more expansive understanding of "villes," or cities, was not entirely correct. Although he was right in saying that Native Americans also built and formed towns, his restrictive definition of cities as concentrations of relatively large populations missed the characteristics that gave New Orleans its urbanity. What made the Louisiana capital an urban place was, not the mere three thousand inhabitants who lived there at the end of the French regime or the stone walls that were never erected, but the function the city came to fulfill in working out the colonial situation in the Mississippi colony as the French were confronted with both Native Americans and African slaves.

In that regard, the Natchez Wars were a turning point. These events fostered the movement of the colonial population to New Orleans and were in-

69. For the completion of the wooden stockade, see Kerlérec to the minister of the navy, Dec. 21, 1760, ANOM COL C13A 42, fols. 83–85. For the failure of the wooden stockade to prevent slave mobility, see RSCL 1764/07/08/01.

70. RSCL 1764/07/10/03, 1764/07/14/04, 1764/09/03/01, 1764/09/03/02, 1764/09/03/03, 1764/09/04/01, 1764/09/04/02, 1764/09/05/01, 1764/09/05/02, 1764/09/07/01, 1764/09/07/03, 1764/09/08/01, 1764/09/08/04, 1764/09/10/01, 1764/09/10/02, 1764/09/10/04, 1764/09/10/05.

The City with Imaginary Walls

strumental in creating a sense of community among white urbanites. Before 1729, the city lacked the municipal institutions that traditionally allowed their French counterparts to function politically, legally, and fiscally, and settlers did not pay taxes anywhere in the colony. For New Orleans's residents, this underdevelopment rendered meaningless the concept of *droit de bourgeoisie,* or legal privileges enjoyed by urban dwellers that distinguished them from those who lived in the countryside. But the high level of anxiety generated by the Natchez conflict—as colonists struggled with the realization that, "all at once, from the friends they [the Natives] were, they become our enemies"—led to the construction of New Orleans as a haven to escape from an uncertainty that could seem unbearable. The measures taken to conduct military operations against the Natchez and to protect the city contributed to strengthening the urban population's civic identity and to illuminating the role played by the capital as the center of colonial power. New Orleans's white settlers became highly conscious that the colonial government and local authorities were one. As Dumont de Montigny highlighted: "The king's governor is Mr. de Bienville. He is the king of the country, and the head of the city." Likewise, he observed, Salmon was not only the commissaire-ordonnateur but also the official who "govern[ed] the city and its *habitants* [permanent residents]." The urban dwellers were also proud of the role played by the newly formed urban militia companies in the expeditions against the Natchez and Chickasaw. According to Dumont de Montigny, "the army (by which I mean the regular soldiers, the Swiss, the militia, and also the negroes) could not stop themselves from joking to one another that it was in celebration of the victory they had just achieved." For once, the slaves who, either voluntarily or under compulsion, helped the French to vanquish the Natchez were included in the festivities, bringing together all of those who had participated in the successful ending of the war—at least in the colonists' perspective—but this circumstantial and limited attempt to bridge the racial divide would not last.[71]

Over the succeeding decades, the nature of the danger that seemed to threaten New Orleans changed. Local authorities and settlers became attuned to the difficulties of controlling the enslaved, who rose up in ever greater numbers, and they increasingly resorted to the police and judicial system to contain and discipline them. Even though the city housed a large segment of Louisiana's population, it was mainly plantation slaves who

71. Sayre and Zecher, eds., *Memoir of Lieutenant Dumont, 1715–1747,* trans. Sayre, 270, 337, 393; Villiers, ed., "L'établissement de la province de la Louisiane," *Journal de la société des américanistes,* XXIII (1931), 420.

were executed with cruelty on the colonial capital's main square. The urban elite's participation in the Superior Council as the court of last appeal in the colony and the punishment of slaves from the surrounding plantations contributed to giving white city dwellers the feeling that they formed a welded community. The unprecedented repressive campaign that fell on runaway and thieving slaves in the early 1760s was a consequence of the first generation of Creole slaveholders' rise to power. During the turmoil of the Seven Years' War and its aftermath, the urban elite sought to claim their political preeminence at a time when New Orleans was becoming increasingly integrated within a greater Caribbean world.

Yet the extreme harshness of judicial violence in the early 1760s could be alternatively seen as an admission of powerlessness. The imaginary walls that whites attempted to erect around New Orleans were continually undermined by slave unrest. For enslaved men and women, the city might have been a site of terrible repression, but it was also a space where they could seek to enjoy an economic and sociocultural autonomy that was out of reach on relatively small plantations. The fantasy of a protected white enclave that the French authorities and colonists entertained in times of ethnic and racial tensions was shaken by the construction of an urban slave counterculture. If whites never built any stone fortifications, it might have been because they knew subconsciously that their so-called enemies were both outsiders and insiders. Within the urban center, they were also prompt to use their daily encounters—in the public space—to maintain racial boundaries.

CHAPTER THREE

The Hustle and Bustle of City Life

The Politics of Public Space and Racial Formation

On July 24, 1768, around 7:00 P.M., an altercation broke out on the corner of Bourbon and Dumaine streets that pitted two white neighbors against each other. Afterward Sieur Roth, a wigmaker, sued Sieur Pierre Olivier dit Percheret, a disabled former serviceman and trader, and his wife, Marie Cordier, in front of the Superior Council to obtain moral reparation and financial damages. The first series of testimonies from people present in the neighborhood depicted a solely white urban scene: a few white persons were relaxing on their porches at the end of the day, and a small group of three white men were strolling in the street, while others were passing by on their way back from the Bayou. Given the nature of the incident that provoked the confrontation, however, a multiethnic community soon came into view.

According to the defendants' interrogatories, the episode began when Percheret's son, named Pierre, bumped into an enslaved woman on the bridge covering the drainage ditches at the crossroads where he was playing. The woman had a basket full of jars of jam on her head that fell and broke. Pierre's mother, who had watched the collision, blamed the slave, at which point an enslaved man intervened. He was described by the couple as the *"sauvage"* ("savage" or "Native") or the "mulatto of Mister Foucault" but was never interrogated.[1] This slave, who had also witnessed the accident, claimed that the white child was guilty, and a quarrel quickly ensued.

---

1. We only learn the name of Foucault's slave incidentally, when Marie Cordier, Percheret's wife, recounted the words she had pronounced during the altercation before the court: "Go, Pierrot, tell your master to have the bridge repaired, he has more authority in the Council than me." See RSCL 1768/08/05/01.

Pierre's mother accused the slave of lying, while the latter retorted that she was the liar, a remark that, significantly, incited Percheret, and not his wife, to enter the fray and slap the man. At this juncture, the Percherets' neighbor, Sieur Roth, stepped in. He had observed the wrangle from his porch and threatened to testify in the slave's favor. During her interrogatory, Pierre's mother presented a different scene than that described in the opening testimonies. In an attempt to exonerate her son, she insisted on the presence of "two negroes sitting on the bridge" and "two or three others standing around" before the collision. She implied that any of these slaves could have been responsible for the fall of the basket. For his part, Percheret claimed that his son was having fun *("badiner")* with three "mulatto[e]" children, suggesting that any of them could have pushed the enslaved woman. Slaves only entered the picture because the couple needed them to exculpate their son.[2]

As this trial exemplifies, what defines any city is the "culture of the public arena" *("culture de la place publique")*. The public space is characterized by both its accessibility and its visibility. Passersby are also spectators. They form the necessary audience to urban scenes where social relationships and hierarchies within a city can be worked out. People not only interact with but also observe one another. In ancien régime societies, this practice of watching one another in public was of crucial importance. Since these societies were highly unequal and worked mainly through oral communication, they were characterized by an exaggerated "culture of appearances" *("culture des apparences")*. Public buildings and spaces (that is "public" in the sense of "open to the public") served as theatrical stages on which historical actors projected their vision of the social order, negotiated their social position, and displayed power struggles with a finely tuned sense of representation. People's behavior and interactions in public were conditioned by the fact that they were under the scrutinizing gaze of others. Public space shaped social encounters, and individuals used the public space both to give a symbolic meaning to their interactions and to negotiate the power dynamics within their relationships.[3]

2. RSCL 1768/07/30/03, 1768/08/02/01, 1768/08/05/01, 1768/08/06/07, 1768/08/09/03.

3. On the "culture of the public arena," see Daniel Roche, *La France des Lumières* ([Paris], 1993), 595. See also Isaac Joseph, *La ville sans qualités* (La Tour d'Aigues, France, 1998). I borrow the expression "culture of appearances" from Roche, who used it for clothing and material culture, but it can be extended to all sorts of symbolic expressions of social distinction. See Roche, *La culture des apparences: Une histoire du vêtement (XVIIe–XVIIIe siècle)* ([Paris], 1989). For the conception of social life as a complex

The Hustle and Bustle of City Life

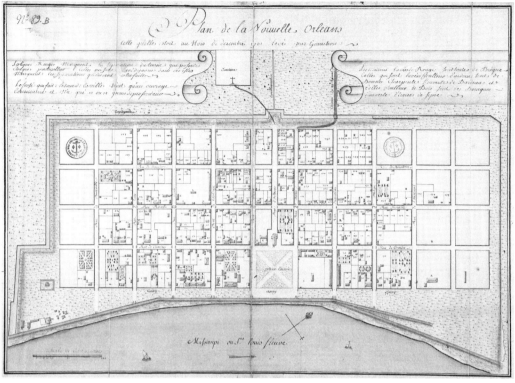

Figure 7: *Plan de la Nouvelle Orl[é]ans telle qu'elle estoit au mois de dexembre 1731 levé par Gonichon.* ANOM France 04 DFC 89 B. Courtesy of Les Archives nationales d'outre-mer. Aix-en-Provence, France

The urban milieu favored all kinds of interactions across social boundaries. The agglomeration of people living in close quarters generated daily encounters in the public space. These meetings included "encounters of proximity," involving people living in the same neighborhood, and "chance encounters," related to people's movements within the city. This collective public life was further enhanced by urban planning. On the 1731 map meticulously drawn by the engineer Gonichon, New Orleans was measured by the number of its built parcels. The materialization of the grid reflected the emergence of a public space constituted by streets. Except for Orleans Street, at the back of Saint-Louis Church, all the streets were 6 toises wide (12 meters), which allowed three carts to pass at the same time. The width

set of performances, see Rhys Isaac, *The Transformation of Virginia, 1740–1790* (Chapel Hill, N.C., 1982), esp. 5–6, 232–257.

The Hustle and Bustle of City Life   { 145

of the streets and the city's regular plan in the form of a grid were intended to facilitate both movement and social control. The levee, the main square at the top of the bend in the Mississippi at the city's center, and the many crossroads with their bridges at each intersection of two streets created many natural places for people to stop and congregate. It was not only the movement of individuals but also the gathering of crowds that made New Orleans alive and complicated its social dynamics.[4]

In this urban environment, no social fault line, including the racial divide, was absolute. Children of all conditions, for instance, could play together in the streets. These boundaries, however, could be immediately reactivated in the event of conflict. Pierre's parents used their position of authority as white *habitants* (permanent residents) belonging to the middling sorts (both men bore a title of civility, "Sieur") to defend their son, a strategy that might have worked if a heckler had not muddied the waters. Foucault's "savage" or "mulatto" was a slave, but he belonged to Denis-Nicolas Foucault, the *commissaire-ordonnateur*. His position in the socioracial hierarchy was modified by the status of his master, who was the second most important official in the colony after the governor. Among several prerogatives, the commissaire-ordonnateur was responsible for civilian justice and chaired the Superior Council as first judge. Anything that came to Foucault's ears could end up in front of the court. His slave seemed fully aware of the power he benefited from as a result and did not hesitate to question a white woman's word. Nevertheless, the man was quickly put back in his place when Percheret slapped him. Even though he belonged to Foucault, the neighbor who watched the scene from his porch, Sieur Roth, must have thought that the slave's version would be questioned because of his status and race. Otherwise, he would not have intervened and offered to testify on his behalf. The wigmaker might have also wanted to please the commissaire-ordonnateur.

The whole conflict, which involved the successive interventions of different spectators who, in their turn, became actors, raises the issue of the relationship between observing and power. Who was watching whom, and who had the means to be more than a mere spectator but also a witness and potential arbiter of the social order? Obviously, the public space was not

4. For the distinction between "encounters of proximity" and "chance encounters," see Maurice Garden, "Histoire de la rue," *Pouvoirs*, no. 116, *La rue* (January 2006), 5–17. The entirety of the city grid was supposed to measure 650 x 230 toises (1300 x 460 meters) in its full extension. See Gilles-Antoine Langlois, *Des villes pour la Louisiane française: Théorie et pratique de l'urbanistique coloniale au 18e siècle* (Paris, 2003), 338.

The Hustle and Bustle of City Life

socially undifferentiated: not every member of the audience held the same rank or the authority to impose his or her social sanction. In this configuration of powers, the state was paramount even though many things escaped its notice, as it could not be everywhere or impose a panoptic monitoring through its agents. In the end, white people's ability to resort to royal justice, which was free and accessible in New Orleans, potentially gave the state the role of final arbiter. Ultimately, it was the judges of the Superior Council who decided not to hear or record the testimony of Foucault's slave and to exclude him from the trial. According to Article 24 of the Louisiana Code Noir promulgated in 1724, slaves could not serve as witnesses except in cases of necessity and if there were no whites available, and they could never testify against their masters.

The discretionary power of judges to decide whether they would consider slaves' testimonies or not impacted the way white people observed, memorized, and recounted what they saw in the public space, for, most of the time, the enslaved would not serve as witnesses. The stories whites told in court offer a window into a mental urban landscape in which only the individuals and groups who were socially significant for them featured. White hegemony not only resulted in the physical exclusion of slaves from some public places and the implementation of some forms of segregation but also enabled whites to socially ignore them even when they were physically present. This exclusively white imaginary representation of the sociospatial world constituted the utmost symbolic violence inflicted on slaves.

Although the series of conflicts that led to this fascinating trial happened in 1768, at the time of the transition between French and Spanish rule, tensions over precedence among local authorities and settlers had occurred continuously throughout the French period. The culture of the ancien régime had made officials and colonists highly sensitive to the issue of maintaining rank in public from the outset of French settlement in Louisiana. Yet this does not mean that the politics of the public space did not evolve over time, leaving questions about how the process of racialization intersected with the colony's "culture of appearances." In the first decades after New Orleans's founding, local authorities mostly ignored the enslaved when they dealt with the organization of public space, but, in 1751, a local ruling promulgated by Governor Pierre de Rigaud de Vaudreuil de Cavagnal and Commissaire-ordonnateur Honoré-Gabriel Michel included two provisions related to racial precedence and segregation in urban public settings. What had happened that could explain why they felt compelled to legislate on this issue whereas the 1724 Code Noir had not addressed it?

Racial formation made the use and control of public space a crucial priority for whites and, over time, strengthened the need for them to publicly display and instill a socioracial hierarchy. The urban milieu forced whites and blacks to live in even closer physical proximity and intimacy than on plantations, while the power struggles between them were exacerbated by the social diversity that existed only within the city. The dialectical "racialization of space and spatialization of race" manifested in various ways, including the exclusion of slaves from rituals and festivities that gave the white community some degree of social cohesion, racial segregation in some public places and buildings, and the urge for whites, especially nonslaveholders, to retain some appearance of social superiority in public in the event of conflict. In part, this racial tension over the material and symbolic control of public space was the result of slaves' actions, for they never ceased to try to take advantage of the subversive potential of the urban milieu and to contest their domination, relegation, and invisibility. As the enslaved increased in number, they made their presence felt in every public space. They also fought to construct their own physical and mental urban landscape in which they could negotiate their own social control over each other.[5]

ON THE SQUARE AND IN CHURCH:
A WHITE CIVIC AND RELIGIOUS COMMUNITY

New Orleans was organized around a central square that opened onto the levee and the river. This square measured 62 x 60 toises (that is, 124 x 120 meters). At the back of the square, facing the Mississippi River, was Saint-Louis Church, which had been dedicated on its completion in 1727. A spectator looking at the square from the levee would have seen the Capuchins' convent on the right of the church and the city's main guardroom and jail, finished in 1730, on its left. The Company of the Indies's or king's buildings (the seat of the Superior Council on one side and some lodgings for various officials and stores on the other, or, after the colony's retrocession to the crown, the governor's quarters on one side and the office of the intendant and king's stores on the other) were built within the two blocks located on the two sides of the square perpendicular to the river, but they did not border it. From 1737 to 1739, the square was lined by brick barracks constructed

5. For a study that analyzes the interweaving of space and race mostly in relation to segregation and ghettoization in the modern period by using the concepts of white or black "spatial imaginary," see George Lipsitz, "The Racialization of Space and the Spatialization of Race: Theorizing the Hidden Architecture of Landscape," *Landscape Journal*, XXVI, no. 1 (2007), 10–23. See also Brooke Neely and Michelle Samura, "Social Geographies of Race: Connecting Race and Space," *Ethnic and Racial Studies*, XXXIV (2011), 1933–1952.

The Hustle and Bustle of City Life

to replace the first ones made of wood previously situated on the edge of the urban center. As the location of these religious and military buildings at the heart of the city testifies, the church and the military were the principal pillars on which French New Orleans society was based. Although the levee was appropriated by all social actors, the main square seems to have been symbolically invested solely by the state and the church.[6]

Space was instrumental in the way the two institutions fulfilled separately and together their function of social engineering. They enacted practices and rituals whose spatial deployment conveyed their sociopolitical messages. Initially, the main preoccupations of the various authorities in relation to these spatialized civic and religious ceremonies and festivities exclusively concerned whites. As in the metropole and in other colonies, conflicts over rank and precedence were common. References to such disputes or to rulings promulgated to impede them are numerous in the *Annales du Conseil Souverain de la Martinique* and the *Loix et constitutions des colonies françoises de l'Amérique sous le vent,* the collection of laws of Martinique and Saint-Domingue. The Louisiana situation was in no way singular in that regard, and the colony's officials tried to solve their problems by drawing on rulings and practices established in Canada or in the Antilles. Consequently, they displayed and helped to strengthen an imperial culture. This shared political and institutional framework left no room for slaves. In the authorities' view, the latter did not belong to the civic and religious community that made the city or, at least, not on the same footing as whites. Over time, however, they were forced to take the enslaved into account in their conception of the sociospatial order. Still, they tried to confine them to a subordinate and separate position.[7]

6. For the map of the first New Orleans church, see "Plan, profils, et élévation de l'église projetée à faire à La Nouvelle-Orléans," May 29, 1724, ANOM COL 04DFC 70B. At the end of the French regime, this church threatened to collapse. A temporary church was set up in the king's general warehouses until a new one could be constructed. See "Inventaire général et estimation de toute l'artillerie, armes, munitions, effets, magasins, hôpitaux, bâtiments de mer appartenant à sa majesté très chrétienne dans la colonie de la Louisiane," 1766, ANOM COL C13A 46, fol. 131. On the main square, see Langlois, *Des villes pour la Louisiane française,* 339; Marcel Giraud, *A History of French Louisiana,* V, *The Company of the Indies, 1723–1731,* trans. Brian Pearce (Baton Rouge, La., 1991), 235–237, 252; Jean M. Farnsworth and Ann M. Masson, eds., *The Architecture of Colonial Louisiana: Collected Essays of Samuel Wilson, Jr., F.A.I.A* (Lafayette, La., 1987), 1–23, 41–68, 109–147, 387–389. Nothing in the judicial records indicates that the main square was used as a privileged site of public sociability across all kinds of social boundaries.

7. On the importance of holding rank in public in the metropole and at the royal court in particular, see Fanny Cosandey, *Le rang: Préséances et hiérarchies dans la France*

Some of the most important public ceremonies to take place in early Louisiana were those organized to celebrate the arrival of new officials. They were staged on the levee, the main square, and in the public buildings on the three sides surrounding the city center. These rituals were essential to both legalize and legitimize the political succession at the head of the colonial government. They also served to establish good relationships between the company's or king's representatives and the other powers with which they had to negotiate. Furthermore, they helped to create a connection between the political authorities and the lower sort *("petit peuple")*, who were conceived of as being exclusively white. The protocol started with an exchange of gun salutes between the shore batteries and the incoming vessel. The number and kinds of salutes were highly codified. Afterward, the new representative landed in front of all the corporate bodies of the colony. In the next few days, he had to be officially welcomed. The ritual included three stages: a review of the troops on the main square, a homily by the priest in church, and the recording of the official's commission by the Superior Council. The ceremony fostered tensions at times. When the *Galathée* arrived carrying the king's commissioner, Jacques de La Chaise, to Louisiana in 1723, for instance, the latter immediately felt resentful when the ship rendered the commandant general Jean-Baptiste Le Moyne de Bienville the honors due a governor. He condemned the action because the salute suggested that Bienville was the single top official in the colony at the same time that the nomination of a civilian royal commissioner in charge of finances and trade had imposed a dyarchic system of government.[8]

The need to cultivate the image of the crown also led to the regular organization of festivities celebrating events related to the royal family or the kingdom's military victories, although they seem to have been less frequent

---

d'Ancien Régime ([Paris], [2016]). For colonial laws related to spatial arrangements in official ceremonies in the Caribbean, see P. F. R. Dessalles, *Les annales du Conseil souverain de la Martinique,* Tome I, Vol. I, *Réédition,* ed. Bernard Vonglis (1786; rpt. Paris, 1995), 246–250, 479–454, 530–533; [Médéric Louis-Élie Moreau] de Saint-Méry, *Loix et constitutions des colonies françoises de l'Amérique sous le vent,* 6 vols. (Paris, 1784–1790), II, 28, 66, 108–109, 302–303, 392–393, 536–537, 578–579, III, 258–263, 636–637, IV, 384. See also the collection of documents related to honors in various colonies gathered by Moreau de Saint-Méry: "Pièces diverses ayant trait aux honneurs," 1681–1779, ANOM COL F3 91, fols. 264–316.

8. For an example of a ceremonial for the arrival of a new governor, see Louis Billouart de Kerlérec to the minister of the navy, Mar. 8, 1753, ANOM COL C13A 37, fols. 34–35. For the incident over the gun salute when Jacques de La Chaise arrived in New Orleans in 1723, see Giraud, *History of French Louisiana,* trans. Pearce, V, 26.

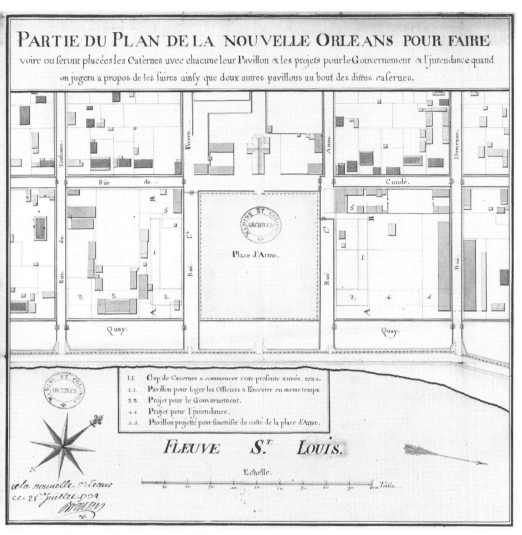

Figure 8: [François Ignace] Broutin. *Partie du plan de la Nouvelle Orléans … et les projets pour le gouvernement et l'intendance …*. July, 25, 1734. ANOM France 04 DFC 95bs B. Courtesy of Les Archives nationales d'outre-mer. Aix-en-Provence, France

than in the metropole. In 1753, for example, Governor Louis Billouart de Kerlérec set up a Te Deum and bonfire to rejoice over the dauphin's convalescence. He told the minister that:

This ceremony, My Lord, was followed by a party at my place and a supper for 113 ladies of all ages, accompanied by nearly 200 partners, including all the members of the Council, all the officers of the regular

troops, and of the militias, of the city and of the countryside, the habitants of the first estate [the nobility], and the main merchants. I also
had two wine fountains installed, one on the square of the barracks
for the troops and the other on the levee for the town-dwellers and the
sailors. The whole event ended with some rather splendid fireworks.

Such rituals were integrative in the sense that all the various white corporate bodies convened to celebrate the royal event. At the same time,
their spatial organization aimed at separating the elite and the *"peuple"*
("people"), that is those who exercised power and those who were supposed
to obey. Kerlérec took pains to detail to the minister all the various sociopro-
fessional categories forming the upper classes and to mention elite women
first, for mixed-gender sociability played a crucial role in creating a sense of
unity and solidarity among the elite. In contrast, he described the "peuple"
as a class- and gender-undifferentiated mass, although he segregated servicemen from civilians since, in the colony, the former were in charge of
policing the latter. This divide seemed more important than the one between all the settlers and the transient population of sailors who took part
in the celebrations. These performances left no room for the enslaved. Despite their demographic weight, they were excluded from the ceremonies
that bound the white civic community. Slaves, nevertheless, could attend
these festivities uninvited.[9]

9. For the 1753 festivities and their significance, see Kerlérec to the minister of the
navy, May 5, 1753, ANOM COL C13A 37, fols. 37, 52–53r; Michèle Fogel, *Les cérémonies de l'information dans la France du XVIe au milieu du XVIIIe siècle* (Paris, 1989);
Fogel, *L'État dans la France moderne: De la fin du XVe au milieu du XVIIIe siècle* (Paris,
1992), 40. Te Deum and other festivities were organized to celebrate the peace at the
end of the War of the Austrian Succession in 1748, the birth of the Duke of Burgundy
in 1751, the recovery of the dauphin in 1753, and victories in Germany during the Seven
Years' War. See Pierre de Rigaud de Vaudreuil de Cavagnal to the minister of the navy,
Aug. 26, 1749, ANOM COL C13A 33, fol. 55rv; Honoré-Gabriel Michel to the minister
of the navy, July 20, 1749, ANOM COL C13A 34, fols. 71–72r, 73–74r, 75–76r; Vaudreuil
to the minister of the navy, Jan. 26, 1752, ANOM COL C13A 36, fols. 23–24r; Vaudreuil
to the minister of the navy, Apr. 8, 1752, ANOM COL C13A 36, fols. 85–87r; Vaudreuil to
the minister of the navy, Apr. 28, 1752, ANOM COL C13A 36, fols. 94–95r; Michel to the
minister of the navy, Jan. 27, 1752, ANOM COL C13A 36, fol. 236; the minister of the
navy to Vincent-Gaspard de Rochemore, Apr. 17, 1762, ANOM COL C13B 1, fol. 340;
and A. Baillardel and A. Prioult, eds., *Le chevalier de Pradel: Vie d'un colon français en
Louisiane au XVIIIe siècle; d'après sa correspondance et celle de sa famille* (Paris, 1928),
209–212. Rather than an indication of a weaker relationship to royal power, the relative
infrequency of royal ceremonies in the colony as compared with the metropole might
have been related to the rhythm of transatlantic communications. See Kenneth J. Banks,

Once the new officials had been settled in, the recognition of their rank in the sociopolitical hierarchy and institutional system had to be reenacted by other regular spatialized rituals on the main square and in church. These repetitive formalities also generated trouble when people thought that the rank they deserved was not acknowledged and, consequently, that their position was not appropriately honored. The conflicts over precedence always reflected power struggles over political prerogatives and institutional remits. Although much has been written about the recurring tensions between the governor and the commissaire-ordonnateur—the two highest ranking officials in the colony following Louisiana's retrocession to the crown in 1731—the preeminence of the governor was never contested in the disputes over the spatial order. Rather, the competition between the sword and the pen expressed itself in the rivalry between the commissaire-ordonnateur and the *lieutenant de roi* or the *major* for second place in the sociopolitical hierarchy. In the metropole, the office of lieutenant de roi had been established to counterbalance the power of the governor, but, in the colony, he assisted the king's first representative, who had much more power than a governor in a metropolitan province; as for the *major*, he was responsible for the New Orleans garrison. They fought with the commissaire-ordonnateur about the delimitation of their prerogatives concerning the management of the troops and the responsibility of the police within the city. However, the latter kept the upper hand because he controlled the distribution of goods from the king's stores and could demand the payment of debts owed to the crown.[10]

The competition between the commissaire-ordonnateur, the lieutenant de roi, and the major often played out in the public sphere, especially with regard to military exercises and honors. The weekly reviews of the troops and, after 1731, the urban militia companies took place on the main square. They served different goals. They constituted a show of force that the state could use to impress or frighten Native Americans, slaves, and whites of lower means when necessary. They also allowed the authorities to count the number of able-bodied soldiers, control desertions, and evaluate the quantity of food, clothes, and arms required to supply the garrison. For this very reason, after 1731, the review was the responsibility of the commissaire-

---

Chasing Empire across the Sea: Communications and the State in the French Atlantic, 1713–1763 (Montreal, 2002), 101–126, esp. 107–114.

10. For the role of governors and lieutenants de roi in the metropole, see Bernard Barbiche, *Les institutions de la monarchie française à l'époque moderne: XVIe–XVIIIe siècle* (Paris, 1999), 328–329.

ordonnateur. His prerogative in the matter was contested by the major. In April 1734, Henry de Louboey, then serving as major, refused to let Edmé Gatien Salmon, the commissaire-ordonnateur, fulfill the task. Bienville recounted to the minister of the navy that de Louboey "fought with him [Salmon] for precedence on all occasions with ridiculous affectation." Then, a few months later, when Salmon was in Mobile, the officers garrisoned in New Orleans did the same with his subdelegate, claiming that only officers holding a *brevet* (the document officially recognizing their incorporation within the navy) from the king were qualified to do so. In the end, the crown responded in the commissaire-ordonnateur's favor, citing other outposts where reviews were the responsibility of storekeepers as a precedent.[11]

Conversely, in 1749, Commissaire-ordonnateur Michel wrote to the minister of the navy to complain about the honors due him when he passed by the guardroom on the main square in comparison with those rendered to the lieutenant de roi and the major. He first recalled that the ruling assigning lesser honors to the commissaire-ordonnateur had been adopted just after the colony's retrocession. At the time, Salmon, who fulfilled the function of *ordonnateur,* only held the rank of *commissaire.* Consequently, it was decided that the troops would present arms and sound a drumroll to recognize the preeminence of the governor whenever he passed by but that the soldiers would only form a guard of honor, without presenting arms or a drumroll, for both the ordonnateur and the lieutenant de roi. Since Michel held the double rank of commissaire and commissaire-général, however, he argued that it was inappropriate for him to be treated in the same way as the lieutenant de roi. He requested that the troops should present arms without a drumroll when he passed by, observing that he had witnessed such a ritual performed for Mr. Hocquart when he was in Canada, even though the latter was only a commissaire-général. Governor Vaudreuil agreed to his proposal, but the lieutenant de roi and major refused, prompting Michel to ask for the king's consent. Yet Louis XV also declined to grant the request on the basis that a pen officer was not entitled to military honors, to which

11. For authorities staging military reviews for the purpose of constituting a show of force, see, for instance, the review of the various military units after the arrival of reinforcements from the metropole and before the departure of the great expedition against the Natchez in December 1730 as described in [Marc-Antoine Caillot], "Relation de voyage de la Louisianne ou Nouvlle. France; fait par le Sr. CAILLOT en l'année 1730," HNOC, MSS596, fol. 178. For the 1734 conflict between the commissaire-ordonnateur and the major, see Jean-Baptiste Le Moyne de Bienville to the minister of the navy, Apr. 23, 1734, ANOM COL C13A 18, fols. 166–170r; and Edmé Gatien Salmon to the minister of the navy, Sept. 6, 1734, ANOM COL C13A 19, fols. 99–100.

The Hustle and Bustle of City Life

Michel countered that he did not claim the enforcement of a right but of a custom. His defense implicitly called for local accommodations against general rules of precedence imposed without discernment throughout the Empire and based on what was enforced in the metropole.[12]

The same argument in favor of local accommodations was used in the numerous conflicts over precedence in church. In the Catholic French Empire, the religious, social, and political spheres intersected. Sunday Mass allowed attendants to practice their faith, socialize, and take part in the political and civic life of the city. After 1731, celebrations of Mass were preceded by the review of militia companies and followed by the promulgation and reading of royal ordinances and local rulings as well as by public auctions for the sale of property and goods. Although the whole congregation was welcome to attend Mass, the place of parishioners within the church depended on their position within the sociopolitical hierarchy. The elite attached great importance to the public display and recognition of their social rank within the religious space. Securing space in church appropriate to one's social status was considered crucial as it was believed to legitimize the sociopolitical order: it reflected the divine order decreed by God.[13]

A series of disputes over church precedence took place at an early stage in New Orleans's development that brought both officials and settlers into opposition with one another within their own groups, even though those concerning the military and administrative elite are better documented. The so-called pew rage that marked the first fifteen years after the city's founding was particularly vigorous because the politico-administrative and social order was fragile and unstable. The social hierarchy that existed among the metropolitan elite could not be reproduced in the colonial capital. In addition, the personality and backgrounds of ranking officials, the simplifica-

---

12. The navy distinguished between ranks (*écrivain, écrivain principal, commissaire,* and *commissaire-général*) and functions (*ordonnateur, contrôleur,* and *intendant*). On the career of pen officers, see Alexandre Dubé, "Making a Career out of the Atlantic: Louisiana's Plume," in Cécile Vidal, ed., *Louisiana: Crossroads of the Atlantic World* (Philadelphia, 2014), 44–67. For the 1749 conflict between the commissaire-ordonnateur and the lieutenant de roi, see Michel to the minister of the navy, July 30, 1749, ANOM COL C13A 34, fols. 100–101r; Michel to the minister of the navy, May 22, 1751, ANOM COL C13A 35, fols. 211–212; and Vaudreuil and Michel to the minister of the navy, May 27, 1751, ANOM COL C13A 35, fols. 37–38.

13. On conflicts over church precedence in the metropole, see Laurence Croq, "Les mutations de la distinction sociale dans les églises paroissiales à Paris (des années 1680 à la Révolution)," in Laurence Jean-Marie and Christophe Maneuvrier, eds., *Distinction et supériorité sociale (Moyen Âge et époque moderne)* (Caen, France, 2010), 81–104.

tion of the institutional framework in comparison with the metropole, and the constant transformation of the administrative organization and balance of power, especially during the Company of the Indies's monopoly, created tensions between various factions and parties. In 1723, La Chaise was sent to the colony as a king's commissioner to seek out all kinds of abuses. He tried to impose his ascendency over the council that governed the colony, the Conseil de Régie. This council was composed of sword officers, including the commandant general, or governor, and company directors, chosen among civilians. The military officers and councillors (only civilians bore this title) also maintained difficult relationships. All these rivalries fueled an extreme sensitivity over church seating arrangements. The disputes were further spurred on by the behavior of Father Raphaël, the Capuchin priest in charge of the New Orleans parish, who took sides in these personal and institutional rivalries.

Incidents among officials over rank in church broke out in 1723, 1725, 1727, 1728, and 1734. The last episode serves as a representative of the conflicts of the 1720s and early 1730s as a whole and explains the reason underlying their repetition. It broke out during Easter Mass in 1734, when Governor Bienville took the initiative of having the councillors' pew moved so that the military officers could sit on the same side as the lieutenant de roi and the major. The councillors protested to the minister that they had been driven out of their traditional place in a particularly humiliating way, "which made the people laugh." Obviously, the elite's dramas over pews had to do with their social standing and the legitimacy of their authority in the eyes of the whole urban population. Although various rulings promulgated for other colonies in Canada and in the Antilles were used in many of these disputes, they only stopped when the crown issued a specific ordinance on all matters of precedence for Louisiana in 1734. Areas covered in the ordinance included precedence at church, the order in which consecrated bread was to be presented and distributed, and rank during processions and bonfires. The publication of this ordinance coincided with the relative stabilization of the political and administrative system and the social order after the retrocession of the colony to the king.[14]

14. Charles Edwards O'Neill, *Church and State in French Colonial Louisiana: Policy and Politics to 1732* (New Haven, Conn., 1966), 152–153, 239–246; and Giraud, *History of French Louisiana*, trans. Pearce, V, 40, 291–299, 312–313. For the 1734 conflict over rank in church, see Salmon to the minister of the navy, Apr. 29, 1734, ANOM COL C13A 19, fols. 53–53bis; Jean-Louis Prat, Jean-Baptiste Claude Raguet, Jacques Fazende, and François Fleuriau to the minister of the navy, May 1, 1734, ANOM COL C13A 19, fols. 180–181. For the use of other colonial models, see Report by Fleuriau, Dec. 29, 1727,

Conflicts over church precedence, among colonists as well between officials, were exacerbated by the multiplication of actors and, in particular, the involvement of women. Religion was their specific domain, as they seem to have been more regular churchgoers than men and to have been in charge of handling their families' religious affairs. They took part in the battle for the places reserved for the military and administrative elite in the chancel and the transept as well as the front pews in the nave. Until 1723, ordinary parishioners stood in the nave during Mass, unless they brought their own chairs. After that time, the priest and churchwardens decided to auction the renting of pews to raise the money necessary for the support of religious services and the church building. After the first auction, Madame Trudeau, who was the wife of a carpenter employed by the company and the mother-in-law of a company cashier, realized that she had arrived too late to get a front pew. Since she believed that she was entitled to such a place of honor because of her social connections, she complained to the councillor in charge of church affairs, who tried to use her case against Father Raphaël.[15]

In 1725, it was the military officers themselves who not only protested their placement outside the chancel but also claimed front pews in the nave for their wives without paying rent. They sought to benefit from the same privileges as nobles in France. At the request of the councillors, the company put a stop to this practice with an ordinance reminding military officers that they were not entitled to any special treatment in church. Apparently annoyed by their social pretensions, the minister of the navy approved the ordinance. As for the matter of women, a comment in the margin of the councillors' letter, probably made by an employee of the Bureau des colonies, asserted that "women have no rank at all." Yet, despite the crown's disapproval, women were locally included in the hierarchy of honors. A map of the church, drawn in 1732, shows the place of the governor, the

---

ANOM COL C13A 10, fols. 302–303; and Salmon to the minister of the navy, Apr. 29, 1734, ANOM COL C13A 19, fols. 53–53bis. For the Louisiana ruling, see "Règlement sur les honneurs dans les églises, processions, et autres cérémonies publiques à la Louisiane," Aug. 17, 1734, ANOM COL A 22, fols. 139–140v.

15. Jacques de La Chaise to the company commissioners, Oct. 18, 1723, ANOM COL C13A 7, fols. 79v–85; O'Neill, *Church and State in French Colonial Louisiana*, 152–153. On the conflicts related to the auctions of pews in France, see Stéphane Gomis, "Tenir son rang à l'église: Le rôle des bancs et des chaises en France sous l'Ancien Régime," in Michel Cassan and Paul d'Hollander, eds., *Temporalités: Revues de sciences sociales et humaines*, no. 6, *Figures d'appartenances (VIIIe–XXe siècle)* (Limoges, France, 2010), 124–134.

commissaire-ordonnateur, the military officers, the councillors, the governor's wife, the commissaire-ordonnateur's wife, the churchwardens, and the other parishioners. The social hierarchy was reflected by an individual's proximity to the Blessed Sacrament and position within the chancel, the transept, or the nave. Even though wives of the king's representatives held no official positions, they were honored in conformity with their role in religious matters and the importance of family relationships in the symbolic expression of power.[16]

Although structural divisions within the elite generated intense tensions that were dramatized in the public space, the opposition between the sword officers and the councillors, or, after 1731, the pen officers, in particular, should not be overestimated. The church was also the place where they displayed the numerous alliances connecting them, especially during weddings or baptismal ceremonies. Marriage witnesses or godparents were chosen to fortify vertical relationships of patronage as well as horizontal ones between friends and relatives. In February 1766, for example, Sieur Charles Auguste de La Chaise married Demoiselle Marie Catherine de Moleon, joining two prominent families active in both the civil and military service. The groom was the grandson of Jacques de La Chaise, the royal commissioner, and the son of Jacques de La Chaise, the assessor councillor of the Superior Council and storekeeper. His mother, Marguerite Darensbourg, was the daughter of the commandant of the German Coast. The bride was the daughter of the deceased military officer Sieur Henry de Moleon *écuyer* (a qualification that identified him as noble) and Dame Marie Elizabeth de Gauvery, herself a military officer's daughter. Those present at the ceremony included the groom's father and maternal grandfather; the commandant of the province, Charles-Philippe Aubry; the commissaire-ordonnateur, Foucault; the treasurer of the navy, Jean-Baptiste Destréhan; the attorney general, Nicolas La Frénière, and several officers and merchants. Such events allowed sword and pen officers to set aside their antagonism as they celebrated their shared membership in the colonial elite.[17]

The ascendancy of the elites was further enhanced by their funeral practices. They were distinguished by their burial in the sanctuary of Saint-

16. Their husbands agreed to pay rent for the pews. See La Chaise and four councillors to the minister [of the navy], Apr. 26, 1725, ANOM COL C13A 9, fol. 138, quoted in O'Neill, *Church and State in French Colonial Louisiana*, 242. For the 1732 map of New Orleans's church, see [De Batz], "Plan du bâtiment de l'église paroissiale de cette ville … levé et dessiné à La Nouvelle-Orléans le 29 juillet 1732," ANOM COL C13A 15, fol. 241.

17. AANO, Saint-Louis Cathedral Marriages, 1764–1774, 02/04/1766; Giraud, *History of French Louisiana*, trans. Pearce, V, 282.

The Hustle and Bustle of City Life

Louis Church, although the custom seems to have been less widespread than in the Antilles. In Louisiana, the privilege was only granted to a small minority of eligible persons. Between 1721 and 1752, only twelve individuals benefited from such a favor: all were male, except for Madame de Noyan, the lieutenant de roi's wife, and they were either priests or higher-ranking lay officials. The rest of the population, whatever their ethnic background and status, were buried in the cemetery located in the rear of the city. There is no information available on the way the graveyard was organized according to status, class, or race.[18]

Even though the rest of the population was legally required to be buried within the cemetery, slave funerals and burials appear to have served to keep them in a subordinate position within society. Slave funerals were probably more expeditious than those of whites. In Saint-Domingue, priests were not paid for conducting these ceremonies (nor baptisms or marriages), whereas they received curial rights when funerals concerned free people. The same practice might have been followed in New Orleans. Likewise, the enslaved were very likely buried in separate sections of graveyards, as became the case in the Antilles throughout the eighteenth century. Furthermore, the number of slave funerals and burials seems low with respect to the size of the slave population in the city and on the surrounding plantations. The 1728 sacramental records include 102 funeral certificates, but only 14 (13.7 percent) relate to slaves of African or Native American descent. In 1738, the New Orleans priest, Father Mathias, complained to the Superior Council that Mr. de La Pommeray, treasurer of the navy, had asked his slaves to bury the corpse of a deceased *"négritte"* ("pickaninny") outside the cemetery. Because the practice was forbidden by the Code Noir, Salmon ordered the corpse to be exhumed and buried in sanctified ground. If a member of the elite such as Mr. de La Pommeray felt he could do such a thing, however, such burials were probably common. Hence, it is not surprising that an anonymous commentator made marginal notes regarding slave burials in a copy of the Code Noir that was included in a compilation of all the legal texts promulgated in Louisiana between 1714 and 1746. "Bad weather and

18. On burial practices in Louisiana, see "Arrêt du Conseil Supérieur de la Louisiane qui ordonne aux habitants d'enterrer les morts dans le lieu destiné pour être le cimetière," June 27, 1724, ANOM COL A 23, fol. 48v; Roger Baudier, *The Catholic Church in Louisiana* (New Orleans, La., 1939), 84–85; and Claude L. Vogel, *The Capuchins in French Louisiana (1722-1766)* (Washington, D.C., 1928), 169–170. On the burial practices of elites in the Caribbean, see P. F. R. Dessalles, *Les annales du Conseil souverain de la Martinique,* Tome II, Vol. II, *Notes et index,* ed. Bernard Vonglis (1786; rpt. Paris, 1995), 250–251.

distance," he stated, specifically with regard to Article 11, which dealt with slave funerals, "often impede the enforcement of this article, and sometimes the settlers are also guilty of neglect."[19]

Two other religious ceremonies brought the enslaved either within or just outside the doors of the church in a manner that reinforced their subservient status—rituals of penance during the enactment of some criminal sentences and collective baptisms. Slaves who had been convicted by the Superior Council were brought to the church door to beg both God's and the king's forgiveness in front of the assembled community before being executed or punished on the main square. This location was used to punish all criminals, not only slaves, but the latter quickly became the main target of royal justice. Moreover, twice a year, on Easter and Whitsun eve, collective baptisms of adult slaves were organized within or just outside the church. These public ceremonies integrated the enslaved into the Christian community, but the way they were structured and the visual juxtaposition of the black catechumens and their white godparents conveyed the idea of a subordinate place for slaves within the church. The number of baptisms of enslaved adults started to rise in the 1740s, possibly as a result of the joint action of Governor Vaudreuil, who arrived in the colony in 1743, and Father Dagobert, who had been stationed in New Orleans since 1744 and became both the Superior of the Capuchins and the priest in charge of the New Orleans parish in 1749. They found a receptive audience among slaves who had been exposed to the Gospel for decades. Nevertheless, it was only during the following decade that people of African descent, free or enslaved, started to serve more frequently as godparents for one another's children.[20]

19. For slaves' funeral and burial practices in Louisiana, see "Extrait des registres mortuaires de La Nouvelle-Orléans de l'année 1728," ANOM COL G1 12, fols. 72–93; RSCL 1738/06/14/02; and "Édit du roi, ou Code noir, qui concerne entièrement les esclaves de la Louisiane …," March 1724, ANOM COL A 23, fols. 50–57. For slaves' funeral and burial practices in Saint-Domingue, see "Ordonnance des administrateurs, concernant les droits curiaux et de fabrique," Apr. 26, 1712, in [Moreau] de Saint-Méry, *Loix et constitutions des colonies françoises de l'Amérique sous le vent*, II, 318–321; and Gabriel Debien, "Petits cimetières de quartier et de plantation à Saint-Domingue au XVIIIe siècle," *Revue française d'histoire d'outre-mer*, LXI (1974), 522–541. Jean-François Niort mentions two local rulings promulgated in Martinique in 1765 and Guadeloupe in 1769 that legally instituted racial segregation within specific cemeteries: they provisioned that slaves and free people of color had to be buried together and separately from whites. See Niort, "La condition des libres de couleur aux îles du vent (XVIIe–XIXe siècles): Ressources et limites d'un système ségrégationniste," *Bulletin de la société d'histoire de la Guadeloupe*, CXXXI (2002), 10.

20. Unlike what took place in Saint-Domingue under the influence of the Jesuits,

As the New Orleans congregation gradually transformed itself into a religious community with a black majority, it became more difficult to ignore the presence of slaves in the religious public space. Therefore, Governor Vaudreuil's and Commissaire-ordonnateur Michel's 1751 local ruling on taverns, markets, and slaves included an article about the seating of slaves in church. Until then, the church had been one of the main public places in which the white elite had projected their vision of the social order and had fought over their own social positions as if slaves did not exist. For the first time, in 1751, an official document recognized that the church was no longer an exclusively white imaginary space. To fight against the social implications of such an acknowledgment, local officials tried to impose a system of racial segregation similar to the one already in place for both the enslaved and free people of color in Saint-Domingue and in the Lesser Antilles, although it was never legally sanctioned in Martinique or Guadeloupe. They ordered that "all the negroes and other slaves who go to church will hear, in the morning, the first mass, those of the countryside will be taken there by the driver of each gang, who will then take them back to their master's. And if there are some enslaved domestics who are in the habit of following their masters to the other masses, they will withdraw to the church door to wait for them, on pain of punishment." If the colony's top officials felt the need to regulate the presence of slaves within the religious space, it is certainly because more fluid practices of attendance and seating must have previously taken place. Yet no other document reveals whether the new ruling was ever implemented. In comparison, local government seems to have been much more successful in its exclusion of slaves from the taverns, the other main places of public sociability in cities, which were viewed as competitors of the church.[21]

---

there was no distinct "priest for negroes" *("curé des nègres")* in New Orleans; the same priest took care of both whites and slaves, and their sacraments were recorded in the same registers, although not in the same way. See G[abriel] Debien, "La christianisation des esclaves des Antilles françaises aux XVIIe et XVIIIe siècles," *Revue d'histoire de l'Amérique française,* XX, no. 4 (March 1967), 551–554; and Sue Peabody, "'A Dangerous Zeal': Catholic Missions to Slaves in the French Antilles, 1635–1800," *French Historical Studies,* XXV (2002), 61–62. On the role of women in the religious life of the enslaved in Louisiana, see Emily Clark and Virginia Meacham Gould, "The Feminine Face of Afro-Catholicism in New Orleans, 1727–1852," *William and Mary Quarterly,* 3d Ser. LIX (2002), 409–448.

21. "Règlement sur la police pour la province de la Louisiane," Article 29, Feb. 28–Mar. 1, 1751, ANOM COL C13A 35, fols. 47r–48v. For segregation in Caribbean churches, see Laënnec Hurbon, "The Church and Slavery in Eighteenth-Century Saint-Domingue,"

In the early modern period, drinking houses were an essential feature of urban culture on both sides of the Atlantic. According to Carl Bridenbaugh, "The tavern was the most flourishing of all urban institutions." British North American and French Caribbean alehouses were sites of social transgression and mixing across class, status, and racial boundaries. In contrast, the small size of French New Orleans seems to have facilitated the social control and racial order that the local authorities, elite, and the rest of the slaveholders tried to impose on the drinking houses that were locally designated as *"taverne"* (tavern), *"cabaret"* (cabaret) and *"auberge"* (inn). Although they could not prevent the out-of-doors sale of alcohol to slaves and Native Americans, they apparently succeeded in keeping taverns as spaces of almost exclusively white male sociability, at least at times. As a result, the enslaved fought hard to create their own places of recreation away from the gaze of whites.[22]

In New Orleans, drinking houses were the sole "sources of secular diversion and amusement." Because the young city did not have any ballrooms, racetracks, theaters, operas, or other fashionable centers of entertainment, they were the only public meeting places specifically devoted to collective leisure outside the home. There white urban dwellers could share a meal, drink, and play pool, cards, and dice as well as gamble. For the numerous

---

in Marcel Dorigny, ed., *The Abolitions of Slavery: From Léger Félicité Sonthonax to Victor Schœlcher, 1793, 1794, 1848* (New York, 2003), 57; Peabody, "'Dangerous Zeal,'" *French Historical Studies,* XXV (2002), 61; and Niort, "La condition des libres de couleur aux îles du vent," *Bulletin de la société d'histoire de la Guadeloupe,* CXXXI (2002), 11.

22. Carl Bridenbaugh, *Cities in Revolt: Urban Life in America, 1743–1776* (New York, 1955), 156, quoted in Anne Pérotin-Dumon, *La ville aux îles, la ville dans l'île: Basse-Terre et Pointe-à-Pitre, Guadeloupe, 1650–1820* (Paris, 2000), 555. On drinking houses and culture in Europe, see Thomas Brennan, *Public Drinking and Popular Culture in Eighteenth Century Paris* (Princeton, N.J., 1988); Peter Clark, *The English Alehouse: A Social History, 1200–1830* (London, 1983); and Beat Kümin and B. Ann Tlusty, eds., *The World of the Tavern: Public Houses in Early Modern Europe* (Aldershot, U.K., 2002). In North America, see, among other studies, David W. Conroy, *In Public Houses: Drink and the Revolution of Authority in Colonial Massachusetts* (Chapel Hill, N.C., 1995); Sharon V. Salinger, *Taverns and Drinking in Early America* (Baltimore, 2002); and Peter Thompson, *Rum, Punch, and Revolution: Taverngoing and Public Life in Eighteenth-Century Philadelphia* (Philadelphia, 1999).

The Hustle and Bustle of City Life

transient and single white men, both civilian and military, taverns were even more important, since they did not possess adequate domestic space in which they could socialize privately. Drinking houses allowed soldiers, sailors, *"voyageurs"* (travelers), and indentured servants to assemble when they were not working or in service.[23]

Because of the need to oversee and control this transient population, public authorities on both sides of the Atlantic developed an impressive legal arsenal against drinking houses during the early modern period. These laws were justified by a socially exclusive discourse about the disorder associated with urban life that taverns came to embody: they were conceived of as places of drunkenness, debauchery, physical violence, and excessive and useless expense that went against the civility, self-restraint, and temperance increasingly associated with elite culture. New Orleans was no exception to this repressive tendency. Besides the marketplace, drinking houses were the main object of those ordinances specifically related to urban life. As in all American colonies, however, law in the Louisiana capital targeted not only the white lower classes, both civilian and military, but also slaves of African descent and Native Americans. Local authorities felt that selling tafia to the enslaved enticed them "to become libertines, steal from their masters and from others to get money for drink." They also believed that it was impossible to make laborers of African descent work after they had participated in drinking parties: "It is easy to see that they won't be good for much when the time comes to set them to work as they are stupefied by tiredness and debauchery."[24]

Ordinances aimed at limiting the number of inns and taverns and regulating their opening hours. They were supposed to remain closed on Sundays and holidays, or at least to stop their activities during Mass, a stipulation that implicitly posited drinking houses as the site of a counterculture for nonpracticing Catholics. These regulations also tried to segregate places where alcohol was sold by their clientele, designating the canteen for the military and taverns for the civil population, and forbade the sale of alcohol to Native Americans and slaves who did not have a note from their masters. Various officials in charge of the police sometimes organized patrols or surprise visits to enforce the different prohibitions. But their control does not seem to have always been consistent or systematic. Phases of tolerance and

23. Salinger, *Taverns and Drinking in Early America*, 57.
24. RSCL 1728/06/05/02; Kerlérec to the minister of the navy, Mar. 30, 1760, ANOM COL C13A 42, fols. 22–25.

repression alternated, even though it is impossible to provide explanations for the changes in policy.[25]

The authorities also tried to curb the illicit sale of alcohol outside licensed taverns and inns that took place in private houses, out-of-doors, and in the military canteen. Selling alcohol was an easy and profitable trade for nearly everyone, although it was essentially a white business. Because the population of free people of color was so small in New Orleans, there are no examples of free blacks running alehouses, although they started to account for a large proportion of tavern and innkeepers in the Lesser Antilles beginning in the middle of the eighteenth century. In the Louisiana capital, many poor white civilians and soldiers sold tafia and wine clandestinely to their counterparts as well as slaves and Native Americans.[26]

The elite did not stay out of the lucrative business of selling alcohol either. Running the canteen, in particular, was the privilege of the major and generated all kinds of abuses. In 1750, the major allegedly organized nighttime visits to private homes in order to force civilians to buy alcohol at the canteen, which was supposed to be restricted to servicemen. If people were found drinking and having fun, even quietly, they were taken to prison until they paid a fine. Several inhabitants, including a woman, are reported

25. For regulations related to the sale of alcohol, see RSCL 1725/10/05/01, 1728/06/05/01, 1746/08/24/01; and various rulings and ordinances promulgated by the Conseil de Régie, the Superior Council, the governor, and commissaire-ordonnateur, or by the commissaire-ordonnateur alone, about the sale of alcohol and the running of taverns, Apr. 11, 1725, ANOM COL A 23, fol. 58, Oct. 5, 1726, fols. 79v–80, Mar. 29, 1727, fol. 84, Mar. 26, 1733, fol. 111v, Dec. 19, 1733, fol. 114v, Dec. 7, 1736, fol. 122, Jan. 7, 1741, fols. 125v–126, Aug. 19, 1746, fols. 151v–152. For measures taken to enforce regulations related to the sale of alcohol, see RSCL 1725/11/01/01, 1725/11/05/01, 1725/12/21/01, 1725/12/22/01; 1726/03/24/01, 1726/03/27/01; 1743/09/16/01; 1764/07/08/01; 1764/10/24/06, 1764/10/24/07; 1765/11/20/02; 1767/04/25/01; Michel to the minister of the navy, May 18, 1751, ANOM COL C13A 35, fols. 206v–207v; "Arrêt du Conseil Supérieur de la Louisiane du 17 août 1726 qui nomme le Sr. Rossard pour veiller à la police de la ville," ANOM COL A 23, fols. 74–75; Michel to the minister of the navy, Jan. 8, 1752, ANOM COL C13A 36, fol. 193r; Vaudreuil and Michel to the minister of the navy, Sept. 28, 1752, ANOM COL C13A 36, fols. 17–18v; and "État des dépenses à faire à la Louisiane pour le service du roi pendant l'année 1764," ANOM COL C13A 44, fols. 39–46.

26. For a rare mention of slaves selling alcohol to white settlers, see RSCL 1767/04/25/01. For the sale of alcohol by free people of color in the Lesser Antilles, see Pérotin-Dumon, *La ville aux îles, la ville dans l'île*, 561. For the role of soldiers and poor whites in selling alcohol in Louisiana, see Michel to the minister of the navy, July 20, 1751, ANOM COL C13A 35, fol. 329; and Michel to the minister of the navy, Jan. 8, 1752, ANOM COL C13A 36, fol. 192v.

The Hustle and Bustle of City Life

to have spent many hours in jail. Yet it is difficult to be sure what happened because Commissaire-ordonnateur Michel was then engaged in a never-ending dispute with the major. It was in the aftermath of this scandal that the governor and commissaire-ordonnateur enacted their 1751 local ruling on markets, taverns, and slaves, but Michel complained that the bylaw was ineffective. Although it was in his interest to exaggerate the level of disorder, alcohol was such a profitable business that it must have been impossible to control its trade.[27]

Both legal prohibitions and social constraints had an impact on the sociology of customers. Taverns were spaces of predominantly white male sociability. One of the main social functions of drinking houses was to impose a gender order in New Orleans that excluded women. This exclusion was the result of social convention rather than legal prescription. In the trials generated by cases of violence that took place in these establishments, most of the defendants, victims, and witnesses were white men: women never appeared as patrons. Female presence in drinking houses was restricted to tavern keepers' wives, who were only incidentally mentioned in a few testimonies; they never served as witnesses, as if it was not proper for them to do so. However, it was often white women belonging to the middling or lower sort who earned their own money or supplemented a couple's income by selling alcohol, although it is not always clear if they actually ran clandestine or licensed taverns where people could stay or only sold alcohol out-of-doors.[28]

27. On the involvement of white elites in the alcohol trade, see Baillardel and Prioult, eds., *Le chevalier de Pradel*, 212; Michel to the minister of the navy, July 20, 1751, ANOM COL C13A 35, fol. 329r; and Sophie White, "'A Baser Commerce': Retailing, Class, and Gender in French Colonial New Orleans," *William and Mary Quarterly*, LXIII (2006), 517–550. On the scandal around the sale of alcohol at the military canteen, see Michel to the minister of the navy, Jan. 17, 1750, ANOM COL C13A 34, fols. 287–289v; Vaudreuil and Michel to the minister of the navy, Jan. 19, 1750, ANOM COL C13A 34, fol. 354; Vaudreuil and Michel to the minister of the navy, May 27, 1751, ANOM COL C13A 35, fols. 37–38v; "Règlement sur la police pour la province de la Louisiane," Feb. 28–Mar. 1, 1751, ANOM COL C13A 35, fols. 39–52; and Michel to the minister of the navy, Jan. 8, 1752, ANOM COL C13A 36, fols. 192–193.

28. For taverns as a "predominantly male space" in early modern Europe and North America, see Brennan, *Public Drinking and Popular Culture in Eighteenth-Century Paris*, 146–151 (quotation, 147); Michel Heichette, *Société, sociabilité, justice: Sablé et son pays au XVIIIe siècle* (Rennes, France, 2005), 117–118; A. Lynn Martin, *Alcohol, Sex, and Gender in Late Medieval and Early Modern Europe* (Houndsmills, Basingstoke, Hampshire, U.K., 2001); Salinger, *Taverns and Drinking in Early America*, 50, 55, 220–226, 243; and Marc Vacher, *Voisins, voisines, voisinage: Les cultures du face-à-face à Lyon à*

The role of women in taverns became an even more important issue after the Spanish takeover. In 1769, one of the first measures Governor Alejandro O'Reilly took after imposing the sovereignty of the Spanish crown was to restrict the number of inns in the city to six, pool halls to six, and taverns to twelve. This means that their number had considerably increased since the auction of six licenses in 1751, two of which were won by women. For the first time, the 1769 ruling provisioned that only men or married couples could run such establishments. The involvement of single or widowed women in tavern businesses was seen as a moral and social problem. But the documentation remains silent about the possible link between those places where white men drank and gambled and prostitution. Although rulings on prostitution were as numerous as those regulating drinking and gambling in the metropole, none were ever promulgated in Louisiana, probably because, after the disappearance of the white women of ill repute sent to the colony with convicts between 1717 and 1721, prostitution was mainly associated with interracial sexuality.[29]

Compared to other locations in the eighteenth-century Atlantic world,

la veille de la Révolution (Lyon, France, 2007), 134–138. For other studies that highlight the presence of women in Parisian drinking houses, see Arlette Farge, _Vivre dans la rue à Paris au XVIIIe siècle_ ([Paris], 1979), 75–76; and Daniel Roche, _Le peuple de Paris: Essai sur la culture populaire au XVIIIe siècle_ (Paris, 1981), 261–262. For the role of social conventions in the exclusion of women from taverns in British North America, see Salinger, _Taverns and Drinking in Early America_, 23. For the presence of women in trials dealing with violence in taverns, see RSCL 1737/07/24/01; 1740/11/07/01, 1740/11/05/01, 1740/11/05/02, 1740/11/08/03, 1740/11/11/02, 1741/02/08/01, 1741/04/19/01, 1741/04/19/02; 1743/09/16/01; 1767/11/06/01, 1767/11/06/02, 1767/11/08/01, 1767/11/09/01, 1767/11/09/02, 1767/11/10/01, 1767/11/10/02, 1767/11/11/01, 1767/11/12/01, 1767/11/12/02. For the mention of tavern keepers' wives in trials, see RSCL 1725/11/01/01; "Procédure contre Gauvin," 1740, ANOM COL F3 242, fols. 308–316; and RSCL 1743/09/16/01. For women selling alcohol, see RSCL 1725/11/01/01, 1746/08/24/01, 1751/04/14/01, 1753/04/24/01, 1764/07/14/04, 1764/10/24/06, 1764/10/27/02, 1766/07/23/03, 1766/11/14/01, 1767/08/12/01, 1767/09/04/02; Bienville and Salmon to the minister of the navy, Apr. 18, 1735, ANOM COL C13A 20, fols. 65–66; and "Venue avec la lettre de Périer et de La Chaise du 26 août 1729, procédure contre Bernaudat," ANOM COL F3 242, fols. 149–178v.

29. For the regulations on the sale of alcohol in the 1750s and 1760s, see RSCL 1751/04/14/01; and RSCL "Ordonnance de Don Alexandre O'Reilly du 21 septembre 1769." On the silence of the archival documentation about prostitution in drinking houses in Guadeloupean cities, see Pérotin-Dumon, _La ville aux îles, la ville dans l'île_, 558. On the importance of the repressive policy toward prostitution in the metropole from the late seventeenth century, see Érica-Marie Benabou, _La prostitution et la police des mœurs au XVIIIe siècle_ (Paris, 1987).

The Hustle and Bustle of City Life

slaves in New Orleans had a complex relationship with taverns and the sale of alcohol. In most large port cities in British North America, such as New York, Philadelphia, and Charleston, drinking houses admitted slaves despite legal prohibitions. Likewise, the enslaved were the main customers of Martinique's taverns. The situation was diffcrent in New Orleans, whose small size made control and repression easier. Although slaves were present in such establishments, since tavern keepers employed them, they do not seem to have been genuine patrons, even though local authorities sometimes displayed a greater leniency toward their gathering in drinking houses. After the authorities decided to curb this tolerance, the enslaved, fearing that they could be caught, probably went to licensed or clandestine taverns to purchase alcohol but did not spend time there, which means that the legislation was partially effective. Marie Langlois, the wife of Bousquet, revealed that, "when the negroes drank a shot, they gave him a small coin, when they took away a bottle twenty-five sols, and that they sometimes bought two that they took away on Sunday." Sometimes, slaves did not even dare to go themselves. During his interrogation, Baptiste, a fifteen-year-old Natchez belonging to the Capuchins, confessed that he had not purchased alcohol at Lemaire's but had asked a soldier to do so for him. Likewise, when François alias Cariton, who was accused of having killed another slave with whom he was wrestling amicably while intoxicated, was questioned by the judge about where he had gotten his alcohol—the trial took place just after officials had promulgated the 1751 ruling—he replied that he had not purchased any alcohol "since the prohibitions to go and buy some at La Carpentras's, La Gautreau's and at Perrot's" and that he drank only what was given to him. The judge then asked him "whether he used some soldiers or sailors to go to the taverns to get drink for him, since he did not dare to go himself" or "through the means of some negresses," which François denied. Slaves and poor whites could not easily share a common sociability in taverns, but they often cooperated to buy alcohol.[30]

30. The judicial archives seldom mention the presence of slaves in taverns. The same was truc of free people of color, who are even more invisible. It is only incidentally in one case that we learn that a tavern was kept by a slave while the owner, his family, and most of the customers were at Mass because one of the latter came back earlier than the others. See "Venue avec la lettre de Périer et de La Chaise du 26 août 1729, procédure contre Bernaudat," ANOM COL F3 242, fol. 153. In the margins of a copy of the Code Noir that was part of a compilation of all the legal texts promulgated in Louisiana between 1714 and 1746, a comment on Article 13, which dealt with slave gatherings, asserted that "in this matter we are too tolerant with slaves' meetings in the city's taverns." See "Édit du roi, ou Code noir, qui concerne entièrement les esclaves de la Louisiane . . . ," March

The exclusion of slaves from white male sociability in drinking houses was the result of legal prohibitions but also of the social monitoring and sanctions exercised by private individuals. During the trial of Jupiter, a plantation slave who was known to most urban dwellers because his master Jean-Charles de Pradel sent him to New Orleans every day to sell produce, a white settler named Jacques Judice told the judge that he had taken advantage of a business meeting with Pradel to warn him about his slave's activities in the city. While at Pradel's estate, he told him: "Your negro is on familiar terms with the sailors of the small ship before Mr. Prévost, I have seen them together round the table, they eat cabbages, say *tu* to each other, and he behaves with them as if they were relatives or friends. Keep an eye on him and don't trust him." The report is not clear enough to ascertain whether Jupiter and the sailors drank together on board ship or in taverns. Regardless, Pradel replied that he was not the kind of man to take offense when told such news, that Jupiter brought him the right amounts of money back, and that he was satisfied with him. He believed that his peddler was not robbing him to buy alcohol, which was the abuse most feared in public rulings prohibiting the sale of alcohol to slaves. Sociability across status and race was not impossible although it is difficult to evaluate its prevalence. Its existence was constrained by the debate that developed among whites about the threat it posed to the system of racial slavery.[31]

Sociability between whites of the lower sort and free people of color might have been more common than with slaves. Yet the crossing of racial barriers did not erase them; people were well aware of what they were doing, and the color line could be reactivated when necessary. In 1744, a white cooper who was accused of having given alcohol from the king's warehouses to slaves claimed that he had spent the night of the robbery "at La Hamelin with his wife, his mother-in-law La Guidon, his son Bidau, Marly negro, La Drouillon his sweetheart, Benoît from the *Lyodon*, Mr. Jaubet from the said ship, Gomier and others." The white defendant felt compelled to mention the racial identity of the free black socializing with them. In the 1740s, the man in question, Jean-Baptiste Marly, seemed well integrated

---

1724, ANOM COL A 23, fols. 50–57. For slaves mentioning the purchase of alcohol during their trials, see RSCL 1766/11/14/02; 1728/06/02/05; 1751/04/14/01. On the presence of enslaved customers in taverns in British North America and in the French Antilles, see Philip D. Morgan, *Slave Counterpoint: Black Culture in the Eighteenth-Century Chesapeake and Lowcountry* (Chapel Hill, N.C., 1998), 414; Salinger, *Taverns and Drinking in Early America*, 128–136, 220–239, 243; and Dessalles, *Les annales du Conseil souverain de la Martinique*, Tome I, Vol. I, ed. Vonglis, 183.

31. RSCL 1744/04/24/01.

within the population of white laborers. He was allowed to bear a surname, knew how to sign his name, and owned several urban parcels that he sold in 1745. Nevertheless, he only served as godfather for enslaved or free infants of color. Cross-racial sociability did not necessarily imply that whites of the lower sort were color blind or that race did not matter to them. They could have fun and share a drink with a free black, but they would not maintain a relation of symbolic kinship with him.[32]

Since slaves could not always spend time in taverns as patrons, they had to find alternative venues to develop their own sociability, which was closely associated with the nighttime world. The 1751 local ruling explained that the main source of disorder came from slaves "who were left to roam at all hours and *most of all during the night*." It also denounced "the city negroes [who] took the liberty of going out *at night* from their masters' house which they leave open and unattended at the risk of any event, to meet up with those from the countryside who come to the city to commit many crimes, and then drink what they have stolen from the public and their masters." The same concern appeared in Article 7 of a 1758 bylaw on policing the enslaved in the district of Cap-Français, which forbade urban slaves from going out after 10:00 p.m. and from being found in the streets unaccompanied by a free person. The enslaved gathered at night because it was the only time they could escape and meet away from the vigilance of owners and authorities. In New Orleans, the large gardens at the back of each urban parcel, where slave cabins were located, offered places were the enslaved could meet relatively undisturbed. They were appropriated by slaves as their own space. In the early 1760s, for instance, some enslaved women organized, with or without the approval of their masters, large dinner parties at night in such gardens, cooking turkey or gumbo while men brought the alcohol. Slave sociability was mixed gender, which means that black men apparently did not develop their own distinct practices of leisure, unlike white men in taverns.[33]

Apart from eating and drinking parties, balls must have also been arranged. Pradel punished his right-hand man, St. Louis alias La Nuit (The

32. For the white cooper's trial, see RSCL 1744/02/22/01. For a similar case, see RSCL 1738/04/12/01. On Jean-Baptiste Marly, see NONA Feb. 2, 1745; and AANO, Saint-Louis Cathedral Baptisms, 1731–1733 and 1744–1753, 03/16/1733, 09/16/1744, 10/24/1746, 03/05/1747, 03/26/1747.

33. "Règlement sur la police pour la province de la Louisiane," Feb. 28–Mar. 1, 1751, ANOM COL C13A 35, fols. 40v, 48v–49r (my emphasis); [Moreau] de Saint-Méry, *Loix et constitutions des colonies françoises de l'Amérique sous le vent*, IV, 227; RSCL 1764/07/14/01, 1764/07/14/04, 1764/09/04/01, 1764/09/08/01.

Night), because he left the plantation at dawn for the city where he "danced all night long at some free negroes' places with the male and female negroes of the city and paid for violins and refreshments costing 150 livres." According to Commissaire-ordonnateur Michel, who was in conflict with Jean-Baptiste de Membrède, major of New Orleans, over their respective prerogatives, the military officer took responsibility for the "ruling of slaves" at the end of the 1740s and authorized slaves "to gather to dance on Sundays." Consequently, the 1751 local ordinance mentioned once again that such gatherings were prohibited. To escape from the repression of authorities, urban slaves might have started to go to plantations to dance more often than rural slaves came to the city for that purpose.[34]

The space that slaves created through their nighttime sociability was neither public nor private but secret. At least, they tried to keep it secret, but the urban milieu tended to expose their so-called clandestine behavior. Slave meetings and entertainments after sundown did not totally escape whites' monitoring. In 1764, for example, when some slaves met in the back of Sieur Boissinot's parcel, a conflict broke out between Narcisse, a twenty-five-year-old man, and a girl, named Marianne, who slapped each other. A slave named Jean, a pastrycook who had just left a wedding party for which he must have worked, joined them and tried to separate them with the help of other enslaved women, but the fight only stopped with the intervention of Sieur Belache, a white merchant. He brought the three protagonists to the house of Sieur Berthelot, the white settler who had hired Jean for the year. When Jean left, he passed in front of Louis Duchesne's inn, and the tavern keeper's wife warned him that the guard was out because a shot had been fired. In fact, an inquiry was opened because a soldier had been injured by an unknown man. During the investigation, the pastry tools and shoes belonging to Jean were found abandoned on Sieur Boissinot's parcel, but Sieur Belache backed up Jean's story about where he had been and what he had done the night of the incident.[35]

34. On slaves' dancing practices in New Orleans, see Jean-Charles de Pradel to his brother, Apr. 10, 1755, HNOC MSS 589, Chevalier de Pradel Papers, 62; Michel to the minister of the navy, Sept. 15, 1749, ANOM COL C13A 34, fol. 173v; and "Règlement sur la police pour la province de la Louisiane," Feb. 28–Mar. 1, 1751, Article 20, ANOM COL C13A 35, fol. 47r. On "calinda," dancing, and balls on plantations, see RSCL 1743/06/26/01; 1744/03/11/01; 1766/07/29/04; and [Antoine-Simon] Le Page du Pratz, *Histoire de la Louisiane* ..., 3 vols. (Paris, 1758), I, 351–352.

35. I borrow the idea that slaves' nighttime sociability was not public or private but secret from Pascal Brioist, Hervé Drévillon, and Pierre Serna, *Croiser le fer: Violence et culture de l'épée dans la France moderne, XVIe–XVIIIe siècle* (Seyssel, France, 2002), 481.

The Hustle and Bustle of City Life

In a society as small as French New Orleans, interpersonal relationships were essential to alleviate the severity of the slave system and to give slaves some space for social autonomy. Some white urban dwellers tolerated this slave sociability; they only intervened in the event of conflict to end violent disputes and to restore calm to the neighborhood, but they did not systematically call for the guard. As the 1751 ruling testifies, local authorities were well aware that masters themselves had a responsibility in what they qualified as slave unrest. Although urban slaveowners and nonslaveholders did not always cooperate with royal justice and tolerated these wanderings and nightly leisure activities, they nonetheless kept a close eye on the enslaved.

STREET FIGHTS AND THE CONSTRUCTION OF WHITENESS

In contrast with taverns, which were the site of a predominantly white male sociability, genuinely public spaces such as the streets and the levee remained defined by their accessibility to all social and ethnic groups. Streets constituted "place[s] of close conviviality" where people from various backgrounds interacted in many ways. But they were also places of distinction and contention. Violence was a crucial component of street culture in ancien régime societies, even though it tended to decline over the eighteenth century as people increasingly resorted to courts to settle their conflicts. Verbal and physical violence continued to be seen as legitimate ways of defending a person's physical integrity, interests, and, in particular, honor. As in the metropole, however, physical violence among whites almost always involved individuals of the same social rank. Only the elite could assault those they considered inferior to them.[36]

––––––

These authors used the idea of secrecy to denote the space where duels took place clandestinely after the crown had managed to exclude them from the public space without having eradicated the practice. For Jean's trial, see RSCL 1764/06/20/01, 1764/06/20/05, 1764/06/20/06, 1764/06/21/01, 1764/06/22/01, 1764/06/22/02, 1764/06/24/01, 1764/06/25/01, 1764/06/25/03, 1764/06/27/01, 1764/06/27/03. For another case of white urban dwellers helping slaves escape from the guard, see Michel to the minister of the navy, Jan. 8, 1752, ANOM COL C13A 36, fols. 187–193.

36. For the qualification of the street as a "space of close conviviality," see Pierre Chaunu, "Introduction," in Annik Pardailhé-Galabrun, *La naissance de l'intime: 3000 foyers parisiens, XVIIe–XVIIIe siècles* (Paris, 1988), 15. Among many works on violence in the metropole, see Brioist, Drévillon, and Serna, *Croiser le Fer;* Jean-Clément Martin, *Violence et Révolution: Essai sur la naissance d'un mythe national* (Paris, 2006), 15–50; Robert Muchembled, *Une histoire de la violence: De la fin du Moyen Âge à nos jours* ([Paris], 2008); and Michel Nassiet, *La violence, une histoire sociale: France, XVIe–XVIIIe siècles* (Seyssel, France, 2011). On the decline of violence over the eighteenth century, see also Robert B. Shoemaker, "The Decline of Public Insult in London 1660–1800,"

In the Louisiana capital, the privilege of asserting one's superior status through physical violence seems to have been extended to all whites in their dealings with slaves. According to the lawyer Michel-René Hiliard d'Auberteuil, the same phenomenon took place in Saint-Domingue. There, he observed: "Anyone who is White mistreats the Blacks with impunity. Their situation is such that they are slaves to their masters and the public." In cases of conflict with slaves in New Orleans, whites felt all the more powerful in using physical force as slaves could not strike back without risking terrible punishment. Not only were the enslaved victims of abusive mistreatment, but they were also excluded from the culture of violence that was shared by all whites across social boundaries. Because of this unequal relationship, blacks never initiated physical confrontations in the streets. Slaves were left with only words and body language to defend themselves. Free men of color living in the city also kept a low profile, whereas those who did not reside there permanently sometimes replied to provocation from whites with their fists.[37]

Like any other form of social interaction, violence in ancien régime societies was ritualized. Social norms governed the way people expressed their aggression and entered into conflict. According to Pascal Brioist, Hervé Drévillon, and Pierre Serna, "Violence is a travesty of politeness. It works in tandem with social etiquette." Street violence was most of the time only expressed symbolically. The way passersby of various social conditions shared the street, moved around, and came into contact was highly codified and orchestrated according to social status. Individuals could deliberately use such encounters to publicly display existing tensions and to offend their opponents. In 1751, for example, the commissaire-ordonnateur Michel was engaged in a conflict with a military officer named Pierre Henri d'Erneville and his father-in-law, François Fleuriau, who was the royal attorney, over a case involving a ship's officer named Battar, who was being prosecuted at the request of d'Erneville. In his official capacity as first judge of the Superior Council, Michel took Battar's side, an action for which d'Erneville, backed by Fleuriau, criticized him. The hostility between Michel, Fleuriau,

---

Past and Present, no.169 (November 2000), 97–131; and Shoemaker, "Male Honour and the Decline of Public Violence in Eighteenth-Century London," *Social History*, XXVI (2001), 190–208. On violence among peers or against social inferiors, see Vacher, *Voisins, voisines, voisinage*, 305–308.

37. [Michel-René] H[iliard] d'[Auberteuil], *Considérations sur l'état présent de la colonie française de Saint-Domingue: Ouvrage politique et législatif; Présenté au Ministre de la Marine* (Paris, 1776), 145.

The Hustle and Bustle of City Life

and d'Erneville was reflected in the way they interacted in public. In a long letter to the minister of the navy detailing the whole story, Michel complained that Fleuriau "has worked up such animosity against me that he refused to greet me, even at church." Likewise, when Michel met d'Erneville on horseback on the levee, he recounted that: "I stepped aside to let him pass. He stared at me in a manner that was improper in all respects, and passed by without doffing his hat, which he has continued to do ever since." The sword officer's reaction was particularly discourteous because, on meeting him, Michel had acknowledged his social preeminence by letting him go first. Since the head was associated with the individual's identity, a hat was seen as a symbol of honor. Deliberately not doffing his hat was a sign of offense.[38]

Other conflicts that mixed verbal and physical violence were no less ritualized. They took place in public to serve different purposes. Although private houses were not deprived of their share of violence, the streets were considered the proper place to express and solve disputes between people who did not live together. Assaulting someone in his home constituted a social transgression that was rarely committed (*his* home, because most cases in the judicial archives concerned men). In 1746, an argument between Pierre Ferrand and Nicolas Judice started in Ferrand's house. Ferrand had recognized a piece of stolen sailcloth in the hands of one of his slaves, who confessed that he had obtained it from one of Judice's brother's slaves. He then had the two slaves put in jail. When he learned about the imprisonment, Nicolas Judice came to see Ferrand at his house. Judice admitted that the slave was a thief, but he explained that his brother refused to hand his slave over to royal justice because some Frenchmen begged him not to do so. A witness recounted to the judge that "Ferrand replied 'if your brother said that, he is a rascal because if there were no fences, there would be no thieves'" to which Nicolas Judice retorted "I am surprised that you are saying that to me, his brother, tell other people if you want, but don't say that in my presence, you are lucky to be at home, and you would not say that in

38. Brioist, Drévillon, and Serna, *Croiser le fer*, 483. On the conflict between Michel, Pierre Henri d'Erneville, and Fleuriau, see Michel to the minister of the navy, July 15, 1751, ANOM COL C13A 35, fols. 294v, 299. For the symbolism of hats in ancien régime societies, see Arlette Farge, *Effusion et tourment: Le récit des corps: Histoire du peuple au XVIIIe siècle* (Paris, 2007), 96; and Frédérique Pitou, "Violence et discours au XVIIIe siècle: 'Si je ne t'aimais pas je te tuerais tout à fait . . . ,'" *Annales de Bretagne et des pays de l'Ouest*, CV, no. 4 (1998), 7–35. For two cases of a hat thrown on the ground to infringe on a person's identity and honor among whites who did not belong to the elite in Louisiana, see RSCL 1744/02/22/01; 1767/04/27/01.

the street." Although he felt insulted, Judice left without further ado, but the next morning, when he met Ferrand in the street, he attacked him with his cane, and a fight ensued.[39]

The streets were also a privileged place for the expression of verbal and physical violence because they could be deliberately used to implicate bystanders as witnesses and arbiters who could give their social sanction to help resolve a conflict. In 1747, Baptiste Barbot spent an entire day chasing his stepfather, Jean-Pierre Hardy alias La Vierge, with whom he did not live, everywhere La Vierge went, except at home, to provoke him verbally and physically. The precise reason for the quarrel between the two male relatives is not known, but Barbot had already been sent to jail once for having assaulted his stepfather. Barbot's mother had married La Vierge but obtained a judicial separation from him because he used to beat her severely. When, at one point, La Vierge threatened to send him back to jail, Barbot retorted that he "could only press charges and could not defy him, that he was only a woman and an old one, unable to stand up arms in hand, whatever arms he chose."[40]

The opposition between the two men resulted in an argument over the legitimate source of social order—justice or *"infrajustice"* (the public or semipublic settlement of a conflict outside court)—interwoven with a competition for virility. Although La Vierge tried to remind Barbot of the respect that he owed him as his stepfather, he was unable to impose his paternal authority to confront his aggressive, young stepson. His masculinity threatened, La Vierge turned to the Superior Council to stop the violence and to have his honor restored. The plaintiff and a witness insisted that the public insults were inacceptable, for some had been pronounced "on the bridge of the street where Mr. Bénac spends time in the company of some of his friends," Mr. Bénac being the city's major at the time. Because of La Vierge's treatment of his mother, Barbot felt no family obligation to him, and he deliberately used the streets to win over public opinion. Even as Barbot's behavior flouted the traditional patriarchal order, he secured a partial victory before the court, which decided for a *décret d'ajournement personnel* (a type of summons), suspending its judgment for lack of information.[41]

39. RSCL 1746/05/17/02, 1746/05/18/01.

40. RSCL 1743/08/30/01, 1743/09/02/01, 1743/09/07/03, 1743/09/10/04, 1744/07/17/01, 1744/07/31/01, 1746/07/07/02, 1747/08/07/01, 1747/08/07/02, 1747/08/09/01, 1747/08/14/01, 1747/09/02/06.

41. RSCL 1743/08/30/01, 1743/09/02/01, 1743/09/07/03, 1743/09/10/04, 1744/07/17/01, 1744/07/31/01, 1746/07/07/02, 1747/08/07/01, 1747/08/07/02, 1747/08/09/01, 1747/08/14/01, 1747/09/02/06. On "infrajustice," see Benoît Garnot, "Justice, infra-

The Hustle and Bustle of City Life

Conversely, streets were sometimes chosen as sites of violence to escape from notice and prosecution. In 1747, Commissaire-ordonnateur Sébastien François Ange Le Normant de Mezy was attacked in the street at night by a man wearing a mask. He had spent the day at the government house working with Governor Vaudreuil. He left at 9:00 P.M., after dinner, accompanied by César, his domestic slave. On his way back to his residence, he met Polydor, another of his enslaved domestics, who had come to ask him if he was going to have dinner at home, but he sent him on ahead. It was at this moment that the official was assaulted. A sword fight followed, and Le Normant sent César to the government house to call for a sentinel. Several men came to help him, including Sieur Olivier, who was the governor's secretary and was accompanied by his own enslaved domestic, René. Le Normant was unable to identify his assailant, and an investigation was organized. The anonymous duelist was recognized by some slaves while he was strolling on the levee the following day at dawn. Le Normant's domestic slaves were called on to confirm that the man who had been arrested, the chevalier de Taillefer, was the culprit. The commissaire-ordonnateur's insistence that Taillefer pay his debt of three thousand livres to the king had apparently struck a blow to the military officer's honor, which sparked off his violent and desperate reaction.[42]

The affair between Le Normant and de Taillefer reveals how the elite exhibited their social superiority in the streets of New Orleans, where walking was the most common way of circulating. Carts were used to move goods, but carriages that served to transport passengers were not common. Likewise, individuals do not seem to have ridden on horseback within the city, except on the levee. In contrast with the metropole, the urban elite could not distinguish themselves by the use of fancy carriages and horses. Instead, they adapted metropolitan practices related to walking as an important source of social distinction and symbolic violence. Apart from shoes with gold or silver buckles, they wore a sword or carried a cane when walking as a sign of social superiority and authority. A goldsmith named Prévost even possessed a stick with the top in the shape of a "negro head." Moreover,

justice, parajustice, et extrajustice dans la France d'Ancien Régime," *Crime, Histoire, et Sociétés/Crime, History, and Societies*, IV, no. 1 (2000), 103–120.

42. RSCL 1747/03/24/01; Sébastien François Ange Le Normant de Mezy to the minister of the navy, Mar. 24, 1747, ANOM COL C13A 31, fols. 155–156v; Pierre Rigaud de Vaudreuil de Cavagnal to the minister of the navy, Apr. 25, 1747, ANOM COL C13A 31, fols. 56–58v; Le Normant to the minister of the navy, May 15, 1747, ANOM COL C13A 31, fols. 153–154v; Vaudreuil to the minister of the navy, May 16, 1747, ANOM COL C13A 31, fol. 93.

following the example of aristocrats who were preceded by their valet or coachman in European cities, the New Orleans elite, like their counterparts in the Antilles, were attended by one or several enslaved domestics in all their movements around the city. Although they also occasionally employed white servants, they chose enslaved men of African descent to accompany them. In so doing, they displayed slaveownership as the main source of social distinction.[43]

The functions fulfilled by enslaved domestics at their masters' sides put them in a position to observe and acquire personal knowledge of the elite's world. Usually, their presence was seen by whites in a utilitarian way, both on a material and symbolic level. They were not supposed to let their owners know that they were watching them or to intervene except to do their duty. Because, in the above-mentioned case, they helped to save Le Normant's life and to recognize and condemn his assailant, the officials let those slaves have a voice. Authorities were compelled to acknowledge their social agency and their participation in the social game of observing one another in the public space. But the exceptionality of the case signifies that most of the time slaves were objectified and exploited by the elite. They included them in their imaginary world only as symbolic reminders of their social superiority.[44]

The reverse was true for nonslaveholders. The ubiquity and relative autonomy of urban slaves in the public space reminded the former of their own social inferiority within the white social hierarchy. The streets of New Orleans were the site of many public confrontations related to race. Those incidents seemed to have multiplied from the late 1740s, even though this impression might be only the result of the lack of evidence for the earlier period. Yet it is possible that the rise in the number of slaves and the massive influx of armed forces in 1750 and then again in 1762 in wartime created racial tensions. Because soldiers lived in proximity with slaves and

43. On carts and horses, see Michel to the minister of the navy, July 15, 1751, ANOM COL C13A 35, fol. 299r; NONA Kernion Oct. 18, 1764, Dec. 20, 1764, Mar. 11, 1765, Mar. 25, 1765; and "Copie d'une lettre écrite par M. de Rochemore à M. de Vergès ingénieur," Aug. 11, 1760, ANOM COL C13A 42, fols. 135–138v. On the use of canes by the elite while walking in Paris, see Farge, *Vivre dans la rue à Paris au XVIIIe siècle*, 100–102. For Prévost's cane, see NONA Kernion Jan. 13, 1767, Jan. 26, 1767. On the practice of walking accompanied by enslaved domestics in the Antilles, see Pérotin-Dumon, *La ville aux îles, la ville dans l'île*, 550–551.

44. On the objectification of domestics by masters in France, see Sarah C. Maza, *Servants and Masters in Eighteenth-Century France: The Uses of Loyalty* (Princeton, N.J., 1983), esp. 199–243.

The Hustle and Bustle of City Life

were socially despised by the elite, they tried to distinguish themselves and to assert their racial preeminence when interacting with people of African descent in public. As objects of social contempt, servicemen might have felt a greater inclination to use violence against slaves, since their only claim to social respect, honor, and power was their virility as men of war.

In 1747, three sick soldiers who were taking a walk in front of the king's hospital engaged in an argument with Étienne Larue, who afterward presented himself to the judge as being "born in Senegal, of the Roman and apostolic Catholic religion, around twenty-two years old, pilot on the ship *L'Unique* come to this colony from St. Louis on the coast of St. Domingue, natural son of Sr. Larue, free negro commandant of the vessels of the Company of the Indies." Other documents show that he had served as a pilot and then as a captain on ships circulating in the greater Caribbean from the early 1720s. During his stay in New Orleans, Larue crossed paths with the three men on the quay near the hospital. He politely greeted them by doffing his hat. But the servicemen felt offended by this gesture, which they believed failed to acknowledge the free black's subaltern position and suggested that he considered himself their equal. One of the soldiers ironically retorted with a "Good Evening, Mi'lady Pickaninny," intending to strike a blow at Larue's masculinity and lower him socially. Larue, however, did not allow himself to be goaded into physical retaliation but contented himself with a reply of "Good Evening, Mi'lord Bugger." The soldiers slapped him in the face, and a fight followed. In their testimonies, the three men explained the defendant's behavior by stating that he was intoxicated. They implied that Larue would not have behaved the way he did if he had not been drunk. They could not otherwise comprehend his pretensions toward equality. As for Larue, his social background, professional occupation, and transient life gave him a social pride and self-respect that empowered him to push back against the servicemen's racial prejudice with physical violence when irony failed. No doubt because his father had served the Company of the Indies and because the plaintiffs were only soldiers, Larue was not sentenced to any corporal punishment. Since he had fired several shots during his arrest so as not to be jailed with loaded pistols in his pockets, he was nevertheless admonished in the court chamber, his pistols were confiscated, and he was ordered to pay fines of one hundred livres to the poor and ten livres to the king.[45]

45. On Larue's career as a pilot and then ship's captain in the Caribbean, see "Campagne du Maréchal d'Estrées," June 16, 1723, AN MAR 4JJ 27, fol. 4; and Jacques-Charles Bochart, marquis de Champigny de Noroy, and Jacques Pannier, seigneur d'Orgeville, to

Larue responded to the soldiers' provocations with verbal and physical violence because he was a free man of color who was an outsider. By contrast, local slaves knew that they could not strike back when they were caught in a street incident, as shown by the altercation between an enslaved woman and a serviceman that led to the discovery of the 1731 slave conspiracy. In his travel account, Antoine-Simon Le Page du Pratz recounted that in June 1731: "A Negress attached to the brick factory, although she belonged to the Company, came back at noon for dinner. A soldier who needed wood tried to force her, by paying her, to look for some for him; she refused to go, as she was pressed for time. The lazy soldier got very mad, and slapped her so violently that the Negress claimed in her anger that the French would not strike the Negroes for long. Those of the French who heard these threats arrested her and brought her to the governor who ordered to throw her in jail." The reason for the conflict was closely related to the status and social identity of the two protagonists. People of African descent furnished most of the laborers in colonial New Orleans, whereas enlisted men were characterized as a social group by the fact that most of them did not own slaves and could not benefit from their work unless they hired or paid them. Soldiers were also bachelors who did not have wives they could rely on to take care of their domestic needs. They were thus deprived of the social preeminence associated with mastery while being doubly dependent on slaves' goodwill. The enslaved woman's refusal appeared to be a reminder of the serviceman's precarious social position. He must have felt even more humiliated since the rejection was expressed in public and came from a woman. Consequently, he used violence to restore what he believed to be the rightful racial and gender order. Despite the social contempt the woman might have felt for the soldier, she knew that she could not fight back. Finding herself powerless in the face of his physical violence, she revealed the plot.[46]

The violence of nonslaveholders, servicemen in particular, against the enslaved was such that local authorities felt compelled to legislate on the subject and to distinguish it from vigilantism. Like the 1724 Code Noir, the 1751 ruling ordered white private individuals to arrest slaves found cir-

the minister of the navy, Dec. 13, 1735, ANOM COL C8A 46, fol. 60. On Larue's trial, see RSCL 1747/05/05/01, 1747/05/05/02, 1747/05/06/04, 1747/05/06/07, 1747/05/18/01, 1747/05/18/02, 1747/05/18/03, 1747/05/18/04, 1747/05/19/05, 1747/05/19/06; and Shannon Lee Dawdy, "La ville sauvage: 'Enlightened' Colonialism and Creole Improvisation in New Orleans, 1699–1769" (Ph.D. diss., University of Michigan, 2003), 300.

46. Le Page du Pratz, *Histoire de la Louisiane* ..., III, 304–305.

The Hustle and Bustle of City Life

culating, gathering, bearing arms, or trading without a note of authorization from their masters. It is impossible, however, to assess to what extent whites actually complied, especially when they were confronted, not with strangers, but with slaves they knew personally. In any case, Vaudreuil and Michel added one last article that sought to curb the propensity all whites displayed for punishing slaves, even when they did not belong to them. In Article 30 of their 1751 bylaw, they decreed:

> We have just exposed all the obligations and the deference that negroes need to show towards whites, masters in particular. It is a good thing to instruct the public that this does not apply to everybody indiscriminately. A private individual, a soldier or anyone else, does not have the power to abuse a negro who has done nothing to him and is not disrespectful towards him. He can arrest him in some circumstances and ask for justice, as the negro is only subjected to that of his master and that of the police. Consequently, and following the king's orders, we forbid anyone to take these liberties, on pain of punishment chosen according to what the cases require.

Apart from defending the state monopoly on legitimate violence, the article aimed at protecting the material and social prerogatives of masters over their human property. Behind any slave stood his or her owner, as any non-slaveholder who attacked an enslaved man or woman knew.[47]

The inclusion of Article 30 was motivated by an incident that involved Claude Joseph Dubreuil, one of the richest planters in the colony and a former militia captain. In a letter recounting the case to the minister of the navy, Commissaire-ordonnateur Michel complained about "the many soldiers who don't abide by the retreat but go out at night to visit the plantations near the city, consort with the negresses, and trouble the settlers' rest." Dubreuil caught one such a serviceman on his plantation late at night.

---

47. The judicial records include few cases of vigilantism. See RSCL 1764/07/24/02, 1764/07/26/01, 1764/07/26/02, 1764/07/26/05, 1764/07/28/04, 1764/07/28/05; 1765/10/15/01, 1765/10/16/01, 1765/10/16/02. In the margins of a copy of the Code Noir included in a compilation of all the legal texts promulgated in Louisiana between 1714 and 1746, an anonymous commentator noted regarding Article 17, dealing with the right of settlers to seize the goods or arms of slaves without a certificate from their masters, that "this article is not enforced." See "Édit du roi, ou Code noir, qui concerne entièrement les esclaves de la Louisiane . . . ," March 1724, ANOM COL A 23, fols. 50–57. For Article 30 of the 1751 ruling, see "Règlement sur la police pour la province de la Louisiane," Feb. 28–Mar. 1, 1751, Article 30, ANOM COL C13A 35, fols. 50r–51v.

But, when the planter brought him back to the barracks, the sentinel seized Dubreuil by the collar, instead of arresting the soldier. It was only with the arrival of the major that the civilian was freed. Although Dubreuil did not lodge a complaint against the soldiers, they plotted to take their revenge. Apart from breaking down the planter's doors at night, they assaulted one of his most valuable slaves, a blacksmith who was estimated as worth more than ten thousand livres. They caught the man while he was walking past a billiard room, attacked him, and beat him so severely that the slave was unable to work for three months. The servicemen were arrested on the governor's orders. According to Michel, the major maneuvered to impede a trial; after he failed, he forged testimonies to prove that "this negro was a rascal who had dared to raise his hand against a white man." Yet the judges acknowledged that the slave had not initiated the dispute and sentenced the defendants to a fortnight in jail.[48]

Enacted in response to the prevalence of violence against slaves by non-slaveholders in the public space, Article 30 of the 1751 ruling sought to resolve the tensions between the necessary solidarity among all whites on which white hegemony was based and the rights of property owners. The anonymous commentator of the 1751 ordinance—probably a member of the Bureau des colonies in the metropole—believed that the text failed to solve this problem. He pointed out its contradictions about vigilantism, stating "It both authorizes and prohibits at the same time!" He nonetheless approved Articles 28 and 29, which were the two main departures from the 1724 Code Noir introduced by the 1751 ruling. Their content demonstrates that local authorities were becoming increasingly aware of the importance of controlling the public space to enforce the racial order. Article 29 dealt with seating in church, while Article 28 was concerned with the behavior of slaves in the streets and country lanes. It provisioned that:

> Any negro and other slaves, either in the city or in the countryside, who will not be very considerate and will not show the submissiveness he owes to whites, meaning that he will be impertinent enough to elbow them out of the way to make room for himself, and that, forgetting that he is a slave, will be disrespectful towards them, will be punished with fifty lashes of whip and branded with a fleur-de-lis on the buttock so that the nature of his crime can be ascertained if needed.

If local authorities felt the need to write and promulgate such an article, it must have been because some slaves turned the streets into a place of

---

48. Michel to the minister of the navy, Sept. 29, 1750, ANOM COL 34, fols. 333v–343v.

The Hustle and Bustle of City Life

protest. Because slaves were unable to use physical violence, they must have resorted to symbolic and verbal violence to assert their dignity.[49]

The racialization that French New Orleans experienced made the use and control of public space a crucial priority for all social actors. It strengthened even more, if possible, the "culture of appearances" that characterized ancien régime societies. Since the disruptive potential of the urban milieu made the project of a strict racial order difficult to enforce in the city, most whites quickly became aware of the need to maintain some appearance of social superiority and to display and instill the socioracial hierarchy by their public behavior. Through segregation in church, exclusion from taverns, and one-sided violence in the streets, they tried to teach slaves the deference that—they believed—befit their station. Whites' ability to make slaves invisible, to segregate them, or to undermine both their physical integrity and dignity in the public space fueled the construction of whiteness. The racialization of space contributed to giving white people a shared sense of belonging to an exclusive racial community, despite class and gender fault lines. Whiteness was primarily an experience that was performed and exhibited by the social actors it defined. It was nonetheless also vigorously contested by some of the very people of African descent that it tried to subordinate and exclude. As local authorities implicitly acknowledged, some slaves fought back for every inch of the streets. The small size of French New Orleans and the proximity of repressive forces, however, facilitated social control, even as authorities and colonists were never able to completely overpower slaves' fight for autonomy and dignity.

Race came to play a crucial role in the politics of public space over time. Yet it collided with other categories of difference such as status, class, and gender. The racial divide intersected with various power relationships, which complemented or contradicted one another. The social diversity that characterized the urban milieu and the demographic and social importance of male nonslaveholders among whites, in particular, complicated the way the system of racial slavery worked in the city in comparison with on plantations. When slaves and white nonslaveholders interacted in the public space, three or four parties were really involved. Behind every slave, there was a master, and local authorities were never far away. The interests of the state, slaveowners, and nonslaveholders sometimes came into conflict.

49. "Règlement sur la police pour la province de la Louisiane," Feb. 28–Mar. 1, 1751, Article 28, ANOM COL C13A 35, fols. 49r–50v; Anonymous comments on the 1751 ruling, May 27, 1751, ANOM COL C13A 35, fols. 53–55.

When the state and the elite tried to subjugate both soldiers and slaves and to defend the rights of property owners, they undermined the cohesion of the white community. As soldiers were deprived of the attributes that gave the elite their authority—marriage, property, and mastery over other human beings—competing models of white masculinity were put in tension. Still, even though all whites might not have benefited from the system of racial slavery to the same extent nor had the same individual motivations and interests, they all shared the same commitment to the perpetuation of the racial order. They might have disagreed on the way white supremacy should be achieved, but they all sought to enforce the racial line in the public space as well as in the intimacy of their domestic households.[50]

50. On competing models of masculinity in colonial and slave societies, see Thomas A. Foster, Mary Beth Norton, and Toby L. Ditz, eds., *New Men: Manliness in Early America* (New York, 2011).

The Hustle and Bustle of City Life

CHAPTER FOUR

"The Mulatto of the House"

The Racial Line within Domestic Households
and Residential Institutions

In 1766, a slave named Valentin intervened to separate two white men who were fighting in his master's residence. The incident led to a trial. In his complaint, the accusant referred to Valentin as "the mulatto of the house" instead of using his name, emphasizing the central role that this enslaved man born in Martinique played in his owner's home. The conflict happened within an atypical household composed of two brothers and two sisters who were between the ages of twenty and thirty-six: Isaac Rodriguez, Manuel, Gracia, and Angélique Monsanto. The eldest brother, Isaac Rodriguez, was the head of the family. Born in the Netherlands, he had first moved to Curaçao before settling with his siblings in New Orleans in 1757. From the Louisiana capital, he operated a prosperous business enterprise trading with the greater Caribbean and the Atlantic world. Apart from nine slaves, the two white men involved in the fight also lived with the family, even though they were unrelated to them. Jean-Baptiste Marcelain Lhomer, a thirty-five- or forty-year-old weaver who had arrived in the colony from Veracruz seven years earlier, had been staying with the Monsantos for the previous six years, and Abraham Robles, a thirty-two-year-old merchant from Bordeaux, had been with them for a month. While Marcelain was Catholic, the Monsanto family and Robles were Jewish, though the court records only formally identified Robles's faith. Robles might have been only passing through Louisiana, for he was apparently unconcerned by the Code Noir's prohibition against the settlement of Jews and Protestants in the colonies. As for the Monsantos, they were tolerated as long as they displayed Catholicism in public and allowed their slaves to participate in Catholic rituals.[1]

1. For the expression "the mulatto of the house," see RSCL 1766/09/08/01. The

The case was prosecuted at Robles's request. He complained that he had been stabbed four times with a knife by Marcelain and that, without the intervention of Valentin, Marcelain would have killed him. The incident had started as a conflict involving Marcelain and the women of the household. Between eight and nine in the morning, a young "negress" was cleaning the downstairs rooms, including Marcelain's bedroom. He decided to punish her because the dirt she was sweeping in the gallery had fallen into a barrel of water that was used for cooking. When Gracia, the eldest Monsanto sister, heard Marcelain scolding the young "negress" in the courtyard, she went upstairs to look for a "mulattress" named Fanchonette, whom she sent to enquire what he wanted. Although she must have played the role of hostess, she apparently did not want to interact directly with him and used a female slave as an intermediary. Marcelain pursued the young "negress" to beat her. In his rage, he hit not only the slave but also her mistress with a stick. Hearing the women screaming, the Monsanto brothers intervened and with great difficulty disarmed Marcelain. After their departure, Gracia locked herself in her room. It was at this moment that Robles came home and found Marcelain trying to smash in the door of Gracia's room with a knife in his hand. Marcelain threw himself at Robles. Hearing people shouting, Valentin tried to rescue Robles, but Marcelain turned against the slave. Alarmed by the cries, the two Monsanto brothers returned. Unable to restrain Marcelain, they called for the guard.[2]

The issue at the heart of the original conflict was a question of authority: who was entitled to punish the household's slaves? When Monsanto asked Marcelain "why he had the audacity to beat his sister who had been kind enough to let him beat her slaves," he replied, "why didn't she command her slaves better and that he did not have to explain himself to anyone." Marcelain defended himself, arguing that he had never intended to beat Gracia, that he respected her, and that the stick only inadvertently touched her. He explained that he had decided to chastise the young "negress" himself because he had not dared to bother Monsanto with such small matters. To justify himself in front of the magistrate, he added: "That besides as he

———
court records only mentioned three slaves in the Monsanto household, but the 1766 census counted nine. See "Padron y lista de las quatro compañias de milicianos y habitantes en la Ciudad por quarterles, segun revista passada en 27 de Mayo 1766," AGI, Audiencia de Sto Domingo, Luisiana y Florida, Años 1766 a 1770, 2595–588. For Monsanto slaves acting as godfathers, see AANO, Saint-Louis Cathedral Baptisms, 1763–1767, 1767–1771, 03/22/1767, 04/26/1767. For baptisms of Monsanto slaves, see ibid., 06/06/1767 (2 baptisms), 02/04/1768.

  2. RSCL 1766/09/10/01.

was Sr. Monsanto's creditor and therefore had an interest in the household, he could inflict these small punishments without complaints especially regarding slaves." Marcelain was not a mere lodger; he was staying with Monsanto because the merchant owed him several thousand piastres that he could not repay as a result of financial complications from what would become known as the Seven Years' War (1756–1763). Owing to the international conflict, the minister of the navy had suspended the settlement of all bills of exchange.[3]

All the members of the Monsanto family testified that Marcelain was a lunatic, though he had been pretty harmless until then. The eldest brother explained to the judge "that when this man arrived in the country, he found him a little deranged, but that for the last three years he had found him pretty quiet, only sometimes playing by himself, laughing at table for no reason, and arguing with the sun and the moon, that he had never known him to act as a bad fellow, although he often beat slaves when they did not serve him according to his whim." Because of his situation as creditor, the Monsanto family had overlooked Marcelain's breaches of the exclusive authority masters held to punish their slaves. For his part, Marcelain also drew on his masculinity to infringe on the prerogatives of the hostess, who was, furthermore, only the sister and not the wife of the eldest Monsanto brother.[4]

A common understanding about who was legally and legitimately entitled to exercise authority and ultimately settle all conflicts within the household united all the protagonists—even Marcelain, once he had calmed down after his fits of anger—the male head. The white protagonists also shared the same acceptance of daily violence against slaves. That enslaved laborers could have a different point of view is revealed by Valentin's testimony. He must have occupied a particular place within the household, since he was asked to provide evidence against Marcelain. At the end of his statement, he added that "the defendant had more wickedness than madness in him." He contested the way whites tended to minimize the importance and significance of daily acts of violence against slaves.[5]

Marcelain tried to exonerate himself with regard to his actions not only during the original incident with the women of the household but also his stabbing of Robles. He claimed that Robles had initiated the violence between them, shouting that he was going to cut his nose and crucify him. In-

3. Ibid.
4. Ibid.
5. Ibid.

stead of saying that Robles had wanted to kill him, he deliberately used the verb "crucify," alluding to the traditional Christian and anti-Semitic accusation that Jews were responsible for the crucifixion of Jesus. Robles denied having been there at the time of the original incident and explained that, when he had returned home from an encounter with another merchant, he had tried to open a door without knowing that Marcelain was behind it. The latter then attacked him with a knife for no reason. The Superior Council recognized Robles's good faith, sentencing Marcelain to perpetual banishment from the colony. After paying eight hundred *livres réelles* (real pounds) to Robles for civil damages, the accused was sent back to his family to be locked up as "raving mad." In this particular case, the Monsantos' and Robles's Jewish religion did not work against them, even though anti-Semitism against Jewish merchants was an acute reality that had surfaced only a few years earlier during the conflict between Governor Louis Billouart de Kerlérec and *Commissaire-ordonnateur* Vincent-Gaspard-Pierre de Rochemore that came to be known as the Louisiana Affair. The Monsanto family and their allies had succeeded in integrating themselves with and being accepted into this Catholic society because they were prominent merchants.[6]

Apart from questions of religious pluralism, the suit brought by Robles raises the issue of the place and treatment of slaves within domestic households. Besides family, the household serves as a crucial category of analysis to determine how New Orleans's slave society became racialized. Most of the time, historical actors used the same word, "family," to designate what historians distinguish as "household" and "family," meaning alternatively all the people residing within a household or only blood relatives. If domestic households and (conjugal) families intersected as analytical and not ver-

6. For the whole trial, see RSCL 1766/09/08/01, 1766/09/08/02, 1766/09/09/01, 1766/09/10/01, 1766/10/01/01, 1766/10/02/01, 1766/10/02/02, 1766/10/02/04, 1766/10/03/02, 1766/10/03/03, 1766/10/10/02, 1766/10/10/03, 1766/11/05/03, 1766/11/05/04, 1766/11/07/03, 1766/11/08/01, 1766/11/08/04, 1766/11/08/07, 1767/05/02/03. On anti-Semitism at the time of the Louisiana Affair, see [Jean-Bernard] Bossu, *Nouveaux voyages dans l'Amérique septentrionale* ... (Amsterdam, 1772), 307–310. In contrast with the tolerance extended toward the Monsantos under French rule, the Spanish governor Alejandro O'Reilly expelled them after his arrival in the colony. Yet, the reason given for their banishment was their participation in illegal trade with nearby Spanish colonies, rather than their Jewish faith. See Emily Ford and Barry Stiefel, *The Jews of New Orleans and the Mississippi Delta: A History of Life and Community Along the Bayou* (Charleston, S.C., 2012), chapter 1; and John G. Clark, *New Orleans, 1718–1812: An Economic History* (Baton Rouge, La., 1970), 175.

"The Mulatto of the House"

nacular categories, at least for whites, they did not overlap, for the former were made up of all kinds of persons. Like all slave societies, New Orleans was characterized by an increasing number of dependents, mainly slaves, within households. Unlike the conjugal families of white settlers, though, those of urban slaves were marked by the residential separation of their various members between households headed by different masters. Moreover, though the community that the Ursulines formed can be viewed as an alternative kind of family, a large minority of the total urban population did not live in domestic households. Some also lacked kinship relationships, as was the case for the nuns and orphans at the convent and most of the soldiers housed in barracks. The patients at the city's hospitals were also temporarily removed from their barracks or domestic households and placed in a distinctive kind of communal setting, often for long periods. Therefore, both domestic households and residential institutions need to be examined in their diversity.[7]

Residential units in this early urban slave society based on a household economy were privileged sites for the implementation of authority and hierarchy and the production and reproduction of social difference, especially race and gender. The urban milieu brought people of all conditions and backgrounds together within relatively small domestic spaces and residential institutions. In comparison with life on plantations, the intimate co-existence between masters and the enslaved—and also a few freed men and women—within domestic households tempered the slave system, which always involved personal interactions in the city. But this closeness did not entirely protect urban slaves from exploitation, violence, and subordination. In spite of slaves' physical proximity, the law and racial prejudice combined to create social distance and produce discrimination. The way censuses were taken reflected local authorities and settlers' growing efforts to establish a racial line between people of European and African descent within domestic households while the violence that was inflicted on domestic slaves constituted the means by which this racial divide was created and maintained. Unlike domestic households, the slaves who lived and worked at the hospitals and the convent did not necessarily belong to those in charge of running these residential institutions; slaves also occa-

7. On households in Europe and the Americas, see Peter Laslett, ed., with Richard Wall, *Household and Family in Past Time: Comparative Studies in the Size and Structure of the Domestic Group over the Last Three Centuries in England, France, Serbia, Japan, and Colonial North America* ... (Cambridge, 1972); and Carole Shammas, *A History of Household Government in America* (Charlottesville, Va., 2002).

sionally visited the barracks where soldiers lived. Yet various mechanisms in all of these places ensured that the enslaved were always kept in a subordinate position.[8]

A CITY OF HOUSEHOLDERS WITH SLAVES:
CENSUSES AND RACIAL FORMATION

Alongside maps, censuses constituted one of the primary ways the imperial state gathered information about French overseas territories. Through censuses, the central government hoped to broadly measure the progression of settlement and the size of militia forces. In addition to being used for purposes of planning and evaluation in the metropole, these documents served colonial authorities as instruments of communication and negotiation with Versailles, on the one hand, and social engineering with local ends in view, on the other.[9]

The way censuses were taken varied greatly from one colony to another. In New Orleans, eight censuses were conducted during the French regime (before 1769). Although local authorities were supposed to send a new census to the metropole every year, they did not comply with this obligation systematically as they were busy with other matters. Furthermore, the making of censuses rested on the active participation of those who were recorded. Depending on the period, New Orleans's residents were to go to the clerk's office (in 1724), to the war commissioner (in 1732), or to their militia captain (sometime between 1732 and 1744) to make statements about the composition of their households and property. Given such haphazard methods of collecting data, censuses could not but be incomplete. The partial informa-

8. On households as privileged sites for the implementation of authority and hierarchy and the production and reproduction of social difference, see Nara Milanich, "Whither Family History? A Road Map from Latin America," *American Historical Review*, CXII (2007), 439–458. See also Julie Hardwick, *The Practice of Patriarchy: Gender and the Politics of Household Authority in Early Modern France* (University Park, Pa., 1998).

9. Censuses counted the number of habitants in French overseas territories. This term should not be translated as "inhabitants" but as "settlers," meaning individuals who established themselves permanently in a colony and had put down local roots. Most often, "habitant" was synonymous with "landowner," but the term could also designate a "land-keeper" (someone who did not own land but rented it or was in charge of running an estate). Therefore, the large floating population of unsettled men who rented rooms in inns, boarded and lodged in private houses, or were given places to sleep by their employers often went unrecorded. Moreover, while censuses were supposed to focus on the civilian population, they occasionally listed military officers or soldiers who were married or who did not live in the barracks and owned or rented urban parcels.

tion obtained in this flawed manner was then compiled and synthesized by the secretary of the Superior Council or by employees of the commissaire-ordonnateur, who made several copies of each census. Although censuses always took the form of a table followed by a general summary, they were not standardized in any way. Census takers changed, and rulings on censuses did not contain detailed recommendations on what they should count and how they should present the data. The social representativeness of censuses—who was included or excluded—and the way census takers gathered, aggregated, and summarized information never ceased to evolve.[10]

10. These nominative censuses were taken in November 1721, January 1726, July 1727, January 1732, 1737, September 1763, May 1766, and June 1766. The first five are kept in ANOM COL G1 464; the last three in AGI, Audiencia de Sto Domingo, Luisiana y Florida, Años 1766 a 1770, 2595—588 and 589. Only the general summary remains for the 1737 census. See "Récapitulatif du recensement général de la Louisiane en 1737," ANOM COL C13C 4, fol. 197. Other censuses were probably taken, but no copies have been kept. The administrative correspondence mentions such a census in 1735. See Jean-Baptiste Le Moyne de Bienville and Edmé Gatien Salmon to the minister of the navy, June 27, 1736, ANOM COL C13A 21, fol. 77. The Company of the Indies first mentioned colonial authorities' obligation to take a census each year in rulings related to the administration of Louisiana in the early 1720s. See "Règlement sur la régie des affaires de la Louisiane ...," Sept. 5, 1721, ANOM COL C13A 6, fols. 196–236. They repeated this order over and over. See Étienne Périer and Salmon to the minister of the navy, Jan. 19, 1732, ANOM COL C13A 14, fol. 168; and the minister of the navy to Bienville and Salmon, Oct. 10, 1736, ANOM COL B 64, fols. 508v–509r. For the ways censuses were taken, see "Arrêt du Conseil supérieur de la Louisiane du 10 juin 1724 concernant les recensements," ANOM COL A 23, fol. 48v; "Ordonnance de Ms. Périer et Salmon du 24 décembre 1732 pour faire faire la déclaration des maisons, blancs, sauvages, nègres, bestiaux, et armes des habitants," ANOM COL A 23, fol. 111; and "Ordonnance de Messieurs Vaudreuil et Salmon du 13 juin 1744 pour les recensements," ANOM COL A 23, fol. 148v. Taxation, combined with a general mistrust toward the state and a lack of acculturation to this kind of governmental practice might explain settlers' reluctance to supply local authorities with information on their families and property. Slaveholders were asked to provide slaves for the corvée and to contribute to public funds used to reimburse the owners of slaves brought to justice. An unwillingness to serve in militia companies, established in the early 1730s, might have played a role as well. This phenomenon could explain the statistical gap between the 1763 and 1766 censuses and the 1770s rosters of white militiamen. See "Arrêt du Conseil supérieur de la Louisiane du 5 octobre 1726 qui enjoint aux habitants de s'assembler pour élire un syndic pour leurs affaires générales," ANOM A 23, fol. 80; Salmon to the minister of the navy, Aug. 16, 1734, ANOM COL C13A 19, fols. 75v–76r; "Milices Nelle Orléans, le 25 janvier 1770," AGI, Correspondencia de los Gobernadores de la Luisiana y la Florida Occidental, Años 1766–1824, Session Papeles de Cuba, legajo 188-A, and "État des quatre compagnies de milice de La Nouvelle-Orléans, 12 février 1770." For previous analyses of French censuses that have not paid much attention

TABLE 2. Census Categories, 1721–1763

November 1721	January 1726	July 1727
"Names of the *habitants* and concession holders" (*"Noms des habitants et des concessionnaires"*)	"Names of the *habitants*" (*"Noms des habitants"*)	"Names of the *habitants*" (*"Noms des habitants"*)
"Number of men" (*"Nombre des hommes"*) "Number of women" (*"Nombre des femmes"*) "Number of children" (*"Nombre des enfants"*)	"Masters" (*"Maîtres"*)	*"Masters"* (*"Maîtres"*)
"French domestics" (*"Domestiques français"*)	"Indentured servants or domestics" (*"Engagés ou domestiques"*)	"Indentured servants or domestics" (*"Engagés ou domestiques"*)
"Negro slaves" (*"Esclaves nègres"*)	"Negro slaves" (*"Esclaves nègres"*)	"Negro slaves" (*"Esclaves nègres"*)
"Native slaves" (*"Esclaves sauvages"*)	"Native slaves" (*"Esclaves sauvages"*)	"Native slaves" (*"Esclaves sauvages"*)

Sources: "Recensement des habitants et concessionnaires de La Nouvelle-Orléans …" 1721, ANOM COL G1 464, "Recensement général des habitations et habitants de la colonie de la Louisiane ainsi qu'ils se sont nommés au 1er janvier 1726," "Recensement des habitations le long du fleuve," 1731, "Recensement général de la ville de la Nvelle Orléans … fait au mois de janvier 1732"; "Récapitulatif du recensement général de la Louisiane en 1737," ANOM COL C13C 4, fol. 197; "Recensement général 1763," AGI, Audiencia de Sto Domingo, Luisiana y Florida, Años 1766 a 1770, 2595–589. Only a general summary is left of the 1737 census.

Note: Of the eight censuses taken in New Orleans before the end of the French period in 1769—November 1721, January 1726, July 1727, January 1732, 1737, September 1763, May 1766, and June 1766—I have

January 1732	1737	September 1763
"Homeowners" ("Propriétaires des maisons") "Names of the bourgeois and of those who lived with them" ("Noms des bourgeois et de ceux qui logent chez eux")		"Heads of family" ("Chefs de famille")
"Men bearing arms" ("Hommes portant les armes")	"Men and boys bearing arms" ("Hommes et garçons portant armes")	
"Women" ("Femmes")	"Women" ("Femmes")	"Women" ("Femmes")
"Children" ("Enfants")	"Boys" ("Garçons")	"Boys under 14" ("Garçons au dessous de 14 ans") "Boys over 14" ("Garçons au dessus de 14 ans")
	"Girls" (Filles)	"Girls under 12" ("Filles au dessous de 12 ans") "Girls over 12" ("Filles au dessus de 12 ans")
"Orphans" ("Orphelins")		
		"Slaves" ("Esclaves"):
"Nègres"	"Nègres"	"Negro" ("Nègre")
"Négresses" "Négrillons" or négrittes"	"Négresses" "Négrillons" "Négrittes"	"Négresses" "Négrillons" "Négrittes" "Mulâtres" "Mulâtresses"
"Sauvages" "Sauvagesses" "Mulâtres" or mulâtresses"	"Sauvages" "Sauvagesses"	"Sauvages" "Sauvagesses"
		"Freed people" ("Affranchis"): "Nègres" "Négresses" "Négrillons" "Négrittes"

elected to use the first six, taken in French; the last two censuses were taken in Spanish, even if the French legally still ruled the colony in 1766.

Censuses always took the form of a table. In the nominative censuses, each row represented one household. The first column was usually text based, recording the names of the household head and sometimes white family members. The remaining columns were numerical in value, indicating the number of men, women, children, slaves, and so on who lived in a household. In the table above, I have reoriented the headings of the columns that followed each other from left to right in the original censuses to appear from top to bottom so as to better show changes in general census categories over time.

Censuses convey the idea that the most basic unit of social organization was the household. Each row of census tables represented a household
unit, rather than an individual. Censuses also offer a window into the socioracial psyche of census takers, which informed the documents they produced both voluntarily and unconsciously. Officials and employees forged
a statistical culture at the same time as they adapted to colonial realities.
When they experimented with the collection and treatment of information,
they necessarily simplified the complexity of social reality. Censuses did not
strictly mirror lived experience but expressed the state project for modeling local society. The textual information in the first column of each census,
which named the heads of the households, compared with the various categories counted in subsequent columns reveals census takers' conceptions of
households and families in relation to their vision of the sociracial order.
At stake in the evolution of these categories were the meanings attached to
household and family, household authority, and the nature of the relationships among the various members within each household, especially the
place of enslaved or free people of color. Incidentally, these transformations
also followed the progression of family life over the French period. Most of
all, they highlight the choice local authorities and settlers made to develop
a system of racial slavery.[11]

Classifying the Population and Institutionalizing Racial Slavery
The first census taken in Louisiana in 1721 reflected the slow process involved in establishing New Orleans as a city. The names of household heads
were listed in the first column, and the number of men, women, children,
French domestics, "negro slaves," and "native slaves" residing within each
household were recorded in subsequent columns without naming them.
Unlike later censuses, the document was further divided into four distinct
sections. The names of the "habitants and concession holders," which in-

---

to the way these documents were produced, see Jennifer M. Spear, *Race, Sex, and Social
Order in Early New Orleans* (Baltimore, 2009), 94–96; and Shannon Lee Dawdy, *Building the Devil's Empire: French Colonial New Orleans* (Chicago, 2008), 153–162, 178–181.

11. Daniel Scott Smith, "The Meanings of Family and Household: Change and Continuity in the Mirror of the American Census," *Population and Development Review*,
XVIII (1992), 421–456. On the statistical culture related to demography during the early
modern period, see Éric Brian, *La mesure de l'État: Administrateurs et géomètres au
XVIIIè siècle* (Paris, 1994); Alain Desrosières, *La politique des grands nombres: Histoire
de la raison statistique* (Paris, 1993), 37–43; and Jacques Dupâquier and Éric Vilquin,
"Le pouvoir royal et la statistique démographique," *Pour une histoire de la statistique*
(1977; rpt. Paris, 1987), 83–101.

"The Mulatto of the House"

cluded military officers, civil employees of the Company of the Indies, and independent settlers who maintained their own households, were listed first, together with their household information, followed by the company's indentured servants, male convicts, and, lastly, female convicts. The city's first residents had been company workers, either indentured servants or convicts, employed to clear the land and build the city. They were lodged in barracks. The number of independent settlers who were granted urban concessions only rose slowly.[12]

Later censuses in the 1720s continued to evolve along with New Orleans's development. Once the heavy work for the construction of the urban center (clearing land, laying out a grid, creating drainage systems, and constructing the levee) had been completed, the company turned its attention to peopling the city with permanent settlers. Whereas many of the individuals who had been first granted urban lots were rural concession holders who resided in the countryside and only came to town on business matters, more colonists began to make their primary home in town. In addition, the contracts of many indentured servants employed by the company came to an end, and many convicts died or deserted. Consequently, local authorities stopped listing company workers after household heads and dividing censuses into sections based on people's status and place of residence.[13]

Patriarchy fueled the dominant conception of household authority. In most censuses taken during the French period, the first column included only the name of the head of the household (with the form of address, sometimes the first name, always the surname, and occasionally nickname). The individual's profession, status, and ethnic origins were occasionally specified but never in a systematic way. Most heads of household were men, although a few widows and single women also appeared (some soldiers' wives in the 1721 census were also mentioned by name, since their husbands were not included in the document). In the list of "habitants and concession holders" on the 1721 census, only three households did not follow this model. Apart from Commandant general Jean-Baptiste Le Moyne de Bienville's household, which might have included his nephew, one was composed of two brothers and another of two associates. In each case, the

12. "Recensement des habitants et concessionnaires de La Nouvelle-Orléans . . . ," 1721, ANOM COL G1 464.

13. In November 1727, Périer and Jacques de La Chaise wrote to the directors of the Company of the Indies in the metropole that they were sending an account of the company's employees with their letter and that it would be followed by a census of the colony. See Périer and La Chaise to the Company of the Indies, Nov. 2, 1727, ANOM COL C13A 10, fols. 184–200.

census takers mentioned the names of both men, implicitly signifying that household authority was shared equally. Except for the three households with two male habitants, the second column counting men only mentioned one man for each household. Although it was not explicitly specified, it was presumed that most households were made up of blood relatives and formed a nuclear family. Households and families were often conflated, and the husband was considered to rule alone over his dependents, representing them to the outside world.[14]

Family life quickly thrived as people embraced marriage as a necessary condition to survive, take root, and prosper. The composition of households in the 1721 census was typical of a nascent migratory society with a strong gender imbalance (Table 3). Many migrants had come to Louisiana as indentured servants and could not wed before the end of their contracts. Yet, once freed from indentured servitude, they seem to have rushed into marriage. After a few years, the kinds of households diversified (Table 4). Kin relationships quickly developed among people of European descent. Marriage took precedence, but households were not confined to nuclear families, as social actors implemented various arrangements to take care of other kinds of relatives, siblings, or in-laws. The number of single men living by themselves was also reduced thanks to a diversity of strategies. Many married, while others lived with one another. This type of arrangement was practical as long as it lasted but could raise difficulties on the death of an associate. When they could not find someone to live with, single men resided in inns or took board and lodging in someone else's household. The censuses explicitly mention several lodgers.[15]

Two main social divisions quickly emerged in New Orleans's censuses,

14. On patriarchy and household, see Smith, "Meanings of Family and Household," *Population and Development Review*, XVIII (1992), 430. Likewise, the Superior Council's 1724 ruling about censuses ordered habitants to make declarations about the various members "whom their families comprise." The French word used to designate the unit of analysis in the Louisiana censuses was "family" *("famille")* and not "homestead" *("feu")* or "household" *("ménage")*. See "Arrêt du Conseil supérieur de la Louisiane du 10 juin 1724 concernant les recensements," ANOM COL A 23, fol. 48v.

15. In the tables, I have not taken into account indentured servants, domestics, and slaves in habitants' households. The categories of family households are those established by Peter Laslett. See Laslett, "La famille et le ménage: Approches historiques," in "Famille et société," special issue, *Annales: Économies, sociétés, civilisations*, XXVII (1972), 847–872; and Laslett, "Introduction: The History of the Family," in Laslett, ed., *Household and Family in Past Time*, 31. For difficulties in case one associate died, see La Chaise to the Company of the Indies's Directors, Oct. 18, 1723, ANOM COL C13A 7, fol. 66.

"The Mulatto of the House"

TABLE 3. Family and Household for White Settlers and
Company of the Indies Indentured Servants, 1721

Family and Household	White settlers		Company indentured servants	
	N	%	N	%
Solitaries				
Single men	27	44.3	30	62.5
Single women	0	0.0	3	6.3
Widows	1	1.6	0	0.0
Households Without a Family Structure				
Two male relatives	2	3.3	0	0.0
Two male associates	1	1.6	0	0.0
Simple Family Households				
Couples	15	24.6	8	16.7
Couples with children	13	21.3	6	12.5
Married women with children	0	0.0	1	2.1
Widows with children	2	3.3	0	0.0
Total	61	100.0	48	100.0

Source: "Recensement des habitants et concessionnaires de La Nouvelle-Orléans ..."
1721, ANOM COL G1 464.
Note: The different types of family units are those established by Peter Laslett. See Laslett, "La famille et le ménage: Approches historiques," XXVII, "Famille et société," special issue, *Annales: Économies, Sociétés, Civilisations* (1972), 847–872; and Laslett, "Introduction: The History of the Family," in Laslett, ed., with Richard Wall, *Household and Family in Past Time: Comparative Studies in the Size and Structure of the Domestic Group over the Last Three Centuries in England, France, Serbia, Japan, and Colonial North America* ... (Cambridge, 1972), 31. The table does not include data regarding the indentured servants, domestics, and slaves living within households.

those of status (master, indentured servant, or slave) and race (white or black). The way these categories were conflated with one another evolved over time. The 1726 and 1727 censuses draw a line between masters, on the one hand, and indentured servants and slaves, on the other. They only provided nominal information on independent white men in the first column. Most of the residential units included only one white man, whether single or married, but a few were composed of several white men. When one of the independent white men was married, the column also described in

TABLE 4. Family and Household for Whites Categorized and Counted as "Masters," 1726

Family and Household	N	%
Solitaries	55	23.6
Single men	50	
Single women	5	
Households Without a Family Structure	16	6.9
Two brothers	2	
Two or more unrelated men (a craftsman with a lodger; a sword or pen officer and his employee; or two or several men sharing the same profession)	14	
Simple Family Households	153	65.7
Couples	51	
Couples with children	76	
Married women	2	
Married women with children	2	
Unmarried women with children	4	
Widows with children	9	
Couples with or without children and one unrelated man (probably a lodger)	9	
Extended Family Household	4	1.7
Couples with children and another relative (in-laws or siblings)	4	
Multiple Family Households	2	0.9
Widows with married daughters and son-in-laws	1	
Men (probably widowers) with daughter-in-laws	1	
Households with an Indeterminate Composition	3	1.3
Couples with one unrelated widow	1	
Men (probably widowers) with children and one unrelated man	1	
Single man with his nephew and his secretary	1	

Source: "Recensement général des habitations et habitants de la colonie de la Louisiane ainsi qu'ils se sont nommés au 1er janvier 1726," ANOM COL G1 464.

Note: The different types of family units are those established by Peter Laslett. See Laslett, "La famille et le ménage: Approches historiques," XXVII, "Famille et société," special issue, Annales: Économies, Sociétés, Civilisations (1972), 847–872; and Laslett, "Introduction: The History of the Family," in Laslett, ed., with Richard Wall, Household and Family in Past Time: Comparative Studies in the Size and Structure of the Domestic Group over the Last Three Centuries in England, France, Serbia, Japan, and Colonial North America … (Cambridge, 1972), 31. The households related to the hospital and the Capuchins have been excluded.

detail his relationships with the rest of the family members. For instance, in 1727, "Pierre Thomelin, a joiner his wife and two children" were mentioned as living on Chartres Street. This mode of presentation clearly distinguished the white and independent members of households: instead of being reduced to statistics like indentured servants and slaves, white family members were individualized and characterized by their relationships to their heads of household. The Superior Council's clerk who compiled the data seems to have tried to retain the detailed information he received from statements about the composition of households and property while synthesizing the data in a table.[16]

The 1726 and 1727 censuses placed an emphasis on the household, not so much as a family in the sense of a group of blood relatives, but as a unit of economic production and social control whose members held different positions according to their status as property holders and employers or laborers. Whereas the first column of these censuses listed the "names of the habitants," the following ones simply counted "masters," "indentured servants or domestics," "negro slaves," and "native slaves." The column related to "masters" was not divided by age and gender according to "men," "women," and "children," as in the 1721 census. It is not surprising that such innovations were introduced in the 1726 census. Three years after Louisiana's slave trade with Africa resumed, the Company of the Indies was increasingly intent on replacing white laborers with slaves. Its main preoccupation no longer seemed to be the peopling of the colony by white settlers and the natural increase of the white population but the economic development of the colony through the expansion of the slave system. Even as early as 1721, commandants had been ordered to take annual censuses "distinguishing ages and sexes, the French and Whites, from the Indian and Negro slaves." Likewise, in its 1724 ruling regarding censuses, the Superior Council had recalled that on several previous occasions it had asked colonists "to provide a signed statement of the number of free persons and slaves who compose their families." These injunctions only partially materialized in the 1726 and 1727 censuses: mastery still prevailed over whiteness, as a distinction was made between white independent settlers and indentured servants. It took local authorities a few more years to make the fault line between freedom and slavery the most important principle organizing and dividing society and households.[17]

16. "Recensement général ... de la Nouvelle Orléans ... au 1er juillet 1727," ANOM COL G1 464.

17. "Recensement général ... au premier janvier 1726," ANOM COL G1 464, "Re-

The 1732 census was a mixture of the methods used to represent the white population in the 1721 census and that of the 1726 and 1727 censuses while also introducing original data. The first column innovated by listing the names of homeowners. The second column, devoted to the "names of the *bourgeois* [urban dwellers who owned or rented houses] and of those who lived with them," did not systematically specify the nature of the relationships between the various white members of households, but it did name every adult, even the wives and sometimes daughters, of elite households. The house owned by Brouet on Royal Street, for example, was made up of Brouet cartwright, Plaisance, and the Widow Sans Chagrin. The subsequent columns provided the total number of "men bearing arms," "women," "children," and "orphans" in each household. The new category devoted to orphans was linked to the Natchez Wars that took place in late 1729. The white adults who were murdered left many children who were split between the Ursulines' convent (for the girls) and urban settlers (for the boys).[18]

Apart from the new column listing orphans, the most important innovation of the 1732 census was the disappearance of the column that counted French indentured servants and domestics separately. This was an effect of the Natchez Wars and the need to assess the number of possible militia men who could be recruited among habitants, workers, and servants. The result of this departure was that indentured servants and domestics were named with other white and independent settlers in the second column. The presentation of the census reveals how common service in the militia companies blurred status and class boundaries among whites and fueled the construction of whiteness.[19]

———

censement général ... de la Nouvelle Orléans ... au 1er juillet 1727." For early company rulings about censuses establishing a line between free and enslaved people, see "Règlement sur la régie des affaires de la Louisiane ... ," Sept. 5, 1721, ANOM COL C13A 6, fols. 196–236; and "Arrêt du Conseil supérieur de la Louisiane du 10 juin 1724 concernant les recensements," ANOM COL A 23, fol. 48v. Two years later, the Superior Council also ordered settlers to elect a *syndic* (a person chosen to represent a community, here the habitants, and take care of their collective rights and obligations) whose functions were all related to the management of slaves. Among other tasks, the syndic had, "when the need arises, to take the necessary censuses to record the number of slaves and more generally everything related to the public good." See "Arrêt du Conseil supérieur de la Louisiane du 5 octobre 1726 qui enjoint aux habitants de s'assembler pour élire un syndic pour leurs affaires générales," ANOM COL A 23, fol. 80.

18. "Recensement général de la ville de la Nvelle Orléans ... fait au mois de janvier 1732," ANOM COL G1 464.

19. In two of the copies made of the 1721 census, the summary, located at the end

"The Mulatto of the House"

After 1732, the local government presented New Orleans (and more generally Louisiana) as primarily a slave society. Censuses reflected not only a rise in the proportion of legal dependents within households in comparison with the metropole but also of slaves among these dependents. Slaves were included in more than 40 percent of households in 1732, accounting for 28.9 percent of the population. Local authorities used the census taken that year to try to persuade the king to favor the slave trade from Africa to Louisiana. In 1744, Governor Pierre de Rigaud de Vaudreuil de Cavagnal and Commissaire-ordonnateur Edmé Gatien Salmon probably had the same motivation when they asked the settlers to make declarations about "the number of slaves, white or black, livestock, arpents of land, arms, munitions and provisions of the country that they currently possess." No census for 1744 has survived in the archives, but the next remaining census from 1763 also concentrated on slaves, who were present in more than half of the city's households, making up as much as 45.4 percent of the urban population. Although other sources testify to the lasting demographic and economic importance of white indentured servants and domestics, they became invisible in censuses. Likewise, white lodgers ceased to be mentioned. With a focus on slavery and race, the 1763 census greatly simplified the composition of households with respect to their white components. The "heads of family" who represented these households ruled over people who, according to the census, seemed to be either part of the head of household's white nuclear family or part of the enslaved or free laborers of African, Native American, or mixed descent who served him or her.[20]

---

of the document after the table and presenting the total numbers for each category, had already combined the number of "men" and "French domestics" (presented in two distinct columns in the table). By naming this new category "men both masters and domestics," they created a category counting all white men, whatever their status as habitants or indentured servants and domestics, without using a racial label. See "Recensement des habitants et concessionnaires de La Nouvelle-Orléans …," 1721, ANOM COL G1 464.

20. On the importance of slaves among dependents in North America, see Carole Shammas, "Anglo-American Household Government in Comparative Perspective," *William and Mary Quarterly*, 3d Ser., LII (1995), 104–144, esp. 121–128. For the use of the 1732 census to convince the king to renew the international slave trade, see Périer and Salmon to the minister of the navy, Jan. 19, 1732, ANOM COL C13A 14, fols. 168–169. The expression "white slaves" in the 1744 ordinance is confusing and must be a mistake. See "Ordonnance de Messieurs Vaudreuil et Salmon du 13 juin 1744 pour les recensements," ANOM COL A 23, fol. 148v. For the 1763 census, see "Recensement général fait à La Nouvelle-Orléans … au mois de septembre 1763," AGI, Audiencia de Sto Domingo, Luisiana y Florida, Años 1766 a 1770, 2595–589.

As in mainland British America, "The population most affected by the expansion of Euro-American household authority were Africans ... and descendants of these forced immigrants." Not only did the number of slaves rise, but the way they were integrated into households set them apart. In the first censuses taken during the 1720s, slaves were distinguished solely according to their ethnic origins. The documents counted them in columns of "negro slaves" and "native slaves," with indigenous slaves always enumerated after those of African descent. Enslaved Africans and Native Americans were not viewed and valued in the same way by local authorities and settlers. Besides ethnicity, censuses also began to sort slaves according to gender, age, and race from 1732 onward. Columns for various racial categories came to include: *"nègres"* ("negroes"), *"négresses"* ("negresses"), *"négrittes ou négrillons"* ("female or male pickaninnies") *"sauvages"* ("male savages," or Native men and boys), *"sauvagesses"* ("female savages," or Native women and girls), and *"mulâtres ou mûlatresses"* ("mulattoes or mulattresses"). Given the partial cessation of the slave trade after the colony reverted to the crown, local authorities started to pay attention to enslaved children as well, for they were anxious to see the slave population of African descent experience some natural growth. Yet they did not show the same concern for slaves of Native parentage. Likewise, the census did not add a column to enumerate the offspring of mixed couples of European and Native descent, whereas sacramental records reveal that enslaved *"métis"* infants were born and categorized as such when they were baptized. Most probably died while very young, and those who survived were not seen as a problem.[21]

Unlike unions between individuals of European and Native American descent, the rise of *métissage* between people of European and African descent worried local authorities, who began to measure its progression in censuses as well as in sacramental records. A by-product of the introduction of a new column for "mulâtres ou mulâtresses" was that it was impossible

21. Shammas, "Anglo-American Household Government in Comparative Perspective," *William and Mary Quarterly*, LII (1995), 122. For the ethnic and racial categorization of slaves, see "Recensement général ... au premier janvier 1726," ANOM COL G1 464, "Recensement général ... de la Nouvelle Orléans ... au 1er juillet 1727," and "Recensement général de la ville de la Nvelle Orléans ... fait au mois de janvier 1732." The natural increase of the slave population of African descent was already a preoccupation of local authorities in 1724. They asked settlers to make declarations about their "slaves, old and young." See "Arrêt du Conseil supérieur de la Louisiane du 10 juin 1724 concernant les recensements," ANOM COL A 23, fol. 48v.

"The Mulatto of the House"

to presume that the recorded slaves within any particular household maintained kin connections with one another, as was the case for most whites. Slave families were a reality that censuses deliberately chose to ignore. Since enslaved persons were reduced to property, they were never named, and they were counted in a column between the free, white members of households and the property owner's animals. At the same time, the column "mulâtres ou mulâtresses" highlighted that slaves could be born out of interracial and illegitimate sexual relations. On the one hand, the way censuses presented the various categories of household members tended to create a strong divide between whites and slaves; on the other, they acknowledged that racial boundaries were crossed, while trying to closely associate slaves categorized either as "negro" or "mulatto."

"Free negroes" were also first acknowledged in the 1732 census. The document identified some free men and women of color in the general list of householders, but it did not include a specific column under which to count this population. Although a separate column for "free negroes" had been introduced in the censuses of the French Antilles in the late seventeenth century in the midst of a debate about extending the discriminative capitation on slaves to free people of color, the reason for this innovation in New Orleans is to be found in the military context. During the Natchez Wars, officials manumitted a few slaves who had supported the French against the Natchez. For the first time, they also thought of creating a free colored militia company. They did not immediately act on the idea, but the conflict gave local authorities and settlers a new racial consciousness that profoundly shaped the sociopolitical and administrative culture. State representatives began to consider free blacks as a group that could be socially engineered in the service of colonial policy. Consequently, free men and women of African descent might have been less reluctant to establish an administrative existence and to willingly offer declarations about their household and property to the troop commissioner.[22]

After the 1730s, Lower Louisiana's population was not counted again until 1763. The long-awaited 1763 census introduced one new category to count "freed people," divided into four columns. Whereas columns for slaves had to do with age, gender, ethnicity, and race—with a distinction made between "negroes," "mulattoes," and "natives"—those for "freed people"

22. Recensement général de la ville de la Nvelle Orléans ... fait au mois de janvier 1732," ANOM COL G1 464. For the creation of a category listing free blacks in Martinique's censuses, see Léo Élisabeth, *La société martiniquaise aux XVIIe et XVIIIe siècles, 1664-1789* (Paris, 2003), 246-252.

concerned only "negro" men, women, boys, and girls. Only one location covered by the census, a small outpost downriver from New Orleans called the English Turn, distinguished between freed "negroes" and "mulattoes." But, even when there was no specific column for freed "mulattoes," the census taker still noted whether a person was a freed "mulatto" in the column listing "negroes" according to age and gender. Although the racial categories reveal a preoccupation with métissage, the expression used to designate the group was not "free mulattoes and negroes" but generally "freed people" *("affranchis")*, and, in one case, at the English Turn, "free negroes and freedmen." Moreover, the columns related to "freed people" occupied the next to last position in the census, after those related to slaves and before that devoted to cattle. This collective designation as "freed," even when they had been born free, and the position of the columns pertaining to free blacks within the table reinforced the barrier between them and whites, not only along the color line but with regard to the servile stain that allegedly remained with them well into the first generation after they achieved their freedom. Likewise, from the 1770s in Saint-Domingue, free people of color were often called freedmen or freedwomen, even when they were born free.[23]

The free blacks who were counted in the 1763 and 1766 censuses were either listed as independent heads of household or as members of white households. Except for one man named Jean, those mentioned as heads of household in New Orleans were all women. They numbered three in 1763 and six in 1766. More free blacks were very likely living on their own in the Louisiana capital, but they might have been less familiar with the militia captain of their urban district. As nonwhite and in many cases female members of the community, they would not have had much contact with this military institution and could have been much more reluctant than whites to make a statement about the composition of their households and property. Additionally, in the 1763 census, nine households headed by white settlers included one or two freed men or women, four in New Orleans, two at the English Turn, two below the city, and one in the Chapitoulas district. Most freed men or women were probably too poor and economically insecure to live on their own immediately after having obtained their freedom.

23. "Recensement général fait à La Nouvelle-Orléans … au mois de septembre 1763," AGI, Audiencia de Sto Domingo, Luisiana y Florida, Años 1766 a 1770, 2595—589. For the use of the expression "freed people" in Saint-Domingue's censuses, see John D. Garrigus, *Before Haiti: Race and Citizenship in French Saint-Domingue* (New York, 2006), 4, 167, 170.

"The Mulatto of the House"

Their daily lives and fates remained necessarily entwined with those of their former owners.

Given the small number of free blacks included in New Orleans's 1763 census, it is not clear why the state representatives felt the need to count them separately or to constitute them as a special group to administer. All in all, out of an urban population of 2,460 inhabitants, only 19 free blacks were enumerated (6 men, 8 women, 3 boys, and 2 girls). Apart from 19 freed persons of African descent, 1,305 whites, 1,099 slaves of African descent, and 37 Native American slaves also lived in the city. Once again, local authorities' primary motivation in counting them probably had to do with military matters. It was during the Seven Years' War that the first permanent free colored militia company, based at the English Turn, was created.[24]

Another reason the colonial government might have felt compelled to count free blacks separately might have had to do with the control of the frontier between freedom and slavery. Local authorities were highly preoccupied by this problem in the Antilles, and their efforts to impede the growth of the free population of color in the islands might help to explain why so few free blacks appear in Louisiana's censuses. Caribbean officials tried to counteract the illicit integration of those who were called *libres de fait* or *libres de savane* within the group of free people of color. These "libres de fait," "libres de savane," or *"soi-disant libres"* (quasi free) were former slaves who lived as if they were free without having been freed officially. They could be runaway slaves passing as free people of color or slaves who had received their certificate of manumission from their masters but whose manumission tax, which had become mandatory in 1745, had not been paid or whose freedom had not been confirmed by the governor and the *intendant* (the second most important official). In 1758, in the context of a slave rebellion, the Superior Council of Cap-Français began ordering free people of color to present their manumission papers to a specially appointed pen officer within a three-month period and threatened that those who did not would be sold as slaves. The governor and intendant of Martinique did the same in 1761.[25]

24. The areas with "concentrations" of free people of color in Louisiana were at the English Turn and Chapitoulas. The former location's population of 544 inhabitants was made up of 125 whites, 381 slaves of African descent, and 38 freed persons of African descent while the latter's population of 1,181 inhabitants included 150 whites, 1,005 slaves of African descent, and 26 freed persons of African descent. There is a mistake in the report of the number of freed women at the English Turn in the 1763 census's final summary: 34 instead of 38, as listed in the table.

25. On the status of the so-called quasi free in the Antilles, see Bernard Moitt, "In

Such an ordinance requiring free blacks to register their manumission papers with local authorities was never promulgated in French New Orleans, but a comparison between the 1763 and 1766 censuses and four lists of free people of color drawn up in 1770 by the Spanish governor Alejandro O'Reilly suggests that the status of quasi free also constituted an important social reality in the Louisiana capital. At least two men, Charles d'Erneville and Noël Carrière, were listed respectively in the 1770 "roll of the free mulattoes of New Orleans" and "list of free negroes . . . in New Orleans," even though the reconstitution of their lives over the French and Spanish periods demonstrates that they had not yet, in fact, been officially manumitted by that time. Instead, their masters let them live as libres de fait. Very likely, this situation was shared by many other men listed in 1770. Their masters probably did not seek to obtain formal approval of their manumission from the colonial administration because these slaves might have redeemed themselves, a practice forbidden by law. They were not declared in censuses for obvious reasons. Such a situation also existed in the Antilles. Article 7 of the 1786 ordinance on censuses in those islands dealt with the failure of census takers to include "libres de fait," often owing to the complicity of their *"patrons,"* as former masters were called.[26]

------

the Shadow of the Plantation: Women of Color and the *Libres de fait* of Martinique and Guadeloupe, 1685–1848," in David Barry Gaspar and Darlene Clark Hine, eds., *Beyond Bondage: Free Women of Color in the Americas* (Urbana, Ill., 2004), 37–59; and Dominique Rogers, "Statu Liberis: Une condition intermédiaire dans les Antilles françaises esclavagistes (XVIIe–XVIIIe siècles)," unpublished paper, conference on "Cadre juridique et pratiques locales de l'esclavage du XIVe au XIXe siècle," University Cheikh Anta Diop, Dakar, Senegal, April 2010. For the Caribbean rulings ordering free people of color to record their freedom papers, see Auguste Lebeau, *De la condition des gens de couleur libres sous l'Ancien Régime: D'après des documents des Archives coloniales* (Paris, 1903), 61–62; and Garrigus, *Before Haiti*, 167.

26. "État des mulâtres et nègres libres," 1770, AGI, Correspondencia de los Gobernadores de la Luisiana y la Florida Occidental, Años 1766–1824, Session Papeles de Cuba, legajo 188-A, "Liste des nègres libres établis tant à quatre lieues de cette ville en remontant le fleuve, que ceux de la ville dénommés cy-après comme suit," 1770, "Rôle des mulâtres libres de La Nouvelle-Orléans," 1770, "Liste de la qualité des nègres libres de La Nouvelle-Orléans fait par moi Nicolas Bacus capitaine moraine," 1770. On Charles d'Erneville, see Kimberley S. Hanger, *Bounded Lives, Bounded Places: Free Black Society in Colonial New Orleans, 1769–1803* (Durham, N.C., 1997), 65; and Spear, *Race, Sex, and Social Order in Early New Orleans*, 82–84, 89. On Noël Carrière, see Emily Clark, *The Strange History of the American Quadroon: Free Women of Color in the Revolutionary Atlantic World* (Chapel Hill, N.C., 2013), 74–84. For the 1786 ordinance on censuses in Martinique, see Élisabeth, *La société martiniquaise aux XVIIe et XVIIIe siècles*, 431–432.

"The Mulatto of the House"

Because of the importance of libres de fait in Louisiana at the end of the French regime, it is impossible to measure the size of the population of free blacks accurately. Whatever the exact number of free people of African descent, many of them still lived with their former masters. For the most part, within the city, domestic households headed by white settlers were the privileged sites of negotiation over the boundaries between freedom and slavery.[27]

PATRIARCHAL SLAVEHOLDERS, THEIR KIN, AND THEIR DEPENDENTS

In most cases, New Orleans households were governed by their male heads. As in the metropole and other colonies, men enjoyed a wide degree of latitude in the exercise of their patriarchal authority, including recourse to violence toward their kin and dependents. But the threat of physical force was not the only dynamic that governed relationships within households. The need for mutual support not only held white couples together but also generations of white relatives within and between households. Aging parents of some means were less dependent on their children than in the metropole, however, since they could rely on slaves to take care of them in their old age. As a result, some domestic slaves were set free on the condition that their manumission would not take effect until the death of their owners. Besides solidarity among white kin, gratitude was sometimes felt and expressed by settlers toward some of their domestic slaves. Urban households fostered intimate relationships that allowed a few enslaved laborers to obtain their freedom but were not devoid of ambiguity. Still, these demonstrations of personal feeling should not be overinterpreted. Even as masters negotiated the conditions of manumission with favorite slaves, they sought to maintain control; when negotiations over manumission did not suffice, they did not hesitate to employ coercion.[28]

Violence among all household members, white and black, should not be minimized, but practices of punishment contributed to racially distin-

27. For other points of view on the evaluation of the number of free blacks, see Hanger, *Bounded Lives, Bounded Places*, 113–114; Thomas N. Ingersoll, *Mammon and Manon in Early New Orleans: The First Slave Society in the Deep South, 1718–1819* (Knoxville, Tenn., 1999), 137–138; Dawdy, *Building the Devil's Empire*, 178–179; and Spear, *Race, Sex, and Social Order in Early New Orleans*, 96–97.

28. Household violence might have also been a sign of the fragility of patriarchal authority. See Joanne Bailey, *Unquiet Lives: Marriage and Marriage Breakdown in England, 1660–1800* (Cambridge, 2003), 112–114.

guish slaves from kin and other dependents. This difference becomes espe-cially evident in the court records. White wives could obtain assistance from relatives, friends, and neighbors as well as local ecclesiastical and state au-thorities, and they sought separations of person and property before the Superior Council. These judicial procedures attest that the power of male heads of households was never absolute and that white women were able to negotiate their positions and fates to some extent. In contrast, slaves had much less leverage to defend themselves. Violence against urban slaves is almost invisible because, in practice, they had no judicial recourse against abuse from their masters. They faced a universal and systemic violence, whereas conjugal violence against white spouses remained contingent albeit frequent. In addition, slaves were confronted not only with the au-thority of the household head but also with possible violence from all white members of the household of which they were a part. Furthermore, people of African descent who obtained their freedom remained vulnerable, too, since most of them continued to live for years with their former owners and were caught in relationships of patronage and dependency.

Domestic Slavery: Intimacy, Negotiations, and Dependency

Owing to spatial proximity, masters and slaves in urban households lived in greater intimacy than those on plantations. With the exception of those slaves serving as domestics, segregation more clearly prevailed on the latter. Plantation slave quarters were composed of a more or less greater number of cabins at a distance from the master's or overseer's house. These dwell-ings sometimes formed a camp that was enclosed by a fence. That was, in particular, the case on the Company of the Indies's and, later, the king's plantation. In the city, the situation was rather different. Some slaves lived in their own cabins at the back of urban parcels or slept in the kitchen, which was built outside the main house because of the risk of fire. Others were lodged in their master's house. They probably bedded down in the main room or in a corridor on a mattress unrolled for the night, as in the Antilles. Some young female slaves might have slept in one of the house's bedrooms or even in their master's bedroom.[29]

29. For slaves' lodging on plantations, see [Antoine-Simon] Le Page du Pratz, *His-toire de la Louisiane* ..., 3 vols. (Paris, 1758), I, 341, III, 227; Shannon Lee Dawdy, "Proper Caresses and Prudent Distance: A How-To Manual from Colonial Louisiana," in Ann Laura Stoler, ed., *Haunted by Empire: Geographies of Intimacy in North American History* (Durham, N.C., 2006), 140–162; and Gilles-Antoine Langlois, "De la case au grenier: Bref aperçu des habitats ruraux des 'nègres' et des maîtres dans la Louisiane

"The Mulatto of the House"

The kind of labor urban slaves performed also fostered intimacy. Many served as domestics, and they attended to all the basic physical needs of their masters: eating, dressing, washing, making beds, changing linens, and so on. This situation could create close personal relationships. If owners were satisfied with the service provided by their slaves, some individuals could work in their domestic capacities for long periods of time. The officer Joseph Delfau de Pontalba was so pleased with the slave he hired out to help him move and cook for him at twenty livres a month that he wanted to buy him and take him to France.[30]

Enslaved women who served as wet nurses occupied particularly intimate positions within their master's households. Originally, settlers resorted to white women to nurse their children, but they quickly turned to enslaved women, despite the belief that their milk was impure. In the subsequent debate about wet nursing that developed among the colonial elite, on the model of the one that existed on wet nurses in the metropole, Antoine-Simon Le Page du Pratz condemned couples, mothers especially, who put their children in the care of black nurses:

From what I have said, I conclude that a French father and his wife are great enemies to their posterity when they give their children such nurses. For the milk being the purest blood of the woman, one must be a step-mother indeed to give her child to a negro nurse in such a country as Louisiana, where the mother has all conveniences of being served, of accommodating and carrying their children, who by that

---

coloniale des années 1720–1740," *In Situ: Revue des patrimoines*, XXI (2013), http://insitu.revues.org/11893. For the lodging of urban slaves, see NONA Feb. 26, 1765 ("building used by domestics"), Jan. 31, 1766 ("lodging for domestics" near the kitchen); and RSCL 1752/06/13/01, 1764/07/14/01, 1764/09/04/01. The drawing that Dumont de Montigny made of his house in New Orleans shows a building on the front side of the lot that was, according to the caption, the "kitchen and house for the Negroes." See Jean M. Farnsworth and Ann M. Masson, eds., *The Architecture of Colonial Louisiana: Collected Essays of Samuel Wilson, Jr., F.A.I.A.* (Lafayette, La., 1987), 105–107. When interrogating a slave named Jassemin during the trial of another slave who had run away, a judge asked Jassemin if he had housed César in his cabin, and the former replied in the negative, explaining that "his mistress did not have a kitchen and that he slept within the house where his mistress sleeps." See RSCL 1764/07/10/03. For other evidence on slaves' lodgings, see RSCL 1748/06/10/03; 1764/07/08/01. For slaves' sleeping arrangements in the Antilles, see Anne Pérotin-Dumon, *La ville aux îles, la ville dans l'île: Basse-Terre et Pointe-à-Pitre, Guadeloupe, 1650–1820* (Paris, 2000), 464.

30. "Declaration in Registry," Aug. 23, 1736, in Heloise H. Cruzat, ed., "RSCL XVII: Supplement Index, no. 4," *LHQ*, VIII (1925), 491.

means may be always under their eyes. The mother then has nothing else to do but to give the breast to her child.

He argued that white infants could be looked after by black slaves but that their mothers should nurse them to avoid contamination from the milk of women of African descent, which was thought to play the same role as blood. If it was impossible to do without a black nurse, he recommended couples use Senegalese women who had, among all the "negroes," the "purest blood." Despite these racist condemnations, the practice of resorting to black nurses did not cease.[31]

Wet nurses could appear as privileged slaves at first sight, but they sometimes had to pay a high price for their position. In 1737, Dame Chamilly lodged a complaint with the Superior Council because a planter named Chaperon had hired out an enslaved woman from the estate of the deceased Jacques Larché to serve as a wet nurse for Dame Grandpré, Dame Chamilly's daughter. Apparently, Chaperon prevented the slave from taking care of her own infant, who was fifteen months old. A doctor's certificate testified to the baby's poor health because he was not well looked after. Other wet nurses, however, seem to have been treated with more gratitude. In 1737, the councillor François Trudeau requested confirmation of the freedom he had given to his "negress" Jeanneton, "whom he bought from Sieur Graveline 23 years ago, she has always served him with zeal and loyalty, as she breast-fed four of his children." There was, nevertheless, a condition to the manumission: Jeanneton was to serve him until his death. Such caveats often appeared when freedom was granted in wills. They allowed owners to benefit from their slaves' labor and ensured that the latter would take care of them in their old age.[32]

As with wet nurses, masters sometimes decided to reward their domestics with their freedom. In 1735, Governor Bienville manumitted a couple named Jorge and Marie "in recognition of good and faithful services for 26

31. For evidence of the existence of wet nurses of European descent, see ANOM COL G1 412, Burials, 10/14/1727; and ANOM COL G1 412, fol. 60. For the condemnation of the practice of resorting to black wet-nurses, see *The History of Louisiana, or of the Western Parts of Virginia and Carolina ... Translated from the French of M. Le Page Du Pratz ...*, new ed. (London, 1774), 362–363, 382–383. See also [Jean-Bernard] Bossu, *Nouveaux voyages aux Indes occidentales ...*, 2 vols. (Paris, 1768), I, 201–202.

32. For Chaperon's trial, see RSCL 1737/03/08/01, 1737/03/08/02. For a case of manumission of a black wet nurse, see RSCL 1737/07/11/01. See also Dumont de Montigny, *Regards sur le monde atlantique, 1715–1747*, transcribed by Carla Zecher (Sillery, Québec, 2008), 289.

"The Mulatto of the House"

years." It is difficult to guess the true nature of the relationship that was behind such language and to evaluate the number of domestic slaves who were freed. Sexual partners and mixed children were often freed on the premise of "good service." The majority of manumissions might have been of the latter kind. Additionally, gratitude was not always the main or only impetus that prompted owners to free their slaves. For some masters, negotiations over freedom, sometimes conducted over years, constituted "an incentive or mechanism of social control."[33]

The case of St. Louis, an enslaved domestic who belonged to Jean-Charles de Pradel, testifies to the lengthy negotiations over freedom that some enslaved individuals had to endure. St. Louis alias La Nuit (The Night) was one of the few slaves whom the former military officer mentioned by name in his letters to his family in France, the first time being in 1755. Pradel considered him his right-hand slave on his plantation located across from New Orleans, on the other side of the Mississippi River. Every day at dawn, the planter sent St. Louis to the city to make purchases. But he realized that his slave took advantage of the situation to leave early, during the night, to dance and give meals to urban slaves and free people of color with sheep and poultry he stole from Pradel. According to Pradel's commentary in a letter to his brother, St. Louis could "behave as a little master" among the people of African descent in the city. Without whipping his faulty laborer or saying a word to him, the slaveowner decided to punish him by sending him to work on his plantation. After two and a half years, however, Pradel started to occasionally use St. Louis as a cook, which allowed the slave "to pay his respects" to his master. Sometime between 1755 and 1763, St. Louis came back into favor. In 1763, Pradel decided to free him. St. Louis was then in his mid-thirties. This decision was apparently the result of a complex interpersonal relationship consisting of coercion and violence but also trust, respect, and even some kind of affection that was worked out over the space of many years.[34]

Yet manumission did not put an end to the ambiguous relationship between Pradel and St. Louis. The slaveholder's sense of ownership did not disappear when he set St. Louis free: he wrote to his brother about "my freed man." This dynamic created another kind of obligation between the

33. RSCL 1735/06/04/01, 1735/06/04/02; Robin Blackburn, "Introduction," in Rosemary Brana-Shute and Randy J. Sparks, eds., *Paths to Freedom: Manumission in the Atlantic World* (Columbia, S.C., 2009), 1–13 (quotation, 5).

34. Jean-Charles de Pradel to his brother, Apr. 10, 1755, HNOC, MSS 589, Chevalier de Pradel Papers, 62.

two men. Pradel also reported in his letters that St. Louis wanted to assure him that "although he had his freedom he is much too grateful for all the kindness I showed him during his slavery to abandon me at a time when I have need of his help." St. Louis then served as Pradel's overseer and purchasing agent. Although the relationship between Pradel and St. Louis seems to have evolved in a more balanced way, it is impossible to know if St. Louis really experienced the feelings his former master said he did or only bore a mask of obedience and deference.[35]

A few months after Pradel's death, St. Louis still remained in the family's service. Pradel's daughter-in-law, who did not know St. Louis personally but had heard a lot about him from her husband, wrote from France to recommend the former slave to the newly appointed general director Jean-Jacques Blaise d'Abbadie (he acted as a governor but did not hold the title), asking him to offer him a present and to assure him that if he wanted to come to France she would help him secure a position. In 1765–1766, the widow Pradel sent St. Louis to the metropole on a mission to convince her two daughters to come back to Louisiana to marry. In her letters, she describes "la Nuit" as a "man one can trust, if only one can have trust in this skin . . . ." The inclusion of St. Louis within the planter's small family circle was not totally devoid of suspicion and mistrust; an affectionate and intimate relationship could not completely overcome racial prejudice. The former slave eventually came back to New Orleans, but it took him a few more years to become economically independent, presumably thanks to his wages and possible donations from his master's family. It was only in the early 1770s, when St. Louis was in his early forties, that he finally became a property holder, owning both slaves and land. His life history testifies to the many twists and turns black men could face on the path to freedom and economic independence. Even though a minority of urban slaves achieved freedom after a long process full of pitfalls, violence remained a daily experience that most shared.[36]

35. Pradel to his brother, Oct. 26, 1763, HNOC, MSS 589, Chevalier de Pradel Papers, 72. On slave psychology, see Alex Bontemps, *The Punished Self: Surviving Slavery in the Colonial South* (Ithaca, N.Y., 2008), 137–179; and Bertram Wyatt-Brown, "The Mask of Obedience: Male Slave Psychology in the Old South," *American Historical Review*, XCIII (1988), 1228–1252.

36. A "negro" named La Nuit is mentioned as having been granted his freedom at the top of the list of ninety-seven slaves who lived on Pradel's plantation that was included in his probate record. See NONA Kernion, Mar. 30, 1764. For Pradel's daughter-in-law's letter, see Melle Cacqueray de Pradel to her uncle, Sept. 5, 1764, HNOC, MS 589, Chevalier de Pradel Papers, 153. For Pradel's widow's letters, see Mrs. Pradel to her brother-in-

Domestic Violence: Helpless Slaves and Protected Wives

Physical violence was commonplace for urban slaves. An enquiry conducted by the Superior Council to collect testimonies from people who had complaints against the first Spanish governor Antonio de Ulloa during the 1768 revolt strongly hints at the ubiquity of violence toward the enslaved within New Orleans. René Gabriel Fazende, a navy scrivener born in the colony, reported that, when "he [Fazende] had a negress whipped at his place, Aubry [the French commandant] asked him to come and see him and told him to whip his negroes further away since Lady Ulloa fainted, and Ulloa said that he would jail all those who had their negroes whipped, especially next to his place. Since then he [Fazende] has been forced to have his domestics chastised two leagues from here, which causes him great inconvenience." Ulloa and his wife's reaction to the corporal punishment of slaves was typical of a new sensitivity to and condemnation of harsh violence in public that would fuel the abolitionist movements in Europe. At the same time, the Spanish governor's prohibition of all whippings and the use of the plural by Fazende to speak of the punishment of his domestic slaves can be regarded as evidence of a different relation to violence locally. Urban slaves do not seem to have been spared from mistreatments. Likewise, the prohibition of whipping slaves in the streets promulgated by the judge of police in Cap-Français in 1763 was not motivated by a desire to restrict violence but by the need to maintain public order. The ordinance testifies to the same prevalence of violence against the enslaved in Saint-Domingue's main port city.[37]

The way urban slaves were treated in New Orleans was very likely influ-

law, Aug. 12, 1765, HNOC, MSS 589, Chevalier de Pradel Papers, 139, Mrs. Pradel to her brother-in-law, Sept. 30, 1765, 141, and Mrs. Pradel to her brother-in-law, May 11, 1766, 142 (quotation). For Saint Louis's land and slave deeds, see NONA Almonester Apr. 8, 1771, fols. 59–60; NONA Almonester Apr. 8, 1771, fols. 64–65; NONA Almonester July 20, 1772, fols. 203–205; NONA Almonester Jan. 13, 1774, fols. 8–9; NONA Almonester Apr. 29, 1775, fols. 259–260; NONA Garic May 12, 1777, fols. 207–208; NONA Garic Aug. 22, 1778, fol. 392; NONA Garic Dec. 23, 1774, fols. 244–245; NONA Garic Dec. 16, 1777, fols. 489–490; NONA Garic Apr. 8, 1777, fols. 156–158; and NONA Garic Sept. 15, 1778, fols. 427–428. See also Sylvia R. Frey, "The Free Black Militia of New Orleans in the Mississippi River and Gulf Coast Campaigns of the American Revolution," unpublished paper, Sons of the American Revolution Annual Conference: "Slavery and Liberty: Black Patriots of the American Revolution," Baltimore, Md., June 24–26, 2011.

37. "Procès-verbal d'information contre M. Ulloa," Nov. 8, 1768, ANOM COL C13A 48, fol. 117r. For Saint-Domingue's ordinance, see "Ordonnance du juge de police du Cap, qui défend aux habitants de la même ville de faire fouetter leurs esclaves dans les rues," Mar. 24, 1763, in [Médéric Louis-Élie Moreau] de Saint-Méry, *Loix et constitutions des colonies françoises de l'Amérique sous le vent*, 6 vols. (Paris, 1784–1790), IV, 566.

enced by what happened on nearby plantations. The use of chastisement in slave societies distinguished the colonies from the metropole. Violence within private households, by masters against servants in particular, existed and was accepted in early modern Europe. On plantations, this violence was amplified, intensified, and systematized. Specific forms of corporal punishment were chosen to enforce and display a racial divide and were intended to debase and even dehumanize the enslaved. For example, a planter's manual published in Guadeloupe explained that slaves had to be woken up by a bell and that, after thirty minutes, they had to exit their cabins once the drivers had cracked their whips. Admittedly, the kind of labor that slaves performed in New Orleans did not require the same level of brutality to compel them to follow rapid cadences for long periods of time, but urban slavery also relied on a regime of terror to force enslaved persons to accept their condition.[38]

The complex composition of urban households, which included many people who had no kin relationship with the head of the household, meant that slaves could face abuse at the hands of multiple white individuals, not just their masters. Disputes over who had the right to punish domestic slaves, like the one that took place at the Monsantos', could break out. A similar conflict happened in 1735 at Dame Buffon's. She ran a boarding house for single white men. Because her lodgers kept their own slaves, domestics belonging to several masters lived together. At the end of the day, Théodore Baldic, a surgeon in New Orleans, went back to the house to find his domestic hurt and dripping with blood. The slave "had only bantered" *("n'avait fait que badiner")* with a four-year-old enslaved girl belonging to a white settler named Filand. The word "badiner," which appears recurrently in interrogations and testimonies, meant that they bodily squabbled for fun, though the banter could quickly turn into a fight. Spurred on by the other slaves of the household, who shouted at them, Baldic's slave had seized the little girl's hands, at which point Filand drove a broomstick into his forehead and other parts of his body and kicked him in his ribs and stomach. No one took the trouble to bandage him. Baldic requested that Filand pay him the price of the slave if the latter died. Although various white persons might dispute who had the right to punish certain enslaved

38. [Jean-Baptiste Poyen Sainte-Marie], *De l'exploitation des sucreries, ou conseils d'un vieux planteur aux jeunes agriculteurs des colonies* (Basse-Terre, Guadeloupe, 1792), 52; Cécile Vidal, "Violence, Slavery, and Race in Early English and French America," in Robert Antony, Stuart Carroll, and Caroline Dodds Pennock, eds., *The Cambridge World History of Violence*, III, *AD 1500–AD 1800* (Cambridge, forthcoming 2019).

"The Mulatto of the House"

men and women, slaves themselves had little recourse to contest the violence perpetrated against them. Only slaveowners, not slaves, could turn to justice to obtain reparation, and these cases were prosecuted as civil, not criminal, most of the time.[39]

Trials for the separation of person and property involving white wives and their husbands underscore the prevalence and acceptance of violence in New Orleans's domestic spaces while at the same time reinforcing slaves' relative powerlessness before the law. These cases concerned all social groups, from military officers and surgeons to craftsmen and laborers. Besides insults, women were kicked, beaten, hit with all kinds of tools (sticks, hammers, fire shovels), or burned with irons. This violence was not without a public audience, as the number of witnesses in these trials demonstrates. Sometimes these incidents happened in front of relatives or friends. Neighbors often witnessed this domestic violence, which was hard to ignore. They occasionally intervened, though it is impossible to know how often they did so. Their efforts to help nevertheless indicate that, even if some violence on the part of husbands was usually accepted, there was a limit to it. Extreme violence that maimed and endangered white women was condemned.[40]

White women who experienced domestic abuse had a number of options available to them. Before taking judicial action, they typically sought assistance from a priest or sometimes even the attorney general or commissaire-ordonnateur. They could also take refuge at the Ursulines' convent or with relatives. Starting in the 1740s, the Charity Hospital (also known as the Poor Hospital) was also a possible place of safety for women of the lower sort. Only after a long period of time, when violence was repetitive and reached

39. RSCL 1735/10/31/01.
40. For cases that concerned couples living in New Orleans or abused women who took refuge in the Louisiana capital, see RSCL 1727/07/31/01; 1728/02/15/01, 1728/03/13/01, 1728/03/13/02, 1728/03/13/03, 1728/03/20/01, 1728/04/19/01, 1728/04/27/01, 1728/05/22/04, 1728/05/25/01, 1728/06/16/01, 1728/06/18/01, 1728/06/19/01, 1728/06/22/01, 1728/06/23/01, 1728/07/08/01, 1728/07/09/01, 1728/08/02/01, 1728/08/07/01, 1728/08/07/02, 1728/08/11/01, 1728/08/11/03, 1728/08/12/01, 1728/08/20/01, 1728/08/23/01, 1728/08/28/02, 1728/09/04/01, 1728/09/06/01; 1737/05/16/01; 1743/08/30/01, 1743/09/02/01, 1743/09/07/03, 1743/09/10/04, 1744/07/17/01, 1744/07/31/01, 1746/07/07/02, 1769 ND no. 84 July 7, 1746; 1745/01/30/01; 1745/02/06/01, 1745/02/25/05, 1745/03/06/01, 1745/03/06/03, 1745/03/06/05, 1745/03/06/06, 1745/09/02/01, 1745/10/02/04; 1753/08/04/05; 1769/06/12/02. For a case concerning a woman separated from her husband who was abused by the man who was his curator (person charged with managing her property), see RSCL 1768/05/20/01, 1768/05/24/01, 1768/05/26/05, 1768/08/31/03, 1768/09/03/03, 1768/09/17/01, 1769/01/21/021.

a level that put their health and even lives at risk, did some women resolve to lodge a complaint with the Superior Council.

In terms of the number of cases, the kind of violence, and the response of society and justice, domestic abuse in Louisiana appears similar to what women of European descent experienced in the metropole or in other French colonies. When husbands had to defend themselves before the Superior Council, they either denied the facts or placed the blame on their wives, alleging that they refused to work or to fulfill their conjugal duty. The response of the council was moderate. On occasion, husbands were only admonished after the first complaint, and years passed with the same abuse before a second complaint was lodged and the council agreed to a separation. Trials for separation were always long and required many witnesses. Judges sometimes decided in favor of women, but not always. Instead of the separation of both person and property, diverse compromises were made.[41]

The meaning of domestic abuse trials in Louisiana differed from that of those in the metropole, however, because they took place in the context of a slave society. The interventions of neighbors and trials for separation show that there was a moral economy of physical abuse against white women, with a bottom line not to be crossed when lives were at risk, that had no equivalent with regard to violence against slaves. Although it is impossible to produce figures, not all white women were victims of the extreme violence that most slaves experienced at least once. Abused women very likely represented a minority, and they benefited from a possible window for negotiation that was denied to slaves. Doors open to white women in distress, such as the Capuchins and the Ursulines, did not exist for slaves.

THE HOSPITALS AND CONVENT:
SOCIORELIGIOUS ASSISTANCE, SLAVERY, AND RACE

Although few in number, the male and female missionaries who lived in the Louisiana capital played a crucial role in the lives of the city's residents that was both religious and social. They not only inspired and headed religious life but were also commissioned and financed by the Company of the Indies and later the crown to run the institutions providing medical treatment, education, and social assistance to New Orleans's inhabitants. Under

41. On separations in France and in Canada, see Julie Hardwick, "Seeking Separations: Gender, Marriages, and Household Economies in Early Modern France," *French Historical Studies*, XXI (1998), 157–180; Sylvie Savoie, "Les couples séparés: Les demandes de séparation aux 17e et 18e siècles" in André Lachance, ed., *Les marginaux, les exclus, et l'autre au Canada aux 17e et 18e siècles* ([Ville Saint-Laurent, Quebec], 1996), 245–259, and "Les attentes des épouses et de la société," 260–282.

the supervision of the Capuchins and the Ursulines, the military hospital, the convent, and, later, the Charity Hospital were transformed by racial slavery, even though whites were supposed to be the exclusive beneficiaries of social and medical assistance. Since the company's and, subsequently, the king's allowances were inadequate, the convent and the Charity Hospital partially drew their income from plantations. All these institutions also increasingly relied on slave labor to perform various functions. Yet the presence of slaves within the walls of the convent or the hospitals was not restricted to their employment as laborers. The military hospital treated the company's and, then, the king's slaves, and the convent took in day pupils and a few boarders of Native American or African descent. These residential institutions were multiethnic places where people of various statuses interacted under diverse circumstances that were to a large extent different from those between masters and slaves within domestic households. However, the human, material, and spatial organization of the hospitals and the convent sought to contravene the blurring of racial boundaries that these intimate relationships could have fostered.[42]

The Military Hospital: Interracial Intimacy and Alienation in Sickness

Originally founded by the Company of the Indies to shelter and cure soldiers who were ill, the military hospital, later known as the King's Hospital after the retrocession of the colony to the crown, should have developed as an institution reserved for whites. However, slaves belonging to the company and then the king were also admitted as patients, although in segregated facilities. Black people could nurse and even treat whites as long as they remained slaves, and servicemen interacted with those who nursed, cleaned, and fed them while they were weak and suffering, but black and white bodies could not be mixed when both were reduced to the same condition as patients. Since most soldiers were not slaveholders and slaves do not seem to have worked at the military barracks, the hospital was the only place where they interacted on such intimate terms. New Orleans's hospi-

42. On the Capuchins, see Roger Baudier, *The Catholic Church in Louisiana* (New Orleans, La., 1939), 69–85, 90–99, 117, 152–159; Pierre Hamer, *Raphaël de Luxembourg: Une contribution luxembourgeoise à la colonisation de la Louisiane* (Luxembourg, 1966); Charles Edwards O'Neill, *Church and State in French Colonial Louisiana: Policy and Politics to 1732* (New Haven, Conn., 1966); Claude L. Vogel, *The Capuchins in French Louisiana (1722-1766)* (Washington, D.C., 1928); and Marcel Giraud, *A History of French Louisiana*, V, *The Company of the Indies, 1723-1731*, trans. Brian Pearce (Baton Rouge, La., 1991), 61–84.

tal was also exceptional within the French Empire for its use of an enslaved apothecary and surgeon, who must have saved the lives of many patients. Nevertheless, the intimacy that servicemen and slaves shared within the hospital seems to have had no impact on the conflicting relationships they often maintained outside the medical institution.

The military hospital was one of the first public buildings erected in the Louisiana capital, opening as early as 1722–1723. The Company of the Indies's general rulings of 1720 and 1721 called for the construction of a hospital in each of the colony's main outposts, and the city's swampy environment made such a facility a high priority. Until land for the urban center had been cleared and a drainage system completed, high mortality rates prevailed. Less than ten years later, a new hospital had to be erected. Its opening took place in 1734. Despite the construction of new facilities, each hospital quickly became obsolete, as the buildings fast deteriorated in the subtropical climate and the military population increased with the renewal of imperial wars by midcentury. In 1753, Governor Kerlérec pleaded for yet another expansion of the hospital and the construction of a separate ward for officers. The construction of a large new military hospital with separate facilities for officers and soldiers started in the late 1750s. Although the complex was not entirely finished by the end of the French regime, it was used to lodge some of the troops garrisoned in New Orleans.[43]

43. "Règlement sur la régie des affaires de la colonie de la Louisiane du 5 septembre 1721," ANOM COL C13A 6, fols. 199v–200v; Pierre Le Blond de La Tour, "Plans, profils, et élévations des bâtiments et casernes faits pour la Compagnie depuis le 1er août 1722 jusqu'au 3 janvier de la présente année 1723," Jan. 3, 1723, ANOM COL 4DFC 67A; Le Blond de La Tour to the Company of the Indies, Oct. 21, 1723, ANOM COL C13A 7, fol. 193v; Adrien de Pauger to the Company of the Indies, Feb. 9, 1724, ANOM COL C13A 8, fol. 24; Pauger to the Company of the Indies, June 3, 1725, ANOM COL 8, fols. 251v–252r; Salmon to the minister of the navy, Dec. 8, 1731, ANOM COL C13A 13, fol. 121v; Salmon to the minister of the navy, Mar. 30, 1732, ANOM COL C13A 15, fols. 74–76; Salmon to the minister of the navy, Aug. 12, 1734, ANOM COL C13A 19, fols. 71–73; Salmon to the minister of the navy, Aug. 19, 1734, ANOM COL C13A 19, fols. 78–79r; Bienville and Salmon to the minister of the navy, Aug. 31, 1735, ANOM COL C13A 20, fols. 105–109; Bienville and Salmon to the minister of the navy, June 20, 1736, ANOM COL C13A 21, fols. 62–74r; "Plan d'un bâtiment projeté à faire en aile à l'hôpital de La Nouvelle-Orléans," June 6, 1737, ANOM COL F3 290, fol. 28; Louis Billouart de Kerlérec to the minister of the navy, Apr. 28, 1753, ANOM COL C13A 37, fol. 48rv; Kerlérec to the minister of the navy, Dec. 6 1758, ANOM COL C13A 40, fols. 128–130; Kerlérec to the minister of the navy, Dec. 6, 1758, ANOM COL C13A 40, fols. 131–132r; Vincent-Gaspard-Pierre de Rochemore to the minister of the navy, June 23, 1760, ANOM COL C13A 42, fols. 118v–119r; and "Inven-

"The Mulatto of the House"

The military hospital did not remain devoted solely to soldiers, sailors, and company workers for long. A 1725 ordinance on the "domestic negroes of the Company" ordered the first councillor "to send all who were sick to the hospital where he will devote a separate place from the whites to have them treated." This policy of treating enslaved patients was continued after the retrocession of the colony. According to the contract signed with the Ursulines in 1744, the hospital was supposed to take in "soldiers, bargee officers and sailors, and workers in the king's service, and the negroes belonging to his majesty in this colony, as well as ship crews."[44]

As the company's ordinance on its domestic slaves reveals, segregation and differing levels of care differentiated white and black patients from the start. A separate room must have been reserved for the enslaved in the first hospital. Mattresses and woolen blankets were also used for soldiers, while slaves had to make do with straw mattresses and covers made of dog hair. As the slave trade resumed in 1723 and the number of enslaved captives brought to New Orleans greatly increased, local authorities took measures to put those who arrived sick, needing care before being sold, in a separate hospital within the city. It might have been the building described by Marc-Antoine Caillot: "You will also find two hospitals, which are each 135 feet long and 45 feet wide, each having 25 beds. At the end of the quay you can observe the large quarters (formerly belonging to the deceased Monsieur de La Tour, . . .), which are used today as a hospital for Negroes." In 1728, another hospital was constructed on the company's plantation to take care of newly arrived slaves. At the end of the French regime, within the old New Orleans hospital, the "hospital for the king's negroes" was a separate, di-

---

taire précis des emplacements, terrains, et bâtiments appartenant au roi en cette ville de La Nouvelle-Orléans, joint à la lettre de M. Foucault du 2 avril 1766," ANOM COL C13A 46, fols. 47–49. For the period during the Company of the Indies's monopoly, the best account of the creation and management of the military hospital (the buildings, the staff, and the finances) can be found in Giraud, *History of French Louisiana*, trans. Pearce, V, 216–223, 250, 304–305, 310, 438. On the architectural history of the military hospital, see Farnsworth and Masson, eds., *Architecture of Colonial Louisiana*, 161–220. For an overview of the medical structures in the French Empire, see James E. McClellan, III, and François Regourd, *The Colonial Machine: French Science and Overseas Expansion in the Old Regime* (Turnhout, Belgium, 2011), 245–255. For environmental circumstances, see Marion Stange, "Governing the Swamp: Health and the Environment in Eighteenth-Century Nouvelle-Orléans," *French Colonial History*, XI (2010), 1–21.

44. "Ordonnance pour les nègres domestiques de la Compagnie," July 25, 1725, ANOM COL F3 242, fols. 56–57; "Marché avec les Dames religieuses ursulines pour les malades de l'Hôpital du roi à La Nouvelle-Orléans," Dec. 31, 1744, ANOM COL C13A 28, fols. 343–345.

lapidated building at the back, between the pharmacy and the building for patients suffering from venereal diseases. In the large new military hospital, whose construction started in the late 1750s, there was no specific building for slaves, who were left in the old one.[45]

Similar to their status as patients, slaves made up the lowest category of the hospital staff, which was racially organized. The hospital was first managed by a private overseer or director under contract. The Ursulines took over in 1734, but few of the nuns actually worked there. According to an inventory taken in 1766, the pavilion next to the ward for patients served as a retreat for both the sole Ursuline *hospitalière* (a nun specialized in the care of sick patients and working in a hospital) and the chaplain. With regard to medical staff, the hospital started out with only one doctor but gained three surgeons by 1754. Ten years later, the medical staff was composed of one doctor, two surgeons, two surgeon's apprentices, and one surgeon's assistant. All of them were white. In contrast, the nursing and domestic workforce was composed of people of various statuses and ethnic backgrounds. The 1726 census listed "three [male] nurses, including the domestic of Mr. Prat the doctor, a gardener, a laundress, two negroes and two negresses." The employment of slaves as nurses and domestics was not unusual; the same practice also existed in Saint-Domingue and other French slave societies. In the 1740s, the king gave rations and paid daily allowances for white male nurses, both assistants and apprentices, and he also granted the nuns seventeen slaves. Seven of them were attached to the hospital: Jean-Baptiste (around thirty years old), his wife Louison (thirty), and their two children, Nicolas (five and a half) and Marie-Joseph (two and a half); Pierrot (fifty) and his wife Jeanneton (forty); and Louis dit Sansquartier

45. Périer and La Chaise to the Company of the Indies, Apr. 9, 1727, ANOM COL C13A 11, fol. 28r; Périer and La Chaise to the Company of the Indies, July 31, 1728, ANOM COL C13A 11, fols. 51–52, 59v; "Inventaires et ustensiles qui se sont trouvés à l'hôpital au mois de novembre 1731," ANOM COL C13A 13, fols. 23–24; [Alexandre de Batz], "Plan du bâtiment servant d'hôpital pour les nègres malades, construit sur l'habitation de la compagnie, levé et dessiné sur les lieux le 9 janvier 1732," ANOM COL 04DFC C92C; [De Batz], "Plan du bâtiment de l'hôpital des nègres construits sur l'habitation de la compagnie levé et dessiné sur les lieux," Jan. 13, 1732, ANOM COL F3 290, 36; Erin M. Greenwald, ed., *A Company Man: The Remarkable French-Atlantic Voyage of a Clerk for the Company of the Indies: A Memoir by Marc-Antoine Caillot*, trans. Teri F. Chalmers (New Orleans, 2013), 79; "Inventaire général et estimation de toute l'artillerie, armes, munitions, effets, magasins, hôpitaux, bâtiments de mer appartenant à sa majesté très chrétienne dans la colonie de la Louisiane," 1766, ANOM COL C13A 46, fols. 131–278; and Giraud, *History of French Louisiana*, trans. Pearce, V, 318.

(fifty). In 1760, the king's slaves who worked for the hospital were roughly the same as in 1744, although they were much older. Only Louis had been replaced by a slave named Jacques. They were lodged together in two dingy cabins in the hospital courtyard. They were employed mainly as domestics: Louison served as a cook, while Pierre, Jeanneton, Louis, and Jacques were used for heavy work.[46]

Jean-Baptiste was the only slave to work in a position of higher status in the hospital. He was described variously as a surgeon, an assistant surgeon, or an apothecary. In Louisiana, as in Saint-Domingue, enslaved surgeons seem to have been exceptional figures. Jean-Baptiste was trained as a surgeon while he was a teenager on the company's plantation. When Le Page du Pratz first arrived there as the new director, he recounted: "I also had two cabins built outside this door, one for the white overseer and the other to secure the medicine and do dressings: a young Negro who followed the surgeon slept and stayed in this cabin, in order to be able to bleed a patient or to apply first aid in cases of emergency. I heard several years ago that this Negro was one of the good surgeons in the colony." Jean-Baptiste and his wife, Louison, had at least one other child named Joseph, who started working at the age of ten and was also trained as a surgeon and apothecary.

46. "Recensement général … au premier janvier 1726," ANOM COL G1 464, "Recensement général … de la Nouvelle Orléans … au 1er juillet 1727," "Recensement général de la ville de la Nvelle Orléans … fait au mois de janvier 1732"; Salmon to the minister of the navy, Dec. 8, 1731, ANOM COL C13A 13, fol. 121r; "Marché avec les Dames religieuses ursulines pour les malades de l'Hôpital du roi à La Nouvelle-Orléans," Dec. 31, 1744, ANOM COL C13A 28, fols. 343–345; "Inventaire général de tous les meubles et ustensiles appartenant à l'Hôpital du roi à La Nouvelle-Orléans," Dec. 31, 1744, ANOM COL C13A 28, fols. 346–351; Sébastien François Ange Le Normant de Mézy to the minister of the navy, Oct. 17, 1745, ANOM COL C13A 29, fols. 116–118r; "Toutes les dépenses de la Louisiane de l'année 1754," ANOM COL C13A 37, fols. 164–174; "État des nègres, négresses, négrillons, et négrittes du roi au 1er janvier 1760," ANOM COL C13A 42, fols. 66–67; "État des dépenses à faire à la Louisiane pour le service du roi pendant l'année 1764," ANOM COL C13A 44, fols. 39–46; RSCI, 1765/10/30/01; "Inventaire précis des emplacements, terrains, et bâtiments appartenant au roi en cette ville de La Nouvelle-Orléans, joint à la lettre de M. Foucault du 2 avril 1766," ANOM COL C13A 46, fols. 47–49; Emily Clark, *Masterless Mistresses: The New Orleans Ursulines and the Development of a New World Society, 1727–1834* (Chapel Hill, N.C., 2007), 104. On the employment of slaves as nurses and domestics in Saint-Domingue, see Gabriel Debien, *Les esclaves aux Antilles Françaises (XVIIe–XVIIIe siècles)* (Basse-Terre, Guadeloupe, 1974), 92, 105, 323, 330; and C[harles] Frostin, "Les 'enfants perdus de l'État' ou la condition militaire à Saint-Domingue au XVIIIe siècle," *Annales de Bretagne et des pays de l'Ouest,* LXXX (1973), 335.

With their knowledge of medicinal plants, both Jean-Baptiste and Joseph helped to cure not only the king's slaves but also soldiers, sailors, and other whites of the lower sort, both within and outside the hospital.[47]

Le Page du Pratz's travel account gave Jean-Baptiste some Atlantic visibility, but local authorities were reluctant to officially acknowledge his position in their correspondence with the metropole. In the same way, the only advantage the slave received from his training and standing in the hospital was a ration similar to the one given to soldiers. Nevertheless, he might have taken pride in his profession and enjoyed a prominent social position among the slave community, for he served as godfather in many baptisms of infants of African descent, sometimes signing his name as Jean Baptiste, "king's negro." Yet his position did not spare his family the hardships associated with the slave system. His son Joseph was described as a "mulatto," which means that he might have been born of a forced sexual relationship. Moreover, in 1750, Joseph was convicted of having forged some banknotes and deported to Saint-Domingue. Even with a privileged position, Jean-Baptiste never obtained his freedom. Except for the executioner, Louis Congo, none of the company's or king's slaves were ever manumitted during the French regime. Only in 1769, as Commandant Charles-Philippe Aubry was making preparations to hand the colony over to the Spanish, were some royal slaves freed, while the others were left to be sold.[48]

47. For enslaved surgeons in Saint-Domingue, see McClelland, III, and Regourd, *Colonial Machine*, 252; Karol K. Weaver, *Medical Revolutionaries: The Enslaved Healers of Eighteenth-Century Saint Domingue* (Urbana, Ill., 2006); and Weaver, "Surgery, Slavery, and the Circulation of Knowledge in the French Caribbean," *Slavery and Abolition*, XXXIII (2012), 105–117. Jean-Baptiste helped Le Page du Pratz look for the culprits of the Bambara plot, translating the words of the leaders of the revolt when they gathered at night in June 1731. See Le Page du Pratz, *Histoire de la Louisiane*, III, 227–228 (quotation, 227), 306–308. For other documents on Jean-Baptiste and his son Joseph, see RSCL 1748/02/10/01; and "Procédure contre Joseph esclave mulâtre chirurgien à l'hôpital du roi ayant falsifié des billets à partir du 30 novembre 1750, joint à la lettre de Michel du 18 mai 1751," ANOM COL F3 243, fols. 48–74. Another Creole slave in Lower Louisiana named Louis, who belonged to Dubreuil, was also trained as a surgeon at the King's Hospital (the name given to the hospital after 1732), but he probably served as a surgeon on his master's plantation. See RSCL 1748/06/09/01, 1748/06/10/06.

48. Salmon to the minister of the navy, Nov. 25, 1738, ANOM COL C13A 23, fol. 137; "Marché avec les Dames religieuses ursulines pour les malades de l'Hôpital du roi à La Nouvelle-Orléans," Dec. 31, 1744, ANOM COL C13A 28, fol. 343v; "Inventaire général de tous les meubles et ustensils appartenant à l'hôpital du roi à La Nouvelle-Orléans," Dec. 31, 1744, ANOM COL C13A 28, fols. 346–351; AANO, Saint-Louis Cathedral Baptisms, 1744–1753, 08/23/1744, 07/13/1745, 09/25/1746, 12/04/1746, 11/12/1746,

An incident that took place in 1752 involving Jean-Baptiste and his wife, Louison, suggests that the intimacy shared by soldiers and slaves at the hospital was not strong enough to erase all racial antagonism. A soldier named Pierre Antoine Pochenet was convicted for having attacked several slaves in the street while he was intoxicated. Among them were several enslaved women from the convent and the hospital who were busy washing laundry in the Mississippi near the barracks. They had refused to wash a handkerchief for Pochenet and had apparently rejected his sexual advances. In addition to assaulting the women, he also fought a male slave from the hospital who rushed up to provide assistance when some of the women cried for help. The man was the enslaved surgeon Jean-Baptiste, and one of the women, seriously injured, was Louison. Although the soldier served in the Arkansas garrison, he had spent a long time at the New Orleans hospital when he was sick, and he knew them well. During his trial, he asserted that "these negresses are not his enemies, on the contrary, when he was sick at the hospital they took care of him." He also apologized, telling the judge that he was "sorry to have hit Baptiste because he owes him much, saved his life several times at the hospital," and he expressed some gratitude as well as a sense of indebtedness toward both the women and Jean-Baptiste, even though he only named the surgeon.[49]

It is not insignificant that the soldier felt he could attack slaves who refused to execute his orders in the street. Unable to recognize slaves he knew personally because he was drunk, he evidently felt entitled to make any slave a victim of his rage and lack of inhibition. He might have been all the more offended by the women's refusal as he might have interpreted it as a sign of social contempt for his military condition. They obviously thought that they could say no to him, but, in so doing, they struck a blow at both his white supremacy and male preeminence. White domination over enslaved women was peculiar in the sense that females were exploited for both the work and the sex they could provide to men. When Louison and Babet re-

---

03/10/1748, 01/26/1749, ??/??/1751, 11/30/1751; RSCL 1748/02/10/01; "Procédure contre Joseph esclave mulâtre chirurgien à l'hôpital du roi ayant falsifié des billets à partir du 30 novembre 1750, joint à la lettre de Michel du 18 mai 1751," ANOM COL F3 243, fols. 48–74; Jean-Baptiste Claude Bobé-Descloseaux to the minister of the navy, Nov. 29, 1769, ANOM COL C13A 49, fol. 160.

49. RSCL 1752/06/08/01, 1752/06/08/02, 1752/06/12/01, 1752/06/12/02 (quotation), 1752/06/13/01, 1752/06/12/05, 1752/06/13/02, 1752/06/17/01, 1752/06/17/02, 1752/06/19/01 (quotation), 1752/06/20/01, 1752/06/26/01, 1752/06/26/02, 1752/06/28/01; Honoré-Gabriel Michel to the minister of the navy, Sept. 20, 1752, ANOM COL C13A 36, fol. 267.

fused him both, the soldier resorted to violence to restore what he believed to be the proper racial and gender hierarchy.

At the trial, the Ursulines chose to privilege the cohesion of the white community over their interests as slaveholders. The nuns who employed Louison refused to take part in the case. They told the judge that if they could save the serviceman's life they would do so, and they even went so far as to state that they preferred to lose their slave than to do something uncharitable toward their fellow human being. The soldier was not sentenced to the death penalty and was only condemned to the galleys. In contrast to the slaves who labored at the military hospital, the Ursulines developed a more complex attitude toward female slaves within their convent.[50]

The Convent: Socioreligious Integration and Racial Subordination
Although the Ursulines, drawn from a Rouen convent, arrived in 1727, they did not take over the running of the military hospital until 1734. They had been chosen to oversee the management of the military hospital over Gray Nuns, who specialized in nursing, on the suggestion of Jesuit Father Ignace de Beaubois, who was trying to improve the position of his own order. The Ursulines signed a contract with the Company of the Indies that made managing the military hospital their primary duty but succeeded in postponing the fulfillment of the obligation until the completion of the convent, which was finished at the same time as the second hospital structure. During that time, they concentrated on female education, the exclusive focus of their order. Housed in a temporary building on the other side of the city, they provided social services and supervised the religious devotion of women. They not only instructed the girls and women of the city but also sheltered orphan girls and a few destitute or battered women.[51]

50. Pochenet's trial contrasted with an earlier case that had taken place in 1736, not because of the sentence, but because the Ursulines pressed charges against the defendant. In the earlier case, a man named Jean Gambert, whom Salmon described as a "disreputable young libertine," shot two of the nuns' slaves twice, and they were hurt. Gambert was sentenced to three years in the galleys and required to pay five hundred livres in damages to the nuns. See "Extrait des registres des audiences criminelles du Conseil supérieur de la Louisiane pendant l'année 1736," ANOM COL F3 242, fols. 234–237v; and Salmon to the minister of the navy, Feb. 10, 1737, ANOM COL C13A 22, fols. 124–125v.

51. "Brevet en faveur des religieuses ursulines qui autorise leur établissement à la Louisiane du 11 septembre 1726," ANOM COL A 23, fols. 75r–76v; "Traité fait par La Compagnie des Indes avec les religieuses ursulines, du 11 septembre 1726," ANOM COL A 23, fols. 76r–79v; Sœur Tranchepain to Abbé Raguet, Jan. 5, 1728, ANOM COL C13A

"The Mulatto of the House"

By 1734, when the nuns took possession of the new convent and started managing the military hospital, they had already become valued members of the community. Four years after Governor Étienne Périer's wife laid the cornerstone for the new hospital and convent in 1730, Salmon recounted to the minister of the navy how the convent was delivered to the sisters: "They were conducted there ceremoniously by the clergy, the Superior Council, and the whole city attended this procession. The Blessed Sacrament was held, there was a sermon on the way in the parish, and the Te Deum was sung in the chapel." The city as a body seems to have wanted to pay homage to the important role the nuns had played for the city dwellers since their arrival in the capital. From 1734 onward, the Ursulines, like their religious sisters in Canada, found themselves at the very center of the city's system of socioreligious assistance. According to the Ursuline Marie Madeleine Hachard, the nuns fulfilled "the functions of four different Communities, that of the Ursulines, that is our first and main Order; that of the Hospitallers, that of Saint-Joseph and that of the Refuge, we will do our best to carry them out as faithfully as possible." Like the nuns of the Congrégation de Notre-Dame in Cap-Français, who welcomed free women or girls of color as day pupils and boarders, the New Orleans nuns especially sought to take care of women and girls of various statuses and ethnic backgrounds, even though they did not have the same expectations for all of them. The convent developed as a multiethnic place that was nevertheless hierarchically organized according to status, class, and race.[52]

Although the Ursulines were always too few in number to fully satisfy their multiple obligations, they remained an order of almost exclusively white

---

11, fol. 273v; Sœur Tranchepain to Abbé Raguet, Apr. 20, 1728, ANOM COL C13A 11, fol. 274.

52. On the 1730 and 1734 ceremonies, see O'Neill, *Church and State in French Colonial Louisiana*, 242; Salmon to the minister of the navy, Aug. 2, 1734, ANOM COL C13A 19, fol. 72r; and Clark, *Masterless Mistresses*, 59–64. On the various functions fulfilled by the Ursulines, see "Lettre à la Nouvelle Orleans, ce premier Janvier 1728" in [Marie Madeleine] Hachard, *Relation du voyage des dames religieuses Ursulines de Rouen à La Nouvelle-Orléans* (1728) (Paris, 1872), 86. On the role of nuns in Canada, see Dominique Deslandres, *Croire et faire croire: Les missions françaises au XVIIe siècle (1600–1650)* (Paris, 2003), 370. On the nuns of the Congrégation de Notre-Dame in Cap-Français, see Dominique Rogers, "Les libres de couleur dans les capitales de Saint-Domingue: Fortune, mentalités, et intégration à la fin de l'Ancien Régime (1776–1789)" (Ph.D. diss., Université Michel de Montaigne, 1999), chapter 9, 519, 522–525.

nuns. Twelve of them came to Louisiana in 1727, even though the contract signed with the company stipulated six, but four died and two went back home as they did not adapt to life in the colony. The nuns were quickly reduced to six. More arrived sporadically over the years. Yet, at a time when the Catholic Reformation had lost its momentum, they experienced difficulty in recruiting new members in the metropole. In the colony, it is possible that they did not even actively try to convince the girls they educated to take their vows, for Christian brides and mothers were considered more useful for the religious and moral supervision of colonial society. The social demand for brides was all the greater since Louisiana's sex ratio was unbalanced. Throughout the French regime, the Ursulines let only eight local young women take their vows, and one was sent back to her brother because she was not "considered proper for religion." Exceptionally, in 1758, they also gave their consent to take a *"Demoiselle"* as a "perpetual boarder" against a large dowry comprising a slave couple on condition that she lodge in the corner of the infirmary set aside for orphans. In the early 1760s, the convent only housed seventeen aging Ursulines: fourteen choir nuns and three converse nuns. Except for Marie Turpin, all were white women.[53]

Traditionally, the Ursulines were divided between choir nuns, who came from the nobility and were given that title because they recited the office daily in choir, and converse nuns, who had an inferior status, served as domestics, and were recruited among working-class people in the metropole. Among the local recruits, six were accepted as choir nuns and came from the upper or middling sorts, including two boarders belonging to the elite and two newly arrived Acadian women in the 1760s. As for the two converse nuns, one was the daughter of a carpenter, and the other was a *"métisse"* girl born to a mixed marriage in the Illinois Country. The latter, Marie Turpin, was not received as a choir nun, although she had the means to do so, probably out of racial prejudice. Moreover, her arrival was incidental. Unlike the

53. On the evolving number of nuns and their recruitment, see "Délibérations du Conseil 1727–1902," HNOC, Archives of the Ursuline Nuns of the Parish of Orleans, Microfilm 1 of 19, fols. 9, 11; "Registre pour écrire les réceptions des religieuses de France et postulantes (4 mars 1726–20 septembre 1893)," HNOC, Archives of the Ursuline Nuns of the Parish of Orleans, Microfilm 2 of 19; "Recensement général de la ville de la Nvelle Orléans … fait au mois de janvier 1732," ANOM COL G1 464; "Recensement général fait à La Nouvelle-Orléans … au mois de septembre 1763," AGI, Audiencia de Sto Domingo, Luisiana y Florida, Años 1766 a 1770, 2595–589; and Clark, *Masterless Mistresses*, 53, 64–74. On the role of religious and moral supervision of Christian brides and mothers, see "Lettre à la Nouvelle Orleans, ce vingt-quatrième Avril 1728," in Hachard, *Relation du voyage des dames religieuses Ursulines*, 98.

Ursulines and Hospitaliers of Quebec who, for the first thirty years of their apostolate, devoted most of their time and energy to evangelizing about a hundred free Native girls admitted as seminarists, the New Orleans sisters never planned to open a seminary for indigenous girls destined to become nuns. The failure of the Canadian experience might have motivated this choice. Sister Hachard also believed that Native Americans, women in particular, were less easy to convert than slaves of African descent, and she compared them to "savage beasts."[54]

The Ursulines did not need as many converse nuns in New Orleans as in the metropole because they could rely on slaves. They immediately became slaveholders who carefully managed their human property to make the most of their enslaved laborers and to impose their social control. The company initially granted them eight slaves, two of whom immediately escaped. Although they kept "a beautiful one" to serve them, they sent most of their slaves to their plantation. The first reason for this organization might have been related to racial prejudice. In 1755, when a poor white widow whose husband had died at the hospital and whose daughter was already at the convent with the orphan girls asked to stay and work for the nuns in exchange for food and lodging, the Ursulines unanimously agreed "to do her this favor to serve our community and to avoid having slaves as far as possible there." The nuns were also probably motivated by economic reasons. They needed slaves to work on their plantation to produce foodstuffs and other products that they could consume or sell, since the company's and the king's allowances were not sufficient to support all of them and cover the expenses incurred by patients and orphans. Their fragile financial situation worsened after 1744, when Commissaire-ordonnateur Sébastien François Ange Le Normant de Mézy negotiated a new contract with them for the management of the military hospital. This prompted the Ursulines to purchase more land and slaves and to increase their participation in the slave

---

54. On the social and ethnic origins of nuns, see Clark, *Masterless Mistresses*, 71–72, 211; and Sophie White, *Wild Frenchmen and Frenchified Indiuns: Material Culture and Race in Colonial Louisiana* (Philadelphia, 2012), 149–175. In contrast with the Ursulines, at the beginning of the French regime, Father Raphaël thought of establishing a seminary to train young Native Americans who could afterward help the Capuchins to evangelize their nations on the model of what the Spanish had done in Mexico. See Father Raphaël to Abbé Raguet, May 26, 1725, ANOM COL C13A 8, fol. 407v; and Father Raphaël to Abbé Raguet, Sept. 15, 1725, ANOM COL C13A 8, fols. 410v–411r. For Native girls as seminarists in Canada, see Deslandres, *Croire et faire croire*, 364–366. For the New Orleans Ursulines' conception of Native American women, see "Lettre à la Nouvelle Orléans," Apr. 24, 1728, in Hachard, *Relation du voyage des dames religieuses Ursulines*, 91.

system. From then on, successive commissaires-ordonnateurs always tried to convince the Ursulines to use more of their plantation slaves to work at the King's Hospital. In 1763, the convent housed sixteen slaves, although it is impossible to know how many worked at the hospital and how many served the nuns as domestics. The slaves were lodged in cabins located in the courtyard of the convent.[55]

With their educational mission, the Ursulines developed a policy of universal socioreligious integration among girls and women of all conditions and backgrounds. Their conceptions of and behavior toward non-European people were, nonetheless, highly ambivalent. The differentiated incorporation the nuns sought to enforce respected the dual logic of ancien régime societies, which was both inclusive and unequal; at the same time, it helped establish whiteness as the ultimate fault line in New Orleans's society. The girls at the convent were divided into three categories: orphans, boarders, and day pupils. Only orphans of European descent were received at the

55. The nuns' register of deliberations shows how they carefully decided to purchase and sell slaves. In 1756, they did not hesitate to sell two couples and a teenager "as thieves and capable of having a bad influence on the others" from their plantation. See "Délibérations du Conseil, 1727–1902," 1756, HNOC, Archives of the Ursuline Nuns of the Parish of Orleans, Microfilm 1 of 19, fol. 44. The Ursulines bought a plantation not too far from New Orleans in 1736. See RSCL 1736/02/08/01. For the Ursulines' various motivations to send most of their slaves to their plantation, see "Délibérations du Conseil 1727–1902," Dec. 13, 1755, HNOC, Archives of the Ursuline Nuns of the Parish of Orleans, Microfilm 1 of 19, fol. 43; P. d'Avaugour to the minister of the navy, Oct. 30, 1731, ANOM COL C13A 13, fols. 265–266r; Pierre de Rigaud de Vaudreuil de Cavagnal and Michel to the minister of the navy, May 17, 1751, ANOM COL C13A 35, fols. 5–6r; "Suite des extraits des nouvelles lettres que l'abbé de l'Isle Dieu a reçu de La Nouvelle-Orléans, capitale de la Louisiane," December 1752, ANOM COL C13A 36, fol. 330–335v; Emily Clark, "Patrimony without Pater: The New Orleans Ursuline Community and the Creation of a Material Culture," in Bradley G. Bond, ed., *French Colonial Louisiana and the Atlantic World* (Baton Rouge, La., 2005), 95–110; and Clark, *Masterless Mistresses*, 195–210. For official pressure on the Ursulines to employ more of their slaves at the King's Hospital, see Kerlérec and Vincent Guillaume Le Sénéchal d'Auberville to the minister of the navy, Apr. 20, 1753, ANOM COL C13A 37, fols. 41–43r; and "Délibérations du Conseil 1727–1902," July 22, 1762, HNOC, Archives of the Ursuline Nuns of the Parish of Orleans, Microfilm 1 of 19, fol. 49. For the number and lodging of the Ursulines' slaves in their convent at the end of the French regime, see "Recensement général fait à La Nouvelle-Orléans … au mois de septembre 1763," AGI, Audiencia de Sto Domingo, Luisiana y Florida, Años 1766 a 1770, 2595–589; "Inventaire précis des emplacements, terrains, et bâtiments appartenant au roi en cette ville de La Nouvelle-Orléans, joint à la lettre de M. Foucault du 2 avril 1766," ANOM COL C13A 46, fols. 47–49; and Clark, *Masterless Mistresses,* 169.

"The Mulatto of the House"

convent, but the nuns agreed to take enslaved girls and women of Native American and African descent as day pupils and a few as boarders.[56]

Despite providing education and assistance across racial lines, the Ursulines were not devoid of race-thinking. The education of slaves was seen as an ordeal that would testify to the nuns' devotion and humility and eventually bring salvation in return. When Hachard mentioned the first enslaved boarders of African descent whom the Ursulines agreed to take care of, she also noted: "We are accustomed to see people who are entirely black, we have been recently given two negro boarders, one six years old and the other seventeen years old, to teach them our Religion, and they will stay in our service; if it was in fashion here for negresses to wear patches on their face, they should be given white ones, which would have a pretty funny effect." The ironic tone hardly hid the feeling of estrangement the nuns felt when faced with black slaves. Moreover, these girls were destined to remain enslaved in their service. In contrast, although officials had initially envisioned using orphans to produce silk, they do not seem to have been put to work. Hence, it is not surprising that when the Ursulines spoke about their community, they emphasized boundaries of status, class, and race between the different women and girls. When the death of Madeleine Mathieu de St. François Xavier was announced, another sister reported in a letter that it caused "screams and sobs both from us and from our boarders, orphans, negresses and day pupils."[57]

56. Originally, the convent only housed a few orphans. Their number greatly increased after the Natchez Wars, rising to twenty-seven in 1732. In 1763, the convent still cared for thirty orphans. See "Recensement général de la ville de la Nvelle Orléans ... fait au mois de janvier 1732," ANOM COL G1 464; and "Recensement général fait à La Nouvelle-Orléans ... au mois de septembre 1763," AGI, Audiencia de Sto Domingo, Luisiana y Florida, Años 1766 a 1770, 2595–589. In late 1728, Hachard counted seven enslaved and twenty white boarders. See "Lettre à la Nouvelle Orleans," Apr. 24, 1728, in Hachard, *Relation du voyage des dames religieuses Ursulines*, 97–98. In 1731, around forty day pupils came to the school. See P. d'Avaugour to the minister of the navy, Oct. 30, 1731, ANOM COL C13A 13, fols. 265–266r.

57. For the Ursulines' vision of black people, see Rev. Mère St. Augustin de Tranchepain, Supérieure, *Relation du voyage des premières Ursulines à La Nouvelle Orléans et de leur établissement en cette ville ...* (New York, 1859), 44, 46; and "Lettre à la Nouvelle Orleans," Apr. 24, 1728, in Hachard, *Relation du voyage des dames religieuses Ursulines*, 98. In 1741, the Ursulines sent a young slave back to her owner claiming that she was a lunatic. See RSCL 1741/08/11/01, 1741/08/14/01, 1741/08/30/01, 1741/08/31/05. For the treatment of white orphans, see Périer to the minister of the navy, Jan. 19, 1732, ANOM COL C13A 14, fols. 45v–46r. For the Ursulines' emphasis on status, class, and

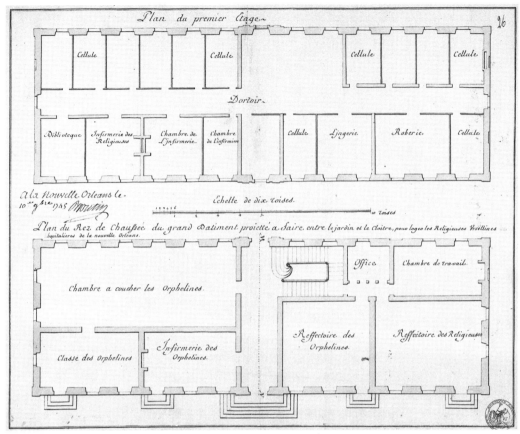

Figure 9: [François Ignace] Broutin. *Plan du premier Étage [et] du rez-de-chaussée du grand bâtiment projetté à faire entre le jardin et le cloître, pour loger les Religieuses Ursulines hospitalières de La Nouvelle Orléans.* Nov. 10, 1745. ANOM France COL F3 290/26. Courtesy of Les Archives nationales d'outre-mer. Aix-en-Provence, France

The organization of activities and space within the convent reflected the social and racial hierarchy the nuns intended to implement. Except for the Jesuit father, who visited the Ursulines every day as their spiritual director, and the male gardener, who had a shack in the garden, the convent was an exclusively female space. The enslaved day pupils of Native American and African descent came every day at lunchtime for one to two hours of instruction. They were taught apart from the white day pupils. Likewise, the instruction of orphans and boarders was conducted separately. They also

---

racial boundaries, see "Délibérations du Conseil 1727–190, July 6, 1728," HNOC, Archives of the Ursuline Nuns of the Parish of Orleans, Microfilm 1 of 19, fol. 11.

"The Mulatto of the House"

slept in different dormitories. In the second convent, inaugurated in 1734, orphans, boarders, and day pupils were entirely segregated. It is unknown where the few free or enslaved boarders of African and Native American descent lived. Aside from the chapel and the convent, which had been rebuilt in the late 1740s, the Ursulines' urban parcel at the end of the French regime included two separate buildings: one which served as a "free school for the day pupils" and one which had fallen into disrepair and was previously used for the lodging and schooling of boarders. Another old building served as a refectory for both the boarders and orphans. Apparently, the segregated organization had somehow relaxed because of material problems. The convent itself was a two-story brick building. It housed only the nuns and the orphans who were destined to stay permanently or until they got married or took their vows. The hierarchy between them was expressed by the fact that the nuns occupied the second floor, though their separate refectory was downstairs. The first floor also included bedrooms, an infirmary, refectory, and classroom for orphans. Although the convent took in and housed people of African descent who were not there to work, the organization of activities and space within the religious institution aimed at maintaining socioracial hierarchies. The situation of slaves was different at the Poor Hospital.[58]

58. The Jesuit father said High Mass and instructed the nuns daily. See "Lettre à la Nouvelle Orleans," Apr. 24, 1728, in Hachard, *Relation du voyage des dames religieuses Ursulines*, 95; and "Inventaire précis des emplacements, terrains, et bâtiments appartenant au roi en cette ville de La Nouvelle-Orléans, joint à la lettre de M. Foucault du 2 avril 1766," ANOM COL C13A 46, fols. 47–49. On the convent building and its spatial organization, see "Lettre à la Nouvelle Orleans, ce premier Janvier 1728," in Hachard, *Relation du voyage des dames religieuses Ursulines*, 85, "Lettre à la Nouvelle Orleans," Apr. 24, 1728, 97; Batz, "Façade et élévation du bâtiment et monastère des d. religieuses Ursulines," Jan. 14, 1732, ANOM COL F3 290 6; "Mémoire pour servir à l'établissement de la Louisiane," ANOM COL C13C 1, fol. 98r; François Ignace Broutin, "Plan du premier étage, plan du rez-de-chaussée du grand bâtiment projeté à faire entre le jardin et le cloître pour loger les religieuses Ursulines," Nov. 10, 1745, ANOM COL F3 290 26; "Inventaire précis des emplacements, terrains, et bâtiments appartenant au roi en cette ville de La Nouvelle-Orléans, joint à la lettre de M. Foucault du 2 avril 1766," ANOM COL C13A 46, fols. 47–49; Clark, *Masterless Mistresses*, 150–155; White, *Wild Frenchmen and Frenchified Indians*, 166–167; and Farnsworth and Masson, eds., *Architecture of Colonial Louisiana*, 161–220. In Quebec City, unlike New Orleans, Native American and French girls were always taught separately, but it was only in the last decades of the seventeenth century that they were segregated when sleeping, eating, and socializing. See Deslandres, *Croire et faire croire*, 372–373; and White, *Wild Frenchmen and Frenchified Indians*, 166–167.

The Charity Hospital: Poor Whites and Black Nurses

Unlike the convent, the only free or enslaved people of African descent who lived at the Poor Hospital were those who worked there. At the time of the Company of the Indies's monopoly, the poor were accepted at the military hospital, but, after the retrocession of the colony, the crown tried to end this practice. It partially succeeded thanks to the creation of the Charity Hospital on private initiative in 1736. In comparison, such an institution was only created in Cap-Français in 1741, albeit on a more ambitious scale and with greater means. The elite played an important role in the founding, financing, and management of the hospital. They used the money they earned from the exploitation of slaves to assist poor whites. Their charitable activity consolidated the sociopolitical position of the slaveholding elite and strengthened the cohesion of the white population. When local authorities and white settlers denied people of African descent admission to the Charity Hospital, they constructed the category of "the poor" as being exclusively white. The same process took place in Saint-Domingue, where institutions of assistance were reserved for whites. A free black man in Cap-Français nonetheless succeeded in founding a "providence house" for free people of color in the middle of the eighteenth century. But free blacks in the Louisiana capital were too few in number and did not yet have the financial means to organize their own system of assistance. The only free or enslaved people of African descent who lived at the Poor Hospital were those who worked there. The reliance on black laborers to assist poor whites who did not have to work at the Charity Hospital throws light on how the meaning of public care was changed by the system of racial slavery.[59]

59. John Salvaggio, *New Orleans' Charity Hospital: A Story of Physicians, Politics, and Poverty* (Baton Rouge, La., 1992). On Saint-Domingue's Poor Hospital and the exclusion of nonwhites, see "Arrêts en règlement du Conseil du Cap, touchant l'établissement et l'administration de la Maison de Providence de la même ville," Nov. 12, 1740, and Jan. 7, 1741, in [Moreau] de Saint-Méry, *Loix et constitutions des colonies françoises de l'Amérique sous le vent*, III, 641–648; and Laënnec Hurbon, "The Church and Slavery in Eighteenth-Century Saint-Domingue," in Marcel Dorigny, ed., *The Abolitions of Slavery: From Léger Félicité Sonthonax to Victor Schœlcher, 1793, 1794, 1848* (New York, 2003), 57. On the founding of a poor hospital for free people of color in Saint-Domingue, see "Pièce concernant le nommé Jasmin, nègre libre, fondateur d'une maison de la Providence pour les gens de couleur au Cap," Mar. 31, 1736, ANOM COL F3 95, fols. 153–158, "Mémoire sur le nommé Aloou Kinson, baptisé sous le nom de Jean Jasmin," fols. 159–160; and Rogers, "Les libres de couleur dans les capitales de Saint-Domingue," chapter 8, 482. The idea that the category "poor" was constructed as being exclusively white contradicts Philip Morgan's proposal to consider slaves as the genuine poor in the slave societies of America. See Morgan, "The Poor: Slaves in Early America," in David Eltis,

"The Mulatto of the House"

New Orleans's nascent urban society endured many hardships, and local authorities could not easily escape the issue of providing medical and social assistance for the destitute. Although the company initially intended the military hospital as a facility for its soldiers, sailors, and laborers, it eventually admitted some poor civilians, including women, out of charity. Yet the minister of the navy pressured Commissaire-ordonnateur Salmon to reduce the cost of the medical institution and to exclude indigent settlers in order to do so. As it was difficult to completely abandon a policy of assistance, Salmon asked the Capuchins to collect money so that the poor could be assisted at home. Three years later, the Poor Hospital was founded in an effort to find a better solution.[60]

The Charity Hospital should have been called Saint Jean after its founder, a man named Jean-Louis who used to work as a sailor for the Company of the Indies and earned a small fortune trading. When Jean-Louis died without heirs, he left a will drafted in 1735 that bequeathed ten thousand livres to the city for the construction of a medical facility offering treatment to New Orleans's impoverished community. The donation was managed by Jean-Baptiste Claude Raguet, the colony's attorney general and the executor of Jean-Louis's estate, and by the New Orleans priest. The first hospital was located in the house that had been rented to the Ursulines from 1728 to 1734. In 1743, the crown selected an urban parcel located on the edge of the city to build a new one for the poor. Originally, the institution seems to have been run by the superior of the Capuchins or one of the churchwar-

---

Frank D. Lewis, and Kenneth L. Sokoloff, eds., *Slavery in the Development of the Americas* (Cambridge, 2004), 288–323.

60. The wives of soldiers, in particular, were accepted at the military hospital. See the list of twenty-five patients in the 1727 census: "Recensement général ... de la Nouvelle Orléans ... au 1er juillet 1727," ANOM, G1, 464. For charitable motivations behind the admission of indigent people at the military hospital, see ANOM COL C13A 8, Dec. 23, 1724, fols. 162r–163r; "Mémoire de la Compagnie des Indes servant d'instruction pour M. Périer nouvellement pourvu du commandement général de la Louisiane," Sept. 30, 1726, ANOM C13B 1, fol. 89r; and the Superior Council to the Company of the Indies's Directors, Feb. 27, 1725, ANOM COL C13A 9, fol. 69v. For the end of this policy and the implementation of alternative measures, see Salmon to the minister of the navy, Dec. 8, 1731, ANOM COL C13A 13, fols. 121r–123r; Salmon to the minister of the navy, July 16, 1732, ANOM COL C13A 15, fols. 164v–165r; Bienville and Salmon to the minister of the navy, Apr. 1, 1734, ANOM COL C13A 18, fol. 33; Salmon to the minister of the navy, Apr. 6, 1734, ANOM COL C13A 19, fol. 28; Salmon to the minister of the navy, May 4, 1737, ANOM COL C13A 22, fol. 149v; and Salmon to the minister of the navy, May 3, 1735, ANOM COL C13A 20, fol. 229v. On the creation of the Poor Hospital, see Bienville and Salmon to the minister of the navy, May 20, 1737, ANOM COL C13A 22, fols. 30–31.

dens, who served as director. The king approved the founding of the Poor Hospital, but he did so at a late juncture and did not support it financially. The royal surgeon in charge of the military hospital, however, also took care of the charitable institution.[61]

Local authorities immediately supported the proposal to establish a poor hospital because they believed it would solve the problem of poverty in the city, in keeping with policies adopted toward indigent people in the metropole. Since the early modern period, the crown had encouraged the confinement of impoverished persons in France in "general hospitals," where they were forced to labor. As Louisiana's governor and commissaire-ordonnateur wrote:

> By this means there will be no beggars any more, they will all be locked away and they will be kept busy in accordance with their skills. This will even contribute to diminishing their number because most of those who beg and who are able-bodied, once they are locked away, will prefer to work to obtain their freedom.... At the same time it will relieve the King's Hospital where we are often compelled to take in the poor destitutes who would otherwise perish without this assistance.

Contrary to expectations, the hospital neither succeeded in solving the problem of poverty nor forced those who were institutionalized to work, maybe because bound labor came to be associated with racial slavery in the colony. Assistance was also only provided for a limited period, as Jacqueline Chaumont, the wife of a soldier, learned the hard way. The couple had been separated for ten years by a judicial decision, but they apparently maintained a relationship. After her husband violently beat her once again, she was unable to lodge a formal complaint because the Capuchins put her in the Charity Hospital to be treated. She was taken care of there by two missionaries for three weeks. Nevertheless, she had to leave the place when she ran out of foodstuffs, which suggests that the hospital did not provide sustenance for all its patients. Because she had lost her sight, she was reduced

61. For the bequest at the origins of the founding of the Charity Hospital, see "Autograph Will of Jean Louis," Nov. 16, 1735, in [Henry P. Dart], ed., "RSCL XV," *LHQ*, V (1922), 275; and RSCL 1736/05/10/01, 1736/06/10/01. The hospital lost part of its parcel when some wooden fortifications that crossed the lot were erected in the early 1760s. See RSCL 1764/10/01/01; 1769/01/15/01, "Registre de l'Hôpital de la Charité." On the Poor Hospital's direction and medical personnel, see RSCL 1752/08/05/04; Father Dagobert and Delaunay to the minister of the navy, Dec. 18, 1759, ANOM COL C13A 41, fols. 372–373; and Vaudreuil and Salmon to the minister of the navy, July 21, 1743, ANOM COL C13A 28, fols. 22–23.

"The Mulatto of the House"

to begging. In her testimony, the Poor Hospital does not appear as a place of confinement and forced labor. Rather, it appears to have operated as a shelter where the sick, crippled, or old could find temporary relief.[62]

The Charity Hospital never had the financial means to take care of all the destitute people in New Orleans. The funding that came from collections, donations, fines, and the income from a plantation owned by the charitable institution remained inadequate. According to an anonymous memorandum written in the late 1750s or early 1760s, "The Poor Hospital supported by the donations of private individuals is itself so poor that it is possible to shelter there only one tenth of the poor people who perish for lack of assistance, this establishment deserves his majesty's attention." It was not long before the King's Hospital once again found itself admitting some of the city's poor. In 1764, an arrangement was even proposed between the Charity Hospital and the Ursulines. The former admitted "the elderly, cripples and foundlings," while the King's Hospital took care of the poor patients against an indemnity. Out of financial insecurity and racial prejudice, free people of color seem to have been excluded from both places.[63]

By the end of the French regime, what had started as a charitable institution became an instrument of racial domination. In 1764, at the request of the new attorney general, Nicolas La Frénière, the Superior Council took some measures to impose better management and control of the expenses of the Poor Hospital. This initiative, taken by La Frénière, who was to play a crucial role in the 1768 revolt, was one among many that sought to increase the local elite's power and control. The council nominated four directors and a treasurer and organized a general assembly to be called twice

62. Bienville and Salmon to the minister of the navy, May 20, 1737, ANOM COL C13A 22, fols. 30–31; RSCL 1745/01/30/01.

63. On the Charity Hospital's finances, see NONA Garic Apr. 21, 1767; RSCL 1737/11/06/05, 1737/11/20/02; 1769/02/23/02, 1769/02/28/02. On the distribution of indigent people between the King's Hospital and the Charity Hospital, see "Mémoire pour servir à l'établissement de la Louisiane," ANOM COL C13C 1, fols. 99v–100r; "Marché avec les Dames religieuses ursulines pour les malades de l'Hôpital du roi à La Nouvelle-Orléans," Dec. 31, 1744, ANOM COL C13A 28, fols. 343–345; RSCL 1769/01/15/01, "Registre de la Maison de Charité"; and "État des dépenses à faire à la Louisiane pour le service du roi pendant l'année 1764," ANOM COL C13A 44, fol. 45v. An unusual labor contract seems to indicate that free people of color were not accepted at either the Poor Hospital or the King's Hospital. A free black man named Pierre Almanzou, who suffered from a venereal disease and did not have the means to pay for his cure, engaged himself as a cook to Mr. Prat, the royal doctor, for five years against food, drugs, and medical treatment. The contract specified that he would serve in all capacities, except "working with an axe or a spade," which meant heavy work. See RSCL 1737/03/02/03.

a year. Apart from the directors and treasurer, those who participated in these meetings included either the commissaire-ordonnateur or the commandant of the colony as well as the superior of the Capuchins, the attorney general, and some prominent residents. The directors were chosen among the elite, either merchants or planters, who were also often churchwardens, or former ones, and militia officers. The Poor Hospital became the main object of the elite's charitable activity. It allowed them to publicly express their devotion and philanthropic spirit toward whites of the lower sort and their sense of belonging to a civic community restricted to white people.[64]

The registers kept by the Charity Hospital provide information on the mixed labor force who served there. They mention hiring a white worker as well as the sale and purchase of slaves. Over time, enslaved laborers very likely made up most of the staff. One of the women was Jeannette, a free black who had been convicted for theft and sentenced to reenslavement at the Poor Hospital. In 1750, the overseer was a free black man named François. He was probably François Tiocou, the Senegalese slave who had won his freedom in the Natchez Wars and had worked for years to purchase his wife from the hospital. But the intimacy that was shared by these black workers and white patients or boarders did not necessarily do away with the racial hierarchy that separated them. In a trial involving male runaways who came to visit the enslaved women working at the Poor Hospital, Jacques Langlois dit Lajoye, a fifty-three-year-old white man who lived there, testified that he did not know Louis, one of the accused. He told the judge that "several negroes go to see the negresses, but he does not know their names." Of course, the witness might have sought to escape from any possible accusation of complicity. Even so, his testimony might also highlight the social distance that existed between not only the missionaries and the slaves in their service but also the white patients or boarders and their enslaved caretakers. Just because enslaved laborers interacted with white patients in close quarters at the Poor Hospital does not mean that they lived in the same social worlds. The same was true for slaves and soldiers within the city.[65]

64. "Extrait du registre des audiences du Conseil supérieur de la province de la Louisiane, remontrances du procureur général du roi sur fonctionnement et contrôle de l'hôpital de la Charité," Mar. 1, 1764, ANOM COL F3 243, fols. 250–252; RSCL 1768/12/10/04; 1769/01/15/01, "Registre de l'hôpital de la Charité."

65. On the oversight of Charity Hospital and its nurses, see NONA Garic Oct. 13, 1764; RSCL 1747/04/11/01; 1769/01/15/01, "Registre de l'hôpital de la Charité"; and AANO, Saint-Louis Cathedral Baptisms, 1744–1753, 10/14/1750. For Jacques Langlois dit Lajoye's testimony, see RSCL 1764/09/03/01.

"The Mulatto of the House"

Whereas the Ursulines were praised for their vows of poverty and chastity and their enclosed life, soldiers were despised on both sides of the French Atlantic for their status as enlisted men. Louisiana governors repeatedly complained about the military recruits sent to the Mississippi colony, denouncing their inadequate physical condition, cowardice, debauchery, and dubious social backgrounds. The traditional contempt felt for servicemen was aggravated in Louisiana, as in other slave societies, by the fact that most of them stood at the bottom of the white social ladder, just above slaves, and could not rely on slave labor at a time when slaveownership was increasingly becoming the ultimate social fault line among whites. Soldiers were sometimes compared to slaves because of the harsh discipline and hard labor imposed on them by the military. Redon de Rassac, the author of a memorandum on Louisiana, reported that officers at the English Turn "used them [servicemen] as negroes or galley slaves." Despite their exploitation, enlisted men cannot be likened to "white negroes," and their service in the military cannot be equated to a kind of bondage. The social positions of soldiers were much more diversified, and those who remained socially the closest to slaves fought hard not be conflated with them. They played a crucial role in the construction of whiteness.[66]

66. By soldiers or servicemen, I mean both soldiers and noncommissioned officers, such as sergeants and corporals, unless otherwise stated. On enlisted men in the metropole, see André Corvisier, *L'armée française de la fin du XVIIe siècle au Ministère de Choiseul: Le Soldat*, 2 vols. (Paris, 1964); Jean Chagniot, *Paris et l'armée au XVIIIe siècle: Étude politique et sociale* (Paris, 1985); Anne Blanchard et al., *Histoire militaire de la France*, II, *De 1715 à 1871*, ed. Jean Delmas (Paris, 1992); and Stéphane Perréon, *L'armée en Bretagne au XVIIIe siècle: Institution militaire et société civile au temps de l'intendance et des États* (Rennes, France, 2005). For a rare study on troops within an imperial framework, see Boris Lesueur, *Les troupes coloniales d'Ancien Régime: Fidelitate per Mare et Terras* (Paris, 2014). For complaints by officials against soldiers, see, for instance, Bienville to the minister of the navy, June 28, 1736, ANOM COL C13A 21, fol. 203; and Vaudreuil and Michel to the minister of the navy, May 20, 1751, ANOM COL C13A 35, fols. 13–17. For the comparison between soldiers and slaves, see "Plan pour rendre la Louisiane la plus riche et la plus puissante de toutes les colonies françaises, par Redon de Rassac," Aug. 15, 1763, ANOM COL C13A 43, fols. 378r–379r; and Frostin, "Les 'enfants perdus de l'État,'" *Annales de Bretagne et des pays de l'Ouest*, LXXX (1973), 343 (quotation). In contrast with scholars who argue that the presence of soldiers aided in the construction of whiteness, historians who make the biggest claims about the disorder and chaos that would have prevailed in Louisiana's society underline solidarities among the lower classes, soldiers, and slaves in particular. If they mention cases of verbal and physi-

Soldiers were an important demographic and social minority group in the Louisiana capital, even though New Orleans housed a relatively small garrison since it had a limited defensive role. During the French regime, the number of *compagnies franches de la Marine* garrisoned in the city constantly evolved. After the company's withdrawal, the king sent new recruits to fill four companies in 1731–1732. In theory, each company was made up of 50 men, but they were often incomplete because of disease, death, and desertion. Between December 1731 and May 1732, the four companies, which should have comprised 200 men but in actuality numbered 118, lost 19 other men, reducing their number to 99. Of these 99 soldiers, 14 were being looked after at the hospital. From the early 1750s, the number of compagnies franches de la Marine in wartime increased to six. Yet, of these six companies, Honoré-Gabriel Michel complained that no less than 90 to 100 soldiers were sick at the hospital. In 1760, Commissaire-ordonnateur Rochemore reported that there had never been more than 600 soldiers garrisoned in New Orleans and that they were reduced to 150 at the time. In addition to the compagnies franches de la Marine, there were also one or two Swiss companies garrisoned in the capital. The first company of Swiss worker-soldiers, sent in 1720–1721, was dismantled in 1725, as it was considered useless, but new Swiss troops from the Karrer Regiment were sent after the crown took over management of the colony from the company. In 1732, Commissaire-ordonnateur Salmon counted 140 Swiss soldiers.[67]

---

cal violence among soldiers and slaves, they overemphasize a shared sociability around alcohol, a common criminality, and joint attempts at escaping. They explain these phenomena by arguing that soldiers and slaves would have found themselves in a similar position. They assimilate military service to a kind of bondage and stress that soldiers were exploited, mistreated, and socially despised, suggesting that class solidarities would have been stronger than race antagonisms. See Gwendolyn M. Hall, *Africans in Colonial Louisiana: The Development of Afro-Creole Culture in the Eighteenth Century* (Baton Rouge, La., 1992), 19–27, 146–179; Dawdy, *Building the Devil's Empire*, 93, 147–150, 174–175, 185–186, 200–213, 287n; and Daniel H. Usner, Jr., *Indians, Settlers, and Slaves in a Frontier Exchange Economy: The Lower Mississippi Valley before 1783* (Chapel Hill, N.C., 1992), 219–243.

67. La Chaise to the Company of the Indies's Directors, Mar. 8, 1724, ANOM COL C13A 7, fol. 18; "Compagnies détachées de la Marine, garnison de la Nvelle Orléans," Dec. 2, 1731, ANOM COL D2C 51, fols. 81–83; "La Louisiane, revue de mai 1732, Garnison de la Nvelle Orléans," May 4, 1732, ANOM COL D2C 51, fols. 92–95r; Salmon to the minister of the navy, July 16, 1732, ANOM COL C13A 15, fol. 160; Michel to the minister of the navy, July 20, 1750, ANOM COL C13A 35, fol. 328; "Revue générale des Compagnies franches de la marine en garnison à La Nouvelle-Orléans durant l'année 1759," ANOM COL D2C 52, fol. 88; Rochemore to the minister of the navy, June 23,

"The Mulatto of the House"

Many phenomena set the military apart from the civilian population, but they also formed an integral part of the city's community. Officers exploited enlisted men, using them in their private service; public authorities employed them alongside slaves on public works projects; they lived in harsh material conditions; and they formed, alongside slaves, the main target of royal justice throughout the French regime. In addition, the way soldiers were recruited in the metropole should have made them transient and extraneous members of the local population. Still, not all soldiers were young, unruly, and displaced single men. Even though most of them remained single, the long duration of their service in Louisiana allowed them to put down roots. A minority also arrived already married or succeeded in marrying in the colony. They were able to become socially integrated and experience some kind of social mobility. Consequently, New Orleans's population was composed of many former servicemen. Because soldiers and indentured servants also shared common geographical and social origins, the social distance between the civil and military populations might have been less significant than in other places. This social proximity might have developed to the detriment of the military esprit de corps, yet it likely made it easier for civilian whites of the lower sort and soldiers to unite and identify with each other.[68]

1760, ANOM COL C13A 42, fols. 118v–119r; Giraud, *History of French Louisiana*, trans. Pearce, V, 231–232; Khalil Saadani, *La Louisiane française dans l'impasse, 1731-1743* (Paris, 2008), 200–201; René Chartrand, "The Troops of French Louisiana, 1699–1769," *Military Collector and Historian*, XXV, no. 2 (Summer 1973), 58–65; David Hardcastle, "Swiss Mercenary Soldiers in the Service of France in Louisiana," in Alf Andrew Heggoy and James J. Cooke, eds., *Proceedings of the Fourth Meeting of the French Colonial Historical Society, April 6-8, 1978, University of Mississippi; Oxford, Mississippi*, [IV] (Washington, D.C., 1979), 82–91; Susan Gibbs Lemann, "The Problem of Founding a Viable Colony: The Military in Early French Louisiana," in James J. Cooke, ed., *Proceedings of the Sixth and Seventh Annual Meetings of the French Colonial Historical Society, 1980-1981*, [VI/VII] (Washington, D.C., 1982), 27–35; Bernard Lugan, *La Louisiane française, 1682-1804* (Paris, 1994), 165–181, 244–249; Carl A. Brasseaux, *France's Forgotten Legion: A CD-ROM Publication: Service Records of French Military and Administrative Personnel Stationed in the Mississippi Valley and Gulf Coast Region, 1699-1769* (Baton Rouge, La., 2000); Arnaud Balvay, *L'Épée et la plume: Amérindiens et soldats des troupes de la marine en Louisiane et au Pays d'en Haut (1683-1763)* (Sillery, [Québec], 2006).

68. The groom was a soldier in 34 out of a total of 441 marriages in the sacramental records kept from 1720 to 1733. From 1759 to 1768, the groom was a soldier in 36 out of 227 marriages. Far from insignificant, this marriage rate reveals that soldiers were not social outcasts. See Archdiocesan Archives, New Orleans, Saint-Louis Cathedral,

To foster the military esprit de corps, prevent desertion, and impose discipline, soldiers were housed in barracks. The idea of building barracks instead of billeting soldiers with the local population was difficult to put into practice in the metropole during the eighteenth century, but officials immediately resorted to this solution in Louisbourg and New Orleans, the two colonial cities created ex nihilo in the first decades of the eighteenth century. Because the Louisiana capital was initially built by slaves, soldiers, and indentured servants, separate barracks for workers employed by the Company of the Indies and the Swiss troops, who were located on the edge of the city, were among the first buildings erected in the new city, whereas the company's slaves were housed on two plantations outside New Orleans. Officials tried to segregate the living spaces of the various workforces who labored together to build the city out of cypress forests and swamps. Yet there were initially no barracks for the French soldiers. They either camped out or were lodged by settlers for a heavy rent. Additional wooden barracks were raised for them near the first ones that had been built for the company's workers and Swiss troops, which were then falling into ruins, on Toulouse Street, sometime prior to 1732. A few years later, local authorities persuaded the king to spend the money necessary to build new barracks in brick. Besides health concerns, their main target was discipline: "Finally when the garrison is barracked it will be possible to contain and discipline it, in fact this is the only way to achieve this. The officer will live in the barracks' wings and will be able to continuously watch the soldiers and to prevent them from going out at night to steal or to get debauched, which has been impossible until now whatever precautions we take." The new barracks, which were located on two sides of the main square at the center of the city, were completed between 1737 and 1739. But, even after the con-

<hr />

BMF (Baptisms, Marriages, Funerals), Vol. A 1731–1733; Baptisms / Marriages, Vol. IV, Whites FPC / Slaves, Jan. 1, 1759, to Nov. 15, 1762; Baptisms / Marriages, Vol. V, Whites FPC / Slaves, Jan. 1, 1763, to June 21, 1767; and Marriage Registers, Vol. A (July 1, 1720, to Dec. 4, 1730) and Vol. B (Jan. 17, 1764, to Jan. 22, 1774). The significant numbers of former servicemen among the city's population were acknowledged by officials. See Périer to Philibert Ory, Aug. 1, 1730, ANOM COL C13A 12, fol. 329v; and Salmon to the minister of the navy, Oct. 10, 1739, ANOM COL C13A 24, fols. 168–169. For more details about the social origins and living conditions of servicemen, see Cécile Vidal, "The Streets, the Barracks, and the Hospital: Public Space, Social Control, and Cross-Racial Interactions among Soldiers and Slaves in French New Orleans," in Emily Clark, Ibrahima Thioub, and Vidal, eds., *New Orleans, Louisiana, and Saint-Louis, Senegal: Mirror Cities in the Atlantic World, 1659–2000s* (Louisiana State University Press, forthcoming 2019).

"The Mulatto of the House"

struction of the barracks, some soldiers who were married continued to live on their own. As early as 1753, Governor Kerlérec argued that it was necessary to demolish the buildings. Because their quarters were falling into ruin at the end of the Seven Years' War, many of the troops were lodged in the new Hôtel de Mars, destined to serve as a hospital for officers, and in the new military hospital for soldiers.[69]

Intended to create separation between enlisted men and the rest of the city's inhabitants, the barracks were nonetheless places of porous boundaries. Although discipline within the barracks could be harsh—a serviceman in 1747, for example, was sentenced to the galleys for life because he had not only insulted his sergeant, addressing him with "tu," but also attacked his superior while intoxicated when the latter attempted to break up a fight between him and a fellow soldier in the room they shared—the military hierarchy did not manage, or maybe even try, to confine soldiers within the walls of the barracks. According to Commissaire-ordonnateur Michel, "disregarding the retreat, soldiers left at night to go to the plantations in the vicinity of the city, chase the negresses, and disturb the rest of the urban dwellers." Furthermore, contrary to what seems to have happened in Louisbourg, where A. J. B. Johnston has argued that "civilians never ventured into one of the strictly military zones—the guardhouses, barracks, or parade

69. "Plans, profils, et élévations des bâtiments et casernes faits pour la Compagnie depuis le 1er août 1722 jusqu'au 3 janvier de la présente année 1723," ANOM COL 04DFC 67A; Le Blond de La Tour to the Company of the Indies, Oct. 21, 1723, ANOM COL C13A 7, fols. 193–199r; La Chaise to the Company of the Indies's Directors, Mar. 8, 1724, ANOM COL C13A 7, fols. 22–23, 34; "Plan de La Nouvelle Orléans telle qu'elle était le 1er janvier 1732," HNOC; Bienville and Salmon to the minister of the navy, May 12, 1733, ANOM COL C13A 16, fols. 50–91v; Bienville and Salmon to the minister of the navy, June 20, 1736, ANOM COL C13A 21, fol. 62; Kerlérec to the minister of the navy, Apr. 28, 1753, ANOM COL C13A 37, fol. 48; "Mémoire pour servir à l'établissement de la Louisiane," ANOM COL C13C 1, fol. 98r; "Inventaire précis des emplacements, terrains, et bâtiments appartenant au roi en cette ville de La Nouvelle-Orléans, joint à la lettre de M. Foucault du 2 avril 1766," ANOM COL C13A 46, fols. 47–49; and Dawdy, "Proper Caresses and Prudent Distance," in Stoler, ed., *Haunted by Empire*, 140–162. For various maps or drawings of the barracks, see ANOM COL 4DFC 74A (Dec. 24, 1726), C78C (Mar. 30, 1729), 79C (Mar. 30, 1729), C77B (Mar. 31, 1729), 95bsB (July 25, 1734); and ANOM COL F3 290, 29 (Oct. 26, 1732), 30 (Oct. 26, 1734). For married soldiers living on their own, see, for instance, the will of a Swiss sergeant, drawn up in his own house: "Nuncupative Will of Antoine Joly," Mar. 11, 1748, in Heloise H. Cruzat, ed., "RSCL LXVII: February–March, 1748," *LHQ*, XIX (1936), 499. On the history of barracks in the metropole, see François Dallemagne, *Les casernes françaises* (Paris, 1990); and Blanchard et al., eds., *Histoire militaire de la France*, II, 47–48.

squares," slaves could easily enter New Orleans's barracks. Jupiter's trial reveals that the enslaved children who helped Pradel's peddler sell his baskets of herbs and vegetables often came into the barracks to sell or give produce to the soldiers. In return, servicemen gave them pieces of bread or bacon and let them stay all day to keep warm. Apparently, Jupiter felt that he could not do what the enslaved children were allowed to do and did not venture into the barracks himself; however, in another case, a slave named Sozie entered the rooms where soldiers slept in the barracks to buy some shirts. Both enslaved adults and children seem to have been regular visitors of the military quarters.[70]

Soldiers and slaves had many other places to meet and interact than the barracks: within and outside the military hospital, at the marketplace, in the streets, and when they labored together rowing upriver in convoys or building levees and fortifications. These daily encounters contradicted the socioracial order that authorities were trying in vain to implement by segregating soldiers in the barracks and canteens. This proximity could favor exchange, cooperation, and assistance. For instance, soldiers and slaves sometimes deserted together. However, servicemen also kidnapped slaves who were then forced to follow them in their desertion, and runaways and deserters could have conflicting relationships. The use of soldiers to prevent criminal activity by patrolling and serving as sentinels in the gatehouses around the city, especially at night; to pursue runaway slaves; and to arrest slaves accused of criminal behavior might have fueled social antagonism between them as well. Not only might slaves have resented soldiers as the instrument used by authorities and masters to impose their power over them, but servicemen might also have been angry because their police function was seen as a dishonorable activity, contrary to military service. This is the argument that Commissaire-ordonnateur Michel put forward to justify his proposal to create a *maréchaussée* (a rural police force) in 1751:

70. The soldier's use of the informal *"tu"* instead of the formal *"vous"* is what made the exchange between the soldier and his sergeant disrespectful. For the serviceman's trial, see RSCL 1747/04/19/02, 1747/04/20/01, 1747/04/20/02, 1747/04/20/03, 1747/04/21/01, 1747/04/21/02, 1747/04/22/01, 1747/04/22/02, ND no. 116 Apr. 20, 1747; and Vaudreuil to the minister of the navy, May 16, 1747, ANOM COL C13A 31, fol. 93. For the differentiated control of the barracks boundaries in Louisbourg and New Orleans, see Michel to the minister of the navy, Sept. 29 1750, ANOM COL C13A 34, fols. 333v–334r; and A. J. B. Johnston, *Control and Order in French Colonial Louisbourg, 1713-1758* (East Lansing, Mich., 2001), 174. For slaves entering the barracks, see RSCL 1744/04/24/01; 1764/07/17/01, 1764/07/17/02, 1764/07/18/02, 1764/07/19/01, 1764/07/19/02, 1764/07/20/01, 1764/07/28/01, 1764/07/28/02, 1764/07/28/06, 1764/07/28/07.

"The Mulatto of the House"

Troops should give a helping hand, but they are not accustomed to do so, and they are extremely reluctant to accomplish this kind of service. If order has to be enforced and we ask the troops for assistance, soldiers secretly warn the innkeepers and other culprits; if arrests have to be carried out there are always some arguments; soldiers are happy to bear arms but none of them want to have anything to do with criminal matters for fear of losing their honor. Every day we have runaway slaves who gather together in the woods around the city, they insult passersby, and often come out at night to raid plantations that they ransack. If it is necessary to track them down in their hiding place, the soldiers retort that it is not their role, that at least they have to be paid, and indeed it has always been done that way.

Hence it comes as no surprise that, within the city, servicemen fought hard to keep some appearance of social superiority over slaves, men in particular, and repeatedly reasserted the color line in public spaces through violence. Soldiers' daily lives were too harsh, the discipline and violence that their officers imposed on them too strict, and the social contempt they suffered from the elite too acute for them to accept being compared to slaves.[71]

French New Orleans was different from the colonial cities created after the revolutionary era in Africa and Asia, which were characterized by the segregation of European and indigenous districts and households. In early American urban slave societies such as the Louisiana capital, masters and slaves not only lived in the same districts and in the same buildings but they also shared the same households. The relative democratization of slave-ownership during the French regime meant that slaves were present in half of the city's domestic households by the early 1760s. New Orleans households experienced the same increase in the number of dependents as all slave societies in the Western hemisphere, which distinguished them from metropolitan societies. Yet the inclusion of slaves within this category of dependents could be misleading. Admittedly, urban slaves could be compared to metropolitan servants and workers on the basis of the kind of labor they performed as domestics, artisans, and traders and the material conditions in which they lived. Urban slavery was certainly less harsh and exploitative than plantation slavery, which does not mean that slaves did not labor very hard. Still, their status set them apart. Slaves had to face violence on a daily basis, and they could not turn to justice to defend themselves against abu-

71. RSCL 1739/10/10/01, 1765/09/09/02, no. 11; Michel to the minister of the navy, May 18, 1751, ANOM COL C13A 35, fols. 207v–209r.

sive owners. The way censuses were taken clearly expressed a consciousness that the enslaved constituted a different type of dependent and that slavery and freedom had become the main fault line that divided households. In censuses, slaves became distinguished not only from the head of the household's blood relatives but also from other dependents of European descent. The classification of freed men and women in the same group as slaves in the 1760s censuses also confirms that race had become more important than status. Most free people of color lived in the privacy of their former master's house, with whom they maintained patron-client relationships; even so, this proximity did not prevent their racial subordination.[72]

Racial prejudice also explains the way enslaved and free people of color were integrated within residential institutions, although their situation was different in the barracks, the convent, and the hospitals. The military quarters exclusively housed white men. Despite the regular presence of slaves who frequently visited the place, it was the only institution within the city that did not rely on slave labor. Precisely because servicemen were collectively defined as a group of nonslaveholders, they resisted being compared to slaves. The convent was the female counterpart of the barracks, but, unlike the military buildings, it was a multiethnic enclave. Alongside the church, the convent constituted the only space where the enslaved were not reduced to their function as laborers as they were considered as catechumens, or Christians. They were nonetheless integrated in a discriminative way that partook of the construction of whiteness. Lastly, in contrast with the convent, most of the people of African descent who stayed at the military hospital or at the Charity Hospital were individuals who worked there as nurses and domestics. The fact that slaves constituted a different kind of dependent within domestic households resulted in their being excluded from the category of the poor. Neither slaves nor free people of color could benefit from public assistance. In this hierarchical and unequal Catholic society, people of African descent were included in the religious community, but they were excluded from the civic body, which only supported its members.

Within domestic households, the intimacy of living under the same roof informed the way the slave system worked at the individual level. The personal knowledge enslaved domestics acquired about their owners during moments of intimate care gave them an instrument of leverage. Conversely, the promise of freedom could also be used by masters to control enslaved

72. On nineteenth- and twentieth-century colonial cities, see Carl H. Nightingale, *Segregation: A Global History of Divided Cities* (Chicago, 2012).

"The Mulatto of the House"

laborers and reduce the subversive potential of urban life. This contradiction turned urban households into privileged spaces of interpersonal negotiations, which explains why manumissions were always more numerous in cities. However, black wet nurses, who were often freed, are a good example of the violence that was inflicted on domestic slaves, since they had to center their daily lives around the families of their owners and could not take care of their own children in the same way, being often separated from their loved ones.

Living under the perpetual gaze of masters could also expose slaves to the mood swings of their owners and to potentially greater daily physical violence. It could facilitate sexual exploitation as well. In the trial centered on the Monsanto household, Valentin was presented as "the mulatto of the house." One cannot presume that he was related to his master or one of his owner's brothers, but the racial category used by the white members of the household to designate him identified him as the offspring of a mixed union. The full expression illuminates how domestic slavery both included and excluded at the same time. Although Valentin was evidently a special member of this household and family, he remained in a subordinate position owing to his status and race. Intimate coexistence both mediated and embedded race in the fabric of everyday life. In the same way as households, the family institution was transformed by its embroilment in the system of racial slavery.

CHAPTER FIVE

"A Scandalous Commerce"

The Disorder of Families

Angst over Louisiana's future peaked during the Natchez Wars.[1] In this climate of anxiety, Company of the Indies employee Marc-Antoine Caillot described the Mississippi colony as a new Sodom and Gomorrah:

> There are also among the Natchez women those who go so far in their debauchery that they go to find the French, even in their beds, to assuage their ardent passion. They do not let you rest unless you have satisfied them. Most of the inhabitants buy only female slaves, Indian as well as Negro, in order to more conveniently lie with them.
>
> The French women of this country follow the native women around quite a bit, because even the girls, who should maintain some kind of chastity, act completely to the contrary and do not make a secret of losing it. You see them brag in public about their wicked conduct. Thus, you can quite easily understand, for the reasons I state, that this colony's upsets and frequent wars derive only from the wicked life that the people there lead, and that the punishments God has sent to us are only too just, as you will see later.

The American environment, the bad example set by Native women, and the development of slavery were believed to have turned what historical actors qualified as "debauchery" into an infectious disease that caused conflict with indigenous peoples. In keeping with a trope commonplace to lit-

---

1. Chapter Five's subtitle is borrowed from Arlette Farge and Michel Foucault, *Le désordre des familles: Lettres de cachet des archives de la Bastille au XVIIIe siècle* (Paris, 1982). Some lettres de cachet sent young men of means and money into exile in Louisiana at the request of their families. More broadly, the title conveys the idea that any major social transformation or establishment of a new social order necessarily transforms family structures, relations, and dynamics.

erature on the Americas—that the so-called weaker sex was more likely to be debased by life in the New World than men—Caillot identified women in particular, both Natchez and French, as the ultimate culprits behind the colony's perceived degeneracy. His travel account may be the first in a long series of texts ascribing the responsibility for the hardships suffered by New Orleans and Louisiana to the misconduct of their inhabitants. This providentialist interpretation was not only reflected in discourse, it also led to the creation of a female congregation by some women and girls of the city soon after the Natchez attack. Called the Congrégation des dames enfants de Marie ("Ladies congregation of the children of Mary") and placed under the Ursulines' patronage, the consorority aimed at maintaining moral rectitude, supporting the poor and dying, and converting slaves. Accused of being the source of social disorder, women decided to play a special role in the spreading of the Gospel and the moralization of society.[2]

Caillot's description was also the apex in a long series of lamentations in travel accounts and in ecclesiastical and secular authorities' correspondence giving voice to more general anxieties about the religious and moral

2. Erin M. Greenwald, ed., *A Company Man: The Remarkable French-Atlantic Voyage of a Clerk for the Company of the Indies: A Memoir by Marc-Antoine Caillot*, trans. Teri F. Chalmers (New Orleans, La., 2013), 97–98. On European views of Native American women's sexuality and their sexual freedom, see Gilles Havard, "Les 'Champs de Vénus': L'hospitalité sexuelle amérindienne (XVIIe–XIXe siècle)," in Alain Beaulieu and Stéphanie Chaffray, eds., *Représentation, métissage, et pouvoir: La dynamique coloniale des échanges entre Autochtones, Européens, et Canadiens (XVIe–XXe siècle)* ([Quebec], 2012), 205–235; Havard, "Des femmes-sujets? La question du consentement sexuel des Amérindiennes dans le contexte de la rencontre avec les Européens (XVIIe–XIXe siècle)," in Havard and Frédéric Laugrand, eds., *Éros et tabou: Sexualité et genre chez les Amérindiens et les Inuits* (Quebec, 2014), 320–358. On the debate over the theory of degeneracy in the New World, see Antonello Gerbi, *The Dispute of the New World: The History of a Polemic, 1750–1900*, trans. Jeremy Moyle (Pittsburgh, Pa., 1973 [1955]). For the gender dimension of this debate, see Kathleen Wilson, *The Island Race: Englishness, Empire, and Gender in the Eighteenth Century* (London, 2003), 6, 18–27. For moralist and providentialist interpretations of Hurricane Katrina and for ecclesiastical reactions to the storm, see Randy J. Sparks, "American Sodom: New Orleans' Past as Prologue," paper presented at the American Historical Association, San Diego, Calif., Jan. 9, 2010, and Southern Historical Association, New Orleans, La., Oct. 12, 2008; and Sparks, "'An Anchor to the People': Hurricane Katrina, Religious Life, and Recovery in New Orleans," in "After the Storm: A Special Issue on Hurricane Katrina," *Journal of Southern Religion* (2009), http://jsreligion.org/Katrina/Sparks.pdf. On the female congregation formed after the Natchez attacks, see Emily Clark, "'By All the Conduct of Their Lives': A Laywomen's Confraternity in New Orleans, 1730–1744," *William and Mary Quarterly*, 3d Ser., LIV (1997), 769–794.

disorder that was thought to prevail in the colony. In that regard, Louisiana was no different from Saint-Domingue and other Caribbean islands, which were also associated with libertinage in colonial narratives. During the first fifteen years after New Orleans's founding, life in the colony was marked by many hardships and uncertainties, including a devastating crisis of mortality among whites in particular. In various ways, authorities and settlers expressed fear that they would not be able to create a viable society. In their opinion, social stability necessarily rested on a moral and religious order based on Christian marriage. In the mid-1720s, for instance, Father Raphaël, the Capuchins' superior, accused white people of being guilty of concubinage, bigamy, and sexual intercourse with slaves of African and Native American descent.[3]

After the early 1730s, the trope regarding the debauchery of colonial life became less frequent in administrative and ecclesiastical correspondence but still resurfaced from time to time, albeit in a more pragmatic way devoid of the intensity of earlier anxieties, to promote marriage among whites. In a report on the administration of Louisiana dated 1749, the navy officer Vincent-Gaspard-Pierre de Rochemore claimed that: "Nothing goes more against the development of the colony and the population than licentiousness with slaves and native women; this is aggravated by people being widely scattered and by their mobility. We cannot take enough precautions in this matter, nor be careful enough to urge young people to get married early on to ensure that they settle down . . . ." The officer, who would later become *commissaire-ordonnateur* in Louisiana, established a link between the weak peopling of the colony, the dispersion and mobility of settlers, and the propensity of white men to maintain liaisons across status and race.[4]

3. The Capuchins of Louisiana (Father Raphaël) to the Company of the Indies's Directors, May 16, 1724, ANOM COL C13A 8, fols. 416–420r; Father Raphaël to Abbé Raguet, May 15, 1725, ANOM COL C13A 8, fols. 399–406. See also "Lettre à la Nouvelle Orléans, ce vingt septième Octobre 1727," in [Marie Madeleine] Hachard, *Relation du voyage des dames religieuses Ursulines de Rouen à La Nouvelle-Orléans* (1728) (Paris, 1872), 36, "Lettre à la Nouvelle Orleans, ce vingt-quatrième avril 1728," 91, 99–100. For an article that takes these lamentations over the religious and moral disorder at face value, see Carl A. Brasseaux, "The Moral Climate of French Colonial Louisiana, 1699–1763," *Louisiana History*, XXVII (1986), 27–42. For the association between the Antilles and libertinage in colonial narratives, see Doris Garraway, *The Libertine Colony: Creolization in the Early French Caribbean* (Durham, N.C., 2005).

4. [Vincent-Gaspard-Pierre de Rochemore], "Mémoire sur l'administration de la Louisiane," ANOM COL C13A 33, fol. 156v. See also "Plan pour rendre la Louisiane la plus riche et la plus puissante de toutes les colonies françaises, par Redon de Rassac," Aug. 15, 1763, ANOM COL C13A 43, fols. 377–389v.

Whether these various commentators intended to denounce the religious and moral climate of the colony or to propose pronatalist measures to expand the colonial population, they acknowledged the transformations experienced by sexual and family norms as they were transferred from Europe to Louisiana. At stake was the containment of sexuality and family within the framework of Christian marriage. Local demographic and social circumstances made it difficult for the population of European descent to maintain this ideal and to impose it on African and Native American slaves. Still, the ideal of Christian marriage remained powerful. The development of a colonial and slave society might have weakened the institution, but it continued to determine what was deemed honorable and respectable in the eyes of white officials and settlers. Christian marriage contributed to the construction of a hierarchical socioracial order, since not all members of the urban population were expected to follow the same religious and moral standards. Sexuality and family played a crucial role in the segmentation of New Orleans's society.[5]

Despite the Code Noir's stated goal "to maintain the discipline of the Roman Apostolic Catholic Church," the colony lacked the ecclesiastical forces to evangelize the growing slave population. Missionaries received no assistance from central or local authorities or from lay masters, who did not show much interest in integrating the black majority within the Christian community, except for the female congregation. Even when slaveholders incited or allowed their laborers to be baptized, they were reluctant to let them wed in church. Moreover, the Code Noir also outlawed interracial marriage and concubinage. This early prohibition was respected most of the time. Consequently, *métissage* developed outside the framework of Christian marriage.[6]

Louisiana's demographic and social makeup was such that métissage could not but thrive. The discrepancy between law and social practice has

5. This chapter focuses on the transfer, appropriation, and transformation of family norms from Europe to Louisiana for two main reasons. First, Europeans were in a position, at least partially, to impose their norms on slaves of African and Native American descent. Second, the documentation does not provide enough material to study the transfer and survival of matrimonial practices from Africa. Moreover, even if African kinship structures and relations were transferred and reproduced in the New World, their meanings would have necessarily undergone change, since they were implemented in a different social context marked by chattel slavery.

6. "Code Noir ou édit du roi servant de règlement pour le gouvernement et l'administration de la justice, police, discipline, et commerce des esclaves nègres de la province et colonie de la Louisiane," March 1724, ANOM COL B 43, fols. 388–407.

often been interpreted as a sign of a lenient racial regime. What has been overlooked is the various forms interracial sexuality could take, from rape to marriage, and what they reveal about the ways the phenomenon was perceived and handled. The association of métissage with either coerced or consensual sex, illegitimate or legitimate unions, or private, hidden relationships versus public, open ones changes its social significance. To understand how institutional and social actors viewed and used interracial sexuality to negotiate power relationships, it is necessary to place mixed unions within a broader study of sexuality and family among and between the urban population's various components.[7]

Rather than a general moral and religious disorder, what developed in New Orleans was a multifarious set of sexual and family values and practices that differed according to status, gender, and race. Even though not all bachelors could marry, marriage remained the norm for whites. In contrast, illegitimate unions constituted the standard for slaves. Widespread interracial sexuality also led to the formation of invisible mixed families, but most of the numerous children born to mixed unions remained enslaved and were not acknowledged by their white fathers. Métissage in Louisiana, as in Saint-Domingue, did not undermine racial formation; on the contrary, it contributed to reinforcing a system of racial domination.[8]

7. For specific studies on métissage in Louisiana, see Guillaume Aubert, "'The Blood of France': Race and Purity of Blood in the French Atlantic World," *William and Mary Quarterly,* LXI (2004), 439–478; Aubert, "'To Establish One Law and Definite Rules': Race, Religion, and the Transatlantic Origins of the Louisiana Code Noir," in Cécile Vidal, ed., *Louisiana: Crossroads of the Atlantic World* (Philadelphia, 2014), 21–43; Jennifer M. Spear, "'They Need Wives': Métissage and the Regulation of Sexuality in French Louisiana, 1699–1730," in Martha Hodes, ed., *Sex, Love, Race: Crossing Boundaries in North American History* (New York, 1999), 35–59; Spear, "Colonial Intimacies: Legislating Sex in French Louisiana," *William and Mary Quarterly,* LX (2003), 75–98; and Spear, *Race, Sex, and Social Order in Early New Orleans* (Baltimore, 2009), 17–99. In the historiographies on families in the Americas, the white family, slave family, and métissage are too often examined separately. See Julie Hardwick, Sarah M. Pearsall, and Karin Wulf, "Introduction: Centering Families in Atlantic History," *William and Mary Quarterly,* LXX (2013), 205–224; and Nara Milanich, "Whither Family History? A Road Map from Latin America," *American Historical Review,* CXII (2007), 439–458.

8. In her study of the discourse on libertinage in Saint-Domingue, Doris Garraway explains that, "rather than viewing the coincidence of racially exclusionary law and interracial libertinage as a contradiction, I consider these phenomena to be mutually reinforcing and constitutive of the system of white supremacy and racial domination that shaped French slave societies." See Garraway, *Libertine Colony,* 30. See also Rashauna Johnson,

Despite lamentations about the moral and religious disorder in the colony, marriage was instrumental in the establishment of a viable settler society. Colonists and soldiers rushed into marriage when they could, and these unions lasted, since they were not weakened by high mortality rates, unlike in the West Indies. Encouraged by the state's pronatalist policies, marriage thrived among whites because migrants came with a marital culture inherited from the Catholic Reformation; Louisiana's demographic and environmental circumstances were not as unfavorable as in the islands; and surviving, putting down roots, and forming a cohesive society demanded it. Although solemnized unions remained standard practice among whites, concubinage also existed, but it was not widespread. Even among whites, only the male elite could display their white concubines in public. Regardless of Caillot's statement, moral concerns over sexuality quickly came to focus on métissage, and the virtue of white women ceased to be a social issue after the 1730s.[9]

Whites' Marital Culture

Imperial officials adopted a pronatalist policy in Louisiana early on, modeled on that followed in France and Canada from the late seventeenth century onward that encouraged marriage among whites. After noting a high number of boys and girls of marriageable age in the 1736 census, the minister of the navy stressed to Governor Jean-Baptiste Le Moyne de Bienville and Commissaire-ordonnateur Edmé Gatien Salmon that it was "important for the good of the colony that you encourage marriage as much as you can." Public authorities, nevertheless, had very few means at their disposal to enforce such a plan. The crown first urged settlers to wed at the age of twenty for boys and sixteen for girls, whereas in practice the age at first marriage in the metropole was late (around twenty-nine years old for men and twenty-seven for women in cities in the mid-eighteenth century). The monarch also sent 120 *filles du roi*, or king's daughters (young single women whose migration was sponsored by the crown), to the colony between 1717 and 1721 with the only migratory wave ever organized to Louisi-

---

Slavery's Metropolis: Unfree Labor in New Orleans during the Age of Revolutions (Cambridge, 2016), 16–17.

9. On the fragility of white marriages in the West Indies, see Trevor Burnard, "A Failed Settler Society: Marriage and Demographic Failure in Early Jamaica," *Journal of Social History*, XXVIII (1994), 63–82.

ana. Likewise, the female orphans whose parents had been killed during the Natchez Wars became embroiled in the royal program favoring marriage. The king agreed to give the nuns a pension of 150 livres for each orphan, as the Company of the Indies had previously done, but he insisted that these girls were "destined to be married as soon as they reach the age to do so." But, since such a step only concerned a few women, it could have only a limited impact.[10]

Royal pronatalist policy would have been inoperative if colonists had not shared the state's commitment to the institution of matrimony. The sacramental records confirm the eagerness of settlers and soldiers to get married, especially in the early years after the colony's founding. From July 1720 to December 1733, 440 marriages between whites were celebrated in New Orleans, and 175 of these ceremonies, or 40 percent, took place during the first three and a half years. Out of these 440 unions, 170 were second marriages, 30 of which concerned at least one survivor of the Natchez attack. If marriages involving such survivors are not taken into account, the rate of remarriage in New Orleans (32 percent) was close to that of Quebec City (28 percent between 1621 and 1760). This means that mortality in Louisiana was not much higher than in Canada and much less than in the Antilles. Although it is impossible to calculate the average length of marriages, since the sacramental records are incomplete, unions in the Mississippi colony probably lasted much longer than in the islands. Among the 170 second marriages, 91 included a widow, 24 a widower, and 55 both a widow and a widower. This situation was typical of a society with an unbalanced sex ratio

10. For the crown's encouragement of settlers to marry, see the minister of the navy to Jean-Baptiste Le Moyne de Bienville and Edmé Gatien Salmon, Oct. 10, 1736, ANOM COL B 64, fols. 508v–509r; and "Mémoire du roi pour servir d'instruction au Sieur de Kerlérec, gouverneur de la province de la Louisiane," Oct. 17, 1752, ANOM COL B 95, fol. 338. Most royal pronatalist actions related to marriage, but, the crown also paid the wages of one or two midwives in New Orleans throughout the French regime to fight against infant mortality. See Bienville and Salmon to the minister of the navy, Apr. 1, 1734, ANOM COL C13A 18, fol. 35r; "Colonies 1754, Louisiane," ANOM COL C13A 37, fols. 164–174; and "État des dépenses à faire à la Louisiane pour le service du roi pendant l'année 1764," Apr. 6, 1764, ANOM COL C13A 44, fols. 39–46. On the female orphans destined to be married, see the minister of the navy to Bienville and Salmon, Oct. 17, 1736, ANOM COL B 64, fol. 515. For royal pronatalist policy in France and Canada, see Leslie Tuttle, *Conceiving the Old Regime: Pronatalism and the Politics of Reproduction in Early Modern France* (Oxford, 2010); Yves Landry, *Les Filles du roi au XVIIe siècle: Orphelines en France, pionnières au Canada; suivi d'un répertoire biographique des Filles du roi* (Montreal, 1992).

owing to a predominantly male population and benefited widows, who were in a powerful situation to negotiate remarriage.[11]

In the colony's later years, reduced migration resulted in a decline in the marriage rate. Despite the growth of the white population, only 227 marriages were celebrated between 1759 and 1768. The rate of remarriage also decreased to around 24 percent. During the last decade of the French regime, of those spouses for whom information is available 76.3 percent of brides and 27 percent of grooms were born locally. Only 11.5 percent of the women were born in France, compared with 61.4 percent of the men. Although some women continued to arrive in the colony, migrants from France were predominantly male. Women born in Louisiana were instrumental in the social integration of these newcomers, who were much less numerous than in the Antilles and not a serious threat to the social order. Though the marriage rate in New Orleans was probably lower than in the metropole, since less men could marry owing to an unbalanced sex ratio, marriage still played a crucial role among whites, helping to root and stabilize the urban society and increase its cohesiveness.[12]

Judging from the colonists' own words, it was difficult to be fully integrated socially without being married. In 1730, a trial took place over the breaking off of a promise of marriage. Jacques Carrière Malozé, the future groom, ended his engagement to Demoiselle Charlotte Corentine Million after rumors started to circulate accusing his future bride of having given birth to a child out of wedlock in the metropole. During the investigation, the young woman argued that it was particularly harmful to be "viewed as a poor wretch in a country in which she is known by very few people." Her defense underlined the problems caused by having migrated unaccompanied and lacking family support.[13]

11. Although the marriages recorded in these registers were celebrated in New Orleans, they could concern people who lived outside the city. For the rate of second marriage in Quebec City, see Danielle Gauvreau, *Québec: Une ville et sa population au temps de la Nouvelle-France* (Sillery, Quebec, 1991), 122–133, 216. In France, the rate of second marriage in the seventeenth and eighteenth century varied between 15 and 25 percent. See Scarlett Beauvalet-Boutouyrie, *La démographie de l'époque moderne* (Paris, 1999), 121–124. For the social position of widows, see RSCL 1740/05/16/02; 1746/10/18/02; 1746/10/18/03.

12. Among the fifty-five second marriages recorded in New Orleans's church registers, thirty included a widow, eleven a widower, and fourteen both a widow and a widower.

13. RSCL 1730/08/28/01, 1730/09/02/01, 1730/09/05/01, 1730/09/12/01, 1730/09/13/01, 1730/09/16/01, 1730/09/16/02, 1730/09/16/03, 1730/10/24/01, 1730/11/18/03, 1730/11/18/06.

If, for all colonists, getting married was a necessity in order to benefit from some assistance and solidarity, for the elite, taking a wife was also seen as a sign of their commitment to the colony. When François Fleuriau resigned from his position as attorney general, left, and then returned in 1725, he had to provide evidence that he had decided to settle for good. After asking for a royal commission for Fleuriau, the Superior Council's members reassured the Company of the Indies's directors of the attorney's newly formed ties to Louisiana:

> Finally, to give some proof of his attachment and feelings for the colony he got married there, Mr. Bruslé and Fazende did the same, and these three weddings were celebrated the same day, the ceremony taking place on the last day in December; Mr. Fleuriau and Fazende married two daughters of Mr. Desmorières and Mr. Bruslé their first cousin who is the daughter of the deceased Mr. Le Blanc, a storekeeper in New Orleans, a family which you had strongly recommended to us. This triple alliance enhances our society, as all of these three ladies are very pleasant and of good birth, the word is that people hope this will foster a strong unity within the Council and will make the three magistrates settle for good, and [bring] prosperity to the colony.

This spectacular triple ceremony united families headed by men who were all in the company's service.[14]

Marriage for the elite was also a crucial instrument to distinguish themselves and help them to assert their authority over the rest of society. Through their choice of spouse, who had to be "of good birth," men could form multiple alliances and acquire the civility they believed only women could provide. For the same reason, top officials and low-level employees who had left their wives in the metropole felt the need to bring them to Louisiana, even when they knew that their career would take them away from the colony. As Royal Commissioner Jacques de La Chaise explained, "The more men and women of breeding among us, the more we will live in peace and harmony." Despite a shared commitment to marriage among all segments of the white population, sexual relationships outside of wedlock still occurred, although not on a large scale.[15]

14. For the triple marriage, see Pierre Dugué de Boisbriant, Jacques de La Chaise, Antoine Bruslé, and François Fleuriau, Jan. 20, 1725, ANOM COL C13A 9, fol. 14; and Marcel Giraud, *A History of French Louisiana*, V, *The Company of the Indies, 1723–1731*, trans. Brian Pearce (Baton Rouge, La., 1991), 272–273.

15. For wives brought from the metropole, see Étienne Périer and La Chaise to the

Disorder of Families

Sexuality out of Wedlock and Illegitimacy among Whites

Concerns over colonists' morality were first raised by local authorities in connection with 150 women of low repute brought to Louisiana, along with numerous convicts and exiles, in the migratory wave organized between 1717 and 1720. By the early 1720s, La Chaise had proposed "to send them inland among the natives," while the Superior Council had expressed the desire to transport them back to the metropole. Still, they really became an issue in the administrative correspondence when Étienne Périer became governor in 1727. Unlike his predecessor, Bienville, Périer was married, and his wife accompanied him to New Orleans. They arrived at roughly the same time as the Ursulines. Under his spouse's influence, he tried to distinguish himself from Bienville and to assert his authority as governor by presenting himself as a paragon of virtue, which included cracking down on sexual misconduct. In one of Ursuline Marie Madeleine Hachard's letters to her father, she wrote that the governor "declares war on vice" and that the "women of low virtue" were severely punished. Since a few of them gave birth to illegitimate children, Périer and La Chaise promulgated a ruling reminding the population of the Royal Ordinance of Blois (1579), which required unwed pregnant women and girls to declare their pregnancy and the name of their baby's father to the clerk's office. They also planned to build a workhouse. In the meantime, they asked the Ursulines to establish a room to be used as a reformatory, an arrangement the nuns were not happy with.[16]

Over time, prostitution among white women did not entirely disappear, but, as many of these exiled women of low repute died or merged with the population, it no longer caused significant scandal. The concern only resurfaced prominently once. In the 1750s, Governor Pierre de Rigaud de Vau-

---

minister of the navy, Apr. 22, 1727, ANOM COL C13A 10, fol. 176r; and La Chaise to the Company of the Indies's Directors, Apr. 29, 1728, ANOM COL C13A 11, fol. 166.

16. La Chaise to the Company of the Indies, Mar. 8, 1724, ANOM COL C13A 7, fol. 20v; Extracts from the letters of the Council of Louisiana, Aug. 28, 1725, ANOM COL C13A 9, fols. 240r, 249r, 250r; "Relation à la Nouvelle Orléans, ce vingt-septième Octobre 1727," in Hachard, *Relation du voyage des dames religieuses Ursulines,* 79–80, "Lettre à la Nouvelle Orleans, ce premier Janvier 1728," 84–85, "Lettre à la Nouvelle Orleans," Apr. 24, 1728, 97, 101, 110; "Arrêt du Conseil Supérieur de la Louisiane du 29 juillet 1727 sur la grossesse des filles et femmes non mariées," ANOM COL A 23, fol. 86; Périer and La Chaise to the minister of the navy, Nov. 2, 1727, ANOM COL C13A 10, fol. 200; Périer and La Chaise to the Company of the Indies's Directors, Nov. 3, 1728, ANOM COL C13A 11, fol. 145; Father d'Avaucour to the minister of the navy, Oct. 30, 1731, ANOM COL C13A 13, fol. 265–266r; Périer and Salmon to the minister of the navy, Mar. 29, 1732, ANOM COL C13A 14, fols. 8–9.

dreuil de Cavagnal ordered a white woman of the lower sort to be exhibited on a wooden horse and banished to a deserted island on Lake Pontchartrain because she prostituted herself. Her activity disturbed public order, as soldiers did not hesitate to leave the barracks at night to go to see her. Prostitution of white women was likely much more widespread than this one incident would suggest. Free Native and black enslaved women were not the only ones who sold their sexual favors. Yet the practice was apparently tolerated among white women as long as it was confined to private homes and not made public.[17]

Officials originally associated illegitimacy with prostitution because of the women of low virtue sent to the colony in the early 1720s, but sexuality out of wedlock also occurred among whites in other circumstances. Although illegitimate births were not kept as quiet as monetized sex, it is difficult to measure the rate of the phenomenon based on the existing documentation. Despite the 1727 local ruling recalling the Ordinance of Blois, no register of unwed mothers was ever kept. This situation conformed to an evolution that took place in the metropole, where pressure on fathers of illegitimate children to force them to face up to their responsibilities tended to decrease over the eighteenth century. Moreover, keeping such a register would probably have made no sense in a slave society, where illegitimacy among slaves constituted the norm. In the absence of a register of unwed mothers, the sacramental records reveal a few baptisms of natural children born to white parents. Nonetheless, the number of illegitimate births recorded among whites was very likely lower than the actual number. In those documented cases, natural children were presented either by both their unwed parents, their single mother, or even their single father. Illegitimate births were thus related to all kinds of family arrangements and social situations.[18]

17. For the 1750 incident involving the white prostitute, see Honoré-Gabriel Michel to the minister of the navy, Sept. 29, 1750, ANOM COL C13A 34, fols. 339–340, 342. The archives mention only a few instances of prostitutes of African or Native American descent. See Michel to the minister of the navy, July 15, 1751, ANOM COL C13A 35, fols. 287–288; and RSCL 1764/07/10/02.

18. On the declining pressure on fathers of illegitimate children to face up to their responsibilities in the metropole, see Vincent Gourdon and François-Joseph Ruggiu, "Familles en situation coloniale," *Annales de démographie historique*, CXXII, no. 2 (2011), 16; and Marie-Claude Phan, *Les amours illégitimes: Histoires de séduction en Languedoc (1676–1786)* (Toulouse, France, 1986), 119–136. Illegitimacy was also very low in New France, even in cities (less than 2 percent in the three urban parishes before 1730), probably because people married much earlier than in the metropole. See Lyne Paquette and

Whatever the circumstances, the church always condemned illegitimacy. The priests who recorded the baptisms of children born outside of wedlock did not try to hide their religious opprobrium, especially when the parents did not belong to the elite. When Pierre Bernard, a shoemaker in New Orleans, and Toinette Duby, who were not married, presented their son for baptism, the missionary specified on the certificate that "the mother of the child claims she is a widow. Rumor has it that she came from Geneva, which remains to be confirmed. For the sake of the infant, the godfather was Pierre Dégout, a butcher practicing in this city, and the godmother Marie Jean Rivet, a seamstress in this city." In that case, the godparents were chosen among whites of the lower sort, but for the illegitimate infant of Catherine Nodel, "from the English nation," the priest exceptionally resorted to a "mulatto" slave and a free "negress," even though people of African or mixed descent, either enslaved or free, were generally not chosen as godparents for white people.[19]

All illegitimate children, however, were not treated with the same social disgrace. Some, who were presumably born to more fortunate white couples, were publicly recognized and socially integrated, although they remained in an inferior position to legitimate children. In 1746, the Superior Council received a request from a man named François Allevin, who presented himself as the natural son of François Allevin. His father's heirs had agreed to grant him the sum of three thousand livres from the estate, but, since he was only twenty-three years old and wanted to make his property work for him, he asked for emancipation and the nomination of a trustee.[20]

Likewise, some elite individuals were able to publicly maintain informal unions and illegitimate children. Such an unconventional family life distinguished them from the rest of the population. Although marriage remained standard practice, concubines of elite white men were no more overlooked—except by priests—in the colony than in the metropole. Some

---

Réal Bates, "Les naissances illégitimes sur les rives du Saint-Laurent avant 1730," *Revue d'histoire de l'Amérique française*, XL (1986), 239–252. The New Orleans sacramental records also include some funerals of illegitimate children. See ANOM COL G1 412, 1726, Burials, 09/05/1726, 10/26/1726. The mother's name was not always mentioned, and the father's name was recorded as "unknown." See ANOM COL G1 412, 1727, Burials, 09/10/1727. Sometimes only the mother's name was mentioned. See ANOM COL G1 412, 1727, Burials, 05/10/1727, 07/07/1727, 07/19/1727. In the latter cases, the name of the father was mentioned, but neither the mother's nor the child's.

19. For the choice of witnesses for illegitimate infants, see AANO, Saint-Louis Cathedral Baptisms, 1763–1767, 02/18/1763, 10/02/1763.

20. RSCL 1746/08/06/03.

prominent military officers chose not to marry long-standing white partners because these marriages would have constituted a misalliance. According to Father Raphaël, the chevalier de Louboey, for instance, maintained "a
scandalous commerce with Lady Garnier retained in the colony by lettre de
cachet" until his death. A younger son of a family from Béarn, de Louboey
was described by Father Raphaël as a "protestant by birth" who had abjured
Calvinism but only displayed a fake Catholicism. The priest was especially
scandalized since "the two of them take some pride in their concubinage,
they stroll around together and live with such a familiarity in front of everybody as if they were united by a legitimate union." In the mid-1720s, they
already had one illegitimate child, and a second one was on the way. This
unsanctioned but open relationship was concealed from central authorities
and tolerated within the colony, except when the officer was in conflict with
one or several local officials. The concubinage affected de Louboey's career
but only minimally, for he ended his life as the *major* in Mobile and was
granted the cross of Saint-Louis in 1744. After his death, which left his unofficial widow penniless, Governor Vaudreuil interceded in her favor, asking the king to allow her to go back to France, where she intended to retire
to a convent.[21]

In the last decades of the French regime, white elite women who did not
follow the dominant religious and moral norms in the matter of family and
sexuality no longer aroused any particular concerns, and they were not out-
cast. In 1724, Sieur Pantin Cadot was actually sentenced to one month in
jail for having published lampoons and written verse against "the honor of
the ladies of New Orleans." Apart from this case, the records of the Superior
Council include only one other trial for insults challenging the sexual repu-

21. La Chaise and the four councillors to the minister of the navy, Apr. 26, 1725, ANOM
COL C13A 9, fol. 135; Father Raphaël to Abbé Raguet, May 15, 1725, ANOM COL C13A
8, fol. 406r; Father Raphaël to Abbé Raguet, May 18, 1726, ANOM COL C13A 10, fol. 46;
Bienville to the minister of the navy, May 18, 1733, ANOM COL C13A 16, fols. 243–244r;
Bienville to the minister of the navy, Apr. 23, 1734, ANOM COL C13A 18, fols. 166–170r;
Pierre de Rigaud de Vaudreuil de Cavagnal to the minister of the navy, May 15, 1751,
ANOM COL C13A 35, fol. 125; Carl A. Brasseaux, *France's Forgotten Legion: A CD-ROM
Publication; Service Records of French Military and Administrative Personnel Stationed
in the Mississippi Valley and Gulf Coast Region, 1699–1769* (Baton Rouge, La., 2000). A
military officer named Joseph de Bellenos also lived in a state of public concubinage with
a woman from Saint-Domingue. Their relationship was tolerated so as long as the couple
did not pretend to be married. The woman's single status did not allow her to become
fully integrated within Louisiana's society in the same way as a married woman. At the
same time, she was not completely excluded from the social life of the elite. See Rochemore to the minister of the navy, June 22, 1760, ANOM COL C13A 42, fols. 113–114.

tation of a married woman, but it involved settlers living at the Natchez outpost. These two instances are revealing of the climate of suspicion over moral and sexual issues that existed during the first decade after the arrival of a wave of migrants. Afterward, there were surprisingly no suits asking for reparation after sexual insults had been uttered against white women. In that regard, Louisiana stands apart from the common experience of both France and Canada, where verbal violence against women most often challenged their sexual reputation. After the early 1730s, the high rate and solidity of marriages among whites, especially women, and the commonness of métissage, alleviated concerns about white women's respectability and morality. Still, marriage was not a white privilege, as masters also promoted the matrimonial institution among their own enslaved workers.[22]

SLAVE MARRIAGES AS AN INSTRUMENT

OF MASTERS' SOCIAL CONTROL

Whereas the enslaved in the Antilles rarely went to church to get married during the early modern period, the number of slaves marrying in New Orleans and its plantation district started to rise over time. Masters, however, only encouraged such unions if they served their interests and were careful not to let slaves use the institution to their own advantage. Unlike what happened in slave societies under Spanish or Portuguese sovereignty, a church wedding in French New Orleans was not, for the most part, a privileged site for the exercise of agency for enslaved or free people of African descent. Despite the relatively high number of slave marriages in Louisiana compared with that in the islands, most enslaved men and women maintained pseudo-conjugal relationships without exchanging religious vows or sharing the same residency, especially in the city. The matrimonial culture of free people of color was even less developed than that of slaves. Deciphering what meanings enslaved and free people of African or mixed descent attached to their unions remains difficult.[23]

22. For recourse to sexual insults against women in the early 1720s, see RSCL 1724/ 02/01/01, 1724/02/05/02, 1724/02/07/02, 1724/03/28/01. In 1725, a woman was accused of being a whore and having been caught cheating on her husband with a sergeant. See RSCL 1725/06/13/01. For the comparison between Louisiana and Canada or France in the matter of sexual insults against women, see Shannon Lee Dawdy, *Building the Devil's Empire: French Colonial New Orleans* (Chicago, 2008), 169–175; and Peter N. Moogk, "'Thieving Buggers' and 'Stupid Sluts': Insults and Popular Culture in New France," *William and Mary Quarterly*, XXXVI (1979), 524–547.

23. On slave marriages in the French Antilles, see Myriam Cottias, "La famille antillaise du XVIIème au XIXème siècle: Étude anthropologique et démographique; en-

Slave marriages did not increase in number until the last decades of the French regime. It took years of evangelization before the number of solemnized unions in the slave community started to rise. Between 1759 and 1769, the period for which a complete series of marriage records is available, the Capuchins united sixty-seven enslaved couples. The figure might seem insignificant compared with the size of the slave population, but slave marriages accounted for more than 25 percent of all solemnized unions. Moreover, 397 (12 percent) of the 3,226 enslaved infants baptized between 1744 and 1769 had married parents.[24]

It is unclear how many of the slave marriages celebrated in the New Orleans church concerned enslaved individuals actually living in the city. The few probate records listing the property of white urban dwellers seldom mentioned slave couples, with or without children. Most of the time, only single slaves, of either sex, or women with children were listed. In comparison with those residing on plantations, the small number of slaves living within urban households was not favorable to the development of coresidential nuclear families among urban slaves. Even so, life in the city made it easier for couples, married or not, and family members living apart to see each other. Urban slaves did not have to escape the way plantation slaves did to visit their partners, children, and other relatives. Although the judicial archives comprise many trials of slaves who had run away to see loved ones, the accused always lived in the countryside. Nevertheless, even in New Orleans, masters still tried to impede the clandestine circulation of

---

racinements créoles" (Ph.D. diss., École des Hautes Études en Sciences Sociales, 1990); Arlette Gautier, "Les familles esclaves aux Antilles françaises, 1635–1848," *Population*, LV (2000), 975–1002; Bernard Moitt, *Women and Slavery in the French Antilles, 1635–1848* (Bloomington, Ind., 2001); and Vincent Cousseau, *Prendre nom aux Antilles: Individu et appartenances (XVIIe–XIXe siècle)* (Paris, 2012), 168–169. On the use of marriage for the exercise of agency by enslaved or free people of African descent in Iberian colonies, see Charlotte de Castelnau-L'Estoile, "La liberté du sacrement: Droit canonique et mariage des esclaves dans le Brésil colonial," *Annales: Histoire, Sciences Sociales*, LXV (2010), 1349–1383; Castelnau-L'Estoile, "'Les fils soumis de la Très Sainte Église': Esclavage et stratégies matrimoniales à Rio de Janeiro au début du XVIIIe siècle," in Myriam Cottias and Hebe Mattos, eds., *Esclavage et subjectivités dans l'Atlantique luso-brésilien et français (XVIIe–XXe siècles)* (Marseille, France, 2016), http://books.openedition.org/oep/1501; and Herman L. Bennett, *Africans in Colonial Mexico: Absolutism, Christianity, and Afro-Creole Consciousness, 1570–1640* (Bloomington, Ind., 2003).

24. On the evangelization of the slave community, see Emily Clark and Virginia Meacham Gould, "The Feminine Face of Afro-Catholicism in New Orleans, 1727–1852," *William and Mary Quarterly*, LIX (2002), 409–448.

their slaves at night for sexual or family reasons. In 1737, for example, Raymond Amyot d'Ausseville sought to void the rent on one of his old houses to a settler named Tixerant through an intermediary because the latter once had one of d'Ausseville's female slaves whipped for having sex with one of his enslaved laborers.[25]

Masters were supported in their efforts to control their slaves' sexual and family lives by the Code Noir. Even as Articles 7 and 8 forbade owners to compel their enslaved workers to marry, slaves could not do so without their masters' consent. At the same time, the permission of the enslaved couple's parents was not required. It is hard to verify whether the first part of this prohibition was ever respected. In 1759, the Ursulines deliberated over whether they should purchase "a negress to marry one of our negroes since there is an auction sale in the city," without much apparent concern for their slaves' freedom to choose their own marriage partners. In contrast, the second part of the Code Noir's provision was strictly applied. In 1742, a free woman of color named Geneviève Irisse recorded a certificate at the clerk's office attesting that she was not a slave and that she could get married whenever the Capuchins chose. Missionaries would not have celebrated the union of a woman of African descent without being sure of her status and, if she was enslaved, without securing the consent of her master. Requiring authorization from owners in effect made slaves perpetual minors and infringed on their freedom to marry.[26]

The legal requirement to obtain their masters' permission limited slaves' access to the institution of matrimony. After 1759, marriage certificates of enslaved persons often included both the owner's authorization and the mutual consent of the bride and groom, but, none of the spouses, out of all the marriages recorded, belonged to separate owners. This was also true of the married couples involved in the baptisms of the 397 enslaved infants recorded between 1744 and 1769. Although slaves were not passive actors of their own evangelization, masters exercised strict control over their relations to religious sacraments. They likely only encouraged and authorized the formation of unions among their own slaves to favor what they called

25. NONA June 6, 1748; NONA Kernion Apr. 3, 1764; NONA Dec. 20, 1764; NONA June 17, 1765, June 20, 1765, Aug. 26, 1765; NONA Kernion Dec. 12, 1765; NONA Kernion Feb. 4, 1766; NONA Garic Jan. 31, 1766; NONA, Garic Sept. 10, 1766; NONA Garic Jan. 15, 1768; "Inventory of the Estate of Sieur Jean Baptiste Prevost, Deceased Agent of the Company of the Indies, July 13, 1769," trans. and ed. Edith Dart Price and Heloise H. Cruzat, *LHQ*, IX (1926), 486; RSCL 1737/02/12/01.

26. "Délibérations du Conseil 1727–1902," Aug. 6, 1759, HNOC, Archives of the Ursuline Nuns of the Parish of Orleans Microfilm 1 of 19, fol. 47; RSCL 1742/10/17/01.

"production," likely because the slave trade from Africa practically ceased after 1731. The main reason for the rise in slave marriages was a local adaptation to a situation of shortage. The relatively high number of slave marriages in New Orleans had nothing to do with the fact that the Code Noir seemed to promote the institution of matrimony among the enslaved. If this had been the case, the code should have had the same impact in the Antilles that it did in the Mississippi colony. The king and the minister of the navy never displayed any concern about slave marriages in their correspondence with Louisiana's authorities.[27]

Church officials sometimes entered into conflict with slaveholders, condemning owners' frequent laxity in providing religious instruction for their enslaved laborers before such important rites as baptism and marriage. In 1727–1728, Father Raphaël complained to his superior Abbé Raguet that the Jesuits had tried to force him to celebrate the marriage of a slave who had been baptized with another one who was not. He then reported that "the master of the slaves whom I had refused to marry then married them on his own authority, without having taken pains since then to instruct them or have the one who is not baptized instructed so that he could receive this first sacrament." The Jesuits might have celebrated the union, or the owner himself might have performed a kind of profane ceremony. In the chapter of his travel account that served as a sort of planter's manual, Antoine-Simon Le Page du Pratz also insisted on the need "to assign each of them a wife, to keep clear of debauchery and its bad consequences," but he did not specify that such unions be formalized by the sacrament of marriage. Likewise, the Ursuline Hachard was deeply concerned about the lack of religious instruction of enslaved girls who were married at a young age. She observed: "The custom here is to marry girls at the age of twelve and fourteen; before our arrival many had been married without even know-

27. Only five possible exceptions to the rule that parents of enslaved infants who were baptized belonged to the same master exist. They do not indicate the name of the father's owner nor specify whether he or she was the same as the mother's. See AANO, Saint-Louis Cathedral Baptisms, 1744–1753, 1759–1762, 1763–1767, and 1767–1771, 06/16/1749, 02/18/1760, 08/06/1763, 04/05/1765, 01/22/1769. On the need for the "production" of slaves, see Salmon to the minister of the navy, Apr. 25, 1741, ANOM COL C13A 26, fols. 136–138. Despite public authorities' general lack of concern for the evangelization of slaves, the Company of the Indies's ordinance regarding its own domestic slaves, promulgated one year after the Code Noir, included an article about the need to provide for slaves' religious instruction and to encourage marriage, if possible. See "Ordonnance pour les nègres domestiques de la Compagnie," July 25, 1725, ANOM COL F3 242, fols. 56–57.

Disorder of Families

ing how many gods there were, just imagine; but since we have been here, no one can be married unless she has attended our classes in religious instruction." The weakness of slaves' catechism is confirmed by the celebration of a few slave unions immediately after the baptism of one or both of the spouses. These cases most often concerned adults baptized in a group on Easter or Whit Sunday. On two occasions, group baptisms were followed by group marriages.[28]

Both church authorities and masters viewed slave marriages as unions between two individuals only, and not between two families or lineages. Wedding certificates did not provide information on spouses' parents and rarely mentioned the names of witnesses. Neither did they involve the publication of banns. In each of these respects, slave marriages differed from white marriages in that they did not comply with the solemnities prescribed by the Royal Ordinance of Blois (1579) and the Royal Declaration of 1639, which imposed the publication of banns and the use of witnesses. Despite Article 7 of the Code Noir, which called for these provisions to be observed with regard to free persons and slaves, they were not enforced. In the 1730s, missionaries sometimes resorted to white witnesses, but they did not respect the obligation of having four witnesses, and they apparently abandoned requiring witnesses altogether in the 1740s. After this period, the nuptial benediction was almost always given to slaves without witnesses. The Capuchins seem to have progressively realized how the slave system was changing the social significance of marriage for the black majority. Three certificates from the 1760s, however, exceptionally mentioned the presence of "witnesses," "friends," or "parents and friends," probably all of African descent, but without specifying their names or even their number. Even though slave marriages were not always recognized or acknowledged by masters and public authorities, some slaves had started to develop ex-

28. On conflicts between church officials and masters over slaves' matrimonial practices and lack of religious instruction, see Father Raphaël to Abbé Raguet, Apr. 18, 1727, ANOM COL C13A 10, fol. 326; Father Raphaël to Abbé Raguet, May 18, 1728, ANOM COL C13A 11, fol. 268v (quotation); *The History of Louisiana, or of the Western Parts of Virginia and Carolina ... Translated from the French of M. Le Page Du Pratz,...*, new ed. (London, 1774), 365; and "Lettre à la Nouvelle Orleans," Apr. 24, 1728, in Hachard, *Relation du voyage des dames religieuses Ursulines*, 97–98. Some masters were even reluctant to have their slaves baptized. See Father Raphaël to Abbé Raguet, May 15, 1725, ANOM COL C13A 8, fol. 403. For group marriages, see AANO, Saint-Louis Cathedral Baptisms, 1744–1753, 1753–1759, 1763–1767, and 1767–1771, 05/28/1746 (twelve marriages), 05/20/1747 (nine marriages), 03/29/1755 (two marriages), 04/27/1765, 05/27/1765, 10/29/1769.

tended families and larger kinship networks and to appropriate Christian marriage more thoroughly by the last decades of the French regime. They might have organized their own festive rituals in order to give a broader social dimension to their solemnized unions.[29]

Unions from the Perspective of Slaves and Free People of Color
Although whites did not assign the marriages of slaves and free people the same legal value and social meaning they reserved for their own, unions between slaves were still intended to form monogamous, indissoluble relationships. But neither slaves nor whites always respected this prescription. In 1748, two slaves who had been kidnapped and taken to Havana were brought back to New Orleans. When they were interrogated about other slaves who had managed to run away and take refuge on the Spanish island, they not only reported that other Louisiana slaves were living in the large Cuban port city but also revealed that some of them had married in Havana, even though they already had a spouse and, in some cases, children in Mobile or New Orleans. Apparently, they volunteered this information without prompting, which could mean that they had adopted Christian moral values.[30]

If escape from the colony could result in bigamy, the documentation also includes hints of a probable case of polygyny in New Orleans. In 1758, a white woman who wanted to be accepted as a permanent boarder at the Ursuline convent offered some money and a slave named Victoire to the Ursulines as a dowry. To avoid separating Victoire from her enslaved husband, Joseph Léveillé, a third party negotiated the nuns' acquisition of Joseph, instead of money. In the 1760s and 1770s, the Ursulines employed Joseph as an overseer. Although Victoire and Joseph had a legitimate son named Louis, he also fathered five illegitimate children. Their mother was a free woman of color named Marie Thérèse Carrière. Their natural chil-

---

29. In 1727, the priest officiating at a slave wedding notably recorded the first names of the parents of two slaves belonging to Governor Bienville. Bienville's paternalism toward his slaves might explain this departure. See AANO, Saint-Louis Cathedral Marriages, 1720–1730, 08/03/1727. In the 1720s, a priest mentioned the dispensation from banns in two certificates. See AANO, Saint-Louis Cathedral Marriages 1720–1730, 10/28/1727, 11/01/1727. The way missionaries organized and recorded slave marriages apparently differed from what prevailed in the Antilles. See Cousseau, *Prendre nom aux Antilles*, 169–170. For the three certificates in the 1760s listing the presence of witnesses at slave weddings, see AANO, Saint-Louis Cathedral Marriages, 1763–1766, 04/03/1763, 05/26/1765 (2 marriages).

30. RSCL 1748/03/22/01.

dren were born both before and after the celebration of Joseph's marriage to Victoire. Joseph Léveillé was manumitted in 1778, and, in 1786, he married Marie Thérèse Carrière. It is impossible to guess what meaning Léveillé and the two women gave to their triangular relationship.[31]

In addition to polygyny, Joseph Léveillé's and Marie Thérèse Carrière's case also raises the issue of marriage among free people of color and unions across status between people of African descent. Free blacks do not seem to have embraced the institution of matrimony. Over the course of the entire French regime, the sacramental records include only fifteen or so free married couples of color. The number of women of African or mixed descent was scarce, and free men of color also had to compete with white men.[32]

Some of the marriages uniting free people of color concerned slaves who had recently been freed and were still dependent on their former masters. One wedding certificate closely resembled that of a white couple. Atypically, the birthplace of both spouses was specified and the information was presented in the same way as for whites—both of them were "born in this parish." Several witnesses were also mentioned, including the bride's mother and brother. The bride and groom were nevertheless each qualified as a "free mulatto" who had been manumitted, and the names of their respective former masters were included. On the one hand, the marriage certificate acknowledged the kinship relationships that these free people of color had developed over two generations; on the other, it continued to place them in a position of subordination relative to their former owners. Two more typical certificates of free couples of color also mentioned the names of the colonists who had freed them. In one case, the former owners, the Marquis de Fremeur, a military officer, and Madame La Pommeray, attended the ceremony. The union apparently took place not long after the slaves had been freed, and the manumission deeds were presented at the wedding. These members of the colonial elite used their former slaves' nup-

31. "Délibérations du Conseil 1727–1902," Nov. 2 and 3, 1748, HNOC, Archives of the Ursuline Nuns of the Parish of Orleans, Microfilm 1 of 19, 45; NONA Garic VIII, 485, Feb. 15, 1777.

32. For marriages of free men and women of color, see AANO, Saint-Louis Cathedral Marriages, 1720–1730, 1731–1733, 1759–1762, 1763–1766, and 1764–1774, 06/05/1730, 03/19/1731, 05/17/1761, 09/01/1761, 01/07/1763, 07/04/1764, 09/13/1764, 04/??/?? (1767 or 1768). For the baptisms of infants born to legitimate couples who were free people of color, see AANO, Saint-Louis Cathedral Baptisms, 1731–1733, 1753–1759, 1759–1762, 1763–1767, and 1767–1771, 11/11/1731, 06/09/1757, 01/22/1759, 12/15/1759, 08/18/1761, 11/08/1762, 06/24/1764, 01/14/1765, 05/29/1765, 03/30/1766, 03/30/1767, 04/13/1767, 10/11/1767, 04/17/1768, 01/22/1769, 03/26/1769, 05/14/1769, 09/19/1769.

tials to publicly demonstrate their liberality and generosity while at the same time asserting the continuation of a relationship of dependency.[33]

Because most free women of color were out of their reach, some free blacks chose to marry enslaved women. The latter always belonged to white masters. Their male partners often fought hard to obtain their freedom. The process could take years. In the meantime, these families were torn between two worlds, that of free people and that of the enslaved. Any children were born slaves until their mothers were officially manumitted. Marriages involving enslaved women could also slow down a free black family's social ascendency and economic independence. When Tiocou from the "Senegal nation" won his freedom as a result of his participation in the expeditions against the Natchez of the 1730s, for instance, he was already married "before the Church" to a slave named Marie Aram, who belonged to his former master, Mr. de Kolly. It took a long time for Tiocou to redeem his wife, since her owners changed several times. At some point, Marie Aram was probably given to the Charity Hospital, because Tiocou signed a contract with its administrators and the Capuchins to work for the hospital for six years without any wages in order to purchase his wife's freedom. In 1744, her freedom was confirmed by the governor and the commissaire-ordonnateur after a request by the administrators of the hospital. In their demand, the administrators mentioned that the couple intended to remain in the charitable institution's service. It is very likely that the François, "free negro overseer of Charity Hospital," who served as a godfather in a baptism in 1750 was, in fact, Tiocou. Likewise, Marie, a "free negress" who was a servant at the Charity Hospital and acted twice as a godmother in 1747 and 1751, could have been his wife. At one point, they must have stopped working for the hospital, for there is a Tiogous named on one of the 1770 lists of free blacks living at the English Turn.[34]

33. AANO, Saint-Louis Cathedral Marriages, 1763–1766, 07/04/1764, 07/07/1763, 09/13/1764.

34. For examples of unions between free blacks and enslaved women in the sacramental records of marriage and baptism, see AANO, Saint-Louis Cathedral Marriages, 1720–1730, 11/27/1727, 04/04/1728, ??/??/1730; and AANO, Saint-Louis Cathedral Baptisms, 1744–1753, 1753–1759, 1759–1762, 1763–1767, and 1767–1771, 07/20/1746, 11/12/1758, 12/13/1761, 07/16/1765, 05/18/1769, 09/15/1769. On free black men's struggle to obtain their wives' or partners' freedom, see RSCL 1727/11/28/01, 1727/11/28/02, 1727/11/28/03, 1728/11/03/01, 1730/11/21/01, 1730/11/21/03, 1730/11/25/01, 1730/11/25/05; 1742/05/24/01; 1747/06/20/01. For Tiocou and his wife Marie Aram, see RSCL 1730/05/13/01, 1737/06/28/06, 1737/07/12/01, 1744/03/06/03; "Petition of Recovery," Oct. 29, 1737, in [Henry P. Dart], ed., "RSCL XVI," LHQ, V (1922), 418; AANO, Saint-

Disorder of Families

Unions between enslaved men and free women of color were much less common, doubtless because women had more choices than men to find a husband or partner. Yet, in 1758, a New Orleans priest celebrated the baptism of a free child of color born to Louison, a "free negress," and Bacchus, a slave belonging to Mr. Boisclair. They were not married, but the priest acknowledged the permanence of the union, since he qualified the infant with the unusual expression "natural son" and mentioned the father's name whereas most baptismal certificates of enslaved or free children of African or mixed descent typically specified that the father was unknown. Bacchus was apparently an unusual slave who managed to develop personal relationships with key members of the white community. In 1770, he became the *"capitaine moraine"* or captain of the *"moreno"* company of militia instituted by the Spanish in addition to the company formed of *"pardos"* ("moreno" and "pardo" were Spanish racial categories referring to dark or light-skinned persons). While enslaved, Bacchus could not transmit either his name or property to his children. Therefore, marriage might not have appeared to be legally or economically essential for the family.[35]

Among slaves, concubinage or long-term relationships without cohabitation were much more widespread than marriage. The church came to recognize some of these quasi marriages. In the continuous series of baptisms of enslaved infants starting in 1744, missionaries, who had not previously given any information about fathers, started to specify when a father was "unknown." In 138 (4.3 percent) of 3,226 baptismal certificates, the priest, who was often Father Dagobert, the Capuchins' superior, even mentioned fathers' first names in addition to those of mothers, although they were not married. Most of the time, parents of illegitimate children, both of whose names were mentioned in the baptism certificates, belonged to the same master, but there were fifteen cases or so in which the father belonged to another owner. These certificates acknowledged long-term illegitimate unions split between two households. The slaves in question were probably urban slaves benefiting from favorable treatment because they had influ-

Louis Cathedral Baptisms, 1744–1753, 03/17/1747, 10/14/1750, 03/17/1747, 05/30/1751; and "État des mulâtres et nègres libres," 1770, AGI, Correspondencia de los Gobernadores de la Luisiana y la Florida Occidental, Años 1766–1824, Session Papeles de Cuba, legajo 188-A.

35. AANO, Saint-Louis Cathedral Baptisms, 1753–1759, 11/12/1758. Nicolás Bacus Boisclair received a pension and a medal for his military action during the Spanish regime. See Kimberly S. Hanger, *Bounded Lives, Bounded Places: Free Black Society in Colonial New Orleans, 1769–1803* (Durham, N.C., 1997), 118, 121.

ential masters or because they had developed close relationships with the Capuchins.[36]

This attention to the fathers of illegitimate enslaved children defeated the logic of slave law, which imposed matrilineal status on slaves. Unlike the patrilineal system, which governed free people, mothers transmitted slave status to their children, not fathers. In addition to naming a child's owner, which remained crucial, these uncommon baptismal certificates also provided identification through the child's parents. Missionaries might have started to specify the first names of both parents of slave children, whether or not those parents were married, under pressure from slave couples themselves, who came together to church to have their infant baptized. These enslaved parents might have wanted to obtain some kind of protection for their families, which were weakened by their unofficial marital status, especially when the couple belonged to two distinct owners or lived in two separate households. As for indications noting when fathers were "unknown," they might be interpreted as a sign of priests' willingness to impose the patriarchal model of nuclear families on slaves. The rise of métissage might also have played a role.

MÉTISSAGE, ILLEGITIMACY, AND THE SILENCE OF WHITE FATHERS

Whereas solemnized marriage was the norm among whites and informal unions the standard among slaves and free people of color, interracial relationships were closely linked with illegitimacy, as mixed marriages between whites and blacks were outlawed early on. Though this prohibition was generally respected, interracial sexuality was widespread, owing to favorable demographic conditions. People in Louisiana do not seem to have been more inclined to métissage than in the Antilles or other places; they just had more opportunities. The slave system, combined with specific local demographic circumstances, generated a marked increase in extramarital sexual relationships in comparison with the metropole, though France, like most other countries in Europe, also experienced a rise in illegitimacy over the eighteenth century. The numerous illegitimate mixed-race children who resulted from these unions, however, could be the fruit of rape, occasional

36. For the fifteen cases or so in which the father belonged to another owner, see AANO, Saint-Louis Cathedral Baptisms, 1744–1753, 1753–1759, 1763–1767, and 1767–1771, 03/25/1749, 05/03/1759, 04/01/1759, 07/22/1759, 02/20/1763, 10/20/1765 (2 baptisms), 07/05/1766, 12/28/1766, 04/26/1767, 03/20/1768, 04/17/1768, 02/13/1769, 04/23/1769, 04/23/1769.

consensual sex, lasting affective relationships without cohabitation, or quasi marriage. All kinds of relationships existed. Although the exact proportion of violence, resignation, and consent is impossible to determine, the level of sexual exploitation of non-European women should not be minimized. Obtaining consent for sex from any woman, including white women, was not considered a major issue in ancien régime societies. Sexual violence in the colonies must have been all the greater, since sexuality was an effective way for white men to express and show their dominance within the slave system.[37]

All slave and colonial societies of the Americas experienced métissage, which happened whenever Europeans, Africans, and Amerindians met, but these societies differed in the degree of legal, official, and public recognition displayed by the government and society toward its legal authorization or prohibition, its official or unofficial toleration, and its public or private existence. In New Orleans, illegitimate relationships were typically kept secret. As a general rule, white fathers remained silent, deigning to publicly acknowledge their sexual partners or mixed-race children. As in Spanish America, people manipulated the divide between public and private space to deal with the discrepancy between legal or customary norms and social practices. The frequency of métissage should not be read as an absence of race-thinking within New Orleans's society; on the contrary, its restriction to the privacy of domestic homes reflected a process of racialization.[38]

37. Illegitimacy in the metropole was higher in cities and rose over the eighteenth century, from around 4 to 10 percent (and even 20 percent in cities such as Paris and Bordeaux). See Beauvalet-Boutouyrie, *La démographie de l'époque moderne*, 238–239. On rape in Europe and the Americas, see Sharon Block, *Rape and Sexual Power in Early America* (Chapel Hill, N.C., 2006); Stéphanie Gaudillat Cautela, "Questions de mot: Le 'viol' au XVIe siècle, un crime contre les femmes?" *Clio: Femmes, genre, histoire*, XXIV, *Variations* (2006); Phan, *Les amours illégitimes*, 153–192; and Georges Vigarello, *Histoire du viol, XVIe–XXe siècle* (Paris, 1998). One planter produced a letter in a suit against his overseer that he had sent to the latter in which he denounced "his scandalous commerce in the fields with negresses," adding "you probably ill-treat those who refuse to comply with what you want." See RSCL 1730/04/29/01. For the use of sexual violence to impose a master's domination, see Trevor Burnard, *Mastery, Tyranny, and Desire: Thomas Thistlewood and His Slaves in the Anglo-Jamaican World* (Chapel Hill, N.C., 2004), esp. 156–162.

38. This chapter contradicts previous interpretations of French Louisiana society that emphasize French "racial openness." See Gwendolyn Midlo Hall, *Africans in Colonial Louisiana: The Development of Afro-Creole Culture in the Eighteenth Century* (Baton Rouge, La., 1992), xv; and Jerah Johnson, "Colonial New Orleans: A Fragment of the Eighteenth-Century French Ethos," in Arnold R. Hirsch and Joseph Logsdon, eds., *Cre-*

The Frequency of Métissage in the Sacramental Records

Although the 1724 Code Noir prohibited mixed marriages and most people adhered to the law, it does not mean that interracial sex did not occur. The demographic balance among whites and blacks in New Orleans from the 1730s onward combined with a disproportionate sex ratio among whites made it all the more likely to thrive. That many bachelors among the settlers and soldiers could not marry constituted another favorable circumstance, even though married white men also had sex with women of African or Native American descent. The New Orleans baptismal registers kept by the Capuchins in charge of Saint-Louis Parish reveal widespread interracial sexuality. It was not long before priests began recording the imagined degree of métissage of free or enslaved children of color using a racial taxonomy borrowed from Saint-Domingue, which became more sophisticated over time. Since no ruling ordered them to do so, this attention to métissage might seem surprising at first, but documenting instances of métissage might have been a way for the church to measure and denounce the practice, which they likely became aware of through their knowledge of Caribbean colonies.[39]

Between 1723 and 1726, Father Raphaël complained several times to Abbé Raguet about the numerous liaisons in the colony between masters and slaves of Native American or African descent. Unlike the Dominicans of the Lesser Antilles in 1722, the Capuchins in New Orleans did not try to impose special penance on female slaves who had children with white men. Instead of putting the blame on enslaved women, Father Raphaël argued that, according to the "law recognized by all Christians," those abused by their masters should be freed. This conception of justice was reminiscent of the debate about the status of offspring born to mixed couples across status

---

ole New Orleans: Race and Americanization (Baton Rouge, La., 1992), 12–57. On the manipulation of the divide between public and private space to deal with interracial relationships in Spanish America, see Ann Twinam, *Public Lives, Private Secrets: Gender, Honor, Sexuality, and Illegitimacy in Colonial Spanish America* (Stanford, Calif., 1999).

39. For the few interracial weddings that were celebrated despite their prohibition, see Cécile Vidal, "Caribbean Louisiana: Church, *Métissage,* and the Language of Race in the Mississippi Colony during the French Period," in Vidal, ed., *Louisiana: Crossroads of the Atlantic World,* 127–131. The obligation for priests to record a person's exact phenotype or degree of métissage was not legally imposed in Martinique before 1778. See Vincent Cousseau, "Les stratégies de métissage dans une colonie à esclaves: Le cas de la Martinique (XVIIe–XXe siècles)," in Michel Cassan and Paul d'Hollander, eds., *Temporalités: Revues de sciences sociales et humaines,* no. 6, *Figures d'appartenances (VIIIe–XXe siècle)* (Limoges, France, 2010), 33.

Disorder of Families

and race that had preceded the promulgation of the first Code Noir in the Antilles in 1685. Some had proposed that those children should follow the condition of their fathers and be manumitted. In Martinique, in the early 1680s, some masters who had children with their slaves were actually fined and their mulatto children declared free once they reached their majority. The 1685 code settled the issue by definitively imposing the law of *Partus Sequitrum Ventrem*, assigning the status and race of mothers to their children. The edict provided for fining masters who had children with their slaves and confiscating those enslaved woman and children for the benefit of the hospital. It also added that a master who fathered a child with one of their slaves while they were single would have to marry that slave, who would then become free. These provisions were never enforced in the Antilles, and the second one was removed from the Louisiana code. Father Raphaël was unable to impose such a radical measure, but he claimed implicitly in 1726 that he had succeeded in reducing "the number of those who kept young Native American or Negresses to satisfy their overindulgence" although "there were still enough to scandalize the Church." Judging from the sacramental records, however, interracial sexuality did not disappear or even diminish.[40]

At the end of the 1750s, the rate of métissage in New Orleans (at least as recorded in the parish baptismal registers) was higher than in the Antilles. In 1762, 31 percent of enslaved children baptized bearing a term of color in New Orleans were of mixed origins, as opposed to 4 percent in 1744 and 22 percent in 1759. From 1744 to 1769, when the use of racial categories was more precisely established, the rate for enslaved children of Native descent (70 percent) was higher than for those of African descent (18 percent). Since

40. On the religious punishment of enslaved women involved in interracial unions in the Antilles, see "Négresse pénitence, Martinique," June 28, 1723, ANOM COL F3 94, fol. 59; Léo Élisabeth, *La société martiniquaise aux XVIIe et XVIIIe siècles, 1664–1789* (Paris, 2003), 222–223, 284; and Vincent Cousseau, "La famille invisible: Illégitimité des naissances et construction des liens familiaux en Martinique (XVIIe siècle–début du XIXe siècle)," *Annales de démographie historique*, CXXII, no. 2 (2011), 52. On the evolving regulations related to the status of mixed-blood enslaved children in the Antilles, see Aubert, "'To Establish One Law and Definite Rules,'" in Vidal, ed., *Louisiana: Crossroads of the Atlantic World*, 34–42. On the importance of métissage in New Orleans, see Letter of Father Raphaël, Aug. 30, 1723, in Pierre Hamer, *Raphaël de Luxembourg: Une contribution luxembourgeoise à la colonisation de la Louisiane* (Luxembourg, 1966), 65–70; the Capuchins of Louisiana to the Company of the Indies's Directors, May 16, 1724, ANOM COL C13A 8, fols. 416–420; and Father Raphaël to Abbé Raguet, May 18, 1726, ANOM COL C13A 10, fol. 46v.

most indigenous slaves were women, they did not have many opportunities to have sexual relations with Native men. Settlers from the New Orleans region might have also preferred sexual intercourse with Native women, as was clearly the case in the Illinois Country. Likewise, 71 percent of illegitimate children born to free women of color baptized bearing a term of color from 1744 to 1769 were designated with a mixed racial label, whereas this rate was only 19 percent for slaves. Free women of color who were not married, which was generally the case, were no doubt particularly vulnerable to white men's assiduous attentions.[41]

Under the influence of the Caribbean system of racial domination, Louisiana missionaries displayed a sensitivity to the color or degree of métissage of the infants of color, both enslaved and free, that they baptized, but, unlike their West Indian colleagues, they largely concealed the names of their white fathers. Yet the identity of white fathers was sometimes revealed, even when the mother was enslaved. In 1751, Louis Rançon, a New Orleans merchant, claimed that he was the father of Louis François, who was designated in the margin of the baptismal register as a *"mulâtre libre"* ("free mulatto"). Having only recently arrived in the colony, Rançon was less inhibited about displaying his liaison with an enslaved woman than colonists who had lived there longer, and he granted Louis François "his freedom, being born to Marie-Jeanne negress slave of Mr. Volant captain commanding the Swiss troops." The child, in theory, should have belonged to the Swiss military officer, but the records do not mention if Rançon pur-

41. It is difficult to draw comparisons between Louisiana and other colonies because the rates of métissage are not always calculated in the same way. From 1760 to 1762, 14 percent of the enslaved children of Case-Pilote (Martinique) were born to white fathers. In the 1770s and 1780s, between 12 and 14 percent of the slave population of Guadeloupe were of mixed descent, but this was the case for only 5 percent of the slave community in Saint-Domingue at the end of the eighteenth century. See Gabriel Debien, *Les esclaves aux Antilles françaises (XVIIe–XVIIIe siècles)* (Basse-Terre, Guadeloupe, 1974), 66–67; Gautier, "Les familles esclaves aux Antilles françaises, 1635–1848," *Population*, LV (2000), 25–26; and Nicole Vanony-Frisch, "Les esclaves de la Guadeloupe à la fin de l'Ancien Régime d'après les sources notariales (1770–1789)," *Bulletin de la société d'histoire de la Guadeloupe*, nos. 63–64, special issue (1985), 27–28, 37, 151–152. For the preference for sexual intercourse with Native women in the Illinois Country, see Cécile Vidal, "Les implantations françaises au Pays des Illinois au XVIIIe siècle (1699–1765)," 2 vols. (Ph.D. diss., École des Hautes Études en Sciences Sociales, 1995), 544, 554–557. One hundred one free illegitimate children (of color) born to single free women of color (whether the name of the father was mentioned or not) were baptized in New Orleans between 1744 and 1769; but only twenty-four legitimate children born to married couples, including a free woman of color, were baptized during the same period.

chased him or not. A few years later, Rançon (Ranson) succeeded in having Marguerite, the daughter of one of his slaves, also recorded as "born free." She was designated as a free *"mulâtresse"* on her baptism certificate. But this time, he did not mention that he had manumitted her nor did he claim that he was her father. In fact, he is only referenced on the certificate as her owner, and it is impossible to know if he was even present at the ceremony. Although other masters followed Louis Rançon's example and freed their putative offspring, these public manumissions were rare because they could give the appearance of a disguised confession of paternity.[42]

The names of white fathers of illegitimate children born to free women of color were concealed even more often than those born to enslaved women. Only two cases have been found where the identity of a white father was revealed. Free women of color who appeared as mothers on baptism certificates also usually only had first names. When last names were included, they rarely belonged to one of the colony's white families. The official situation of most free blacks in French New Orleans was different from those in the Antilles, where many free mothers of color in the first half of the eighteenth century still managed to have the names of their children's white fathers recorded in the sacramental records. This practice was so widespread that in 1752 Charles-Martin Hurson, the Martinique *intendant,* ordered that the expression "unknown father" be specified in place of names on the certificates of illegitimate free children of color, unless the white father specifically authorized the use of his name. Three years later, the Superior Council of Port-au-Prince made the same decision. This colonial legislation conformed to a legal evolution in the metropole, where a 1734 ordinance forbade the inclusion of the names of fathers of illegitimate infants on baptismal certificates and prohibited priests from even requesting the names of fathers. The act was not promulgated in Louisiana, but use of the expression "unknown father" became more widespread in the 1750s, and registers ceased to mention the names of white fathers. Previously, only mothers were specifically mentioned in most cases, although "unknown father" appeared as early as 1731 in the New Orleans registers. In 1769, Dagobert,

42. AANO, Saint-Louis Cathedral Baptisms, 1744–1753, 06/19/1751; AANO, Saint-Louis Cathedral Baptisms, 1759–1762, 11/09/1760; AANO, Saint-Louis Cathedral Baptisms, 1753–1759, 1759–1762, and 1763–1767, 07/17/1755, 08/09/1761, 05/07/1766; RSCL 1746/02/01/03, 1767/02/12/01. For more examples where the identity of white fathers was revealed, see Vidal, "Caribbean Louisiana," in Vidal, ed., *Louisiana: Crossroads of the Atlantic World,* 140–143. For the revelation of the names of white fathers of enslaved infants in the Antilles, see John D. Garrigus, *Before Haiti: Race and Citizenship in French Saint-Domingue* (New York, 2006), 60–61.

the Capuchins' superior, wrote down the name and quality of the father of a slave belonging to the missionaries who was brought forward to be baptized then crossed the note out and replaced it with the expression "unknown father."[43]

43. Of the 101 illegitimate children born to free women of color between 1744 and 1769, the sacramental records indicate the names of only nine fathers. Two of the fathers identified were white, and seven were of African or Afro-European descent. Among the latter, at least three were slaves. See AANO, Saint-Louis Cathedral Baptisms, 1744–1753, 1753–1759, 1759–1762, 1763–1767, and 1767–1771, 12/13/1744, 07/20/1746, 12/17/1747, 01/20/1750, 11/12/1758, 12/25/1759, 12/13/1761, 02/24/1765, 05/26/1769. Most of the time, fathers were not mentioned at all, except for the expression "unknown father." In two cases, the priest indicated that unknown fathers were white and in one case *"nègre."* See AANO, Saint-Louis Cathedral Baptisms, 1744–1753 and 1753–1759, 12/13/1751, 04/09/1752, 03/28/1756. For the baptisms of free infants of color whose white fathers' names were revealed, see AANO, Saint-Louis Cathedral Baptisms, 1744–1753, 1753–1759, 12/17/1747, 04/25/1748, 01/20/1750, 06/02/1754, 04/12/1755. However, the fact that the mother of Pierre, the son of Charles Donné, was only called by her first name, Anne Marie, on her son's baptismal certificate could mean that she was nonwhite or of mixed descent. See AANO, Saint-Louis Cathedral Baptisms, 1744–1753, 11/26/1746. Only a dozen certificates out of 101 from 1744 to 1769 included a free single mother of color with a last name. See AANO, Saint-Louis Cathedral Baptisms, 1744–1753, 1753–1759, 1759–1762, 1763–1767, and 1767–1771, 07/31/1746, 10/17/1749, 06/18/1752, 02/15/1753, 03/26/1753, 03/25/1754, 11/14/1757, 12/25/1759, 12/08/1763, 07/29/1767, 09/17/1768, 12/22/1768. Measures to hide the names of white fathers in the islands were not always well enforced, but, when new rulings in Guadeloupe in 1763 and Martinique in 1773 forbade free people of color from taking their white fathers' names, they gained more respect. In Martinique, a 1774 ruling ordered free people of color who had already adopted their white fathers' names to change their last names. One year earlier, in Saint-Domingue, the Superior Council of Cap-Français even tried to create "an onomastic of color" and to compel free people of color (in fact, their natural children and the new and old freed men and women) to take "a nickname from the African idiom or from their profession." But this ruling was only partially applied. Some free people of color circumvented the law, taking a slightly modified version of their white father's last name. See Cousseau, "La famille invisible," *Annales de démographie historique,* CXXII, no. 2 (2011), 47–54; Yvan Debbasch, *Couleur et liberté: Le jeu du critère ethnique dans un ordre juridique esclavagiste,* I, *L'affranchi dans les possessions françaises de la Caraïbe (1635–1833)* (Paris, 1967), 69–71n; Letter, Aug. 22, 1752, ANOM COL C8A 59, fol. 304, quoted in Élisabeth, *La société martiniquaise aux XVIIe et XVIIIe siècles,* 105, 229, 317, 401; Garrigus, *Before Haiti,* 165–167; Stewart R. King, *Blue Coat or Powdered Wig: Free People of Color in Pre-Revolutionary Saint Domingue* (Athens, Ga., 2001), 9–13; Frédéric Régent, *Esclavage, métissage, liberté: La Révolution française en Guadeloupe, 1789–1802* (Paris, 2002), 159–160, 200–201; and Dominique Rogers, "Les libres de couleur dans les capitales de Saint-Domingue: Fortune, mentalités, et intégration à la fin de l'Ancien Régime (1776–

Despite the few cases in New Orleans's baptismal registers where white fathers of children of color were identified, sexual or quasi-conjugal relations between white men and African or Native women were typically not revealed or recognized publicly and officially. Métissage between people of European and African descent in particular was supposed to be kept secret. Only exceptional circumstances brought people to acknowledge illicit mixed liaisons and offspring. Most often, these revelations were motivated by necessity, greed, or retaliation. In 1765, Dame Elizabeth Tomelin, widow of Lavergne, made an unusual request at the clerk's office. She declared that her deceased husband had had two children by their indigenous slave. The children were allowed to work on their own behalf. One of them, François, or Jacob, Lavergne, described as a *"métis,"* was a traveler on the Mississippi River. When he died leaving some goods and game in a pirogue, the white widow claimed that he had never been officially manumitted and that his legacy should be left to her and her children. It was very likely out of poverty that this white woman acknowledged the existence of her husband's second family. On the one hand, he seems to have unofficially recognized his illegitimate enslaved children, as they benefited from special treatment and were able to live as quasi free; on the other, he never formally manumitted them, which put them in a precarious situation. Since François / Jacob Lavergne's property was auctioned, local authorities apparently refused to consider Elizabeth Tomelin's claim.[44]

Not all children born of unions between white men and Native American slaves were treated as liberally by their fathers, even though they still sometimes received special consideration. In 1728, François Guillory, the father of a natural child, Jean Guillory, born from a liaison with an indigenous slave, took measures to distinguish his son but never intended to free him. Jean's family story was only publicly revealed because he ran away with two other Native Americans belonging to other masters. During the trial, the man to whom he had been entrusted, Sieur François Trudeau, testified that Jean Guillory was the son of François Guillory and an indigenous woman

---

1789)" (Ph.D. diss., Université Michel de Montaigne, 1999), chapter 5, sections 1a, 2. For metropolitan legislation on the exclusion of fathers' names on baptismal certificates of illegitimate infants, see Gourdon and Ruggiu, "Familles en situation coloniale," *Annales de démographie historique*, CXXII, no. 2 (2011), 16. On corrections made in the New Orleans sacramental records, see AANO, Saint-Louis Cathedral Baptisms, 1763–1767, 07/03/1765.

44. NONA Garic Mar. 2, 1765, Mar. 4, 1765 (probate record), Mar. 4, 1765 (request), Mar. 6, 1765, Mar. 8, 1765, Mar. 12, 1765.

and that, before his death, the father had verbally asked him to take care of his "bastard," to teach him a trade, and to deliver him to his legitimate son. Jean Guillory explained that he had had no choice but to run away because he was abused at Trudeau's. Although Jean Guillory remained a slave, his origins might explain why he was only sentenced to be publicly flogged whereas one of his companions was condemned to be hanged.[45]

Conflicting interests between settlers often played a role in the public disclosure of mixed unions and families. One colonist, Louis Jourdan, had an affair with a slave named Catherine, whose master was Sieur François Hery Duplanty, a New Orleans resident, but he tried in vain to purchase her for a large sum of money. When the owner refused, the woman ran away. During her escape, which lasted several months, she took refuge in another slave's cabin, and the couple met either there or in the room that Jourdan rented at Dame Brunel's house, where Catherine was ultimately arrested. The innkeeper, Antoine Gauvin, testified that "around eighteen or twenty months ago while lodging at Lady Brunel's where Jourdan also lodged as if at his own place, a negress left the room one morning, and when he learnt that this negress had run away he warned the defendant that if he had negresses who had run away sleep over in his room he would have to expel him." Clearly, the innkeeper was not shocked by the liaison, he was only afraid of the consequences of helping a slave who had run away. The master requested that his slave be saved from corporal punishment but that Jourdan be sentenced to pay a fine of ten livres a day for each day the desertion and concubinage had lasted.[46]

Although long-term unions without cohabitation between whites and

45. RSCL 1728/06/07/03, 1728/06/14/01, 1728/06/14/02; "Capital Sentence on Indian Slave," June 14, 1728, in [Henry P. Dart], ed., "RSCL XII [XIII]," *LHQ*, IV (1921), 489.

46. RSCL 1767/07/09/02, 1767/07/12/01, 1767/07/12/02, 1767/08/08/04, 1767/08/14/01. Sieur André Jung, a militia officer, also appears to have tried to buy his enslaved mistress and their offspring from her master, but, where Jourdan failed, he succeeded. In 1763, he paid Monsieur Benoît Payen de Chavoye, a military officer, 17,500 livres for a "negress" named Jeanne. Her daughter, a "mulâtresse" named Marguerite, fourteen or fifteen years old, was to be delivered to Jung in four years for another 4,000 livres. The prices were so high that the slaves must have had more than an economic value for the buyer. See "Sale of a Negress," Nov. 29, 1762, in G. Lugano, ed., "RSCL LXXXVII: October–December, 1762," *LHQ*, XXIV (1941), 582–583. In a trial for the murder of a sailor named Martin by another sailor, a white man, who earned money "feeding people," testified that Martin "ate at his place, but never slept there, he slept at the house of a negress whom he doesn't know." See RSCL 1767/11/06/02.

Disorder of Families

blacks frequently existed, interracial concubinage does not seem to have been widespread and was even less apparent. All the above cases of interracial relationships concerned white officers or settlers who were either married to a white woman, did not keep their own house and household because they did not have the means to do so, or were only passing through the colony. Judicial proceedings, travel accounts, and private correspondence show that most white men who did not have a white woman (mother, spouse, or daughter) to take care of their house did not rely on a free or enslaved *ménagère* (a female housekeeper who was also often the household head's mistress) but took board and lodging at a white neighbor's or at an inn. The practice of ménagère did not constitute an institution in French Louisiana as in the Caribbean, and the word "ménagère" is even missing from Louisiana documentation.[47]

One case of ménagère, however, has been traced. Even though Marie Angélique, alias Isabelle Chavannes, did not hold the title "ménagère," she clearly fulfilled the same functions. Paradoxically, her status as a slave who was officially manumitted late, despite her relationship with her master, Jean-Baptiste Chavannes, allowed her to accumulate and manage her own property. The son of a war commissioner, Chavannes was born in Paris. He was exiled to Louisiana at the request of his parents in 1719, when he was thirty-five years old, to escape from a trial for dueling. With royal commissioner Jacques de La Chaise's backing, he was named secretary of both the Conseil de Régie (the council governing the colony during the Company of the Indies's monopoly) and the Superior Council in March 1724, but he was forced to resign in March 1726. This hard blow might have been a consequence of the struggle between La Chaise and the other councillors. Jean-Baptiste and Isabelle seem to have maintained a relationship that implied a common strategy to develop their fortune and patrimony. Accord-

47. On ménagères in the Antilles, see Arlette Gautier, *Les sœurs de solitude: La condition féminine dans l'esclave aux Antilles du XVIIe au XIXe siècle* (Paris, 1985), 165–172; Garrigus, *Before Haiti*, 56–58; King, *Blue Coat or Powdered Wig*, 187, 191–193, 196; Anne Pérotin-Dumon, *La ville aux îles, la ville dans l'île: Basse-Terre et Pointe-à-Pitre, Guadeloupe, 1650–1820* (Paris, 2000), 669–674, 704–717; Frédéric Régent, "Structures familiales et stratégies matrimoniales des libres de couleur en Guadeloupe au XVIIIe siècle," *Annales de démographie historique*, CXXII, no. 2 (2011), 69–98; and Rogers, "Les libres de couleur dans les capitales de Saint-Domingue," chapter 10, section 2. For another case that concerned a military officer, Pierre Henri d'Erneville, whose informal family was revealed in administrative correspondence because he was embroiled in a conflict with the commissaire-ordonnateur, see Hanger, *Bounded Lives, Bounded Places*, 65; and Spear, *Race, Sex, and Social Order in Early New Orleans*, 82–84, 89.

ing to the map of New Orleans drawn by Pierre Le Blond de La Tour, by 1722, urban parcel number 95 on Royale Street had been granted to "Marie Angélique alias Isabelle free negress of Chavannes." She was identified as a free black woman at the same time that the name of her former master was mentioned, as if he still owned her. Chavannes did not ask the governor and commissaire-ordonnateur for official approval of her manumission until 1732, and Isabelle, "Mr. Chavannes' negress," waited six more years to record her freedom at the clerk's office. Whatever Isabelle's status, the unofficial couple could not possess property in common. As a result, the documentation variously mentions either him or her as the legal holder of the same urban parcel that was finally sold by the former slave in 1739.[48]

After the sale of Chavannes and Isabelle's house in the city, the couple moved to the north bank of Lake Pontchartrain, where Chavannes ran a tar factory in partnership with Claude Vignon dit La Combe. The latter apparently maintained a sexual relationship with a free woman of color as well. Isabelle participated in the enterprise, purchasing some cattle in 1739. The couple might have had at least one daughter, who was manumitted by her father, but there are no freedom papers for her. In the 1740s, Marie Angélique served several times as a godmother at the baptisms of enslaved infants and was described once as "Mr. de Chavanne's female mulatto." She had two of her own children baptized in 1754 and 1758, and the girl was qualified as a *"quarteronne."* Chavannes would not have met his grandchildren, for he died before they were born. In 1752, Isabelle successfully sued the estate's executor for the wages that were due her. She and Chavannes had maintained the fiction that they had lived together because she worked for him as a de facto housekeeper. She obtained all his property, which did

48. His last name was spelled either Chavannes or Chavanne. A particle (de) was sometimes added to his name. See Glenn R. Conrad, trans. and comp., *The First Families of Louisiana*, 2 vols. (Baton Rouge, La., 1970–1999), I, 54; Dumont de Montigny, *Regards sur le monde atlantique, 1715–1747*, transcribed by Carla Zecher (Sillery, Québec, 2008), 92; La Chaise to the Company of the Indies, Mar. 8, 1724, ANOM COL C13A 7, fol. 43; "Délibérations du Conseil," Feb. 9, 1726, ANOM COL 9, fols. 329r–331v; RSCL 1727/05/09/01, 1727/05/10/01, 1727/05/10/02, 1727/05/11/01, 1727/05/16/01, 1727/05/16/02, 1727/05/17/05; 1738/02/15/03; Map by Pierre Le Blond de La Tour, 1722, HNOC, Vieux Carré Survey, Map by François Ignace Broutin, 1728, and Map by Gonichon, 1731; Censuses of November 1721, January 1726, July 1727, January 1732, ANOM COL G1 464; "Sale of Real Property," Mar. 20, 1739, in Heloise H. Cruzat, ed., "RSCL XIX," *LHQ*, VI (1923), 310; Marcel Giraud, *Histoire de la Louisiane française*, 4 vols. (Paris, 1953–1974), IV, 365; and Giraud, *History of French Louisiana*, trans. Pearce, V, 11, 29, 46–47.

Disorder of Families

not amount to much. That the Superior Council granted her request might be a sign that their hidden relationship was unofficially acknowledged and tolerated, since Chavannes never married a white woman.[49]

Other cases of hidden concubinage might have existed. Some free women of color lived within urban households headed by white men. Half of the manumission deeds recorded were related to enslaved women and their mixed-blood children. Others were granted their freedom and a legacy in their owner's will. Although these documents do not provide positive evidence of affective or kin relationships and no recognition of fatherhood, the presumption that they concerned "invisible families" is high. In 1769, for instance, Mr. Louis Claude Leclert, a former La Balise storekeeper who was then living in New Orleans, wrote a will in which he declared that:

> He had a negress named Nanette, 40 years old, a Creole, who had always been his considerate domestic, and for the great care she took of him whether he was in good health or ill, and also her children Marie Jeanne, 19, Louis who was blind, 17, Charlotte, 14, and Anne Marthe, 2, all mulatto children of the said Nanette and illegitimate, believed that the greatest token of gratitude he could show them for their good and pleasant services was to grant them their freedom from now on.

Leclert asked the Superior Council to confirm their freedom and made them his legatees, as he had no relatives. He did not acknowledge the paternity of the children, but his highly affectionate tone and his insistence on their illegitimate birth looks like disguised social recognition. Other wills such as this one were drawn up, although freedom was most often granted at an owner's death and bequests were much smaller, especially when the testator had an official white family. One will even extended the enslavement of a woman and her young daughter after their owner's death, granting them freedom only on the condition that the mother work in the service of the Charity Hospital for two more years. Sometimes, wills only asked that a woman and her children be taken care of by the estate's executor. These

49. "Power of Attorney," Oct. 9, 1739, in "RSCL XXII: Succession of Francois Trudeau, 1739," *LHQ*, VII (1924), 494, "Agreement in Tar Trade," Oct. 9, 1739, 494; RSCL 1745/02/23/01, 1747/08/16/01; "Acknowledgment by Sr. Claude Reynaud," Aug. 6, 1739, in "RSCL XXII," *LHQ*, VII (1924), 354–355; AANO, Saint-Louis Cathedral Baptisms, 1744–1753 and 1753–1759, 07/16/1746, 09/25/1746, 06/26/1747, 03/25/1754, 03/19/1758; "Isabelle vs. Succession of Jean Baptiste Gon de Chavannes," Dec. 2, 1752, in Heloise H. Cruzat, ed., "RSCL LXXVII: October–December, 1752," *LHQ*, XXI (1938), 1245–1246; Spear, *Race, Sex, and Social Order in Early New Orleans*, 261n.

various provisions reflect great diversity in the kinds of connections uniting white men, their partners of African or, less often, Native American descent, and their mixed-blood children.[50]

Most of the time, manumissions of enslaved women and mixed children in wills seem to have been respected, but conflicts, nevertheless, occasionally arose. In October 1735, Pierre de Saint-Julien privately freed the two daughters of his "negress," stating that he did so "for good and pleasant services which the two said children provided me with" and "for specific reasons." His sole condition was that "it must be understood that they will show the respect they should always exhibit towards whites." He even mortgaged all his property so that no one could try to nullify their freedom in the event of debt as well as to provide for them so that they could establish themselves when they became of age. A few months before drafting his will, he had left one of them, the "mûlatresse" Marie Charlotte, as a school boarder with the Ursulines. This unusual practice seems to confirm a kin relationship. Yet, after Saint-Julien's death in 1737, the attorney for vacant estates, Raymond Amiot d'Ausseville, claimed that the manumission was invalid because it had not been sanctioned by the governor and the commissaire-ordonnateur. The deceased had also left debts amounting to three times the value of the estate. The Ursulines agreed to give Marie

50. For free women of color living within urban households headed by white men, see Tulane University, Howard-Tilton Memorial Library, Louisiana Research Collection, Kuntz Collection, Box I, fol. 165, 09/14/1765, fol. 170, 02/01/1767. For manumission deeds concerning women or their mixed-blood children, see RSCL 1728/07/21/02; 1729/10/22/01; 1735/06/04/01, 1735/06/04/02; 1735/10/09/01; 1736/03/28/01; 1737/07/11/01; 1738/02/15/03; 1740/02/24/02, 1742/05/24/01; 1743/07/16/01; 1743/11/30/02; 1744/07/14/01, 1744/07/14/02; 1745/11/14/01; 1746/02/01/03; 1747/06/20/01; 1757/07/01/01; 1758/07/01/01; 1762/01/22/01; 1762/01/22/02; 1762/02/08/02; 1762/04/10/01; 1767/07/20/03. The expression "invisible families" is borrowed from Cousseau, "La famille invisible," *Annales de démographie historique,* CXXII, no. 2 (2011). For Leclert's will, see RSCL 1769/11/18/01. For other wills granting freedom and bequests to women of color and mixed-blood children on various conditions, see RSCL 1738/08/26/03; 1738/09/05/01; 1736/08/11/03, 1738/09/07/01; 1740/02/24/02, 1740/03/12/02; 1742/05/24/01; 1747/08/16/01; 1766/07/30/04; 1767/02/12/01. The administrator of the Charity Hospital also requested the full execution of the will of Sieur Henry, formerly clerk of the Superior Council. He had bequeathed eighty-eight hundred livres to Vénus, a free "mûlatresse." In the event of her death, the sum was to go to Pierre, her son, and, in the event of his death, to the Charity Hospital. See RSCL 1767/03/24/01. For a probate record that mentioned that a female slave and mixed-blood children were supposed to get their freedom on the death of their owner, see RSCL 1769/01/10/01. For a donation to a freed Native American woman and her child, see RSCL 1744/12/26/02.

Disorder of Families

Charlotte to d'Ausseville after he had paid the price of her board. D'Ausseville then auctioned her off, but she claimed that the debts due by the succession were paid and requested her freedom. When the Superior Council settled the case in her favor, the man who had bought her, Sieur Barbin, demanded that she reimburse the price of her own purchase, fifteen hundred livres. Arguing that it would not be "just that a free woman should have been kept in slavery through a trick," she then requested that the council sentence d'Ausseville's heirs to pay her wages during the time she worked for the attorney for vacant estates. The judgment in this case is not extant, but, most of the time, the Superior Council seems to have adopted a legalistic point of view in such matters. When there were papers attesting to an agreement, the court appears to have forced owners to respect promises made to slaves and free people of color.[51]

Pierre de Saint-Julien was not the only white father who made provisions for the care of his mixed-blood offspring. Although Father Raphaël described Diron d'Artaguiette, general inspector for the Company of the Indies and later commandant of Mobile, as "full of religion and zeal for the success of our ministry, having a edifying behavior," he also fathered two natural children. When he moved to Saint-Domingue in 1739, he did not bring them with him, but he made some dispositions for them to be taken care of in New Orleans. The boy was apprenticed as a shoemaker, and the girl was sent to the convent. They were entrusted to the attendance of a rich planter named Dubreuil, even though it was the commissaire-ordonnateur who partly paid for their pensions. In 1744, the young shoemaker's apprentice—then fourteen years old—testified in a trial, presenting himself as the natural son of the deceased Mr. Diron, whose name he bore. In the documents, the children's ethnic background was never mentioned. A series of deeds contracted in 1747, however, reveals the full story and confirms that Diron d'Artaguiette was the father of these "métis" children. While in Mobile, the commandant had maintained a Native American woman in his service, named Marianne, as his concubine. They had three children. One of them, Marguerite, married Mathias Berthelot, the king's gunsmith. Diron d'Artaguiette granted her ten thousand livres as a dowry, which was a substantial sum, provided that her husband make a donation to his wife's sib-

51. RSCL 1735/10/09/01, 1737/07/29/01; "Petition," Feb. 6, 1745, in Heloise H. Cruzat, ed., "RSCL XLVII: January–February, 1745," *LHQ*, XIII (1930), 517. Saint-Julien had a privileged relationship with the church, since he had served as a beadle during the 1720s. See Charles Edwards O'Neill, *Church and State in French Colonial Louisiana: Policy and Politics to 1732* (New Haven, Conn., 1966), 178.

lings when they came of age. Berthelot fulfilled his obligation in 1747. In Berthelot's first request, he said that the parents of the three children had died when they were still very young, but, in one obligation, he incidentally presented Diron d'Artaguiette as the "father" of Jean Baptiste Pani Ouassa. Officials knew about and tolerated this unconventional situation, probably because Diron d'Artaguiette belonged to the elite and the children were of French-Native descent.[52]

Many illicit relationships took place while their protagonists lived in distant outposts such as La Balise or Mobile or resided on plantations outside New Orleans. Rochemore was right when he wrote that this "scattering of people and the travels" facilitated "debauchery." Outside the Louisiana capital, the practice of concubinage was apparently more open. When fathers moved back to New Orleans or when mixed-blood children had to be taken care of, a lack of public display and official silence once again became the rule. It does not mean that public authorities and people did not know about or suspect the truth. Keeping all these relationships secret was impossible. Still, there was a common understanding that they ought not to be publicly exhibited and officially acknowledged. Although scandal was disapproved of, clandestine liaisons and families seem to have been accepted. Wills granting freedom to slaves of African descent were apparently respected by heirs and confirmed by local authorities, and donations made to free people of color, which were outlawed by Article 52 of the Code Noir, were not invalidated by the Superior Council. That these donations were made openly in wills and officially authorized, even though they contradicted the law, suggests that local authorities and colonists tolerated and even protected these irregular families as long as they remained publicly and officially invisible.[53]

Most enslaved women involved in sexual relationships with white men and their mixed-blood children remained enslaved. The existence of a few exceptions to the prohibition of mixed marriages and the formation of some hidden quasi marriages and genuine mixed families, with white fathers

52. Father Raphaël to Abbé Raguet, May 15, 1725, ANOM COL C13A 8, fol. 406v; RSCL 1744/01/25/01; 1744/02/20/01; 1747/07/01/01, 1747/07/01/02, 1747/07/01/03; "Letter," Nov. 27, 1746, in Heloise H. Cruzat, ed., "RSCL LIX: September–December, 1746," *LHQ*, XVII (1934), 197. When Paul Augustin Le Pelletier de La Houssaye was the commandant of Mobile, he also maintained such a liaison and fathered mixed-blood children. See Salmon to the minister of the navy, Mar. 6, 1741, ANOM COL C13A 26, fols. 115–119.

53. [Rochemore], "Mémoire sur l'administration de la Louisiane," ANOM COL C13A 33, fol. 156v.

caring for children of mixed descent, reveal that some individuals chose not to respect the racial line within their domestic households. All kinds of bonds and feelings could unite people across unequal positions. But, even when consensual and affective long-lasting interracial relationships developed, they were overdetermined by the interplay of gender, status, and race. Moreover, they were far from being the most common situation. Physical violence—that is, sexual exploitation—and symbolic violence—the refusal to legally and socially recognize these mixed unions and their offspring and give them the same rights and protection—remained standard practice. The few cases of open concubinage between white men and women among the elite contrasted with the official silence to which mixed families were confined highlights the power of race. Métissage was kept hidden because it was widespread and held the potential to imperil the binary division on which society was based. In a comparison of slave systems of the Chesapeake and the Lowcountry, Philip D. Morgan has argued that the more balanced the number of blacks and whites, the more frequent interracial relationships became, but, on the same token, the more frequent these mixed unions, the less open and accepted they were, and vice versa. The difference between Louisiana and the Antilles in that regard was comparable to that between Virginia and South Carolina. All these slave societies were no less profoundly shaped by race.[54]

When historical actors, especially missionaries, wanted to condemn what they considered immoral sexual practices, they qualified them as a "scandalous commerce." The expression appears over and over in the documentation to designate all kinds of inappropriate relationships, including métissage, that went against the dominant French norms pertaining to sexuality and family. The word "scandal" implied both the idea of error and sin and of public exhibition. People were scandalized as much by the public display of these behaviors as they were by the behaviors themselves. In an ancien régime society characterized by an exacerbated culture of appearances, it was hardly conceivable not to arouse suspicions in public. While the feeling of general moral and religious disorder in the city's first fifteen years concerned all segments of New Orleans's population, whatever their social con-

54. Philip D. Morgan, "British Encounters with Africans and African-Americans, circa 1600–1780," in Bernard Bailyn and Morgan, eds., *Strangers within the Realm: Cultural Margins of the First British Empire* (Chapel Hill, N.C., 1991), 157–219; Morgan, *Slave Counterpoint: Black Culture in the Eighteenth-Century Chesapeake and Lowcountry* (Chapel Hill, N.C., 1998), 398–412.

dition and ethnic origins, over time, anxieties about promiscuous conduct came to focus on interracial relationships. The public and official silence that confined most of these mixed liaisons and their illegitimate offspring to the privacy of domestic homes was all the more deafening as métissage was more widespread in New Orleans than in the Antilles and the social control exercised by the church and the state was greater in the Louisiana capital than in its surroundings and more distant outposts. A desire to maintain discretion seems to have been widely shared by whites of all statuses and was not restricted to the elite. White men nevertheless appeared more inclined to hide their kinship with women and children of African and Afro-European descent than with Native American ones. The association between people of African ancestry and slavery and the servile stain that allegedly persisted well into the first generation after former slaves achieved their freedom put black people at the bottom of the racial hierarchy, below indigenous individuals.[55]

On the one hand, according to the dominant religious standards of the time, New Orleans was a disorderly society. Although marriage in church was not a white privilege, most slaves were excluded from the white system of honor connected to solemnized unions and legitimate children. Métissage was widespread because of the demographic conditions, and illicit and informal interracial liaisons allowed white male sexuality to be potentially fully disconnected from matrimony. The rate of illegitimacy in the colony was high, especially when infants born to unwed enslaved or free parents of color and to mixed couples are taken into account. Even if family and sexual norms were starting to relax in France, by midcentury, New Orleans's society stood much further away from the strict seventeenth-century society constrained by the impact of the Catholic Reformation than the metropole. It was in the eyes of the church that the scandal of sex out of wedlock was the most outrageous.

On the other hand, Louisiana's lay population, both state representatives and settlers, might have had a different assessment of the colony's situation, even though they could not declare it out loud. They managed to create a viable and cohesive white society that was based on numerous and lasting marriages and did not have to face a massive influx of single male migrants.

55. Father Raphaël denounced "others who lived in scandalous dissoluteness with their slaves." See Father Raphaël to the Company of the Indies, May 16, 1724, ANOM COL C13A 8, fol. 418v. In the first edition of *Le dictionnaire de l'Académie françoise* (1694), the definition of *scandaleux* includes the following example: "A public concubinage is scandalous." In the fourth edition, published in 1762, the expression "scandalous commerce" was even mentioned.

Disorder of Families

After the 1730s, as demographic conditions stabilized, slaveholders were in a better position to enforce their rule over slaves' matrimonial practices. Everywhere in the Americas, slave marriage was a contradiction in terms: the free consent of spouses that constitutes the very substance of marriage always stood to potentially conflict with the authority slaveowners exercised over their human property. For this reason, conjugality among the enslaved in the Antilles was rare. In Louisiana, the quasi ending of the slave trade induced masters to allow some slaves to wed, but masters used slave marriage selectively to obtain more enslaved laborers without allowing their human property to leverage the institution of matrimony as an emancipatory tool. The slave order imposed itself over the religious one. From the masters' point of view, such action, however, was not necessarily seen as a moral and religious failure, for they treated slaves de facto as if the latter did not have the same natural moral dispositions as themselves. The way religion cemented society in the metropole stumbled against the segmentation of the social world in this highly inegalitarian slave society. Pluralism concerned not only law but also moral values and conduct. For their part, slaves and free people of color fought hard to form families and have children within or outside the religious, moral, and legal system imposed on them by whites. It is difficult to know to what extent they appropriated the Christian gospel or how they mixed it with their own conceptions of kinship and sexuality.

The divide between whites' public lives and their private behavior constituted a socioracial order that allowed them to maintain their supremacy while white men could indulge themselves in unrestricted sexuality. One of the major sociocultural consequences of the formation of slave societies was the disconnection between marriage and sexuality for white men. Whereas colonial narratives emphasized female depravity, it was white men, in practice, who deviated more often from the ideal of Christian marriage. Consequently, the colony's socioracial order had a strong gender dimension. As Trevor Burnard has underlined for Jamaica, in early Louisiana, too, "Gender was nearly as important as race in defining social relationships." Over the eighteenth century, illegitimacy in the metropole tended to rise, and fathers of natural children were less and less socially and legally incited to shoulder their responsibilities—a policy that had previously offered some protection to women and had, to a certain extent, corrected their unequal position with respect to birth out of wedlock. But, in the colony, these trends were exacerbated by the slave system and the intersection of gender and race. Men alone had the upper hand in deciding how to treat their sexual or conjugal partners of African or Native American descent and their mixed children. Yet the latter sought to make the most of their fragile position. The most common form of manumission led to colored women's demographic overrepresentation among the population of free blacks and gave them relatively substantial economic power. The hardship of their lives was compensated for by a kind of autonomy unavailable to most white women. Faced with such a situation, it is no surprise that white women quickly felt the need to form a religious congregation devoted to the Virgin Mary. Moral and religious exhortation and education represented the only tools at their disposal to counter white masculine domination. Both the legitimate wives and children of white men who maintained informal families as well as the black partners and children of abused enslaved or free women of color suffered to some extent from this sexual socioracial order, but enslaved women were still the first victims of sexual violence. In contrast, both male and female slaves were overworked.[56]

56. Trevor Burnard, "Evaluating Gender in Early Jamaica, 1674–1784," *History of the Family*, XII (2007), 8; Burnard, *Mastery, Tyranny, and Desire*.

Disorder of Families

CHAPTER SIX

"American Politics"

Slavery, Labor, and Race

In 1764, Attorney General Nicolas La Frénière asked that two men accused of having stolen cows be tortured. His action was in keeping with the intense campaign initiated by the Superior Council in the early 1760s to repress runaways and thieves that started to resort more frequently to question (judicial torture) to extract confession from defendants. Most of the victims were slaves, but, in this exceptional case, torture was inflicted on both a black slave and a white tradesman: Jacob, a "negro" who belonged to Mr. La Chaise and worked as a cowherd, and Pierre Dégouté dit Fleury, a thirty-five-year-old white butcher. The investigation was launched after many people complained that their animals had disappeared. At least twenty-five oxen, cows, and calves had reportedly been killed, and the city was abuzz with rumors. Indeed, it was not a small matter. Meat supply had always been a serious concern, since it was an essential part of the traditional diet of European migrants. Local authorities issued numerous rulings to encourage cattle breeding and regulate the meat trade. Over time, game was increasingly replaced by butcher's meat, which became an important commodity. In the 1750s, the rising demand for meat from New Orleans's growing population and the numerous troops stationed in Louisiana for the war led some settlers to request new lands to open cattle farms in the Attakapas district. Older plantations in the city's immediate vicinity also maintained their own herds, which were overseen by specialized slaves working on foot or on horseback. These planters also sometimes agreed to keep one or two cows for urban dwellers.[1]

---

1. RSCL 1764/03/08/01. For concerns about the meat trade and its management, see "Ordonnances," Aug. 8, Sept. 27, 1721, ANOM COL C13A 6, fols. 148v–149r; various ordinances promulgated by the Superior Council regulating the butchering of cattle,

Slaves were only involved in cattle breeding as cowherds in service to their masters, whereas they raised pigs and poultry to satisfy their own needs and to sell in the urban market. They never ate beef unless they stole some. The consumption of beef was a sign of racial distinction. Likewise, the meat trade was operated solely by white employers and workers. In Martinique, by the mid-eighteenth century, slaves had come to be involved in this important commercial activity, but they were forbidden to exercise the profession of butcher by local authorities from 1763 onward. In the Louisiana capital, white butchers either kept their livestock in the woods surrounding New Orleans or purchased oxen, cows, or calves in small groups. Cattle were brought live to town every day, where they were slaughtered for the residents' consumption. At the time of the case, several butchers ran shops in the city. Apart from Fleury, only three butchers were interrogated in relation to the rash of thefts, even though there were probably more operating in the city.[2]

From the countryside, where slaves kept herds destined for the city's consumption, to butcher shops, run by white settlers, the meat trade connected laborers of various statuses and backgrounds. Still, they were not necessarily united by the same interests, as the theft scheme reveals. Fleury

---

May 20, 1724, ANOM COL A 22, fols. 103v–104v, Aug. 23, 1716, ANOM COL A 23, fol. 6, Sept. 20, 1716, fol. 6v, Jan. 8, 1721, fol. 30v, Dec. 13, 1721, fols. 33v–34r, Apr. 29, 1723, fols. 38v–39, Nov. 13, 1723, fol. 45r, May 20, 1724, fols. 57v–58r, July 24, 1725, fol. 60, Aug. 2, 1727, fol. 70r, Jan. 2, 1735, fol. 118rv, May 18, 1737, fol. 122; and "Complaint," Feb. 7, 1744, in Heloise H. Cruzat, ed., "RSCL XLIV: January–March 14, 1744," *LHQ*, XII (1929), 660. See also RSCL 1744/02/07/02, 1744/02/07/03. Already in the early 1730s, Company of the Indies employee Marc-Antoine Caillot noted that "butcher's meat in New Orleans is quite good, but they do not eat mutton at all because of its rarity." See Erin M. Greenwald, ed., *A Company Man: The Remarkable French-Atlantic Voyage of a Clerk for the Company of the Indies: A Memoir by Marc-Antoine Caillot*, trans. Teri F. Chalmers (New Orleans, La., 2013), 86. For the meat trade in metropolitan France, see Reynald Abad, *Le grand marché: L'approvisionnement alimentaire de Paris sous l'Ancien Régime* (Paris, 2002), 383–392; and Thierry Argant, "L'approvisionnement en viande de boucherie de la ville de Lyon à l'époque moderne," *Histoire urbaine*, VII, no. 1 (2003), 205–231. On enslaved cowherds in Louisiana, see Andrew Sluyter, "The Role of Blacks in Establishing Cattle Ranching in Louisiana in the Eighteenth Century," *Agricultural History*, LXXXVI, no. 2 (Spring 2012), 41–67.

2. For regulation of the meat trade in Martinique, see P. F. R. Dessalles, *Les annales du Conseil souverain de la Martinique*, Tome I, Vol. I, *Réédition*, ed. Bernard Vonglis (1786; rpt. Paris, 1995), 185. Bringing beef to cities fresh on the hoof was a common practice in metropolitan centers, including Paris. See Abad, *Le grand marché*, 111–392. For the three New Orleans butchers' testimonies, see RSCL 1764/03/08/01.

Slavery, Labor, and Race

and his associate Periche, two independent tradesmen, employed a white indentured servant named Jacques to take charge of catching and bringing cows to town. Either in collaboration with his masters, who might not have given him any choice in the matter, or on his own initiative, Jacques stole cattle with the assistance of the enslaved cowherd, Jacob. For his part in the theft, the slave was promised "the paunch and a dribble of alcohol," a reward that reflected his inferior status and subordinate position. He received only a small fraction of the expected benefits and was left with what was considered a cheap cut. Another white indentured servant, employed as a carter by Periche, and an enslaved cowherd named Pierrot, who belonged to Mr. Dorville, refused to participate in the criminal enterprise. Because Pierrot's master punished him for losing cows under his supervision with "four stakes" (a common punishment for slaves that involved being whipped while lying on the ground tied to four stakes), he had to be threatened to let Jacques and Jacob take animals that did not belong to them. Periche and Jacques fled before the opening of the investigation and escaped from justice, though Jacques stole some letters of exchange and clothes from the other white indentured servant before he left.[3]

Periche and Jacques had good reason to fear the Superior Council, which did not display any leniency toward either the remaining white tradesman or the black slave. Since beef was a central component of the white urban population's diet, local authorities had a vested interest in protecting the meat trade. They might have also been afraid that laborers of various conditions who had to collaborate to fulfill their tasks would unite across racial boundaries to the detriment of the elite and middling sorts. Fleury was severely punished for having enrolled a slave in a criminal enterprise. As the prosecutor general argued, at stake was "public safety." Yet the interrogations and testimonies show that the relationships between the various protagonists were made of dependency, constraint, and violence rather than race-blind cooperation and solidarity. The workplace was the site of intense power struggles and generated great tension and conflict between people of

3. RSCL 1764/04/07/03 (quotation). Periche's gift of the paunch to Jacob must be interpreted within the food culture of settlers of European descent. During the eighteenth century, tripe and offal in the metropole were increasingly rejected by the elite and only consumed by the poor. Likewise, butchers stopped selling and preparing what was called the *"cinquième quartier"* (the "fifth hindquarter") which became the specialty of tripe butchers. See Madeleine Ferrières, *Nourritures canailles* (Paris, 2007), 101–127. For another example of an enslaved cowherd threatened with being tied to four stakes and whipped as punishment if he did not bring back all the cows entrusted to his care to their enclosure every night, see RSCL 1748/01/12/01.

different legal statuses, socioeconomic situations, and ethnic backgrounds. Work experiences and relations were central in the construction of a hierarchical socioracial order.[4]

Throughout the American colonies, the resource that people struggled over most was labor. As Stephen Innes has observed, "If colonization represented a search for work to some and for better working conditions to others, it represented a search for workers—particularly unfree ones—to still others." Many Europeans crossed the Atlantic looking for employment, whereas slaves were deported from Africa to fulfill the high demand for workers. As labor was scarce and difficult to control, governments, trading companies, and settlers resorted to various types of bound labor in addition to free labor to obtain, stabilize, and discipline the workforce. Among these various forms of unfree labor, slavery became increasingly important from the late seventeenth century onward alongside the rise of the transatlantic slave trade, especially in tropical and subtropical colonies.[5]

Louisiana did not escape the trend toward slave labor. From the beginning, local authorities repeatedly asked the crown for permission to exchange North American Native captives for black slaves from the Caribbean. Still, when the Company of the Indies took over the colony in 1717, it sought to fulfill its obligation to people the colony as quickly as possible by taking advantage of all the previous forms of labor that had been tried in the Atlantic world during the first centuries of colonial expansion. The company resorted to various kinds of laborers: indentured servants, convicts, soldiers, and slaves. This policy of relying on a mixed-labor force, however, failed in every way possible. Many of the indentured servants who came from Europe with the only migratory wave to the colony ever organized died or fled; the slave trade from Africa practically ceased in 1731; and only scattered free or forced migrants came afterward from Europe or the Antilles. Throughout the French period, the labor market remained small and in a situation of constant shortage.

Louisiana's relatively slow demographic growth and difficult economic development, owing to its late founding and competition from older and

4. RSCL 1764/03/07/01 (quotation), 1764/03/08/01, 1764/03/08/02, 1764/03/09/01, 1764/03/10/01, 1764/03/11/01, 1764/03/11/02, 1764/03/15/01, 1764/03/17/01, 1764/03/18/02, 1764/03/20/04, 1764/03/21/01, 1764/03/21/02, 1764/03/22/02, 1764/03/22/03, 1764/04/04/01, 1764/04/06/01, 1764/04/07/02, 1764/04/07/03, 1764/04/07/04, 1764/04/07/05, 1764/04/07/06, 1764/04/23/01, 1764/04/25/01.

5. Stephen Innes, "Fulfilling John Smith's Vision: Work and Labor in Early America," in Innes, ed., *Work and Labor in Early America* (Chapel Hill, N.C., 1988), 3–42 (quotation, 10).

better located colonies, might have allowed much needed laborers to nego-tiate better working conditions and improve their social standing while the use of workers of all statuses and backgrounds might have further accentu-ated the segmentation of the labor force and fostered the blurring of social and racial boundaries between the various kinds of laborers. Yet, after the collapse of John Law's System and the reorganization of the Company of the Indies in 1723, local authorities and settlers chose to emulate Saint-Domingue. Even when the slave trade from Africa practically ceased after the company abandoned the Mississippi colony in 1731, their commitment to the perpetuation and expansion of chattel slavery did not diminish. As in British America, the main social division in the Mississippi colony quickly became and remained that between the free and the unfree, and a genu-ine slave society took hold over the French regime. Slavery did not consti-tute one form of labor among others; instead, slavery was recognized as a distinctive system that determined not only labor relationships between whites and blacks but also among whites. This was the case throughout the colony, including the capital. Because the production and reproduction of a slave society required the active participation of all free people, labor and race became increasingly entangled.[6]

WHITE LABORERS, OR, "THE BEST PART OF THE CITY'S *BOURGEOIS*"

When Governor Jean-Baptiste Le Moyne de Bienville described New Orleans's white workers as "the best part of the city's *bourgeois*" in 1733, he was not assessing their position on the social ladder. He only meant that they constituted most of the people who rented or owned houses in the capi-tal. Their situation transformed over the French period. Three stages punc-tuated this evolution. Most white laborers initially came to the colony as indentured servants, although a few convicts were also among their num-ber. They were not treated as badly as slaves, but the company did manage these laborers in a coercive way to control their labor and force them to settle. When this experiment with mixed labor did not succeed, as many in-dentured servants and convicts died, ran off, or returned to the metropole, the company decided to expand the slave system on the model of Saint-Domingue. A second stage then started for the former indentured servants and convicts who had managed to survive. Some settled and set up their own businesses in New Orleans, which fostered the growth of an urban economy and a regime of free labor even as the initial system of indentured

6. For the divide between the free and the unfree in British America, see ibid., 18.

servitude never completely disappeared. In the following years, the numbers of white and black workers tended to balance each other. Still, whites remained a large part of the urban labor force. In the last decades of the French regime, a third stage began as the expansion of the slave system allowed some white craftsmen to experience social mobility, though the world of white laborers remained characterized by its great heterogeneity.[7]

Apart from officials, soldiers, and some slaves, most of New Orleans's first inhabitants were indentured servants and convicts either hired or transported by the Company of the Indies. In the early years of its monopoly, the company was a major employer of white craftsmen and unskilled laborers. Between 1717 and 1721, the company recruited 250 indentured servants in Europe. These civilians were assisted by dozens of skilled worker-soldiers. In 1722, 73 of the company's indentured servants worked in New Orleans. The following year, after Law's departure and the collapse of his System, the company was reorganized, and a policy of economy was launched that included the reduction of the number of white craftsmen and laborers in its service. The company's directors, nevertheless, tried to retain the most sought-after workers, those with a skill. They were offered some enticing benefits, including better wages and rations or even the free transportation of their families to the colony. After the company completed its reorganization, indentured servants were recruited once more. Between 1727 and 1730, forty-nine new contracts were signed in the metropole.[8]

7. Jean-Baptiste Le Moyne de Bienville to the minister of the navy, July 25, 1733, ANOM COL C13A 16, fols. 269v–270v. This definition of "bourgeois" appears clearly in the 1732 census of the city, which first mentioned the "owners' houses" and then the "names of the bourgeois and of those who resided at their place." See "Recensement général de la ville de la Nvelle Orléans . . . fait au mois de janvier 1732," ANOM COL G1 464. For another interpretation of "bourgeois," see Thomas N. Ingersoll, *Mammon and Manon in Early New Orleans: The First Slave Society in the Deep South, 1718-1819* (Knoxville, Tenn., 1999), 41.

8. "Liste des officiers, soldats, et autres embarqués sur *La Mutine* à destination de la Louisiane depuis Lorient," Nov. 14, 1720, ANOM G1 464; Pierre Le Blond de La Tour, "État des ouvriers servant la Compagnie en Louisiane," Dec. 9, 1721, ANOM COL C13A 6, fols. 158–161r; "État des ouvriers qui seront entretenus à La Nouvelle-Orléans jusqu'à ce que les maisons et magasins de la Compagnie soient construits tant à La Nouvelle-Orléans qu'à La Balise," May 19, 1722, ANOM COL B 43, fols. 117–120; Le Blond de La Tour, "État des ouvriers conservés pour les travaux et fortifications à faire à la Louisiane et leurs gages par an après la réforme faite, suivant les ordres de M. les commissaires," Jan. 15, 1723, ANOM COL C13A 7, fols. 95–97; "Décision du Conseil," Sept. 17, 1724, ANOM COL C13A 8, fol. 385; "Extraits des lettres du Conseil de Louisiane," Aug. 28,

Slavery, Labor, and Race

While the company continued to employ indentured servants, the company's directors were never comfortable with the convict labor imposed on the colony by the crown. Between 1717 and 1720, thirteen hundred convicts and exiles were deported to the colony. These forced migrants did not suit the company's vision for its new establishment, which is why they were listed separately in all three versions of the 1721 census. Four years later, in May 1725, the Conseil de Régie (the council running the colony during the company's tenure) ordered convicts to be registered at the clerk's office to evaluate their number before deciding what to do with them, suggesting that the authorities must have lost track of them. Many likely died or deserted; others must have been hired by settlers or survived as day laborers or, as was the case for some women, as prostitutes. A few months later, after having informed the crown that an exile named Blanchard had tried to escape to the Spanish, the councillors argued for "the need to purge the colony of these vagrants." When given the opportunity, they did not hesitate to use justice to reach this goal. In 1722, François Fleuriau, the attorney general, demanded the prosecution of Jean Melun / Melin dit Lagrange alias Bourguignon because he allegedly tried to steal a piece of bacon at a friend's and stabbed the man who tried to stop him. Fleuriau described Bourguignon as a man who had been transported as a convict to the colony and had been repeatedly found guilty of drunkenness, violence, and debauchery. Bourguignon's trial, however, revealed that he had come to Louisiana voluntarily as an indentured servant on the Beauregard concession. Despite Bourguignon's poor mental state, the council condemned him to a whipping and perpetual banishment thereafter.[9]

––––––

1725, ANOM COL C13A 9, fol. 252; Marcel Giraud, *A History of French Louisiana*, V, *The Company of the Indies, 1723–1731*, trans. Brian Pearce (Baton Rouge, La., 1991), 257–258.

9. After the first group transportation of convicts to the colony, the king continued to send convicts against the Company of the Indies's wishes on an individual basis throughout the 1720s. See Giraud, *History of French Louisiana*, trans. Pearce, V, 259–260. For the company's policy toward convicts, see "Recensement des habitants et concessionnaires de La Nouvelle-Orléans et lieux circonvoisins avec le nombre de femmes, enfants, de domestiques blancs, hommes, et femmes de force, esclaves nègres, esclaves sauvages, bêtes à cornes, et chevaux," Nov. 24, 1721, ANOM COL G1 464; "Délibérations du Conseil," May 24, 1725, ANOM COL C13A 9, fol. 108r; "Arrêt du Conseil Supérieur du 24 mai 1725 qui ordonne aux gens de force envoyés de force dans la colonie de faire leur déclaration," ANOM COL A 23, fol. 59; Letter by M. de La Tour, Oct. 21, 1723, ANOM COL C13A 7, fol. 194r; Extracts from the letters of the Council of Louisiana, Aug. 28, 1725, ANOM COL C13A 9, fols. 240r (quotation), 249r, 250r. For Bourguignon's trial, see RSCL 1728/05/22/01, 1728/05/22/02, 1728/05/22/03, 1728/05/24/03; and "Decision

Coercion characterized the company's management of all its workers, not only convicts. Because the company did not possess enough horses to occupy their blacksmiths full-time, for example, it was resolved to employ them as edge-tool makers, but turning down such work was not an option. "If they [the blacksmiths] refuse, we have to force them to set up their own business in New Orleans." Even worse, a woman who had been hired in the metropole to labor on a concession by a couple named Moran had her contract sold to the company without her consent. She protested to the Superior Council, claiming that she could not be hired against her will, but the councillors dismissed her plea. Their decision constituted a dramatic change from working conditions in France, where labor contracts could not be sold without the consent of workers and testifies to the deterioration of laborers' rights in the colony. The same process had taken place earlier in the Antilles.[10]

The company's constraining policy also aimed at regulating former indentured servants who had been first employed by private individuals to develop the concessions along the Mississippi River. After completing their time, usually thirty-six-months, or having been abandoned by their masters, they frequently came to the city seeking employment or assistance. In an effort to halt this phenomenon, the company ordered indentured servants to remain in the service of their original masters and forbade their recruitment by other settlers if their former employers had not given them their formal authorization, claiming that the laborers only moved to the city "under the pretext that their time as indentured servants was over, that they were not well fed or for various other bad reasons."[11]

The company also tried to retain laborers in the colony when they desired to leave. During the 1720s, many settlers lived in a state of destitution and insecurity. The primitive conditions of daily life in any nascent colony were aggravated in French Louisiana by the collapse of Law's System, the

against Bourguignon," May 29, 1728, in [Henry P. Dart], ed., "RSCL XII [XIII]," *LHQ*, IV (1921), 486.

10. "État des ouvriers qui seront entretenus à La Nouvelle-Orléans jusqu'à ce que les maisons et magasins de la Compagnie soient construits tant à La Nouvelle-Orléans qu'à La Balise," May 19, 1722, ANOM COL B 43, fols. 117–120; "Petition for Independent Service," July 9, 1726, in "RSCL X," *LHQ*, III (1920), 410–411, "Decision in Civil Suits," July 11, 1726, 411. For the deterioration of laborers' rights in the Antilles, see Philip P. Boucher, *France and the American Tropics to 1700: Tropics of Discontent?* (Baltimore, 2008), 146.

11. "Arrêt du Conseil Supérieur de la Louisiane du 13 novembre 1723 qui défend d'engager aucun domestique et ouvriers sans permission de leur maître," ANOM COL A 23, fols. 44v–45.

Slavery, Labor, and Race

subsequent withdrawal of the company's investments, and the breakup of the concession system. Food and goods from the metropole were lacking and their prices too high for most laborers. In 1723, a year that came to be remembered as the "famine year," it was reported that some of the company's indentured servants who had been employed to build fortifications "implore in tears to be granted their return to France." Given that such requests were not often satisfied, many commoners tried to escape. The company qualified this mobility as "desertion" and criminalized resistance to work discipline and forced settlement. Moreover, it applied such judgments equally to laborers who had completed their contractual time as well as persons who had yet to finish their indentures. In June 1728, a judge from the Superior Council interrogated nine persons who were accused of having organized a plot involving French, Swiss, German, and Irish civilians and servicemen "to escape" to the English. In the end only one individual, twenty-eight-year-old Bonaventure François Langlois, was sentenced to three months in jail for having "made seditious speeches in the taverns and streets of this city inciting people to desert," but the interrogations reveal that most of the suspects dreamed of fleeing Louisiana. One of them was a thirty-year-old Irishman who had been recruited as an indentured servant in Ireland by Sr. de Cantillon, had spent ten years in the Mississippi colony, and was then living with Sr. Darby. He had escaped once to Pensacola, but the Spanish authorities had sent him back with other deserters. He argued that his master, Sr. Darby, had refused several times to discharge him and that he wanted to ask the authorities for his passage back to France.[12]

Despite the severity of these measures, there were limits to the company's ability to control its laborers. The men in its service were not as disciplined as their employer would have liked, and they tried to use the scarcity of labor to their own advantage. The company's carters and other craftsmen, for example, did not hesitate to work for settlers, forcing the Conseil de Régie to issue an ordinance forbidding private masters to poach carters and other

12. On harsh conditions in the colony and requests to return to metropolitan France, see Marcel Giraud, *Histoire de la Louisiane française*, 4 vols. (Paris, 1953–1974), IV, 301–306; Giraud, *History of French Louisiana*, trans. Pearce, V, 115–159, 262–266; "Petition to Recover a Slave," Oct. 28, 1724, in "Abstracts of French and Spanish Documents concerning the Early History of Louisiana, [RSCL, II]," *LHQ*, I, no. 3 (January 1918), 249; and [Adrien de Pauger], "Rôle des ouvriers," Sept. 23, 1723, ANOM COL C13A 7, fol. 170. For the 1728 trial for desertion, see RSCL 1728/06/02/01, 1728/06/01/01, 1728/06/02/02, 1728/06/02/03, 1728/06/02/04, 1728/06/02/06, 1728/06/03/01, 1728/06/03/02, 1728/06/03/04, 1728/06/04/01, 1728/06/04/01, 1728/06/04/02, 1728/06/07/02, 1728/06/03/03.

workers from the company. This ruling notwithstanding, the councillors found it difficult to prevent the company's indentured servants from earning their living with easier jobs or trades. Similarly, although the company employed the port captain or hired foremen to supervise the work of its laborers, they could not convince the latter to respect work hours or increase productivity. As a result, most of the company's coopers were eventually let go.[13]

Although indentured servants were managed harshly by the company, in no way were they considered or treated as enslaved laborers without rights. Indeed, the company sometimes defended the interests of workers against the directors or managers of concessions. In several cases, the Superior Council ordered private employers to settle with their workers and to discharge them when their terms expired. Still, such judicial decisions were not entirely motivated by humanitarian concerns as much as they were by financial considerations. The company often had to deal with indentured servants who had not been paid or took refuge at the company's hospital in New Orleans, where some died. In 1725, the attorney general, Fleuriau, suggested to the Conseil de Régie that the expense generated by such men, who could not be refused out of "humanity" and "justice," should be taken from the accounts of concession owners.[14]

13. Giraud, *History of French Louisiana*, trans. Pearce, V, 259; "Arrêt du Conseil Supérieur du 11 octobre 1725 qui défend aux charretiers et gens de la Compagnie de travailler pour le public," ANOM COL A 23, fol. 64; "Ordonnance du Conseil," Nov. 4, 1724, ANOM COL C13A 8, fols. 139r–140v; Extracts from the register of deliberations of the Superior Council of Louisiana, Sept. 28, 1725, ANOM COL C13A 8, fols. 390–391r.

14. For decisions of the Superior Council regarding labor suits, see "Petition of Recovery," Sept. 26, 1724, in "Abstracts of French and Spanish Documents concerning the Early History of Louisiana, [RSCL, II]," *LHQ*, I, no. 3 (January 1918), 246; "Petition for Supplies," Aug. 22, 1725, in [Grace King], ed., "RSCL VIII," *LHQ*, II (1919), 465, "Memorandum on Petition for Supplies," Aug. 30, 1725, 468, "Memorial of Mr. De Verteuil," Aug. 30, 1725, 468, "Petition for Fair Treatment," Sept. 1, 1725, 468, "Decision in Labor Suit," Sept. 1, 1725, 468, "Petition for Discharge," Sept. 6, 1725, 470, "Remonstrance on Court Ruling," Sept. 6, 1725, 470, "Discharge Granted," Sept. 7, 1725, 470, "Petition to Recover Wages," Sept. 13, 1725, 472, "Petition of Recovery," Oct. 20, 1725, 479, "Decision in Labor Suit," Oct. 22, 1725, 479, "Colonial Jurisprudence," Nov. 5, 1725, 481, "Decision in Labor Suit," Nov. 5, 1725, 481; and "Petition of Recovery," Jan. 13, 1726, in "RSCL IX," *LHQ*, III (1920), 142–143. For another example of indentured servants from the concession belonging to Madame Chaumont who had not been paid and who harassed the director of the concession, who was left without any instructions and assistance from the metropole, see Étienne Périer and Jacques de La Chaise to the Company of the Indies's Directors, Nov. 2, 1727, ANOM COL C13A 10, fol. 197r. For Fleuriau's argument to the Conseil de Régie about the situation of former indentured servants, see RSCL 1725/11/05/02.

Slavery, Labor, and Race

In a context of scarce labor, the company also occasionally protected the rights of free black laborers. In 1725, it became involved in a dispute between the free black Raphaël Bernard and colonist Jean-Baptiste Faucon Dumanoir. Bernard had followed Dumanoir from the metropole and served him as a domestic in the colony since 1723. In July 1728, Bernard, probably inspired by the numerous procedures started by white indentured servants, filed a suit against his master. When the domestic had asked for his discharge after three years, his master stopped paying his wages and giving him his old clothes, locked him up for one month, and beat him severely and repeatedly. The problem was not so much that Dumanoir tried to turn Bernard into a slave as that he tried to force him to stay in his service. The company did not take the master's side nor did it prevent the black man from prosecuting Dumanoir. Rather, the Superior Council ordered Dumanoir to pay Bernard the wages owed him and to let him find another employer, as it had done in other cases related to white laborers. The councillors' principal concern was to hold this free black laborer in the colony. Likewise, a few months earlier, the company had agreed to hire Antoine Beauvais, a "free mulatto," to work as a sailor for fifteen livres a month and rations, since he could no longer exercise his craft as a cooper as he was having problems with his eyesight. Keeping any laborer in the colony was more important than discriminating against free blacks.[15]

From the mid-1720s, a second stage began for laborers of European descent. By then, the company had come to realize that it was difficult to oversee and control indentured servants, but, instead of replacing those whose thirty-six-month contracts had come to an end, the determination was made to privilege chattel slavery. Roughly at the same time, the company became aware of the need to people the city, not only the countryside. Consequently, the company started to somewhat relax its policy of coercion toward white workers. Whereas in the first few years the French and German indentured servants employed to clear and build the city were housed in barracks, the company contributed to New Orleans's demographic and

15. On Raphaël Bernard, see Glenn R. Conrad, trans. and comp., *First Families of Louisiana*, I (Baton Rouge, La., 1970), 25, 71, 117; and RSCL 1724/07/21/01. Raphaël Bernard first resorted to the Superior Council to claim the payment of a debt a few months earlier. See "Petition of Recovery," May 9, 1724, "Abstracts of French and Spanish Documents concerning the Early History of Louisiana, [RSCL, II]," *LHQ*, I, no. 3 (January 1918), 238, "Court Sentence in Discharge of Debt," May 10, 1724, 238; and Jennifer M. Spear, *Race, Sex, and Social Order in Early New Orleans* (Baltimore, 2009), 92–93, 261n. For the hiring of Antoine Beauvais, see "Arrêt du Conseil de Régie de la province de la Louisiane," May 20, 1724, ANOM COL C13A 8, fol. 104r.

economic growth and social stabilization by granting urban parcels to its own workers, to indentured servants from former concessions, and even to migrants who had come as convicts. The change in policy is reflected in the maps and lists of urban proprietors drawn up by engineers at that time. Most of the grantees were whites, but a few free people of color also received urban parcels.[16]

Although local authorities initially had difficulty finding candidates who wanted grants, they eventually succeeded in encouraging this population of workers to settle. In 1725, royal commissioner Jacques de La Chaise reported, with the other councillors of the Conseil de Régie, that "no laborer had requested an urban parcel to settle down since the promulgation of the ruling on this matter," but, by the 1727 census, 141 craftsmen and 9 unskilled workers were listed among the 365 households established in the city. All of these households were headed by a white man or woman. While a few day laborers were able to become property holders, a large proportion of the new urban heads of households were craftsmen working for the company or in business for themselves. Most of them labored in the wood, construction, and metal trades; others were also found in the transport business, food services, and clothing and apparel trades. Their distribution among the various trades was typical of a new city under construction and of a nascent urban society and economy whose basic needs had first to be fulfilled. Only one woman was listed as having a profession, and she was categorized as a "laundress."[17]

16. For the housing of indentured servants of French and German descent in barracks, see [Le Blond de La Tour], "Plans, profils, et élévations des bâtiments et casernes faits pour la Compagnie depuis le 1er août 1722 jusqu'au 3 janvier de la présente année 1723," ANOM 04 DFC 67A; and Giraud, *Histoire de la Louisiane française*, IV, 407–411. For the distribution of urban concessions, see "Plan de la Nouvelle Orléans telle qu'elle était au mois de décembre 1731 levé par Gonichon," ANOM 04 DFC 89B; "État des noms de tous ceux qui ont des emplacements à La Nouvelle-Orléans," 1723, ANOM COL C13C 2, fol. 271v; and "Petition for Building Site," Apr. 3, 1723, in "Abstracts of French and Spanish Documents concerning the Early History of Louisiana, [RSCL, I]," *LHQ*, I, no. 1 (January 1917), 109. See also "The Collins C. Diboll Vieux Carré Digital Survey: A Project on the Historic New Orleans Collection" on HNOC's website, which uses the 1722 map of New Orleans by Le Blond de La Tour, the 1728 map by François Ignace Broutin, and the 1731 map by Gonichon: http://www.hnoc.org/vcs/index.php.

17. La Chaise and the four councillors of the Conseil de Régie, June 2, 1725, ANOM COL C13A 9, fol. 145v; "Recensement général des habitants, nègres esclaves, sauvages, et bestiaux au département de La Nouvelle-Orléans qui se sont trouvés au 1er juillet 1727," ANOM G1 464. In the 1726 census, only one woman was listed as having a profession. She was a seamstress. See "Recensement général des habitations et des habitants de la colonie de la Louisiane ainsi qu'ils se sont nommés au 1er janvier 1726," ANOM G1 464.

Slavery, Labor, and Race

Despite more opportunities opening for white laborers and an increasing reliance on slavery, indentured servitude remained an important part of the city's workforce. Sixty-five "indentured servants or domestics" were listed in the 1727 census, albeit without specific information regarding their name, gender, or occupation. More women might have been included in the group. These "indentured servants or domestics" did not live on their own, unlike the 141 craftsmen and unskilled workers named in the census. These white dependents must have been new indentured servants who had signed contracts in the metropole; others were likely former indentured servants of the company or of the concessions along the river who succeeded in finding new employment locally on a daily basis or for a longer period of time. Apparently, except for trips to hunt, transport goods, or participate in the Native trade, formal labor contracts were not signed before a notary. As was the case in France, local labor agreements between masters and domestics were made verbally and privately, which means that working conditions were defined by custom. These new *"engagés"* (indentured servants) were referred to in the same way as those who had been transported from the metropole with a thirty-six-month contract, but their situation resembled wage labor more than bound labor.[18]

In the late 1720s, interpersonal relationships of dependency among local employers and laborers similar to the ones that existed in the metropole started to replace the general policy of coercion that had characterized the company's early years. Contrary to some contractual indentured servants who went to court over back pay or permission to leave the colony, few laborers among those who were hired locally without a formal contract brought charges against their masters. Likewise, local authorities did not issue any rulings related to wage labor, as the company did in the early 1720s for its own indentured servants, either during the company's tenure or after the colony's retrocession to the crown. Following Christopher Tomlins's insights, it is possible to read this lack of legal activity and reliance on courts to settle labor relations as a sign that authorities had stopped considering indentured servants as one of their main targets requiring discipline and control as free labor came to replace bound labor among whites. From the

18. For verbal agreements instead of formal contracts between masters and servants in France, see Sarah C. Maza, *Servants and Masters in Eighteenth-Century France: The Uses of Loyalty* (Princeton, N.J., 1983), 97. For the content of indentured contracts signed in the metropole, see Marie-Claude Guibert, Gabriel Debien, and Claude Martin, "L'émigration vers la Louisiane: (La Rochelle, Nantes, Clairac) (1698–1754)," in *Actes du 97e. congrès national des sociétés savantes: Nantes 1972; Section d'histoire moderne et contemporaine*, Tome II (Paris, 1977), 97–136.

late 1720s, slavery became the primary if not the sole object of regulation and judicialization of work. As Tomlins has recently reminded historians of early British America, "During the first two centuries of mainland settlement 'free labor' came to mean 'without public or private regulation.'"[19]

The deregulation of wage labor in Louisiana was likewise reflected in the crown's prohibition of privileged guilds in the colony. Nevertheless, the social identity that these corporate institutions gave craftsmen survived for some time in New Orleans, as shown by a list of workers employed by the company in 1722 in which three locksmiths were identified as masters and given a supervisory function. In the sacramental records, craftsmen not only always specified their trade when they had to self-identify but also referred to themselves with the title of master artisan. This identification might have been a way of recalling their prerogatives in the transmission of their trade to apprentices, even though the guild system never took hold in the colony. Some forms of professional organization or cooperation must have survived, since skilled laborers of the same trade often appear as witnesses in the marriage contracts or ceremonies of their colleagues. In November 1728, exceptionally, the four witnesses at "master locksmith" Pierre Paul Loisel's wedding were themselves all "master locksmiths." It was not systematic, however, and witnesses also included craftsmen from other trades, company employees, other white settlers, and even sometimes sergeants and soldiers.[20]

In the 1740s and early 1750s, a third stage began for white labors. Despite

19. For servants' relationships of dependency toward their employers in metropolitan France, see Jean-Yves Grenier, *L'économie d'Ancien Régime: Un monde de l'échange et de l'incertitude* (Paris, 1996), 111. For a few labor suits after the mid-1720s, see "Petition of Recovery," Feb. 23, 1726, in "RSCL IX," *LHQ*, III (1920), 147; "Petition of Recovery," Apr. 17, 1726, in "RSCL X," *LHQ*, III (1920), 404 (quotation), and "Petition of Recovery," June 16, 1726, 409. For the lack of regulation of free labor in British America, see Samuel McKee, Jr., *Labor in Colonial New York, 1664–1776* (New York, 1935), 179, quoted in Christopher Tomlins, *Freedom Bound: Law, Labor, and Civic Identity in Colonizing English America, 1580–1865* (Cambridge, 2010), 294.

20. For the lack of privileged guilds in Canada, see Jean-Pierre Hardy and David-Thiery Ruddel, *Les apprentis artisans à Québec, 1660–1815* (Montreal, 1977); and Peter N. Moogk, "In the Darkness of a Basement: Craftsmen's Associations in Early French Canada," *Canadian Historical Review*, LVII (1976), 399–439. For the use of the title of "master" in early Louisiana, see "État des ouvriers qui seront entretenus à La Nouvelle-Orléans jusqu'à ce que les maisons et magasins de la Compagnie soient construits tant à La Nouvelle-Orléans qu'à La Balise," May 19, 1722, ANOM COL B 43, fols. 117–120. For Pierre Paul Loisel's wedding, see AANO, Saint-Louis Cathedral Marriages, 1720–1730, 11/29/1728.

Slavery, Labor, and Race

the War of the Austrian Succession, these decades marked a time of demo-graphic expansion, economic growth, and social stabilization. Whereas the Natchez Wars, the lack of flour and goods from France, a hurricane, and lack of employment opportunities in the late 1720s and early 1730s prompted many settlers to ask to leave the colony, the following decades saw new ar-rivals, and requests from white laborers to go back to the metropole largely stopped appearing in administrative correspondence. The colony was be-coming attractive, and those who had already settled there did not dream of leaving it anymore.[21]

The social trajectory of Mickael/Michel Zeringue's family highlights opportunities that were opening up for white workers. A master carpenter from Alsace, Zeringue had worked on the fortifications of Huningue before being brought to the colony with his wife and child by de Boispinel, a com-missioned engineer, in 1721. Excelling in his trade, Zeringue was protected by the engineers Pierre Le Blond de La Tour and Adrien de Pauger. The latter had known him since his life in Alsace, where they had been neighbors. Ze-ringue was able to secure employment as the supervisor of the carpentry work on the company's house of directors, the barracks, and the church. In 1726, he was encouraged by Pauger, who claimed he could obtain slaves for him, to settle in the colony for good. At the time, Zeringue and his second wife were living in the city, but, sometime before 1731, he managed to ac-quire a plantation in the Chapitoulas district, which he worked with twelve slaves and one indentured servant. Long after his death in 1738, two of his sons, Joseph and Jean-Louis, married sisters, who were the daughters of a former militia officer, in 1759 and 1763. The two families had been neigh-bors at Chapitoulas, where they ran plantations with dozens of slaves.[22]

21. Bienville nevertheless concealed from the minister of the navy the fact that two families of settlers had moved from Louisiana to Saint-Domingue. See Extract from let-ter by the minister of the navy to Bienville, Jan. 19, 1742, ANOM COL F3 242, fol. 333.

22. "Liste des officiers de la Compagnie, ouvriers pour M. de La Tour, soldats, et autres embarqués sur *Le Dromadaire* commandé par M. de St. Marc pour la Louisiane," Jan. 4, 1720–Jan. 24, 1721, ANOM G1 464; [Le Blond de La Tour], "État des ouvriers servant la Compagnie en Louisiane," Dec. 9, 1721, ANOM COL C13A 6, fol. 158r; Le Blond de La Tour to the Company of the Indies, Jan. 15, 1723, ANOM COL C13A 7, fol. 198; Pauger to the Superior Council, Jan. 3, and May 19, 1724, ANOM COL C13A 8, fols. 46–47; "Gratification en faveur de Mikael Seringue, maître charpentier," Dec. 24, 1724, ANOM COL C13A 8, fols. 164–165r; Pauger to the Company of the Indies's Directors, Mar. 19, 1726, ANOM COL C13A 9, fols. 354v–355v; "Recensement général des habita-tions et des habitants de la colonie de la Louisiane ainsi qu'ils se sont nommés au 1er jan-vier 1726," ANOM G1 464; "Recensement des habitations le long du fleuve," 1731, ANOM G1 464; "Recensement général du quartier des Chapitoulas ... dans la présente année

Regardless of the improvement in the global economic context, a wide diversity of socioeconomic situations nonetheless continued to exist among craftsmen and unskilled workers. The lives of many laborers were still marked by vulnerability and insecurity. At the bottom of the social ladder stood families such as the La Prairies. The lack of information about them alone testifies to the poverty and harshness of their lives. In the mid-1740s, Jean-Philippe La Prairie died, leaving a widow with two children and no income. At that time, his ethnic origins were not mentioned, but he was categorized as a "bohemian" in the 1732 census. He must have come to the colony as a convict. His wife, Marie Jeanne, was constrained to work to earn a living for her family but could not find enough employment to cover the cost of food, which was high in the wartime context. After eighteen months, she had no other choice but to sell part of her urban parcel, located at the corner of Saint Philippe and Royal Streets, to buy food and goods. Since she only owned one-third of a regular urban lot to begin with, she was left with only one-sixth on which to set up her "shack." The mastery of a trade, the way settlers came to the colony, the opportunity to find a spouse and form a family, accidents during people's lifetimes, access to slaves—all these factors greatly influenced the ability of individuals to take root in Louisiana and to benefit from social mobility.[23]

By the end of the French regime, New Orleans's population was still made up of many white tradesmen. Although one of the 1770 militia rolls mentioned ninety-four craftsmen, they might have been even more numerous as the list was incomplete. Their distribution among the various trades had changed. More laborers worked in the food, clothing, and apparel trades

1763," AGI, Audiencia de Sto Domingo, Luisiana y Florida, Años 1766 a 1770, 2595—588 and 589, "Padron y lista de las quatro compañias de milicianos y habitantes en la ciudad por quarterles, segun revista passada en 27 de Mayo 1766"; "État des quatre compagnies de milice de La Nouvelle-Orléans, 12 février 1770," AGI, Correspondencia de los Gobernadores de la Luisiana y la Florida Occidental, Años 1766–1824, Session Papeles de Cuba, legajo 188-A; AANO, Saint-Louis Cathedral Marriages, 1720–1730, 1759–1762, and 1763–1766, 12/26/1726, 05/01/1759, 06/28/1763; "Marriage contract," May 11, 1740, in Alice Daly Forsyth and Ghislaine Pleasonton, eds., *Louisiana Marriage Contracts,* [1], *A Compilation of Abstracts from Records of the Superior Council of Louisiana during the French Regime, 1725-1758* (New Orleans, 1980), 99; "Marriage contract," Apr. 18, 1759, and June 16, 1763, in Alice Daly Forsyth, ed., *Louisiana Marriage Contracts,* II, *Abstracts from Records of the Superior Council of Louisiana, 1728–1769* (New Orleans, 1989), 155–156; NONA Kernion Feb. 20, 1764, Feb. 28, 1764, Mar. 13, 1764; NONA Garic June 9, 1765; Giraud, *History of French Louisiana,* trans. Pearce, V, 233–236, 252, 267.

23. "Recensement général de la ville de la Nvelle Orléans ... fait au mois de janvier 1732," ANOM COL G1 464; NONA Oct. 19, 1745, Oct. 20, 1745.

than in the construction, wood, and metal ones. Commerce and services had become the two most important economic sectors in a society that was much more refined. The militia rolls cannot provide information about white female workers, but the list of names for the only district for which professional activities are mentioned in the 1763 census reveals the presence of two menders and one seamstress. It seems that a few services were the preserve of female laborers. They washed, sewed, and mended clothes and stockings. In so doing, they reoriented the traditional domestic tasks performed by women within their own households to fulfill the needs of a market economy and society that included many transient and single men. Like the sacramental records, which never mention brides' professions, censuses underrepresent the labor of white women, except for single women of adult age living on their own, since women's social identity was defined primarily by their family situation, not their work. Censuses remain silent on what other women, whether they were married or widowed, did to complement their husbands' professional activities or to earn money on their own, particularly in ancillary services, such as running a boarding house or a tavern. The widow Piquery, for instance, is listed in the 1763 census as the head of her household, but her profession is not specified, even though she continued to run her husband's bakery with the help of twelve slaves after his death. Slaveownership must have facilitated this kind of professional continuity.[24]

24. "Milices Nelle Orléans, le 25 janvier 1770," AGI, Correspondencia de los Gobernadores de la Luisiana y la Florida Occidental, Años 1766–1824, Session Papeles de Cuba, legajo 188-A; "Recensement général fait à La Nouvelle-Orléans ... au mois de septembre 1763," AGI, Audiencia de Sto Domingo, Luisiana y Florida, Años 1766 a 1770, 2595–589. On washing, sewing, and mending as specifically female activities in Europe and North America, see George Hanne, "L'enregistrement des occupations à l'épreuve du genre: Toulouse, vers 1770–1821," in "Travail et société, XVIe–XIXe siècles: Angleterre-France-Belgique," special issue, *Revue d'histoire moderne et contemporaine*, LIV, no. 1 (January–March 2007), 81; and Anne Pérotin-Dumon, *La ville aux îles, la ville dans l'île: Basse-Terre et Pointe-à-Pitre, Guadeloupe, 1650–1820* (Paris, 2000), 507–508. On women's invisibility in most records and on their greater involvement in economic life as they worked within or outside their households in France, see Sabine Juratic and Nicole Pellegrin, "Femmes, villes, et travail en France dans la deuxième moitié du XVIIIe siècle: Quelques questions," in "Lectures de la ville: (XVe siècle–XXe siècle)," special issue, *Histoire, économie, et société*, XIII (1994), 477–500; and "Forum: Women and Work," *French Historical Studies*, XX (1997), 1–54. For documents that qualified Madame Piquery as a "baker," see AANO, Saint-Louis Cathedral Baptisms, 1744–1753, 03/16/1750; "Petitions," "Notice," and "Judgments," Aug. 1, Aug. 5, and Sept. 2, 1752, in Heloise H. Cruzat, ed., "RSCL LXXVI: August–September, 1752," *LHQ*, XXI (1938), 876, 879, 882, 884, 900, 903; NONA Kernion Mar. 30, 1764; and NONA Garic Feb. 15, 1768. For the role of slave-

Although artisans and day laborers remained a large part of the white urban population, authorities and settlers repeatedly complained about the "shortage of laborers" and their "exorbitant price." It was mostly white craftsmen who were in high demand and expensive. Some officials and members of the elite chose to invest time and money in the recruitment of these skilled workers in the metropole. In 1729, Jean-Charles de Pradel, for example, used his family connections to hire some clog makers in his native province, while, in 1752, Governor Louis Billouart de Kerlérec spent a lot of time looking for a few tradesmen in Brest before embarking for New Orleans. Others believed that skilled slaves were less expensive and more reliable. In 1753, the Council of the Ursulines met to decide if they should purchase a "negro blacksmith." The result was that "it was unanimously decided that it was better to have one instead of a white and we sent Mr. Barthélémy to purchase one, but as he was too expensive he wasn't bought." Demographic, economic, and sociopolitical circumstances constrained settlers' access to a skilled workforce and influenced the choice between white and black laborers. These trends and events transformed the relationship between labor and race.[25]

"WHITES' INDOLENCE": LABOR AND RACIAL FORMATION

The founding of New Orleans coincided with the beginning of the slave trade to Louisiana from Africa. Slaves played a crucial role in the development of the city. Within the French Atlantic, the rise of the slave trade and the replacement of European indentured servants by African slaves had started in the Antilles in the last decades of the seventeenth century.

---

ownership in maintaining the economic security of widows in Charleston, see Emma Hart, *Building Charleston: Town and Society in the Eighteenth-Century British Atlantic World* (Charlottesville, Va., 2010), 112.

25. "Relation à la Nouvelle Orléans, ce vingt-septième Octobre 1727," in [Marie Madeleine] Hachard, *Relation du voyage des dames religieuses Ursulines de Rouen à La Nouvelle-Orléans* (1728) (Paris, 1872), 79; Bienville and Edmé Gatien Salmon to the minister of the navy, Sept. 10, 1735, ANOM COL C13A 20, fols. 123–125r; A. Baillardel and A. Prioult, eds., *Le chevalier de Pradel: Vie d'un colon français en Louisiane au XVIIIe siècle d'après sa correspondance et celle de sa famille* (Paris, 1928), 30–31, 55, 80–81, 87; RSCL 1730/04/12/01; Louis Billouart de Kerlérec to the minister of the navy, Aug. 4, 1752, ANOM COL C13A 36, fols. 151–152, Aug. 7, 1752, fols. 153–154, Sept. 15, 1752, fol. 157, Sept. 28, 1752, fols. 159–160, Nov. 13, 1752, fols. 170–171; "Antoinette Bigeaud de St Magne pour l'achat d'un nègre forgeron," "Délibérations du Conseil 1727–1902," June 1, 1753, HNOC, Archives of the Ursuline Nuns of the Parish of Orleans, Microfilm 1 of 19, fol. 42.

The decision to further expand the slave system in the Mississippi Valley after 1723 was based on this previous experience in the French Caribbean islands. Local authorities and settlers commonly made comparisons with the Antilles when they argued about the necessity to establish the slave system in Louisiana. The rationale developed by officials in New Orleans to justify this choice drew on both economic and cultural factors. The formation of slave societies in the Lesser Antilles and Saint-Domingue had started to alter the relationship of whites to work. The experience of slavery in Louisiana would only further enhance the links between labor and race. Even when whites and blacks labored side by side within the city, the kind of work people did was determined by race; the organization of labor in the colony fueled the construction of race in turn.[26]

Local authorities defended their decision to rely on slave labor out of economic necessity and racial prejudice. They complained that most settlers would go back to France if they did not obtain slaves to labor on their tobacco and indigo plantations and to produce wood for trade with the Antilles. Immediately after arriving in the colony as the king's commissioner, La Chaise wrote an alarming report conveying the requests of concessions directors: "If we do not continually grant them negroes on credit their concessions will flounder. On his concession this year, Sieur Dubuisson only managed to produce three hanks of silk which weighed two pounds altogether, he cannot keep whites for lack of flour, the others are in the same situation, they demand blacks." Because white laborers fled for many reasons, including the lack of French bread, the system of white indentured servitude did not produce the results authorities and concession holders expected. Slaves were viewed as an absolute necessity to ensure the survival of the nascent colony and the development of a plantation society.[27]

Since importing slaves into Louisiana was expensive and did not immediately yield a high return, local authorities had to develop arguments to explain that whites did not resort to slave labor out of laziness. La Chaise wrote the company's directors:

26. For the growth of the slave trade and the expansion of the slave system in the Antilles, see Boucher, *France and the American Tropics to 1700*, 154–167, 268–300; and David Geggus, "The French Slave Trade: An Overview," *William and Mary Quarterly*, 3d Ser., LVIII, *New Perspectives on the Transatlantic Slave Trade* (2001), 119–138.

27. Extracts from letters from the Council of Louisiana, Aug. 28, 1725, ANOM COL C13A 9, fols. 239–240r; La Chaise to the Company of the Indies's Directors, Mar. 8, 1724, ANOM COL C13A 7, fol. 26 (quotation).

In fairness to our settlers, I have to admit that most of those who can only have one or two negroes far from being served by them they often pound their foodstuffs in order not to divert them, and work as hard as the negroes do; I see with pleasure that no one is inactive, the hope of getting some negroes and securing a small property spurs everybody on to settle on a parcel and to cultivate it; officers, who have the idlest way of life, only stay in New Orleans to fulfill their service, and then go back to their plantations which is their sole occupation, so I do not think that we have more reasons to complain about whites' indolence than anywhere else where there are always some lazy persons among the rest.

The letter was a response to a company order regarding officers who had been forced to retire as a result of changes in the company's economic policies and the subsequent reduction in troops. Périer and La Chaise were asked to encourage them to open plantations in an effort to cease paying their pensions.[28]

La Chaise was trying to impress the company's directors, but his discourse valuing work and condemning idleness should also be framed in the context of shifting European conceptions of labor. Contrary to the old Christian association of work with pain, misery, and redemption, a new narrative had begun to emerge in Europe as early as the sixteenth century that promoted labor as having essential economic and moral value for individuals and society. Work was thought to both fuel economic growth and fulfill individual aspirations to happiness. "Nobody should be idle" was the wish Law had expressed in 1719, with the implication that everybody ought to be working. Colonies were seen as a solution to the problems of poverty and vagrancy, and bound labor was conceived of as a legitimate way of forcing the poor to work. The crown did not hesitate to deport convicts to the Mississippi colony.[29]

28. La Chaise to the Company of the Indies's Directors, Apr. 29, 1728, ANOM COL C13A 11, fols. 162v–163r (quotation); "Mémoire de la Compagnie des Indes servant d'instruction pour M. Périer nouvellement pourvu du commandement général de la Louisiane," Sept. 30, 1726, ANOM COL C13B 1, fols. 96v–97r; Giraud, *History of French Louisiana*, trans. Pearce, V, 117.

29. John Law quoted by Jean-Claude Perrot, *Une histoire intellectuelle de l'économie politique, XVIIe–XVIIIe siècle* (Paris, 1992), 155. For European conceptions of work, see Steven Laurence Kaplan and Cynthia J. Koepp, eds., *Work in France: Representations, Meaning, Organization, and Practice* (Ithaca, N.Y., 1986); Josef Ehmer and Catharina Lis, eds., *The Idea of Work in Europe from Antiquity to Modern Times* (Farnham, U.K., 2009). For colonies and bound labor as solutions to poverty, see Alain Clément, "Oisiveté,

Yet the establishment of plantation societies that increasingly relied on African slaves laboring under the supervision of settlers, first in the Antilles and later in Louisiana, contradicted this trend. How could the new injunction that everybody should work be reconciled with the divide concerning labor that informed social dynamics in new slave societies? This divergence between theory and practice led to accusations of excessive idleness against slaveholders. In the section of Marc-Antoine Caillot's travel account devoted to his stay in Saint-Domingue, en route to Louisiana, he portrayed "Creole" women as lacking in industry owing to their status as slaveholders. They "have many slaves," he observed, "and this is the reason they are so lazy, even to the point that if they drop something on the ground, they have the patience to call a slave five or six times to come pick up what is just at their feet."[30]

When La Chaise wrote about "whites' indolence" using a category related to race and not status, he was thus alluding to the reputation of extreme laziness that settlers first acquired in the islands. He emphasized that, on the contrary, in Louisiana, all white people, from the top of the social ladder (the military officers) to the bottom (the settlers with only one or two slaves), "worked," even if they did so according to their ranks. The officers ran plantations whereas settlers, or the lower sort, pounded rice or corn to feed their slaves. Only the latter performed manual work, but they were spared toiling on the land. La Chaise was trying to reconcile the traditional ethos of ancien régime societies that distinguished between noblemen and commoners with the new values attached to labor and race-thinking that were developing in the colony alongside the slave system. Despite La Chaise's claims, however, all kinds of heavy work, including pounding rice, would quickly become the sole domain of slaves.[31]

Already in 1721, local authorities commenting on the census taken that year had begun to press for the necessity of slave labor in the colony based on an argument first advanced in the Antilles regarding the fitness

contrainte, et travail obligatoire dans la pensée mercantiliste (XVIe–XVIIe siècles)," in Christophe Lavialle, ed., *Le travail en question, XVIIIe–XXe siècle* (Tours, France, 2011), 25–44; and Jean-Pierre Gutton, *La société et les pauvres en Europe (XVIe–XVIIIe siècles)* (Paris, 1974), 101.

30. Greenwald, ed., *Company Man*, trans. Chalmers, 53. Anne Pérotin-Dumon has suggested that, despite their reputation for idleness, work became a central value organizing the socioeconomic system in colonial societies earlier than in metropolitan societies. See Pérotin-Dumon, *La ville aux îles, la ville dans l'île*, 570–574.

31. La Chaise to the Company of the Indies's Directors, Apr. 29, 1728, ANOM COL C13A 11, fols. 162v–163r.

of African slaves to perform manual labor in the tropics. In their report, they stated: "It is absolutely necessary to send many Negroes to the colony. They are better suited than whites to work the land. And, as the American islands have been developed by enslaved Negroes, Louisiana will never be well developed if we do not send enough of them. They adapt very well to the climate, and the only obligation is to provide them with clothing in winter, the expense is small." After 1731, the governor and the *commissaire-ordonnateur* continually resorted to this line of reasoning, contending that slaves were "better suited" for the work of plantations, especially in the summer. Jean-François-Benjamin Dumont de Montigny likewise drew on this same discourse in his poem about the establishment of Louisiana: "Yet very few Frenchmen themselves work / At cultivating land, as the heat is extreme. / Hence it must be known that negroes do it, / Working under the sun, without fearing its beams; . . . ." Implicit in his poem, as well as in his travel account, was the belief that the exhausting work of pounding rice and corn ought to be done by slaves, an opinion in which he was not alone. In the context of colonies, "work" for white people increasingly meant the act of making slaves toil, not engaging in physical labor themselves. In 1725, the Conseil de Régie justified its demand for slaves by claiming that "every settler asks for nothing else [than slaves] to be able to work."[32]

As Louisiana's leading slaveholders, the Company of the Indies and later the crown played a crucial role in promoting the slave system and transforming the relationship between race and labor in New Orleans and its environs. When the colony came back under the king's tenure in 1731, the trading corporation possessed "148 male negroes, 68 female negroes, 18 negro boys or girls and a few infants." After a dozen slaves were sold to private individuals to pay debts, the crown took the company's place as the

32. "La Louisiane, Recensement," 1721, ANOM COL G1 464 (quotation); "Mémoire de Charles LeGac ci-devant directeur pour la Compagnie des Indes à la Louisiana," 1721, Manuscrits de la Bibliothèque de l'Institut de France, MS 487 Mélanges historiques, Recueil A, fol. 550r; Périer and Salmon to the minister of the navy, Dec. 5, 1731, ANOM COL C13A 13, fols. 9v–10r; Périer to the minister of the navy, Dec. 10, 1731, ANOM COL C13A 14, fols. 168–169; Marc de Villiers, ed., "L'établissement de la province de la Louisiane: Poème composé de 1728 à 1742 par Dumont de Montigny," *Journal de la société des américanistes*, New Ser., XXIII (1931), 387–388 (quotation), 422; Dumont de Montigny, *Regards sur le monde atlantique, 1715-1747*, transcribed by Carla Zecher (Sillery, Quebec, 2008), 287; Baillardel and Prioult, eds., *Le chevalier de Pradel*, 224; M. G. Musset, ed., "Le voyage en Louisiane de Franquet de Chaville (1720–1724)," *Journal de la société des américanistes*, IV (1902), 135–136, 142; Extracts from the letters of the Louisiana Council, Aug. 28, 1725, ANOM COL C13A 9, fol. 239.

colony's preeminent slaveowner, purchasing its remaining 225 slaves for 157,500 livres as well as acquiring its plantation. Although the monarch expressed concern over the expense generated by the slaves belonging to the royal domain five times, in 1734, 1739, 1745, 1754, and 1759, sometimes to the point of ordering them all to be sold, each time, the commissaire-ordonnateur in charge managed to convince Versailles that keeping them was an absolute necessity and agreed to sell only a few. The number of royal slaves gradually declined, owing to sales, but, by 1760, the crown still retained 84, along with a commitment to the slave system that did not waver, regardless of pecuniary concerns.[33]

As the management of the company's slaves reveals, the heavy work of plantations was not the only form of labor transformed by the implementation of the slave system in Louisiana. Commissaire-ordonnateur Edmé Gatien Salmon, attempting to convince the crown to purchase the company's slaves, listed the various tasks they performed:

> Some of these negroes, as already mentioned, are employed to build fortifications, and for water transport as sailors, others chop firewood for the barracks or guardrooms, and the women produce foodstuffs and pound the rice for their subsistence, these various tasks would cost the king as much as 25 or 30 thousand livres based on the price of a workday for a unskilled laborer, furthermore we would not find any and the service would inevitably be faulty, hence if we acquired this

33. Salmon to the minister of the navy, Jan. 16, 1732, ANOM COL C13A 15, fols. 13r–14r; Salmon to the minister of the navy, Jan. 17, 1732, ANOM COL C13A 15, fol. 22; Salmon to the minister of the navy, Sept. 3, 1739, ANOM COL C13A 24, fols. 159v–160r; Kerlérec to the minister of the navy, Aug. 15, 1760, ANOM COL C13A 42, fols. 64–65; "État des nègres, négresses, négrillons, et négrittes du roi au 1er janvier 1760," ANOM COL C13A 42, fols. 66–67. For an example of the sale of royal slaves, see "Adjudication of Negress Bradiguine," Mar. 23, 1740, in Heloise H. Cruzat, ed., "RSCL XXXIV: (January, 1740, to April, 1740)," *LHQ*, X (1927), 272. For arguments from commissaires-ordonnateurs against the sale of royal slaves, see Salmon to the minister of the navy, Apr. 24, 1734, ANOM COL C13A 19, fol. 52; Salmon to the minister of the navy, Sept. 3, 1739, ANOM COL C13A 24, fols. 158–160; Sébastien François Ange Le Normant de Mézy to the minister of the navy, Oct. 21, 1745, ANOM COL C13A 29, fols. 139r–140v; Vincent Guillaume Le Sénéchal d'Auberville to the minister of the navy, July 4, 1754, ANOM COL C13A 38, fols. 147–149r; and the minister of the navy to Kerlérec and d'Auberville, Nov. 27, 1759, ANOM COL B 97, fol. 13rv. In contrast, governors were sometimes inclined to sell royal slaves. See Salmon to the minister of the navy, Sept. 3, 1739, ANOM COL C13A 24, fols. 158–160; and Kerlérec to the minister of the navy, Aug. 15, 1760, ANOM COL C13A 42, fols. 64–65.

bunch of negroes who would cost no more than 30 thousand livres based on the price that the Company sells them for, the capital would be amortized in four or five years. In the future, it would even be possible to train negro boys to the trades of blacksmith, locksmith, carpenter, mason, and other trades, to profitably use them and reduce the expenses we have to incur for the wages of those sorts of workers.

The company used slaves to fulfill its administrative, military, and commercial responsibilities at a lesser expense than it would have cost to hire white laborers but never became a planter producing indigo or tobacco for exportation. The king did the same.[34]

The idea of training male slaves as sailors and craftsmen dated from the late 1720s, when Périer and La Chaise headed the colony. The goal was to reduce the number of white laborers as much as possible because they were more expensive and more difficult to control. In 1728, local authorities informed the company's directors that "we apprentice Negroes to all the workers we believe to be good and honest, and if this practice had been implemented when the colony started to receive slaves, we would at present be able to do without several whites, even though the workers are reluctant to teach the Negroes how to master their trades because they realize that it will hurt their interests in the future." In their letter, Périer and La Chaise clearly expressed the project of turning the colony into a genuine slave society.[35]

As in all urban slave societies, the practice of training slaves as skilled laborers in Louisiana became commonplace. Local white master craftsmen from all trades, including that of the goldsmith, one of the most prestigious trades, agreed to train slaves for material and financial incentives. They used the privilege of training new skilled workers and the labor culture inherited from the metropolitan guild system to keep and assert their dominant position in the hierarchy of laborers and in the socioracial order within the city.[36] As a result of this system of slave apprenticeship, few

34. Salmon to the minister of the navy, Jan. 16, 1732, ANOM COL C13A 15, fols. 13r–14r.

35. "Mémoire de la Compagnie des Indes servant d'instruction pour M. Périer nouvellement pourvu du commandement général de la Louisiane," Sept. 30, 1726, ANOM COL C13B 1, fols. 87r–88r; Périer and La Chaise to the Company of the Indies's Directors, Nov. 2, 1727, ANOM COL C13A 10, fols. 192r–193v; Périer and La Chaise to the Company of the Indies's Directors, Nov. 3, 1728, ANOM COL C13A 11, fols. 142r–143v, 146r (quotation).

36. For the training of slaves as craftsmen in slave societies, see Mariana L. R. Dantas,

whites learned a trade. Nearly all of those who signed apprenticeship contracts were orphans who had lost their father or both parents and whose mother or other relatives, if they had any, could not take care of them. Some of them were also natural sons. The group of white craftsmen was renewed mainly thanks to new migrants from the metropole and, very likely, the sons of craftsmen trained at home.[37]

Black Townsmen: Urban Slavery and Freedom in the Eighteenth-Century Americas (New York, 2008), 73–84; Neville A. T. Hall, *Slave Society in the Danish West Indies: St. Thomas, St. John, and St. Croix,* ed. B. W. Higman (Mona, Jamaica, 1992), 92; Hart, *Building Charleston,* 102–106, 110–111; and Frédéric Régent, *Esclavage, métissage, liberté: La Révolution française en Guadeloupe, 1789-1802* (Paris, 2004), 101–102. For an enslaved goldsmith in New Orleans, see NONA Jan. 13, 1767; and NONA Garic Jan. 15, 1768. For the hierarchy of crafts in European cities, see Olivier Zeller, "La ville moderne," in Patrick Boucheron et al., *Histoire de l'Europe urbaine,* I, *De l'antiquité au XVIIIe siècle: Genèse des villes européennes,* ed. Jean-Luc Pinol (Paris, 2003), 700–701. For apprenticeship contracts for slaves in New Orleans, see RSCL 1740/04/26/04, 1763/08/29/01; "Apprenticed Slave," Oct. 5, 1727, in "RSCL XI," *LHQ,* IV (1921), 230–231; "Francois Brunet, Blacksmith, Agrees to Teach His Trade …," Apr. 26, 1740, in Cruzat, ed., "RSCL XXXIV," *LHQ,* X (1927), 279; and "Madame Marie Anne Hoffman,… Sues to Recover from Dupare Her Young Negro …," Aug. 9, 1741, in William Price and Heloise H. Cruzat, eds., "RSCL XXXVII: July–November, 1741," *LHQ,* XI (1928), 131. See also the mention of the apprenticeship contract of Paul, an eighteen-year-old slave, to Desjean, a blacksmith, dated Feb. 16, 1767, in "Inventory of the Estate of Sieur Jean Baptiste Prevost, Deceased Agent of the Company of the Indies, July 13, 1769," trans. and ed. Edith Dart Price and Heloise H. Cruzat, *LHQ,* IX (1926), 479, 486; and Giraud, *History of French Louisiana,* trans. Pearce, V, 258.

37. For the period between 1718 and 1745, only fifteen apprenticeship contracts have been found for whites. See RSCL 1737/12/09/02, 1762/07/12/02; "Contract of Apprenticeship," May 7, 1737, in Cruzat, ed., "RSCL XXIX: February–May 1737," *LHQ,* IX (1926), 135; "Contract of Apprenticeship," June 25, 1737, in Cruzat, ed., "RSCL XXX: Supplemental Index, no. 7 (June, 1737, to August, 1737)," *LHQ,* IX (1926), 297; "Contract of Apprenticeship," Oct. 6, 1738, in Cruzat, ed., "RSCL XVIII," *LHQ,* VI (1923), 127, "Apprenticeship of Pierre Fion," Nov. 17, 1738, 141; "Olivier Dormoy, Minor Orphan, Authorized by His Uncle … to Continue Learning the Shoemaker's Trade …," May 22, 1740, in Cruzat, ed., "RSCL XXXV: May 1st, to December 30th, 1740," *LHQ,* X (1927), 414; "Act of Apprenticeship," Jan. 7, 1744, in Cruzat, ed., "RSCL XLIV: January–March 14, 1744," *LHQ,* XXII (1929), 649; "Act of Apprenticeship," Mar. 31, 1744, in Cruzat, ed., "RSCL XLV: March–September, 1744," *LHQ,* XIII (1930), 125, "Act," Apr. 15, 1744, 127, "Contract of Apprenticeship," July 20, 1744, 142, "Contract for Apprenticeship," Aug. 31, 1744, 155, "Contract of Apprenticeship," Aug. 31, 1744, 155, "Act of Apprenticeship," Sept. 7, 1744, 157; "Act of Apprenticeship," Feb. 4, 1745, in Cruzat, ed., "RSCL XLVII: January–February, 1745," *LHQ,* XIII (1930), 511; and "Act of Apprenticeship," Apr. 12, 1745, in Cruzat, ed., "RSCL XLIX: March–May, 1745," *LHQ,* XIV (1931), 104. For the mention

Although some slaves were trained as skilled laborers and white and black craftsmen worked together (which does not mean that an egalitarian relationship existed between them), slave labor quickly became associated with heavy and degrading work. In one of the efforts made by local officials to convince the crown to retain its slaves, Commissaire-ordonnateur Salmon insisted in 1739 that they were also employed "in cleaning and clearing the ditches, latrines, wells and other vile tasks, and their women were busy producing tow, carrying wood to the hospital, sweeping, and washing dishes." When the ships did not bring wheat flour from the metropole in times of war, enslaved women were forced to do the arduous work of pounding rice and corn to make bread for the troops. Salmon insisted that slaves could not be replaced by soldiers because the latter could not be trusted in the stores or on journeys and would steal merchandise. He also stressed that it would be difficult to find white laborers that would produce half the output of slaves and contended that they would be sick all the time. His ultimate argument in favor of retaining the king's slaves was that they had no choice but to carry out "all the vile tasks that whites will refuse to accomplish."[38]

Workers of European descent quickly started to refuse to do the heavy labor that was increasingly becoming associated with slaves. As early as 1724, Jacques Fazende asked the company to sell him an enslaved woman whom he could employ to accomplish "the heavy kitchen work," claiming that it was impossible "to use male or female whites, because of their idle-

---

of an apprentice locksmith and an apprentice shoemaker who was the natural son of Mr. Diron d'Artaguiette in two judicial cases, see RSCL 1744/01/25/01; 1744/02/20/01. Another apprenticeship contract has been found relating to the natural son of a settler holding a farm in Lower Louisiana and a blacksmith in the Illinois Country. See RSCL 1739/07/04/02. In colonial New York City, likewise, "Apprenticeship had become little more than a facade for labor agreements and the putting out of orphans and paupers, in which the provision for induction into craft skill and mysteries figured scarcely if at all." See Simon Middleton, *From Privileges to Rights: Work and Politics in Colonial New York City* (Philadelphia, 2006), 156–159 (quotation, 159). At least one family of carpenters appears in the documentation relating to eighteenth-century New Orleans. Charles Lavergne, fifty years old, was probably the father of Nicolas, nineteen years old, and Jean, fifteen. They were recorded together as carpenters living on Dauphine Street in the 1770 muster roll of the New Orleans militia companies. Another carpenter named Alain Lavergne, twenty-two years old, who was probably another brother, lived on his own on Saint-Anne Street. See "Milices Nelle Orléans, le 25 janvier 1770," AGI, Correspondencia de los Gobernadores de la Luisiana y la Florida Occidental, Años 1766–1824, Session Papeles de Cuba, legajo 188-A.

38. Salmon to the minister of the navy, Sept. 3, 1739, ANOM COL C13A 24, fols. 158–160.

Slavery, Labor, and Race

ness as well as their debauchery." This so-called laziness might have been a way for white laborers to resist exploitation. Another case of whites' reluctance to perform painful and dirty work happened in 1752. Sent to Louisiana in preparation for the next anticipated war, Mr. de Gamon, a captain, brought with him a white servant whom he had hired as a valet and barber in the metropole. Once in the colony, the domestic agreed to serve as a cook, although he had no training in this trade. White domestics, such as this cook, did not completely disappear over the French regime. Like Mr. de Gamon, the transient military officers sent to the colony for the duration of the international wars of midcentury always brought their white servants with them. The top officials also continued to employ both white and black domestics, especially male ones, as was the case in the Antilles. This practice of distinction allowed them to display their fortune and their connections with the metropole. But these servants were not asked to fulfill the same tasks as slaves. When Governor Bienville, for example, returned from France in 1743, he brought with him two white domestics, a maître d'hôtel and a valet de chambre (manservant), and two slaves, a cook and a governess. This racial differentiation did not go unnoticed by Mr. de Gamon's white domestic. After his master asked him to go to the riverbank every day to chop down and transport wood on his back, he answered that "this is the job of the negroes in this country, and that he will not do it; that he had not been hired for that." The expression "in this country" suggests that the man might have agreed to perform such tasks in the metropole but that he realized, once in New Orleans, that the meaning of heavy labor was different in the colony. The officer put him in jail, the commissaire-ordonnateur obtained his release, and the valet entered the governor's service.[39]

39. For Jacques Fazende's 1724 request to the company, see "Décision du Conseil de Régie," Nov. 4, 1724, ANOM COL C13A 8, fol. 139r. On domestics in France, see Jean-Pierre Gutton, *Domestiques et serviteurs dans la France de l'Ancien Régime* (Paris, 1981); and Jacqueline Sabattier, *Figaro et son maître: Maîtres et domestiques à Paris au XVIIIe siècle* (Paris, 1984). According to Sarah Maza, in France, "The ideal aristocratic household was characterized by the employment of large numbers of men." See Maza, *Servants and Masters in Eighteenth-Century France*, 205–206. For military and civil officials employing white domestics in Guadeloupe, see Régent, *Esclavage, métissage, liberté*, 99. For mentions of white domestics in New Orleans, see "Recensement général de la ville de la Nvelle Orléans ... fait au mois de janvier 1732," ANOM COL G1 464; "Procès-verbal de l'enlèvement de M. Belot, secrétaire de Rochemore, joint à la lettre de Rochemore du 28 avril 1759," Apr. 27, 1759, ANOM COL F3 243, fol. 141v; "Liste des personnes à qui il a été accordé le passage de la Louisiane en France sur *La Somme*," May 14, 1732, ANOM COL F5B 34, "Liste des personnes à qui il a été accordé le passage de la Louisiane en France sur *La Gironde*," 1733, "Passagers sur *La Charente*," 1743, "Liste des passagers pour *La*

Racial prejudice against heavy work was shared not only by domestics but also by craftsmen. In 1754, four indentured servants who had been hired in Bordeaux to work as pit sawyers for four years by a merchant who wanted to open a plantation in Louisiana and develop a lumber trade with the Antilles complained to the Superior Council that they had been hired out for six months to other settlers who made them work with their bodies half in the water and did not provide them with adequate food, clothes, or bedding. When they finally started to work directly for the commissioner of the merchant who had hired them in the first place, they claimed they were not treated "as Frenchmen should be." The Superior Council refused to cancel their contract but ruled that its terms should be respected, especially those related to food, and that they could not work for other colonists. Though the proprietors' interests were nearly always defended, the judges seemed to believe that white craftsmen ought to be distinguished from African slaves.[40]

The differentiation between slaves and laborers of European descent was less obvious when it came to white convicts who performed the same kind of work and were treated as badly as the enslaved. Yet even convicts sought to be distinguished from the latter. In the early 1740s, the trial of Jean-Baptiste Chevalier dit Lachaume, specifically addressed the issue. A twenty-nine-year-old man, he identified himself as coming from the "bohemian nation." According to the attorney general, he was a "rascal" who had been sentenced by the Superior Council to forced labor in December 1741. He was then sent to the Natchez outpost to work in the service of its commandant, Mr. Dorgon. Lachaume told the judge that he labored incessantly cultivating tobacco and vegetables and serving as a domestic in Dorgon's household. His master frequently beat him and had him punished for stealing goods and trying to convince soldiers to run away.[41]

The case started in June 1743 with a conflict between Lachaume and a soldier named Masson, who served as cook for Dorgon. The serviceman ordered Lachaume to clean the kitchen, but the convict refused, arguing

Pie," Nov. 17, 1748, "Liste des passagers sur *Le Rhinocéros*," Oct. 4, 1752, and "Liste des officiers et autres personnes de la Louisiane qui passent en France sur les vaisseaux du roi *L'Opale* et *La Fortune*," Dec. 31, 1758. For the 1752 case, see Michel to the minister of the navy, Jan. 15, 1752, ANOM COL C13A 36, fols. 222v–224r (quotation).

40. "Extrait des registres des audiences du Conseil Supérieur de la province de la Louisiane, joint à la lettre de Ms. de Kerlérec et d'Auberville du 24 septembre 1754," Mar. 2, 1754, ANOM COL F3 243, fols. 106–108v; Kerlérec and d'Auberville to the minister of the navy, Sept. 24 1754, ANOM COL C13A 38, fols. 37–38r.

41. RSCL 1743/07/06/01, 1743/07/06/02.

Slavery, Labor, and Race

that he was overworked and did not even have time to eat, adding that it was Masson's task. The cook then beat him, and Lachaume fought back, as "he could not stand to be abused by a man who had no authority over him." Masson complained to Dorgon, who gave Lachaume two hundred strokes with a cane and asked the storekeeper to send a slave belonging to the king to tie him up. The officer likened the convict to a "slave" when he argued that "a slave was not allowed to hit a free man." As the royal slave tried to bind Lachaume, the latter stabbed himself several times with a knife. When the convict was asked the reason for his failed attempt at suicide, he claimed that "it was to get away from slavery and that it was what several great men had done before him," alluding to the suicides of prominent figures in antiquity. He later explained to the magistrate in New Orleans "that it was in anger when he heard that Mr. Dorgon wanted him to be attached by a negro, it was what drove him to despair as he had not deserved that and should not be abused by negroes." He had no intention of killing himself, but he wanted to find a way to be delivered from the cruelty of his master and to be sent to the capital. He described Dorgon as an abusive officer and master and claimed that he would prefer to be commanded by a "negro" than by him. Despite these contradictory statements, the convict refused to be abused, chastised, or treated like a slave of African descent. His main motivation was to reduce the harshness of his working conditions, but racial prejudice also informed his behavior and discourse.[42]

The development of a slave society and economy also changed the relationship of white women to labor, at least among the upper and middle classes. In 1739, an orphan girl presented a request to the Superior Council asking to be placed at the Ursulines' convent. She decided on this course of action because her female tutor forced her to perform labor, such as "plowing the garden and running errands in town," that would have been considered proper for a domestic in the metropole but that seemed inappropriate for a white girl of her condition in the colony. Likewise, over time, laundering, which was one of the most strenuous domestic activities, became a chore for female slaves, as was the case in Charleston.[43]

The association between slavery and heavy labor informed the organization of the colony's corvée. Statute labor was never imposed on white civilians nor, once white militia companies had been established during the Natchez Wars, on militiamen. In contrast, in Canada, the peasants, who all

42. RSCL 1743/06/18/01, 1743/07/06/01, 1743/07/06/02.
43. RSCL 1739/05/07/02; 1743/09/11/01, 1744/05/18/01, 1748/06/10/06, 1752/06/13/01, 1764/09/04/01, 1765/10/30/01.

had to serve as militiamen, were the major source of labor for public works. The corvée constituted the principal royal imposition in the Saint Lawrence Valley. The same was true in Louisiana, but, in New Orleans, as in the Antilles, settlers sent their slaves to work for the public good, rather than laboring themselves. Governor Périer first resorted to using slaves for the corvée to construct the levee and the canal at Bayou Saint John in 1724. In so doing, he introduced the only form of gang labor that existed for slaves in the city. Throughout the French regime, local authorities called for this peculiar kind of imposition each time they needed labor for public works, but it was never institutionalized on a yearly basis. The colonists resented and resisted the corvée, and the central government did not favor this practice because they preferred slaves to be employed on plantations. The governor and the commissaire-ordonnateur had to offer settlers some incentives to convince them to send their slaves for the corvée.[44]

The corvée allowed urban development to be subsidized by the planta-

44. On the corvée in Canada, see Louise Dechêne, *Le peuple, l'État, et la guerre au Canada sous le Régime français,* ed. Hélène Paré et al. (Montreal, 2008), 259–286. On the corvée in Martinique, see Dessalles, *Les annales du Conseil souverain de la Martinique,* Tome I, Vol. I, ed. Vonglis, 481–482. Slaves were also employed in public works in other empires, see Laird W. Bergad, *The Comparative Histories of Slavery in Brazil, Cuba, and the United States* (Cambridge, 2007), 194; and Pedro L. V. Welch, *Slave Society in the City: Bridgetown, Barbados, 1680–1834* (Kingston, Jamaica, 2003), 154. For the introduction of the corvée in New Orleans, see "Memorandum of Labor Squads," Mar. 21, 1724, in "Abstracts of French and Spanish Documents concerning the Early History of Louisiana, [RSCL, II]," *LHQ,* I, no. 3 (January 1918), 234, "Regulation Ordering Levees," Mar. 21, 1724, 234, "Levee Labor Enjoined under Due Penalty," Mar. 31, 1724, 236, "Levee Labor Decreed Binding," Mar. 31, 1724, 236, "Revised Enactment on Flooded Lands," Apr. 3, 1724, 236, "Revised Ruling on Flooded Lands," Apr. 3, 1724, 236; and Périer to the Company of the Indies's Directors, Nov. 15, 1727, ANOM COL F3 24, fol. 164. On the negotiations over the government's and slaveholders' obligations with regard to the corvée, see "Arrêt du Conseil Supérieur de la Louisiane du 28 février 1728 sur les journées des nègres à fournir par les habitants pour les travaux des nègres," ANOM COL A 23, fols. 87v–88; "Contract to Buy Slave," Mar. 23, 1728, in "RSCL XI," *LHQ,* IV (1921), 249; Périer and La Chaise to the Company of the Indies's Directors, Aug. 18, 1728, ANOM COL C13A 11, fols. 63–64r; Périer and La Chaise to the Company of the Indies's Directors, Nov. 2, 1727, ANOM COL C13A 10, fols. 185r, 200r; Périer and La Chaise to the Company of the Indies's Directors, Nov. 3, 1728, ANOM COL C13A 11, fol. 134, 146r; Bienville and Salmon to the minister of the navy, May 12, 1733, ANOM COL C13A 16, fols. 64v–65v; "Relation du massacre des Natchez arrivé le 29 novembre 1729," Mar. 18, 1730, ANOM COL C13A 12, fol. 40r; "Report on Sick Slave," Apr. 15, 1730, in [Dart], ed., "RSCL XII [XIII]," *LHQ,* IV (1921), 519, "Petition to Recover Value of Slave," Apr. 15, 1730, 519–520, and "Mortuary Certificate," Apr. 15, 1730, 520.

Slavery, Labor, and Race

tion economy. This form of urban levy on the countryside continued until the end of French rule, despite a project to reform the system of imposition. In 1747, after having tried in vain to gather slaves belonging to private owners to build two new forts at the English Turn, Governor Pierre de Rigaud de Vaudreuil de Cavagnal and Commissaire-ordonnateur Honoré-Gabriel Michel denounced the lack of productivity and efficiency of the corvée and tried to replace it with a system of monetary taxes imposed on all free civilian residents of the city and ship's captains who traded in New Orleans. The white, civilian, and permanent elements of the city's population were classified in five groups according to their work, profession, property, or economic dependency: (sword or pen) officers, merchants, *habitants* (the inhabitants who owned or rented property), *ouvriers* (workers), and day laborers. The goal of the reform was to spare plantation owners and their slaves. But it was never enforced. In 1764, the lease of a plantation with its slaves still included a clause stipulating that the renter had to send slaves for the corvée. In such a new and fragile economy, it was difficult to ask settlers to pay any kind of taxes, and the proposed system would have also transferred the burden of paying for public works to all whites, regardless of their slaveholdings. The next time that local authorities tried to introduce taxes to reduce the king's expenses, they proposed a system of capitation that would take slaveholding into account. This new tax plan confirms that slaveownership had become the main fault line dividing Louisiana society. As Dumont de Montigny underlined in his vivid style, "Those who have many enslaved negroes . . . are considered as the noblemen of this country." If all whites supported the slave system, the sharing of slaves and the profits they brought nevertheless remained an object of contention among colonists.[45]

45. On the construction of two new forts at the English Turn in 1747, see Carl J. Ekberg, "The English Bend: Forgotten Gateway to New Orleans," in Patricia K. Galloway, ed., *La Salle and His Legacy: Frenchmen and Indians in the Lower Mississippi Valley* (Jackson, Miss., 1982), 218. For the tax reform, see "Règlement de Vaudreuil et Michel sur l'entretien des chemins, de la levée, des clôtures, et l'enfermement des bestiaux," Nov. 13, 1747, ANOM COL F3 243, fols. 33v–34v. Military officers were included among potential taxpayers, but not soldiers. For the plantation lease mentioning the corvée, see NONA Sept. 18, 1764. The idea of introducing the capitation on slaves first appeared in 1728 and was considered several times during the French regime but never enforced because the central authorities thought that the economy was too weak and fragile to bear it. See Giraud, *History of French Louisiana*, trans. Pearce, V, 124–125; "Ordonnance de Ms. Bienville et Salmon du 24 décembre 1742 concernant l'imposition de 50 sols par tête de nègre pour la bâtisse de l'église de La Nouvelle-Orléans," ANOM COL A 23, fol. 129v;

Settlers actively sought to acquire slaves out of both economic and socio-cultural motivations, but becoming a slaveowner was not an easy process. The scarcity of slave labor in the colony aggravated the competition to obtain slaves. During the eleven years from 1719 to 1731 during which Louisiana received slaves from Africa, the Company of the Indies controlled the slave trade and discriminated between potential buyers according to their financial solvency and social connections, which aroused a great deal of tension. Holding the monopoly on the slave trade enabled the company to exert powerful leverage on social structure. Over time, slaves became the main source of labor in New Orleans, and the last decades of the French regime saw a relative democratization in slaveholding. As slaveownership became the necessary condition for climbing the social ladder, many settlers experienced some social mobility thanks to increasing slaveholdings.

While the development of a slave society benefited many white settlers, the situation did not necessarily benefit enslaved workers. Urban slaves were used in many different capacities to fulfill the needs of the growing population and to take advantage of all the possibilities offered by the port city's expanding economy. Slave hiring, in particular, helped diversify the urban economy and complicated social relationships based on slavery. The practice, in fact, continued in another way the struggle between slaveowners and nonslaveholders, as it was in the interest of the latter to exploit hired slaves without any consideration for their preservation. Although urban slaves profited from more autonomy and the labor they performed was less exhausting than that done by slaves on plantations, they could still be overworked and abused.

Because slaves were considered essential for both economic and cultural reasons, all settlers tried to obtain some. Slaveownership gradually became more widespread, but this process took time. Since less than six thousand slaves were deported from Africa to Louisiana before the retrocession of the colony to the crown in 1731, their distribution led to many abuses and created accusations of favoritism. First, incoming slaves had to pass a medical

---

and Kerlérec to the minister of the navy, Aug. 15, 1760, ANOM COL C13A 42, fol. 64. For slaveownership as the main fault line dividing Louisiana society, see Dumont [de Montigny], *Mémoires historiques sur la Louisiane ...*, ed. [Jean-Baptiste Le Mascrier], 2 vols. (Paris, 1753), II, 242 (quotation).

examination. If slaves were not needed for public work on the levee, they were then offered for sale. To determine the order of distribution, lots were drawn among the settlers who had requested slaves and had been chosen by company officials. In most cases, the price of slaves was fixed by the company. Only the slaves who were ill were auctioned. After 1722, the company increased the price of a *pièce d'Inde* (a man in his prime, considered the most valuable kind of slave) from six hundred to one thousand livres, the same price slaves sold for in the Antilles, even though Caribbean planters had greater economic means. The company favored settlers who could pay in cash up front or easily make payments and who were most likely to contribute to the colony's economic development. In 1726, a list was compiled of all permanent residents who had asked for slaves that included detailed comments not only on their socioeconomic situation and financial solvency but also on their character. Would-be purchasers of slaves were supposed to conform to an ideal type of colonist, enterprising and hardworking. Moreover, the company threatened to seize and auction the slaves of bad debtors and forbade the distribution of new slaves to settlers who had not paid for those already bought from previous distributions. It also tried to control the resale of slaves acquired from the company by making it mandatory to obtain permission to sell any slaves and prohibiting the resale of slaves who had not yet been paid for. Consequently, colonists who were unable to purchase slaves tried to hire enslaved labor from the company or other slaveholders, especially on Sundays and holidays.[46]

46. "Ordre que la Compagnie d'Occident veut être observé pour la vente des nègres qu'elle enverra à la colonie de la Louisiane," May 27, 1718, ANOM COL F3 241, fol. 211; "Règlement de la Compagnie des Indes du 2 septembre 1721 sur la vente des nègres, marchandises, et autres affaires de Louisiane," ANOM COL A 23, fols. 31v–33v; [Montigny], *Mémoires historiques sur la Louisiane*, ed. [Mascrier], II, 240–241; Giraud, *History of French Louisiana*, trans. Pearce, V, 125; Périer and La Chaise to the Company of the Indies's Directors, Nov. 2, 1727, ANOM COL C13A 10, fols. 185–186r; Périer and La Chaise to the Company of the Indies's Directors, Nov. 3, 1728, ANOM COL C13A 11, fol. 135; "État des habitants qui ont fait au greffe du Conseil leurs soumissions pour avoir des nègres et du nombre qu'ils en demandent payables aux termes réglés par la Compagnie," Oct. 30, 1726, ANOM COL G1 464; Périer and La Chaise to the Company of the Indies's Directors, Apr. 22, 1727, ANOM COL C13A 10, fol. 176v; Périer and La Chaise to the Company of the Indies's Directors, Nov. 3, 1728, ANOM COL C13A 11, fol. 135; "Ordonnance des directeurs de la Compagnie à la Louisiane du 12 mars 1722 sur la vente des nègres," ANOM COL A 23, fol. 36; "Arrêt du Conseil Supérieur du 22 avril 1725 qui défend la vente des nègres, maisons, terrains, et autres immeubles sans permission," ANOM COL A 23, fol. 59; "Extrait des Registres du Conseil d'État, Arrêt concernant la revente des nègres par les habitants de la Louisiane," Dec. 11, 1725, ANOM COL A 23,

Since not all demands for slaves could be fulfilled, the distribution of slaves always left some settlers unsatisfied and discontented. Unsurprisingly, local authorities were accused of favoring their friends and clients. Dumont de Montigny complained that, in the early 1720s, slaves were only given to "cronies" and that, during Bienville's first term as commandant, slave acquisition was even further limited to Canadians. But he admitted that the difficulties in obtaining slaves lessened for a time with the arrival of Périer, who did not hesitate to grant slaves to the "poor." When Salmon took up his post as commissaire-ordonnateur in 1731, however, he did not draw a picture of the situation much better than the one described by Dumont de Montigny the previous decade. He referred to the same fault line between "little" and "big habitants":

> The allotment of slaves has been made mainly to settlers who behaved as landlords and who, for most of them, did not take advantage of them as they could have done, while if we had granted a few slaves to the little habitants and to soldiers who settled here, at present this colony, which is very poor for this reason, would be much stronger .... I realized that through the great number of little habitants and workers who asked for their passage back to France and if I had granted their request the colony would be empty.

The expression "behave as landlords" helps to explain the elite's attitude. At stake was the reproduction of the main social division between nobles and commoners that existed in France in the new social and economic circumstances of the colony. Although slavery had completely disappeared from the metropole, the institution allowed the colonial elite to embrace the traditional aristocratic ethos associated with the seigniorial system and the power of commanding vassals and peasants while providing them with the means to improve their economic fortunes.[47]

---

fol. 67, or ANOM COL F3 242, fols. 71–72r; and various ordinances promulgated by the Company of the Indies about the sale or hiring of slaves, Nov. 13, 1723, ANOM COL A 23, fols. 43v–44, Oct. 17, 1725, fols. 63v–64r, Aug. 31, 1726, fol. 75, July 25, 1725, ANOM COL F3 242, fols. 56–57.

47. Extracts from the letters of the Council of Louisiana, Aug 28, 1725, ANOM COL C13A 9, fol. 250; Pauger to the Company of the Indies's Directors, Apr. 6, 1726, ANOM COL C13A 9, fols. 378–379r; Dumont de Montigny, *Regards sur le monde atlantique*, 212–213 (quotation); Villiers, ed., "L'établissement de la province de la Louisiane," *Journal de la société des américanistes*, XXIII (1931), 422–423; Salmon to the minister of the navy, Dec. 14, 1731, ANOM COL C13A 15, fols. 186v–187r (quotation); Périer and Salmon to the minister of the navy, Dec. 5, 1731, ANOM COL C13A 13, fol. 10v; "Mémoire con-

The socioeconomic trajectory of Pierre Delille dit Dupart, a shoemaker, testifies to both the hardships some settlers experienced in their attempts to acquire slaves and the social mobility that slaveownership could offer whites of the lower or middling sorts. In 1736, Dupart fell victim to the social superiority and economic intransigence of the company agent named Jean-Baptiste Prévost, the man left responsible for collecting debts still owed the company following the colony's retrocession to the crown. According to Dumont de Montigny, Prévost had a reputation for targeting the "little habitants," asking them to give back their pièces d'Inde when they could not pay their debts. He then used those slaves to work his own plantation until he resold them or purchased them for himself at half the price. Through such actions, Prévost managed to accumulate a large fortune, securing a place among the colony's elite. Dupart's troubles with Prévost began when the latter sent his domestic slave to summon Dupart to his office. When the craftsman entered, Prévost demanded the bill that Dupart owed him. When Dupart replied that he had not realized that it was for this reason that Prévost had asked for him but that he would bring the bill to him as soon as possible, the company's agent started to beat him violently with his cane, whereupon the artisan seized the cane to defend himself and left. Prévost's behavior made it clear that he considered Dupart his social inferior, for he did not hesitate to humiliate him in public. Nevertheless, Dupart was eventually able to benefit from some social mobility as he diversified his economic activities, although he did not abandon his trade and continued to train white and black apprentices. In 1737, he signed several contracts with Salmon to buy or supply goods to the king's stores. These contracts might have helped him to accumulate the capital to open a cattle farm on the road to Bayou Saint John, which he worked with the labor of one slave. This enterprise, in turn, likely enabled him to obtain more slaves. By 1763, Dupart's urban household included seven slaves, signifying his success in integrating himself within the ranks of the city's slaveholders. Dupart's upward mobility might have been a struggle, but his socioeconomic progression through the acquisition of slaves was not an exceptional case.[48]

---

cernant les services que Raymond Amyault écuyer Sr. d'Ausseville a rendus à l'État . . . , joint à la lettre de M. Amyaut au 20 janvier 1732," ANOM COL C13A 14, fols. 246r–247v.

48. On Prévost, see Dumont de Montigny, *Regards sur le monde atlantique*, 399–400; Villiers, ed., "L'établissement de la province de la Louisiane," *Journal de la société des américanistes*, XXIII (1931), 423; "Inventory of the Estate of Sieur Jean Baptiste Prevost, July 13, 1769," trans. and ed. Price and Cruzat, *LHQ*, IX (1926), 411–498. For Dupart's request against Prévost, see RSCL 1736/10/24/01. For Dupart's social mobility, see RSCL 1740/04/26/04; RSCL 1744/05/18/01; "Madame Marie Anne Hoffman . . . Sues to

A comparison between the censuses drawn up in 1732 and 1763 reveals the relative democratization of slaveholding over time, documenting transformations in slaveownership that occurred in the last decades of the French regime. In 1732, the number of slaves of African descent in New Orleans had increased as the colonial capital took advantage of the second wave of Louisiana's participation in the slave trade from Africa. Yet slaves still represented only 28.9 percent of the urban population. The rate of slaveownership in the city amounted to 40 percent, with 85 houses out of 212 recording the presence of slaves of African descent. But the census continued to reflect the inequality of the general population's access to slaves that had characterized the period when the Company of the Indies controlled the colony. Of the 85 houses distinguished by slaveownership, 54 percent included only one or two slaves, 32 percent between three or five, and 14 percent more than six. A pattern in the concentration of the slave labor force was developing. If slaves belonging to the company, the king, or the church are excluded, the most important urban slaveholders were military and pen officers, members of the Superior Council, surgeons, engineers, and employees of the company, and, later, the king. A few ship's officers, merchants, and craftsmen also managed to accumulate slave property.[49]

In contrast, by 1763, slaveownership had become more widespread, although it remained a dividing line within New Orleans society. Slaves of African descent accounted for 45.4 percent of the overall urban population, which made the Louisiana capital comparable to other urban slave societies of the greater Caribbean. Native slaves still appeared on the census, but they only numbered 37 out of a total of 1,135 slaves. Black slaves were included

---

Recover from Dupare Her Young Negro Slave," Aug. 9, 1741, in Price and Cruzat, eds., "RSCL XXXVII: July–November, 1741," *LHQ*, XI (1928), 131; "Contract," Jan. 7, 1737, in Cruzat, ed., "RSCL XVIII: Supplemental Index, no. 5 (October 20, 1736, to Feb. 13, 1737)," *LHQ*, VIII (1925), 688; "Contract Passed," Sept. 5, 1737, in [Henry P. Dart], ed., "RSCL XVI," *LHQ*, V (1922), 411; and "Deposit," Jan. 26, 1745, in Cruzat, ed., "RSCL XLVII: January–February, 1745," *LHQ*, XIII (1930), 506. His son, Sieur François Delille Dupart fils, became a planter. See FRLG Oct. 21, 1765.

49. I use the term "house" instead of "household" because of the way the 1732 census was taken. The census included buildings belonging to the king. See "Recensement général de la ville de la Nvelle Orléans ... fait au mois de janvier 1732," ANOM COL G1 464. In 1732, most of New Orleans's urban slave population was of African descent. There were only 9 Native slaves in comparison with 258 black ones. Most houses with indigenous slaves only had one, and all but one of those households also included slaves of African descent who were overwhelmingly preferred in the city to Native slaves. The latter were employed as hunters or rowers whereas the former served as domestics or craftsmen.

Slavery, Labor, and Race

in 192 out of 371 households, which made them present in more than half the households in the city. As in most urban slave societies, a large majority of slaveholders did not keep more than four slaves on their urban properties: 25.5 percent of all slaveowning households listed only one slave, 37 percent between 2 and 4, 25 percent between 5 and 9, and 9 percent between 10 and 19. Seven households had an exceptionally large number of slaves, housing between 28 and 62, but most of the latter lived on plantations at Gentilly, on the outskirts of the city, with the exception of those belonging to two prominent planter-merchant-entrepreneurs, Joseph Dubreuil and Gilbert-Antoine de Saint Maxent. The existence of these concentrations of slaves points to another major fault line separating urban slaveholders whose property was entirely confined to New Orleans and those who possessed land and slaves in the city's surroundings. Plantation holders can also be differentiated according to the number of slaves they kept on their rural estates.[50]

Because most domestics were enslaved, their presence in New Orleans's households was much more common than in metropolitan cities, where the employment of servants only started to spread in the late eighteenth century

50. "Recensement général fait à La Nouvelle-Orléans ... au mois de septembre 1763," AGI, Audiencia de Sto Domingo, Luisiana y Florida, Años 1766 a 1770, 2595—589. In Guadeloupe, slaves represented between 45 and 55 percent of the urban population between 1772 and 1820; in Saint-Domingue, this rate reached 57 percent in Cap-Français in 1771; and in the cities of the Danish West Indies in the second half of the eighteenth century it fluctuated between 55 and 73 percent. See David Geggus, "The Major Port Towns of Saint Domingue in the Later Eighteenth Century," in Franklin W. Knight and Peggy K. Liss, eds., *Atlantic Port Cities: Economy, Culture, and Society in the Atlantic World, 1650–1850* (Knoxville, Tenn., 1991), 104–105; Hall, *Slave Society in the Danish West Indies*, ed. Higman, 87–89; and Pérotin-Dumon, *La ville aux îles, la ville dans l'île*, 330. In eighteenth-century British North America, Charleston had a majority of slaves (around 50 percent in 1774), contrary to most cities in the Chesapeake (9 percent in Baltimore in 1790), while in the 1740s slaves accounted for 8 percent of the population of Boston, 10 percent in Philadelphia, and 20 percent in New York. See Dantas, *Black Townsmen*, 54–59; Thelma Wills Foote, *Black and White Manhattan: The History of Racial Formation in Colonial New York City* (Oxford, 2004), 68–70; Philip D. Morgan, *Slave Counterpoint: Black Culture in the Eighteenth-Century Chesapeake and Lowcountry* (Chapel Hill, N.C., 1998); 663–664; Gary B. Nash, "Slaves and Slaveowners in Colonial Philadelphia," *William and Mary Quarterly*, XXX (1973), 223–256; and Trevor Burnard, "Towns in Plantation Societies in Eighteenth-Century British America," *Early American Studies*, XV (2017), 835–859, esp. 845, 849. For the limited number of slaves within urban households in slave societies, see Hart, *Building Charleston*, 103–105; and Pérotin-Dumon, *La ville aux îles, la ville dans l'île*, 551.

but mostly during the nineteenth century. Moreover, enslaved female domestics often stayed in service until more advanced ages than their counterparts in France, since most of the latter remained under thirty because they left service to get married. As in most urban slave societies, female slaves outnumbered male slaves, although in New Orleans the imbalance was not great (441 women to 416 men). The probate record of Bernard de Vergès, a former chief engineer, reflects the typical prominence of enslaved women in urban households in comparison with the countryside. In his town house, he kept only two slaves, both categorized as "negress": Marie-Jeanne, around twenty-five years old, probably a domestic, and, Julie, twenty-eight to thirty years old, described as a laundress, which means that she not only took care of the household's washing but also earned money for her master by washing other people's clothes. He also owned a slave family (a couple with an adult child) and seven male slaves, but he kept them on his plantation. A greater number of slaves within an urban household allowed for more diversity in gender as well as specialization. At his death, Dominique Bunel, who was probably a goldsmith, owned five slaves: Jacob, *"nègre,"* apprentice goldsmith, twenty-eight to thirty years old; François, "nègre," hunter, thirty years old; Françoise or Angélique, *"négresse,"* cook, fifty years old; Mariane, the cook's eight-year-old daughter; and Marie Poupone, *"mulâtresse,"* fifteen years old.[51]

The significance of slaveownership for each household's socioeconomic

51. On servants in the metropole, see Maza, *Servants and Masters in Eighteenth-Century France,* 60–74, 266–278. For the 1763 census, the slaves who were categorized separately as "mulatto" with the mention of their gender but not of their age have been counted as adults. There were also 117 "negro" boys and 124 girls. See "Recensement général fait à La Nouvelle-Orléans ... au mois de septembre 1763," AGI, Audiencia de Sto Domingo, Luisiana y Florida, Años 1766 a 1770, 2595–589. The slight imbalance between men and women could have been related to the fact that female heads of households were not as numerous in New Orleans as in older urban slave societies. See Bergad, *Comparative Histories of Slavery in Brazil, Cuba, and the United States,* 195; Hall, *Slave Society in the Danish West Indies,* ed. Higman, 88–89; Philip D. Morgan, "Black Life in Eighteenth-Century Charleston," *Perspectives in American History,* New Ser., I (1984), 190; Régent, *Esclavage, métissage, liberté,* 97; and Welch, *Slave Society in the City,* 98–99. In contrast, enslaved men outnumbered women in Cap-Français in the 1770s See David P. Geggus, "The Slaves and Free People of Color of Cap Français," in Jorge Cañizares-Esguerra, Matt D. Childs, and James Sidbury, eds., *The Black Urban Atlantic in the Age of the Slave Trade* (Philadelphia, 2013), 107–108. For Bernard de Vergès's probate record, see NONA Garic Jan. 31, 1766. On Dominique Bunel, see "Contract of Apprenticeship," Oct. 6, 1738, in Cruzat, ed., "RSCL XVIII," *LHQ,* VI (1923), 127. For his probate record, see NONA Kernion Apr. 03, 1764.

situation varied. For some, a single slave represented their only source of income and means of survival. Others entered into slaveownership with an entrepreneurial spirit, seeking to take advantage of any opportunity to make a profit and diversify activities to achieve not only security but also prosperity. In 1737, Commissaire-ordonnateur Salmon wrote to the minister of the navy to ask for his approval of a decision he had taken in favor of a widow. He had agreed to deliver a slave belonging to the king to a craftsman as an advance on payment for some work the latter had promised to do in the barracks. Although the artisan died before he could complete his task, Salmon decided to leave the slave with his widow because she could not survive without the revenues drawn from her husband's work. In contrast with this widow, Dumont de Montigny chose to keep only one female domestic slave to make rice bread for his household during his tenure in New Orleans in the early 1730s but leased five other slaves to a settler who produced pitch and tar on the other side of Lake Pontchartrain for fifteen or sixteen livres a month. The former military officer also cultivated his garden and had his vegetables sold at the market.[52]

A slave hiring system gave a much larger segment of New Orleans's population access to slave labor while allowing masters to obtain "capital returns on slaves without the necessity of relinquishing title to them." Slaves could be hired out within or outside the city. Apart from working in the tar production units on the northern bank of Lake Pontchartrain, New Orleans slaves could also be leased out for journeys to the Illinois Country. Within the city, those working as craftsmen, such as carpenters, pastry-cooks, carters, domestics, or wet nurses, could be rented out on a task basis or for a certain period of time, which could range from a month to a year. Both men and women as well as children could be hired out. In 1765, Babet, an eleven-year-old girl belonging to Sieur Fleuriau, a military officer and the son of a former attorney general, was presented to the Superior Council's clerk as a "slave hireling" by the jailer, who had rented her labor and accused her of having stolen some piastres.[53]

52. Salmon to the minister of the navy, Dec. 16, 1737, ANOM COL C13A 22, fol. 213. Dumont de Montigny also worked as an unofficial lawyer. See Dumont de Montigny, *Regards sur le monde atlantique*, 287–288, 396. See also Edwin J. Perkins, "The Entrepreneurial Spirit in Colonial America: The Foundations of Modern Business History," in "Entrepreneurs in Business History," special issue, *Business History Review*, LXIII (1989), 160–186.

53. On the importance of slave hiring in the colonial and antebellum South, see, among many studies, Jonathan D. Martin, *Divided Mastery: Slave Hiring in the American South* (Cambridge, Mass., 2004) 18 (quotation). For another case of slaves hired out

Hiring out slaves as craftsmen or domestics could be both a potentially lucrative but sometimes risky business for masters, but, for slaves, the experience could turn into a nightmare. Unless slaves were hired out at auctions, most rental agreements were made privately among people who knew each other. In the late 1760s, the military officer Favrot leased the slaves from his grandmother's estate to members of the city's elite circle. According to his accounts, female domestics at the time were hired out from 25 to 30 livres a month, which could amount to an annual income of 300 to 360 livres a year for an owner. This sum corresponded to one-third the price of renting a house in his social milieu. The price for men was higher. In 1767, a "mulatto" slave was hired out at an auction for 600 livres a year. Usually, renters were responsible for providing food, lodging, and medical care for hired slaves. Depending on the agreement, they might or might not be required to compensate owners if slaves ran away or died of an "inflicted death." Because renters did not own leased slaves outright, they often felt under no restraint and had a tendency to exploit the slaves they hired forcibly. Some contracts included a clause specifying that those hiring slaves ought to "treat" the latter "as good pater familias," but this legal precaution did not entirely prevent abuses. In 1741, Bernard Alexandre Vielle, a surgeon, hired out fifteen slaves to Gérard Péry, a New Orleans merchant. After the death of François, one of Vielle's best carpenters and pit sawyers, his master asked for compensation amounting to 2,500 livres, since the slave had committed suicide while in Péry's charge. Vielle might have presumed that François killed himself because he had been mistreated.[54]

------

for the production of pitch and tar on the banks of Lake Pontchartrain, see "Lease of Slaves for Tar Industry," Apr. 29, 1735, in [Dart], ed., "RSCL XV," *LHQ*, V (1922), 264; RSCL 1736/03/27/01; "Partnership," June 20, 1736, in Heloise H. Cruzat, ed., "RSCL XXVI: Supplemental Index no. 3," *LHQ*, VIII (1925), 296; "Petition to Superior Council," Apr. 26, 1737, in Cruzat, ed., "RSCL XXIX: February–May 1737," *LHQ*, IX (1926), 128; and "Partnership Agreement," Apr. 26, 1739, Cruzat, ed., "RSCL XX," *LHQ*, VI (1923), 500. For contracts to rent slaves for journeys to the Illinois Country, see RSCL 1736/08/21/03, 1737/08/15/03, 1737/08/16/02, 1737/08/16/04, 1737/08/17/03, 1738/04/09/01. For a few examples of rented slaves working in town, see RSCL 1736/10/15/01, 1737/03/08/02, 1740/02/04/ ??, 1748/06/10/03, 1764/06/22/01, 1764/07/10/03, 1764/07/26/01, 1767/08/12/01. For Babet's trial, see RSCL 1765/10/09/01, 1765/10/10/01.

54. For the price of renting slaves, see [Alexandre] De Clouet, "État des loyers de la succession tant maisons que domestiques," circa June 1, 1767–Jan. 1, 1778, in *Transcriptions of Manuscript Collections of Louisiana: No. 1, The Favrot Papers*, II, *1769–1781* (New Orleans, 1941), 2–3 (59-R76); and NONA Feb. 12, 1767. For the idea that renters had a tendency to exploit slaves they hired, see Martin, *Divided Mastery*, 73–74, 86–104. For contracts with clauses related to the way that slaves should be treated, see NONA

A few years earlier, in 1736, another desperate hired slave named Marianne looked for a less extreme solution to end her misery. After the death of her master, she had been leased out with the rest of her master's former property to take care of the young widow and her children, who were living with the hirer, Joseph Chaperon, but Marianne only served to feed Chaperon's slaves and was continuously manhandled. She ran away and took refuge at the house of her former owner's brother. Her move illuminates the "triangularity of hiring arrangements," which "made it easier for slaves to appeal to the authority of their owners in dealings with the men and women who hired them." Marianne told her master's brother that he should be sensitive to the abuse of slaves who had been hired out since he had one in his own household who was dying after having worked at the tar production unit at Saint-Julien's. She was leased at auction to another settler.[55]

Most slaves seem to have been rented out by their masters and had no choice over who hired them, but they were sometimes allowed to choose whom they worked for, provided they brought back their earnings to their owners. During a conflict with some military officers in the early 1750s, Michel reported to the minister of the navy that Madame d'Erneville sent her slave Charlotte to work every day in the city on condition that she brought back fifty sols. Charlotte reportedly earned this money by prostituting herself. Whereas some slaves were transformed into day laborers and had the responsibility to find their own jobs, this practice of self-hire does not seem to have been prevalent during the French regime. Moreover, self-hired slaves were not always in a privileged situation.[56]

Apart from these few hints about hired slaves, little information is available regarding the working conditions of enslaved laborers within the city. Except for the company's and later the king's slaves—who toiled as packers in the harbor and stores; as workers at the mill, the brick factory, and the earthenware factory; or as surgeons, nurses, and domestics at the hospital—most slave labor took place within private households, which were

---

Feb. 02, 1767; and NONA Kernion Mar. 13, 1769. For Bernard Alexandre Vielle's request against Gérard Péry, see RSCL 1741/10/06/01.

55. RSCL 1736/09/18/01, 1736/09/29/01/ 1736/10/15/01; Martin, *Divided Mastery*, 131–132, 138–160.

56. Michel to the minister of the navy, July 15, 1751, ANOM COL C13A 35, fols. 287–288. The daily wage had increased since 1737. In a request by Dumont de Montigny to the Superior Council, he asserted that it then cost twenty sols a day to hire a slave in New Orleans. See "De Montigny Represents to the Superior Council," May 4, 1737, in [Dart], ed., "RSCL XVI," *LHQ*, V (1922), 399. For a more finely nuanced reconsideration of the practice of self-hire, see Martin, *Divided Mastery*, 161–187.

the main units of production and consumption in New Orleans's domestic economy. Most urban slaves worked under the close supervision of their masters, either their owners or those who hired them, or of white laborers. Yet they were not trapped in their residential and working units, as were most slaves on plantations. The most mobile slaves were the ones employed as sailors, carters, hunters, and hucksters or peddlers. Still, even more mobile jobs did not always lead to pleasant experiences. In 1764, an enslaved carter belonging to the Capuchins was brutally assaulted by a white settler who had refused to let him drive his cart through "his" street the day before. He could not work for forty-seven days. Those who were confined the most within their households were domestics. Alexandre, a slave accused of theft, defended himself by telling the judge that he did not have the time to go out since he worked all day long in his master's house. But even domestics could receive visits. Prévost once returned home to find Pradel's slave, Jupiter, who used to sell his master's plantation products at the levee but also door to door, in his house crawling under his bed in his room upstairs. Jupiter had come to *"badiner"* (fool around) with the household's female enslaved servants, Angélique, Thérèse, and Louison, and he hid when he heard that Prévost had come back. Some domestics also had opportunities to move around when they accompanied their masters, washed the laundry in the river, ran errands, did the shopping, or sold fruit and vegetables grown in urban gardens. Except for construction workers, who were sent to other people's urban parcels to perform work, slaves employed as craftsmen also worked within their owners' shops, but they could interact with clients. Some slaves belonging to merchants did the same.[57]

After 1731, the better working conditions and greater autonomy that most enslaved laborers benefited from in all urban slave societies were further enhanced in New Orleans by the quasi ending of Louisiana's slave trade with Africa. Since the sporadic arrival of slaves from the Caribbean islands prevented owners from easily replacing their slaves, masters had a vested interest in not overworking them. A metropolitan merchant named Henry Pouillard, who visited Louisiana in the early 1760s, underscored that the enslaved there were not as badly abused as in the Antilles, even though their owners wanted to make the most of them: "Its residents who comprise around 1,500 masters and from 5 to 6,000 negroes at the most, are generally very active in promoting their interests, industrious, hard-working, and business-oriented, they know perfectly well how to take advantage of their negroes whom they treat more leniently than in Saint-Domingue and Mar-

57. RSCL 1764/06/11/04; 1744/03/13/01; 1744/03/03/01.

Slavery, Labor, and Race

tinique." He understood that a relatively milder regime of labor in comparison with the Antilles did not prevent New Orleans and its plantation region from becoming a genuine slave society.[58]

Paradoxically, the fact that masters in Louisiana treated their slaves less harshly than in the Antilles in the 1760s testifies to their continuing commitment to the perpetuation and expansion of racial slavery throughout the French regime. This engagement could have waned when the Company of the Indies decided to abandon its trade monopoly, causing Louisiana's slave trade with Africa to almost completely cease. At the time, the king was reluctant to invest much in the colony, and he told local authorities that if the inhabitants wanted slaves "they should acquire them by their own means." This withdrawal did not deter the colony's settlers. Not only did they manage their enslaved laborers in such a way that the slave population was able to grow through natural increase, but they actively sought to purchase slaves from the Caribbean and even tried to organize slaving expeditions to Africa. The competition among settlers to acquire as many slaves as they could and the rise of slave hiring as a practice also attest to their desire to develop and give preeminence to slave labor. Likewise, the model offered by the company and later the king as slaveholders, the regulation and judicialization of slave labor, the way white craftsmen used what was left of their guild culture to maintain their dominant position in the hierarchy of laborers, the proceedings white domestic and indentured servants brought against their employers so as not to be considered or treated as slaves of African descent, the violence of soldiers against slaves, and the development of the corvée, which relied solely on slave labor all confirm that New Orleans had become a slave society powerfully tormented by the interrelated issues of work and race.[59]

Although the Company of the Indies had initially envisioned the colony's

58. "Mémoire concernant la population et le commerce à la Louisiane et Cayenne par H.P.," 1761, ANOM COL C13A 42, fol. 294r.

59. The quotation from the king corresponds to a note in the margin of a letter in which the governor and the commissaire-ordonnateur asked for the importation of slaves. See "Habitations, cultures, et commerce," ANOM COL C13A 14, fol. 168. On the crown's responsibility in the quasi ending of the slave trade from Africa after 1731, see John G. Clark, *New Orleans, 1718–1812: An Economic History* (Baton Rouge, La., 1970), 128–135. On the attempt by Louisiana planters to organize slaving expeditions to Africa, see Salmon to the minister of the navy, June 5, 1737, ANOM COL C13A 22, fols. 173–174r; and Bienville and Salmon to the minister of the navy, Feb. 20, 1738, ANOM COL F3 24, fols. 307–309.

development as a product of a mixed labor force of indentured servants, soldiers, convicts, and slaves, by the end of the French regime, the priority given to slave labor and the need to sustain the system of racial domination that helped legitimize the slave system led to the dismissal of the idea that white convicts could be sent to the colony to labor side by side with black slaves. The metropolitan merchant Pouillard, who knew the colony well and proposed a plan to develop both Louisiana and Guyana to the minister of the navy in the early 1760s, argued that:

> American politics demand that negroes be kept in the strictest subordination and the harshest obedience, it is imperative to have them fear us, and to instill into them that we are as much above them as they are above beasts, they are so utterly convinced of this that they say in their language to horses (Me be a slave to whites and you be a slave to negroes). How can we maintain them in this opinion if, unfortunately, we associate them with some of our fellows who are enchained or who they learn once were? By this misconceived operation we will work at dissipating their fear, and at weakening their ideas about us, which will make them so bold as to shake off the yoke. Torture and death will only inflame their fickleness and love of liberty which we informed them about. We know only too well how dangerous their plots are.

In this merchant's view, slaves were not to be likened to animals, rather, they were to be considered as intrinsically inferior to whites, occupying an intermediate position between whites and animals. His argument, expressed at a time of intense slave unrest in the French Empire and, more globally, the greater Caribbean, presented labor as a crucial tool of social engineering in the implementation and internalization of racial prejudice. As work intertwined with race in New Orleans, the meaning of labor underwent a profound change. The same phenomenon happened with trade.[60]

60. "Mémoire concernant la population et le commerce à la Louisiane et Cayenne par H.P.," 1761, ANOM COL C13A 42, fol. 290r; "Mémoire de M. Henry Pouillard, négociant," 1761, ANOM COL F3 21, fol. 265.

CHAPTER SEVEN

"Everybody Wants to Be a Merchant"

Trade, Credit, and Honor

After having spoken about Indians, let's talk
About what our Frenchmen are in these districts.
Yet, we need to distinguish those who remain in the city,
From those who are not there; it is easy
To guess why I say that:
One has a good time and the other does not.
Indeed, in the capital, we sell to each other,
One is a wine merchant, the other, like a good apostle,
Retires to his place, living alone out of his property;
We often find ourselves in a good situation.
One provides food, the other sells eau-de-vie;
Almost everybody is full of envy;
Everyone would like to earn, everybody is a merchant,
Officers, soldiers, councillors, *habitants* [permanent residents],
...
That's the way we spend our time in the city
Always working, selling, and trafficking.

Under Jean-François-Benjamin Dumont de Montigny's pen, New Orleans
appears as a great marketplace, where interest in trade has risen to a fever
pitch. Commerce and the general ease it brought over time distinguished
the city from the countryside. In that regard, New Orleans was a typical
port city of the greater Caribbean; the development of a large commercial
sector partially disconnected from the plantation economy was a shared
feature of all these urban centers. Yet, in France and in Europe, all individuals, whatever their social standing, were also involved in the market,
especially in cities. Commerce was the "mainspring of the urban economy,"

and the image of what constituted a city in the eighteenth century was increasingly becoming associated with trade. Does this mean that there was nothing peculiar in the Louisiana situation or, more globally, the greater Caribbean experience, that Dumont de Montigny's statement was only a truism, or that his astonishment was overstated? His insistence on the engagement of every white city dweller in trade points to a singularity of all colonial settler societies. Founded by Europeans for "commerce and agriculture," colonies attracted European migrants who were motivated by a strong desire to make their fortune.[1]

Beyond this search for wealth and social elevation common to all colonists, there is more to Dumont de Montigny's flight of oratory over commerce. Having suffered a drop in status, this former military officer felt the need to collectively make sense of his own social trajectory and to justify his behavior. He was one of the younger sons of an *avocat* (lawyer) in the Parlement of Paris. After a year as a cadet in the Auxerrois Regiment, he joined the *gardes-marines* (navy guards), a favor that his father obtained from the war minister, Louis-Claude Le Blanc. Dumont was sent to Quebec City where he spent three years, from 1715 to 1717, learning the trade of an engineer. Thanks to the intervention of his brother, an avocat in the Conseil

1. For Jean-François-Benjamin Dumont de Montigny's quotation, see Marc de Villiers, ed., "L'établissement de la province de la Louisiane: Poème composé de 1728 à 1742 par Dumont de Montigny," *Journal de la société des américanistes*, XXIII (1931), 419–420, 422. On urban economy in the greater Caribbean, see Trevor Burnard and Emma Hart, "Kingston, Jamaica, and Charleston, South Carolina: A New Look at Comparative Urbanization in Plantation Colonial British America," *Journal of Urban History*, New Ser., XXXIX (2013 [2012]), 214–234; and Anne Pérotin-Dumon, *La ville aux îles, la ville dans l'île: Basse-Terre et Pointe-à-Pitre, Guadeloupe, 1650–1820* (Paris, 2000), 532–544. On the rising role of commerce in Europe, especially in cities, see Laurence Fontaine, *Le marché: Histoire et usages d'une conquête sociale* ([Paris], 2014), 70–78. See also Anne Montenach, *Espaces et pratiques du commerce alimentaire à Lyon au XVIIe siècle: L'économie du quotidien* (Grenoble, France, 2009), 174–190; Jean-Claude Perrot, *Genèse d'une ville moderne: Caen au XVIIIe siècle*, 4 vols. (1975; rpt. Paris, 2011), II, 440 ("mainspring"); Roger Chartier et al., eds., *Histoire de la France urbaine*, III, *La ville classique de la Renaissance aux Révolutions*, ed. Georges Duby (Paris, 1981), 16–20; and Bernard Lepetit, *Les villes dans la France moderne (1740–1840)* (Paris, 1988), 52–81. For the role of commerce in colonies, see François Veron de Forbonnois, "Colonie," in [Denis] Diderot and [Jean Le Rond] d'Alembert, eds., *Encyclopédie ou dictionnaire raisonné des sciences, des arts, et des métiers, par une société de gens de lettres*, 28 vols. (Paris, 1751–1772), III, 650 ("commerce and agriculture"); and Edwin J. Perkins, "The Entrepreneurial Spirit in Colonial America: The Foundations of Modern Business History," in "Entrepreneurs in Business History," special issue, *Business History Review*, XLIII (1989), 160–186.

Trade, Credit, and Honor

du roi, he was granted a *brevet* (the document that officially recognized his incorporation within the navy) as a sublieutenant to serve the Company of the Indies in the Mississippi colony. In May 1720, he was promoted to the rank of lieutenant and attached to the military companies in charge of the protection of the concessions held by the war minister and his economic partners in Louisiana. After the collapse of the concession system, however, he was "demoted as a bad subject" by Commandant general Jean-Baptiste Le Moyne de Bienville, with whom he had maintained a conflictual relationship and who described him as "a dishonest fellow." From 1724, he lived by his wits as a mere habitant, first in the countryside and then in the city. He could not maintain his rank or conform to the social behavior expected from an individual of his social background, which involved not publicly engaging in retailing. His description of New Orleans thus implicitly emphasized that the general embracing of trade in the colony went against the infamy traditionally associated with commerce in ancien régime societies. A constant tension existed between two economic cultures: an aristocratic culture based on gift giving and paternalism and a mercantile and capitalist culture. In the Louisiana capital, as in the metropole, the growing role played by market exchanges throughout the eighteenth century did not take place without arousing conflict among whites.[2]

In his poem and travel account, Dumont de Montigny chose to underscore the widespread participation of city dwellers of European descent in trade, but slaves were also imbued with the mercantile spirit that characterized colonial societies, even though they had no choice in their migration. To improve their living conditions and social positions, many took part in various kinds of commercial activities. Influenced by the slave system that

2. On Dumont de Montigny's career, see "Passagers sur la flûte *La Somme*, commandée par le chevalier de Querlérec, partie de La Nouvelle-Orléans le 15 juin 1737," ANOM COL F5B 34; Jacques de La Chaise to the Company of the Indies's Directors, Mar. 8, 1724, ANOM COL C13A 7, fols. 36r–37r; and Gordon M. Sayre and Shannon Lee Dawdy, "Introduction," in Dumont de Montigny, *Regards sur le monde atlantique, 1715-1747*, transcribed by Carla Zecher (Sillery, Quebec, 2008), 1–41. On the dual economic culture in ancien régime societies, see Laurence Fontaine, *L'économie morale: Pauvreté, crédit, et confiance dans l'Europe préindustrielle* ([Paris], 2008); and Jean-Yves Grenier, *L'économie d'Ancien Régime: Un monde de l'échange et de l'incertitude* (Paris, 1996). For the French debate on "noblesse commerçante," see Jay M. Smith, "Social Categories, the Language of Patriotism, and the Origins of the French Revolution: The Debate over *Noblesse Commerçante,*" *Journal of Modern History*, LXXII (2000), 339–374; and John Shovlin, *The Political Economy of Virtue: Luxury, Patriotism, and the Origins of the French Revolution* (Ithaca, N.Y., 2006).

had first developed in the Caribbean islands, authorities and slaveholders both encouraged and resisted the participation of enslaved individuals in the market economy. Two of the few innovations included in the 1724 Code Noir in comparison with the 1685 West Indian edict, which are rarely discussed, related to trade. The Louisiana code softened Article 5, which forbade masters from making their slaves work on Sundays and holidays, by permitting them to send their slaves to the marketplaces. It also added any kind of grain, wares, old clothes, and rags to the list of goods specified in Article 15 that slaves could not sell without a certificate from their owner. Previously, the article had focused on foodstuffs, including fruit and vegetables, firewood, and hay for cattle fodder. Buyers of said products could face a heavy fine of fifteen hundred livres as well as criminal prosecution. These changes were adopted in response to the rise of enslaved people in the islands as crucial actors in the circulation and exchange of both local products and European merchandise imported from the metropole. In Louisiana, as in the Caribbean, their participation in the market economy disturbed the slave order and created antagonisms among whites.[3]

While much attention has been given to labor in shaping American colonial and slave societies, the significance of commerce has been underestimated, even though it informed social dynamics, including racial formation, in a crucial way, especially in port cities. Trade became the most important economic sector, source of income, and means of social mobility within New Orleans. During the Company of the Indies's monopoly, everyone had been desperate to find any means to earn money. For the lower sort, it was a question of sheer survival, whereas most of the elite tried to maintain a semblance of social standing, even as some sought to benefit from the situation by profiteering. Still, after the retrocession of the colony to the king, commerce experienced a surge. Urban settlers of all social conditions took advantage of the opening of trade to French merchants after 1731 to seize new opportunities to engage in mercantile activities and improve their socioeconomic status. They also profited from the growth of the city, which created additional needs that had to be satisfied.[4]

3. "Code Noir ou édit du roi servant de règlement pour le gouvernement et l'administration de la justice, police, discipline, et commerce des esclaves nègres de la province et colonie de la Louisiane," March 1724, ANOM COL B 43, fols. 388–407.

4. Whereas studies by Sophie White and Alexandre Dubé have offered insightful approaches to commerce in the Mississippi colony, one based on cultural history and the other on economic and political history, the focus here encompasses all forms of trade and the social relationships that commerce shaped, and was shaped by, within the port

The general involvement of all urban dwellers in trade, from white elites to slaves, had important social effects. Commercial exchanges increased social cohesion as they created social ties. Through trade and credit, most people were trapped in a chain of creditors and debtors and connected by relationships of dependency and obligation. At the same time, participation in the market was largely determined by status, race, class, and gender and contributed to segmenting the urban population. Not all categories of commerce (the import and export trade, wholesaling within the colony, and retailing in shops, in the marketplace, or on the streets) were open to all social actors. Likewise, while illicit trade was not restricted to whites of the lower sort and slaves, it had a greater importance for them. Furthermore, as Dumont de Montigny's focus on white colonists in his poem testifies, even though people of all social statuses were involved in commerce, the participation of slaves in the market economy, either on their master's behalf or for their own benefit, was viewed as a completely different matter to that of free people.

Even so, the rise of commercial activities produced a set of circumstances in which social and racial boundaries were more easily negotiated. By the end of the French regime, the quest for fortune, dignity, and independence that animated many participants in the market had given birth to a distinct, powerful corporate body of self-identified white merchants and traders and a much smaller, discreet group of quasi-free persons of color who had been able to illicitly purchase their freedom. More globally, the importance of trade had succeeded in challenging, if not completely eradicating, the traditional conception of commerce as an infamous occupation. In contrast, the participation of the enslaved in the market and cash economy necessarily integrated them within the economy of honor and credit—in the sense that trade operated on the basis of trust, reputation, and power—but their involvement did not weaken the long-lasting association whites made between slavery and dishonor.

---

city. See Dubé, "Les biens publics: Culture politique de la Louisiane française, 1730–1770" (Ph.D. diss., McGill University, 2009); White, "'A Baser Commerce': Retailing, Class, and Gender in French Colonial New Orleans," *William and Mary Quarterly*, 3d Ser., XLIII (2006), 517–550; and White, "Slaves and Poor Whites' Informal Economies in an Atlantic Context," in Cécile Vidal, ed., *Louisiana: Crossroads of the Atlantic World* (Philadelphia, 2014), 87–102. This chapter only deals with the commerce of goods, but New Orleans was also the site of an intense urban housing and real estate market. Renting rooms and houses constituted a growing business as well.

"EVERYONE MAKES A BUSINESS AS BEST HE CAN TO SUPPORT HIMSELF": MERCANTILE PRACTICES AND SOCIAL IDENTITIES

After having described how many settlers took refuge in New Orleans following the Natchez attack and survived by growing their own food, selling
their fruit and vegetables, and hiring out their slaves, as he did himself,
Dumont de Montigny explained in his travel account: "Other Frenchmen
will be cloth merchants, drapers, etc. Still others are wholesalers of wine,
eau-de-vie, or beer brought from France .... Finally, some are keepers of
dining halls, bakeries, or taverns. In short everyone makes a business as
best he can to support himself." Once again, his description insisted on the
involvement of all urban dwellers in commercial activities, but it also highlighted two other related phenomena. First, a heterogeneous group of self-
identified merchants and traders had developed that only differed from one
another by the kind of trade they did (wholesaling or retailing) and the
variety of products they sold or the type of services they provided. Second,
the way people traded was constrained: their engagement in mercantile activities depended on what they could afford. What is missing in Dumont de
Montigny's description, however, is the idea that, besides regulation, fortune, connections, and education, social conventions were a powerful factor
influencing trading practices. Commerce was not considered a neutral activity but one having as much to do with moral and social values as with the
economy. People were highly self-conscious about the kind of business they
participated in; they were also selective about whether or not they chose to
identify themselves as a merchants or traders, whatever the extent of their
commercial activities. Yet, over time, a genuine local mercantile community arose, self-identified merchants gained a social preeminence they did
not enjoy earlier, and commerce started to be viewed as a more honorable
condition.[5]

That commerce would be so vigorously embraced by all social actors could
not have been foreseen in the colony's early days, since the Company of the
Indies restricted the freedom of trade within the French Empire. Private
wholesaling merchants should not have existed in Louisiana. They nonetheless appeared almost immediately. Unable to fulfill the basic needs of
the first settlers and to offset their difficult economic situation, the com-

5. Gordon M. Sayre and Carla Zecher, eds., *The Memoir of Lieutenant Dumont,*
1715–1747: A Sojourner in the French Atlantic; Jean-François-Benjamin Dumont de
Montigny, trans. Sayre (Chapel Hill, N.C., 2012), 374.

pany could not help but allow a few privileged individuals to import goods on its ships on condition that they paid freight costs. Instead of consuming their wares, some of those who had the means to import merchandise established a profiteering trade. For instance, Jean-Daniel Kolly, the owner and manager of a concession, maintained a shop in New Orleans, with the assistance of a member of the Superior Council, where he sold the goods that he had brought in his personal luggage on his initial voyage and that his wife sent him afterward, making a one hundred percent profit. In the same way, ship's captains were authorized to transport some goods free of freight, but royal commissioner Jacques de La Chaise reported many complaints against this *"pacotille des vaisseaux"* ("vessels' trade in trinkets") and the exorbitant prices practiced by speculators.[6]

Since metropolitan commodities were scarce and expensive, contraband trade boomed. Many inhabitants purchased goods directly from ship's captains and unloaded merchandise before company employees could inspect newly arrived ships. The few prosecutions launched by the Superior Council did not succeed in halting this smuggling. According to company employee Marc-Antoine Caillot, the practice was so widespread that in New Orleans: "There are also several shops selling various types of merchandise that they buy from the ships, no matter that it is against company orders. These traders have wives who sell in the streets." Lacking the means to satisfy the needs of the local population, the company could not but tolerate breaches of its monopoly.[7]

6. The Company of the Indies also authorized the concession Sainte-Reyne to trade with Saint-Domingue for three years. See "Ordonnance qui accorde à la concession Sainte-Reyne la liberté de commerce de la Louisiane à Saint-Domingue," July 11, 1725, ANOM COL F3 242, fols. 54–55; Marcel Giraud, *A History of French Louisiana*, V, *The Company of the Indies, 1723–1731*, trans. Pearce (Baton Rouge, La., 1991), 149; and La Chaise to the Company of the Indies's Directors, Mar. 8, 1724, ANOM COL C13A 7, fol. 27.

7. For the legislation on trade downriver, see "Ordonnance des directeurs de la Compagnie à la Louisiane du 1er octobre 1722 qui défend d'aller à bord des vaisseaux qui arrivent dans la colonie sans la permission du commandant," ANOM COL A 23, fol. 37r; and "Arrêt du Conseil Supérieur de la Louisiane du 26 mai 1723 qui défend d'aller à bord des vaisseaux qui arrivent dans la colonie sans une permission du Conseil," ANOM COL A 23, fols. 40v–41r. On the repression of contraband, see "Contraband Trade Reported," Mar. 24, 1724, in "Abstracts of French and Spanish Documents concerning the Early History of Louisiana, [RSCL II]," *LHQ*, I, no. 3 (1918), 235, "Contraband Goods Pursued," Mar. 24, 1724, "Remonstrance against Seizure of Goods," Mar. 24, 1724, "Attachment Ruling Reversed," Mar. 27, 1724; RSCL 1724/09/06/01; "Attachments of Funds in Contraband Trade," Sept. 3, 1729, in "RSCL XI [XII]," *LHQ*, IV (1921), 347, "Prosecution for Contraband Trade," Sept. 5, 1729, 347, "Seizure of Ship *St. Michel*," Sept. 5, 1729, 347, "Sum-

After 1731, the opening of Louisiana's trade to metropolitan merchants progressively strengthened the local mercantile community, which was nevertheless characterized by its heterogeneity and volatility. From the late 1730s, this community grew with the sporadic arrivals of new merchants from France and the Caribbean. Some of the partners or agents who had been sent to New Orleans by metropolitan merchants to take care of their economic interests and who were often family members sometimes settled in the colony, married there, and also traded on their own account. After establishing himself in New Orleans in 1736, Paul Rasteau, the son of a prominent La Rochelle merchant, married the daughter of engineer and planter François Ignace Broutin. Likewise, in February 1762, Louis Rançon, a merchant from Saintonge who was engaged in a trading partnership with a cousin in La Rochelle, abjured Protestantism and married Demoiselle Marie Françoise Gallot, the daughter of a deceased employee of the navy office and merchant. He then obtained the rank of militia captain in New Orleans. In 1770, he became the *síndico procurador general* (public advocate) of the *cabildo* (town council).[8]

Apart from the crown, those who imported merchandise from the metropole were not restricted to men who self-identified as merchants, that is, professional merchants who ran a warehouse or a shop. Sword or pen officers, including top officials, religious communities, and planters also participated in trade. They had their merchandise transported freely on royal

---

mons to Testify," Sept. 15, 1729, 349–350, and "Testimony in *St. Michel* Affair," Sept. 15, 1729, 350. On the failure to repress contraband, see Erin M. Greenwald, ed., *A Company Man: The Remarkable French-Atlantic Voyage of a Clerk for the Company of the Indies: A Memoir by Marc-Antoine Caillot*, trans. Teri F. Chalmers (New Orleans, La., 2013), 83.

8. On the mercantile community, see Dubé, "Les biens publics," 343–344. On Paul Rasteau, see Marriage contract between Paul Rasteau and Suzanne Seignel, Oct. 7, 1746, in Alice Daly Forsyth and Ghislaine Pleasonton, eds., *Louisiana Marriage Contracts*, [I], *A Compilation of Abstracts from Records of the Superior Council of Louisiana during the French Regime, 1725–1758* (New Orleans, 1980), 165; John G. Clark, *New Orleans, 1718–1812: An Economic History* (Baton Rouge, La., 1970), 61–106; Clark, *La Rochelle and the Atlantic Economy during the Eighteenth Century* (Baltimore, 1981); and Dubé, "Les biens publics," 274–275. On Louis Rançon, see AANO, Saint-Louis Cathedral Marriages, 1759–1762, 02/01/1762. For the social and professional identification of Rançon's bride's father, see "Procuration Granted," Jan. 15, 1748, in Heloise H. Cruzat, ed., "RSCL LXVI: January, 1748," *LHQ*, XIX (1936), 229; Earl C. Woods and Charles E. Nolan, eds., *Sacramental Records of the Roman Catholic Church of the Archdiocese of New Orleans*, II, *1751–1771* (New Orleans, 1988), 234; Dubé, "Les biens publics," 274–275; and Gilbert C. Din, *Spaniards, Planters, and Slaves: The Spanish Regulation of Slavery in Louisiana, 1763–1803* (College Station, Tex., 1999), 44–47.

Trade, Credit, and Honor

ships or paid freight on private ones. Both professional merchants and non-professionals residing in the colony were enmeshed in relationships of solidarity and interdependence. Since all merchants who had moved to the colony invested in plantations and some officer-planters and planters engaged in maritime trade, they are sometimes hard to distinguish from one another if one considers only their behavior and property. Augustin Chantalou, for instance, was, according to John Clark, "one of the more active businessmen in New Orleans between 1740 and 1765, combining widespread mercantile operations with official positions as Attorney of Vacant Estates, Chief Clerk of the Superior Council, and Royal Notary after 1754." Most nonprofessionals, however, were usually not as heavily implicated in maritime trade as professional merchants.[9]

Whatever their degree of involvement, the common economic interests of those engaged in trade resulted in family alliances and common belonging to institutions of sociability. Professional merchants and the daughters of pen officers and employees often wed. In 1747, Sieur Jean-Baptiste Bancio Piemont, a merchant, married Dame Jeanne Raguet, the daughter of Jean-Baptiste Raguet, a notary and clerk of the Superior Council, and Dame Jeanne Marie Corbin de la Touche. In January 1762, the union of Sieur Nicolas Forstall, an Irish merchant who settled in Louisiana after having spent time in Martinique, and Demoiselle Pélagie de La Chaise, the daughter of the New Orleans royal warehouse manager Jacques de La Chaise and the granddaughter of royal commissioner Jacques de La Chaise, was celebrated in Saint-Louis Church. One of the witnesses was Pierre Hardy de Boisblanc, a subdelegate of the *commissaire-ordonnateur* and navy scrivener. Likewise, in 1764, Jean-Baptiste Garic, the chief clerk of the Superior Council, and Demoiselle Marie Anne Testar, the daughter of a prominent merchant from La Rochelle, served together as godparents in the baptism of an enslaved infant. In addition, several professional merchants and employees of the commissaire-ordonnateur belonged to the masonic lodge founded in the early 1760s.[10]

The only difference between professional merchants and nonprofession-

9. On the involvement of the Capuchins, Jesuits, and Ursulines in trade, see Dubé, "Les biens publics," 330–333. On Augustin Chantalou, see Clark, *New Orleans, 1718–1812*, 99–102.

10. For family alliances between professional merchants and king's officers or employees, see "Marriage Contract," Jan. 14, 1747, in Heloise H. Cruzat, ed., "RSCL LX: January–February, 1747," *LHQ*, XVII (1934), 369; AANO, Saint-Louis Cathedral Marriages, 1759–1762, 01/25/1762; AANO, Saint-Louis Cathedral Marriages, 1763–1766, 15/07/1764; and Dubé, "Les biens publics," 279. For members of the masonic lodge, see ibid., 170n.

als was the way they chose to self-identify. Those sword officers, pen officers, and employees of the king who were also planters and acted as merchants almost always primarily defined their social identity as being in the king's service, which remained the most honorable estate. Their way of life also associated them with the class of planters and slaveholders. Chantalou never identified himself as a merchant in any of the economic deeds or letters kept in the records of the Superior Council. In the same way, his occupation was usually not specified on the many baptism certificates where he appeared as godfather or owner, which constituted a way of asserting his identity as a slaveholder; when it was, he was identified as clerk of the Superior Council. Likewise, the former officer Jean-Charles de Pradel, who self-identified most of the time as an officer or a retired captain and sometimes habitant but never as a merchant, chose to reside on his plantation and devoted much time and energy to embellishing his "big house." Beyond the economic investment it represented, his estate had a strong symbolic and sentimental value. As for the professional merchants who owned plantations, most chose to put forward commerce as their main social identity. A few others, like Louis Rançon, had a less consistent way of presenting themselves; they most often self-identified as merchants, but they occasionally qualified themselves as both merchants and habitants, or as mere habitants. Rançon's dual social identity is reflected in his marriage contract, which was executed on his plantation but whose male witnesses were all merchants. Because it was apparently important for him to assert his identity as a slaveholder, he frequently appeared at the Saint-Louis church to baptize his slaves.[11]

Local merchants, both professional and nonprofessional, who imported European and Caribbean merchandise into Louisiana and traded with Spanish colonies held the most powerful socioeconomic position in the New Orleans mercantile community. Still, they were not the only

11. For Chantalou's self-identification, see AANO, Saint-Louis Cathedral Baptisms, 1744–1753, 1753–1759, and 1759–1762, 01/01/1745, 03/28/1750, 12/27/1755, 02/15/1756, 12/25/1756 (clerk), 07/24/1757, 12/19/1757, 11/12/1758, 06/24/1759 (clerk), 08/27/1759, 02/03/1760, 04/06/1760, 05/05/1760, 11/23/1760, 02/07/1762 (clerk). For Rançon's self-identification, see "Marriage Contract," Jan. 30, 1762, in Heloise H. Cruzat, ed., "RSCL LXXXIII: January–February, 1762," *LHQ*, XXIII (1940), 605; AANO, Saint-Louis Cathedral Baptisms, 1744–1753, 1753–1759, 1759–1762, 1763–1767, and 1767–1771, 06/19/1751 (merchant), 01/23/1752 (merchant), 04/17/1756, 05/28/1757, 01/14/1759, 11/09/1760, 01/18/1761 (habitant), 03/27/1761, 05/19/1765 (2 baptisms), 09/22/1765, 03/16/1766, 07/13/1766, 02/08/1767 (merchant), 10/11/1767, 04/02/1768, 04/21/1768, 11/13/1768, 05/14/1769, 05/15/1769.

ones who practiced wholesaling. Some individuals also purchased European and Caribbean wares from ships once they arrived in New Orleans. They then took advantage of the complex fluctuation of prices to supply the king's warehouses or trade with other outposts in the colony, such as Mobile and the Illinois Country. They also retailed goods in the capital. The opening of wholesale operations to these smaller traders was fiercely contested. Some people tried to bypass them by purchasing whole cargos before ships even reached New Orleans. This practice allowed speculators to sell European and Caribbean commodities at prohibitive prices. Consequently, Commissaire-ordonnateur Honoré-Gabriel Michel included an article in the 1751 local ruling on police that ordered ships to unload and sell their cargoes on the levee and prohibited purchases that took place before ships entered the port. The bylaw nevertheless did not succeed in halting the trade downriver.[12]

The people who engaged in a mix of wholesaling and retailing within the colony were either professionals or occasional traders who seized an opportunity to make a profit. The place that trade occupied in their professional activities and incomes varied greatly. Two men who signed several trading agreements with Edmé Gatien Salmon in 1736–1737, Jean Merle alias Grandjean and Jacques Ozanne, are representative of this kind of commercial actor. Although they were acquaintances, and perhaps friends, who lived on the same street (Royal), and shared the same employer and place of work, their involvement in the wholesale trade had different economic meanings. A native of Savoy, Merle was an employee in charge of the distribution of foodstuffs at the company's and then king's warehouses. At the time of his death in 1745, his wages only amounted to 360 livres a year, and he had remained a bachelor. The contracts he signed with Salmon probably constituted a circumstantial attempt to improve his difficult daily life. In comparison, Jacques Ozanne was in a better situation. Originally, he was a master cooper who first came to the colony as an indentured servant in the company's service and was able to marry the daughter of a blacksmith, named Joseph Moreau, in 1727. He started to retail merchandise from the metropole and the Antilles, brandy and wine in particular, early on. In 1728, he and another man, named Lemaire, were sentenced to a lenient fine of

12. Caillot, for instance, formed a partnership with an associate for trade upriver. See [Marc-Antoine Caillot], "Relation du voyage de la Louisianne ou Nouvlle. France; fait par le Sr. CAILLOT en l'année 1730," HNOC, MSS596, fols. 142–143. For the ruling prohibiting trade downriver, see "Règlement sur la police pour la province de la Louisiane," Feb. 28–Mar. 1, 1751, Article 18, ANOM COL C13A 35, fol. 46r; and Dubé, "Les biens publics," 291–296.

20 livres for having sold some brandy to two Native American slaves. The contracts he signed with Salmon to supply brandy, rum, and coffee to the king's warehouses very likely represented a new stage in his career, since he then began to purchase larger quantities from Gérard Péry, a prominent merchant who imported goods from the metropole. He must have managed to accumulate enough property for his widow to be in a suitable social position to marry Sieur Claude Trenaunay Chanfret, the subdelegate of the commissaire-ordonnateur at Pointe Coupée, in 1743.[13]

The occasional or regular participation of all kinds of people, professional merchants and traders as well as nonprofessionals, in the purchase of goods from ships coming from the metropole or the Caribbean contributed to blurring the frontiers between wholesaling and retailing. Professional merchants' shops were used for both, while nonprofessionals resorted to various means to retail their merchandise. In his commercial correspondence, Terrisse de Ternan, a storekeeper in the Illinois Country, informed Michel Rossard, the Superior Council's clerk, that he had sent tobacco, flour, hams, onions, and pelts to the latter in exchange for alcohol, metropolitan goods, and wares for the fur trade. Terrisse de Ternan asked his New Orleans partner "to have it [the tobacco] sold by shop traders or by retailers of the city." Apart from a few pounds bought by a military officer, Rossard sent a large quantity to be sold at La Mobile; the rest was retailed in New Orleans by the clerk's wife.[14]

13. For Jean Merle and Jacques Ozanne's contracts with Salmon and social proximity, see "Petition to Mr. de Salmon," Aug. 11, 1736, in Heloise H. Cruzat, ed., "RSCL XVII: Supplemental Index, no. 4," *LHQ*, VIII (1925), 479; "Recensement général de la ville de la Nvelle Orléans … fait au mois de janvier 1732," ANOM COL G1 464; and "Sale of Lot," May 4, 1734, in Cruzat, ed., "RSCL: Supplemental Index, no. I: 1718 to 1734," *LHQ*, VII (1924), 701. On Merle's life, see "Recensement général des habitations et des habitants de la colonie de la Louisiane ainsi qu'ils se sont nommés au premier janvier 1726," ANOM G1 464; "Last Will," Jan. 24, 1745, and other acts related to his succession, Jan. 24–Feb. 11, 1745, in Cruzat, ed., "RSCL XLVII: January–February, 1745," *LHQ*, XIII (1930), 500–503. On Ozanne's life, see AANO, Saint-Louis Cathedral Marriages, 1720–1730, 11/10/1727; "Petition of Recovery," Nov. 9, 1728, in [Henry P. Dart], ed., "RSCL XII [XIII]," *LHQ*, IV (1921), 502, "Memorandum of Accounts," Nov. 19, 1728, 504; RSCL 1728/06/05/02; "Contract," June 1, 1737, in Cruzat, ed., "RSCL XXIX, February–May, 1737," *LHQ*, IX (1926), 140; "Contract," Aug. 23, 1737, in Cruzat, ed., "RSCL XXXI, Supplemental Index, no. 8," *LHQ*, IX (1926), 504; "Bond," Nov. 5, 1737, 523; and Marriage Contract, Dec. 30, 1743, in Forsyth and Pleasonton, eds., *Louisiana Marriage Contracts*, [I], 113.

14. RSCL 1727/05/21/01, 1729/03/15/01, 1729/07/05/02, 1729/11/20/01, 1730/04/14/01, 1730/05/23/02, 1730/09/30/03, 1731/03/04/02, 1731/06/10/02, 1731/06/13/01, 1731/06/13/02, 1731/09/10/01. On Terrisse de Ternan, see Carl J. Ekberg, "Terrisse de Ter-

As in most cities in Europe and Anglo-America, women were often engaged in retailing. This petty trade allowed those of middling and lower sort to escape from wage labor. They often breached the law. In 1738, the wife of Laboissière, an earthenware maker and seller, consigned one *ancre* (a unit of measurement) of bear oil to Marie Anne, wife of Nicolas Dartel alias Francœur. She was supposed to sell twenty-eight *pots* (a unit of measurement) at three livres per pot while keeping the proceeds from the sale of the rest of the oil for herself. When a woman named La Prairie came to Marie Anne's to buy one *quart* (a unit of measurement), the two realized that the container was half full of water. Besides fraud, theft was a frequent component of this petty trade. In 1743, Sieur Brosset lodged a complaint at the clerk's office of the Superior Council against a woman named La Clef, wife of Fontanne. Because she had offered him some vermillion at a lower price than that sold in the king's warehouses, he suspected that the vermillion had been stolen. Although she claimed that her husband had given her the product to sell and that she had already sold some to Durantais, a traveler, Brosset still did not trust her.[15]

Free women of color also participated in this kind of petty trade. In 1738, the free black woman known as "Marie the Negress" purchased two lots of handkerchiefs at the auction of the movable property of a deceased settler with the intent to resell them. Yet women such as Marie were too few in number and too fragile economically to take on the economic role that free women of color played in French Saint-Domingue or, later, in Spanish New Orleans. Moreover, they were expected to keep a low profile. Otherwise, they could risk much, as the case of another free woman of African descent named Jeannette demonstrates. She had been manumitted as a child along with her parents and siblings by her former master, officer Jacques de Coustilhas, in his will. By 1746, she apparently lived on her own, as she was summoned and admonished by the Superior Council because she organized dinners with several of the city's domestic slaves at night. A few months later, she was sentenced to reenslavement for theft. One of the reasons for her reenslavement was the considerable debts she owed. Her sale was sup-

---

nan: Epistoler and Soldier," *Louisiana History*, XXIII (1982), 400–408; and Cécile Vidal, "Les implantations françaises au Pays des Illinois au XVIIIe siècle (1699–1765)," 2 vols. (Ph.D. diss., École des Hautes Études en Sciences Sociales, 1995), 131, 140, 351, 413, 513.

15. For the implication that women participated in retailing to escape from wage labor, see Seth Rockman, *Scraping By: Wage Labor, Slavery, and Survival in Early Baltimore* (Baltimore, 2009), 23. For cases of fraud in petty trade, see RSCL 1738/07/05/01; and "Declaration," Dec. 5, 1743, in Heloise H. Cruzat, ed., "RSCL XLIII: November–December, 1743," *LHQ*, XII (1929), 488.

posed to cover her debts, the rest being granted to the Charity Hospital. Part of these debts came from the estate of her deceased sister Marguerite, also a free woman of color, to whom merchandise had been sold and money had been loaned for commerce in 1745 by a white settler who was never paid back.[16]

In contrast with these free women of color, who could not but remain petty traders, a few white women managed to reach an enviable economic and social independence by wholesaling and retailing. They were often single or widowed or traded on behalf of themselves when married. One of them, Dame Marie Catherine Beaudrau, later known as the Widow Gervais, had been residing in the Illinois Country at the time of her marriage. Once widowed, she earned her living as a "public trader" in Louisiana's capital. Although she occasionally traded on her own behalf, she mainly ran her shop, with the assistance of two female slaves and their children, on a consignment basis, retaining a five percent commission. The list of creditors in her probate records shows that nonprofessionals of all sorts, both men and women, used her to both wholesale and retail.[17]

16. For Marie's purchase, see NONA Feb. 25, 1738, Succession of Georges Amelot, quoted in Sophie White, "Cultures of Consumption in French Colonial Louisiana: Slaves' Informal Economies in an Atlantic Context," unpublished paper presented at the workshop "Louisiana and the Atlantic World in the Eighteenth and Nineteenth Centuries," Tulane University, New Orleans, April 2008. For Jeannette's life, see RSCL 1738/08/26/03, 1739/03/04/04, 1746/09/03/05, 1747/04/11/01; "Sale of a Free Negress," Apr. 8, 11, 1747, in Heloise H. Cruzat, ed., "RSCL LXII: April, 1747," *LHQ*, XVIII (1935), 168, and "Petition," Apr. 27, 1747, 189. For the involvement of free women of color in trade in Saint-Domingue and Spanish New Orleans, see Dominique Rogers and Stewart King, "Housekeepers, Merchants, Rentières: Free Women of Color in the Port Cities of Colonial Saint-Domingue, 1750–1790," in Douglas Catterall and Jodi Campbelle, eds., *Women in Port: Gendering Communities, Economies, and Social Networks in Atlantic Port Cities, 1500–1800* (Leiden, Netherlands, 2012), 357–397; and Kimberly S. Hanger, "Landlords, Shopkeepers, Farmers, and Slave-Owners: Free Black Female Property-Holders in Colonial New Orleans," in David Barry Gaspar and Darlene Clark Hine, eds., *Beyond Bondage: Free Women of Color in the Americas* (Urbana, Ill., 2004), 219–236.

17. According to the Coutume de Paris, a married woman could not benefit from the legal power to conclude a contract or to institute proceedings without her husband's authorization except when she was "considered a public merchant if she sold merchandise separate from her husband's." See [Robert-Joseph] Pothier, *Traité de la Puissance du Mari*, VII, 9, quoted in Vaughan B. Baker, "'Cherchez les Femmes': Some Glimpses of Women in Early Eighteenth-Century Louisiana," *Louisiana History*, XXXI (1990), 21–37. The widow Gervais was described at least once as a *"marchande publique"* ("public trader"). See RSCL 1747/12/02/03. For a different view, see White, "'Baser Commerce,'" *William and Mary Quarterly*, XLIII (2006), 517–550, esp. 523, 528, 550.

The Widow Gervais is one of the few female merchants who surfaces from the documentation in the 1740s; two decades later, more women were publicly recognized as *"marchandes"* (female merchants). Among them were Marie Pascal Dame Goudeau, Demoiselle Marie-Rose Lange, and Dame Anne Testar. None were widows. One was a single woman who ran a shop, and two of them were married. Their titles of civility indicate that they belonged to the upper classes. Dame Goudeau's spouse, François Goudeau, was a royal surgeon. Marie-Rose might have been the Demoiselle Lange who came to join her brother, possibly the militia captain Guillaume Jacques Nicolas Lange serving on the German Coast, in Louisiana in 1734, bearing a letter to Paul Rasteau from his cousin bespeaking his good offices on her behalf. Testar's husband was a merchant of La Rochelle who had started a highly profitable partnership with Chantalou at midcentury. Dame Testar had also engaged in commercial activities on her own behalf prior to her arrival in the colony. While living in La Rochelle, she began trading with Dame Songy, the wife of Chantalou. She moved to Louisiana at the end of the Seven Years' War to obtain the settlement of a case the couple had pending with a local merchant named Jean-Baptiste Grevenberg dit Flamand. Her husband joined her some time later.[18]

Unlike their male counterparts, female merchants were identified by

18. For female merchants in the 1760s, see RSCL 1763/08/30/03, 1762/02/08/01, 1768/09/28/05, quoted in White, "'Baser Commerce,'" *William and Mary Quarterly*, XLIII (2006), 523n. For Demoiselle Lange's shop, see also "Procédure contre Joseph esclave mulâtre chirurgien à l'hôpital du roi ayant falsifié des billets à partir 30 novembre 1750, joint à la lettre de Michel du 18 mai 1751," ANOM COL F3 243, fols. 48–74. Because women needed the agreement of their husbands to obtain the status of "public merchants," such status was uncommon throughout the French Empire. On Île Royale, as in Louisiana, a few married women traded independently from their husbands, but most women who engaged in trade either assisted their husbands or were widowed. See Josette Brun, "Les femmes d'affaires en Nouvelle-France au 18e siècle: Le cas de l'Île Royale," *Acadiensis: Journal of the History of the Atlantic Region / Revue d'histoire de la région atlantique*, XXVII, no. 1 (Autumn 1997), http://journals.hil.unb.ca/index.php /acadiensis/article/view/10856/11687. For female merchants' social position, see "Letter of . . . to Paul Rasteau," Aug. 5, 1738, in "RSCL XVIII," *LHQ*, VI (1923), 124; RSCL 1753/11/20/01, Letter of Testar to Chantalou, quoted in Dubé, "Les biens publics," 275; "Petition of Madame Testar," Sept. 27, 1763, in G. Lugano, ed., "RSCL XCIII: September, 1763," *LHQ*, XXV (1942), 1181, "Citation," Sept. 29, 1763, 1181; Clark, *New Orleans, 1718-1812*, 99–102; and Dubé, "Les biens publics," 268–272, 281–289. In 1766, Maurice Testar signed the request of the merchants to the Superior Council against Antonio de Ulloa's legislation on trade. See "Réquisitions au Conseil supérieur par les négociants," Sept. 12, 1766, ANOM COL C13A 46, fols. 300r–301r.

their trade in notarial deeds or judicial records that directly concerned their mercantile activities but lost their professional identity in other kinds of documentation. In 1764 and 1765, Dame Testar leased and then sold a house in New Orleans, but she did not self-identify as a merchant in the deeds. Instead, she appeared as Dame Anne Recoquille, wife of Sieur Maurice Testar, a merchant of La Rochelle or New Orleans. Likewise, no profession was mentioned with regard to Dame Anne Recoquille on her daughter Marie Pascal's marriage contract or wedding certificate nor to that of Mademoiselle Marie-Rose Lange on the baptism certificates of slaves in which she appeared as godmother or owner. Even as these women earned greater social recognition for their engagement in business, they remained defined mainly by their family situation rather than by their profession.[19]

By the end of the French regime, commerce had become a more honorable activity. The growing acceptance of merchants as members of the elite is reflected in their nomination as captains of the New Orleans militia companies. In 1763, the militia captains were Sieurs St. Martin, Villars, Braquier, and Guinault; in 1766, Joseph Milhet replaced St. Martin; in 1770, only Joseph Villars was left from the French period, and the three new militia captains were Gilbert-Antoine de Saint Maxent, Barthélémy Macnemara, and Louis Rançon. Among these eight men, only two were not chiefly identified as merchants, St. Martin and Villars. Yet these two men also drew some of their fortune from commerce. These merchants occupied the top of Louisiana's social hierarchy, being outstripped only by royal officials and military officers.[20]

The social elevation of merchants and the new leading role they came to fulfill in the last decade of French rule marked a rupture from what had gone before. Until the mid-eighteenth century, state representatives did not explicitly recognize merchants as one of the main social categories among the white population most of the time. When Dumont de Montigny and Salmon decried the discriminatory distribution of slaves in the early 1730s,

19. Testar's house was located next to Madame Goudeau's in New Orleans. The site shows once again the importance of relationships of neighborhood and friendship among female merchants and traders. For female merchants' self-identification, see NONA Garic Mar. 8, 1764, Mar. 28, 1765; Alice Daly Forsyth, ed., *Louisiana Marriage Contracts*, II, *Abstracts from Records of the Superior Council of Louisiana, 1728–1769* (New Orleans, 1989), 78; and AANO, Saint-Louis Cathedral Baptisms, 1744–1753, 1763–1766, and 1767–1771, 08/09/1746, 10/18/1746, 08/01/1750, 06/06/1763, 05/14/1769.

20. Merchants were already chosen as militia officers in the 1750s in Canada. See Louise Dechêne, *Le peuple, l'État, et la guerre au Canada sous le Régime français*, ed. Hélène Paré et al. (Montreal, 2008), 230.

they contrasted the "big" and "little habitants," who were distinguished by their fortune, connections, and slaveownership. Likewise, when Governor Louis Billouart de Kerlérec complained about Commissaire-ordonnateur Vincent-Gaspard-Pierre de Rochemore in the late 1750s, he reported that "The murmur of public discontent is already loud enough, the good habitant and the common people are already disheartened," implicitly positing landownership as the main factor of social distinction. Into this binary conception, Rochemore introduced a third category when he complained in 1760 that the governor "has often deprived officers, habitants, the common people, and myself of even the tranquility of sleep." Previously, the attorney general François Fleuriau had also taken into account members of the church in his complaints against Michel in 1752: "I would have many things to say about it but we have enough other complaints, all the estates of the colony in general, ecclesiastics, militaries, habitants, he [Michel] is hated and detested as much as he himself is offensive, brusque, and unapproachable." When these officials wanted to underline the unanimity of the social orders or estates, they did not allude to trade as a professional activity that had given birth to a corporate body.[21]

From the late 1750s, merchants started to be collectively distinguished as a specific estate. They already formed one of five categories into which Governor Pierre de Rigaud de Vaudreuil de Cavagnal and Commissaire-ordonnateur Michel divided the urban population in their 1747 project of taxation; whether foreigners or locals, they were defined by the holding of a warehouse or store in the city. But, since the project was abandoned, this first opportunity for official recognition of New Orleans's merchants as a corporate body was lost. They had to wait for the clash that broke out in 1759 between Governor Kerlérec and Commissaire-ordonnateur Rochemore regarding the authorization of the British ship *Le Texel* to trade in the colony during the Seven Years' War to be able to appear publicly as a political force of their own. When the latter accused the former of corruption and abuse of power, what later became known as the Louisiana Affair turned into a major political scandal. In 1759 and 1760, a few self-identified merchants signed two declarations with other "citizens" against Rochemore. In

---

21. Dumont de Montigny, *Regards sur le monde atlantique*, 212–213; Edmé Gatien Salmon to the minister of the navy, Dec. 14, 1731, ANOM COL C13A 15, fols. 186v–187r; Louis Billouart de Kerlérec to the minister of the navy, Oct. 4, 1758, ANOM COL C13A 40, fol. 91r; Vincent-Gaspard-Pierre de Rochemore to the minister of the navy, June 22, 1760, ANOM COL C13A 42, fol. 106r; François Fleuriau to the minister of the navy, Feb. 1, 1752, ANOM COL C13A 36, fol. 316r.

April 1763, nearly thirty of them signed a new declaration in favor of Ker-lérec. A few months later, in November 1763, the governor received fare-wells from the "Commerce" in the name of five merchants "acting for lack of a *Chambre de Commerce* [chamber of commerce] on behalf of all the merchants in New Orleans." Starting in the early 1700s, the merchants of most of the main port cities in the metropole were organized in chambres de commerce. Four *chambres d'agriculture et de commerce* (chambers of agriculture and commerce) were established in the colonies in 1759: two in Saint-Domingue (in Cap-Français and in Port-au-Prince), and one each in Martinique and Guadeloupe. The Louisiana merchants might have felt dis-appointed at not having been included in this reform and possibly looked to the Louisiana Affair to make their voices heard in the metropole.[22]

In the kingdom, the aftermath of the Seven Years' War was a crucial time for the chambres de commerce, marking a moment when they began to ex-change and coordinate their action. The first occasion to present a united front was in their common opposition to the "Mémoire sur l'étendue et les bornes des lois prohibitives du commerce étranger dans nos colonies" ("Memoir on the extent and limits on prohibitive laws on foreign commerce in our colonies") written by Jean-Baptiste Dubuc in 1764. A planter from Martinique, Dubuc had been nominated as head of the Bureau des colonies by the minister of the navy, Étienne-François de Choiseul, the previous year, and he proposed measures to make the Exclusif (the restriction of com-merce within imperial boundaries) more flexible. In Louisiana, in contrast, the merchants used some of Dubuc's arguments to collectively defend their

22. For Vaudreuil's and Michel's project of taxation in the 1740s, see "Règlement de Vaudreuil et Michel sur l'entretien des chemins, de la levée, des clôtures, et l'enferme-ment des bestiaux," Nov. 13, 1747, ANOM COL F3 243, fols. 33v–34v. On the Louisiana Affair, see Dubé, "Les biens publics." For the statements and petitions produced on the occasion of the Louisiana Affair, see "Copie de la déclaration des négociants et habi-tants sur les séditieux propos tenus par le Sr. Mandeville lieutenant au peuple assemblé le 22 juillet 1759," ANOM COL C13A 46, fols. 115v–116r; "Copie de la déclaration de 57 citoyens des plus notables et de différents états sur l'administration de M. de Roche-more ...," 1760, ANOM COL C13A 46, fol. 114; "Copie de la déclaration des négociants de la Louisiane en faveur de M. de Kerlérec qui justifie la protection constante et décidée que ce gouverneur a toujours accordée au commerce et l'injustice des calomnies répan-dues contre lui à cette occasion," Apr. 29, 1763, ANOM COL C13A 46, fol. 111; and "Ex-trait des adieux faits par le commerce à M. de Kerlérec gouverneur de la Louisiane à son départ pour la France," Nov. 4, 1763, ANOM COL C13A 46, fol. 112. For the creation of chambres de commerce in metropolitan France, see Jean Tarrade, "Chambres de com-merce," in Lucien Bély, ed., *Dictionnaire de l'Ancien Régime: Royaume de France, XVIe-XVIIIe siècle* (Paris, 2002), 224–226.

Trade, Credit, and Honor

own colonial economic agenda. The attempts of General Director Jean-Jacques Blaise d'Abbadie (who acted as the colony's governor although he did not hold the title) to solve the currency crisis and to impose an official monopoly on the Indian trade in 1763–1764 followed by the first reforms of transatlantic trade introduced by Governor Antonio de Ulloa in 1766 after the Spanish gained control of the colony gave merchants fresh opportunities to mobilize as a corporate body as they collectively presented requests to the Superior Council. By the end of the French regime, merchants were able to mobilize to defend their interests. The fortune and the social recognition they benefited from, which fueled an assertive sense of self-identity, gave them the means to lobby successfully. They were all the more powerful because other elites shared their economic interests, even though they refused to self-identify as merchants.[23]

"THE FEAR OF LOSING MY CREDIT": NOBILITY, CREDIT, AND COMMERCE

Apart from colony officials, sword officers stood at the top of Louisiana's social ladder. Many belonged to the nobility or second estate. As a result of the recruitment of military officers in the metropole or in other overseas territories to serve in the *compagnies franches de la Marine*, members of fifty-three noble lineages were present in the Mississippi colony at various times during the French period, whereas noblemen in the Antilles were more numerous among civilians who had not served in the navy or the army. Another difference with the Caribbean had to do with the more modest origins of New Orleans's noblemen, as most of them descended from families of the minor provincial nobility. When Kerlérec sent his recommendations

23. For the participation of the chambres de commerce in the debate on "free trade" after 1763 and the "Mémoire sur l'étendue et les bornes des lois prohibitives du commerce étranger dans nos colonies" ("Memoir on the extent and limits on prohibitive laws on foreign commerce in our colonies") written by Jean-Baptiste Dubuc in 1764, see Jean Tarrade, *Le commerce colonial de la France à la fin de l'Ancien Régime: L'évolution du régime de "l'Exclusif" de 1763 à 1789*, 2 vols. (Paris, 1972), 165–372; and Tarrade, "Les chambres de commerce à la fin du XVIIIe siècle: La naissance d'un réseau portuaire," in Michèle Collin, ed., *Ville et port, XVIIIè-XIXè siècle* (Paris, 1994), 273–285. For merchants' petitions against Jean-Jacques Blaise d'Abbadie's and Antonio de Ulloa's legislation on trade, see "Requête des négociants de la Louisiane à d'Abbadie," June 7, 1764, ANOM COL C13A 44, fols. 63–68r; "Supplique des négociants de la Louisiane," Sept. 8, 1766, ANOM COL C13A 46, fol. 298; "Supplique des capitaines de navire," Sept. 10, 1766, ANOM COL C13A 46, fol. 299; and "Réquisitions au Conseil supérieur par les négociants," Sept. 12, 1766, ANOM COL C13A 46, fols. 300r–301r.

for promotions for military officers to the minister of the navy in 1758, he emphasized their qualifications, not their birth: "I will add to the present list of proposed promotions only the recommendations about the character and way of thinking, and the varying degree of zeal and exactitude of Misters the officers. As for the recommendations related to their birth, I believe that the information I could give on this occasion would mortify many of them." Just as titles of nobility remained important in the islands, where colonists recorded them at the clerk's office, having a noble lineage did not lose its significance in Louisiana. The divide between noblemen and commoners was nevertheless challenged by the growing importance of trade. Military officers found themselves in a paradoxical position; they could not hold their rank without being involved in commercial activities, but their growing reliance on trade challenged their social preeminence. The debate about the infamy of commerce that raged in the kingdom resonated with force in New Orleans.[24]

Military service remained the most honorable estate in the eyes of the colonial elite, and sword officers fought hard to preserve their social preeminence, despite the growing role played by commerce in redefining social positions and values. The tension between these two ethos might have been at stake in a 1751 conflict between a military officer and a ship's officer who navigated between Martinique and New Orleans. According to Commissaire-ordonnateur Michel, events unfolded as follows: "In a small room where Mr. de Sabran, a lieutenant, entertained guests, Sr. Battar absent-mindedly put his hat on. Sr. Sabran took the hat off his head and

24. For Louisiana's nobility, see Yves Drolet, *Dictionnaire généalogique de la Noblesse de la Nouvelle-France*, new ed. (Montreal, 2017): http://numerique.banq.qc.ca/patrimoine /details/52327/2785738; and Giraud, *History of French Louisiana*, trans. Pearce, V, 276– 285. On the colonial nobility in the French Empire, see Lorraine Gadoury, *La noblesse de Nouvelle-France: Familles et alliances* (Quebec, 1991); and François-Joseph Ruggiu, "Une noblesse atlantique? Le second ordre français de l'Ancien au Nouveau Monde," in "L'Atlantique Français," special issue, *Outre-mers: Revue d'histoire*, XCVII, nos. 362–363 (2009), 39–63. On the low origins of military officers, see Kerlérec to the minister of the navy, Sept. 15, 1758, ANOM COL C13A 40, fol. 37v. For the significance of nobility in the Antilles, see P. F. R. Dessalles, *Les annales du Conseil souverain de la Martinique*, Tome II, Vol. II, *Notes et index*, ed. Bernard Vonglis (1786; rpt. Paris, 1995), v–x, 55–56; and [Médéric Louis-Élie Moreau] de Saint-Méry, *Loix et constitutions des colonies françoises de l'Amérique sous le vent*, 6 vols. (Paris, 1784–1790), III, 650–651, 670–671, 853–854, IV, 139, 573.

threw it on the ground. [Sr. Battar] did the same to Sr. Sabran who left to look for the guard; and as he could not find Sr. Battar when he returned he chased him all over the city, and finally found him in his room where he besieged him at the head of the guard even though he did not have an order to do so. Sr. Battar forced him to fight, they crossed swords, and both were hurt. Finally, Battar was arrested and taken to prison." Notwithstanding his belonging to the world of maritime commerce, the ship's officer had behaved as if he and the lieutenant were on equal footing and shared the same dueling culture. This behavior had offended the military officer who, after having chased and attacked Battar, lodged a complaint with the attorney general Fleuriau, who refused to begin an investigation. The case was settled by the governor outside the court system. Battar was left in jail until he agreed to go to Mr. de Noyan, the *major*, and to apologize to Sabran on his knees in the presence of all the military officers. Even though Fleuriau himself had "been deeply offended last year by an officer who publicly treated him as a negro and had not obtained reparation," he took the side of the sword officer. No one was shielded from the violence of military officers, which was compared to the extreme violence the slave system allowed masters to use against their enslaved laborers.[25]

For military officers, and noblemen in particular, recognition of their social superiority was a matter of crucial importance. They needed to keep up appearances to hold their rank, which entailed ostentatious modes of consumption, practices of liberality, and the financial means to support such a lifestyle. Yet most of them were likely younger sons, like Pradel, or belonged to impoverished families. They had chosen the navy precisely because they did not have to purchase an officer's commission and had come to the colony to make their fortune. Given that their salaries were not high enough to meet their needs, these sword officers actively engaged in all kinds of commercial activities. In so doing, they displayed an entrepreneurial spirit. They did not wish to accumulate and hoard money but to make it work for them. Captain Jean-Baptiste Benoît de Saint-Clair clearly expressed such an intention in a letter to the Widow Gervais with whom he had concluded a trading agreement before he left for the Illinois Country where he served as commandant between 1742 and early 1749: "If you think that I can make some profit if the price of the goods falls, send some, otherwise sell them at sea. As I told you when I left, money in a chest profits no-

25. Honoré-Gabriel Michel to the minister of the navy, July 15, 1751, ANOM COL C13A 35, fols. 291, 294, 307.

one." According to the aristocratic ethos, profit, however, was not supposed to be sought after for its own sake but as a means to promote advancement in the hierarchy of rank.[26]

Like Benoît de Saint-Clair, military officers could take advantage of the great variations in prices between New Orleans and the outposts of the interior, or they could take part in the fur or pelt trade. The most enterprising ones, such as Pradel, engaged in transatlantic commerce. They typically entered into partnerships with metropolitan merchants and freighted merchandise on royal or private ships. One captain named de Coustilhas distinguished himself by the scale of his business. Already in possession of a plantation with many slaves, he organized a slave trading trip to Africa via Martinique in partnership with the merchant Péry. Even though the expedition failed, as the ship's captain died in Martinique and de Coustilhas lost his life in the last expedition against the Chickasaw in 1739, it was one of the first attempts by a Louisiana colonist to renew the slave trade with Africa after its quasi cessation in 1731.[27]

26. The financial duress of officers was particularly dramatic during the 1720s. See La Chaise to the Company of the Indies's Directors, Mar. 8, 1724, ANOM COL C13A 7, fol. 22; and "Mémoire de la Compagnie des Indes servant d'instruction pour M. Périer nouvellement pourvu du commandement général de la Louisiane," Sept. 30, 1726, ANOM COL C13B 1, fol. 97. The financial and material situation of officers improved somewhat afterward. Still, their needs exceeded their salaries. For instance, Kerlérec repeatedly complained that his annual salary of twelve thousand livres was not sufficient to meet his expenses, which amounted to thirty thousand livres. See Kerlérec to the minister of the navy, Sept. 15, 1758, ANOM COL C13A 40, fol. 48v. For Jean-Baptiste Benoît de Saint-Clair's letter, see RSCL 1746/08/04/02. On aristocratic ethos, see Grenier, *L'économie d'Ancien Régime*, 101.

27. Salmon to the minister of the navy, June 5, 1737, ANOM COL C13A 22, fols. 173–174r; "Judicial sale of *The Marie Elisabeth*," Nov. 17, 1736, in Heloise H. Cruzat, ed., "RSCL XVIII: Supplemental Index, no. 5 (October 20, 1736, to Feb. 13, 1737)," *LHQ*, VIII (1925), 682, "Engagements," Jan. 31–May 15, 1737, 696–699, "Declaration," Feb. 6, 1737, 699; "Acknowledgment," Apr. 1, 1737, in Cruzat, ed., "RSCL XXIX, February–May, 1737, Supplemental Index, no. 6," *LHQ*, IX (1926), 119, "Contract for a Voyage after Slaves," Apr. 24, 1737, 126–127, "Contract to Serve as Surgeon on Slave Trader," May 15, 1737, 137; NONA Jan. 17, 1738, Jan. 23, 1738. For the will de Coustilhas made before his departure on the expedition against the Chickasaw, see RSCL 1738/08/26/03, 1739/03/04/04. For the settlement of his estate, see "Succession of Jacques de Coustilhas," Feb. 21, 1739, in "RSCL XXII," *LHQ*, VII (1924), 334–336; "Estate Accounts Filed," Feb. 25, 1739, in "RSCL XIX," *LHQ*, VI (1923), 301; "Petition of Recovery," Mar. 7, 1739, 305; "Petition of Recovery," Mar. 23, 1739, in "RSCL XX," *LHQ*, VI (1923), 482, "Petition of Recovery," Mar. 26, 1739, 482, "Slave Deal Reversed," Mar. 30, 1739, 483; "Maritime Accounting," Sept. 27,

Trade, Credit, and Honor

Transatlantic trade was considered a legitimate commercial activity for noblemen whereas retailing was viewed as problematic, since it constituted a reason for derogation in the kingdom. The crown had authorized the Canadian nobility to engage in both wholesale and retail trade in 1685, but this royal edict had not been promulgated in Louisiana. Furthermore, the social standards on which the colonial elite based their judgment on the appropriateness of social behavior were those of the metropole. The reputation of these transatlantic families had to be preserved on both sides of the ocean. Throughout the French Empire, most noblemen continued to develop strategies to hide their participation in retailing. In 1733, Commissaire-ordonnateur Salmon reported that in order to compensate for their low salaries, "Some others [military officers] purchase goods and have someone sell them in a shop but few do this, such a trade does not create much emulation, the officer gets rusty and lives like scum."[28]

Few military officers displayed the energy that Pradel showed to both expand his commercial activities and conceal his involvement in retailing. He first wrote his brother in 1729 how he intended to use one of his white servants to run a tavern on his behalf. He had gotten the idea from Governor Étienne Périer whose maître d'hôtel had made a lot of money that way the previous three years. Officially, Pradel discharged his servant, but he left the house, with the wine and liquor he had bought, in her care. He planned to keep supplying her with alcohol, in partnership with a member of the Superior Council, Nicolas Chauvin de La Frénière. Worried that his commercial activities might become known in the colony as well as in the metropole, he closed his letter by cautioning his brother: "I am telling you, my dear brother, about all my small businesses, but I beg you not to communicate my letters to anyone except the most important members of the family. And besides you are wise enough not to talk about these kinds of things which there is no need for everybody to know about." Then, in

---

1739, in "RSCL XXI," *LHQ*, VI (1923), 681; and "Sale of Cattle," Jan. 9, 1740, in Cruzat, ed., "RSCL XXXIV: (January, 1740, to April, 1740)," *LHQ*, X (1927), 254.

28. For the relationships between nobility and commerce in metropolitan France and its North American colonies, see Henri Lévy-Bruhl, "La noblesse de France et le commerce à la fin de l'Ancien Régime," *Revue d'histoire moderne*, New Ser., II, VIII (1933), 209–235; Guy Richard, *La noblesse d'affaires au XVIIIe siècle*, 2d ed. (Paris, 1997), 15–32; Guy Chaussinand-Nogaret, *La noblesse au XVIIIe siècle: De la Féodalité aux Lumières* ([Bruxelles], 2000), 119–161; and White, "'Baser Commerce,'" *William and Mary Quarterly*, XLIII (2006), 543–545. For noblemen's strategies to hide their engagement in trade, see Salmon to the minister of the navy, Jan. 31, 1733, ANOM COL C13A 17, fols. 23–24.

late April 1731, Pradel decided to purchase another town house and some slaves with the intent of using a man named Ceirac as a straw man to sell metropolitan goods both wholesale and retail. Ceirac would receive five percent of the profits and losses. The shop and store needed to be located at a certain distance from Pradel's home, but he nevertheless intended to visit them several times a day. Once again, he felt the need to justify himself to his brother: "It is the only means I have to earn enough to spend my old age with you. This, my dear brother, is my plan. May God bless it. If I fail, it won't be my fault. If I have taken such pains to hide the financial straits in which I was here it was for fear of losing my credit; because, if I had been compelled to sell some of my goods it would have been known without fail and it would have hurt me because people believe I am richer than I am; and people might have ceased to trust me." Pradel's prestige rested on his fortune and ability to pay his debts, not just his family background, military service, and social connections.[29]

Over the eighteenth century, noblemen apparently started to give more importance to the idea that they needed to pursue both reputation and fortune to hold their ranks. A tension nonetheless developed between these two imperatives. In another letter, Pradel reported the compliment Kerlérec paid him when he visited his plantation named Monplaisir. The governor said "that he did not consider my house as a provincial castle but as one belonging to a farmer general in the outskirts of Paris ...." The chevalier felt flattered by this comparison at the same time that the comment insinuated that the magnificence of Monplaisir did not correspond to the taste and ethos of the provincial nobility—the social world to which Pradel's family belonged—but of the parvenus who made their fortunes in finance. The former military officer could take pride in his social ascendency above a kind of provincial mediocrity. Yet his rise was at the cost of a more refined way of life associated with the high nobility. Had fortune become an end it itself?[30]

29. A. Baillardel and A. Prioult, eds., *Le chevalier de Pradel: Vie d'un colon français en Louisiane au XVIIIe siècle; d'après sa correspondance et celle de sa famille* (Paris, 1928), 56–57 ("I am telling"), 96 ("It is the only means"). The 1732 census recorded Madame Pradel as living with an unrelated man named Sieur Layrac (Ceyrac?) in a rented house. See "Recensement général de la ville de la Nvelle Orléans ... fait au mois de janvier 1732," ANOM COL G1 464. According to Governor Bienville, who had been himself actively engaged in all kinds of trade, his predecessor, Périer, entered into a partnership with Pradel that centered on this shop. See White, "'Baser Commerce,'" *William and Mary Quarterly*, XLIII (2006), 545–546.

30. Pradel to his brother, Apr. 10, 1755, HNOC, MSS 589, Chevalier de Pradel Papers 62; Dubé, "Les biens publics," 346.

The same debate that split the second estate in France, regarding the *"noblesse commerçante,"* meaning the possibility for noblemen to engage in trading activities without losing their honor, also raged among the colonial elite, particularly the sword officers, whether they were of noble descent or not. In 1756, the very year Abbé Coyer published his essay entitled *La Noblesse commerçante,* which provoked the metropolitan controversy, Governor Kerlérec ordered Captain Jean-Bernard Bossu to head a convoy for the Illinois Country. When Kerlérec asked Bossu what kind of *pacotille* (goods carried free of freightage) he intended to take, the officer reportedly replied "that I knew nothing about trade; as a military man his Majesty sent me to Louisiana to serve him, that service was my sole source of glory." Bossu's answer, included in his travel account in 1768, was intended for a metropolitan audience at a time when Kerlérec was being examined by the magistrates of the Châtelet Court for the Louisiana Affair. The captain wanted to distinguish himself from the former governor, with whom he had maintained a tense relationship. Even so, Bossu's statement can also be read as a response to Abbé Coyer's comments on glory: "Glory, this passion that characterizes elevated souls, this motive for grand actions, is not always well understood.... And without doubt, it is admirable to suffer and die for one's *patrie* [fatherland]. But do you think that commerce does not have its own services, its own dangers, its own combats?" In contrast with Coyer's unconventional view, Bossu exhibited a strict military ethos that could help his advancement.[31]

In the 1750s, not only was the appropriateness of noblemen engaging in trade up for debate but so was the criteria used to promote military officers to higher rank. Over the eighteenth century, military merit was increasingly starting to become judged according to a new set of professional standards related to talent, application, exactitude, and personal sacrifice, rather than birth. At stake in Bossu's interchange with Kerlérec were both his reputation and his ability to climb the military hierarchy. In the early 1730s, Pradel had already been evaluated by his superiors as "more attached to commerce than to service" for his failure to display the indifference to mundane mone-

31. For the French debate on nobility and commerce, see Smith, "Social Categories, the Language of Patriotism, and the Origins of the French Revolution," *Journal of Modern History,* LXXII (2000), 339–374; and Shovlin, *Political Economy of Virtue,* 58–65. For the relationships between Bossu and Kerlérec, see [Jean-Bernard] Bossu, *Nouveaux voyages aux Indes occidentales ...,* 2 vols. (Paris, 1768), I, 181. For Coyer's statement about glory, see Abbé [Gabriel François] Coyer, *La noblesse commerçante* (London, 1756), 141, 161, quoted in Smith, "Social Categories, the Language of Patriotism, and the Origins of the French Revolution," *Journal of Modern History,* LXXII (2000), 351–352.

tary matters that was expected from military officers, whether belonging to the nobility or not. Two decades later, Bossu's display of this military ethos was a way to promote a new vision of the social order that was based on the opposition between "the corrupt and idle rich and the 'useful classes' among whom poorer nobles—gentlemen farmers and military officers in particular—might count themselves," rather than on the traditional distinction between nobility and commoners. Since Bossu was not of noble descent, defending a military ethos might have appeared particularly crucial for him.[32]

Still, the captain missed one important dimension of the favor extended to him by Kerlérec. In the metropole, the king's favor played a crucial role in the preservation of the fortunes of noble families, paying their debts and giving them pensions. In Louisiana, the crown replicated this policy through its representatives, although it was adapted to fit the financial, economic, and social circumstances of the colony. Since the salaries of military officers were so low, local authorities enabled officers to maintain their position at the top of the social hierarchy by providing them with the means to keep and increase their fortune. Apart from inviting them to dine at their table, they appointed them as commandants of the interior outposts where they could more easily engage in the fur trade. Likewise, they ordered them to command Illinois convoys and extended them free freight on the king's boat, since metropolitan goods were sold at prices from fifty to one hundred percent higher in the Illinois Country than in Louisiana. They also afforded officers large amounts of credit at the royal warehouses in New Orleans.[33]

Like other sword and pen officers, top officials were similarly involved in commerce, a practice that Commissaire-ordonnateur Michel denounced

32. On the new culture of merit in the French army, see Rafe Blaufarb, *The French Army, 1750–1820: Careers, Talent, Merit* (Manchester, U.K., 2002); and Jay M. Smith, *The Culture of Merit: Nobility, Royal Service, and the Making of Absolute Monarchy in France, 1600–1789* (Ann Arbor, Mich., 1996), 42–49, 191–261. For the governor's evaluation of Pradel, see "Liste apostillée des officiers des troupes entretenues à la Louisiane," ANOM COL D2C 51, fol. 106, quoted in Marcel Giraud, *Histoire de la Louisiane française,* 4 vols. (Paris, 1953–1974), III, 358. For the debate on luxury in metropolitan France, see John Shovlin, "The Cultural Politics of Luxury in Eighteenth-Century France," *French Historical Studies,* XXIII (2000), 577–606 (quotation, 579).

33. On the king's favor in metropolitan France, see Laurence Fontaine, "Pouvoir, relations sociales, et crédit sous l'Ancien Régime," *Revue française de socio-économie,* IX, no. 1, *Crédit à la consommation: Une histoire qui dure* (2012), 101–116. On the governor's practice of inviting military officers to dine at his table, see Salmon to the minister of the navy, Jan. 31, 1733, ANOM COL C13A 17, fol. 23. Bossu was particularly grateful to Vaudreuil for his liberality. See Bossu, *Nouveaux voyages aux Indes occidentales,* I, 24–25.

to the minister of the navy because of the ways it could lead to corruption and abuses of power. At the time Michel entered into this conflict with Vaudreuil, he was also engaged in multiple struggles with other military officers on various grounds related to power and honor. Although the governor and commissaire-ordonnateur (or intendant) in every colony often maintained tense relationships, Michel went further than any of his predecessors when he criticized the governor's wife in his acrimonious letters to the minister. Aristocratic women were special targets for critics of the highest nobility because they "encapsulated the misuse of power and wanton extravagance associated with the order as [a] whole." Michel explained that Vaudreuil needed to handle the corporate body of officers carefully as his wife had too many interests in the outposts and in town. He especially denounced the involvement of the governor and his spouse in the fur and pelt trade, alleging that Vaudreuil protected his interests by appointing his fellow countrymen and relatives or those of his wife as commandants of the interior outposts instead of choosing them by drawing lots. Michel claimed that Madame Vaudreuil was directly involved as she held half of the trade of Pointe Coupée in partnership with Joseph Delfau de Pontalba, the only commandant who was not allied to the couple and who, he alleged, owed his nomination to this business partnership. As if that was not enough, Michel also wrote about a more serious offense:

> Madam his spouse is capable of a viler commerce than this. She does business with everybody here and she forces merchants and private individuals to accept her goods and sell them at the price that she imposes. She has a shop in her home with all kinds of drugs, that her maître d'hôtel sells; and when he is not there she measures the goods out herself. Her husband is in the know. It brings him a good income, and that is the motivation for all his desires and occupations.

The governor's wife not only consigned goods with merchants—she was one of widow Gervais's consigners—and used domestics as straw men to retail merchandise, she herself was said to handle and sell goods to customers in her shop.[34]

34. For noblewomen as the focus of criticism, see Mita Choudhury, "Women, Gender, and the Image of the Eighteenth-Century Aristocracy," in Jay M. Smith, ed., *The French Nobility in the Eighteenth Century: Reassessments and New Approaches* (University Park, Pa., 2006), 167–188 ("encapsulated," 169). For Michel's criticisms against Vaudreuil and his wife, see Michel to the minister of the navy, July 15, 1751, ANOM COL C13A 35, fol. 311r; and Michel to the minister of the navy, July 20, 1751, ANOM COL

Commissaire-ordonnateur Michel's accusation against Madame Vaudreuil took place in the late 1740s, at a time when the debate on luxury in France had intensified. According to John Shovlin, the condemnation of the effects of commercialization on French society and culture and the hostility to luxury "resonated with the ethos and interests of important sections of the middling elite, especially elements of the provincial nobility, and some of the *rentiers*, professional, and office-holders who enjoyed a position of respectability in provincial cities." Although Michel had intended to improve his fortune through trade when he arrived in the colony, he was representative of these social categories in the colonial world. He seems to have shared the same fear that commerce and luxury could imperil the dominant social position of noblemen and women.[35]

It is hard to know if Madame Vaudreuil really acted as a shopkeeper and compromised herself in retail trade, but what could have been an exaggeration reveals that her fault was not to keep up appearances. In France, it was not uncommon for nobles to engage in wholesale and even retail trade through straw men and women. In Brittany, in particular, many noblemen involved in the maritime trade also retailed all kinds of goods using the names of their wives. What was distinctive about the colony, however, was the extent of their involvement, which shook the moral and social values transferred from the metropole. In addition to arousing tension at the top of the social ladder, commerce created conflicts at the bottom.[36]

"MONEY DOES NOT HAVE A MASTER": CROSS-RACIAL EXCHANGE IN THE MARKETPLACE

Slaves were no less involved in mercantile activities than white settlers. In that regard, the Louisiana situation was similar to what took place in other slave societies. The enslaved's participation in trade took two forms. They openly sold and bought commodities for their masters or for themselves, and they fueled an informal market economy based on theft. In so doing, they contributed to the circulation of both goods and currencies. In 1765,

---

C13A 35, fols. 322–336v. Similar accusations were made by Rochemore against Kerlérec, who allegedly used his secretary, Thiton, as a straw man. See Rochemore to the minister of the navy, Oct. 15, 1759, ANOM COL C13A 41, fol. 305r.

35. On the French debate on luxury, see Shovlin, *Political Economy of Virtue*, 38–44. On Michel's motivations, see White, "'Baser Commerce,'" *William and Mary Quarterly*, XLIII (2006), 517–550.

36. For the use of strawmen by noblemen to trade in metropolitan France, see Chaussinand-Nogaret, *La noblesse au XVIIIe siècle*, 129.

a trial revealed that Cupidon, a sixty-five-year-old slave, had apparently convinced another slave named Louis, belonging to the same owner, Sieur Carlier, to steal some coins, piastres, and letters of exchange. He was reported to have said that "money does not have a master." The statement was particularly powerful since their master was a royal scrivener who had served as the navy's comptroller of Louisiana between 1759 and 1761. Slaves seemed well aware that their participation in the cash and market economy empowered them, but they also knew that their position was fragile. At one point during a trial for several thefts, Pradel's peddler Jupiter admitted that "a servant is not a master." He acknowledged the limits that his slave status imposed on his agency. Commerce and credit illuminate more than any other social practice the ambiguous position of enslaved men and women in urban settings, in between greater autonomy and greater repression.[37]

The wholesale trade might have been the exclusive domain of whites, but slaves participated in the retail trade. During a period when wheat flour was so scarce in New Orleans that local authorities gave soldiers their ration in

37. On slaves' economy, see among other studies Hilary McD. Beckles, "An Economic Life of Their Own: Slaves as Commodity Producers and Distributors in Barbados," *Slavery and Abolition*, XII (1991), 31–47; Ira Berlin and Philip D. Morgan, eds., *The Slaves' Economy: Independent Production by Slaves in the Americas* (London, 1991); Robert Olwell, "'Loose, Idle, and Disorderly': Slave Women in the Eighteenth-Century Charleston Marketplace," in David Barry Gaspar and Darlene Clark Hine, eds., *More than Chattel: Black Women and Slavery in the Americas* (Bloomington, Ind., 1996), 97–110; and Betty Wood, *Women's Work, Men's Work: The Informal Slave Economies of Lowcountry Georgia* (Athens, Ga., 1995). On the importance of theft in the circulation of garments or food products in France, see Daniel Roche, *La culture des apparences: Une histoire du vêtement (XVIIe–XVIIIe siècle)* (Paris, 1991), 313–345; and Montenach, *Espaces et pratiques du commerce alimentaire*, 195–201. For the trial of Sieur Carlier's slaves, see RSCL 1765/07/06/01, 1765/07/13/01, 1765/07/15/02, 1765/07/17/01, 1765/08/02/04, 1765/08/27/03, 1765/09/07/01, 1765/09/07/03, 1765/09/08/02, 1765/09/08/03, 1765/09/09/01, 1765/09/09/02, 1765/09/18/02 (quotation), 1765/09/20/02, 1765/09/20/03, 1765/09/21/01, 1765/09/21/02, 1765/09/21/03, 1765/09/21/04, 1765/09/21/05, 1765/03/01/03, 1765/03/02/01; and NONA Garic Sept. 23, 1765. For an interpretation of the market as emancipatory in early modern Europe, see Fontaine, *Le marché*, esp. 193–240. For Jupiter's trial, see RSCL 1744/02/26/01, 1744/02/29/01, 1744/03/02/01, 1744/03/03/01, 1744/03/05/01, 1744/03/07/02, 1744/03/11/01, 1744/03/11/02, 1744/03/12/01, 1744/03/12/02, 1744/03/13/01, 1744/03/14/01, 1744/03/14/02, 1744/03/16/01, 1744/03/17/01, 1744/03/18/01, 1744/03/18/02, 1744/03/19/01, 1743/03/21/01, 1743/03/21/02, 1744/03/21/03 (quotation), 1744/03/21/04, 1744/03/21/05, 1744/04/23/01, 1744/04/24/01, 1744/10/03/01.

rice and hulled grain instead of bread, Rochemore reported an incident to the minister of the navy that testifies to the role domestic slaves played in shopping for urban households. Lieutenant Chabillard "waited at noon for the domestic negroes as they came back from the bakery where they had gone to get the bread for the houses they serve, he asked mine who was his master, and on the basis of what he replied, he took part of his provisions." Because domestic slaves appearing in public were seen as a social extension of their masters, the military officer felt he could offend the commissaire-ordonnateur and send him a message of protest by attacking his slave. Although Chabillard's violence toward the slave in this case had nothing to do with the shopping itself, commercial interactions still occasionally fostered disputes.[38]

Far from being a place of fluid and peaceful encounters among all social and ethnic groups, the urban marketplace could be a site of contested social hierarchy and (petty) violence. As domestic slaves shopped for their masters, they sometimes got involved in more serious conflicts. "Go f. yourself you and your master," yelled Pierrot, a white butcher, to Scipion, the enslaved cook of Mr. le chevalier de Morand, in his New Orleans shop in June 1737. According to Scipion's master's complaint, he had sent the slave to the butcher's to buy some meat. After having asked for a specific cut, Scipion then watched François de Bellisle's "negress" being given the very same beefsteak. All the other slaves present in the shop apparently made a grab for the piece of meat, but, when Scipion followed suit, the butcher stabbed his finger with a knife. The slave, "who appeared offended," must have replied with a stream of abuse to prompt the butcher to insult him and his master in return. Domestic slaves knew that they could take advantage of the social position of prominent masters in their dealings with whites of the lower sort, but the white butcher's retort clearly put Scipion on notice. Whoever his owner was, the slave was not allowed to challenge the tradesman's authority in his own shop. For his part, Mr. de Morand merely asked for financial compensation for lost work owing to Scipion's injured hand. His argument that "everybody has only slaves to serve them" sounded like a disguised apology. He seemed to imply that he was not responsible for the unruly behavior of his slave, which was inherent in his nature. He claimed nevertheless that the butcher should have waited on the slave without manhandling him or insulting his master. The power of money and the market held the potential to blur all social boundaries, in-

38. Rochemore to the minister of the navy, July 12, 1760, ANOM COL C13A 42, fols. 128–130r.

cluding race, yet, as the butcher's reaction demonstrates, people engaged in commercial transactions with one another did not see each other as mere sellers or customers.[39]

Unlike shops, which were run by white merchants and artisans—sometimes with the assistance of enslaved laborers—the levee constituted an interracial place of commerce where slaves were both customers and sellers. Located in front of what would become the intendancy, the levee had become the marketplace as early as 1724, after an episode where a crowd violently seized foodstuffs brought by German farmers from upriver before they could unload their pirogues. The company then institutionalized a formal marketplace that was supervised by soldiers. Dumont de Montigny testified to this close surveillance by authorities: "The settler comes to sell his provisions on it. / If it comes to blows because of a disagreement, / The culprit is immediately brought to jail." On Sundays, distant farmers from the German Coast and the English Turn, either white settlers or free people of color, came to sell their products on the levee, but the location was also used as a marketplace on weekdays. There were no market days officially fixed by local authorities, as was the case for most metropolitan cities. Although the levee was used every day, permanent facilities were apparently not built. Despite a belated project to construct a public covered market on Saint-Louis Street three blocks from the river, where the first barracks had been erected, the levee remained the only marketplace in New Orleans up to the end of the French regime.[40]

As the slave system expanded, slaves became a major feature of the market that took place on the levee, although it did not become the "Negroes market" like the one that operated in Clugny Square in Cap-Français starting in the 1760s. Masters, both within and outside the city, increasingly relied on slaves

39. RSCL 1737/06/03/03.

40. "Arrêt du Conseil Supérieur du 20 septembre 1724 concernant les denrées qu'on apporte à la ville pour vendre," ANOM COL A 23, fol. 49v; Villiers, ed., "L'établissement de la province de la Louisiane," *Journal de la société des américanistes*, XXIII (1931), 307; Rochemore to the minister of the navy, June 22, 1760, ANOM COL C13A 42, fols. 111v–112v; "Copie d'une lettre en réponse écrite à M. de Rochemore par M. de Vergès," ANOM COL C13A 42, fol. 135; "Copie d'une lettre écrite par M. de Rochemore à M. de Vergès ingénieur," ANOM COL C13A 42, fol. 137v; "Plan de La Nouvelle-Orléans," ANOM COL C13A 42, fol. 139r. A map dated 1755 shows the planned location of a "small marketplace" and a "big marketplace." See [Thierry], "Plan de La Nouvelle-Orléans capitale de la province de la Louisiane," 1755, HNOC. For marketplaces in metropolitan France, see Dominique Margairaz, *Foires et marchés dans la France préindustrielle* (Paris, 1988), 169–189.

to buy and sell foodstuffs and other commodities. Sending slaves to engage in market activities on a master's behalf was not seen as poor behavior on the part of owners, even though retailing was a reason for derogation for noblemen. In any case, controlling peddlers was not an easy task for local authorities. As in Europe or in other colonies such as Saint-Domingue, they tried to prohibit the trade of foodstuff brought from the surrounding farms or plantations outside the marketplace. Yet slaves also hawked goods to potential buyers from door to door. During his daily trading trips to the city, Jupiter, who was Pradel's huckster, always visited many private houses to offer his produce, and he sent enslaved children into the barracks to sell vegetables to soldiers since he did not dare to enter their quarters himself. Furthermore, he took advantage of his presence in the city to do many other things besides sell his master's vegetables: he purchased alcohol for the plantation's overseer; he served as a peddler for another white man who gave him one-third of the resulting profits; he sold his own poultry and eggs; he bought food, clothes, and jewelry for himself; and he occasionally stole.[41]

Apart from hucksters who were sent by their masters to trade in the city, other slaves took the initiative to sell their own produce on Sundays. The practice seems to have been fairly common and accepted by authorities and planters, even though it was forbidden by the Code Noir. Unlike what happened in Charleston and other slave societies, where urban markets were dominated by female traders of African descent, men also acted as vendors in the Louisiana capital. One Sunday in 1766, a slave named Paul, a "Creole of Guadeloupe" who grew corn and raised poultry on his individual lot, came to New Orleans to sell his products on the levee. With the money he earned, he bought alcohol and got intoxicated. He also purchased some tobacco and shirts and took advantage of his visits to various shops to steal two handkerchiefs, a snuffbox, and some bills. During his trial, four prominent merchants, who all lived on Royal Street, testified but none were prosecuted for having sold goods to a slave without a certificate from his master, despite the heavy restrictions and constraints on slaves' commercial activities imposed by law.[42]

41. For the slaves' marketplace in Cap-Français, see [Moreau] de Saint-Méry, *Loix et constitutions des colonies françoises de l'Amérique sous le vent*, IV, 535, 639–641, V, 2–3, 150–152. For the prohibition of selling anything outside marketplaces, see "Arrêt du Conseil du Cap, sur la police des marchés," Feb. 7, 1707, in [Moreau] de Saint-Méry, *Loix et constitutions des colonies françoises de l'Amérique sous le vent*, II, 90–91; and Fontaine, *Le marché*, 92–95. On the informal food trade outside authorized marketplaces in France, see Montenach, *Espaces et pratiques du commerce alimentaire*, 80–100.

42. For the role of enslaved women in Charleston's marketplace, see Olwell,

Trading with slaves without proper authorization was considered a serious matter. Articles 15, 16, and 17 of the 1724 Code Noir dealt with the issue of slaves at the marketplace. The Superior Council also promulgated several specific regulations prohibiting slaves from engaging in trade without requisite certificates from their masters both before and after the publication of the code. Authorities were afraid that slaves might be incited to steal from their masters or others. The high level of theft seems to have triggered obsession over potential slave involvement in such crimes, and, from the 1730s, slaves were almost systematically suspected of this felony.[43]

According to the many trials where slaves were brought up on charges of theft, they stole to resell stolen goods or to pay for other goods or services just as much as to meet their immediate needs. In so doing, they participated in an informal market economy that linked slaves, free people of color, soldiers, and other whites of the lower sort. In 1729, François was sent by his master to get some salt at La Goupillon, where he found and stole some bacon (lard). He then exchanged it for tobacco with another slave. Likewise, Sozie was caught on the levee while trying to resell a blanket he had just stolen from the barracks. He had come to the barracks to buy shirts, but the sale did not take place because the slave did not have the cash on him. The soldiers did not believe that he would come back to pay his debt as other servicemen told them that they knew him as a rascal who did not keep his word. Contrary to François, Sozie was not an incidental buyer but regularly participated in this illicit market economy.[44]

Slavery complicated the relationship between sellers and customers, since trade and credit were necessarily based on trust. When Pradel's enslaved peddler Jupiter stood trial for having burgled several urban houses, he perfectly understood the foundations of his social position. Faced with the death penalty, which he ultimately incurred, the slave endeavored to defend himself in the strongest terms possible by dwelling on the "trust" he earned from most whites. Although he did not use the same word as his master, Jupiter's insistence on "trust" echoed Pradel's concern over "credit,"

"'Loose, Idle, and Disorderly,'" in Gaspar and Hine, eds., *More than Chattel*, 97–110. For Paul's trial, see RSCL 1766/07/21/07, 1766/07/23/03, 1766/06/25/01, 1766/06/25/03, 1766/06/25/04, 1766/08/02/04.

43. Various ordinances promulgated by the Superior Council or by the colony's top officials prohibiting commercial transactions with slaves, May 20, 1714, ANOM COL A 23, fol. 4v, Apr. 29, 1723, fols. 38v–39, Nov. 13, 1723, fol. 43, July 20, 1726, fol. 68v.

44. On the merging of the formal and informal trade economy in metropolitan cities, see Montenach, *Espaces et pratiques du commerce alimentaire*. For François's trial, see RSCL 1729/09/05/04. For Sozie's trial, see RSCL 1764/07/17/01, 1764/07/28/01.

when the officer revealed his participation in retail trade in his letters to his brother. In ancien régime societies, credit, reputation, and trust went together.[45]

Pradel himself recognized that he had chosen to trust Jupiter when he made him his peddler. What his slave was doing when he sent him to the city did not interest the planter much. The only thing that mattered was that he "came back with the sum that was expected." Yet trust was not the only component of their relationship; violence also played a major role. Pradel expected Jupiter to come back from the market with a certain amount of money, and, when he failed, Pradel whipped him. As part of his defense, Jupiter told the story of a young female slave who belonged to his master's economic partner. Her owner forced her to swallow the vegetables she had not managed to sell. Jupiter justified his thefts by explaining to the judge that Pradel gave him too much produce and that it was impossible for him to sell all of it; therefore, he had no other choice but to steal to bring back the money his master expected and to avoid violent punishment. Despite the autonomy they enjoyed, enslaved hucksters were no less brutalized and exploited than other plantation slaves working in the fields.[46]

To instill trust in his peddler, Pradel gave Jupiter a certificate stating, first, that he was authorized to sell and buy on his master's behalf and, second, that larger bills could be given to him and that change would be returned. Since there were not enough coins in circulation, people used cash vouchers and card money issued by local authorities as well as private bills and bonds. The certificate also set a limit on the price of commercial transactions that Jupiter could engage in. Although Jupiter's certificate was confiscated by the plantation's overseer one year before the slave was caught, Jupiter admitted that it did not matter, since everybody "trusted" him even without the certificate. It was apparently common for masters not to give one to slaves who served them as hucksters, and, over time, Jupiter had built up interpersonal relationships with his customers. Most people in the city knew him as Pradel's vendor. Still, not all whites trusted Jupiter. The *voyageur* (traveler) Étienne Durantais told the judge of an incident where

45. RSCL 1744/03/21/01; Baillardel and Prioult, eds., *Le chevalier de Pradel*, 96. On the historiographical silence on urban microcircuits of credit in early modern Europe, see Fontaine, *L'économie morale*, 101–133. For a rare study on the subject, see Montenach, *Espaces et pratiques du commerce alimentaire*, 339–350. On the relationships between credit, reputation, and trust in ancien régime societies, see Fontaine, *L'économie morale*; and Pierre Gervais, "Crédit et filière marchandes au XVIIIe siècle," *Annales: Histoire, Sciences Sociales*, LXVII (2012), 1048.

46. RSCL 1744/03/05/01, 1744/03/12/01, 1744/03/21/03, 1744/04/24/01.

Trade, Credit, and Honor

he refused to give Jupiter a bill that the slave had asked for on his master's behalf because he did not trust him and only agreed to give it to him after seeing Pradel in the distance on the levee sending Jupiter back. Likewise, Louis Quesle, a tailor, who served as a witness, told the magistrate that he knew Jupiter because the slave frequently came to the boarding house where he lived to sell his vegetables. He reported that Jupiter always had money and asked him to buy goods all the time, but he added "that he would have sold if he had been in the mood to sell to negroes." Not only did Quesle refuse to purchase vegetables from Jupiter for reasons specific to him, but he was also against trading with slaves on principle. Of course, such a statement might have been a defense against the accusation of exchanging goods with slaves without certificates from their masters, since Jupiter had claimed that he had borrowed money from him and gave him some earrings as guarantee. At the same time, Quesle's statement confirms that the practice of trading with slaves aroused tension and disagreement among whites in Louisiana, as in other slave societies.[47]

While most slaves stole to gain access to money, one used a more exceptional method to reach his ends. During the fall of 1750, the commissaire-ordonnateur was informed that forged bills were circulating among the public. After a quick investigation, he learned that several had been given out by Joseph, a nineteen-year-old "mulatto" slave who belonged to the king. A "Creole of the colony," he was the son of Jean-Baptiste, the enslaved surgeon at the King's Hospital. He had been raised in the medical institution, where he started to work when he was around ten. He was trained as a surgeon and helped to look after sick patients. He also attended whites of the lower sort outside of the hospital. Joseph had forged some bills to pay for cufflinks, garters, and shoe buckles that he had purchased from two transient Spanish passengers and to reclaim the ruffled shirt he had given

47. For Jupiter's trial, see RSCL 1744/03/21/01, 1744/04/24/01. On monetary problems in Louisiana, see N. M. Miller Surrey, *Commerce of Louisiana during the French Regime, 1699–1763* (New York, 1916), 107–125; Clark, *New Orleans, 1718–1812*, 97–154; Giraud, *Histoire de la Louisiane française*, III, 353–356, IV, 321–331; Giraud, *History of French Louisiana*, trans. Pearce, V, 152–154; and Dubé, "Les biens publics," 384–386. On the 1724 Code Noir kept in the Bureau des colonies, commented on by an anonymous author, Article 15, related to this issue, bears the following marginal note: "The settlers neglect to give a certificate or known mark to their slaves." See "Code Noir," March 1724, ANOM COL A 23, fols. 50–57. In Georgia, the debate over whether to allow slaves to participate in the marketplace only developed in the late eighteenth century. See Betty Wood, "'White Society' and the 'Informal' Slave Economies of Lowcountry Georgia, c. 1763–1830," *Slavery and Abolition*, XI (1990), 313–331.

a soldier as a deposit. Since he was a valuable slave, Joseph was not sentenced to the death penalty but ordered to be whipped at all the crossroads of the city and then banished and sold in Saint-Domingue. He was indeed atypical: his literacy, his trade, and the connections he was able to maintain because he cured soldiers and sailors at the King's Hospital set him apart from most urban slaves.[48]

Slaves like Jupiter or Joseph often took part in a system of pawnbroking with soldiers and other poor whites. In 1743, a free black named Jean-Baptiste, who worked as an indentured servant for a military officer heavily involved in all kinds of commercial activities, acknowledged that he had pawned shirts for forty livres to a soldier because he needed money. Pawnbroking was an operation of credit that worked through sale and repurchase and was commonly practiced among the lower sort and in cities in Europe. The person who needed money sold a commodity at a price below its value and committed to buying it back some time later at a price that corresponded to the capital plus interest. Since the buyer, or creditor, was in a position to impose a lower price, the seller, or debtor, was in a position of dependency that was moral as well as economic. At first sight, soldiers and slaves might have appeared socially close, as the former often agreed to engage in a pawning system with the latter. However, far from representing a form of solidarity and cooperation, the practice helped servicemen to maintain their social superiority over free and enslaved people of color, causing the latter to be obliged to them.[49]

Whites were less at risk than slaves when they engaged in illicit trade with the latter. The prosecution and sentencing of settlers for having traded with slaves without a certificate from their master varied greatly over time and with the social position of the defenders. According to the Code Noir, offenders could be sentenced to a heavy fine and incur criminal charges, but few whites were sued for this offense. When they were, they were only sentenced to a fine. In 1744, the white couple who sold some jewelry to Jupiter only had to pay fifty livres. Yet, in the 1760s, at the time of the repressive campaign against slaves who ran away and stole, royal justice came to show less leniency. In 1766, a destitute couple was sentenced to pay a fine

48. Michel to the minister of the navy, May 18, 1751, ANOM COL C13A 35, fols. 205–210r; "Procédure contre Joseph esclave mulâtre chirurgien à l'hôpital du roi ayant falsifié des billets à partir du 30 novembre 1750, joint à la lettre de Michel du 18 mai 1751," ANOM COL F3 243, fols. 48–74.

49. For Jean-Baptiste's interrogatory, see RSCL 1743/08/19/03. On pawnbroking in metropolitan France, see Fontaine, L'économie morale, 101–133.

of twenty livres to the king and to lifetime banishment from the colony for selling tafia to slaves and taking some turkeys stolen from the commissaire-ordonnateur in exchange.[50]

Two generations after New Orleans's founding, the engagement of slaves in commercial activities to earn money on their own account had become common and was widely accepted among settlers. Already by midcentury, Dumont de Montigny had reported that the slaves who "reside in the capital or in the surroundings ordinarily take advantage of the two hours of rest they are given at noon to pick up firewood that they then sell in town; others sell ashes, or fruit from the countryside when it is the season. Some of these negroes have done so well that they have earned enough to purchase their freedom, and have opened plantations in imitation of the French in this province." This extract is the only allusion to a practice that was strictly forbidden by the Code Noir. Among the additions made to the 1685 code before it was promulgated in the Mississippi colony in 1724, one concerned the manumission of slaves. Article 50 of the Louisiana code authorized owners to free their slaves but imposed some new restrictions: "And yet, as some masters are mercenary enough to set a price on their slaves' freedom, which prompts slaves to steal and plunder, no person, whatever his rank and condition, shall be permitted to set his slaves free, without obtaining a decree of permission to that effect from the Superior Council." Despite the prohibition on slaves paying to purchase their own freedom, this practice must have thrived with the demographic and economic growth of the port city and could explain the number of quasi-free people who lived in New Orleans and its surroundings by the end of the French regime. Urban circumstances favored the participation of slaves in the market and cash economy. With the money they earned, the ultimate investment they could make was their own freedom.[51]

Just as commerce greatly contributed to shaping and transforming New Orleans's society, it was also the mainspring of the 1768 revolt against the first Spanish governor. Although many American colonies experienced one or several changes of sovereignty, Louisiana is the only one where a diplomatic cession was followed by an uprising. Exceptional circumstances

---

50. RSCL 1744/03/10/01, 1744/03/21/01, 1744/03/21/05; 1766/11/14/01, 1766/11/14/02, 1766/11/20/04.

51. Dumont [de Montigny], *Mémoires historiques sur la Louisiane,...*, [ed. Jean-Baptiste Le Mascrier], 2 vols. (Paris, 1753), II, 243; "Code Noir," March 1724, ANOM COL B 43, fols. 388–407.

might partly explain this uncommon event. The treaties of Fontainebleau and Paris divided Louisiana between the Spanish and the English in 1762–1763, but the former did not arrive in New Orleans until 1766, whereas the latter immediately took possession of the left bank. Even then, the first Spanish governor Ulloa delayed holding a formal ceremony imposing the sovereignty of the Catholic Monarchy on the former French colony owing to a lack of military force. For several years, the French captain Charles Philippe Aubry, who had acted as governor since February 1765, ruled the colony "in the name of the king of France ... as if it belonged to the king of Spain." In this highly ambiguous political context, aggravated by a heavy financial crisis, the Spanish promulgated a new ordinance forbidding settlers to trade freely with metropolitan France and the French Antilles. In response, a large section of the Louisiana capital's white population and that of its surroundings, headed by the magistrates of the Superior Council and other members of the elite, rose up in revolt. In a few days, without causing bloodshed, they expelled Ulloa.[52]

Commercial issues were what both sparked and kept the fire of rebellion going for months. The insurgents' main demand was "freedom of trade." They denounced the restrictions and prohibitions imposed on the transatlantic trade with metropolitan France and the French Antilles, the slave trade within the whole Caribbean basin, and the local Indian trade as forms of bondage. Since these infringements potentially affected everybody, from the most prosperous merchant engaged in maritime trade to the most destitute soldier bartering his pay in goods with local Native Americans, around six hundred persons, out of a total population of around fifteen hundred white civilian inhabitants, signed the initial petition to the Superior Council. Directly or indirectly, the mercantile sector sustained most of the colonial population. The merchants and the rest of the elites, among whom the leaders of the uprising were recruited, were defending their own economic interests and, more broadly, those of the whole colony. The cession and its consequences not only imperiled Louisiana's economic and financial situation but also shook the sociopolitical organization on which it was founded.

52. Charles Philippe Aubry to the minister of the navy, Jan. 20, 1768, ANOM COL C13A 48, fol. 8r; Carl A. Brasseaux, *Denis-Nicolas Foucault and the New Orleans Rebellion of 1768* (Ruston, La., 1987); David Ker Texada, *Alejandro O'Reilly and the New Orleans Rebels* (Lafayette, La., 1970); John Preston Moore, *Revolt in Louisiana: The Spanish Occupation, 1766–1770* (Baton Rouge, La., 1976); Marc de Villiers du Terrage, *Les dernières années de la Louisiane française: Le Chevalier de Kerlérec, D'Abbadie-Aubrey, Laussat* (Paris, [1903]).

Trade, Credit, and Honor

The shock of the cession must have been felt all the more violently as the king was a central economic actor.[53]

The consensus among the colonial population over the role commerce should play within the socioeconomic system, however, was not universal. After Ulloa had been expelled and the insurgents were in the midst of creating an independent republic, an anonymous author reported that he had left the city for his plantation because he could not:

> suffer anymore the tedious acts of bravado of so many dumpy shop-keepers who make a hundred European families bemoan the complete loss of their fortune that they dissipate in this colony with a degree of smugness and arrogance which would revolt the most in-different and phlegmatic person, indeed we see now some parvenu craftsmen who fight with prominent people for the consideration due to their rank and position; all the estates are mixed, everything is in a state of indescribable chaos and disorder; the vilest dregs of the people believe that they can demand satisfaction from officers and other distinguished persons, for the contempt in which we hold their testimony and their temerity to vote on all kinds of matters in general; these poor people want to pass off as doctors and create, so to speak, a new world; they draw up plans for legislation to which they want to submit this colony.

The man, who was very likely a military officer, despised the leaders of the revolt, whom he compared to shopkeepers. Inveighing against their modest social backgrounds, he condemned their engagement in trade, retailing

53. For the rebels' complaints about "freedom of trade," see "Arrêt du Conseil supérieur," Oct. 29, 1768, ANOM COL C13A 48, fols. 233v–244v; "Mémoire des habitants et négociants de la Louisiane sur l'événement du 29 octobre 1768," ANOM COL C13A 48, fols. 245v–255v; "Représentations du Conseil supérieur au roi," Nov. 12, 1768, ANOM COL C13A 48, fols. 149v–158v; "Le Conseil supérieur au ministre de la Marine," Nov. 22, 1768, ANOM COL C13A 48, fols. 195v–199r; "Les habitants de la Louisiane au ministre," Mar. 20, 1769, ANOM COL C13A 49, fol. 190; "Observations du Conseil supérieur de la province de la Louisiane faite au Parlement séant à Paris," 1768, Favrot Papers, S-3; "Mémoire sur la révolution arrivée à la Louisiane le 29 octobre 1768 pour être présenté à son A.R. Monseigneur le duc d'Orléans," 1768, Favrot Papers, S-4; and "Lettre des habitants, négociants, et colons de la Louisiane à Monseigneur le duc d'Orléans," 1768, Favrot Papers, S-6. On the support of the revolt, see Aubry to the minister of the navy, Nov. 25, 1768, ANOM COL C13A 48, fols. 24, 28v; Aubry to the minister of the navy, Dec. 23–24, 1768, ANOM COL C13A 48, fol. 40r; and Copy of the letter by Aubry to Alejandro O'Reilly, Aug. 20, 1769, ANOM COL C13A 49, fol. 32v.

in particular, as a degrading activity incompatible with their pretensions to political leadership and authority, and he lamented the perturbations caused by the insurrection to the traditional social order, the confounding of ranks, and the mixing of estates in particular. Not all local elites were in agreement with the social preeminence acquired by merchants by the end of the French regime or the way commerce was increasingly becoming an honorable estate in the colony, a process that imperiled the ancien régime culture.[54]

Slaves might have developed their own critical point of view on the rebellion, for slavery was another object of contention with the Spanish governor. Among other grievances, leaders of the revolt condemned the mixed marriage that Ulloa's personal chaplain celebrated between a white Spaniard and a black slave, the refuge offered to fugitive slaves, and the protection given to "negroes who have not been maimed." The Superior Council described mixed marriage as a "humiliation" to the "French nation" and summarized their complaints for the king, claiming "Your subjects were threatened with slavery, and their negroes were acquiring the status of free men." Such laments very likely explain why enslaved and free people of color do not seem to have taken part in the rebellion. Given the close ties the French had maintained with nearby Spanish settlements and possible interactions with the slaves who arrived with the first Spanish officials and settlers in 1766, Louisiana's population of African descent might have been aware that, thanks to the system of *coartacion* (a legal mechanism enabling slaves to enter into an agreement with their masters to acquire their freedom for a fixed price with installments paid over a set period of time), freedom could be more easily purchased under Spanish rule. As the Spanish, unlike the French, did not prohibit the possibility of redeeming oneself, slaves might have forged for themselves another interpretation of what "freedom of trade" meant.[55]

54. Favrot Papers, S-7 (1768).

55. The Code Noir authorized masters to punish their slaves, but they were forbidden to torture, mutilate, or kill them. On the rebels' complaints about Ulloa's actions related to racial slavery, see "Mémoire des habitants et négociants de la Louisiane sur l'événement du 29 octobre 1768," ANOM COL C13A 48, fol. 252r; and "Représentations du Conseil supérieur au roi," Nov. 12, 1768, ANOM COL C13A 48, fol. 154v. See also Cécile Vidal, "Francité et situation coloniale: Nation, empire, et race en Louisiane française (1699–1769)," *Annales: Histoire, Sciences Sociales*, LXIII (2009), 1019–1050.

Trade, Credit, and Honor

CHAPTER EIGHT

Lash of the Tongue, Lash of the Whip

The Formation and Transformation of
Racial Categories and Practices

In 1768, a *"garçon charretier"* ("carter boy") named Jean-Pierre Phénard boldly proclaimed to three upper-class men with whom he was engaged in a dispute that justice in Louisiana was in the service of everybody. The incident took place just outside New Orleans on a spring day. Wanting to go on a picnic lunch in the countryside, Sieur Saint-Pé, a merchant, and Sieurs Lacoste and Milhet, two ship's officers, secured transportation in carts from Phénard and a soldier named Maréchal. After journeying to a *"métairie"* (a small farm) on the other side of the Bayou Saint John, they asked the two carters to wait for them to help them cross the bayou on their return. In the meantime, Phénard and Maréchal had more than a few drinks, as did, apparently, the merchant and the ship's officers. On the latter's return, they got into an argument with Maréchal, prompting Phénard to intervene. He threatened to report the way they abused the serviceman to Mr. de Grand-maison, the *major* of New Orleans. Declaring that they could care less about Mr. de Grandmaison, the three men set on Phénard with their canes, then ordered him to drive them back to the city. When Phénard refused, shouting that he would not transport any "bugger," they started beating him again, but he managed to flee to the other side of the bayou, leaving his rig behind him. The three men told the slaves who were accompanying them to drive the cart, crossed the bayou, and abandoned the vehicle. Meeting with them again near the city, Phénard asked them who would be answerable for his horses and equipment. According to a witness, "Sieur Lacoste replied 'I am not the keeper of your cart, you yokel'"; he then "took his cane and told him 'you have not yet found your criminal judge,' to which Phénard retorted that 'justice would decide, that it was made for him as for everybody.'" Once again, the three men attacked the carter, this time with their fists and a sword. He only managed to escape when some bystanders stepped in, an indication that they disapproved of the violence.[1]

The affair led to a trial, for Phénard sought to obtain justice and procure damages. He was the main plaintiff, but Jean-Louis Vills, a thirty-year-old mason, also made a request on behalf of his mother, Phénard's mistress. She owned the lost cart with its four horses, and Phénard was her indentured servant. Since the fight, he had lain dangerously ill. She asked for reimbursement for the equipage as well as Phénard's daily takings, three to four piastres a day, until such time as he recovered. Unlike slaves, poor whites had the right to sue men of the upper class, who, consequently, could not always get away with using violent behavior to assert their social superiority. By contrast, the enslaved domestics who had accompanied the merchant and ship's officers were barely mentioned by the parties involved on either side and were not even asked to testify, contrary to many white witnesses, despite being present throughout the event. They were excluded from the judicial arena by their status and race.[2]

Forty years earlier, Ursuline Marie Madeleine Hachard had already begun to interrogate the question of equality before Louisiana's judicial system. Commenting on the Superior Council's efforts to curb the debauchery and disorder that prevailed in the late 1720s with the summary exercise of justice, she exclaimed: "A thief is tried in two days, he is hanged or punished on the wheel, White, Savage or Negro there is no distinction or mercy." The nun evidently expected magistrates to dispense justice in a prejudiced way, which they did in the kingdom, and registered astonishment when they did

1. Metairie has become the name of a district on the southern shore of Lake Pontchartrain. Milhet was very likely one of the two brothers who featured among the leaders of the 1768 revolt. On transportation by carts between the lake, the bayou, and the city, see Dumont de Montigny, *Regards sur le monde atlantique, 1715-1747,* transcribed by Carla Zecher (Sillery, Quebec, 2008), 204. For the narrative of the incident between Jean-Pierre Phénard and the three men from the upper and middle class, see RSCL 1768/05/13/01 (quotation), 1768/05/16/01, 1768/05/18/02 (quotation), 1768/05/19/03.

2. On Jean-Louis Vills, see "Padron y lista de las quatro compañias de milicianos y habitantes en la ciudad por quarterles, segun revista passada en 27 de Mayo 1766," AGI, Audiencia de Sto Domingo, Luisiana y Florida, Años 1766 a 1770, 2595−588; "Milices Nelle Orléans, le 25 janvier 1770," AGI, Correspondencia de los Gobernadores de la Luisiana y la Florida Occidental, Años 1766–1824, Session Papeles de Cuba, legajo 188-A, and "État des quatre compagnies de milice de La Nouvelle-Orléans, 12 février 1770." For the complete trial on Phénard's behalf, see RSCL 1768/05/11/02, 1768/05/13/01, 1768/05/13/03, 1768/05/16/01, 1768/05/16/02, 1768/05/16/03, 1768/05/18/02, 1768/05/19/01, 1768/05/19/02, 1768/05/19/03, 1768/05/19/04, 1768/05/19/05, 1768/05/19/06, 1768/05/19/07, 1768/05/30/01.

not. Nevertheless, rather than class or gender distinctions, she emphasized racial differences among culprits. On the one hand, her letter indicates that race had already become the most important fault line at the heart of white settlers' conception of the social order; on the other, it reveals that, although clearly a topic of debate, an obvious relationship did not yet exist between racial discrimination and racial nomination, categorization, and identification. A comparison between her description of the judicial system in 1728 and the trial in 1768 also highlights transformations in the way people of African descent were treated by the judicial system over the course of the French regime. What took place that could explain why magistrates prosecuted everyone at the beginning of the period equally yet shifted at some point to start predominately taking action against the enslaved?[3]

The field of justice seems to suggest a hardening of the racial regime, whereas that of military defense conveys, at first sight, the opposite impression. Introduced by the Code Noir, the categories "freed" or "free negro," like "white," "savage," and "negro," were already in circulation very early on. The royal edict granted freed slaves the same rights as French "naturals" (nationals) but asked them to show respect to their former masters and provisioned severe punishment if they stole or helped runaways. It also prohibited mixed marriages and donations made by whites to free blacks. The law presumed that a natural solidarity existed between free and enslaved people of color and sought to create a racial divide among persons of free status. Therefore, it is not surprising that, while local authorities used free and enslaved people of color for military support in times of war, they never envisioned integrating free blacks within white militia units. By the end of the French period, they had nevertheless established a free colored militia company. In so doing, they helped free black men to distinguish themselves from slaves and included them in the economy of honor. Racial discrimination seems to have relaxed somewhat for free people of color by the close of the Seven Years' War, though they remained segregated from whites. The system of racial domination underwent, not so much a loosening, but a more complex transformation.

Looking simultaneously at the evolution of the language of race and the racialization of both the judicial and militia systems raises questions

3. For the Ursuline's statement, see "Lettre à la Nouvelle Orleans, ce vingt-quatrième avril 1728," in [Marie Madeleine] Hachard, *Relation du voyage des dames religieuses ursulines de Rouen à La Nouvelle-Orléans* (1728) (Paris, 1872), 96–97. For justice in metropolitan France, see Benoît Garnot, *Histoire de la justice: France, XVIe–XXIe siècle* (Paris, 2009), 157–171.

about how racial categories were formed, inhabited, and refashioned over time. It challenges the idea that race is above all a language or a discourse, even though the words used to designate racialized individuals or groups also have a history. The same racial categories can give birth to very different racial regimes depending on the forms of discrimination, exploitation, and violence with which they are associated. Like racial vocabulary, these practices never cease to shift with changing local and global circumstances. Moreover, the degree of oppression and severity of a racial regime cannot be measured by a single factor. Different dimensions of racialization need to be examined together.[4]

In New Orleans, representations of the social order that fueled the language of race both informed and were shaped by a discriminatory system of public justice that increasingly targeted slaves as well as by the exclusion of free blacks from institutions established for the colony's military defense and the belated creation of a segregated free colored militia company. Physical violence—the lash of the whip—and symbolic violence—the lash of the tongue—combined to produce, reproduce, and transform the system of racial domination throughout the French regime. When the Spanish took over Louisiana in the late 1760s, they found a society in which race was more firmly embedded than in the 1720s. At the same time, the racial regime in constant flux fostered more tensions and contradictions.

"WHITE, SAVAGE OR NEGRO": THE LANGUAGE OF RACE AND THE BIRACIAL ORDER

In 1763, Nicolas Verret, an inhabitant of New Orleans, stated in his testimony regarding a settler's murder that, when a rumor circulated within New Orleans about a corpse that had been found on an island, "He ran to the place with many other people, negroes and savages and whites." He described the urban population according to a ternary divide based on race and ethnicity, a vision of the social order that, as Hachard's comment demonstrates, had prevailed since the early days of the port city. Institutional

---

4. This chapter draws on both work by Ann Laura Stoler and criticisms that have been made regarding her approach to race. See Stoler, "Racial Histories and Their Regimes of Truth," *Political Power and Social Theory*, XI (1997), 183–206; and Loïc J. D. Wacquant, "For an Analytic of Racial Domination," *Political Power and Social Theory*, XI (1997), 221–234. On the necessary "social etymologies" that "trace the career of words" in imperial formations, see Stoler and Carole McGranahan, "Introduction: Refiguring Imperial Terrains," in Stoler, McGranahan, and Peter C. Perdue, eds., *Imperial Formations* (Santa Fe, N.Mex., 2007), 4; and Stoler, *Along the Archival Grain: Epistemic Anxieties and Colonial Common Sense* (Princeton, N.J., 2009), 35.

and social actors who lived in Louisiana did not invent racial categories such as *"nègres"* ("negroes"), *"sauvages"* ("savages"), *"blancs"* ("whites"), or *"mulâtres"* ("mulattoes"), nor the race-thinking that these categories reflected and enacted. From the start, they had at their disposal the instruments of racial domination—not only the language but also the law—that had already been forged in the metropole and in the Antilles to respond to the formation of slave societies in the islands. Under the influence of the Caribbean, race and status quickly became the primary markers of identification. This process of racialization affected all three populations brought into contact with one another by the colonial situation—European, African, and Native American—albeit in different ways. Whiteness was constructed in relation to both blackness and "savageness" as well as in reaction to *métissage* and the rise of a population of free people of color, two phenomena which blurred the boundaries that racial categories sought to create. Yet, by the 1760s, free blacks were still viewed as an anomaly that only slowly started to disturb what had amounted to a biracial order—whites and blacks—for much of the French regime, despite the common use of three major racial categories ("blancs," "nègres," "sauvages").[5]

In New Orleans, the presence of Native Americans coming from nearby indigenous villages or from further away remained significant throughout the eighteenth century. In contrast, only a few Native slaves lived in the city permanently, and their number rapidly decreased. As had been the case since the beginning of French colonization in North America, Native Americans, either enslaved or free and independent, were sometimes called *"Indiens"* ("Indians") but more often "sauvages." The latter category emphasized cultural differences and conveyed the idea that indigenous people could be civilized. From the early eighteenth century, a third category, "red," based on color, also appeared in travel accounts and administrative correspondence dealing with French-Native interactions in Indian Country. The military officer Jean-Bernard Bossu often labeled Natives as "red men" when he wrote about diplomatic and military relationships. He also mentioned a "red woman," a "swarthy, or red ... slave," and a "red or copper-skinned mother" in reference to wet-nursing, alluding to the impurity of blood, and with regard to mixed unions, reporting stories of indigenous women giving birth to twins, one being white and the other black. For him, "red" was not only a color but also a racial category.[6]

5. RSCL 1763/07/04/05.
6. For the naming of Native Americans in New France, see Olive Patricia Dickason,

Bossu's hesitation in the way he qualified Natives' skin color suggests that the use of the category "red" did not originate with the French. First Nations probably forged the label themselves, albeit without a racial connotation. Adapting previous indigenous conceptions of human diversity in reaction to the arrival and settlement of Europeans in their midst, they resorted to color vocabulary, juxtaposing "white," "black," and "red," to make sense of their sociopolitical position toward the newcomers. In 1725, Father Raphaël, the first superior of the Capuchins, visited the Taensa living in the vicinity of New Orleans to preach the gospel. He reported that one chief explained his enthusiasm for conversion by way of a tale accounting for man's place in the world based on differences of color:

> Long ago,... there were three men in a cave, one white, one red, and one black, the white man went out first and he took the good road that led him to a fine hunting ground.... The red man who is the savage, for they call themselves in their language red men, went out of the cave second, he went astray from the good road and took another which led him into a country where the hunting was less abundant. The black man, who is the negro, having been the third to go out, got entirely lost in a very bad country in which he did not find anything on which to live. Since that time the red man and the black man have been looking for the white man to show them the way to the good road. That is more or less the traditional fable of our Indians, which may have some foundation in the story of the three sons of Noah, as they have some knowledge of the Flood.

Le mythe du sauvage, trans. Jude Des Chênes (1995; rpt. Paris, 1993); and Cornelius J. Jaenen, "'Les Sauvages Ameriquains': Persistence into the 18th Century of Traditional French Concepts and Constructs for Comprehending Amerindians," *Ethnohistory*, XXIX (1982), 43–56. For the use of "red" to describe Natives in Louisiana's travel accounts and administrative correspondence, see Jennifer M. Spear, "Colonial Intimacies: Legislating Sex in French Louisiana," *William and Mary Quarterly*, 3d Ser., LX (2003), 95; and Gilles Havard, "'Nous ne ferons plus qu'un peuple': Le métissage en Nouvelle-France à l'époque de Champlain," in Guy Martinière and Didier Poton, eds., *Le Nouveau Monde et Champlain* (Paris, 2008), 93–94. On the use of racial categories to designate Indians in British North America, see Alden T. Vaughan, "From White Man to Redskin: Changing Anglo-American Perceptions of the American Indian," *American Historical Review*, LXXXVII (1982), 917–953. For Bossu's usage of "red" man or woman, see [Jean-Bernard] Bossu, *Nouveaux voyages aux Indes occidentales ...*, 2 vols. (Paris, 1768), I, 40, 68, 71, 137, 139, 159, 201; and Bossu, *Nouveaux voyages dans l'Amérique septentrionale ...* (Amsterdam, 1777), I, 194, 214, 345.

The Taensa understood and tried to manipulate the conception of the colonial order that French authorities and settlers sought to implement. Father Raphaël, for his part, read the story through biblical history, sharing in the debate about the origins of Native Americans that had begun with the European conquest of the New World. Since he had to provide translations for "red" and "black," they must have been Native categories. The French always labeled indigenous men and women living within New Orleans as "savages" in the censuses, parish registers, notarial deeds, and court records.[7]

In contrast, slaves of African descent were hardly ever called "blacks." They were generally described as "nègres" or *"nègres esclaves"* ("enslaved negroes"). The term *"noir"* ("black") was not widespread, although it was inscribed in the title and content of the Code Noir. It also surfaces in one of the first reports written by a Company of the Indies director in 1721: "It was stated that in the whole colony of Louisiana there may be around 6,000 French persons and 600 blacks"; or, "It would be opportune to send the royal ordinance, which was promulgated to contain blacks in the French islands of America, so that it could be followed for the blacks in Louisiana." Moreover, when slaves were identified, their status was not always mentioned. Instead of being qualified as a "nègre esclave" or *"mulâtre esclave"* ("enslaved mulatto"), as customary, a color term, or degree of métissage, like nègre" or "mulâtre," was sometimes employed alone. Still, the use of "nègre" implicitly indicated an enslaved person, as evidenced by the expression *"nègre mulâtre"* ("mulatto negro"), which appears in a few baptism certificates and in court records. "Nègre" was first a depreciatory color term applying to people of African descent without any white ancestry, but "nègre" could also mean "slave." When the term was combined with "mulâtre," which meant a person of mixed descent, "nègre" indicated an en-

7. For the tale told by the Taensa chief, see Father Raphaël to Abbé Raguet, May 15, 1725, ANOM COL C13A 8, fols. 404v–405r. The administrative correspondence includes other discourses by Native American chiefs using the same expression "red men." See, for instance, "Joint à la lettre de M. de Rochemore, parole pour la nation tchatka de la part de Tchacta Youtakty matachito père des hommes rouges et grand ami des Tchactas," June 22, 1760, ANOM COL F3 25, fols. 142–144. For a detailed analysis of Father Raphaël's letter, see Nancy Shoemaker, "How Indians Got to Be Red," *American Historical Review*, CII (1997), 624–644 (partial translation of quotation, 627); and Shoemaker, *A Strange Likeness: Becoming Red and White in Eighteenth-Century North America* (Oxford, 2004). For the debate on Native Americans' origins, see Giuliano Gliozzi, *Adam et le Nouveau Monde: La naissance de l'anthropologie comme idéologie coloniale; Des généalogies bibliques aux théories raciales (1500–1700)* (Lecques, France, 2000).

slaved status. This linguistic practice conveyed the idea that most people of African and mixed descent were or must be slaves.[8]

Racial labels referring to a person's color or degree of métissage were in use in Louisiana from the earliest days of settlement. Besides "nègre," the most common racial category employed to identify people of African or mixed descent, either enslaved or free, was "mulâtre." At the beginning of the period, the term was also occasionally used alternatively alongside *"métis"* to indicate the offspring of French-Native couples. "Mulatto" even cropped up before New Orleans's founding in local authorities' correspondence with the minister of the navy in relation to a debate about French-Native marriages. In 1715, *Commissaire-ordonnateur* Jean-Baptiste Dubois-Duclos opposed missionary Henri Roulleaux de La Vente's proposal to authorize and encourage such alliances out of concern for "the alteration such marriages would cause in the whiteness and purity of blood of the children; since, whatever M. de La Vente says, experience reveals every day that the children born from that kind of marriage are extremely swarthy, so much so that, if French men and women were no longer to come to Louisiana, the colony would become a colony of mulattoes who are naturally lazy, dissolute scoundrels, as those from Peru and Mexico and other Spanish colonies demonstrate." The commissaire-ordonnateur linked having a non-white phenotype with pejorative moral traits, essentializing mixed-blood individuals. Natives were increasingly viewed through the lens of race-thinking.[9]

Over time, "mulâtre" started to be reserved for the offspring of interracial unions between people of European and African descent. The term

8. For the use of the category "black," see "Code noir ... donné à Versailles au mois de mars 1724," ANOM COL A 22, fols. 110–128; and "Mémoire de Charles LeGac cy devant directeur pour la Compagnie des Indes à la Louisiane," 1721, Manuscrits de la Bibliothèque de l'Institut de France, MS 487 Mélanges historiques, Recueil A, fols. 508–559, esp. fols. 540, 549. For the use of the expression "nègre mulâtre" in a few baptism certificates and in the court records, see AANO, Saint-Louis Cathedral Baptisms 1744–1753, 1753–1759, 01/25/1746, 11/26/1750, 12/30/1755, 03/14/1756; and RSCL 1743/09/04/01.

9. Jean-Baptiste Dubois-Duclos to the minister of the navy, Dec. 25, 1715, ANOM COL C13A 3, fols. 815–820. On the racialization of Native Americans, see Guillaume Aubert, "'The Blood of France': Race and Purity of Blood in the French Atlantic World," *William and Mary Quarterly*, LXI (2004), 439–478; Havard, "'Nous ne ferons plus qu'un peuple,'" in Martinière and Poton, eds., *Le Nouveau Monde et Champlain*, 85–107; Spear, "Colonial Intimacies," *William and Mary Quarterly*, LX (2003), 75–98; and Saliha Belmessous, "Assimilation and Racialism in Seventeenth and Eighteenth-Century French Colonial Policy," *American Historical Review*, CX (2005), 322–349.

was pervasive in administrative correspondence as well as all other kinds of documentation. The introduction of "mulâtre" in the sacramental records from the mid-1720s onward was followed very quickly by the inclusion of a column counting "mulatto slaves" in the New Orleans census of 1732. Following the example of the church, the state concerned itself with the progression of métissage early on. The category was mobilized not only by churchmen and administrators but also by notaries. In New Orleans, the latter seem to have systematically mentioned the color or degree of métissage in cases of both slaves and free blacks, while, in the Lesser Antilles, notaries were only compelled to add racial labels after the names of free people of color starting in the 1770s.[10]

Requests, interrogatories, and testimonies in court records reveal that a person's color or degree of métissage quickly became inescapable identifiers in New Orleans's society. From the late 1730s, the term "mulâtre" occurs repeatedly in the narratives of defendants and witnesses, both slaves and settlers: "left his plantation with a Spanish mulatto"; "Lamoureux shot some negroes and mulattoes he claims to have found fishing"; "has learnt from a slave named François, mulatto negro"; "it was Mr. de La Chaise's mulatto who arrested him"; "having seen a young mulatto"; "he sold it to her at the mulatto Marie Louise's instigation"; "had an affair with a mulatto woman ... unaware that his master had also an affair with her"; "the negro ... grabbed a stick from the hands of a mulatto"; "Marcelain left Sr. Robles and wanted to attack the mulatto with a knife"; "a mulatto named Jos belonging to Sr. Stuart woke him up"; "has learnt that Sieur Desruisseau put a mulatto woman to whom the negro was attached on an island"; "his son called Pierre and three mulattoes played together"; "Mr. Foucault's mulatto who was seated told him that it was his son who ... made the negro woman fall." "Mulâtre" was a category used in everyday language, and both settlers and slaves apparently paid attention not only to the status of the individuals

10. The first instance of the label "mulâtre" has been found in burial registers for 1726 and baptism registers for 1730, but the sacramental records are incomplete. See "Extraits des registres pour les inhumations de l'église paroissiale de La Nouvelle-Orléans," 07/03/1726, ANOM COL G1 412, and "Extraits des registres pour les baptêmes de l'église paroissiale de La Nouvelle-Orléans," 01/16/1730. On the racial categorization of free people of color in the Antilles, see Léo Élisabeth, *La société martiniquaise aux XVIIe et XVIIIe siècles, 1664-1789* (Paris, 2003), 413; Stewart R. King, *Blue Coat or Powdered Wig: Free People of Color in Pre-Revolutionary Saint Domingue* (Athens, Ga., 2001), 8; and Frédéric Régent, "Couleur, statut juridique, et niveau social à Basse-Terre (Guadeloupe) à la fin de l'Ancien Régime (1789-1792)," in Jean-Luc Bonniol, ed., *Paradoxes du métissage*, (Paris, 2001), 41-42.

they interacted with or talked about but also to their racial categorization as a matter of course.[11]

Preoccupation with a person's color or degree of métissage was particularly acute in parish registers, leading the church to introduce an even greater variety of racial categories than those recorded by state authorities. In addition to "nègre" and "mulâtre," the more elaborate racial taxonomy developed by missionaries included two other terms: *"quarteron"* ("quadroon"), indicating a third degree of métissage, between whites and blacks, and *"griffe"* ("sambo"), pertaining to unions between people of Native American and African descent. These racial terms were specified on baptism certificates in conjunction with the increase of métissage in the colony, or, at least, authorities', missionaries', and settlers' perception of the practice (Tables 5 and 6).[12]

Although the vocabulary of métissage throughout the American colonies drew its inspiration from the one first developed in the Spanish Americas, the taxonomy used in French New Orleans—"nègre," "mulâtre," "quarteron," "métis," "griffe"—was to a large extent based on that of Saint-Domingue. In Martinique and Guadeloupe, a child born to a white and a "nègre" or *"négresse"* was called a *"métis(se),"* that of a white and a "métis(se)," a "quarteron," and that of a "nègre" or "négresse" and a "mulâtre" or *"mulâtresse,"* a *"câpre."* In eighteenth-century Spanish colonies and, later, Spanish Louisiana, the words *"pardo"* (light-skinned) and *"moreno"* (dark-skinned) were preferred to "mulatto" and "negro," which first emerged in the sixteenth century and inspired the vocabulary of the French West Indies in the seventeenth century. Racial categories used in New Orleans in the first half of the eighteenth century, however, were less numerous than in the Antilles (the West Indian terms *"tierceron,"* a person born to a white and a "quadroon";

11. RSCL 1739/11/07/02, 1741/01/11/01, 1742/03/13/01, 1743/09/10/03, 1743/09/04/01, 1744/09/01/01, 1764/07/06/02, 1765/09/09/02, 1765/10/11/02, 1765/11/13/01, 1766/06/04/03, 1766/06/05/01, 1766/06/05/03, 1766/06/05/04, 1766/09/10/01, 1767/04/25/01, 1767/07/04/01, 1767/07/11/01, 1768/08/05/01.

12. For a limited use of the New Orleans sacramental records to study racial categorization and métissage, see Thomas N. Ingersoll, *Mammon and Manon in Early New Orleans: The First Slave Society in the Deep South, 1718–1819* (Knoxville, Tenn., 1999), 111–115, 139–140; Spear, "Colonial Intimacies," *William and Mary Quarterly*, LX (2003), 92–94; and Jennifer M. Spear, *Race, Sex, and Social Order in Early New Orleans* (Baltimore, 2009), 79–82, 97–99. For more details on the way missionaries recorded racial categories in sacramental records, see Cécile Vidal, "Caribbean Louisiana: Church, *Métissage*, and the Language of Race in the Mississippi Colony during the French Period," in Vidal, ed., *Louisiana: Crossroads of the Atlantic World* (Philadelphia, 2014), 125–146.

"mamelouk," a person born to a white and a "métis"; and *"sang-mêlé,"* a person of "mixed-blood," were absent), in part because slaves had only been in the colony in great numbers for less than two generations. The categories were also more confused because slaves could be of either African or Native American descent. Racial taxonomy in the Mississippi colony nonetheless partook of the same racist and discriminatory conceptions toward nonwhites as in the Caribbean and elsewhere.[13]

It is difficult to determine how New Orleans priests acquired this racial vocabulary and consciousness. Little information is available on their origins, with the exception of Father Raphaël. They were the first Capuchins from the province of Champagne to serve in an overseas colony, since those in the West Indies came from the province of Normandy. Yet missionaries from the islands and the continent apparently had some contact. In one diatribe against the Jesuits, Father Raphaël—who had arrived in the colony on *La Galathée,* which stopped on its way from France at Cap-Français in 1723—explained that he had himself seen that they gave some parishes in Saint-Domingue to vessel's chaplains because they lacked missionaries. Likewise, in the early 1750s, an anonymous report compared the New Orleans church with that of Cap-Français.[14]

Besides "nègre," "mulâtre," "quarteron," "métis," and "griffe," the racial category "white" also appears in the sacramental records, not in relation to a white settler who was baptized, married, buried, or served as a witness or a godparent, but to qualify the "unknown father" of an enslaved or free child of color. Generally, the administrative methods used to identify persons of

13. For racial categories in Saint-Domingue and the Lesser Antilles, see Frédéric Régent, *Esclavage, métissage, liberté: La Révolution française en Guadeloupe, 1789–1802* (Paris, 2004), 14–18. For racial categories in Spanish Louisiana, see Gwendolyn Midlo Hall, "African Women in French and Spanish Louisiana: Origins, Roles, Family, Work, Treatment," in Catherine Clinton and Michele Gillepsie, eds., *The Devil's Lane: Sex and Race in the Early South* (New York, 1997), 26on; and Kimberly S. Hanger, *Bounded Lives, Bounded Places: Free Black Society in Colonial New Orleans, 1769–1803* (Durham, N.C., 1997), 15–16.

14. On Capuchins, see Pierre Hamer, *Raphaël de Luxembourg: Une contribution luxembourgeoise à la colonisation de la Louisiane* (Luxembourg, 1966), 53; and J[oseph] Rennard, *Histoire religieuse des Antilles françaises: Des origines à 1914 ...* (Paris, 1954), 127. All the archives of the Capuchin province of Champagne were destroyed during the French Revolution. On connections between missionaries in Louisiana and Saint-Domingue, see Father Raphaël to Abbé Raguet, May 18, 1726, ANOM COL C13A 10, fol. 45v; and Claude L. Vogel, *The Capuchins in French Louisiana (1722–1766)* (Washington, D.C., 1928), 41–42.

TABLE 5. Ethnic and Racial Labels of Enslaved Children Recorded in New Orleans Baptism Certificates, 1729–1733 and 1744–1769

Year	"Négrillon," "Négritte" ("Negro" boy or girl)	"Mulâtre," "Mulâtresse," "Mule" ("Mulatto")	"Quarteron," "Quarteronne" ("Quadroon")	"Sauvage," "Sauvagesse," "Indien" ("Indian")	"Métis," "Métisse" ("Mixed-blood")	"Griffe" ("Sambo")	Without any term of color	Total
1729*	71	0	0	2	0	0	0	73
1730*	37	3	0	3	0	0	1	44
1731	97	0	0	1	2	0	0	100
1732*	72	1	0	2	0	0	0	75
1733	112	1	0	2	4	0	0	119
Total	389	5	0	10	6	0	1	411
1744	77	3	0	1	0	0	2	83
1745	82	4	0	0	0	0	5	91
1746*	65	5	0	0	0	0	9	79
1747	66	6	0	3	0	0	20	95
1748	54	3	0	1	1	0	26	85
1749	64	7	0	1	1	0	23	96
1750	96	6	0	4	0	0	15	121
1751	74	3	0	2	0	0	9	88

Year								
1752	84	6	1	1	1	0	21	114
1753	82	9	0	0	1	0	9	101
1754	67	12	0	2	0	0	30	111
1755	70	12	2	0	0	0	25	109
1756	93	17	0	1	3	0	20	134
1757	88	17	1	0	4	0	11	121
1758	82	18	4	0	2	0	9	115
1759	103	21	3	1	5	0	3	136
1760	107	27	4	0	0	1	10	149
1761	81	28	1	0	5	0	3	118
1762	93	37	0	0	5	0	1	136
1763	88	28	0	0	3	0	5	124
1764	58	32	1	0	2	1	84	178
1765	74	24	0	0	5	0	76	179
1766	101	25	1	1	1	7	23	159
1767*	63	28	7	1	1	1	93	194
1768	16	10	1	1	1	0	87	116
1769	34	8	0	2	1	0	148	193
Total	1962	396	26	22	42	10	767	3225

*Incomplete data are due to missing pages from the registers.
Source: Sacramental records, AANO.

TABLE 6. Ethnic and Racial Labels of Illegitimate Children Born to Free Women of Color Recorded in New Orleans Baptism Certificates, 1744–1769

Year	"Négrillon," "Négritte" ("Negro" boy or girl)	"Mulâtre," "Mulâtresse" ("Mulatto")	"Quarteron," "Quarteronne" ("Quadroon")	"Sauvage," "Sauvagesse" ("Indian")	"Métis," "Métisse" ("Mixed-blood")	"Griffe" ("Sambo")	Without any term of color	Total
1744	1	1	0	0	0	0	0	2
1745	1	0	0	0	0	0	0	1
1746*	1	2	0	0	0	0	1	4
1747	1	0	0	0	0	0	1	2
1748	0	0	0	0	0	0	2	2
1749	1	0	0	0	0	0	0	1
1750	0	1	0	0	0	0	2	3
1751	0	2	1	0	0	0	0	3
1752	2	1	0	0	0	0	0	3
1753	2	1	0	0	0	0	3	6
1754	3	0	0	0	0	0	1	4

Year							Total
1755	1	0	0	0	0	1	2
1756	0	0	0	0	0	2	2
1757	2	1	0	0	0	0	3
1758	0	2	0	0	0	2	4
1759	0	1	0	0	0	0	1
1760	0	5	0	0	0	1	6
1761	2	6	1	0	0	1	10
1762	0	1	0	0	0	0	1
1763	1	5	0	0	0	0	6
1764	0	5	1	0	0	2	8
1765	1	0	0	0	0	3	4
1766	0	4	0	0	0	0	4
1767*	0	0	0	0	0	0	0
1768	0	2	0	0	0	7	9
1769	0	3	0	1	0	6	10
Total	19	43	2	2	0	35	101

*Incomplete data are due to missing pages from the registers.

Source: Sacramental records, AANO.

European descent followed a strictly metropolitan model. When white individuals had to officially self-identify or be identified, whether in a notarial deed, at the beginning of a testimony or interrogation in a trial, in a request to the Superior Council, or in a religious ceremony registered in the sacramental records, they were never described by the terms "white" or "free." Being white meant having no race and being presumed free.[15]

For the same reason, the label "white" seldom showed up in censuses. Most often administrative documents used the following expressions to categorize free persons of European descent: *"habitants"* (permanent resident), "concession holders," "masters," "bourgeois," "heads of family," "indentured servants," "domestics," and so on and so forth. A few exceptions, nevertheless, where census takers incidentally used the category "white" reveal that racial consciousness was already embedded in their psyche. The census of "New Orleans and its surroundings" taken November 24, 1721, was presented in different ways and duplicated in at least three copies. The titles of two copies, which listed the various column headings, mention "French servants," while the third refers to "white servants." These documents represent the first known written instances of the term "white" in Louisiana, three years before the Code Noir was promulgated in the colony. The category "white employees, laborers or servants" was also used in a census dated December 20, 1724, spanning the territory from New Orleans to the "German village" (the German Coast). Finally, in the summary table of the census of the department of New Orleans, finished July 1, 1727, individuals were classified in two general categories subdivided in three subcategories: "whites" ("masters," "children," "indentured servants or domestics") and "slaves" ("negroes," "female or male negro children," "savages").[16]

Although "white" was not an administrative category, it belonged to the language of daily life. The term repeatedly shows up in interrogatories and testimonies of both settlers and slaves: "mistreat them violently without any

15. Contrary to what Shannon Lee Dawdy asserts, the category "white" was used in all kinds of official documents in French New Orleans early on. See Dawdy, *Building the Devil's Empire: French Colonial New Orleans* (Chicago, 2008), 201, 231. The expression "unknown father" to designate the father of enslaved infants became common in baptism certificates starting in the mid-1740s. For the first instance of "unknown father" in New Orleans sacramental records, see AANO, Saint-Louis Cathedral Baptisms 1744–1753, 02/17/1744.

16. "Recensement de La Nouvelle-Orléans et lieux circonvoisins du 24 novembre 1721," ANOM COL G1 464, "Recensement des habitants depuis la ville de La Nouvelle-Orléans jusqu'au village des Allemands du 20 décembre 1724," "Recensement général du département de La Nouvelle-Orléans du 1er juillet 1727."

whites present"; "to see if there were some negroes, or whites, foreigners";
"François the white overseer of his plantation"; "when a slave lays hands on
a white he deserves the death penalty"; "questioned as to whether he knew
if it was some negroes or some Frenchmen who had committed the theft, he
said that he was not sure it was anyone, either white or black"; "he did not
want to fire on the whites"; "he had bought it from a white man he does not
know"; "there was a white witness he does not know"; "a young white man
Sr. Piqueneau left at her place opened the door." Whether it was necessary
to mention the overseer and craftsmen of French descent on a plantation, to
identify a corpse, to guess the perpetrators of a theft, or to recall the law related to the relations between masters and slaves, New Orleans's residents
resorted to "white" as a useful identifier in a variety of situations.[17]

"White" was first introduced as a legal category by the 1724 Code Noir.
The term "white," which is missing from the 1685 text, is repeated several
times in the Louisiana edict. Article 6, prohibiting mixed marriages, states
"We forbid our white subjects, of both sexes, to marry with the blacks. . . .
We also forbid our white subjects, and even the manumitted or free-born
blacks, to live in a state of concubinage with blacks." Article 24 affirms that
slaves shall not "be called upon to give their testimony either in civil or
criminal cases, except when it shall be a matter of necessity, and only in
default of white people." And, finally, Article 52, declares free blacks "incapable of receiving donations, . . . from the whites." The introduction of
the category "white" aimed at distinguishing settlers of European descent
among the free population. It was forged in opposition to both "negroes"
and "blacks."[18]

Outside the Code Noir, "white" was used in the legislation produced
locally with regard to mixed marriages between Frenchmen and Native
women. This issue principally concerned the Illinois Country, where the

17. For "white" in court records, see RSCL 1726/10/14/02; 1730/09/05/02; 1739/
10/10/01; 1739/10/26/01; 1739/12/14/05; 1742/01/09/04; 1742/03/13/01; 1743/09/04/01;
1744/01/25/01; 1745/02/25/02; 1748/01/10/01; 1748/05/18/03; 1752/03/26/01, 1764/
07/24/03; 1765/02/26/01; 1766/06/04/03; 1766/11/14/01; 1767/02/21/01, 1767/04/25/01.
One can also find the similar use of "white" in private correspondence and in notarial
documentation. In 1729, the officer and planter Jean-Charles de Pradel wrote to his
brother in the home country that he was going to send "two negroes and a white" to
gather some wood on his plantation. See A. Baillardel and A. Prioult, eds., *Le chevalier de
Pradel: Vie d'un colon français en Louisiane au XVIIIe siècle d'après sa correspondance et
celle de sa famille* (Paris, 1928), 55. A succession deed also mentions that "the heirs only
provide a white mason and carpenter to conduct these works." See NONA Apr. 19, 1764.
18. "Code noir," March 1724, ANOM COL A 22, fols. 110–128.

Jesuits and priests of the Seminar of Foreign Missions celebrated such unions as a circumstance they deemed preferable to concubinage. On the occasion of an inheritance case related to a Frenchman who had been married to an Illinois woman, the New Orleans Superior Council promulgated a regulation "prohibit[ing] moreover the French or other white subjects of the King from marrying female savages." Despite this prohibition, Commissaire-ordonnateur Edmé-Gatien Salmon found it necessary to denounce the situation in the Illinois Country once again in a letter to the minister of the navy in 1732: "I have learned that these kinds of marriage had been authorized by missionaries who claimed that there was no difference between a Christianized savage and a white." In all the rest of the literature produced by the debate on French-Amerindian marriages, however, as well as the whole of the colony's administrative correspondence more generally, officials wrote about "the French" or the "habitants" rather than about the "whites," suggesting that, even though French-Native relationships contributed to the construction of whiteness, blackness was more important than nativeness in shaping white identity. Natives were not racialized to the same extent as people of African descent because the majority were not enslaved and lived independently. Not only were indigenous slaves within colonial settlements few in number, but native enslavement was minimized by central and local authorities. The Code Noir only dealt with black slaves. Likewise, even though the sacramental records mentioned a few *"sauvagesses libres"* ("free savage women") or *"métisses libres"* ("free mixed-blood women"), there was no equivalent to the expression "free blacks" to collectively identify the few indigenous slaves who had been manumitted and still lived in New Orleans. Free natives never became a legal, administrative, and social category. Race had to do first and foremost with African slavery.[19]

The close association between blackness and whiteness was further reinforced by law with the passing of generations. In 1751, Governor Pierre de Rigaud de Vaudreuil de Cavagnal and Commissaire-Ordonnateur Honoré-Gabriel Michel promulgated a local ruling that addressed all matters related to public order, including slaves and slavery. The bylaw respected the

19. On French-Native mariages in the Illinois Country, see Cécile Vidal, "Les implantations françaises au Pays des Illinois au XVIIIe siècle (1699–1765)," 2 vols. (Ph.D. diss., École des Hautes Études en Sciences Sociales, 1995), 485–502. For the use of "white" in the debate about French-Native mariages, see "Arrêt du Conseil supérieur de la Louisiane concernant le mariage des Français avec les sauvagesses," Dec. 18, 1728, ANOM COL A 23, fols. 102–103; and Edmé Gatien Salmon to the minister of the navy, July 17, 1732, ANOM COL C13A 15, fol. 166r.

spirit of the 1724 Code Noir and used the term "white" in the same manner as the royal edict. Article 29, for instance, insisted on "the submissiveness [slaves] owe to whites." This deference was also required of freed persons. Previously, in 1735, a manumission deed concerning two *"négrittes"*("pickaninny girls") had qualified their freedom, stating that it was granted on the understanding that they would "maintain the respect they shall always show to whites," a condition that went a step further than Article 53 of the Code Noir, which only insisted on the "profoundest respect" owed by manumitted slaves to "their former masters, their widows, and their children."[20]

A comparison of the terms employed to mention free individuals in the 1724 Code Noir and 1751 local ruling reveals that white identification grew in importance and took on a new political meaning from midcentury as it became closely associated with freedom and citizenship. This evolution imposed itself to the detriment of free people of color. Whereas the 1724 Code Noir mentioned the "habitants," "masters," "subjects," "white subjects," "settled subjects," "whites," and "free persons," the 1751 regulation referred to "masters," "French," "private individuals," "citizens," "habitants," "habitants and citizens," "whites," and the "public." In the articles of the 1724 Code Noir sanctioning the seizure of goods from slaves attempting to trade without certificates from their masters or the arrest of slaves who assembled, moved around, or bore arms without written permission, the king not only authorized but enjoined his "subjects" or "settled subjects" to intervene; in the 1751 local bylaw, however, the governor and commissaire-ordonnateur specifically exhorted and ordered "whites" and "citizens" to behave in this manner. The switch from subjects to citizens reflected the ongoing debate about the relationships between the monarch and civil society and the new political meaning attached to nation, which was increasingly viewed as a political community over the eighteenth century. Yet the promotion of colonists to citizens only concerned whites. As the 1751 ruling equated the categories of "French," "citizens," and "whites," it implicitly excluded free people of color from the civic and national community. Such an evolution not only affected language but was also translated into violent measures against free blacks. The 1724 edict conveyed the image of an inclusive monarchy that automatically granted French *naturalité* (nationality) to freed slaves despite some discriminatory provisions. By contrast, the 1751 bylaw was not interested in free people of color anymore except to order their automatic reenslavement

20. "Règlement sur la police pour la province de la Louisiane," Feb. 28–Mar. 1, 1751, ANOM COL C13A 35, fol. 47r; RSCL 1735/10/09/01; "Code Noir," March 1724, ANOM COL B 43, fols. 388–407.

if they assisted runaway slaves. The potential for free blacks to be returned to slave status further weakened their social position.[21]

Throughout the French regime, free people of color remained associated with slaves. When the 1760s censuses first introduced a column to count them separately, it was located after those related to the enslaved. Still, the expression used to designate people of African or mixed descent who had been freed or were born free was not yet "free people of color." The expressions *gens de couleur* (people of color) and *gens de couleur libres* (free people of color) apparently only emerged in the Lesser Antilles and Saint-Domingue in the aftermath of the Seven Years' War and did not start to be commonly used in Louisiana until the 1820s. In the 1724 Code Noir, free persons of African or mixed descent were identified as "freed or free-born blacks" or "freedmen or free negroes." In the 1763 census, they were labeled as "free negroes and mulattoes" and "freed." The latter term was used in a generic way to describe all free blacks, even when they were born free, and points to servile origins. In other kinds of sources, individuals were always categorized as "free negro / negress" or "free mulattress." When a free person of color had to be classified, the individual was sometimes only noted as "free," without reference to his or her color. Since people of European descent were never identified individually as "free" or "white," the use of the adjective "free" to categorize a person meant that she or he was not white and could have a pejorative connotation.[22]

21. "Code Noir," March 1724, ANOM COL B 43, fols. 388–407; "Règlement sur la police des cabarets, des esclaves, des marchés en Louisiane," Feb. 28–Mar. 1, 1751, ANOM COL C13A 35, fols. 39–52r. For the politicization of citizenship throughout the eighteenth century, see David A. Bell, *The Cult of the Nation in France: Inventing Nationalism, 1680–1800* (Cambridge, Mass., 2001). On "naturalité" in metropolitan France, see Peter Sahlins, *Unnaturally French: Foreign Citizens in the Ancient Regime and After* (Ithaca, N.Y., 2004), 182–183.

22. For one of the few historians of Louisiana who has analyzed the way the free population of color was historically labeled over time, see Spear, *Race, Sex, and Social Order in Early New Orleans*, 14–15. The expression "gens de couleur" was ambiguous because it could embrace both slaves and free people of African or mixed descent, only the latter, or only free people of mixed descent, known as "sang-mêlé." It could also imply a pejorative connotation or, on the contrary, be used positively by free people of color themselves in defense of their rights. The designation, however, only appears in ordinances, administrative correspondence, legal treatises, philosophical or historical essays, and political pamphlets. Free people of African or mixed descent were never identified individually in front of judges, notaries, and priests as *"homme / femme de couleur (libre)"* ("free man / woman of color") but always as *"nègre / mulâtre / quarteron, etc. libre"* ("free negro / mulatto / quadroon, etc."). "Gens de couleur" was used for the first time in 1782

Although the idiom "free people of color" was not yet in use, the racial idea it conveyed already informed legal practices and social relations in Louisiana in the first half of the eighteenth century. During the antebellum period, the term was a kind of oxymoron that combined two concepts that were seen as antithetical: freedom and color. Together, they contradicted the association between freedom and whiteness, on the one hand, and slavery and blackness, on the other, and the opposition between these dual phenomena around which the colony's slave society was organized. Although "color" in "free people of color" puts the emphasis solely on phenotype, the variety of racial labels in use during the French period ("nègre" and "mulâtre" and, in the sacramental records, "métis," "quarteron," and "griffe") indicated both an individual's phenotype or color and degree of métissage. They reflected an anxiety over métissage and a desire to measure a person's distance or proximity to whites. A term that encompassed all people

---

in the summary of a census for the western and southern provinces in Saint-Domingue to designate only "mulattoes" and other people of mixed descent. The multiple definitions and boundaries given to the category reflect a tension between two visions of the social world, either as a triracial or biracial society. For instances of "gens de couleur," see Auguste Lebeau, *De la condition des gens de couleur libres sous l'Ancien Régime: D'après des documents des archives coloniales* (Paris, 1903); Léo Élisabeth, "The French Antilles," in David W. Cohen and Jack P. Greene, eds., *Neither Slave nor Free: The Freedmen of African Descent in the Slave Societies of the New World* (Baltimore, 1972), 135; Dominique Rogers, "Les libres de couleur dans les capitales de Saint-Domingue: Fortune, mentalités, et intégration à la fin de l'Ancien Régime (1776–1789)" (Ph.D. diss., Université Michel de Montaigne, 1999), section II, chapter 4; and John D. Garrigus, *Before Haiti: Race and Citizenship in French Saint-Domingue* (New York, 2006), 19, 142, 163, 168. In 1806, the first American census for the Territory of Orleans had a single heading for "Free men, and women, and children of Colour," instead of the two columns for "pardos" and "morenos" that appeared in the Spanish censuses. See Paul Lachance, "The Louisiana Purchase in the Demographic Perspective of Its Time," in Peter J. Kastor and Francois Weil, eds., *Empires of the Imagination: Transatlantic Histories of the Louisiana Purchase* (Charlottesville, Va., 2009), 145. Two years later, territorial legislation decreed that a free person of African or mixed descent had to be referred to either as a "free man of color or a free woman of color" in all public documents. See "An Act to Prescribe Certain Formalities Respecting Free Persons of Colour," Mar. 31, 1808, in L[ouis] Moreau Lislet, ed., *A General Digest of the Acts of the Legislature of Louisiana: Passed from the Year 1804, to 1827, Inclusive, and in Force at This Last Period ...*, 2 vols. (New Orleans, 1828), I, 499–500. But the expression only became common in New Orleans's sacramental records from 1820 on. See AANO, Libro primero de matrimonios de negros y mulatos en la parroquia de Sn. Luis de la Nueva-orleans. This usage coincided with the introduction of the category "free colored persons" in the federal census the same year. See Paul Schor, *Compter et classer: Histoire des recensements américains* (Paris, 2009), 40.

of African descent, including those of mixed race, in order to preserve the purity of the white race, had not yet been invented, as became the case with "colored." But, since "mulâtres" and "nègres" were systematically combined under French rule, individuals categorized as "mulâtres" remained closely associated with people of African descent. Despite their "white blood," they were not considered a distinct racial group. "Savages," the third category of people besides whites and blacks brought into contact by French colonization, remained separate. The language designating free people of African or mixed descent reflected a biracial system in which free blacks were seen as an anomaly. Likewise, the latter also rarely went as plaintiffs or defendants before the Superior Council. Most of them were invisible in the eyes of judges; in that regard, they were much better off than slaves, who could not escape the sword of royal justice.[23]

JUDICIAL VIOLENCE IN THE SERVICE OF RACIAL SLAVERY

Despite possible circumstantial tensions over the way slaves should be individually punished, a large collective consensus quickly formed among whites with regard to the administration of justice. Central authorities, local officials, and settlers all shared the belief that the Superior Council should support the consolidation of the slave system and the enforcement of a strict racial order. As evidenced by the social identities of the individuals who were brought before the bench, the crimes for which they were prosecuted, the punishments to which they were sentenced, and the status of the executioners who carried out sentences, the court succeeded over time in implementing a biracial judicial order that largely spared whites, targeted black slaves, and mostly ignored free people of color. Judicial violence was staged to imprint terror and instill obedience among the slave majority while saving the lives of most enslaved laborers, who were much needed in a colony where hardly any slave ships arrived from Africa after 1731. It was only in the early 1760s that the level of judicial repression reached a new stage, when magistrates, led by a new attorney general, multiplied convictions, resorted to judicial torture without hesitation, and condemned slaves to some of the most terrible forms of death sentences. This theater of legal violence expressed ambitions on the part of the colony's local elite to assume a greater role in the administration of New Orleans and of Louisiana as a whole.[24]

23. On the biracial system in the U.S., see Schor, *Compter et classer*, 75–76, 145–158.
24. The administration of justice and its early racialization reflected metropolitan views as well as those of Louisiana's local elites. For an opposite view arguing that the

An Early Turn in the Regime of Judicial Violence against Whites

When the Ursuline Hachard wrote to her father about the equality of "White, Savage or Negro" before the judicial system in 1728, the situation was already quickly evolving. In the early years after New Orleans's founding, people of all statuses and backgrounds were prosecuted, convicted, and punished, yet, shortly after the slave trade resumed in 1723, enslaved outlaws of African descent became judges' primary focus. Most criminal trials, especially those concerning theft, involved black slaves as defendants, even though soldiers, sailors, and other whites of the lower sort were also severely punished. Whites were nonetheless spared corporal punishment and the cruelest forms of the death penalty since extreme violence had started to become closely associated with the domination and subordination that linked masters and slaves. In most cases, magistrates also refused to allow slaves to testify against whites. This discriminatory justice was instrumental in the construction of whiteness.

White civilians seem to have been more frequently brought up on charges before the court in the 1720s than in later decades. The convicts who had been deported to the colony were the principal victims of this repression. In September 1724, the attorney general Jean-Baptiste Claude Raguet petitioned the Superior Council regarding these men and women. He accused them of being responsible for all the disorder in the colony: "robberies, sedition, conspiracies and thefts of ferryboats, rowboats, and longboats." According to Raguet, they had no trades but lived by all kinds of illicit commercial activities, including prostitution, and they incited the "French domestics, savages, and negroes" to steal from their masters. He proposed to expel them from the city and to force them to settle in a remote outpost. One month later, when merchandise was lacking and food prices were extremely high, the attorney general requested that two women named La Flamande and La Chevalier, who had come to the colony as convicts, be sentenced to a fine of one hundred livres, two weeks in jail, and banishment from the city for having sold eggs at more than ten sols each to a soldier and a domestic. In the event of relapse, they would be exposed to public scorn and forced to wear an iron collar around their neck. In the end, they were only sentenced to a heavy fine. Still, such forms of shaming were not uncommon in the early 1720s. The year before, a man had been convicted for having sold cats and dogs instead of regular meat to the hospital, and

---

judicial system was only influenced by the local elite, see Dawdy, *Building the Devil's Empire*, 198–204.

he was sentenced to ride the wooden horse with a sign around his neck on which was written "dog and cat eater." According to Hachard, loose women were also severely punished "by tying them to a wooden horse and having them whipped by all the Soldiers of the Regiment which guards our city."[25]

Justice during this early period appears to have principally concerned those of the lower sort, regardless of status, gender, or race. A few individuals brought up on charges of theft demonstrate the range of persons who came before the magistrates. They all belonged to the bottom rungs of the social hierarchy. These cases concerned a soldier, a young orphan who served as domestic, a free "negress" married to a white locksmith, and three slaves. As in the metropole, justice showed more mercy toward people belonging to the upper and middling classes. Even so, most of the individuals who were convicted of theft or robbery were probably not sentenced to the death penalty, as the colony lacked laborers. One defendant, however, the soldier, for whom a sentence has been kept, was condemned, among other punishments, to be whipped. The whip was often used in France and in Canada, but, in Louisiana, this punishment was increasingly seen as a specific form of violence used by masters to punish their slaves.[26]

25. During the Company of the Indies's monopoly, most of the records of the Superior Council relate to civil affairs and suits. There are few criminal trials left. However, extracts from letters of the Superior Council in the administrative correspondence reveal that two men, whose trial records have not been found, were sentenced to the death penalty in 1725. Many more cases were probably prosecuted, but it is impossible to determine how many are missing or how representative the trials are for which records have survived. See "Extraits des lettres du Conseil de Louisiane," Nov. 21, 1725, ANOM COL C13A 9, fols. 267–268. For Jean-Baptiste Claude Raguet's petition against convicts, see RSCL 1724/09/02/01. For La Flamande and La Chevalier's trial, see RSCL 1724/10/23/02; and Jacques de La Chaise to the Company of the Indies's Directors, Mar. 8, 1724, ANOM COL C13A 7, fols. 48–49. For the use of shaming as punishment, see RSCL 1723/09/10/01; and "Lettre à la Nouvelle Orleans," Apr. 24, 1728, in Hachard, *Relation du voyage des dames religieuses ursulines*, 96–97.

26. For early trials for theft, see RSCL 1720/02/23/01; 1723/05/20/01, 1723/05/22/02, 1723/05/22/03; 1723/07/13/01, 1723/07/14/01, 1723/07/15/01; 1723/12/02/01, 1723/12/02/03, 1723/12/03/02, 1723/12/03/03, 1723/12/03/04. Unfortunately, the sentences for most criminal trials during this early period have disappeared, so it is impossible to verify Hachard's statement about the equal severity of justice. In 1728, a company employee was sentenced to make honorable amends after being tortured for having counterfeited bills and to serve on galleys for life. The council, however, requested his pardon for three reasons: "He is said to have family"; he had been brought to Louisiana by one of the company's directors; and "it was due to youthful folly that he would quickly grow out of." See Étienne Périer and La Chaise to the Company of the Indies's Directors, July 31, 1728, ANOM COL C13A 11, fols. 54–55. For the case of a man sentenced to being beaten

After the mid-1720s, white civilians seem to have rarely been prosecuted for theft. Although plots of desertion by indentured servants or former indentured servants led to some investigations, most white civilians no longer had to fear criminal justice. When the slave trade resumed in 1723 and the number of slaves started to increase, local authorities quickly redirected their attention to slaves. They used the court to help masters control their enslaved laborers, prosecuting cases of marooning, theft, and rebellion. In 1726, the attorney general Raguet petitioned the Superior Council to alert the judges about a band of armed Native deserters who lived outside the city, robbing plantations. He requested that the runaways be tracked down and sentenced to death. Referring to the Code Noir that the king gave to Louisiana in March 1724, out of his "paternal kindness ... despite our remoteness from him," he argued that, while the law did not prescribe the death sentence for desertion only, it did so for gathering and bearing arms, concluding that "we will never manage to contain slaves unless we threaten them with death." This band of indigenous deserters was apparently scattered, and unorganized slaves of African descent who ran away individually or in small groups quickly replaced them at the center stage of royal justice. In the late 1720s, the number of trials of black slaves for marooning and theft started to multiply, as magistrates tried to curb rising slave unrest. In one case, the attorney general cited continual thefts in the city to justify the prosecution. Likewise, in another trial, he pointed out that the behavior of the slave in question was "a rebellion against his master that deserves to be punished all the more since with the increase in the number of negroes in this colony we would not be safe in the distant plantations."[27]

----

with a stick, see RSCL 1728/05/22/01, 1728/05/22/02, 1728/05/22/03, 1728/05/24/03, 1728/05/29/01, 1728/05/29/02, 1728/05/29/08. On the use of whipping in metropolitan France and Canada, see Pascal Bastien, *L'exécution publique à Paris au XVIIIe siècle: Une histoire des rituels judiciaires* (Seyssel, France, 2006), 107–108; and André Lachance, *Le bourreau au Canada sous le régime français* (Quebec, 1966), 34–51.

27. On the lack of prosecution of white people from the mid-1720s, see Sophie White, "Slaves and Poor Whites' Informal Economies in an Atlantic Context," in Vidal, ed., *Louisiana: Crossroads of the Atlantic World*, 96. Only one investigation of a white person for theft has been found for the period spanning the 1730s, 1740s, and 1750s. See RSCL 1744/01/25/01. Yet, later, in the early 1760s, two trials were organized to judge whites of the lower sort who had stolen cattle. On the repression of Native American deserters, see RSCL 1726/08/17/03. In 1741, several settlers also complained that some runaways flocked together behind and below the city. A troop composed of soldiers, free blacks, and Native Americans was sent to address the situation. They reported that the enslaved driver of a man named Chaperon was sheltering and giving food to maroons. See RSCL 1741/01/10/01. For African slaves prosecuted for desertion or theft in the late 1720s, see

As black slaves continued to be tried for desertion and theft in growing numbers over the following decades, white settlers increasingly came to view them as responsible for all the thefts committed, whether on plantations or in the city. When a white urban dweller lodged a complaint concerning stolen clothes in 1738, she told the clerk that she only suspected some "negroes" and asked their masters to pay her back. In the same way, the previous year, the attorney general attributed the blame for several cattle thefts to slaves despite the lack of any concrete evidence. Although he reported that the incident had been investigated "without having succeeded in finding out by whom," he determined "that it must have been runaway negroes who looted the plantations." The black slave had become the archetype of the thief.[28]

The transformation in the social identities of criminals that began in the late 1720s was accompanied by changes in the kinds of punishment whites received. By the early 1730s, the practice of whipping people of European descent to punish and shame them had disappeared because it was now considered unacceptable. The forms of violence masters inflicted on their slaves quickly influenced notions of violence among settlers, even before it impacted methods of judicial repression. In the minds of some whites, the relationship of domination, superiority, and authority that existed in slavery was expressed through the mistreatment owners meted out to their slaves. When one colonist inflicted excessive or unjustified violence on another, the victim often felt reduced to the status of a slave, the lowest rung of society to which a person could fall. Whites saw extreme violence as more than an attack on an individual's physical integrity; rather it was also a blow to someone's honor and called into question the victim's status and condition. Such violence seemed unbearably humiliating.

In 1741, the Superior Council in New Orleans judged in appeal a case involving two whites, connected by friendship or family ties, in Pointe Coupée. Louis Faugère had entered Joseph Herbert's house to do him a small service. Suddenly, Herbert forced Faugère onto a bed, took off his trousers, and spanked him. Then, he put Faugère in a barrel full of tar in which an accomplice tried to plunge him up to his shoulders while Herbert forced

<hr />

RSCL 1728/07/08/03, 1728/07/10/01, 1728/07/10/02; 1729/09/05/02, 1729/09/05/03, 1729/09/05/04, 1729/09/05/05, 1729/09/05/06; 1729/09/27/01; 1729/11/16/01. A trial for poisoning was also organized, which shows that the level of anxiety among planters was increasing as they encountered difficulties controlling their slaves. See RSCL 1729/10/21/03, 1729/10/25/01. On the feeling of disorder in relation to slave unrest, see RSCL 1729/09/05/02; 1728/07/10/02.

28. RSCL 1738/02/24/02; 1737/03/19/02.

him to drink alcohol. The assailant called in all his neighbors, inviting them to laugh at his victim's expense. One of the bystanders told the judge that at one point Herbert "took the whip for Negroes to use it against Faugère, the Canadian called Abel said 'Stop this Mr. Herbert, one doesn't whip the French like the negroes,' and he grabbed the whip and threw it in the attic." In fact, two other men also chose that moment to intervene, even though no one had lifted a finger before, despite Faugère's calls for help. Herbert prevented anyone from interceding by insisting that he was the master in his house, but, clearly, in the eyes of Abel and the two bystanders who stepped in, Herbert's decision to beat Faugère with an instrument usually reserved for black slaves marked the instant when the situation became intolerable and the violence excessive.[29]

By the mid-1730s, the forms of violence slaves endured from their masters seem to have had an impact on the kinds of punishment inflicted on white criminals as well. In 1737, Commissaire-Ordonnateur Salmon sent the proceedings of seven suits that had taken place between July 1736 and January 1737 to the metropole (see Table 7). In contrast with the 1720s, when the repressive policy against convicts concerned both men and women, all the defendants were men, which fit the typical type of criminal in the early modern period. Royal justice's scrutiny especially fell on male slaves, although the Superior Council also set their sights on the transient white male population—unsettled young men, soldiers, and sailors. Among the white convicts, one "dissolute young vagrant" was severely condemned because he had permanently crippled a slave who did not belong to him. In comparison, throughout the French regime, most whites who inflicted temporary or permanent wounds on slaves whom they did not own merely incurred civil suits and financial damages, and only two soldiers were sentenced to be hanged for having killed one or several slaves. Among the convicts in the seven suits Salmon forwarded to the metropole, only one, a slave, was condemned to the death penalty. The commissaire-ordonnateur wanted to obtain a death sentence for the overseer on the king's vessel, but he lacked proof. The whites were severely punished with galley sentences, though, unlike the slaves, none were sentenced to other forms of corporal punishment, such as flogging, branding, or mutilation. From the early 1730s, whites in French Louisiana were hardly ever whipped, beaten with a stick, branded, or cut on their ears or hands, even as these forms of punishments were still meted out in the metropole. In Jamaica, in contrast, "flogging was not re-

29. RSCL 1741/01/17/02, 1741/01/18/01, 1741/01/23/01, 1741/02/04/03, 1741/02/04/05.

TABLE 7. Judicial Punishments, 1736–1737

Date	Defendant(s)	Crime	Sentence(s)
July 12, 1736	1 overseer on a king's vessel and 2 sailors	Tried to set a ship on fire with two barrels of gunpowder	Galley for life and confiscation of all property for the overseer; 2 sailors exculpated
Sept. 18, 1736	1 black slave	Rebellion against his master	Beaten with a stick or whipped and sent back to his master
Sept. 18, 1736	1 black slave	Repetitive rebellion against his master, whom he attacked with a knife	Right hand cut, broke on the wheel, body exposed on the road to Bayou Saint John. *Retentum**: strangled after the third hit
Sept. 18, 1736	1 white "dissolute young vagrant"	Shot at two slaves belonging to the Ursulines from whom he wanted to take a pirogue; left one slave crippled	3 years in the galleys in the metropole and 500 livres of damages to the Ursulines
Nov. 7, 1736	1 black slave	Repetitive running away	Right ear cut, branded on the right shoulder
Dec. 13, 1736	7 soldiers	Theft of merchandise the soldiers had helped to save from a shipwreck	2 soldiers sentenced to 10 years in the galleys in the colony, a fine of 10 livres, and the costs of the trial; 1 soldier left and was tried in absentia; 4 soldiers exculpated
Jan. 12, 1737	1 black slave	Repetitive running away	Two ears cut, branded with a fleur-de-lis on the right shoulder, and sent back to his master

Retentum: a secret measure decided by judges to shorten the sufferings of the convicted felon.
Sources: Edmé Gatien Salmon to the minister of the navy, Feb. 10, 1737, ANOM COL C13A 22, fols. 124–125; "Extrait des registres des audiences criminelles du Conseil Supérieur de la Louisiane pendant l'année 1736," ANOM COL F3 242, fols. 234–237v.

served for slaves"; rather, "the assize courts awarded sentences of flogging to free people until slavery ended," maybe because separate courts judged enslaved and free people.[30]

Just as the attorney general and the magistrates of the Superior Council quickly started to treat whites and slaves differently with regard to prosecution and punishment, they also began to make distinctions about who could testify in court, respecting the stipulations of the Code Noir related to the use of slaves as witnesses in all cases involving white defendants. The 1685 code had completely forbidden the testimony of slaves in civil and criminal suits, but Article 24 of the 1724 Louisiana edict introduced an exception, "when it shall be a matter of necessity, and only in default of white people." In no circumstances, however, could slaves testify against their masters. In 1738, the crown promulgated an ordinance repeating the content of Article 24 of the Louisiana code and extending it to the Antilles. Likewise, in the metropole, over the eighteenth century, judges increasingly had the freedom to decide whether a testimony could be received, despite the legal inca-

30. For the proceedings of the seven suits Salmon sent to the metropole, see Salmon to the minister of the navy, Feb. 10, 1737, ANOM COL C13A 22, fols. 124–125; and "Extrait des registres des audiences criminelles du Conseil Supérieur de la Louisiane pendant l'année 1736," ANOM COL F3 242, fols. 234–237v. Only one of the judicial proceedings has been found in the records of the Superior Council, which confirms once again that the extant collection is incomplete. See RSCL 1737/01/04/02, 1737/01/10/01, 1737/01/12/01. For the social identities of criminals in metropolitan France, see Garnot, *Histoire de la justice,* 157–171. Most of the affairs concerning whites who injured slaves probably did not lead to a suit but were settled outside court, since many of these documents are only declarations. See RSCL 1731/10/13/01, 1731/10/13/02, 1731/10/31/02; 1731/12/29/02; 1737/06/03/03; 1739/04/10/01; 1742/03/15/01; 1743/11/04/02; 1745/03/15/02; 1745/06/11/01; 1746/08/23/02; 1747/12/16/03, 1747/12/17/01, 1747/12/26/01, 1748/02/23/02; 1764/06/11/04. In one case, two slaves killed by a soldier belonged to the king and worked for the Ursulines, who refused to lodge a complaint against the soldier. See RSCL 1752/06/08/01, 1752/06/08/02, 1752/06/12/01, 1752/06/12/02, 1752/06/13/01, 1752/06/12/05, 1752/06/13/02, 1752/06/17/01, 1752/06/17/02, 1752/06/19/01, 1752/06/20/01, 1752/06/26/01, 1752/06/26/02, 1752/06/28/01; and Honoré-Gabriel Michel to the minister of the navy, Sept. 20, 1752, ANOM COL C13A 36, fol. 267. The other case involving a soldier sentenced to hang for injuring a slave took place in Pointe Coupée, and the soldier was tried in absentia. See RSCL 1764/02/21/01, 1764/02/22/01, 1764/02/24/03, 1764/02/27/02, 1764/02/29/01, 1764/03/14/01, 1764/04/07/01, 1764/04/14/03, 1764/05/26/01. On the use of beating, branding, and mutilation in metropolitan France, see Bastien, *L'exécution publique à Paris au XVIIIe siècle,* 150–159. For the punishment of whites in Jamaica, see Diana Paton, "Punishment, Crime, and the Bodies of Slaves in Eighteenth-Century Jamaica," *Journal of Social History,* XXXIV (2001), 936–942 (quotation, 939).

pacity of a witness as a relative, woman, convict, lunatic, and so on. In New Orleans, some slaves served as witnesses in trials of whites right up until the end of the French regime, but, as in Saint-Domingue, their depositions only supplemented those of whites and were not used to establish proof of guilt. When there were plenty of white witnesses, enslaved individuals were not heard. In the affair between the military officer Pierre Henri d'Erneville and the ship's captain Battar, who had allegedly kidnapped one of d'Erneville's female slaves with whom he had fallen in love, the former, "after having called nine white witnesses, wanted, against the spirit of the ordinance, to call some negroes and negresses to testify, which was rejected."[31]

In many cases, local authorities refused to allow slaves to testify even when there were no white witnesses and when they wanted them to testify. In 1730, a member of the Superior Council, Raymond Amyault d'Ausseville, lodged a complaint against his overseer, Jacques Charpentier dit Le Roy, who overexploited, battered, and abused his slaves. But, as d'Ausseville explained in one of his requests, he had difficulties proving his accusations, "for the Code Noir does not admit slaves as witnesses." Consequently, apart from trying to find white witnesses, he produced letters he had written to his overseer in which he reported accusations made by his slaves about the latter and a letter from a surgeon who had visited his plantation and had warned him regarding Le Roy. Likewise, in 1747, Governor Vaudreuil had first believed that the masked officer who had attacked Commissaire-Ordonnateur Sébastien François Ange Le Normant de Mézy in the street at night could not be prosecuted because the domestics who had identified the man were slaves, stating they "cannot prove anything against a white because they are black." A few years later, a soldier garrisoned in Mobile was tried in New Orleans for bestiality. Given that the only testimony available came from a slave, however, the soldier was only sentenced to one year of prison until more evidence could be found. Governor Louis Billouart de Kerlérec assured the minister of the navy that the serviceman would have

31. For the legislation on slaves' testimonies, see "Arrêt qui admet que les nègres esclaves puissent être reçus comme témoins à défaut de blancs sauf s'ils parlent contre leurs maîtres," July 15, 1738, ANOM COL A 27, fol. 87. For witnesses' social identities in metropolitan France, see Benoît Garnot, "La justice pénale et les témoins en France au 18e siècle: De la théorie à la pratique," *Dix-huitième siècle*, no. 39, *Le témoignage* (2007), 99–108. For the issue of slaves' testimonies in Saint-Domingue, see Malick W. Ghachem, *The Old Regime and the Haitian Revolution* (Cambridge, 2012), 181–187. For Pierre Henri d'Erneville vs. Battar, see Michel to the minister of the navy, July 15, 1751, ANOM COL C13A 35, fol. 293r. For a different interpretation of slaves' testimonies that relies on less evidence, see Spear, *Race, Sex, and Social Order in Early New Orleans*, 70.

been convicted "if the testimonies of the negroes who testified against him were admissible." He also asked the minister if servicemen could be tried for desertion in order to obtain the death penalty. Local authorities behaved as if Louisiana was governed by the original 1685 Code Noir.[32]

Although slave testimony could not be used to prove the guilt of white defendants, all condemned men and women—including whites—were punished by a black executioner who was either a slave or a former slave. Throughout the French regime, following a practice established in the Antilles, the New Orleans executioner was always a slave who either remained in bondage or was granted his freedom as a reward for his work. At first sight, this practice seems to contradict the racial order on which slave societies were based. The power the black executioner exercised, however, was only a delegation of the king's power. The monarch himself held his judicial power from God, which the coronation ceremony symbolized with the gift of the hand of justice and the sword. Inflicting corporal punishment, death in particular, transgressed the frontier between the sacred and the profane; hence, the executioner was considered impure and infamous. His touch polluted the convict, thereby corporal punishment both brought pain and conveyed shame. Far from being a sign of racial blindness, the use of a black man as an executioner, enslaved or freed, reflected the early embedding of race in this new slave society. Racial slavery did not contradict the inner workings of the French ancien régime society; rather, it pushed them to their logical extreme. Local authorities in Louisiana increasingly

32. For Jacques Charpentier's trial, see RSCL 1730/04/06/01, 1730/04/29/01, 1730/09/05/02, 1730/09/05/05, 1730/09/07/01, 1730/09/18/01. For the prosecution of the masked officer who attacked the commissaire-ordonnateur, see RSCL 1747/03/24/01; Sébastien François Ange Le Normant de Mézy to the minister of the navy, Mar. 24, 1747, ANOM COL C13A 31, fols. 155–156v; Pierre de Rigaud de Vaudreuil de Cavagnal to the minister of the navy, Apr. 25, 1747, ANOM COL C13A 31, fols. 56–58v; Le Normant to the minister of the navy, May 15, 1747, ANOM COL C13A, fols. 153–154v; and Vaudreuil to the minister of the navy, May 16, 1747, ANOM COL C13A 31, fol. 93. For the soldier's trial for bestiality, see RSCL 1753/08/12/01, 1753/08/14/01, 1753/08/14/02, 1753/08/14/03, 1753/08/14/04, 1753/08/16/02, 1753/08/16/03, 1753/08/17/02, 1753/08/17/03, 1753/08/18/02, 1753/08/18/02, 1753/08/16/01, 1753/08/17/01, 1753/08/18/01, 1753/08/18/04, 1753/08/20/01, 1753/08/21/01, 1753/08/27/02, 1753/08/27/03, 1753/08/28/01, 1753/08/28/02, 1753/08/29/01, 1753/08/20/02, 1753/08/20/03, 1753/08/22/01, 1753/08/27/01, 1753/08/28/02, 1753/08/29/02, 1753/08/29/03, 1753/08/29/04, 1753/08/29/05, 1753/08/29/06, 1753/08/29/07, 1753/08/29/08, 1753/08/29/10, 1753/08/30/01, 1753/09/09/01, 1753/09/10/01, 1753/10/05/01, 1753/10/06/08, 1753/09/10/02, 1753/09/10/03; and Louis Billouart de Kerlérec to the minister of the navy, Nov. 16, 1753, ANOM COL C13A 37, fols. 92–93v.

targeted slaves as criminals, but they never considered resorting to anyone but a slave as public executioner.[33]

An Increasingly Merciless Justice against Slaves

The judicial system sustained the collective interests of slaveholders who wished to preserve their authority over their enslaved laborers but needed the assistance of royal justice to control and discipline the most rebellious ones and to arbitrate conflicts regarding their punishment among settlers. The domestic sovereignty of masters was respected, as they were never prosecuted for abusing their slaves. Likewise, when justice had to be served, owners who lost a slave sentenced to the death penalty received financial compensation. During the three decades after the retrocession of the colony to the king, relatively few enslaved outlaws were tried. Justice in New Orleans was not different from that in the metropole; there, too, for various reasons, only a small percentage of crimes were investigated and prosecuted, which explains why justice aimed at setting examples with harsh sentences. Depending on the circumstances, masters in the Louisi-

33. For more details on black executioners, see Cécile Vidal, "Public Slavery, Racial Formation, and the Struggle over Honor in French New Orleans, 1718–1769," *Anuario Colombiano de historia social y de la Cultura*, LXIII, no. 2, *Raza: Perspectivas trans-atlánticas* (July–September 2016), 155–183. Contrary to what Shannon Lee Dawdy asserts, there is some evidence in the documentation about the use of a black executioner up to the end of the French period. See Dawdy, *Building the Devil's Empire*, 189–192, 201. This chapter's interpretation of the employment of black executioners is also different from that put forward by Gwendolyn Midlo Hall. See Hall, *Africans in Colonial Louisiana: The Development of Afro-Creole Culture in the Eighteenth Century* (Baton Rouge, La., 1992), 131–132. On executioners in the Antilles, see P. F. R. Dessalles, *Les annales du Conseil souverain de la Martinique*, Tome I, Vol. I, *Réédition*, ed. Bernard Vonglis (1786; rpt. Paris, 1995), 169; [Jean-Baptiste] du Tertre, *Histoire générale des Antilles habitées par les François*, 4 vols. (Paris, 1667–1671), I, 534; and Gene E. Ogle, "Slaves of Justice: Saint Domingue's Executioners and the Production of Shame," *Historical Reflections/Réflexions historiques*, XXIX, *Interpreting the Death Penalty: Spectacles and Debates* (2003), 275–293. On the infamous character of executioners in the French kingdom, see Florence Renucci, "L'exécuteur des sentences criminelles en France au dernier siècle de l'Ancien Régime," *Tijdschrift voor Rechtsgeschiedenis/Revue d'histoire du droit/The Legal History Review*, LXXVI (2008), 384–388; Pascal Bastien, "'La mandragore et le lys': L'infamie du bourreau dans la France de l'époque moderne," *Histoire de la justice*, XIII, *La Cour d'assises: Bilan d'un héritage démocratique* (2001), 223–240; and Michel Porret, "Corps flétri—corps soigné: L'attouchement du bourreau au XVIIIe siècle," in Porret, ed., *Le corps violenté: Du geste à la parole* (Geneva, Switzerland, 1998), 103–135.

ana capital cooperated with or tried to shield their slaves from royal justice, since they had to balance the need for discipline with the desire to preserve their labor force, which was a crucial issue. Consequently, the level of repression was mild. Yet the few enslaved defendants who were convicted were condemned to severe corporal punishment, even though few were sentenced to the death penalty. During the 1760s, the Superior Council not only started to prosecute a rising number of slaves, but the magistrates, under the leadership of the attorney general, often ordered the use of judicial torture and issued more death penalty sentences. This outburst of repression against slaves by royal justice was linked to an increasing fear of the pernicious influence exercised by creolized slaves brought from the Antilles and the desire of local elites to play a greater role in the colony's government.[34]

The judicial machine mainly worked in the service of the slave system and to the benefit of slaveowners. From the late 1720s onward, the majority of criminal trials involved slaves as defendants. They hardly ever appeared before judges as plaintiffs or victims. Despite Article 20 of the Code Noir, which allowed for slaves to resort to the judicial system in cases of abuse, no procedure was apparently started as a result of a complaint made by a slave to the attorney general that he or she was not well fed, clothed, or taken care of. In one exceptional case, an enslaved woman was confiscated from her owner by the Superior Council and sold at auction to benefit the Charity Hospital because her master had repeatedly mistreated her. Nevertheless, he was not prosecuted in a criminal court. By comparison, a few masters were condemned in the Antilles during the eighteenth century, even though such trials were extremely rare. Plantation management and the treatment of slaves only became a subject of concern and debate in the French Empire after 1763.[35]

Because city dwellers were slaveholders who were considered responsible for the punishment of their slaves both individually and collectively, they were afforded recognition as a community with some form of political representation. In the mid-1720s, local authorities established a syndic

34. On judicial repression in metropolitan France, see Garnot, *Histoire de la justice,* 104–187.

35. For the unique case of a slave confiscated for mistreatment, see RSCL 1737/11/06/05, 1737/11/20/02. On the prosecution of abusive masters in the Antilles, see Yvan Debbasch, "Au cœur du 'gouvernement des esclaves': La souveraineté domestique aux Antilles françaises (XVIIe–XVIIIe siècles)," *Revue française d'histoire d'outre-mer,* LXXI (1985), 31–54; and Ghachem, *Old Regime and the Haitian Revolution.*

elected by a meeting of the settlers. While the syndic was also assigned the mission "of attending to and following all the general matters of the habitants either at the Council or elsewhere and, when required, of taking the necessary censuses to record the number of slaves and generally everything relating to the public good," his first task, as stipulated by the regulation, was to take care of the "distribution that must be made on each head of negro for the payment of the executed slaves whose reimbursement is due to their masters." When slaves were executed, their masters were granted financial compensation, which was intended to come from taxes paid by all slaveholders. Whereas the practice of electing a syndic apparently quickly disappeared, that of reimbursing masters who lost their slaves to justice did not, even though taxes for the purpose were never levied. According to Commissaire-ordonnateur Salmon, tax arrears needed to pay for the "*esclaves justiciers*" ("slaves brought before justice") amounted to twenty thousand livres in 1734. Afterward, the king seems to have taken over the responsibility for reimbursing the owners of executed slaves.[36]

The administration of justice often generated tension among settlers and also between local authorities and certain slaveholders. Although slaveowners collectively supported the repressive policy implemented by local officials and judges of the Superior Council against slaves who ran away or stole in general, it was another matter when their own slaves were concerned. They did not always fulfill their obligation to report their runaways to royal authorities. Some masters also tried to hide slaves who were accused of theft, as Jean-Charles de Pradel did with his peddler Jupiter. Another slave named Joseph, who was put in jail for theft, managed to escape and return to his master, Claude Joseph Villars Dubreuil, one of Louisiana's most prominent planters and the king's building contractor. Dubreuil forgave him, since he was the son of his driver, and sheltered him, but, two months later, Dubreuil ultimately decided to send Joseph back to prison to be tried, after the slave repeated his misdemeanors. Owners were reluctant to turn slaves over to judicial authorities because they were obliged to

36. "Arrêt du Conseil supérieur de la Louisiane du 5 octobre 1726 qui enjoint aux habitants de s'assembler pour élire un syndic pour leurs affaires générales," ANOM COL A 23, fol. 80; Salmon to the minister of the navy, Aug. 16, 1734, ANOM COL C13A 19, fol. 76r. For documents asking for the evaluation of or evaluating convicted slaves, see RSCL 1742/01/20/02; 1744/10/03/01; 1748/01/10/02, 1748/01/10/03, 1748/01/10/04; 1748/05/03/02; 1764/06/23/02, 1764/06/23/07; 1764/07/21/03; 1764/09/10/04; 1765/09/21/08. In 1735, a slave known for his reputation as a thief was evaluated at only five hundred livres. However, the demand for slaves was so high that he was auctioned at one thousand livres. See NONA Jan. 8, 1735.

pay all costs incurred, including jail and legal fees and possibly damages. They were also conscious of the fact that their enslaved laborers lost value if mutilated. When slaves were executed, the financial compensation provided to masters was lower than the price at which these men or women could have been sold, and owners had difficulty replacing them.[37]

Masters usually took the punishment of their slaves into their own hands, especially when they suspected them of lesser offenses such as theft, but they sometimes initiated proceedings of royal justice. They typically appealed to the law when they were unable to manage their slaves on their own, such as when the latter became uncontrollable by running away for extended periods of time, frequently, or in a group. In 1737, Sieur Lange, the overseer on Governor Étienne Périer's plantation, sent Gueula to jail because he had run away several times and demanded that justice be meted out according to the Code Noir. Owners also sent their slaves to prison in more serious cases where slaves physically attacked them or when they murdered one another. They resorted to royal justice because they needed to eliminate dangerous elements who posed a threat or who might serve as a bad example to fellow slaves. They let the state punish such individuals publicly and solemnly to dissuade other slaves from doing similar things. In this way, planters and authorities collaborated to prevent further disorder.[38]

Settlers seem to have frequently argued about how slaves suspected of crimes should be punished and whether they should be turned over to local authorities to be tried. Tensions became all the more intense when they in-

37. In the margin of the Code Noir, a commentator noted beside Article 32: "Masters seldom declare their slaves who have run away." See "Édit du roi, ou Code noir, qui concerne entièrement les esclaves de la Louisiane . . . ," March 1724, ANOM COL A 23, fols. 50–57. Pradel seems to have tried to hide Jupiter and to address the issue privately with the settler who had been robbed before having Jupiter arrested and sent to jail. See RSCL 1744/03/02/01, 1744/03/03/01. For Joseph's trial, see RSCL 1753/04/23/01, 1753/04/03/02, 1753/05/02/01.

38. Runaway slaves interrogated by judges often told stories about being punished by their masters for theft. See RSCL 1738/04/11/02, 1741/01/16/01, 1753/03/13/01, 1764/07/31/01, 1764/08/04/01. For Gueula's trial, see RSCL 1737/01/04/02. For a similar case of a slave sent to prison for repetitive desertion, see RSCL 1764/10/23/01. For slaves sent to prison by their masters for assaulting whites or murdering fellow slaves, see RSCL 1728/07/08/03; 1729/09/27/01; 1729/10/21/03; 1736/07/06/05; 1743/06/27/03; 1743/08/24/02; 1745/02/09/01; 1745/04/01/01; 1751/04/14/01; 1756/07/29/01; 1764/06/10/02. Some masters resorted to other strategies to get rid of dangerous slaves. In 1756, the Ursulines sold six of their plantation slaves "because they were thieves and likely to have a bad influence on the others." See "Délibérations du Conseil 1727–1902," HNOC, Microfilm 1 of 19, Archives of the Ursuline Nuns of the Parish of Orleans, 44.

volved slaveholders of unequal conditions, means, and influence. In 1747, a planter named Henry Buquois dit Plaisance lodged a complaint against slaves who belonged to Raguet, the attorney general, stating that they had killed and ate some of his cattle. Rather than concede any wrongdoing on the part of his slaves or assume responsibility for the missing animals, Raguet replied that Plaisance let his cattle graze on his plantation and should not have entered his property to search his slave cabins or harass his slaves. Quoting Article 29 of the Code Noir about the theft of cattle, he said that he would reimburse the value of the cattle when he had been paid damages. He also managed to have Plaisance's sons sentenced to a week in jail for assaulting his slaves.[39]

Few slaves ended up before the Superior Council before the 1760s. Only three criminal suits of slaves are extant for the 1730s, eight for the 1740s, and five for the 1750s. The vast majority involved plantation workers of African descent, whose labor regime and material conditions were much harsher than those of urban slaves. They were most often tried for marooning or theft, as in other slave colonies. Judges took pains to enquire about the circumstances under which crimes were committed, asking many questions and letting slaves reply at great length. They often tried to understand the defendants' motivations and whether the crime had been caused by a master's mistreatment. Because looking for runaways was a financial burden, local authorities had an interest in understanding and limiting this form of evasion.[40]

For their part, slaves actively tried to defend themselves. Gueula, who had run away several times, explained that his master beat him and did not

39. For Henry Buquois dit Plaisance vs. Raguet, see RSCL 1747/12/31/01, 1748/01/27/07. For other cases involving similar conflicts, see RSCL 1745/06/11/01; 1746/05/17/02, 1746/05/18/01; 1748/06/09/01, 1748/06/24/01.

40. For a list of documents initiating court proceedings involving criminal suits against slaves, see RSCL 1737/01/04/02, 1738/04/11/01, 1738/04/24/01, 1741/01/10/01, 1742/01/09/04, 1743/06/26/01, 1744/03/02/01, 1748/01/03/07, 1748/02/09/02, 1748/05/18/03, 1748/06/09/01, 1751/04/14/01, 1751/06/21/01, 1752/02/17/01, 1752/03/26/01, 1753/04/23/01. Each case, however, could involve many documents, sometimes up to twenty-five. Documents regarding many trials are likely missing, especially for the 1750s. Native American slaves were rarely prosecuted. For rare cases involving indigenous slaves, see RSCL 1728/06/07/03, 1728/06/14/01, 1728/06/14/02; 1748/05/18/02, 1748/05/18/03, 1748/05/22/01, 1748/05/22/02, 1748/05/26/01. For the prosecution of slaves for marooning or theft in Jamaica, see Paton, "Punishment, Crime, and the Bodies of Slaves in Eighteenth-Century Jamaica," *Journal of Social History*, XXXIV (2001), 928–932, 945. For the state's burden to look for runaways, see Périer and La Chaise to the Company of the Indies's Directors, Mar. 30, 1728, ANOM COL C13A 11, fols. 66–103.

give him enough food. Lafleur argued that he had been wrongly accused of theft and had been whipped and clapped in irons with no food to eat. A young Creole slave named François left because his master sold him to another settler, severing him from his mother. It is difficult, however, to assess how judges took into account mitigating circumstances or mistreatment when deciding on sentences. What is certain is that masters were never prosecuted for cruelty or neglect toward their slaves. By contrast, managers or overseers could sometimes run afoul of justice as owners did not hesitate to turn against them. In 1736, an investigation was launched into one plantation manager to determine whether a group of slaves had run away because of abuse, but the charges were dropped. Decades later, in 1764, another overseer was also interrogated because a group of runaways accused him of mistreatment, yet the slaves in question were severely punished.[41]

Although enslaved defendants were sentenced to terrible corporal punishments, most of them were spared the death penalty. In 1733, Commissaire-ordonnateur Salmon explained to the minister of the navy why two slaves belonging to Governor Périer had not been sentenced to death, even though they had stolen rice from the king's warehouses:

> Strictly speaking, according to the Code Noir they deserved the death penalty, but the Council considered that if all negro thieves were hanged none of them would be spared the gallows because all of them are more or less thieves, and, on the other hand, they declared that they had only stolen to avoid dying of hunger, they were sentenced to the whip and the fleur-de-lis, Mr. Périer's overseer is more blameful than them for he did not give them enough food because at that time there was rice to be sold at 5 livres the quart which weighs 180 livres; thus even though it is expensive for poor habitants this overseer was not excusable for having let these negroes perish of hunger.

41. For slaves' defending themselves, see RSCL 1737/01/10/01; 1738/04/11/02; 1748/05/18/03. Some masters lodged complaints against their overseers because they had overworked, abused, or mistreated slaves, but their suits were always "civilized" (overseers were prosecuted according to civil procedure) and usually resulted in financial damages only. See RSCL 1727/09/02/03, 1727/09/04/01, 1727/09/21/01, 1727/09/21/02, 1727/09/21/03, 1727/09/27/01, 1727/10/22/01, 1727/11/03/01; 1730/04/06/01, 1730/04/29/01, 1730/09/05/02, 1730/09/05/05, 1730/09/07/01, 1730/09/18/01; 1741/02/04/02. For other prosecutions of managers or overseers, see RSCL 1736/08/04/01; 1764/01/01/01, 1764/01/04/01, 1764/01/04/02, 1764/01/25/01, 1764/01/28/01, 1764/01/31/01, 1764/01/31/02, 1764/01/31/03, 1764/02/04/01, 1764/02/05/01, 1764/02/10/01, 1764/02/14/01, 1764/02/14/02, 1764/02/14/03, 1764/02/14/07.

Runaways like thieves were also protected. Before the early 1760s, only one slave convicted of marooning or theft was sentenced to be hanged, despite the fact that the Code Noir prescribed the death penalty for running away on the third offense. Likewise, apart from Pradel's huckster Jupiter, who committed multiple robberies and break-ins, only two other slaves were sentenced to hang, for murdering their wives, and one young slave was condemned to the wheel, for having killed a soldier. In 1742, the attorney general also asked for a slave who had badly injured a soldier to be hanged, but the judges voted a different sentence: the slave was condemned to be flogged, have his ears cut, and wear a chain with a ball weighing six pounds for the rest of his days. They found a way to make him pay until his death while sparing his life. Since settlers could not acquire new slaves easily, masters could not afford a royal justice that was too merciless.[42]

This lack of severity in the implementation of the Code Noir should not be read as a sign that the Superior Council dismissed and was not attached to the royal edict. Although magistrates were reluctant to strictly implement its criminal provisions because they wanted to preserve the plantations' labor force, they tried to teach slaves the code's content at their trials. Slaves were well aware that they were supposed to show that they did not ignore the law. In 1748, one slave acknowledged during his interrogatory that he knew that runaways were severely punished and could even be hanged for having deserted three times. Before the last years of the French regime, the code was mobilized more as an arm for instilling fear rather than for carrying out an implacable judicial vengeance.[43]

In the early 1760s, repression against slaves entered a new stage. Two lists were drawn up of seventeen "esclaves justiciers" chastised or executed from March 1764 to October 1765. Nearly as many slaves were prosecuted and convicted during these twenty months as those whose trials remain extant for the three decades spanning the 1730s to the 1750s. From 1764 to 1767, thirty-three slave trials took place, which means that the repressive campaign stopped only a few months before the 1768 revolt. The harshest years were 1764 and 1765. Although women were rarely prosecuted, two female slaves were tried during this period. Justice was hastier, with fewer interrogatories and generally more severe sentences, even though they still

42. For Salmon's explanation of the Superior Council's clemency in 1733, see Salmon to the minister of the navy, Jan. 18, 1733, ANOM COL C13A 17, fols. 152–153r. For slaves sentenced to be hanged (not taking into account the leaders of the 1730 slave rebellion), see RSCL 1723/10/01/01, 1744/03/21/05, 1748/01/10/03, 1748/05/04/09. For the case of a slave who was spared the death penalty, see RSCL 1742/01/20/02, 1742/01/20/03.

43. For a slave's knowledge of the Code Noir, see RSCL 1748/05/18/03.

varied according to the crimes committed and their circumstances. Prepubescent children and old slaves were spared the usual forms of corporal punishment, and, in four cases, slaves were even set free.[44]

Even so, the rate of convictions in slave trials during this period was extremely high, and corporal punishments were chosen to teach slaves a lesson. Before being executed, César had to make honorable amends for having committed several armed robberies and shooting at settlers and members of the urban militia as well as submit to having his right hand cut. César, like four other slaves, was sentenced to the death penalty. Of these five, three were condemned to be hanged, and two, Louis and César, were to be broken on the wheel. A *retentum* (a secret provision included in the sentence), however, ordered Louis to be strangled before any stroke was given. White convicts, by contrast, were always hanged. Previously, the wheel had been used only once in 1748, to punish a slave who had killed a soldier. The sentence constituted a terrible way to die. After having their arms and legs broken by the executioner, convicts were left to agonize for hours on the wheel. Slaves accused of complicity, such as female partner, in one case, or an old man who was like a father to one convict, in another, could also be ordered to attend and watch executions. Judicial shows were intended to terrorize and educate the slave population. For the same purpose, judges ordered the sentence of another slave, condemned to be hanged in 1764 because he had murdered a fellow slave, to be published in all the outposts of the colony.[45]

44. For different interpretations of this repressive campaign, see Mathé Allain, "Slave Policies in French Louisiana," *Louisiana History*, XXI (1980), 127–137; Carl A. Brasseaux, "The Administration of Slave Regulations in French Louisiana, 1724-1766," *Louisiana History*, XXI (1980), 139–158; and Thomas N. Ingersoll, "The Law and Order Campaign in New Orleans, 1763-1765: A Comparative View," in Sally E. Hadden and Patricia Hagler Minter, eds., *Signposts: New Directions in Southern Legal History* (Athens, Ga., 2013), 45–64. For lists of "esclaves justiciers," see RSCL 1764/97/24/01, 1765/10/10/02, 1766/08/02/04, 1767/09/05/03. For a list of references of the first document pertaining to each of the thirty-three trials from 1764 to 1767, see RSCL 1764/01/01/01; 1764/02/17/01; 1764/04/12/01; 1764/04/23/02; 1764/05/17/01; 1764/06/10/02; 1764/06/20/01; 1764/07/05/03; 1764/07/06/02; 1764/07/08/01; 1764/07/17/01; 1764/07/24/02; 1764/07/31/03; 1764/08/01/01; 1764/08/10/01; 1764/09/03/01; 1764/10/18/01; 1764/10/23/01; 1764/11/14/01; 1765/02/16/01; 1765/02/25/03; 1765/06/03/03; 1765/07/06/01; 1765/10/09/01; 1765/10/20/02; 1766/06/03/01; 1766/06/04/03; 1766/07/21/07; 1766/11/03/03; 1767/02/21/01; 1767/04/24/01; 1767/06/10/01; 1767/08/12/01. For women's trials, see RSCL 1764/09/10/02; 1764/10/23/01. For clemency toward prepubescent children or old slaves, see 1765/09/21/05, 1765/09/21/06; 1765/10/12/01. For slaves who were discharged, see RSCL 1764/05/26/01; 1764/07/28/05.

45. For severe corporal punishments against slaves, see RSCL 1764/06/23/07;

Torture also came to be used relatively frequently during this repressive campaign, though it was never employed lightly. Throughout the French regime, all the members of the Superior Council—the governor and the commissaire-ordonnateur, the other sword officers, and the permanent and assessor councillors—generally attended sessions, while regular investigations were the responsibility of a single judge chosen among the councillors. During the 1740s and 1750s, the court had resorted to preparatory questioning (torture imposed before the final sentence in order to elicit a defendant's confession) and preliminary questioning (torture applied before the execution of the sentence to obtain the confession of other crimes or the denunciation of accomplices) in only three trials, and they all involved slaves. The magistrates behaved in conformity with French judicial culture. Despite the dramatic decline in judicial torture in the metropole over the seventeenth century, its use continued to be legitimated and validated for longer and only came under attack from Enlightenment thinkers during the 1760s. In French New Orleans, it was precisely during this decade that defendants, including one woman, were tortured in twelve trials. Seven of these trials took place in 1764, the same year that Cesare Marquis Beccaria-Bonesana published his treatise on legal reform *On Crimes and Punishments* in which he advocated the ending of torture and the death penalty. Translated first into French and then several other languages, the book quickly gained considerable influence all over Europe. Nonetheless, the use of judicial torture in the colonies against the enslaved was not questioned. The Louisiana Superior Council might have been influenced once again by recent events in Saint-Domingue, where torture was inflicted on Macandal, an infamous slave poisoner and leader of a group of maroons, during his trial in 1758. One case of judicial torture in New Orleans in the 1760s even involved two whites of the lower sort. Although the repressive campaign mainly targeted slaves of African descent, a few poor whites were prosecuted and convicted for cattle theft for the first time since the 1740s,

---

1764/07/21/08, 1764/07/21/09; 1764/09/10/02, 1764/09/10/05; 1765/09/21/06, 1765/09/21/07; 1767/03/14/07. Another slave, Francisque, escaped the death penalty demanded by the attorney general when judges condemned him to be flogged, branded with a letter "V" on the cheek, and then banished, an unusual punishment for a slave. They might have reached this decision because Francisque was an Anglophone slave of high value. See RSCL 1766/07/31/06, 1766/08/02/04. For a white sentenced to the wheel, see RSCL 1748/01/10/03. For enslaved accomplices sentenced to watch the execution of the main criminal, see RSCL 1764/09/10/02, 1765/09/21/06. For the publication of a sentence, see RSCL 1764/06/23/07, 1764/06/23/08.

Formation and Transformation of Racial Categories and Practices

and a white couple was sentenced to banishment outside the colony for having sold alcohol to slaves in exchange for stolen geese.[46]

46. In 1748, a missionary also attended a session of the Superior Council. See RSCL 1748/01/10/01. For early cases of torture, see RSCL 1744/03/21/01, 1744/03/21/02, 1744/03/21/03, 1744/03/21/05; 1748/05/04/03; 1753/05/05/01. In Canada, by comparison, thirty accused criminals were sentenced to judicial torture during the ninety-six years between the creation of the Sovereign Council and the Conquest of 1760 by the British, the majority being soldiers. Only nineteen, however, were actually subjected to torture, since many of them successfully appealed their sentences before the Superior Council. See Lachance, *Le bourreau au Canada sous le régime français*, 27–34. For the use of judicial torture in metropolitan France, see Lisa Silverman, *Tortured Subjects: Pain, Truth, and the Body in Early Modern France* (Chicago, Ill., 2001). For cases of torture in New Orleans in the 1760s, see RSCL 1764/01/01/01, 1764/01/04/01, 1764/02/04/01, 1764/02/05/01, 1764/02/14/02; 1764/04/07/02, 1764/04/07/03, 1764/04/07/04; 1764/07/21/01; 1764/07/24/03; 1764/07/28/01, 1764/07/28/02; 1764/07/26/02; 1764/07/31/02; 1764/09/08/01, 1764/09/10/01; 1765/09/21/01, 1765/09/21/02, 1765/09/21/03, 1765/09/21/04; 1765/11/09/02; 1766/11/14/02; 1766/11/22/01; 1767/08/13/01, 1767/08/13/03; 1767/09/05/01. A major scandal over the torture of two female slaves broke out in Saint-Domingue in 1788, but the issue in contention was, not the use of torture by the state, but by masters. Louis XVI abolished preparatory questioning in judicial procedure in 1780 and extended the prohibition to preliminary questioning in 1788. See Ghachem, *Old Regime and the Haitian Revolution*, 167–210. Macandal was known as François before running away. The plantation on which he was a slave belonged to Le Normant de Mézy, who had served as the commissaire-ordonnateur in New Orleans between 1744 and 1748 after having occupied the position of commissaire-ordonnateur in Cap-Français between 1739 and 1744. Le Normant de Mézy was nominated as intendant of Rochefort in 1750. After having escaped capture for many years while heading various groups of maroons, Macandal was arrested and convicted for having poisoned whites and for spreading knowledge about the use of poison to other slaves in Saint-Domingue. He was burned at the stake in January 1758. See Ghachem, *Old Regime and the Haitian Revolution*, 168, 179–180; and Trevor Burnard and John Garrigus, *The Plantation Machine: Atlantic Capitalism in French Saint-Domingue and British Jamaica* (Philadelphia, 2016), 101–136. For cases of torture of poor whites, see RSCL 1764/03/07/01, 1764/03/08/01, 1764/03/08/02, 1764/03/09/01, 1764/03/10/01, 1764/03/11/01, 1764/03/11/02, 1764/03/15/01, 1764/03/17/01, 1764/03/18/02, 1764/03/20/04, 1764/03/21/01, 1764/03/21/02, 1764/03/22/02, 1764/03/22/03, 1764/04/04/01, 1764/04/06/01, 1764/04/07/02, 1764/04/07/03, 1764/04/07/04, 1764/04/07/05, 1764/04/07/06, 1764/04/23/01, 1764/04/25/01; 1766/09/20/01, 1766/09/11/01, 1766/09/11/02, 1766/09/24/01, 1766/09/24/02, 1766/10/12/03, 1766/10/13/01, 1766/10/13/02, 1766/10/17/01, 1766/10/18/01, 1766/10/18/02, 1766/10/18/03, 1766/10/25/02, 1766/10/25/03, 1766/10/25/01, 1766/11/08/03; 1766/11/08/07; and Denis Nicolas Foucault to the minister of the navy, Nov. 18, 1766, ANOM COL C13A 46, fol. 75rv. For a couple sentenced to banishment, see RSCL 1766/11/22/04.

Judicial action against slaves was supplemented by a series of local regulations related to public order and slave control. They were promulgated by the Superior Council, which also got involved in the management of the Charity Hospital and the prison. Most noticeably, the council prohibited the introduction of creolized slaves from Saint-Dominique in 1763 and from Martinique in 1765 because they were seen as particularly troublesome and dangerous. The Seven Years' War was a period of great slave unrest in the Caribbean. The Macandal poisoning scare in Saint-Domingue of the late 1750s lasted for several years, while massive slave revolts ravaged Jamaica and Dutch Guyana in the early 1760s. To obtain a ban of creolized slaves from Saint-Domingue in 1763, the New Orleans attorney general mentioned the risk of poisoner slaves. This fear was not entirely fantastical: out of the eighteen trials that mentioned the geographic backgrounds of the accused between January 1764 and July 1767, six concerned slaves from the Antilles.[47]

The Superior Council's repressive campaign and pretension to exercise

47. For the Superior Council's repressive legislation against slaves, see "Arrêt du Conseil supérieur de La Nouvelle-Orléans sur les esclaves marrons," Apr. 6, 1763, ANOM COL C13A 43, fols. 304–307; "Arrêt du Conseil supérieur de La Nouvelle-Orléans sur les gens sans aveu," Sept. 3, 1763, ANOM COL C13A, fols. 310–313; RSCL 1763/09/03/01; and "Extrait du registre des audiences du Conseil Supérieur de la province de la Louisiane, remontrances du procureur général du roi, et mesures contre les assemblées d'esclaves (calinda), port d'armes, ventes sans billet des maîtres," Mar. 3, 1764, ANOM COL F3 243, fols. 253–256. For the Superior Council's management of the prison and the Charity Hospital, see "Extrait du registre des audiences du Conseil Supérieur de la province de la Louisiane, sur remontrances du procureur général qui propose un règlement pour les prisons de La Nouvelle-Orléans, approuvé par le Conseil Supérieur qui ordonne son exécution," Feb. 4, 1764, ANOM COL F3 243, fols. 244–246v; and "Extrait du registre des audiences du Conseil Supérieur de la province de la Louisiane, remontrances du procureur général du roi pour le fonctionnement et contrôle de l'hôpital de la charité," Mar. 1, 1764, ANOM COL F3 243, fols. 250–252. For the legislation banning creolized slaves from the Antilles, see "Arrêt du Conseil Supérieur de La Nouvelle-Orléans interdisant l'importation en Louisiane, sous peine d'amendes, de nègres venant de Saint-Domingue," July 9, 1763, ANOM COL C13A 43, fols. 302–303, 308–309; RSCL 1763/07/09/02; and "Arrêt du Conseil Supérieur de la Louisiane autorisant la vente, à la barre de la cour, de 21 nègres arrivés de la Martinique en Louisiane," Nov. 16, 1765, ANOM COL C13A 45, fols. 100–101. Four slaves prosecuted in the 1760s came from Saint-Domingue, one from Martinique, and one from Guadeloupe. They were either Creole (three of them) or African (three). See RSCL 1764/01/01/01, 1764/02/17/01, 1764/05/18/01, 1764/07/06/01, 1764/07/06/02, 1764/07/08/01, 1764/07/19/01, 1764/07/31/02, 1764/08/02/01, 1764/08/10/01, 1764/09/04/02, 1764/10/23/01, 1765/02/26/01, 1765/06/14/01, 1765/09/09/02, 1765/10/10/01, 1766/07/01/07, 1766/07/23/02.

administrative and legislative power coincided with the return of Louisiana native Nicolas La Frénière from the metropole and his nomination as attorney general in 1763. As the first Creole attorney general, he was largely responsible for this major sociopolitical turn. He also later became the principal leader of the 1768 revolt. He was the son of a Canadian who had settled with several of his brothers in the colony early on and had become a rich planter, a militia captain, and a member of the Superior Council. La Frénière had been nominated to serve as an assessor councillor while still a minor, but it was only after he had obtained his law degree in the metropole that he was promoted to the position of attorney general. In June 1764, Jean-Jacques Blaise d'Abbadie, director general of the colony, identified La Frénière as the leader of the Superior Council responsible for its new spirit of independence. In his attempt to increase the prerogatives of the court, La Frénière might have been influenced by the political struggle for legislative power that had stirred up the parlements against the king in the metropole starting in the middle of the century. He might have also drawn his inspiration from the discussions within the two successive *commissions de législation coloniale* (committees on colonial legislation) established in the metropole in 1761, which were working on the reform of the colonial superior councils under the supervision of Émilien Petit, a former councillor of Saint-Domingue.[48]

Although La Frénière provided the impetus, the judicial campaign was apparently backed by the colony's top officials and the other members of the Superior Council. Apart from the epidemic of slave revolts in the Caribbean, the settlers felt particularly vulnerable for a whole series of reasons. First,

48. Governor Kerlérec first began advocating for Nicolas La Frénière's nomination in 1760, after Jean-Baptiste Raguet's death. See Kerlérec to the minister of the navy, Dec. 21, 1760, ANOM COL C13A, fols. 81–82. On the La Frénière family, see Vaudreuil to the minister of the navy, Mar. 18, 1747, ANOM COL C13A 31, fol. 32; and Gary B. Mills, "The Chauvin Brothers: Early Colonists of Louisiana," *Louisiana History*, XV (1974), 117–132. For La Frénière's career, see Vaudreuil and Michel to the minister of the navy, July 24, 1749, ANOM COL C13A 34, fols. 8–9r; and the minister of the navy to Kerlérec and Jean-Jacques Blaise d'Abbadie, Jan. 18, 1762, ANOM COL B 114, fol. 168rv (19r–v). For La Frénière's designation as the leader of the Superior Council, see D'Abbadie to the minister of the navy, June 7, 1764, ANOM COL C13A 44, fols. 58–62r. The commissions de législation coloniale were suppressed in November 1768. Jean Tarrade explains this suppression by the nomination of René Augustin Charles Nicolas de Maupeou as chancellor in September 1768, but it might have also been related to the uprisings led by the superior councils in both Louisiana and Saint-Domingue the same year. See Tarrade, "L'administration coloniale en France à la fin de l'Ancien Régime: Projets de réforme," *Revue historique*, CCXXIX (1963), 103–122.

slaves still outnumbered whites in the lower Mississippi Valley. Second, the English took possession of the left bank of the Mississippi River immediately after peace had been signed, and, by 1764, rumors were also spreading that the king had abandoned New Orleans and the rest of the colony to the Spanish. Most of the troops sent from France during the war went back to the metropole or were transferred to Saint-Domingue, leaving only four *compagnies franches de la Marine* in New Orleans. Last, many local military officers chose to leave and sell their plantations, leading to a dispersal of slaves that forced new planters to impose their authority on recently acquired laborers. La Frénière and the other members of the Superior Council took advantage of these circumstances to advance their own political agenda as they rallied the colony's slaveholders in their efforts to crack down on slaves. One of the "esclaves justiciers" whom the Superior Council punished in 1764–1765 was Marie-Jeanne, a slave who worked at the Charity Hospital. She was probably the same former freed woman who had been sentenced to reenslavement and given to the charitable institution in the 1740s. Royal justice could also be merciless toward free people of color.[49]

Free Blacks before the Superior Council

While the judicial system mainly targeted slaves and largely spared whites, few free blacks ended up before the Superior Council, either as defendants or plaintiffs. Nevertheless, justice was also instrumental in the harsh subordination of free people of color who lived in the city. The Louisiana Code Noir had already toughened the discrimination between whites and free blacks. The 1751 local regulation made the reenslavement of those found guilty of crimes specified under its tenth article compulsory: "All negroes and negresses who had obtained their freedom, and had retired to some corner of the city or the surroundings who housed slaves to serve them and to incite them to steal from their masters, and live a scandalous life contravening royal ordinances and religious rules, will lose their freedom; and will go back to slavery in the king's domain."[50]

49. Ingersoll, *Mammon and Manon in Early New Orleans*, 89–91. For the ordinance reducing the number of compagnies franches de la Marine in New Orleans, see "Ordonnance pour l'établissement de quatre compagnies seulement pour la garde et la police de la ville de la Nouvelle-Orléans," Mar. 16, 1763, ANOM COL F3 243, fol. 287. For court records related to Marie-Jeanne, see RSCL 1746/09/03/05, 1747/04/11/01; 1764/09/05/01, 1764/09/10/02.

50. "Règlement sur la police pour la province de la Louisiane," Feb. 28–Mar. 1, 1751, Article 10, ANOM COL C13A 35, fol. 44r.

Local authorities had begun to impose discriminatory and merciless punishment on free people of color even before the promulgation of the 1751 bylaw. In 1722, they condemned a free black man in Biloxi named Larose to be whipped and forced to labor on a galley or in some other form of service to the king for six years. They also convicted at least two free blacks, including Marie-Jeanne, for theft and sentenced them to reenslavement in the 1740s. In 1763, Sieur Jean Trudeau, *aide-major,* presented a request on behalf of Jean-Baptiste, *"cy-devant libre"* ("formerly free"), who had been reduced by the council to perpetual servitude in 1757. The judges had ordered the convict to be kept in jail until he was sent to another colony to be sold. According to Trudeau, six years later, Jean Baptiste, "repenting of the debauchery for which he had lost his freedom," had begged him to ask the court to commute his punishment and order that he remain a slave in the colony. The magistrates decided to sell Jean-Baptiste to Trudeau for one thousand livres. Since the possibility of reenslavement was not an idle threat, it is not surprising that the only two cases that have been found of assault involving a free black man and a white man concerned transient free men of color who did not live permanently in the colony. Local free blacks would not have dared to attack a white. In contrast, such cases happened in Saint-Domingue, even though judges punished free blacks harshly for such crimes.[51]

Despite the severity of justice, some free blacks also turned to the Superior Council to protect their rights. According to the Code Noir, manumissions had to be confirmed by local authorities in order to be legally valid. Masters often asked for the council's approval, but many owners apparently

51. Although Larose's trial took place in 1722, the sentence was recorded much later at the clerk's office, maybe because he tried to obtain a legal certificate that he had completed his sentence. See RSCL 1730/07/31/03. For free people of color sentenced to reenslavement, see RSCL 1743/08/19/02, 1743/08/19/03, 1743/08/22/01, 1743/08/22/02, 1743/08/22/03, 1743/08/22/04, 1743/08/22/05, 1743/08/24/01, 1743/08/24/04, 1743/08/24/05, 1743/09/10/03, 1743/09/11/01, 1743/09/14/03, 1743/09/14/06; 1746/09/03/05, 1747/04/11/01. For Jean Trudeau's request on behalf of Jean-Baptiste, see RSCL 1763/09/03/08. In Saint-Domingue, cases of assault by free blacks against whites were always criminalized in the second half of the eighteenth century. In contrast, white assaults on free blacks were treated as civil suits giving rights to honor reparations and financial damages for the persons who had brought charges in case the defendant was found guilty. Moreover, free people of color who attacked a white person were often condemned to severe punishment such as banishment, forced labor, or having to wear an iron collar. See Rogers, "Les libres de couleur dans les capitales de Saint-Domingue," chapter 5, 358–363.

just freed their slaves privately and did not make the effort to request official confirmation. Most slaves probably felt that they could not do anything to put an end to their ambiguous and dangerous legal status. Exceptionally, in 1735, Marie, a "négresse," asked the court to legally confirm the freedom that had been privately granted to her and her husband by her master, who happened to be Governor Jean-Baptiste Le Moyne de Bienville. She cited the Code Noir to support her request. The council asked that their freedom be confirmed by Bienville and the commissaire-ordonnateur. In 1737, another free woman of color named Marion also went before the court and cited the code to fight against the attorney for vacant estates, who claimed that her manumission was invalid. Likewise, a few free blacks recorded their freedom papers. Some free men of color presented requests to the Superior Council to obtain the full execution of agreements concluded with their former masters for the manumission of their wives. No free black ever lodged a complaint against a white for violence or theft, but, a few, like the executioner Louis Congo, did so against enslaved or free men of color.[52]

Apart from the exceptional case of Raphaël Bernard in the early 1720s, free blacks rarely went to court to settle affairs related to work or property. Most lived with their former masters and lacked the financial means to act as significant economic actors. In contrast, free people of color in cities on Saint-Domingue in the second half of the eighteenth century constituted a great economic force and did not hesitate to take legal action to obtain the full payment of debts or wages or the execution of contracts for building or repair work, and a significant number of them won their trials. Free blacks maintained a different relationship to justice in Saint-Domingue and Louisiana in correlation with their respective demographic and economic situations. These circumstances also explain why the enrollment of people of African descent in military operations and units followed different paths in the islands and in New Orleans.[53]

52. For Marie's request, see RSCL 1735/06/04/01, 1735/06/04/02. For Marion's case, see RSCL 1735/10/09/01, 1737/07/29/01; and "Petition," Feb. 6, 1745, in Heloise H. Cruzat, ed., "RSCL XLVII: January–February, 1745," *LHQ*, XIII (1930), 517. For the recording of freedom papers, see RSCL 1742/05/24/01, 1742/10/17/01. For Louis Congo, see RSCL 1726/08/17/03, 1737/01/24/04. For other conflicts between free blacks, see RSCL 1745/05/17/01; 1769/03/30/01.

53. For Raphaël Bernard, see Chapter 6. For the relationship of free people of color to the judicial system in Saint-Domingue's cities, see Rogers, "Les libres de couleur dans les capitales de Saint-Domingue," chapter 5, 342–358.

MILITIA SERVICE: THE QUEST FOR HONOR, CIVIC COHESION, AND RACIAL EXCLUSIVENESS

After the relatively long period of peace following the short war against Spain in 1719, the lower Mississippi Valley was disturbed by a series of military events starting in the early 1730s: the Natchez Wars in 1729–1731, the two military expeditions against the Chickasaw in 1736 and 1739, the War of the Austrian Succession (1740–1748), and the Seven Years' War (1754–1763). Although Lower Louisiana was spared actual attacks and battles during the two imperial wars. The need for defense triggered a militarization of New Orleans and Louisiana society that closely paralleled the one experienced earlier by Canada. Apart from the presence of soldiers, the requirements of war influenced governmental organization and increased centralization of power. Louisiana was headed by a governor who was a military officer and represented the king. He ruled the colony, in collaboration with the commissaire-ordonnateur, and he commanded the armed forces, with the assistance of the *lieutenant de roi* and major. The militarization of society also impacted the position of military officers, who occupied the top of the social hierarchy. Their corporate body was open to the sons of the local elite, as the monarch granted them commissions as officers in the Compagnies franches de la Marine. Military service proved to be the easiest way for the monarchy to coopt the colonial elite.[54]

Most of all, the militarization of society took place through the creation of militia companies in which all white men of arms-bearing age were required to serve. After 1729, militia service constituted the only tax that all white settlers had to pay to the crown. Among whites, the universality of militia service and the fact that it was a personal, not communal, obligation made colonial militias an institution with no equivalent in the kingdom. Yet, in practice, more similarities than not existed between New Orleans's *compagnies de milice bourgeoises* (urban militia companies) and those existing in the metropole. The white militia companies contributed to integrating settlers within the French Empire and to connecting the local elite with the king. They also played a crucial role in fostering the cohesion of a white civic community within the city. A free colored militia company was institutionalized by French local authorities at the end of the Seven Years' War. Military service allowed free blacks to gain dignity and honor and to distinguish themselves from slaves, but this social mobility was at the price

---

54. On the militarization of Canadian society, see Louise Dechêne, *Le peuple, l'État, et la guerre au Canada sous le Régime français,* ed. Hélène Paré et al. (Montreal, 2008).

of their segregation from whites. By joining the nonwhite militia, free black men unwillingly helped to perpetuate the racial order.[55]

Militia Service and the Construction of Whiteness

Although the Company of the Indies had envisioned the creation of militia companies on the model of those existing in other colonies early on, it was only after the outbreak of the Natchez Wars that the colony's first four compagnies de milice bourgeoises were established. As in Canada, where the militia was institutionalized to fight the Iroquois, indigenous danger explains their introduction in Louisiana. Their organization in January 1730, followed by the arrival of a royal vessel with reinforcements from the navy and the army in September 1730, brought relief and reassurance to the urban population. Both the troops and the militia companies participated together in a general review that was organized on New Orleans's main square before the troops went to war against the Natchez. The ceremony constituted a show of force intended to threaten Native Americans

55. On the specificity of militia service in colonies, see ibid., 111–119. On militia companies in metropolitan France, see Laurent Coste, "Les milices bourgeoises en France," in Jean-Pierre Poussou, ed., *Les sociétés urbaines au XVIIe siècle: Angleterre, France, Espagne* (Paris, 2007), 175–188; and Serge Bianchi and Roger Dupuy, eds., *La Garde nationale entre nation et peuple en armes: Mythes et réalités, 1789–1871* (Rennes, France, 2006). Most historians of Louisiana, following Roland C. McConnell, believe that "a regular company of free Negroes had become a reality" during the second expedition against the Chickasaw (1739–1740) and that this company remained on active duty during the last decades of the French regime. McConnell also stated that free men of color were "definitely organized into a company with their own officers by the second Chickasaw war." See McConnell, *Negro Troops of Antebellum Louisiana: A History of the Battalion of Free Men of Color* (Baton Rouge, La., 1968), 3–14 (quotations, 13–14); and McConnell, "Louisiana's Black Military History, 1729–1865," in Robert R. Macdonald, John R. Kemp, and Edward F. Haas, eds., *Louisiana's Black Heritage* (New Orleans, 1979), 32–62. Others, however, think that the company was disbanded after 1740 and that the Spanish governor O'Reilly used this "'ghost' free black militia" to create new companies. For historians who claim that "French authorities created a permanent free black military force" during the 1730s, see Caryn Cossé Bell, *Revolution, Romanticism, and the Afro-Creole Protest Tradition in Louisiana, 1718–1868* (Baton Rouge, La., 2004), 16 (quotation); and Daniel H. Usner, Jr., *Indians, Settlers, and Slaves in a Frontier Exchange Economy: The Lower Mississippi Valley before 1783* (Chapel Hill, N.C., 1992). For those who argue that the company was disbanded after 1740, see Kimberly S. Hanger, "A Privilege and Honor to Serve: The Free Black Militia of Spanish New Orleans," *Military History of the Southwest*, XXI (1991), 59–86; Hanger, *Bounded Lives, Bounded Places*, 109–135, esp. 117–118 (quotation, 118); and Thomas N. Ingersoll, "Free Blacks in a Slave Society: New Orleans, 1718–1812," *William and Mary Quarterly*, XLVIII (1991), 180.

and African slaves and to exhibit the unity of white city dwellers, despite their diversity of conditions, under the protection of the king. After the reception of Antoine-Alexis Périer de Salvert, the governor's brother, who had arrived with the troops from the metropole as the new lieutenant general of the province of Louisiana, some drills were performed to display the transformation of the habitants into settler-soldiers. The review was followed by a week of "joy and uninterrupted entertainment." The ceremony constituted a first step in the militarization of Louisiana's society that was further reinforced in the following decades.[56]

Originally, militia companies were mobilized only in times of war and reverted to a dormant state with the return of peace. During the Natchez Wars, the mission of the urban militia companies was to police the city, patrol, and mount the guard. Some militiamen participated in the French-Chickasaw War of 1736, but they were relegated to guarding the city once more during the 1739 campaign. In 1752, however, they became more active when the king instructed the new governor, Kerlérec, to regularly review the companies to see that they were well trained and armed. The goal was to ensure that they were operational, although they were only to be called to serve when absolutely necessary. During the Seven Years' War, they were assigned an actual military role in the defense of the colony. Militiamen were also called to arms with the troops for official ceremonies, such as those organized to celebrate the return of the governor from trips to Mobile or the arrival of a new official in the colony.[57]

56. For the company's early project of creating militia companies, see "Règlement sur la régie des affaires de la Louisiane …," Sept. 5, 1721, ANOM COL C13A 6, fols. 196–236, or ANOM COL F3 241, fols. 303–337, esp. fols. 323–324. For the actual creation of the militia companies during the Natchez Wars, see [Marc-Antoine Caillot], "Relation de voyage du la Louisianne ou Nouvlle. France fait par le Sr. CAILLOT en l'année 1730," HNOC, MSS596, fols. 150–152, 177–180; and Dumont de Montigny, *Regards sur le monde atlantique*, 260.

57. For the role of militia companies during the Natchez Wars, see [Caillot], "Relation de voyage de la Louisianne ou Nouvlle. France fait par le Sr. CAILLOT en l'année 1730," HNOC, MSS596, fols. 150–152, 177–180; and Dumont de Montigny, *Regards sur le monde atlantique*, 269. In 1736, Bienville called for one militia company from New Orleans, another from Mobile, and a third company to be formed of *voyageurs* (travelers) and volunteers who happened to be in New Orleans. Only unmarried men were enlisted in the militia companies. See "Relation de la guerre des Chicachas attaqués par l'armée de La Nouvelle-Orléans commandée par M. de Bienville gouverneur de cette province," 1736, ANOM COL C13A 21, fol. 164; "État des troupes et milices qui ont fait la campagne des Chicachas," ANOM COL C13A 21, fol. 187; Jean-Baptiste Le Moyne de Bienville to

The Seven Years' War seems to have played a crucial role in giving a permanent reality to the militia companies that did not cease with the advent of peace. As early as the late 1750s, Commissaire-Ordonnateur Vincent-Gaspard-Pierre de Rochemore had already pleaded for the expansion of militia companies rather than the regular garrison because he considered the latter prejudicial to the demographic and economic development of the colony. He cited the example of the Antilles to support his claim: "Martinique and Saint-Domingue would very likely be deserted islands if the bourgeois militia were not the main force." After 1763, this policy became a necessity, for the king ordered the general discharge of troops in Louisiana, and they were progressively sent to Saint-Domingue or France. Although the city housed the Angoumois Regiment and extra Compagnies franches de la Marine during the war, the New Orleans garrison was reduced to four companies in 1763. From then on, the city was structured and organized around white militia companies. Because militia captains were responsible for taking censuses, they started to play an administrative role that increased their importance in the eyes of the local population. A review of the militia units apparently took place every Sunday and became a moment of sociability among male city dwellers. Militiamen also assisted soldiers in policing the city against slave unrest. The greater involvement of militia companies in defending and maintaining order in New Orleans coincided with the greater power acquired by the Superior Council in the administration of the city and the colony and with the wave of judicial repression against slaves. It partook of the efforts of the local elite to expand their political autonomy.[58]

---

the minister of the navy, June 28, 1736, ANOM COL C13A 21, fol. 190; and Dumont de Montigny, *Regards sur le monde atlantique*, 269. For the limited role of militia companies in the second campaign against the Chickasaw, see minister of the navy to Salmon, Dec. 20, 1739, ANOM COL F3 242, fol. 300r. For the increasing importance of militia companies beginning in the 1750s, see "Mémoire du roi pour servir d'instruction au Sieur de Kerlérec, gouverneur de la province de la Louisiane," Oct. 17 1752, no. 9, ANOM COL B 95, fol. 338; Kerlérec to François Simard de Bellisle, Feb. 25, 1759, ANOM COL C13A 40, fols. 17–23; Extracts of letters from comte de Fremeur (colonel of the Angoumois Regiment in New Orleans), June 25, 1762, ANOM COL C13A 37, fols. 223v–224r; and Rochemore to the minister of the navy, Aug. 27, 1760, ANOM COL C13A 42, fols. 147–150r.

58. On militia companies in the 1760s, see Rochemore to the minister of the navy, Jan. 2, [1758 or 1759], ANOM COL C13A 40, fols. 174v–175r; and "Ordonnance pour l'établissement de quatre compagnies seulement pour la garde et la police de la ville de la Nouvelle-Orléans," Mar. 16, 1763, ANOM COL F3 243, fol. 287; RSCL 1764/03/08/01, 1764/07/10/02, 1764/07/13/01, 1764/07/21/02. For the removal of troops to Saint-

Members of the upper class coveted appointments as militia officers because they both sanctioned and increased social superiority while creating a direct connection with the king. In 1730, the captains chosen by Governor Périer to head the city's first four militia companies were members of the Superior Council. After the participation of two militia companies in the 1736 Chickasaw War, Commissaire-ordonnateur Salmon attempted to increase the authority of militia officers by asking that they be granted royal commissions, following complaints regarding a lack of discipline among the men, whom militia officers felt they should be authorized to punish. The king agreed, and, afterward, commissions of militia officers were regularly sent from the metropole. The crown, however, apparently did not comply with the militia officers' additional request for uniforms, although the settlers were willing to pay for them. In 1757, Governor Kerlérec went even further in his efforts to secure privileges on behalf of a militia officer by requesting a *brevet* (the document officially recognizing his participation in the king's service and giving rights to a pension from the crown) for Joseph Dubreuil, arguing that such favors existed for militia officers in Saint-Domingue and Martinique. Dubreuil's father, who died in 1757, had been one of the most prominent planters in the colony and the royal contractor of public works.[59]

Despite the apparent universal support for militia service among settlers, the military obligation created social tension and was not accepted by all white civilians. When the militia companies were first established in 1730, only habitants, not company employees, were enlisted, a point which led to contention. The settlers complained that company employees did not have to mount guard in the city, even though they still made patrols. In an effort to maintain their rank above settlers, the company employees, in turn, refused to be enlisted within the same militia companies as the habitants. Governor Périer agreed to let them form their own company of cadets,

Domingue in 1763, see Carl A. Brasseaux, "Introduction: The French and Canadian Precursors of Louisiana's Administrative and Military Institutions," in Brasseaux, *France's Forgotten Legion: A CD-ROM Publication; Service Records of French Military and Administrative Personnel Stationed in the Mississippi Valley and Gulf Coast Region, 1699–1769* (Baton Rouge, La., 2000), 74–75.

59. [Caillot], "Relation de voyage de la Louisianne ou Nouvlle. France," HNOC, MSS596, fols. 151, 179–180; Salmon to the minister of the navy, June 17, 1736, ANOM COL C13A 21, fol. 279; Kerlérec to the minister of the navy, Sept. 19, 1758, ANOM COL C13A 40, fol. 67r; Salmon to the minister of the navy, May 12, 1737, ANOM COL C13A 22, fols. 152–154v; Vaudreuil to the minister of the navy, Mar. 18, 1747, ANOM COL C13A 31, fol. 32; Kerlérec to the minister of the navy, Jan. 31, 1757, ANOM COL C13A 39, fol. 255.

which served as the *"colonelle"* (as the first unit was called); to pick their own captain, the general storekeeper; and to drill and patrol separately. They also wore fancy uniforms to distinguish themselves from the colonists. Although this company seems to have disappeared after the colony's retrocession, pen employees still retained a special status. In the early 1760s, not only were all civilian officers with commissions, brevets, or letters of service exempt from militia service, but employees working for the commissaire-ordonnateur without a brevet also usually benefited from the same privilege. Rochemore vehemently complained to the minister of the navy that, in the absence of the governor, the zealous temporary commandant of the city, Barthélémy, chevalier de Macarty, who had just arrived from the Illinois Country in New Orleans, had thrown all the commissaire-ordonnateur's employees without a brevet into military jail because they had not participated in the ceremony organized for the return of the governor from Mobile. His gardener experienced the same fate in civilian jail, although Rochemore did not know that he had been enlisted. In 1770, "clerks at the French Bureau" still kept their special status and were recorded separately at the end of the roll of militiamen.[60]

Exemption from militia service concerned not only pen employees but also prominent habitants and merchants. At the time of the 1760 incident, Rochemore reported that "Mr. de Macarty also threw into the military prison twenty habitants or merchants and shopkeepers, all of them fusiliers in the militia, and whose occupations in relation with their estate or other reasons had prevented from being under arms the same day for the arrival of the governor." Such indiscipline was not exceptional. In 1758, Kerlérec sent an officer from New Orleans to the Île aux Chats "with a garrison

60. In the metropolitan urban militias, soldiers sometimes participated in the designation of their officers. See Coste, "Les milices bourgeoises en France," in Poussou, ed., *Les sociétés urbaines au XVIIe siècle,* 181–182. On tensions between settlers and company employees over militia service in the early 1730s, see [Caillot], "Relation de voyage de la Louisianne ou Nouvlle. France," HNOC, MSS596, fols. 150–152. For the exemption of civilian officers with commissions, brevets, or letters of service from militia service, see "Mémoire du roi pour servir d'instruction au Sieur de Kerlérec, gouverneur de la province de la Louisiane," Oct. 17 1752, no. 9, ANOM COL B 95, fol. 338; and Dechêne, *Le peuple, l'État, et la guerre au Canada sous le Régime français,* ed. Paré et al., 114. For conflict over the militia service of employees of the commissaire-ordonnateur without a brevet in the early 1760s, see Rochemore to the minister of the navy, Aug. 27, 1760, ANOM COL C13A 42, fols. 149–150; and "Milices Nelle Orléans, le 25 janvier 1770," AGI, Correspondencia de los Gobernadores de la Luisiana y la Florida Occidental, Años 1766–1824, Session Papeles de Cuba, legajo 188-A.

formed of soldiers and habitants from this Capital; but these habitants were all vagrants that the prominent settlers put in their place with the agreement of the Governor, to serve at this outpost. These tramps stayed on the Île aux Chats as long as they were paid by the urban dwellers who were required to mount guard." In 1770, craftsmen and laborers accounted for most of the militiamen recorded in New Orleans.[61]

Seven male *"Bohémiens"* ("Gypsies") were also listed on the 1770 militia rolls but on a separate list from white soldiers. In the last decades of the seventeenth century, Bohemians had suffered from increasing repression at the hands of both royal and local legislation in France, where they were likened to vagrants and criminals. The royal declaration of 1682, in particular, ordered the arrest of all Bohemians. The men were to be sent to the galleys and the women and children to be confined in general hospitals. Some were probably deported as convicts to Louisiana. A few became free settlers after having completed their time. Still, they were unable to completely merge with the French population. They were identified as "Bohémien" in the censuses and court records, even when they served as witnesses. This marginalization had to do with race-thinking. Jean-François-Benjamin Dumont de Montigny did not hesitate to draw a comparison between Bohemians and Native Americans based on their skin color: "All the Indians [savages] in general are ruddy in complexion and, indeed, all over their bodies, nearly like the Bohemians who come to France." Not only were Bohemians marginalized, but they were also the victims of some distinct forms of control and repression. In 1770, it was Governor Alejandro O'Reilly who ordered that militia rolls be drawn up, yet it was French employees who did the job. The treatment of Bohemians testifies to the importance that was given to the racial exclusiveness of white urban militia companies. Not surprisingly, when local authorities decided to include free men of color in the militia on a more permanent basis, they created a segregated unit.[62]

61. Rochemore to the minister of the navy, Aug. 27, 1760, ANOM COL C13A 42, fols. 149–150; Bossu, *Nouveaux voyages aux Indes occidentales*, II, 127; "Milices Nelle Orléans, le 25 janvier 1770," AGI, Correspondencia de los Gobernadores de la Luisiana y la Florida Occidental, Años 1766–1824, Session Papeles de Cuba, legajo 188-A, and "Etat des quatre compagnies de milice de La Nouvelle-Orléans, 12 février 1770."

62. For the distinct listing of "bohemians" on militia rolls, see "Milices Nelle Orléans, le 25 janvier 1770," AGI, Correspondencia de los Gobernadores de la Luisiana y la Florida Occidental, Años 1766–1824, Session Papeles de Cuba, legajo 188-A. For general studies on Bohemians in early modern France, see François de Vaux de Foletier, *Les Tsiganes dans l'Ancienne France* ([Paris], 1961); Henriette Asséo, "Marginalité et exclusion:

The Belated "Company of the Free Mulattoes and Negroes of This Colony of Louisiana"

Local authorities in French Louisiana never envisioned using free or enslaved men in the same military units or capacities as white settlers, whereas mixed units operated at various points in Saint-Domingue. Although fear of a slave revolt or a union between enslaved and free people of color against white settlers prevented the creation of a permanent segregated unit during the Natchez Wars, the event was important because the few slaves who helped the French were freed. Afterward, local authorities started to pay attention to free people of color and to consider how they could be used in matters of colonial policy. But various factors, including the willingness of colonists to serve in white militia companies, the relatively small number of free blacks in the colony, the arrival of military reinforcements from the metropole as needed, the absence of actual battles in Louisiana during imperial wars, and the racial prejudice of local authorities continued to stand in the way of the establishment of a standing free colored militia company on the model of those that existed in the Antilles until the very end of the Seven Years' War. The single unit, finally created in the early 1760s, was based at the English Turn, where Governor Vaudreuil had started to settle free people of color in a segregated district during the 1740s. The military incorporation of free blacks did not contradict the policy of racial exclusiveness that local authorities sought to implement; rather, it served to perpetuate it.[63]

Le traitement administratif des Bohémiens dans la société française du XVIIe siècle," in Asséo, Jean-Pierre Vittu, and Robert Mandrou, eds., *Problèmes socio-culturels en France au XVIIe siècle* (Paris, 1974), 9–87; and David D. Boutera, "Les Bohémiens en Bretagne sous l'Ancien Régime," *Annales de Bretagne et des pays de l'Ouest*, CXIII, no. 4, *Varia* (2006), 135–158, http://abpo.revues.org/546. For conceptions and treatment of Bohemians in French Louisiana, see RSCL 1743/07/06/01; 1744/04/24/01; and Gordon M. Sayre and Carla Zecher, eds., *The Memoir of Lieutenant Dumont, 1715-1747: A Sojourner in the French Atlantic; Jean-François-Benjamin Dumont de Montigny*, trans. Sayre (Chapel Hill, N.C., 2012), 337 (quotation).

63. While free blacks in the district of Cap-Français formed their own militia company early on, free men of mixed ancestry and whites served in the same units there until after 1724. In the South Province, white and free colored militiamen were not separated into distinct companies before the early 1740s. See Garrigus, *Before Haiti*, 95–96. During the Spanish regime in Louisiana, free blacks served in white militia units in Opelousas and Natchitoches. The racial exclusiveness of the free colored militias in Spanish New Orleans was a legacy of the French period, although this kind of organization also existed in other Spanish territories, including Cuba. See Hanger, *Bounded Lives, Bounded Places*, 112.

Given that all imperial powers resorted to black military forces, either enslaved or free, in vulnerable frontier settlements and in periods of war to compensate for the scarcity of manpower, it is not surprising that Louisiana authorities started to occasionally enlist people of African descent for military service in the 1730s, a decade fraught by conflict with Native Americans.[64] In addition to using slaves to dig a ditch and build a stockade around New Orleans, Governor Périer called for their participation in the militia on three occasions during the Natchez Wars (1729–1730), although only a few actually responded. In May 1730, the attorney general, François Fleuriau, proposed to his colleagues on the Superior Council to free those slaves who supported the French, starting with the six slaves who went to the Illinois outpost to warn local authorities of the Natchez attack on the promise that they would gain their freedom. He also suggested the formation of a permanent company of free blacks to be called on for duty when necessary. Similar military units already existed in the Antilles, but it was the intense anxiety and helplessness that New Orleans inhabitants experienced after the Natchez killing that explains the proposal to introduce such an innovation in the Mississippi colony. Nevertheless, only a few slaves were freed, probably no more than a dozen, and a militia company was not created at the time. As Périer underlined, slave labor was too scarce and precious in this nascent colony to dispense with. Furthermore, more slaves seem to have sided with the Native Americans, and a slave conspiracy was discovered in New Orleans in late June 1731.[65]

64. For the circumstantial use of enslaved and free people of color in English colonies, see Maria Alessandra Bollettino, "'Of Equal or of More Service': Black Soldiers and the British Empire in the Mid-Eighteenth-Century Caribbean," *Slavery and Abolition,* XXVIII (2017), 510–533; Roger Norman Buckley, *Slaves in Red Coats: The British West India Regiments, 1795–1815* (New Haven, Conn., 1979); Sylvia R. Frey, *Water from the Rock: Black Resistance in a Revolutionary Age* (Princeton, N.J., 1991), 77; and Peter H. Wood, *Black Majority: Negroes in Colonial South Carolina from 1760 through the Stono Rebellion* (1974; rpt. New York, 1974), 124–130. For Saint-Domingue, see "Ordonnance des administrateurs, touchant les nègres à armer en temps de guerre," Sept. 9, 1709, in [Médéric Louis-Élie Moreau] de Saint-Méry, *Loix et constitutions des colonies françoises de l'Amérique sous le vent,* 6 vols. (Paris, 1784–1790), II, 167, and "Ordonnance des administrateurs, concernant le choix des nègres destinés pour porter les armes contre les ennemis de l'État," Feb. 14, 1759, IV, 244–246.

65. In December 1729, Périer asked a few black men to attack the Chaouacha living in the vicinity of the Louisiana capital during the period of intense panic in the weeks after the attack at the Natchez outpost. In mid-January 1730, the governor also sent a pirogue with a detachment of twenty "men of good will," including six "negroes," to warn the Illinois outpost and to take in voyageurs on the Mississippi. Finally, later that month, fifteen

Free blacks occasionally appear as participants in accounts of military campaigns against Native Americans after 1730, but not as part of a long-lasting militia unit. When Governor Bienville organized his first expedition against the Chickasaw in 1736, he wrote to Versailles that the troops included a "surplus of 140 negroes from which one company of fifty men of those people has been formed, commanded by free negroes." He had decided to gather these 45 or 50 slaves—not free blacks—in a company on the ground once he had arrived at Tombecbe. Three years later, during his second campaign against the Chickasaw, the governor explained to the minister that "I am not ordering any militia to march, I have urged them to supply us with around 250 negroes to assist with the boats that need to be brought up to the warehouse from which I intend to send them back to their masters." Bienville's problem was not the size of his military forces, since he had received reinforcements from the metropole and Canada, but the logistics of moving his army to the interior of the continent, especially because he did not know the way to the Chickasaw towns. Most of the 270

------

black men took part in the first retaliatory expedition against the Natchez led by Pierre Diron d'Artaguiette. See "Relation du massacre des Natchez arrivé le 29 novembre 1729," Mar. 18, 1730, ANOM COL C13A 12, fols. 37–46. The original document manumitting slaves who supported the French during the Natchez War, dated May 13, 1730, is in bad condition, and it is difficult to clearly decipher the names of the six slaves who were freed. The list at the end of the document probably includes Caesar, Crispin, Hardy, Simon, and at least two other names. See RSCL 1730/05/13/01; Fleuriau, "Proposition to Free Negroes for Military Merit," May 13, 1730, in [Henry P. Dart], ed., "RSCL XII [XIII]," *LHQ*, IV (1921), 524; and "Proposal to Free Negroes: Memorial of Mr. de La Chaise," May 16, 1730, in Heloise Hulse Cruzat, ed., "New Orleans under Bienville: Sidelights on New Orleans in Bienville's Time," *LHQ*, I, no. 3 (January 1918), 132–133. Since La Chaise died on February 6, 1730, this memorial was probably written earlier. See Burial of Jacques de La Chaise, Feb. 7, 1730, ANOM COL G1 412, fol. 107r; Marcel Giraud, *A History of French Louisiana*, V, *The Company of the Indies, 1723–1731*, trans. Brian Pearce (Baton Rouge, La., 1991), 107, 110–111; and McConnell, *Negro Troops of Antebellum Louisiana*, 8. On the early use of slaves and free people of color in specific military expeditions and on the permanent employment of free people of color in the *maréchaussée* (rural police force), militia companies, and special regiments in the army in the Antilles, see Élisabeth, *La société martiniquaise aux XVIIe et XVIIIe siècles*, 52, 57, 66–67, 427; King, *Blue Coat or Powdered Wig*, 52–77; Stewart R. King, "The Maréchaussée of Saint-Domingue: Balancing the Ancien Régime and Modernity," *Journal of Colonialism and Colonial History*, V, no. 2 (Fall 2004); and Garrigus, *Before Haiti*, 42–43, 95–139. For reasons not to create a permanent free colored militia company in New Orleans, see "Relation du massacre des Natchez arrivé le 29 novembre 1729," Mar. 18, 1730, ANOM COL C13A 12, fol. 46r; and McConnell, "Louisiana's Black Military History, 1729–1865," in Macdonald, Kemp, and Haas, eds., *Louisiana's Black Heritage*, 33.

slaves who were finally enlisted were not armed. Apart from a few women employed as nurses in the field hospital, enslaved men were used to row boats and to pull carts.[66] The only document that refers to a "company of fifty free negroes" is a "list of the army of Mississippi" drawn up by an officer named Fontaine-Mervé. Neither the governor of the colony, Bienville, the commissaire-ordonnateur, Salmon, the commandant of the metropolitan troops, Louis Aymé de Noailles, nor the engineer in chief, Bernard de Vergès, mentioned it. In their eyes, the unit had no great importance, either on a military or a social level.[67] The company, if it ever existed, was very

66. For the use of enslaved and free people of color in the campaigns against the Chickasaw, see "Relation de la guerre des Chicachas attaqués par l'armée de la Nouvelle-Orléans commandée par M. de Bienville gouverneur de cette province," 1736, ANOM COL C13A 21, fol. 164; Bienville to the minister of the navy, June 28, 1736, ANOM COL C13A 21, fol. 191r; and Bienville to the minister of the navy, Sept. 4, 1739, ANOM COL C13A 24, fol. 93r. For Salmon's figures, see Salmon to the minister of the navy, Jan. 2, 1740, ANOM COL C13A 25, fol. 134r. For references to the way slaves were employed, see Bienville to the minister of the navy, Aug. 30, 1739, ANOM COL C13A 24, fols. 85–87v; "Extrait d'une lettre écrite par M. de Bienville à M. de Louboey du fort de l'Assomption le 8 décembre dernier," [1740], ANOM COL C13A 25, fol. 282r; Extracts from de Vergès's journal, ANOM COL C13A 25, fols. 315–336, esp. 319r; and "Journal de la campagne contre les Chicachas de M. Aymé de Noailles," June 1, 1739–July 8, 1740, AN Marine B4 45, fols. 361–405.

67. For the only document mentioning a free colored militia company, see "Liste de l'armée du Mississippi (Fontaine-Mervé)," Manuscrits de la Bibliothèque de l'Institut de France, MS 487 Mélanges historiques, Recueil A, fol. 562. This list was quoted by Marc Villiers du Terrage, who misspelled the name of the officer. Roland McConnell based his narrative on the creation of the free colored militia company on Villiers du Terrage's book, but he did not check the original document. See Villiers du Terrage, Les dernières années de la Louisiane française: Le Chevalier de Kerlérec, D'Abbadie-Aubrey, Laussat (Paris, [1903]), 22; and McConnell, Negro Troops of Antebellum Louisiana, 13. Another report to the minister of the navy mentions that Bienville "has levied 300 negroes from the habitants, from which a group could be armed, they could always be used to relieve the soldiers from the Marine who are not used to rowing." See "La Louisiane, guerre des Chicachas," Sept. 22, 1739, ANOM COL C13A 24, fol. 101r. For correspondence from Bienville and Salmon, both separately and together, with the minister of the navy, see Bienville to the minister of the navy, Oct. 31, 1738, ANOM COL C13A 23, fol. 99v; Bienville and Salmon to the minister of the navy, June 9, 1739, ANOM COL C13A 24, fol. 3; Bienville and Salmon to the minister of the navy, Aug. 10, 1739, ANOM COL C13A 24, fol. 11; Salmon to the minister of the navy, Aug. 26, 1739, ANOM COL 24, fol. 28; Bienville to the minister of the navy, May 12, 1739, ANOM COL C13A 24, fols. 52r–54r; Bienville to the minister of the navy, Aug. 30, 1739, ANOM COL C13A 24, fols. 85–87v; Bienville to the minister of the navy, Sept. 4, 1739, ANOM COL C13A 24, fols. 89–94r; "La Louisiane, guerre des Chicachas," Sept. 22, 1739, ANOM COL C13A 24, fols. 95–103;

likely dismantled after the second Chickasaw expedition. In any event, no one had the opportunity to prove their military prowess, since the attack never took place. None of the enslaved recruits who served as rowers or soldiers seem to have been manumitted whereas some masters whose slaves died in the campaign asked for financial compensation.[68]

The renewal of imperial wars at midcentury served as the impetus that induced local authorities to finally organize the permanent free colored militia company they had first envisioned in 1730. The institutionalization of this unit was closely linked to the settlement of free people of color as farmers at the English Turn. This outpost was located downriver, eight miles from the city. Local authorities started to fortify the site and to expand its settlement in order to transform it into a crucial element of protection for the capital during the War of the Austrian Succession because the fortifications at La Balise, the outpost which controlled the mouth of the river, had fallen into ruin. Besides troops, habitants, and "Indian volunteers," Governor Vaudreuil specifically mentioned "free negroes" as one of the categories of inhabitants who could be gathered and settled there in 1747. Local authorities used their power to grant land to induce free people

---

"La Louisiane, guerre des Chicachas," Jan. 1, 1739, ANOM COL C13A 24, fols. 104–113; Salmon to the minister of the navy, Oct. 10, 1739, ANOM COL C13A 24, fols. 168–169; Salmon to the minister of the navy, Jan. 2, 1740, ANOM COL C13A 25, fol. 134r; and "Extrait d'une lettre écrite par M. de Bienville à M. de Louboey du fort de l'Assomption le 8 décembre dernier (1740)," ANOM COL C13A 25, fol. 282r. For Bernard de Vergès's journal, see "Extraits de quelques articles des instructions de M. de Coustilhas concernant l'établissement du premier entrepôt et la continuation de la découverte du chemin (avec observations sur les instructions)," ANOM COL C13A 25, fols. 315–336. For Louis Aymé de Noailles's journal and correspondence, see "Journal de la campagne contre les Chicachas de M. Aymé de Noailles," June 1, 1739–July 8, 1740, AN Marine, B4 45, fols. 361–405; and Mr. de Noailles to the minister of the navy, May 10, 1740, AN Marine B4 50, fols. 118–119, May 30, 1740, fols. 120–123, Aug. 26, 1740, fols. 124–127v.

68. For the failure of the 1739 campaign, see Bienville and Salmon to the minister of the navy, Aug. 10, 1739, ANOM COL C13A 24, fol. 11; Salmon to the minister of the navy, Aug. 26, 1739, ANOM COL 24, fol. 28; Salmon to the minister of the navy, Oct. 10, 1739, ANOM COL C13A 24, fols. 168–169; and Bienville and Salmon to the minister of the navy, June 24, 1740, ANOM COL C13A 25, fols. 9–16r. The records of the Superior Council also include several declarations by slaveholders whose slaves came back sick or died in the Chickasaw wars. They wanted the crown to replace them. See "Report of Death of Slave," Aug. 15, 1739, in "RSCL XXII," *LHQ*, VII (1924), 359; "Report of Dead Slave," Dec. 3, 1739, in "RSCL XXII: Succession of Francois Trudeau, 1739," *LHQ*, VII (1924), 514, "Report of Dead Slave," Dec. 4, 1739, 514, "Report in Registry by Françoise Trepagnier," Dec. 5, 1739, 515; and RSCL 1739/12/21/01.

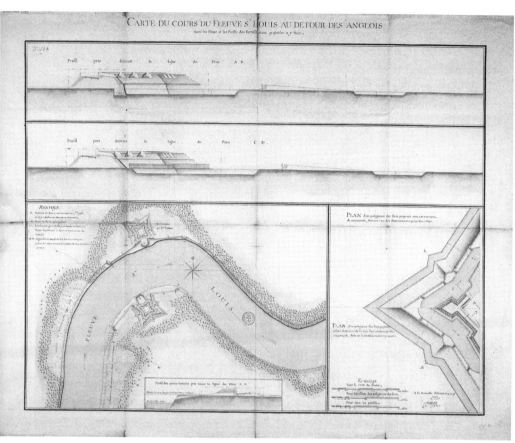

Figure 10: [Bernard] Devergès. *Carte du cours du fleuve St. Louis au détour des anglois avec les plans et les profils des fortifications projettées à y faire.* May 9, 1747. ANOM France 04 DFC 55 A. Courtesy of Les Archives nationales d'outre-mer. Aix-en-Provence, France

of color to settle in a separate district, which was swampy and vulnerable to flooding. According to a series of maps, the "district of the free negroes" was located downriver from the fort, which means that, in the event that enemy forces tried to move upriver to attack the city, free people of color would make up New Orleans's first line of defense. The district was also clearly separated from plantations owned by whites and circumscribed by woods. The 1763 and 1766 censuses taken at the English Turn still mentioned the "district of the free negroes under the Fort Saint-Leon."[69]

69. For the new defense policy that began in the 1740s, see Carl J. Ekberg, "The English Bend: Forgotten Gateway to New Orleans," in Patricia K. Galloway, ed., *La Salle*

Governor Kerlérec visited the new outpost at the English Turn immediately after his arrival in the colony. Then, in 1755, when asked about his preparations in case of attack, he informed the minister of the navy that he could not remove too many white militiamen from their posts because they were needed there to oversee the slaves. To solve a rising problem of slave unrest, which he attributed to the presence of slaves brought from the Antilles, he proposed to manumit slaves on the islands on the condition that they would come to Louisiana to settle and to form a *maréchaussée* (police force) *"à titre de brigade"* ("by way of a brigade"). This measure would have formalized the previous circumstantial use of free blacks against runaways. After this proposal, which was never implemented, Kerlérec concluded that he could add "some detachments of negroes chosen among those who are good hunters and coureurs de bois" to the regular troops and the three hundred white militiamen. According to the military instructions given by Kerlérec to François Simard de Bellisle, the major of New Orleans, in 1759, some of these measures had actually been enforced at the beginning of the Seven Years' War, when the governor had to go to Mobile. The document refers to a note dated July 1, 1756, related to slaves who could be used to cut the wood necessary to fortify the forts at the English Turn. This note also included "the list of the eight free negroes suited to be put at the head of the war parties that could be formed with the negroes who are hunters and coureurs de bois." After having described the artillery that formed part of the defenses at Forts Saint Leon and Sainte Marie at the English Turn, Ker-

---

and His Legacy: Frenchmen and Indians in the Lower Mississippi Valley (Jackson, Miss., 1982), 211–229. For the proposal to settle free people of color at the English Turn, see Vaudreuil and Le Normant to the minister of the navy, Nov. 24, 1746, ANOM COL C13A 30, fols. 3–9; Memorandum to the king, February 1747, ANOM COL C13A 31, fols. 13–16; Vaudreuil to the minister of the navy, May 15, 1747, ANOM COL C13A 31, fols. 87–92 (quotation, fol. 91); and Vaudreuil to the minister of the navy, May 26, 1748, ANOM COL C13A 32, fols. 72–76. For the granting of land concessions to free people of color in a distinct district, see Michel to the minister of the navy, Jan. 18, 1752, ANOM COL C13A 36, fol. 226; Kerlérec to the minister of the navy, Mar. 8, 1753, ANOM COL C13A 37, fols. 35r–36v; and "Plan pour rendre la Louisiane la plus riche et la plus puissante de toutes les colonies françaises, par Redon de Rassac," Aug. 15, 1763, ANOM COL C13A 43, fols. 378r–379r. In the maps, the expressions are *"déserts et habitations des nègres libres"* ("vacant lands and plantations of the free negroes") or *"habitations des nègres libres"* ("plantations of the free negroes"). See *Carte du cours du fleuve Saint Louis au détour des anglois avec les plans et les profils des fortifications projettées à y faire,* May 9, 1747, ANOM 04DFC 55A; and *Carte de la partie du fleuve St Louis nommée le Détour aux Anglais avec les plans de deux batteries de canons,* Nov. 3, 1745, ANOM 04DFC 64B.

lérec warned de Bellisle that "it would be also essential to select and assign some handy negroes to assist with the artillery."[70]

The 1763 and 1766 censuses provide information that suggests that the free blacks assigned military duties for the defense of New Orleans in the mid-1750s must have been organized into a more formal militia company centered around the English Turn between 1759 and 1763. In the 1766 census, a man named Simon Calfat was recorded as *"capitán de los negros libres"* ("captain of the free blacks") in the "district of the free negroes" at the English Turn. He is certainly the same man who commanded the company of fifty slaves that was temporarily formed during the first campaign against the Chickasaw in 1736, and he was also the first to sign the oath of allegiance and fidelity to the king of Spain taken by the free colored militia in 1769. Jacques Zacharie dit Grand Jacquot and Thomas Haultz are listed in both the 1763 and 1766 censuses respectively as *"brigadier"* and *"sous-brigadier,"* ranks belonging to noncommissioned officers, besides being named as the household heads of two families of free people of color living in the free colored district. Jacques Zacharie does not appear among the thirty-four men who took the oath of fidelity to the king of Spain in 1769, but the "Pierre fils de Thomas" ("Pierre son of Thomas") who put his mark on the 1769 oath is very likely the same "Pierre Haultz," twenty-six years old, who lived next to his father, Thomas Haultz, seventy years old, at the English Turn in the 1760s. Since censuses mentioned their militia ranks, their military enrollment must have become a permanent situation that they could take advantage of to negotiate their social standing in their daily relationships. One can assume that the free colored militia company was formally organized after the British took Havana in 1762, when both Louisiana's officials and the colony's entire population expected an attack on New Orleans. The company, called the "Compagnie des mulâtres et nègres libres de cette colonie de la Louisiane" ("Company of the free mulattoes and negroes of this colony of Louisiana"), might have been modelled on the regiment of Chasseurs-Volontaires de l'Amérique that local authorities organized in Saint-Domingue the same year. As its title clearly

70. For Kerlérec's project at the English Turn, see Kerlérec to the minister of the navy, Mar. 8, 1753, ANOM COL C13A 37, fols. 35v–36r; Kerlérec to the minister of the navy, June 26, 1755, ANOM COL C13A 39, fols. 12v–13; Kerlérec to Bellisle, Feb. 25, 1759, ANOM COL C13A 40, fols. 17–23; and Ekberg, "English Bend: Forgotten Gateway to New Orleans," in Galloway, ed., *La Salle and His Legacy*, 225. For the previous use of free men of color, along with white soldiers and Indians, against runaways, see, for instance, RSCL 1741/01/10/01.

indicates, only one free colored militia company must have been formed for the entire Mississippi colony, or at least its lower part. Although the unit's center remained at the English Turn, the militiamen most likely resided in New Orleans and in the smaller settlements surrounding the city extending up to the German Coast.[71]

The formation of this militia company elevated the group of free colored militiamen to the status of a corporate body, that is a group defined by certain privileges, although this would only become more obvious under Spanish rule. Most noticeably, whereas militia reform in Saint-Domingue forbade free black men from serving as officers in 1768–1769, Louisiana's company of free blacks was headed by a captain of mixed ancestry. Nevertheless, the creation of this distinct militia unit only served to reinforce the racial system, which had mainly rested until then on the regulation of marriage and sexuality. In addition to expanding the militia system in a discriminatory fashion, French local authorities began to count free people of color separately in censuses, and they started to grant them land segregated from whites' plantations. Although they were far from successful in implementing this policy of segregation, they were driven by an exclusionary racial vision of the social order. The state policy toward free people of color was characterized by its strong ambivalence. The differentiated incorporation of free blacks into Louisiana society that these measures tried to enforce at once respected the dual logic of ancien régime societies, which were both integrative and unequal, and attempted to innovate, by establishing whiteness as the ultimate fault line that confined nonwhites to the lower ranks of the free population.[72]

71. On Simon's heroic behavior during the Natchez Wars, see Dumont [de Montigny], *Mémoires historiques sur la Louisiane ...*, ed. [Jean-Baptiste Le Mascrier], 2 vols. (Paris, 1753), II, 225–226. For the oath of allegiance, see RSCL 1769/09/20/01. For the regiment of "Chasseurs-Volontaires de l'Amérique," see King, *Blue Coat or Powdered Wig*, 71–72. For the 1770 lists giving information on free blacks, see "État des mulâtres et nègres libres," 1770, AGI, Correspondencia de los Gobernadores de la Luisiana y la Florida Occidental, Años 1766–1824, Session Papeles de Cuba, legajo 188-A, "Liste des nègres libres établis tant à quatre lieues de cette ville en remontant le fleuve, que ceux dc la ville dénommés cy-après comme suit," "Rôle des mulâtres libres de La Nouvelle-Orléans," and "Liste de la qualité des nègres libres de La Nouvelle-Orléans fait par moi Nicolas Bacus capitaine moraine."

72. In Saint-Domingue, the officers of the free colored militia companies were exempted from having to send slaves to labor on public works. See [Moreau] de Saint-Méry, *Loix et constitutions des colonies françoises de l'Amérique sous le vent*, III, 761. In Spanish Louisiana, free colored militiamen were later granted "the right to the *fuero military*." "The fuero was a corporate charter with important implications, for it exempted

The Emergence of a Small Elite Group of Free Black Men

In September 1769, after the Spanish Governor O'Reilly succeeded in re-pressing the 1768 revolt and imposing the sovereignty of the Catholic Monarchy, thirty-four members of the "Compagnie des mulâtres et nègres libres de cette colonie de la Louisiane" took an oath of allegiance and fidelity to the king of Spain. The ceremony marked the first public performance of the free colored militiamen as a corporate body that was recorded and kept in the archives. Their collective biography over the course of the French regime offers insights into the motivations that led them to join the seg-regated militia company. Unlike their counterparts in the cities of Saint-Domingue in the 1760s, free people of color in New Orleans far from con-stituted a great demographic and socioeconomic force. These men seized the opportunity offered by the establishment of the military institution to reduce their socioracial marginalization, lessen their dependency on their former masters, and consolidate their social position within the free popu-lation of color.[73]

Among the thirty-four free colored militiamen, the company's captain, Simon Calfat, was the only one who earned his freedom during the Natchez Wars. Aged sixty-five in 1769, he was the oldest on the list. The others had not been born or were children at the time of the Natchez and Chickasaw campaigns.[74] Consequently, most of the other militiamen owed their free-

------

black militiamen from prosecution in civil courts and put them on equal juridical status with white militiamen. The fuero also granted blacks who served in the military hospi-talization, retirement, and death benefits, as well as the right to wear uniforms and bear arms." See Jane Landers, "Transforming Bondsmen into Vassals: Arming Slaves in Colo-nial Spanish America," in Christopher Leslie Brown and Philip D. Morgan, eds., *Arm-ing Slaves: From Classical Times to the Modern Age* (New Haven, Conn., 2006), 120–145 (quotation, 126–127). For the 1768–1769 militia reforms in Saint-Domingue, see Garri-gus, *Before Haiti*, 95–138.

73. Following the order of the document from top to bottom and left to right, the free black militiamen were: "Simon Calpha, JB Horry, Joseph Lacombe, Jules Csar, St Louis dit La Nuit, Jean Baptiste Hugon, Henry Versailles, François Langes, Pierre fils de Thomas, Jean Baptiste Bienville, René Joseph Vaudreuil, Jean-Louis Meunier, Étienne Maréchal, Jean Baptiste Bertrand, Alexandre Graveline, François Lacombe, Joseph Gutton, Scipion Tatin, Simon, Joseph Lange, Joseph Beaulieu, Jean Baptiste Raphaël, Jacques Raphaël, Jean Baptiste Charras, Jean Grant, Christophe Graveline, George Lacombe, Michel Lacombe, Joseph Casenave, Pierre Gentaud, Alexis Graveline, Louis Casenave, Étienne Ste Thérèse, Pierre Ste Thérèse." The first four signed, the others made their mark. See RSCL 1769/09/20/01.

74. Apart from Simon Calfat, the documentation mentions only one other black

dom to their owners. Although some masters occasionally freed male adult slaves, as was the case with St. Louis alias La Nuit, it was more common for slaveholders to free women who were sexual or conjugal partners and their mixed children. Yet the nature of the relationship between former masters and freed women and children often remained unclear in manumission deeds. In 1753, one of the future thirty-four militiamen, Jean-Louis (later called Meunier), who was categorized as a "mulatto," was freed in his early teens along with his mother for "good and pleasant services provided by the negress." Another, Joseph Lacombe, was probably manumitted with his mother, Marianne, when he was a child. According to Pierre Boyer's will, both Marianne and her two "mulatto" sons, Joseph and Pierre, were living with Claude Vignon alias La Combe in 1745 and had already been freed. Pierre Boyer, their neighbor on Lake Pontchartrain, lived alone without any relatives, and he bequeathed all his cattle to the two boys for "the help they provide him every day." Two years later, in his own will, Claude Vignon alias La Combe confirmed that Marianne and her sons were free and that they owned some cattle in their own right from previous gifts; he also bequeathed one hundred piastres to each of them but reserved the rest of his property for a white man. La Combe did not acknowledge that he was Joseph and Pierre's father.[75]

---

man who won his freedom during the campaign against the Natchez and who was still alive in 1770 but did not join the militia company: François Tiocou of the "Senegal nation," who was then sixty-eight. On Tiocou, see RSCL 1737/06/28/06, 1737/07/12/01, 1744/03/06/03; "Petition of Recovery," Oct. 29, 1737, in [Henry P. Dart], ed., "RSCL XVI," *LHQ*, V (1922), 418; "Negro Diocou [Tiocou] v. D'Auseville," in Helen Tuncliff Catterall, ed., *Judicial Cases concerning American Slavery and the Negro*, III, *Cases from the Courts of Georgia, Florida, Alabama, Mississippi, and Louisiana* (Washington, D.C., 1926), 410; and AANO, Saint-Louis Cathedral Baptisms 1744–1753, 03/17/1747, 10/14/1750, 05/30/ 1751. Simon Calfat's age is mentioned in a survey of plantations drawn up in 1770. See "Année 1770, au moins de janvier, État des habitations de la côte du bas du fleuve à commencer depuis l'habitation de Madame La Chaise jusqu'aux environs de la Prairie aux Moucle tant dessus la rive (droite) que dessus la rive gauche," AGI, Correspondencia de los Gobernadores de la Luisiana y la Florida Occidental, Años 1766–1824, Session Papeles de Cuba, legajo 188-A. In 1770, the youngest militiaman was nineteen years old, and the oldest was forty-seven. The ages are mentioned in one of the 1770 lists of free blacks: "État des mulâtres et nègres libres."

75. In 1744, the planter Joseph Meunier and his wife recorded a certificate to free their slave Françoise and her six-year-old son, Jean-Louis, in the event of Joseph's death. Yet Governor Vaudreuil and Commissaire-ordonnateur Vincent Guillaume Le Sénéchal d'Auberville authorized the manumission of Françoise and Jean-Louis, the boy being then fourteen, in 1753, before the planter's death. See RSCL 1744/07/14/01, 1744/07/14/02.

The only free men of color whose lives were not interlinked with that of their former masters were the few free migrants of color who came to Louisiana from the British or the French West Indies. The militiaman Pierre Thomas was identified as *"Pierre fils de Thomas"* ("Pierre son of Thomas"), that is, Pierre Haultz, in the 1760s censuses. His father was a "free negro of Jamaica" who had married Jeanne Marie, "free negress," in New Orleans under the name "Thomas Hos" in 1730. Another man who made his mark on the oath was himself a migrant: Étienne Maréchal. The son of Jeanne Catherine from Saint Pierre, Martinique, he concluded a marriage contract with Charlotte, a "mulatto" born in New Orleans, in 1767. According to the deed, only the bride possessed some property: a plantation and two slaves, evaluated altogether at six thousand livres. Étienne had to agree that only one-third of her fortune would be included in the community of assets. Marriage allowed some free migrants of color to more easily integrate themselves into Louisiana society and to gain some measure of economic independence. Pierre (Haultz) Thomas and Étienne Maréchal were two of the few militiamen who did not have to keep living within their former owner's household. They also did not have to continue working for them as domestics or craftsmen in the city; as overseers and purchasing agents on their plantations, as St. Louis alias La Nuit did for a long time; or as rowers on trips up the Mississippi River, hunting, trading with Native Americans, or transporting goods to the Illinois Country.[76]

None of the few militiamen who lived independently were recorded as city dwellers. In the 1720s and 1730s, local authorities, anxious to get as

---

It is possible that Joseph Meunier had already planned to free Jean-Louis as an infant in the will he had drawn up before he left for the second war against the Chickasaw. See RSCL 1738/09/05/01. For Joseph Lacombe's manumission, see RSCL 1745/02/23/01; 1747/08/16/01.

76. For Thomas Hos and Jeanne Marie's marriage certificate, see AANO, Saint-Louis Cathedral Marriages, 1720–1730, 06/05/1730. The survey of plantations in 1770 confirmed that Thomas, "free negro," had a wife named Jeanne Marie. The couple had a daughter, Anne Louise, baptized in 1731. See AANO, Saint-Louis Cathedral Baptisms, 1731–1733, 11/11/1731. For Étienne Maréchal and Charlotte's marriage contract, see RSCL 1767/05/25/01. For examples of other free men of color employed as overseers on plantations during the French period, see RSCL 1730/04/21/01, 1731/12/29/02, 1769/03/30/01. For indenture contracts of free black men residing in New Orleans to serve on journeys to the Illinois Country, see RSCL 1736/08/21/01, 1764/04/25/02; and "Contract by Free Negro to Act as Supercargo," Mar. 10, 1739, in Cruzat, ed., "RSCL XIX," *LHQ*, VI (1923), 306. For mentions of free black men employed as indentured servants in the Native trade, see RSCL 1743/08/19/02, 1743/09/10/03.

many inhabitants as possible to settle in New Orleans, did not hesitate to grant urban concessions to some free blacks, both men and women, even though the lots granted were all located on the periphery of the city. In the 1760s, however, the only free people of color mentioned as heads of household in the New Orleans censuses were a few women who lived among white colonists, with the exception of one man named Jean. Jacques Zacharie, the brigadier on the 1763 census, and Joseph Lacombe, who signed the 1769 oath, must have lived in the capital at one point because they both sold an urban parcel in the 1750s. By the early 1760s, they had evidently moved to the English Turn and Chapitoulas, respectively, and each of them owned a small plantation. Together with Simon Calfat, Pierre (Haultz) Thomas, and Jean-Louis Meunier, Lacombe was one of only four militiamen who possessed a plantation in the vicinity of New Orleans. The concentration of free people of color in these two rural districts both fit the policy of separate settlement implemented by local authorities in the late 1740s and the desire of free blacks to possess land and live independently.[77]

Simon Calfat might have been the first of the free black militiamen to become a landowner. According to the 1731 census, he and his wife already held a plantation upriver, below the Chapitoulas district, which was next to the property of another free black named Scipion. At the time, Simon, "free mulatto," squatted four arpents and purchased two from Scipion, "free negro." In the early 1750s, Simon Calfat then moved to the English Turn on a plot of land for which he requested a formal property title in 1767. Ten years before, Thomas Haultz had already settled at the English Turn, with the permission of Governor Bienville, although he only received a formal land grant for this plantation in 1758. Among the younger generations, only Pierre (Haultz) Thomas and Jean-Louis Meunier, at twenty-six and twenty-five years old respectively, were able to exploit their own land at an early age.

77. For urban concessions granted to free blacks in New Orleans, see Vieux Carré Survey, square nos. 48, 55, 58, 71, 77 (based on the 1722 map by Pierre Le Blond de La Tour and the 1731 map by François Ignace Broutin), HNOC. For sales of urban concessions by free blacks, see Vieux Carré Survey, square nos. 78, 813–815 Ursuline Street, lot N° 22982, HNOC; and NONA July 24, 1762. All the information on the plantations belonging to free blacks comes from the 1763 and 1766 censuses and the 1770 survey of plantations as well as the FRLG. For the 1763 and 1766 censuses, see "Recensement général fait à La Nouvelle-Orléans … au mois de septembre 1763," AGI, Audiencia de Sto Domingo, Luisiana y Florida, Años 1766 a 1770, 2595–589; and "Padron y lista de las quatro compañías de milicianos y habitantes en la ciudad por quarterles, segun revista passada en 27 de Mayo 1766," AGI, Audiencia de Sto Domingo, Luisiana y Florida, Años 1766 a 1770, 2595–588.

In contrast, two other men who took the 1769 oath, Jacques and Jean Baptiste Raphaël, forty-seven and thirty-seven years old respectively in 1770, were not as fortunate and still lived on their father's plantation, which was headed by their widowed mother after his death sometime between 1763 and 1766. It was difficult for free blacks, especially for those without any links to white people, to accumulate or obtain enough land to settle all their children or to find partners or spouses with property for their children. While Pierre (Haultz) Thomas possessed his own plantation, his two sisters, who already had children of their own, lived with their old father, Thomas Haultz. In fact, it was common for several generations (grandparents, parents, and children) or siblings to live on the same plantation, whether they were headed by a free man or woman of color. Before marrying Étienne Maréchal, the "mulatto" Charlotte headed a household that included her mother, two brothers, and two sisters on a plantation at Chapitoulas.[78]

In addition to the four men among the thirty-four militiamen who owned land in their own right, three others had relatives (a father or a wife) who were also proprietors. These militiamen and their relatives accounted for most of the few colored landholders in the New Orleans region. In 1770, only 8 out of 131 plantations were occupied by free blacks (four men and four women), but 4 other vacant and uncultivated parcels of land also belonged to colored persons. This high percentage of landholders (20 percent) among the militiamen and their families might indicate that the free men of color who signed or made their mark on the 1769 oath were those who were the most economically successful. Yet few of them were slaveholders. According to the 1766 census, among all the militiamen who owned plantations only Simon Calfat possessed three slaves. Étienne Maréchal's wife, Charlotte, also owned two slaves. Most militiamen who owned a plantation had to work their land themselves and were farmers rather than planters. They probably took advantage of the absolute and relative growth of the urban population after 1731 by participating in the city's food supply networks, growing corn, rice, potatoes, and other vegetables and raising poultry for eggs and meat. They were more favored than most free people

---

78. For Calfat's early plantations, see "Recensement des habitations le long du fleuve Mississippi," 1731, ANOM COL G1 464, fols. 26–27v; and "État des habitants établis le long du fleuve, au-dessous de La Nouvelle-Orléans, et au-dessus jusque et compris le quartier des Allemands à dix lieues de cette ville après 1731," ANOM COL G1 464. Calfat's last plantation was located down the Chaouchas, below and on the other side of the city. See "Concession au S. Simon Calpha mulâtre libre," 1767, FRLG. For Thomas's plantation, see "Requête de Thomas nègre libre," May 15, 1758, FRLG.

of color, but their modest fortune did not allow them to purchase slaves easily.[79]

The lack of access to land constrained the ability of free black men to enter into marriage or long-lasting unions. Jean-Louis Meunier was manumitted with his mother in 1753, while he was still an adolescent, but they apparently continued to live with their former master for some years. In 1756, Jean-Louis served as godfather in a baptism celebrated at Fort Saint Leon, and the priest mentioned specifically that he was a "free mulatto living at Sr. Meunier's place." According to the 1763 census, however, there was an anonymous freed man registered as living in Joseph Meunier's household at the English Turn, whereas a twenty-five-year-old, Jean-Louis, referenced as a "freed mulatto," and his mother were recorded as living independently on a plantation in the "district of the free negroes" of the same outpost. A few years later, in 1770, Joseph still resided there, but he had a wife, named Babé, and two small children, Louis and Marie. Whether for lack of property or other reasons, only a few of the thirty-four militiamen were married (Simon Calfat, Jules César, Jean-Louis Meunier, and Étienne Maréchal), and those who were chose free women of color for their brides.[80]

To compensate for the lack of solemnized unions and to multiply the networks from which they could benefit, militiamen were more willing to serve as godparents. Even men like St. Louis alias La Nuit, who does not seem to have gotten married nor become a father, served eight times as godfather, for six enslaved and two free children of color, after he was manumitted. Unlike St. Louis, most free blacks engaged in fictive kinships both as parents and godparents. Although they could only serve as godparents for slaves and free people of color, they chose godfathers and godmothers for their children among whites, free people of color, and slaves. Simon Calfat and his wife, Anne Marthe, had at least four children between 1759 and 1767, Zacharie, Pierre, Constance, and Geneviève. Their godparents were, respectively, Jacques Zacharie, a "free negro" (whom Calfat later joined at the English Turn), and Marie Jeanne, a "free negress"; Pierre, a "free negro," and Marie Louise, an "enslaved negress" of the hospital; Sieur Jean Bap-

79. On the involvement of the farmers at the English Turn in the city's food supply starting in the late 1740s, see Steve Canac-Marquis and Pierre Rézeau, eds., *Journal de Vaugine de Nuisement: Un témoignage sur la Louisiane du XVIIIe siècle* (Quebec, 2005), 15.

80. For Jean-Louis serving as godfather in 1756, see AANO, Saint-Louis Cathedral Baptisms, 1753–1759, 12/12/1756. In 1764, Joseph Meunier requested a land grant next to Jean-Louis's plantation. See "Concession à Joseph Meunier," Jan. 10, 1764, FRLG.

tiste Augustin de Noyon, a white discharged military officer, and Demoiselle Constance Louise Chauvin Desilles, an elite white woman; and Jean Baptiste (possibly Horry), a "free mulatto," and Louise, a "free mulattress." Apart from serving as godfather for three slave children, Simon Calfat was also the godfather of the son of Pierre, a "free negro," and Marie Jeanne, a "free negress," and of the daughter of Magdelaine Canelle, a "free mulattress," to whom Pierre Canel and the "boy of Pierre Canelle" mentioned in two of the 1770 lists were probably related. This extensive engagement in the system of godparentage helped Simon Calfat to both establish vertical ties between himself and white protectors and between himself and free or enslaved black clients as well as to reinforce horizontal links with free colored friends, neighbors, and allies considered as equals. Multiple networks of alliances constituted a promise for his family's future and reinforced his position of leadership among free people of color and slaves.[81]

Whereas whites could serve as godparents in baptisms of enslaved or free infants of color or as witnesses in marriages uniting free blacks, the reverse was not true. The only exception, over the entire French period, concerned Simon Calfat. In August 1766, the very year he was described as "capitán de los negros libres" in the census, he acted as a witness in the marriage of two whites of the lower sort: Jacques Langliche, whose parents' names were unknown, "they having been killed by the Indians when he was but six years of age," from Barataria, and Elizabeth Pugeo, native of Cannes Bruslée. This exceptional case reflects both the social mobility and the limitations to social ascendency that participation in the militia company offered free men of color.[82]

While most free people of color throughout the French regime did not bear a surname, some free black men who appear as parents or godparents

81. For St. Louis alias La Nuit acting as godfather, see AANO, Saint-Louis Cathedral Baptisms, 1763–1767 and 1767–1771, 07/07/1765, 03/25/1768, 04/17/1768, 07/10/1768, 03/18/1769, 07/05/1769, 12/20/1769, 12/26/1769. For the godparents of Calfat's children, see AANO, Saint-Louis Cathedral Baptisms, 1759–1762 and 1763–1767, 01/22/1759, 08/18/1761, 04/24/1764, 03/30/1767. For Calfat serving as godfather for slaves, see AANO, Saint-Louis Cathedral Baptisms, 1744–1753 and 1763–1767, 03/04/1746, 02/07/1748, 01/27/1765. For Calfat serving as godfather for free people of color, see AANO, Saint-Louis Cathedral Baptisms, 1763–1767 and 1767–1771, 03/30/1766, 09/17/1768. For the significance of fictive alliances through godparenting, see Vincent Cousseau, *Prendre nom aux Antilles: Individu et appartenances (XVIIe–XIXe siècle)* (Paris, 2012), 181–196.

82. Marriage contract between Jacques Langliche and Elizabeth Pugeo, Aug. 14, 1766, in Alice Daly Forsyth, ed., *Louisiana Marriage Contracts*, II, *Abstracts from Records of the Superior Council of Louisiana, 1728–1769* (New Orleans, 1989), 86.

of enslaved or free children of color were allowed to claim one by missionaries in sacramental records because of their integration in the Christian community and their active role in the evangelization of the slave population. Catholicism was a powerful instrument of social ascendency for free people of color, but this favor was not systematic. Many blacks who served as godparents were never granted a last name, and those who received one were not always referred to by their full name. Simon Calfat was sometimes listed only by his first name, but his identity seems certain, as evidenced by his signature on the baptism certificate, something few free people of color could produce as many were not literate, or by the presence of his wife, Anne Marthe, at the ceremony. Simon Calfat's wife was another one of the few free blacks who could write her name. In the same way, the sacramental records include a series of baptism certificates between 1753 and 1769 where the godfather is named simply as Jean Baptiste, a "free mulatto." This godfather stands out, too, since he also knew how to record his name. He is very likely the same man who appears on two baptism certificates, in 1760 and 1769, listed only by his first name but who signed Jean Baptiste Aury / Horry. Simon Calfat and Jean Baptiste Horry were the first two militiamen to affix their names to the 1769 oath, before Joseph Lacombe, whose signature also shows up in the sacramental records, and Jules César. Moreover, three out of the four signers (the others made their mark), Simon Calfat, Jean Baptiste Horry, and Joseph Lacombe, were identified as "mulattoes" by missionaries. Their mixed ancestry suggests that they might have benefited from education from missionaries or within white families.[83]

The majority of the thirty-four free colored militiamen bore a surname affirming a real or symbolic filiation with their former master or presenting the latter as their putative father or patron. In the latter case, the former master could have also been a woman. Many of the last names on the 1769 oath and 1770 lists match those of white settlers. Some free colored militia-

83. For the Calfat couple in the sacramental records, see AANO, Saint-Louis Cathedral Baptisms, 1744–1753 and 1753–1759, 03/04/1746, 12/07/1746, 07/12/1748, 01/22/1759, 08/18/1761, 04/24/1764, 03/30/1766, 03/30/1767, 09/17/1768. A doubt remains for the following certificates: AANO, Saint-Louis Cathedral Baptisms, 1731–1733, 1744–1753, and 1759–1762, 03/27/1733, 09/16/1744, 09/18/1744, 12/07/1746, 09/02/1759. For Jean-Baptiste Horry in the sacramental records, see AANO, Saint-Louis Cathedral Baptisms, 1753–1759, 1759–1762, 1763–1767, and 1767–1771, 05/07/1753, 12/28/1754, 04/12/1757, 12/25/1760 (signature), 03/30/1766, 03/01/1767, 09/25/1768, 03/26/1769, 05/15/1769, 10/08/1769 (signature). A doubt remains for the following certificates: AANO, Saint-Louis Cathedral Baptisms, 1763–1767 and 1767–1771, 10/07/1764, 04/06/1765, 10/05/1765, 09/07/1766, 03/30/1767, 04/23/1769.

men men carried the name of former governors (Bienville, Vaudreuil), military officers (Cazenave, Marie Joseph Hugon, Ste. Thérèse de Langloiserie), employees of the Company of the Indies (Lange), or planters who originally came from Canada (Chauvin de Beaulieu, Jean-Baptiste Baudreau dit Graveline), Martinique (the widow Tatin), or elsewhere (Joseph Meunier). Once again, the last names selected by these free black men illustrates how their lives remained entangled with that of their former owners.[84]

Joining the segregated militia company must have represented a way for free men of color to achieve more autonomy and to distance themselves from their former masters at one jump than they could have normally achieved over a few years or decades, the symbolic ties formed by their surnames notwithstanding. Many had no choice but to live with and work for their former owners or to maintain relationships of patronage with them for years after they had acquired their freedom. Free blacks labored under many constraints making the dream of economic and social independence for themselves and their families difficult to attain. Through military service, the state, albeit moved by its own considerations, offered some of them the possibility of extricating themselves from their former masters' ascendency and control. Previously, participation in the church had been the premium venue for free blacks' autonomous social integration and mobility. Then, from the early 1760s, service in the militia afforded some free men of color the possibility of being recognized as living an honorable life on their own. They achieved honor through both military service to the king and the economic independence associated with landownership. Militia duty also gave them the possibility to activate old networks and create new ones, particularly the most prosperous and socially integrated members of the unit whose signatures or marks appear recorded at the top of the 1769 oath. These men were the officers of the first colored militia company. The incorporation of other militiamen into the company as regular soldiers might have been the result of the mobilization of their own networks of alliances among free men of color, which transcended all differences among them (Creoles and Africans, "negroes" and "mulattos," outsiders and locally born, and so on).

The militia company also helped free colored men negotiate gender tensions and divisions among free blacks in a way that benefited them. The

84. The practice of taking the name of former masters to signify a family connection or as a sign of loyalty was also common in the French Antilles. See Cousseau, *Prendre nom aux Antilles*, 356; Garrigus, *Before Haiti*, 165–167; and Régent, *Esclavage, métissage, liberté*, 159–160, 200–201.

tendency of masters to predominately manumit their enslaved sexual partners led to the demographic overrepresentation of women among the free population of color and gave them relatively substantial economic power. As the example of Charlotte, Étienne Maréchal's wife, testifies, they accounted for many of the household heads and holders of urban lots and plantations, a circumstance favored by local officials who clearly seemed less afraid of free women of color in the city than of men. The hardship of these women's lives was compensated for by a kind of autonomy unavailable to most white women. Against this trend favoring women, the colored militia company constituted a new path to social recognition and collective identity that excluded women, unless they were the mothers, wives, or daughters of militiamen. Although free black women remained important property holders during the Spanish period, the creation of the free black militia company imposed a new patriarchal order on some free women of color.[85]

The oath the free colored militiamen took to the Spanish government in 1769 represented a genuine social event: the public ceremony sanctioned free blacks' place in-between white settlers and black slaves and gave New Orleans society a tripartite structure. Still, the social position free men of color gained with the institutionalization of the militia company was not deprived of ambiguity. On the one hand, the participation of free blacks in the colony's defensive preparations accorded these men the honor associated with military service and immediately enhanced their social standing. This social promotion was reflected in the oath, which acknowledged the militiamen's honor by giving credit to their word. It was also revealed by their signatures or marks on the document, most of which included a surname. Until then, custom deprived most free blacks of the right to have a last name in official documents. Although not dictated by law, this naming practice reveals the subordinate and inferior position in which free blacks had been confined by authorities for most of the French period. In contrast, a surname offered protection, as it helped certify their identity and freedom, and also signaled them as potential owners able to pass on their name and property within their families, unlike chattel slaves. The oath allowed each militiaman to claim a new individual social identity publicly and officially. Together, however, these militiamen also endorsed a collective racial iden-

---

85. On free women of color in Spanish New Orleans, see Kimberly S. Hanger, "Landlords, Shopkeepers, Farmers, and Slave-Owners: Free Black Female Property-Holders in Colonial New Orleans," in David Barry Gaspar and Darlene Clark Hine, eds., *Beyond Bondage: Free Women of Color in the Americas* (Urbana, Ill., 2004), 219–236.

tity as a group of "free negroes and mulattoes" in the public sphere for the first time.[86]

Ultimately, what could be viewed as a social victory for free men of color was also what gave race precedence over class and status in Louisiana society. While the 1724 Code Noir already provided that free blacks did not enjoy the same status as free whites, it was their exclusion from the white militia companies that further actualized racial prejudice; they would never be recognized as the social equals of whites, whatever their fortune or way of life, solely because of their racial categorization. When some free black men decided to join the segregated militia and agreed to take an oath as a corporate body of "free mulattoes and negroes," they could not but contribute to the perpetuation of a social order in which whiteness was the ultimate fault line that restricted access to the top of the social hierarchy. Whatever free men of color thought about race-thinking, their struggle for social dignity and mobility paradoxically forced them to adapt to this system of racial domination.

Even if French Louisiana had not been ceded to England and Spain after the Seven Years' War, the 1760s would have still represented a turning point in the social history of New Orleans. For most of the French regime, New Orleans and its surrounding region of plantations remained a biracial society marked by a divide between white settlers and black slaves. With Saint-Domingue looming large on the horizon, the Mississippi colony quickly became a slave society whose social institutions, including justice, were all devoted to the perpetuation of slavery. However, the racial language and slave code that French New Orleans and Louisiana inherited from the Antilles had been forged in reaction to the development of métissage and to the rise of the free black population in the islands. They did not initially correspond to the demographic and social situation of the lower Missis-

86. Following the perspective of William H. Sewell, Jr., on the relationships between categorization, social change, and events, I argue that the oath can be qualified as a "social event," that is an event able to transform social structures, whereas daily social encounters and interactions only reproduce them. See Sewell, "Three Temporalities: Toward an Eventful Sociology," in Terrence J. McDonald, ed., *The Historic Turn in the Human Sciences* (Ann Arbor, Mich., 1996), 245–280. On the significance of carrying a surname, see Cousseau, *Prendre nom aux Antilles*, 355. On the need to connect "the study of collective identities with that of public spheres," see Luis Roniger and Tamar Herzog, eds., *The Collective and the Public in Latin America: Cultural Identities and Political Order* (Brighton, U.K., 2000), 4.

sippi Valley. The use of racial categories throughout the French regime reveals not only that race mattered and informed representations of the social order from the beginning but that racial dynamics also evolved over the first two generations as Louisiana's local society adapted to circumstances that the Antilles had experienced much earlier. Although some free blacks were present in New Orleans early on, since some came from the Caribbean, it was only in the 1750s and 1760s that their number became more significant, as a result of métissage, and that more of them were able to live on their own, outside their former masters' households. As the emergence of a small elite group of free black men coincided with the renewal of imperial wars, they were able, at the end of the Seven Years' War, to distinguish themselves from slaves, with whom they had been associated for most of the period, and to benefit from some social elevation through the creation of a free colored militia company. A triracial society slowly started to emerge.

Yet the formation of the free black militia company only represented one side of the racial coin. The late institutionalization of the segregated militia unit and the outburst of judicial repression against slaves in the early 1760s was not a mere coincidence. To a large extent, local authorities and the elite had succeeded in enforcing a strict racial order in New Orleans because of the city's small size. Moreover, the colonial population did not have to continually integrate and acculturate new waves of forced migrants to the slave system, since Louisiana's direct access to the slave trade from Africa practically ceased after 1731. The demographic expansion and economic growth the city benefited from during the 1740s and 1750s nevertheless started to create conditions in the Louisiana capital that, by the early 1760s, would make New Orleans a much more dangerous and potentially subversive urban environment. Runaway slaves coming from the plantation world, like César and Louis, could merge with the urban population and survive in the city thanks to the active informal market economy that also allowed some urban slaves to purchase their freedom. At the same time, while local authorities gave some privileges to a few free men of color, they also tried to better control the boundaries between slavery and freedom and to limit the number of slaves passing as free by intensifying and strengthening the judicial repression of slaves. The physical violence that was inflicted on enslaved convicts by black executioners on the city's main square and the symbolic violence that was imposed on free blacks as they were segregated in a distinct rural district and military unit also partook of the very racial system whose goals were to perpetuate the slave order and to assert white domination, despite urban growth.

Louisiana officials had to adapt to the evolution of local circumstances, but they also faced consequences resulting from transformations in the circuits that linked the colony to the rest of the Atlantic world. As transatlantic relationships were heavily disturbed by the English blockade during the Seven Years' War, connections between Louisiana and Saint-Domingue intensified in their stead. The slaves that came in greater numbers to New Orleans from the island during these intercolonial exchanges appeared particularly troublesome, and they started to be identified as agents of disorder. These rebellious slaves brought their own vision of the social order and their own culture of resistance. From Louisiana's founding, Saint-Domingue had fascinated local authorities and settlers; in the twilight of the French regime, the Caribbean colony now also increasingly threatened them.

CHAPTER NINE

From *"Louisians"* to *"Louisianais"*
The Emergence of a Sense of Place and the Racial Divide

In 1728, Abbé Raguet, one of the directors of the Company of the Indies, composed a letter regarding the legal constraints on mobility between Canada and Louisiana. To identify the white inhabitants of Canada, he chose the term *"Canadiens"* ("Canadians"), an ethno-label that had started to come into more common use in the late seventeenth century. But, when he needed to name the settlers of the Mississippi Valley, he was presented with something of a quandary, since no word had yet been invented to designate them. To solve the difficulty, he coined the neologism *"Louisians."* Following his letter, the expression does not appear to have been employed again. For decades, Louisiana colonists were referred to as either French, Canadian, or Creole. Then, in 1768, in the midst of a revolt against the first Spanish governor to arrive following the cession of the western part of the colony and its capital to Spain after the Seven Years' War, the rebels self-identified as *"Louisianais"* ("Louisianan"). Seeking political support in the metropole to remain within the French Empire, they invented the term while writing to the Duc d'Orléans, whose ancestor had played a crucial role in the colony's development and for whom, in fact, New Orleans is named after. With "Louisianais," the insurgents conceived of an ethno-label that not only expressed how their relationship to the place where they lived had evolved but that also allowed for the development of a new kind of patriotism, independent from the metropole, should the crown refuse to grant their demands. At the same time, their decision not to call themselves Creoles signaled a desire to continue to claim their Frenchness.[1]

1. For the history of the term "Canadian," see Gervais Carpin, *Histoire d'un mot: L'ethnonyme Canadien de 1535–1691* (Sillery, Quebec, 1995). For the use of the neologism "Louisian," see Letter from Abbé Raguet, director of the Company of the Indies, Feb. 14,

Although the establishment of the English and the Spanish in the 1760s certainly provoked a crisis that was both political and sociocultural, the change of sovereignty did not alone spark the tensions between Frenchness and Creoleness. The crucial role played by Canadian officers and recruits in founding some of Louisiana's first outposts, the proximity and entanglement of colonial territories in the region belonging to various European powers, imperial rivalries and wars, the desire for the crown to enforce absolute power from afar, the transatlantic migrations of settlers to the colony from all of France's provinces as well as some German and Swiss states, the short duration of the direct slave trade from Africa, the early creolization of the slave population, the arrival of free and forced migrants from Canada and the Caribbean, the expansion of the slave system, and, finally, the development of a multiethnic society in which people of European, African, and Native American descent all lived in proximity within New Orleans meant that ethnic and national identifications became an essential power issue, for all social actors, with multiple political, social, and cultural ramifications, from the start. The points of friction, nevertheless, changed over the period depending on the context.

Most of the various ethno-labels commonly used in French Louisiana referred to "nations." Local authorities and colonists spoke and wrote about the French, Spanish, and British nations; the Breton, Norman, Provençal, Bambara, Mandingue, Poulard, Tonica, Illinois, or Chickasaw nations; and even the Jewish or Bohemian nations. The ubiquity of national categories was linked to an old definition of "nation," borrowed from biblical and legal texts, as a "people, located in a relatively fixed spatial and cultural terrain, that was conceived of geographically and ethnographically (as well as ethnocentrically)." Since each nation was regarded as being located in a specific place, a common belief in the influence of both climate and the environment on a people's character led to the naturalization and essentializing of national identities that brought nation and race together. Afterward, especially from the late seventeenth century on, this ethnic conception competed with another understanding of nation as a territorial and political entity. In 1694, the *Dictionnaire de l'Académie françoise* (Dictionary of the French Academy) defined "nation" as "all the inhabitants of the same state, the same country, who live under the same laws and use the same language." The politicization of nation triggered a debate about sov-

---

1728, ANOM COL F5A 6/2. For the first mention of "Louisianais" in the documentation, see "Mémoire sur la révolution arrivée à la Louisiane le 29 octobre 1768 pour être présenté à son A. R. Monseigneur le duc d'Orléans," 1768, Favrot Papers, S-4.

ereignty and citizenship over the eighteenth century. If the nation formed a political community, who should be included or excluded? Overseas colonization brought the old ethnic model of what constituted a nation and the new political meaning of the concept into conflict with each other; the idea that cultural assimilation should be a prerequisite for political and legal integration emerged earlier on. These discussions raised questions about the relationships between nation, empire, and race as well as the status of colonial territories with respect to their metropoles and that of the various categories of inhabitants living within them.[2]

Yet nation was not the only category employed by social actors to define their ties to the ethnic or political entity or community to which they felt they belonged. *Pays* ("country") was another crucial term employed by both settlers and slaves to designate a more or less large territory that corresponded to their birthplace. When "pays" did not refer to the whole country, as in the present-day sense of the term, but to a province or colony or to a subregion, it reflected an emotional bond to a small *patrie* ("fatherland"). Therefore, the invention of the ethno-label "Louisianais" by the New Orleans rebels revealed the intimate connection they had built with a territory that had become their new fatherland. This relationship was not exclusive and blended with their attachment to France, their larger patrie.[3]

The place to which the insurgents felt they belonged locally was both

2. For the traditional definition of "nation," see Kathleen Wilson, *The Island Race: Englishness, Empire, and Gender in the Eighteenth Century* (London, 2003), 7 (quotation). On the proximity and confusion between the concepts of "race" and "nation," see Nicholas Hudson, "From 'Nation' to 'Race': The Origin of Racial Classification in Eighteenth-Century Thought," *Eighteenth-Century Studies*, XXIX (1996), 247–264; Silvia Sebastiani, "National Characters and Race: A Scottish Enlightenment Debate," in Thomas Ahnert and Susan Manning, eds., *Character, Self, and Sociability in the Scottish Enlightenment* (New York, 2011), 187–205; and Wilson, *Island Race*, 6–14. For the politization of nation, see *Le dictionnaire de l'Académie Françoise …*, 2 vols. (Paris, 1694), II, 110, quoted in Robert Descimon and Alain Guéry, "Fondations: L'État, monarchique, et la construction de la nation française," in Descimon, Guery, and Jacques Le Goff, *Histoire de la France*, IV, *La longue durée de l'État*, ed. Le Goff (1989; rpt. Paris, 2000), 364–369; David A. Bell, *The Cult of the Nation in France: Inventing Nationalism, 1680–1800* (Cambridge, Mass., 2001); and Cécile Vidal, ed., *Français? La nation en débat entre colonies et métropole, XVIe–XIXe siècle* ([Paris], 2014).

3. Yves Durand, *L'ordre du monde: Idéal politique et valeurs sociales en France, XVIe–XVIIIe siècle* (Paris, 2001), 233–238; David A. Bell, "Nation et patrie, société et civilisation: Transformations du vocabulaire social français, 1700–1789," in Laurence Kaufmann and Jacques Guilhaumou, eds., *L'invention de la société: Nominalisme politique et science sociale au XVIIIe siècle* (Paris, 2003), 99–120.

Emergence of a Sense of Place and the Racial Divide

New Orleans and Louisiana. To be sure, the inhabitants living in the colonial settlements never invented a specific ethno-label to designate urban dwellers, but some slaves self-identified as "Creoles of New Orleans" and some colonists presented themselves as "native of New Orleans" or "native of this city" in court or parish records. They also talked and wrote about *"la ville"* ("the city") and constructed it as a distinct territory from the surrounding plantations and the rest of the colony. Likewise, although some rural settlers in the vicinity of the Louisiana capital participated in the 1768 revolt, it was first and foremost an urban uprising. The rebellion reflected the demographic, economic, and sociopolitical importance the port city had acquired. Over the eighteenth century, New Orleans had come to embody Louisiana.[4]

The sense of place Louisiana colonists progressively forged in association with their new fatherland also emerged out of a sense of time as it was felt through the passage of generations, the birth of children, and the burial of parents in the colony. Still, this attachment did not simply impose itself on people through the shared experience of life events; people also constructed their relationships to the territory, although this process was slow. Like "Canadian," the term "Louisianais" did not become prevalent until two generations had succeeded one another, but the meanings settlers gave to the new ethno-label they claimed for themselves expressed their agency in the constrained situation created by the French crown's cession of the colony to Britain and Spain. At the same time, slaves were not included in this process of identification, which only served to strengthen the cohesion of whites. The French regime did not witness the birth of a single Creole identity that would have united all inhabitants across racial boundaries. The use of ethnic and national identities expressed a "process of contention" between social formations. Race shaped the connections that the various individuals and groups developed over time with New Orleans.[5]

4. On the interplay between place, belonging, and identity, see Irwin Altman and Setha M. Low, eds., *Place Attachment* (New York, 1992); Nadia Lovell, ed., *Locality and Belonging* (London, 1998); and Low and Denise Lawrence-Zúñiga, eds., *The Anthropology of Space and Place: Locating Culture* (Malden, Mass., 2003). For the use of the expression "Creoles of New Orleans" by slaves, see note 41 below. For identification by whites as "natives of the city" or "natives of New Orleans," see AANO, Saint-Louis Cathedral Marriages, 1759–1762, 1763–1766, and 1764–1774. For references to "la ville" ("the city"), see note 37 in Chapter 2.

5. For creolization as a process of contention, see O. Nigel Bolland, "Creolisation and Creole Societies: A Cultural Nationalist View of Caribbean Social History," in Verene A.

The meanings attached to Frenchness were redefined several times over the French period through the experience of colonization and changing demographic, social, economic, and geopolitical circumstances. Given that early census takers and the engineers who drew maps listing the grantees of urban parcels in the 1720s and early 1730s assumed that most of the white inhabitants of colonial settlements were French, they did not usually record their ethnic origins. Yet they occasionally specified whether a resident was Provençal, Canadian, German, Swiss, or Bohemian. They did so because these ethnic identities appeared problematic in the eyes of local authorities and most colonists. Frenchness was initially constructed within the colony in opposition to people who came from places outside the kingdom, either another French colony, such as Canada, or a foreign country such as the German or Swiss states. Migrants from metropolitan provinces tended to merge with one another more easily, taking on a collective French identity, although those from Provence remained distinctive for longer. That Canadians were viewed as others suggests that the markers of identity at stake were not limited to subjecthood, language, or religion. A few decades later, Frenchness came to be defined in contrast with the Creole identity that the metropolitan officials and elite imposed on all settlers who were born in the colony, whether they were of Canadian or French parentage. Seldom appropriated by colonists themselves, the Creoleness projected onto Louisiana's white inhabitants played a crucial role in their construction as colonial subjects. The renewal of imperial wars in the 1740s and the cession of the colony to the British and Spanish at the end of the Seven Years' War led to a final shift in national identification, as settlers claimed Frenchness, not primarily in contrast with a Canadian or Creole identity, but in opposition to Britishness and Spanishness.[6]

Shepherd and Glen L. Richards, eds., *Questioning Creole: Creolisation Discourses in Caribbean Culture* (Kingston, Jamaica, 2002), 1–46 (quotation, 38).

6. "Recensement des habitants et concessionnaires de La Nouvelle-Orléans," 1721, ANOM COL G1 464, "Recensement général des habitations et des habitants de la colonie de la Louisiane ainsi qu'ils se sont nommés au premier janvier 1726," "Recensement général des habitants nègres esclaves sauvages et bestiaux du département de la Nouvelle Orléans qui s'y sont trouvés au 1er juillet 1727," and "Recensement général de la ville de la Nouvelle-Orléans ... fait au mois de janvier 1732." For the maps, see "The Collins C. Diboll Vieux Carré Digital Survey: A Project on the Historic New Orleans Collection," on HNOC's website, which uses the 1722 map of New Orleans by Louis Le Blond de La

A person's attachment to place in the kingdom was principally associated with his or her "pays," the province or locality where people were born and lived, but daily life in overseas colonies tended to erase regional differences. It is difficult to evaluate to what extent former regional ethnic identities remained meaningful and informed social practices in Louisiana. Although colonists from Western France and Paris were more numerous, transatlantic migrations mixed together individuals from all over France whose journey to the New World was often preceded by internal moves within the kingdom and prolonged stays in cities. In Canada, the diminutive size of the colonial population, the smallness of the territory occupied by the French, marriages, relationships among neighbors, religious ceremonies, and service in the militia all favored cultural and linguistic homogenization similar to the Anglicization or Hispanization of colonial populations experienced in British or Spanish territories. The same process seems to have taken place in Louisiana. Admittedly, settlers and soldiers still displayed regional identities. Nicknames based on a French city (Le Parisien, Versailles, etc.) or province (Dauphiné, La Provençale, Berry, etc.) appear in colonial records. Belonging to the same "pays" was also presented as a reason for obtaining assistance and maintaining relationships. Most of the marriages celebrated in the New Orleans church during the 1720s and early 1730s nonetheless united people from different French regions. A few colonists chose a spouse born in the same province, but they were a small minority.[7]

Language might have played an important role in helping migrants to construct a collective French identity. With the exception of those from

Tour, the 1728 map by François Ignace Broutin, and the 1731 map by Gonichon: http://www.hnoc.org/vcs/index.php.

7. On subregional identities in the kingdom, see Yves Durand, *Vivre au pays au XVIIIe siècle: Essai sur la notion de pays dans l'ouest de la France* (Paris, 1984). On the relationships between mobility within metropolitan France and migrations to American colonies, see Leslie Choquette, "La mobilité de travail en France et l'émigration vers le Canada (XVIIe–XVIIIe siècle)," in Yves Landry et al., eds., *Les chemins de la migration en Belgique et au Québec, XVIIe–XXe siècles* (Beauport, Quebec, 1995), 201–208. On Frenchification, Anglicization, or Hispanization, see Gilles Havard and Cécile Vidal, *Histoire de l'Amérique française* ([Paris], 2008), 595–603; Jack P. Greene, *Pursuits of Happiness: The Social Development of Early Modern British Colonies and the Formation of American Culture* (Chapel Hill, N.C., 1988); and Jean-Paul Zúñiga, *Espagnols d'outre-mer: Émigration, métissage, et reproduction sociale à Santiago du Chili au XVII siècle* (Paris, 2002). On relationships of solidarity based on common subregional identities, see Alexandre Dubé, "Les biens publics: Culture politique de la Louisiane française, 1730–1770" (Ph.D. diss., McGill University, 2009), 276–282.

Provence, the majority of colonists likely came from urban centers in the metropole and spoke French rather than a regional language, which facilitated the merging together of people. In one of his travel accounts, Jean-Bernard Bossu observed that "New Orleans and Mobile are the only two cities where there is no dialect; people speak quite good French there." Contrary to what Bossu claimed, however, some urban dwellers in the Louisiana capital practiced a *"patois"* (dialect), Provençal in particular, in addition to French. Their Occitan language fueled their alterity. Migrants from Provence started to arrive in the colony early on, well before the 1760s when Marseille was increasingly becoming an Atlantic port city. Although French settlers' regional origins were usually not specified in censuses, a New Orleans inhabitant was identified as "Provençal" in 1727, while a murder trial forty years later, involving a group of friends who got drunk together, also reveals a network of sociability and solidarity among sailors from Marseille and Provence, some of whom spoke Provençal. The regional identity of the protagonists concerned in the murder trial was not the reason for the violence, but people from Provence still seem to have been viewed as somehow different by most white inhabitants, who came from other parts of France, perhaps because the Provençal language was more recalcitrant to the process of linguistic homogenization. When the officer Jean-Charles Pradel wrote about another officer who owed him some money, he displayed some xenophobic hostility: "I suspected that this officer, named Mr. de Mazan, from Provence, would not keep his word," as if people from Provence were naturally inclined to be unfaithful to their word. Nevertheless, aside from occasional prejudice expressed toward people from Provence, identities linked to the various provinces and "pays" of the kingdom seem to have informed relationships of solidarity rather than of antagonism.[8]

8. For the prevalence of the French language in cities, see [Jean-Bernard] Bossu, *Nouveaux voyages aux Indes occidentales* . . . , 2 vols. (Paris, 1768), I, 27 (quotation). For identifications of people from Provence in censuses and court records, see "Recensement général . . . au 1er juillet 1727," ANOM COL G1 464; and RSCL 1767/11/06/01, 1767/11/06/02, 1767/11/08/01, 1767/11/09/01, 1767/11/09/02, 1767/11/10/01, 1767/11/10/02, 1767/11/11/01, 1767/11/12/01, 1767/11/12/02. For the mention of Félix Le Provençal, see also RSCL 1769/03/30/01. The phenotype of people from Provence was also seen as different. In the sixteenth century, Jean de Léry described the skin color of the Tupinamba as "swarthy," comparing them to Spanish and *Provençaux*. See Jean de Léry, *Histoire d'un voyage faict en la terre de Brésil (1578)*, (2d ed., 1580), ed. Frank Lestringant (Paris, 1994), 212, quoted in Gilles Havard, "'Nous ne ferons plus qu'un peuple': Le métissage en Nouvelle-France à l'époque de Champlain," in Guy Martinière and Didier Poton, eds., *Le Nouveau Monde et Champlain* (Paris, 2008), 95. For Jean-Charles de Pradel's

In contrast, interactions between people from France and from Canada often appear much more conflicted. Because Canadian officers and recruits played a crucial role in the colony's founding and development, Frenchness also became meaningful in opposition to Canadianness. Canadians were often labelled as such, even when there was no obvious reason to do so. This was true in censuses and maps as well as in declarations, interrogatories, and testimonies before the Superior Council. In some judicial cases, the specification of a Canadian identity was clearly used to incriminate defendants, as if being born in Canada was proof of a person's guilt. In 1747, when a shooting incident was first brought before the court, for example, only one of a group of four men who were present was identified with an ethno-label, "Moreau," the "Canadien." While passing in a pirogue near the farm of Étienne Degle dit Malborough at the German Coast, one of the four had shouted out Marlborough's name in greeting, whereupon the farmer came out to see what was going on. When one of the travelers insulted him, Malborough got mad and fired a shot, wounding a slave who was with them. Apart from Moreau, the other three men were all German. They accused Moreau of being the one who had offended Malborough, although he denied it. Similarly, in other cases when clothes were stolen and resold by enslaved or free people of African descent, Canadians were often designated as receivers of stolen goods.[9]

A scarcity of resources, especially at the beginning of the Company of the Indies's monopoly, could help to explain some hostility toward Canadi-

---

xenophobic comment about an officer from Provence, see A. Baillardel and A. Prioult, eds., *Le chevalier de Pradel: Vie d'un colon français en Louisiane au XVIIIe siècle; d'après sa correspondance et celle de sa famille* (Paris, 1928), 212.

9. The ethno-label "Canadian" became common in New France in the closing decades of the seventeenth century. The use of this ethnic category, nevertheless, should not be interpreted as a sign that settlers became conscious over time of a new ethnic identity that was distinct from a French identity. In administrative correspondence between Quebec and Versailles or Paris, the colonists of Canada kept a dual identity and were described as both French and Canadian. Officials insisted on either one or both faces of this Janus of the New World, depending on the anxiety they felt about the way settlers embraced or rejected the imperial project. See Carpin, *Histoire d'un mot*; and Thomas Wien, "Quelle est la largeur de l'Atlantique? Le 'François Canadien' entre proximité et distance, 1660–1760," in Vidal, ed., *Français? La nation en débat entre colonies et métropole*, 55–75. For the 1747 case at the German Coast, see RSCL 1747/12/16/03, 1747/12/17/01, 1747/12/26/01, 1748/02/23/02. For Canadians accused of theft, see RSCL 1723/07/15/01; 1752/03/26/01, 1752/03/27/02. For other court records identifying Canadians, see RSCL 1730/04/06/01; 1741/01/23/01; 1748/01/06/02.

ans. All of the colony's early governors were born in Canada, and colonists and officials born in metropolitan France accused them, Jean-Baptiste Le Moyne de Bienville especially, of favoring their fellow countrymen. After his arrival in Louisiana in 1724, the king's commissioner Jacques de La Chaise charged Bienville with privileging Canadians in judicial decisions and in the distribution of merchandise from the company's warehouse. His first report to the minister of the navy was particularly scathing in its commentary:

> All the French are ill-treated, they are refused everything from the warehouses even when they pay cash, and the merchandise is given only to the Canadians, who do nothing here, so that they can trade in the Illinois, they take their merchandise there and sell it for exorbitant amounts, and they come back with bear oil and bills of exchange on the Council from the outpost of the Illinois; a Canadian told me that he had sold one quart of eau-de-vie in this country for 5 000 livres in bills of exchange. This is downright theft; none of these travelers clear ground or run a plantation ... ; I know for sure and I have seen with my own eyes that only soldiers, sailors and Canadians are granted favors by the Council; for the Canadians they do not lack merchandise. Mr. de Bienville is careful to deliver what they ask.

Canadians were looked on with suspicion because many of them were transient travelers and traders who only came to New Orleans to sell furs and pelts, bear oil, and game, not to settle permanently in the lower Mississippi Valley and open plantations.[10]

Jean-François-Benjamin Dumont de Montigny also denounced Bienville, averring that he showed preferment toward Canadians in the distribution of slaves. Claiming that he was the victim of Bienville's partiality, he explained his failure to amass a fortune by stating that the most prominent settlers in Louisiana were "Canadians who have become wealthy under the protection and support of their commandant and countryman. This is the honest truth, although they cannot in good faith call themselves opulent, because they had to repay the Company for their negroes." Unlike La Chaise, Dumont de Montigny targeted those Canadians who had chosen to become planters and slaveholders, rather than transient traders and travelers.[11]

10. Jacques de La Chaise to the Company of the Indies's Directors, Mar. 8, 1724, ANOM COL C13A 7, fols. 15–16 (quotation).

11. Gordon M. Sayre and Carla Zecher, eds., *The Memoir of Lieutenant Dumont, 1715–1747: A Sojourner in the French Atlantic; Jean-François-Benjamin Dumont de Montigny,* trans. Sayre (Chapel Hill, N.C., 2012), 378 (quotation).

Emergence of a Sense of Place and the Racial Divide

After Bienville's final departure, *Commissaire-ordonnateur* Honoré-Gabriel Michel continued the tradition of hostility toward Canadian governors and occasionally accused Pierre de Rigaud de Vaudreuil de Cavagnal of favoring his "Canadian creatures" for nominations as commandants of outposts. This time, it was the Canadian officers sent to the colony by the king who were the main object of the commissaire-ordonnateur's resentment. Overall, the animosity toward Canadians nonetheless diminished in the last decades of the French regime. Some Frenchmen managed to accumulate property and capital, while matrimonial and economic alliances among French and Canadian families also connected their fates.[12]

Before this appeasement in the tensions between the French and Canadians, the criticisms leveled by Bienville's most virulent critic, Father Raphaël, the Capuchins' first superior and New Orleans's priest, are particularly noteworthy for the way they associated Canadian and Native identities. Like Dumont de Montigny, he decried the protection that had enabled some Canadian settlers in Louisiana to succeed over other colonists who had originated in France. But he went even further than the governor's other detractors by denying that Bienville, as a Canadian, had the French political and administrative expertise to rule the colony. He asked Abbé Raguet, one of the company directors, to restrict the authority of military officers "as long as the Canadians are in command, because as they have been so to speak raised among the savages they are unfamiliar with the customs and policy of the kingdom." The tone of his letter echoes metropolitan discourses against Creoles throughout the Americas that claimed that settlers born in the colonies experienced a process of degeneracy that grew out of their ties with Native Americans. Even though other travel accounts, more generally, praised the competence of Canadians in dealing with indigenous populations, the priest condemned Bienville for his close relationships with First Nations. This intimate knowledge of Native cultures, however, did not impede the Canadian-born governor from spending the rest of his life in Paris, where he died, following his last appointment as Louisiana's highest official. He likely thought of himself primarily as an officer in the service of the French king.[13]

12. Honoré-Gabriel Michel to the minister of the navy, July 20, 1750, ANOM COL C13A 35, fol. 325.

13. Father Raphaël to Abbé Raguet, Sept. 15, 1725, ANOM COL C13A 8, fol. 412; Father Raphaël to Abbé Raguet, Oct. 12, 1725, ANOM COL C13A 8, fol. 415. Jean-Baptiste Le Moyne de Bienville was certainly the governor with the greatest knowledge of Native American cultures. He spoke the Mobilian language (the lingua franca of Native Ameri-

Discourses about Canadians and Creoles need to be examined together. People born in Canada were sometimes called *"Créoles"* in the Saint Lawrence Valley, and the sons of Canadian settlers in Louisiana were also described as *"Créoles."* Moreover, Governor Vaudreuil, who was a native of Canada, compared Creoles and Canadians in a letter to the minister of the navy. As he wrote about French-Native American interactions in the Mississippi Valley, he lamented the impossibility of following enemy parties that were able to take refuge "in places inaccessible to people other than savages or creoles from the country accustomed from a young age to running in the woods and making war there like these barbarians do, as it is practiced in Canada, and what cannot be done here as the colony is too new to supply a sufficient number of such warriors capable of fortifying the party of our allies and impressing our enemies." Vaudreuil drew a comparison between creolization and canadianization in connection with indianization. The governor's considerations on Creole and Canadian identities reflected the anxiety generated among Europeans by life in the New World. They feared that they could lose their civility overseas. Besides the natural environment and climate, close relationships with Native Americans or African slaves were viewed as being responsible for the transformation of colonists' French, Spanish, or English identities. Discourses specifically regarding Canadianness in New France, however, diverged from those on Creoleness in the Caribbean in that the former typically centered on concerns over colonists' French identity merging with that of Natives, whereas commentary on Creole identity usually involved worries over the intermingling of Frenchness and Africanness.[14]

In contrast with the documentation produced locally, such as administrative correspondence and judicial proceedings, the term "Creole" took on

<hr/>

cans in the Southeast) and was tattooed. On his knowledge of Native American cultures and his policy toward First Nations, see Havard and Vidal, *Histoire de l'Amérique française,* 254–384. For a positive appreciation of Canadians in their relationships with indigenous populations, see [Antoine-Simon] Le Page du Pratz, *Histoire de la Louisiane* …, 3 vols. (Paris, 1758), II, 214–215, 227.

14. For the use of the term "Creole" in New France, see Carpin, *Histoire d'un mot,* 137–138. For the description of the sons of Canadian settlers as Creoles, see "Liste apostillée des officiers des troupes entretenues à la Louisiane," ANOM COL D2C 51, fols. 104v–112v, "Liste apostillée des officiers de la Louisiane, 1738," fols. 159–162v, "Liste apostillée des officiers et cadets qui servent dans les troupes de la Louisiane, 1740," fols. 171–176, and "Liste des cadets à l'aiguillette," May 9, 1741, fols. 183–184r. For Pierre de Rigaud de Vaudreuil de Cavagnal's comparison between Canadians and Creoles, see Vaudreuil to the minister of the navy, Sept. 22, 1749, ANOM COL C13A 33, fols. 87–87v.

a different meaning in travel accounts to Louisiana published in the metropole. Although these authors occasionally mentioned Canadians, they did not allude to the conflicting relationships between the French and Canadians in the lower Mississippi Valley. Most of the time, they simply designated the local population of European descent as "the French" and restricted the ethno-label Creole to the sections of their books devoted to the Antilles. Nevertheless, they occasionally described people born in Louisiana as Creole. When Antoine-Simon Le Page du Pratz underlined the great physical constitution of Louisiana settlers in his *Histoire de la Louisiane,* he called them the "French Creoles of Louisiana." In addition, he explained in a footnote that "a Creole is a child born in a distant Country, to a father and a mother of the same Nation."[15]

Le Page du Pratz's definition of Creole is interesting because it was broader than the one most commonly accepted at the time (born in the Americas) and conveyed a sense of the Atlantic or global dimension of empire. It also contrasted "nation," as a people or community, with "pays," as a space or territory, and linked them to the language of family, lineage, and blood. On the one hand, Creoles were recognized as French; on the other, their Frenchness was questioned by their identification as Creole. They were both identical to and different from French people. This difference came from their birth and life in a country located overseas. Life at distance from the territorial center of the nation, the different climate and environment to which they were exposed, and their nearness with other nations, it was feared, held the potential to shape them into different people than those who came from the same birthplace, even if they still shared the same blood. Because colonists' place of birth could no longer serve as a common tie, binding them to those born in the kingdom, their blood and race took on greater importance. At the same time, mentioning that a Creole child was born of two parents of the same nation was a way of preventing the suspicion of *métissage,* often associated with Creole identity, and of underlining a person's purity of blood.[16]

15. Le Page du Pratz, *Histoire de la Louisiane,* II, 309.

16. The ethno-label "Creole" (*"Crioulo"* in Portuguese and *"Criollo"* in Spanish) first appeared in the context of Iberian expansion. From Spanish America, it spread throughout the Atlantic world, including the French Empire. See Carolyn Allen, "Creole: The Problem of Definition," in Shepherd and Richards, eds., *Questioning Creole,* 47–63; and Ralph Bauer and José Antonio Mazzotti, "Introduction: Creole Subjects in the Colonial Americas," in Bauer and Mazzotti, eds., *Creole Subjects in the Colonial America: Empires, Texts, Identities* (Chapel Hill, N.C., 2009), 3–7.

In contrast with Le Page du Pratz, Bossu generally used the term "Créole" to designate colonists born in the Mississippi Valley. His travel accounts dealt with a later period, in the 1760–1770s, at a time when people born locally in the colony had become more numerous. The description that he offers of the New Orleans population also raises the issue of métissage:

> The settlers are of four kinds, namely Europeans, Americans, Africans, or Negroes and Mixed-Blood. The Mixed-Blood are those born to Europeans and natives of the country whom we call savages. We name Creoles those who are born to a Frenchman and a French woman, or a European woman. In general, the Creoles are very brave, tall and well-built; they have a special aptitude for arms and sciences; but as they cannot cultivate it to perfection for lack of good teachers, the wealthy and considerate fathers do not fail to send their children to France, as to the first School of the world, in all matters.

Bossu's recourse to ethno-labels related to continents allowed him to implicitly comprise the various national subgroups among Europeans (the French but also the German settlers), Native Americans, and Africans in his description. In so doing, he insisted on the ethnic and cultural divides between the three populations. Moreover, he also referred to Africans with a pejorative term, *"nègres,"* that conveyed both their status and race and that tended to merge them into a single, more homogenous category. In Bossu's consideration of African people, race appears more important than culture and ethnicity. He thus ignored the substantial population of individuals born of unions between people from Europe and Africa, whereas he emphasized métissage among Europeans and Native Americans.[17]

Bossu also restricted the use of the term "Créole" to settlers of European descent. He did not see the ethno-labels French, European, and Creole as being mutually exclusive. As in Le Page du Pratz's definition, Creoles appear in Bossu's reckoning as a variety of French people or Europeans whose only difference from those born in the Old World was their birthplace. The picture he drew of Creoles was a panegyric. A few pages before his description of New Orleans's inhabitants, he talked about the Creoles in the islands in the same generally positive tone. He was responding to the debate about the degeneracy of mankind in the Americas that had started afresh in Europe in the early 1760s with publications by the French naturalist and philoso-

17. Bossu, *Nouveaux voyages aux Indes occidentales*, I, 25–26 (quotation), 132, 201, II, 43; [Jean-Bernard] Bossu, *Nouveaux voyages dans l'Amérique septentrionale . . .* (Amsterdam, 1777), 53, 309, 345, 348–349, 390–392.

Emergence of a Sense of Place and the Racial Divide

pher Georges-Louis Leclerc de Buffon in 1761 and the Dutch philosopher, geographer, and diplomat Cornélius de Pauw in 1768. Although Bossu was mostly opposed to Buffon's theories, he came closer to his point of view when he wrote about settlers of European descent who allowed their infants to be nursed by "a black, swarthy, or red slave ... of tainted blood." The practice of employing wet nurses of African or Native descent was often used against Creoles to prove their degeneracy.[18]

Within the colony, the persons most likely to assign a Creole identity to persons of European descent born in Louisiana were administrative and ecclesiastical authorities. Although some of these officials originated in Canada, not in France, they still expressed the point of view common to the imperial elite regarding the subjects they had to rule over or the parishioners they had to control and assist. In contrast, they did not define their own ethnic identity in relationship to their birthplace but in connection with their status as men in the service of the king or the Gallican Church. In addition to the debate about degeneracy in the New World, their discourse was influenced by the monarch's anxiety over the loyalty of his colonial subjects.

The ethno-label "Creole" frequently appears in administrative correspondence in the context of education. Because local authorities needed the support of the crown to open new educational institutions or finance those that already existed, they insisted on Creoles' intellectual abilities and stressed the risk that they could fall into vice if they did not receive an education. In 1725, Father Raphaël advocated the creation of a college, claiming that "several will succeed, those among the Creoles in particular, they have a good memory and are sharp-witted." Two years later, La Chaise praised the newly arrived Ursulines, adopting a paternalist tone when he mentioned the Creoles with a possessive pronoun: "Those ladies would be highly useful there [in the Hospital], and would not be less so for our Creoles who, for

18. Bossu, *Nouveaux voyages aux Indes occidentales*, I, 17–19, 201–202 (quotation). On the debate about degeneracy in the New World, see, among other studies, Antonello Gerbi, *The Dispute of the New World: The History of a Polemic, 1750–1900*, trans. Jeremy Moyle (1955; rpt. Pittsburgh, Pa., 1973); and Jorge Cañizares-Esguerra, *How to Write the History of the New World: Histories, Epistemologies, and Identities in the Eighteenth-Century Atlantic World* (Stanford, Calif., 2001). On the association between degeneracy and wet nursing of white infants by women of color, see Bernard Lavallé, "Recherches sur l'apparition de la conscience créole dans la vice-royauté du Pérou: L'antagonisme hispano-créole dans les ordres religieux (XVIème–XVIIème siècles)" (Ph.D. Thesis, Université Michel de Montaigne Bordeaux III, 1978), 751–902, https://hal.archives-ouvertes.fr/tel-01585336/document.

lack of education, fall into vice before they know what it is, and get so used to it that it is difficult for them to abandon it."[19]

Louisiana governors also regularly alluded to Creoles when they wrote about tensions with Native Americans. Governor Étienne Périer mentioned that the few "Creoles" in the colony acquitted themselves with bravery in the expeditions against the Natchez in 1730. He also hoped that the "Creoles," if trained correctly, could replace the soldiers sent from the metropole and reduce the colony's dependency on First Nations. Likewise, in 1748, at the end of the War of the Austrian Succession, Vaudreuil recounted in great detail a series of attacks by a small party of "rebellious" Choctaw against some settlers and slaves on the German Coast. He described the Germans as too timorous to defend themselves, whereas some "Creoles of New Orleans," including a "métis" who had gone there to hunt, fought valiantly. The governor found it necessary to draw attention to Creoles' positive conduct in defense of the colony because their loyalty and bravery were typically viewed as questionable in the eyes of both central and local authorities. In the same vein, Bienville thought that he had to defend his decision, in 1736, to entrust the command of a small expedition against the Choctaw to a young "Creole." He emphasized the youth's qualities, explaining that it was in his interest to stop the English fur trade, as it was hurting his own commercial prospects.[20]

Finally, the state's two highest representatives specified the Creole origins of local settlers born in the colony each time they asked a favor from the king on their behalf. They seemed to believe that the monarch would be all the more generous toward his Creole subjects in order to co-opt them within the Empire. The term Creole repeatedly appears on lists of passengers on the king's ships, as if the commissaire-ordonnateur who granted their free passage felt the need to justify doing so. In the same way, the colony's top officials sometimes described officers or employees as "Creoles of this colony" when they wanted to obtain some advancement, a new title, or pension for their clients. As in Canada, the crown allowed the sons of local elites to become sword officers and pen employees in the navy and to serve as councillors on the Superior Council. In fact, in 1762, the min-

19. Father Raphaël to Abbé Raguet, Sept. 15, 1725, ANOM COL C13A 8, fol. 413; La Chaise to the minister of the navy, Aug. 29, 1727, ANOM COL C13A 10, fol. 343.

20. Étienne Périer to the minister of the navy, Apr. 10, 1730, ANOM COL C13A 12, fols. 303–304; Périer to the minister of the navy, Aug. 1, 1730, ANOM COL C13A 12, fols. 329v–330r; Vaudreuil to the minister of the navy, Nov. 16, 1748, ANOM COL C13A 32, fols. 137–144; Jean-Baptiste Le Moyne de Bienville to the minister of the navy, May 10, 1736, ANOM COL C13A 21, fols. 154v–155v.

Emergence of a Sense of Place and the Racial Divide

ister of the navy insisted on the need to recruit assessor councillors for the court among Creoles. The goal was both to cultivate their loyalty and to save money. Unlike what happened in the Spanish Empire, no competition ever developed between metropolitans and Creoles for administrative, ecclesiastical, and military offices. Louisiana colonists were deprived of a powerful incentive for creolism, that is the struggle for the rights of Creoles.[21]

Because identifying as Creole carried negative connotations, Louisiana colonists born in the Americas did not appropriate this ethnic category for themselves. There is only one instance of such self-identification in administrative files, which appears as part of an individual's effort to obtain a pension. Likewise, settlers never used the ethno-label in sacramental records and very rarely in notarial deeds and judicial proceedings. Instead, they presented themselves in the same way people did in the metropole, with their place of origin and family relationships. Significantly, a woman who had come from Cap-Français and who had arrived in New Orleans after a terrible misadventure identified herself to the Superior Council as "Dame Marie Le Veuf, native du Cap françois veuve de défunt Sr. Antoine Denoyer," whereas Bossu described her as a "Créole" several times when he told her story in his travel account. Creoleness was an assigned identity mainly used when metropolitan interlocutors or audiences were involved.[22]

21. For lists of passengers, see "Colonies: passagers embarqués pour France, Louisiane 1732–1765," ANOM COL F5B 34. See also the letters between the minister of the navy and Vaudreuil about a "Creole of this colony" who was in the metropole because of the war: Vaudreuil to the minister of the navy, May 12, 1747, ANOM C13A 31, fols. 79–80; and the minister of the navy to Vaudreuil, Sept. 30, 1747, ANOM COL B 85, fol. 235v (8v). For the documentation about officers and employees, see "Liste apostillée des officiers des troupes entretenues à la Louisiane," ANOM COL D2C 51, fols. 104v–112v; "Liste apostillée des officiers de la Louisiane, 1738," fols. 159–162v; "Liste apostillée des officiers et cadets qui servent dans les troupes de la Louisiane, 1740," fols. 171–176; "Liste des cadets à l'aiguillette," May 9, 1741, fols. 183–184r; Vincent-Gaspard-Pierre de Rochemore to the minister of the navy, Dec. 31, 1758, ANOM COL C13A 40, fol. 201v; and Louis Billouart de Kerlérec to the minister of the navy, June 8, 1761, ANOM COL C13A 42, fol. 215. On the need to recruit Creoles for the Superior Council, see minister of the navy to Kerlérec and Jean-Jacques Blaise d'Abbadie, Jan. 18, 1762, ANOM COL B 114, fol. 168rv (19r–v). On Spanish creolism, see Benedict Anderson, *Imagined Communities: Reflections on the Origin and Spread of Nationalism*, rev. ed. (London, 1991), 47–65; and David Anthony Brading, *The First America: The Spanish Monarchy, Creole Patriots, the Liberal State, 1492–1867* (Cambridge, 1991).

22. On the similar refusal of settlers to adopt this ethno-label in British America, see Joyce E. Chaplin, "Creoles in British America: From Denial to Acceptance," in Charles Stewart, ed., *Creolization: History, Ethnography, Theory* (Walnut Creek, Calif., 2007),

Within the colony, French settlers apparently saw the divide between themselves and foreigners as more meaningful than that between the French and Creoles. This was particularly obvious in relation to the Germans, who formed a large contingent of the transatlantic migrants who arrived in Louisiana in the 1720s. Just as Swiss and French troops were ruled and managed separately, local authorities planned for German migrants to form a distinct outpost in the vicinity of New Orleans. Some single German men and German families nonetheless settled in the capital, while many women of German descent married French colonists in the New Orleans church. These German settlers often integrated themselves with French people of the lower sort, prompting officials to campaign against their assimilation. For example, the Germans were blamed as the persons chiefly responsible for the opening of clandestine taverns in New Orleans, perhaps because it was easier to justify urban disorder if it was caused by foreigners.[23]

Even German or Swiss officers, who served the French crown and who married among the French elite, were sometimes regarded with xenophobia. After Pradel's death, his widow had to see to their daughters' marriages.

46–62; and Bauer and Mazzotti, "Introduction," in Bauer and Mazzotti, eds., *Creole Subjects in the Colonial Americas*, 39–42. For a rare instance of a person identifying as Creole while requesting a pension, see "Mémoire des services du sieur Carrière Monbrun," Mar. 21, 1769, ANOM COL E 64. For a few exceptions where persons self-identified as Creole in court records or notarial deeds, see RSCL 1747/03/10/04; "Procuration," May 12, 1747, in Heloise H. Cruzat, ed., "RSCL LXIII: May, 1747," *LHQ*, XVIII (1935), 445; "Contract of Apprenticeship," Mar. 20, 1748, in Cruzat, ed., "RSCL LXVII: February–March, 1748," *LHQ*, XIX (1936), 502; RSCL 1749/03/29/01; and "Procès-verbal des informations faites contre Ulloa," Nov. 8, 1768, ANOM COL C13A 48, fols. 101v–119v. For the different ways used to identify Dame Le Veuf, see RSCL 1765/10/12/02, 1765/10/12/03; and Bossu, *Nouveaux voyages dans l'Amérique septentrionale*, 62–76. When local officials wrote to the minister of the navy, they did not describe the woman as Creole. See Charles Philippe Aubry and Denis Nicolas Foucault to the minister of the navy, Oct. 19, 1765, ANOM COL C13A 45, fols. 3v–4. In one exceptional letter, Pradel described his daughter born in the colony as Creole because he wanted to convince his brothers not make her travel before the spring, as winter in the metropole was hard to bear for a "créole." See Baillardel and Prioult, eds., *Le chevalier de Pradel*, 213.

23. Reinhart Kondert, *The Germans of Colonial Louisiana, 1720–1803* (Stuttgart, Germany, 1990); René Le Conte, "The Germans in Louisiana in the Eighteenth Century," trans. and ed. Glenn R. Conrad, *Louisiana History*, VIII (1967), 67–84. For local authorities' policy against German settlers of the lower sort, see "Observations sur le règlement de police de Ms. de Vaudreuil et Michel du 6 mars 1751," Article 9, ANOM COL F3 243, fols. 84–89.

Emergence of a Sense of Place and the Racial Divide

When one of them considered marrying a cousin, Antoine de La Chaise, she categorically opposed the union. Among her various objections to the match, she pointed out the foreign origins of both Antoine's mother (Spanish) and stepmother (German) in a deeply xenophobic and even racist tone. Later, at the time of the revolt, which propelled nationalist discourses, this xenophobia against German-speaking people resurfaced and crystallized, in particular, around the former Swiss officer Pierre Marquis. Distinctions between French citizens and foreigners were made only in situations of conflict or tension.[24]

Such circumstantial surges of ethnic prejudice also fell on foreigners who came from European countries other than the German and Swiss states. During most of the French regime, there were so few of them that their foreign origins were rarely mentioned, and they were fully integrated socially. But at least one settler named Jonathan Darby was confronted with xenophobia during the settlement of an inheritance case. Darby was an Englishman educated at Oxford and recruited as an indentured servant by the concession Cantillon in 1719. He became the director of the concession in 1727. He then settled on his own plantation and built a fortune. In the 1750s and 1760s, he served as a churchwarden and militia officer. He married a Frenchwoman and formed profitable matrimonial alliances with prominent families for his children. His English origins appear to have had no impact on his social integration and mobility until a French settler named Jacques Judice designated him as the executor of his will and guardian of his son.[25]

24. Baillardel and Prioult, eds., *Le chevalier de Pradel,* 376, 381–385; Aubry to the minister of the navy, Dec. 23–24, 1768, ANOM COL C13A 48, fol. 40r.

25. In early modern France, the *droit d'aubaine* was "a royal right of escheat inherited from the feudal world that allowed the king to confiscate the property of aliens, foreigners who died in the kingdom without native heirs, as well as French citizens who died having established themselves outside the kingdom." It "became the key legal mechanism for distinguishing foreigners and citizens, and the motive force behind thousands of individual naturalizations from 1660 to 1789." See Peter Sahlins, *Unnaturally French: Foreign Citizens in the Old Regime and After* (Ithaca, N.Y., 2004), xiii. On Darby's life, see Glenn R. Conrad, trans. and comp., *The First Families of Louisiana,* I (Baton Rouge, La., 1970), 41; and Earl C. Woods and Charles E. Nolan, eds., *Sacramental Records of the Roman Catholic Church of the Archdiocese of New Orleans,* 19 vols. (New Orleans, 1987–2003), I, 63, II, 64–65. Some information about Darby also comes from the lawsuit between him and John Mingo, an "English free negro." Mingo had come "from the English" and had taken refuge at Darby's. A national solidarity had prevailed over racial antagonism. See RSCL 1727/11/28/01, 1727/11/28/02, 1727/11/28/03, 1728/11/03/01, 1730/11/21/01, 1730/11/21/03, 1730/11/25/01, 1730/11/25/05.

Issues over Darby's status as a foreigner arose when Nicolas Judice, the child's uncle, decided to protest Jacques's will. Unlike Darby, he had only been named as a surrogate guardian. In his request to the Superior Council, he admitted that "the Sieur Darby [is] known in this colony as being an honest and prominent permanent resident," but he argued that "these qualities … cannot give him the quality of being French, even if he had been granted letters of naturalization by our prince, and even if he peacefully enjoys the privileges of the nation. Nevertheless, customary law makes him incapable of civil effects because of his quality as a foreigner, and if the situation was taken into account by this same law there would not be any difference in the kingdom between foreigners and natives." The Superior Council, in conjuction with a meeting of the minor child's relatives and friends, decided in favor of Judice. Yet they might have been motivated by the desire to privilege family members rather than to discriminate against a foreigner. Because Darby left four living children at his death in 1767, his succession did not raise any difficulty.[26]

The colony's cession to Great Britain and Spain following the Seven Years' War also provided settlers with the opportunity to express their xenophobic impulses. The establishment of the British on the eastern bank of the Mississippi (except for New Orleans) in 1763 sparked a massive flight of French colonists. The testimony of Louis de Populus de Saint-Protais, a military officer garrisoned in Mobile, before the Superior Council hints at the nationalistic reasons that carried the French population away from the British-held territory. Because the court had ordered the separation of person and property between him and his wife, de Populus had to justify his decision "not to remain among foreigners" and his intention of "staying with my nation in this colony or in another country not too distant if necessary." He argued that he did not wish to stay "in a place which would become strange to me because of the foreigners who occupy it. If my wife wants to change religion, that is not my intention. Moreover, I am in the [king's] service, I have two boys, and also a girl, it is not appropriate for her to remain with ~~foreigners~~ Huguenots." His request echoed the new patriotism cultivated by the crown beginning in the 1750s in the context of the imperial conflict. Whereas royal discourse surrounding the defense of the homeland became more secularized, insisting on the barbarism of the English and re-

26. For Nicolas Judice's suit against Darby, see RSCL 1747/03/04/03, 1743/03/04/04, 1743/03/04/05, 1747/03/04/06, 1747/03/08/01, 1747/03/10/01. On the legal incapacities of foreigners, see Sahlins, *Unnaturally French*, 31–42. For Darby's inheritance, see NONA Garic Feb. 19, 1767; and NONA Garic 1767.

Emergence of a Sense of Place and the Racial Divide

maining silent about their Protestant faith, de Populus, however, chose to emphasize religious antagonism.[27]

The British immediately took possession of the eastern bank of the Mississippi River in 1763, but the new Spanish governor, Antonio de Ulloa, did not arrive until March 1766. Since the ceremony of possession was postponed, relationships between the French and Spanish were fraught. According to Charles Philippe Aubry, the French military officer commanding the colony, "Public signs of aversion and hate have been displayed for everything which bore the name Spanish." In the midst of these tense circumstances, an incident occurred between a French settler and an enslaved domestic. *"Perros los Franceses"* are the words Antoine Paul is reported to have shouted at Sieur Rivière, a merchant, on a New Orleans street one Sunday afternoon in 1766. Some neighbors who saw the fight told the judge that Sieur Rivière was hitting the slave with a stick and that Antoine Paul was trying to defend himself while "chattering incessantly." None of them understood what the enslaved man was saying because he spoke in Spanish. Sieur Rivière complained that Antoine Paul not only tried to defend himself but also attacked him. Coughing and spitting on the ground, the slave reportedly made "many silly remarks about the French." In front of the magistrate, Antoine Paul claimed that he had not insulted the French and that he had only said "that the English were dogs, that they did not know the Virgin Mary or anything else, and that the Sieur Rivière had misunderstood if he thought he was talking about the French, that he had nothing wrong to say about them since he was himself a Creole from Martinique."[28]

At first sight, Antoine Paul's decision to defend himself on the grounds of his birth in Martinique and his Catholic baptism in Santo Domingo might seem surprising. In a previous interrogation, he had told the judge about the complex peregrinations his life had taken since his birth in Martinique. Dutch merchants had bought him and took him to Curaçao and then Santo Domingo, where he was baptized. Afterward, he circulated in the Caribbean Sea and the Gulf of Mexico, living in various Spanish settlements be-

27. RSCL 1763/04/16/01 (the deletion is in the original document). See also RSCL 1763/03/16/01. On the new patriotism, see Edmond Dziembowski, *Un nouveau patriotisme français, 1750–1770: La France face à la puissance anglaise à l'époque de la guerre de Sept Ans* (Oxford, 1998); John Shovlin, "Selling American Empire on the Eve of the Seven Years War: The French Propaganda Campaign of 1755–1756," *Past and Present*, no. 206 (2010), 121–149; and Bell, *Cult of the Nation in France*, 78–106.

28. Aubry to the minister of the navy, 1769, ANOM COL C13A 47, fols. 200r–201v; RSCL 1766/06/04/03, 1766/06/05/01, 1766/06/05/02, 1766/06/05/03, 1766/06/05/04, 1766/06/07/06.

fore landing in Havana, where his master at the time of the 1766 incident, Joseph de Loyola, bought him. Antoine Paul's owner was probably the war commissioner who had come from Havana to New Orleans with Ulloa a few months earlier to take possession of the Louisiana capital. The last part of Antoine Paul's life had given him a Spanish culture. During the incident, Antoine Paul was identified as a "Spanish Negro" because he spoke the language of Cervantes, and one witness who testified in front of Superior Council called him that as well. Yet the slave apparently proclaimed in French, before the magistrate in charge of his case, his attachment to the French and to Catholicism. To escape from punishment, he seized on the two attributes—birthplace and religion—that defined Frenchness in the eyes of the French crown. Antoine Paul, however, did not succeed in convincing the court, which sentenced him to make amends and to be put in the stocks and given twenty-five lashes.[29]

Antoine Paul's case is the only one that offers a window into the way Frenchness and other European national identities might have become meaningful for people of African descent, either free or enslaved, although their lives were equally affected by transnational movements, imperial rivalries, and colonial cessions. At the time of the change of sovereignty, free people of color in Louisiana were not numerous enough to claim a French identity to fight racial discrimination. They were also still too socially and economically dependent on their former masters and too poorly educated to have the means to do so. In most of the documentation, the ethnic identities of people of African descent, mostly slaves, seem to have been conceived separately from those of settlers, except in their relationships to the new "pays" in which they lived together.

"FROM MY COUNTRY": THE PLASTICITY OF SLAVES' ETHNICITIES

With respect to the formation and transformation of slaves' ethnic identities, early New Orleans is a paradoxical case study. Contrary to what took place in the French Caribbean and in many other slave societies, the enslaved in Louisiana were rarely categorized with ethno-labels. Because the colony's direct access to the slave trade from Africa ceased early on, race quickly became the most important marker of identification in the Mis-

29. For Paul Antoine's trial, see RSCL 1766/06/04/03, 1766/06/05/01, 1766/06/05/02, 1766/06/05/03, 1766/06/05/04, 1766/06/07/06. For the royal definition of Frenchness, see Peter Sahlins, "Fictions of a Catholic France: The Naturalization of Foreigners, 1685–1787," in "National Cultures before Nationalism," special issue, *Representations*, no. 47 (Summer 1994), 85–110; and Sahlins, *Unnaturally French*, 56–64.

Emergence of a Sense of Place and the Racial Divide

sissippi colony. The judicial archives, however, constitute an extraordinary reservoir of evidence demonstrating that slaves' ethnic identities were mobilized to negotiate power relationships not only among authorities, masters, and slaves but also among slaves themselves. During court trials, ethnicities were discovered, negotiated, assigned, and appropriated, and information about slaves' ethnic makeup circulated from the bottom up as well as the top down. Yet the court records do not merely point to the persistence of African cultural practices and ethnic identities or the late emergence of an Afro-Creole culture. Nor do they simply reveal the late substitution of a racial identity for a plurality of African ethnicities. The French regime did not bear witness to one linear and unique process of ethnogenesis. During that time, the colony experienced the Company of the Indies's decision to end Louisiana's participation in the slave trade from Africa, the succession of two or three generations of slaves, the creolization of the slave population, and the scattered arrival of slaves born in both Africa and the Americas from the Antilles. The appropriation of racial identities by enslaved men and women happened early on and coexisted with the production, reproduction, and transformation of old and new ethnic identities. Slaves did not inherit a single ethnicity nor did they pick one and stick with it; they chose and made sense of several according to circumstances. Moreover, place as much as culture was at stake in the formation and transformation of categories of identification. Slaves not only talked about their "nations" but also about their "pays." By embracing these French terms, they expressed an attachment and sense of belonging to homelands that could be multisituated, both in Africa and in the Americas.[30]

30. On the debate over the transfer, survival, retention, and transformation of African cultural practices and ethnic identities, see Gunvor Simonsen, "Moving in Circles: African and Black History in the Atlantic World," *Nuevo Mundo; Mundos Nuevos*, Colloques, Sept. 19, 2008, http://nuevomundo.revues.org/42303. From the early 1990s, Gwendolyn Hall has made the Louisiana case a paradigmatic one to demonstrate the point of view of the revisionist or Afrocentrist side, arguing fiercely in favor of the transfer and persistence of African cultural practices and ethnic identities. She was the first to discover and analyze fascinating material and has produced an impressive database about slaves transported to Louisiana during the eighteenth and early nineteenth centuries. See Hall, *Africans in Colonial Louisiana: The Development of Afro-Creole Culture in the Eighteenth Century* (Baton Rouge, La., 1992); Hall, *Slavery and African Ethnicities in the Americas: Restoring the Links* (Chapel Hill, N.C., 2005); and Hall, *Afro-Louisiana History and Genealogy, 1719–1820*, http://www.ibiblio.org/laslave. Although this quantitative approach has its advantages, it also aggregates complex information from various sources that requires a more qualitative and detailed treatment in order to propose more

In comparison with other colonies, the French Antilles in particular, few primary sources from French Louisiana mention the African nations to which individual slaves supposedly belonged. There are no lists of captives as they disembarked after the Middle Passage, and, aside from matters related to the Bambara revolt in 1731, the administrative correspondence rarely discussed the issue of specific African nations, even when local authorities wrote about the slave trade. Additionally, slaves were not baptized immediately on arrival, and, when they were, they were not asked about their birthplace or ethnicity. Exceptionally, a few adult slaves who were baptized by a missionary named Stanislas in 1764 were identified as coming from the Guinea Coast, but that was a vague geographical identification. More generally, the sacramental records rarely identified slaves with an ethnic term. The same was true for free people of color. Although the birthplace of free blacks sometimes appears in marriage records from the 1720s and early 1730s, the practice of recording this information almost completely disappeared in the succeeding decades.[31]

---

nuanced interpretations. A more systematic analysis of all the sources in which ethno-labels were recorded or not is necessary to understand what relations of contention and solidarity were at stake for all the historical actors involved in the formation and transformation of slaves' ethnic identities. It is impossible to separate the multiple meanings attached by the various actors to the ethno-labels used to (self-) identify slaves from the conditions of the production of the archival material in which they were recorded. The risk otherwise is to reify ethnicities instead of showing how they made sense only in the specific circumstances in which they were mobilized and how they evolved over time.

31. For slaves' ethnicities in the Antilles, see G[abriel] Debien et al., "Les origines des esclaves aux Antilles," *Bulletin de l'Institut Français d'Afrique Noire*, Ser. B: *Sciences Humaines*, XXIII (1961), 363–387, XXV (1963), 1–41, 215–266, XXVI (1964), 166–211, 601–675, XXVII (1965), 319–371, 755–799, XIX (1967), 536–558; Debien and J[acques] Houdaille, "Les origines africaines des esclaves des Antilles françaises," *Caribbean Studies*, X, no. 2 (July 1970), 18–29; Arlette Gautier, "Les origines ethniques des esclaves déportés à Nippes, Saint-Domingue, de 1721 à 1770 d'après les archives notariales," *Canadian Journal of African Studies / Revue Canadienne des Études Africaines*, XXIII (1989), 28–39; David Geggus, "Sex Ratio, Age, and Ethnicity in the Atlantic Slave Trade: Data from French Shipping and Plantation Records," *Journal of African History*, XXX (1989), 23–44; Roseline Siguret, "Esclaves d'indigoteries et de caféières au quartier de Jacmel (1757–1791)," *Revue française d'histoire d'outre-mer*, LV (1968), 190–230; and Nicole Vanony-Frisch, "Les esclaves de la Guadeloupe à la fin de l'Ancien Régime d'après les sources notariales (1770–1789)," *Bulletin de la société d'histoire de la Guadeloupe*, nos. 63–64, special issue (1985), 3–165. For certificates of baptism of adult slaves with ethnic identification, see AANO, Saint-Louis Cathedral Baptisms, 1763–1767, 22/07/1764, 29/07/1764, 05/08/1764, 05/08/1764 (there were two baptisms on that date). For ethnic identifications of free people of color, see AANO, Saint-Louis Cathedral Marriages, 1720–

Emergence of a Sense of Place and the Racial Divide

In the same way, New Orleans's probate records do not mention the African ethnicities of enslaved workers, even as deceased individuals' property inventories in the Antilles, by contrast, constitute one of the richest source bases for studying African nations. Instead, slaves were identified by their color or degree of métissage ("nègre" or *"mulâtre"*), age, family situation, trade, and occasionally their state of health, that is, the only information local authorities deemed necessary to evaluate their commercial value and assess the legal possibility of selling them. Deeds of sale made privately or at auctions did not mention slaves' ethnicities either. Likewise, individuals in charge of slaves did not always declare runaways at the clerk's office of the Superior Council, even though they were required to do so by law after 1736. Those who did report missing slaves were often trying to protect themselves because they did not own the slaves in question; rather, they managed them as part of their work as the director of a concession or as an overseer of a plantation. Settlers also sometimes oversaw slaves belonging to other masters while taking care of a relative's property, serving as the executor of an estate, or supervising the labor of rented slaves. They sought to escape from any possible accusation of having caused a slave's desertion or from being asked to reimburse their value. Given that these declarations were not principally aimed at searching for and capturing runaways, they often described them with minimal information: their name, color or degree of métissage ("negro" or "mulatto"), and age. In rare instances, they noted their height and sometimes included a physical defect. Only six out of thirty-eight declarations reference a runaway's ethnicity ("Créole" or an African nation). It is thus impossible to exploit these documents in the same fashion as the detailed advertisements for runaway slaves published in the press in British colonies or in Saint-Domingue after 1766.[32]

1730, and 1731–1733, 30/06/1725 (this marriage is the only one that concerned two free Indians: the groom was from the "Appalachian nation" and the bride came from the Black River), 14/08/1725 (in this single mixed marriage, the groom was from Martinique while the bride was born in Bruges), 05/06/1730 (the groom was from Jamaica whereas the bride's nation was not mentioned), 19/03/1731 (the spouses were both from Senegal: the groom was born in Senegal, and the bride was identified as "Senegalese"). In the last decades, only one certificate mentioned that the free people of color who got married were born in the parish. See AANO, Saint-Louis Cathedral Marriages, 1763–1766, 04/07/1764.

32. For the obligation to declare runaways, see "Ordonnance de Ms. Bienville et Salmon pour la déclaration des nègres marrons du 1er septembre 1736," ANOM COL A 23, fol. 121v. This obligation was reenacted in 1763 with provisions regarding the time allotted for a declaration, depending on the distance from the city, and fines, in case the

This general lack of attention to African ethnicities was likely linked to the short duration of the slave trade from Africa that lasted only a few years, from 1719 to 1731, and to the way the Company of the Indies distributed slaves by lottery, which did not allow settlers to develop buying strategies that took into account factors such as ethnicity. Masters had only just started to become familiar with their slaves and the slave system when the slave trade from Africa practically ceased. Though the colony continued to receive African-born slaves from Saint-Domingue and Martinique, the creolization of the slave population happened quickly, by the 1740s. Therefore, markers of status and race, but not ethnicity, appear ubiquitously throughout the colonial records.

Hearings involving slaves who came before the Superior Council make up the only situation where local authorities seem to have deemed identifying slaves' ethnicities as crucial. Combined with hints in travel accounts and administrative correspondence, judicial archives open a fascinating window into the complex process of production, reproduction, and transformation of old and new ethnicities. The judge in charge of each case ordered slaves who appeared as defendants or witnesses to identify themselves. In many instances, the court records open with the same conventional set expression used to interrogate white people: "asked his name, age, quality,

---

ordinance was not respected. See "Arrêt du Conseil supérieur de La Nouvelle-Orléans sur les esclaves marrons," Apr. 6, 1763, ANOM COL C13A 43, fols. 304–307. For declarations of runaways, see RSCL 1736/08/30/08, 1736/09/02/01, 1736/09/02/02, 1736/09/17/01, 1736/11/20/02, 1736/11/20/03, 1737/01/08/01, 1737/11/24/01, 1738/03/07/01, 1738/05/26/01 (Bambara), 1738/12/15/01 (Bambara), 1738/12/22/03, 1739/12/21/01, 1739/12/29/03 (Bambara), 1740/02/04/01, 1740/05/18/02, 1743/12/07/02 (Bambara, Bambara, no mention, Fond), 1744/01/31/01, 1744/06/30/01, 1744/07/17/01, 1744/09/08/01 ("Créole"), 1744/10/20/01, 1745/03/08/03, 1745/03/15/01, 1745/10/01/01, 1746/06/23/01, 1746/08/03/02, 1746/09/28/01, 1746/10/10/01, 1746/12/15/01, 1747/02/18/02, 1747/07/01/01, 1747/07/28/01, 1747/09/13/01, 1747/10/10/01 ("sauvage"), 1748/05/21/01 ("Créole du pays"), 1749/02/11/01, 1754/12/19/01, 1757/08/02/01. The records of the Superior Council also include many declarations of the death of slaves. For the same reasons having to do with runaways, none mention the ethnicities of the slaves concerned. See RSCL 1736/02/13/01, 1737/01/25/02, 1737/02/24/02, 1737/06/12/02, 1738/06/12/01, 1738/09/15/01, 1738/11/15/01, 1738/11/16/01, 1739/02/25/02, 1739/03/22/01, 1739/03/28/01, 1739/05/05/01, 1739/09/15/02, 1739/10/07/05, 1739/10/19/02, 1739/10/19/03, 1740/02/27/01, 1740/04/13/01, 1740/05/18/03, 1740/06/12/02, 1744/12/24/03, 1746/11/28/01, 1747/04/17/02, 1747/06/26/01, 1747/12/26/03, 1759/05/21/01. For the advertisements of runaways in the *Affiches Américaines* (Saint-Domingue) from 1766 to 1790, see the website "Marronnage in Saint-Domingue (Haiti): History, Memory, Technology," http://www.marronnage.info/en/accueil.php.

and residence." The enslaved seem to have supplied the answers to these questions themselves, as owners do not appear to have provided the magistrate with such data in advance. This impression is confirmed by three exceptional trials involving four slaves. Although enslaved men and women did not usually name their place of residence, the four responded to such a line of inquiry literally, specifying Mobile, New Orleans, and Bayou Saint John. Kenet, one of the four slaves, also mentioned her "status" as a *"piocheuse"* (a field hand working the land on a plantation).[33]

In contrast, most slaves did not provide all the information requested from them by the judge because it did not make sense for their situation. Instead, they gave their name, status, and color or degree of métissage as well as their age, master's name, and nation. They also sometimes indicated if they were baptized or Catholic. Pierrot, who listed all these elements of identification except for his ethnicity, was subsequently ordered to specify his nation. Slaves were expected to identify with an ethno-label. In fact, magistrates sometimes modified the customary interrogative sentence used to identify white people when they wanted to be sure that enslaved defendants or witnesses stated their master's name, their religion, and their nation. In 1744, Marie Joseph was "asked her name, age, quality, her nation, to whom she belongs." When slaves were specifically questioned about their nation, most did their best to comply and even anticipate the judge's request. Bassouvant did not initially mention his nation, even when directly ordered to do so during his first interrogatory. Afterward, during a subsequent round of questioning involving the use of torture, the magistrate only demanded "his name, age, quality and to whom he belongs." When he then inquired if Bassouvant was a Christian, the slave not only replied negatively but added "that he was from the Congo [nation]." He had learned that he was supposed to give this information.[34]

33. For a different view on who provided information regarding slaves' identification to magistrates, see Peter Caron, "'Of a Nation Which the Others Do Not Understand': Bambara Slaves and African Ethnicity in Colonial Louisiana, 1718–60," in "Routes to Slavery: Direction, Ethnicity and Mortality in the Transatlantic Slave Trade," special issue, *Slavery and Abolition*, XVIII, no. 1 (April 1997), 108–109. For slaves mentioning their specific place of residence, see RSCL 1764/06/22/01 (François and Narcisse); 1764/11/14/01 (another slave named François); 1767/06/10/02 (Kenet).

34. For Pierrot's interrogatory, see RSCL 1738/04/24/02. For Margot's interrogatory, see RSCL 1744/03/11/02. For other cases in which the judge asked specifically about the slave's nation in his first question related to the identification of the accused or witness, see RSCL 1744/03/18/01; 1748/05/18/03, 1748/05/22/02; 1748/05/26/01; 1748/06/10/03, 1748/06/10/04; 1751/04/23/01; 1752/02/17/01; 1753/04/24/01, 1753/05/02/01; 1764/

Free people of color were not tried in great numbers, and most did not present themselves with an ethno-label. They might have wanted to self-identify before the magistrate in the same way as white people, thereby distancing themselves from the African ethnicities associated with the enslaved. Exceptionally, the clerk recorded that a freed black man named Joseph Pantalon was instructed "to tell us his age, his nation, if he is free or enslaved, and what religion he professes." In the same trial, Joseph Pantalon's wife, Marie, told the judge that she ignored "what her nation is since she came to this country when she was very young." On the one hand, she apparently understood what the magistrate wanted when he interrogated her about her nation; on the other, she could not provide the information, as no one had ever told her what it was. National identifications were not always meaningful for people of African descent, though they could be.[35]

Most slaves who mentioned an African nation in their interrogatories or testimonies specified one among several categories. Those from Senegambia included Bambara, Sénégal, Guinée, Mandingue (Mandingo or Malinke), Poulard (Fulbe), Cerer (Sereer), and Beafada; from the Gold Coast, Mina and Quiamba (Chamba); from the Slave Coast, Arada (Ewe-Fon), Nago (Yoruba), Foëda (Hweda), and Fond (Ewe-Fon); and from Central Africa, Congo. The most common by far was Bambara, followed by Sénégal. A few slaves nevertheless presented themselves in more original ways. Joseph Laoursot self-identified as "a negro slave belonging to the king, from the Turkish nation." Was he a slave who had been purchased in the Mediterranean Sea? In another case, Songot told the judge through a translator that he was "from Mandigo country of Gorée." He might have confused an ethnic affiliation with a geographic one since, unlike most captives who only passed through Gorée or Saint-Louis, he had been a slave in Gorée for some time.[36]

01/25/01, 1764/02/10/01; 1764/06/11/03; 1764/07/06/01; 1764/07/06/02; 1764/07/10/03; 1764/08/02/01; 1764/08/10/01; 1764/09/07/01; 1764/10/23/01; 1765/07/17/01; 1765/09/09/02; 1765/10/16/02; 1765/10/29/02. In one case, the magistrate asked for the slave's "pays," not nation. See RSCL 1741/01/16/03. In the same way, the judge requested the twenty-one slaves who were deported from Martinique and interrogated before being sold to mention their "country of birth." See RSCL 1765/11/12/03. For Bassouvant's interrogatories, see RSCL 1765/10/29/02, 1765/11/09/02.

35. RSCL 1743/09/10/03 (Joseph Pantalon), 1743/08/22/02 (Marie).

36. For original geographic affiliations, see RSCL 1748/02/10/01 (Laoursot); 1723/12/02/01 (Songot). For the ethnic backgrounds of slaves deported from French slave trading outposts in Senegal, see Ibrahima Thioub, "L'esclavage à Saint-Louis du Sénégal au XVIIIe–XIXe siècle," *Jahrbuch 2008/2009* (2010), 334–356. Few slaves of Native

The different meanings attached to ethno-labels need to be retraced with great care. The African ethnicities that appear in various sources were highly polysemic. Moreover, shared ethnicities did not necessarily imply shared cultures. Nations could correspond to ethnic, geographic, or religious categories. In the colony, the term "Bambara," for instance, probably designated non-Muslim slaves and did not refer to a specific ethnicity. The label "Sénégal" was also as vague as that of Bambara. Although authors of travel accounts named and described various Native American nations in detail, they most often used broadly inclusive categories such as "negroes" and "Africans" to designate slaves. One of the few exceptions was Le Page du Pratz in his *Histoire de la Louisiane*. The former director of the company plantation included a kind of planters' manual in his travel account. When he talked about the nursing of white infants by African slaves, he recommended employing Senegal women. He then offered a long panegyric on Senegal slaves, which was not devoid of race-thinking:

> I shall only say, that for any kind of service whatever about the house, I would advise no other kind of negroes, either young or old, but Senegals, called among themselves Diolaufs [Wolofs], because of all the negroes I have known, these have the purest blood; they have more fidelity and a better understanding than the rest, and are consequently fitter for learning a trade, or for menial services. It is true they are not so strong as the others for the labours of the field, and for bearing the great heats.
>
> The Senegals however are the blackest, and I never saw any who had a bad smell. They are very grateful; and when one knows how to attach them to him, they have been found to sacrifice their own life to save that of their master. They are good commanders over other negroes, both on account of their fidelity and gratitude, and because they seem to be born for commanding. As they are high-minded, they may be easily encouraged to learn a trade, or to serve in the house, by the distinction they will thereby acquire over the other negroes, and the neatness of dress which that condition will entitle them to.

This extract recalls the literature on the slave trade in which African nations were identified and classified according to their perceived or imagined attributes. The goal was to evaluate their usefulness or danger to the slave system. But, aside from passages in Le Page du Pratz's travel account, there

American descent were tried, but, of those who were, one was a Chickasaw. See RSCL 1748/05/26/01.

are no other hints of such preoccupation among Louisiana authorities and settlers. Given their limited access to the slave trade, they simply longed for slaves, any slaves.[37]

Le Page du Pratz also pointed out that not everyone resorted to the same ethno-labels to identify the various nations associated with slaves of African descent. He apparently employed the French expression "Sénégal" in a restrictive way to name, as he wrote, those Africans who identified themselves as Wolof. In contrast, Bossu referred to "Negroes from Guinea or Senegal" but probably meant slaves from Senegambia. In court records, Étienne Larue, a free man of color born in Western Africa, who was a ship's pilot, also presented himself as being born in Senegal while Antoine, another transient African sailor, specified that he was from the Senegal nation. The French expression "Senegal nation" was adopted by slaves themselves when they needed to self-identify in front of the Superior Council; no slave ever described himself as a Wolof. Still, it is impossible to know what they meant: should we assume that they were Wolof or came from Senegambia? In one trial, Alexandre first mentioned the Sereer and then the Senegal as his nation. Likewise, some slaves said that they came from Guinea or the Guinea Coast. Two others even claimed to be of the "nation of Guinea." Guinea was a vague geographic term referring probably not only to Senegambia but to the whole of West Africa, even though Bossu conflated "Guinea" with "Senegal." In the same way, a free "mulatto" pilot told the magistrate that he was born in Senegal but that he had lived in Cap-Français "since he left Guinea."[38]

37. For the meaning of Bambara, see Caron, "'Of a Nation Which the Others Do Not Understand,'" *Slavery and Abolition*, XVIII, no. 4 (April 1997), 98–121. For Le Page du Pratz's panegyric on the Senegal, see Le Page du Pratz, *The History of Louisiana, or of the Western Parts of Virginia and Carolina ... Translated from the French of M. Le Page Du Pratz ...*, new ed. (London, 1774), 362–363.

38. For Bossu's conflation of Guinea and Senegal, see Bossu, *Nouveaux voyages aux Indes occidentales*, II, 77. For free people of color self-identifying as Senegal, see RSCL 1747/05/05/01, 1747/05/18/02 (Étienne Larue); 1765/10/16/02 (Antoine). For slaves presenting themselves as Senegal, see RSCL 1738/04/24/02; 1739/11/07/02; 1744/03/13/01; 1748/01/05/02. Gwendolyn Midlo Hall systematically translated *"Sénégal"* as Wolof. See Hall, *Africans in Colonial Louisiana*, 113, 400. David Geggus is much more cautious, stating that "the vague term 'Sénégal' apparently referr[ed] to Wolof and others living along the lower Senegal." See Geggus, "Sex Ratio, Age, and Ethnicity in the Atlantic Slave Trade," *Journal of African History*, XXX (1989), 23–44, esp. 35. According to Philip D. Curtin, "A slave identified as Senegalese might therefore be either (a) an individual shipped from Saint Louis, whatever his nationality, (b) a Wolof of Cayor or Walo in the

Upper Guinea constituted a great cultural and commercial zone. But its diversity, which extended beyond linguistic and political divisions, should not be underestimated. Senegambia was broadly split between hierarchical societies in the North and more egalitarian ones in the South, even though the North included a few societies that were more egalitarian and vice versa. A Wolof slave and a Beafada slave could both be said to have come from Senegambia, yet they would have been exposed to different social organizations in Africa. Among the slaves who originated from hierarchical societies such as the Wolof and the Soninke Sereer, there were probably individuals who belonged to different castes. The focus on slaves' ethnicity that has been so prevalent among historians has often led to an underestimation of the impact religion (Muslim or non-Muslim) or social structures and dynamics also had in shaping slaves' identities. In any case, Louisiana slaves probably found it necessary to adapt their former African experiences to navigate the different power struggles presented by the colonial situation.[39]

As the slave population started to be made up of a growing number of locally born men and women, some self-identified as "Créole" before the court. The first occurrence of this usage of "Créole" appeared in a criminal trial in 1744 with regard to the identification of a female witness. Summoned to indicate her nation, she "said that her name is Marie Joseph, that she was born in the year of the Natchez or Natchitoches War, that she was the slave of Sieur Joseph Carrière, Creole from the Mississippi." Significantly, when, in another case, François described himself as *"Créole du pays"* ("Creole of the country"), the judge also enquired about "the name of his father and mother is and where they are." Creole identity was connected with local birth and kinship networks, though such family relationships could be fragile. Indeed, the slave replied that "he believes that Scipion, Mr.

---

immediate vicinity of the town, or, (c) a Pular-speaker from Futa Toro in the middle valley of the Senegal." See Curtin, *The Atlantic Slave Trade: A Census* (Madison, Wis., 1969), 184. For Alexandre's interrogatories, see RSCL 1744/02/29/01, 1744/03/13/01. For slaves from Guinea, see RSCL 1764/01/25/01, 1764/05/18/01, 1764/07/06/01, 1764/07/10/03, 1764/09/07/01. For a free man of color conflating Senegal and Guinea, see 1747/05/05/01.

39. Boubacar Barry, *Senegambia and the Atlantic Slave Trade*, trans. Ayi Kwei Armah (Cambridge, 1998); Martin A. Klein, "Servitude among the Wolof and Sereer of Senegambia," in Suzanne Miers and Igor Kopytoff, eds., *Slavery in Africa: Historical and Anthropological Perspectives* (Madison, Wis., 1977), 335–363; James F. Searing, "'No Kings, No Lords, No Slaves': Ethnicity and Religion among the Sereer-Safèn of Western Bawol, 1700–1914," *Journal of African History*, XLIII (2002), 407–429; John Thornton, *Africa and Africans in the Making of the Atlantic World, 1400–1800*, 2d ed. (Cambridge, 1998 [1st ed. 1992]), 186–189.

La Frénière's negro, is his father and his mother's name is Digueny or Marie who is at his master's, Sieur Boisclair."[40]

When born in the Americas, many slaves answered that they were "Creole as a nation," an expression reflecting social actors' awareness that a Creole identity had replaced an African ethnicity. As an alternative, they also frequently added their birthplace to their identification as Creole. They were "Creole of this colony," "Creole of the country," "Creole from the Mississippi," "Creole of this city [New Orleans]," "Creole from Mobile," "Creole from Saint-Domingue," "Creole from Cap Français," "Creole from Martinique," or "Creole from Philadelphia." These expressions were referenced to display a sense of local belonging to the colony or, more narrowly, to a colonial town. But they could also serve as a reminder that their bearers came from other places in the Americas and to convey the idea that they were different from locally born slaves. Instead of one unique and general Creole identity that could be advanced in place of a variety of African identities, various Creole identities coexisted.[41]

The primary reason judges asked about slaves' ethnic origins might have been the need to find translators. This was especially the case during Louisiana's participation in the slave trade from Africa. The Superior Council employed a French gunner who had lived in Saint-Louis, Senegal, as a translator. The court also sometimes relied on other slaves. Even at the end of the French regime, a few African slaves who had come through the Antilles did not speak French. In one case, the clerk presented the enslaved translator at great lengths in the records, specifying that the defendant, who was an enslaved woman, understood "his Nago language," while, earlier during the interrogatory, he had referred to "her" or "their language" without identifying it. After 1763, when some English settlers arrived in New Orleans, other slaves only spoke English and needed a translator from English to French.

40. For Creole slaves' interrogatories, see RSCL 1744/03/11/02 (Marie-Joseph); 1748/05/18/03 (François).

41. For the use of the expression "Creole as a nation," see RSCL 1764/01/25/01, 1764/07/08/01, 1764/07/26/01, 1764/08/02/01, 1764/08/10/01. For identifications linking Creole identity with a place, see RSCL 1744/03/11/02, 1747/04/11/01, 1748/01/05/02, 1748/01/06/02, 1748/01/08/01, 1748/05/18/03, 1748/06/10/03, 1748/06/10/06, 1751/04/14/01, 1752/02/17/01, 1752/02/17/02, 1753/04/24/01, 1764/01/25/01, 1764/02/10/01, 1764/02/17/01, 1764/06/14/01, 1764/07/06/02, 1764/07/08/01, 1764/07/19/01, 1764/07/26/01, 1764/08/02/01, 1764/08/10/01, 1764/11/14/01, 1765/06/14/01, 1765/07/17/01, 1765/09/09/02, 1765/09/18/02, 1765/10/10/01, 1766/07/01/01, 1766/07/25/02, 1766/06/05/01, 1766/07/23/03, 1767/08/13/01, 1767/08/13/03.

Emergence of a Sense of Place and the Racial Divide

Still, most of the enslaved in the last decades of the French regime spoke French with few exceptions.[42]

Since magistrates kept asking slaves about their ethnic backgrounds, they must have had other motivations. They might have been reacting to the reputations various ethnic groups held regarding their propensity to commit crimes. In 1729, a planter accused one of his enslaved workers of having poisoned his driver. The attorney general asked for an investigation, arguing that "negroes from his nation are prone to be poisoners and the other negroes believe they are witches." But he did not specify his ethnicity. Among the various African nations present in French Louisiana, historians have argued that the Bambara were particularly troublesome and rebellious. If the French had particularly dreaded this nation, however, they would not have picked a Bambara man to be the driver of the king's slaves in the late 1740s. Although local authorities displayed moments of concern regarding the Bambara over the course of the French regime, they do not appear to have had a constant, long-lasting preoccupation or fear of slaves of that ethnicity.[43]

The first Bambara movement identified by officials and colonists was a 1731 slave conspiracy. Officer Jean Jadard de Beauchamp reported to the minister of the navy that "all the Bambara leagued together to calmly set themselves free from this country with this revolt; the other negroes who are in the colony and who are not of this nation are said to serve them as slaves." Yet according to Périer, the Bambara only ended up leading the insurrection as a result of happenstance. He reported that the event started when the Chickasaw returned a Bambara slave to colonial settlements who had arrived in their villages with the Natchez. "This negro being a Bam-

42. For the use of translators, see RSCL 1729/09/05/03, 1729/09/05/05, 1729/09/05/06; 1723/12/02/01, 1723/12/02/02, 1723/12/02/03, 1728/07/10/01, 1729/11/16/01, 1738/04/24/02; and "Audience criminelle du Conseil supérieur de la province de Louisiane," May 28, 1738, ANOM COL F3 242, fols. 265–290. It is impossible to know what languages slaves spoke. Because the ethnic categories used to identify them were so polysemic, the slaves identified as *"Sénégal,"* for example, could belong to several different ethnic groups and speak several languages. Conversely, slaves who spent time in Saint-Louis, Senegal, or Gorée probably spoke Wolof, which served as the lingua franca in these slave trading outposts. This means that a slave speaking Wolof was not necessarily a Wolof. See RSCL 1765/02/16/01. The English translator was a French settler. See RSCL 1767/04/25/01.

43. For the poisoner's trial, see RSCL 1729/10/21/03, 1729/10/25/01. For the choice of a Bambara slave as the king's driver, see RSCL 1748/02/10/01. For a different view on the Bambara, see Hall, *Africans in Colonial Louisiana,* 96–118.

bara of a nation that the others do not understand had drawn into his party all the negroes from his nation." Although it is not clear whether he meant that the other slaves did not understand the language of the Bambara or that they did not understand the language of a specific nation among the Bambara, the governor pointed out that not all slaves were linguistically intelligible to each other and that the linguistic divide explained conflicting relationships between different groups of slaves.[44]

Concerns over the Bambara arose once again in the mid-1760s during the trials of two enslaved runaways and thieves, César and Louis. That Louis alias Foÿe and several other slaves involved were Bambara did not escape Attorney General Nicolas La Frénière's attention. Unusually, while questioning other enslaved witnesses and writing to General Director Jean-Jacques Blaise d'Abbadie, he described Louis and his accomplices as Bambara. But he also identified Louis as having been deported from Saint-Domingue. Louis's fellow slaves recognized that having Caribbean origins was an issue for La Frénière. Although Mama Comba first admitted that she "knows Louis from the Illinois, whom Mr. Gaillardy sold, that she has known him since the Cap," she later retracted and claimed that "she has known him since he lives in this country and not before." This preoccupation with crimes committed by slaves purchased from the Antilles also comes across in the trial of Jean, a slave accused of desertion and theft. He was depicted as "coming from Saint-Domingue" in both his interrogation under torture and in his sentence.[45]

Because the direct slave trade between Africa and Louisiana practically stopped in 1731, the colony's slaveholders obtained most of their enslaved workers from Saint-Domingue and Martinique. Given that West Indian planters often got rid of unruly slaves who were inclined to steal and run away, slaves from the French Caribbean acquired a bad reputation. In 1755, while writing to the minister of the navy, Governor Louis Billouart de Kerlérec decried "the great number of vicious [slaves] sent to us every day from

44. On the Bambara conspiracy, see Jean Jadard de Beauchamp to the minister of the navy, November 1731, ANOM COL C13A 13, fol. 200; and Périer to the minister of the navy, Dec. 10, 1731, ANOM COL C13A 13, fols. 63v–64r. On the debate about the homogeneity versus the heterogeneity of the slave population in French Louisiana, see Hall, *Africans in Colonial Louisiana*, 28–55; and Thomas N. Ingersoll, "The Slave Trade and the Ethnic Diversity of Louisiana's Slave Community," *Louisiana History*, XXXVII (1996), 133–161.

45. For Louis's trial, see RSCL 1764/07/10/03, 1764/07/10/06, 1764/07/14/01. For Mama Comba's interrogatories, see RSCL 1764/07/10/03; 1764/09/04/01. For Jean's trial, see RSCL 1764/07/31/02, 1764/09/01/01.

Emergence of a Sense of Place and the Racial Divide

Saint-Domingue and Martinique [who] had already perverted the Creoles from the country and the others." He then proposed to prohibit the slave trade from the Antilles, but slaves were too much in demand for his plan to be implemented. Less than a decade later, at the end of the Seven Years' War, the new attorney general La Frénière put forward the Macandal poisoning conspiracy in Saint-Domingue in 1758 to justify his request to the Superior Council for a ruling that would prohibit the introduction of "negroes having resided or having been creolized in Saint-Domingue" into the colony. His targets were not just slaves from the French section of the island, though, only the "creolized ones"; in contrast, African slaves, who had just been brought to the Caribbean territory, were most welcome. In July 1763, the court forbade the importation of "creolized" slaves and provided for the arrest and expulsion of offending slaves in La Balise at their owners' expense. Their masters were to also pay a fine. A trial that took place in 1765 confirms that officials paid attention to slaves' origins: at the beginning of the proceeding, the judge asked François, who had volunteered that he had been baptized in Martinique, to specify the length of his stay "in this country [Louisiana]" and, in a subsequent interrogatory under torture, he also inquired about the name of the ship that had brought François to the colony. Three years later, the Superior Council took advantage of the arrival of twenty-one slaves from Martinique who were suspected of being ex-convicts "bought at the Court's bar in the civil prisons of Martinique" to extend the ruling prohibiting the importation of creolized slaves from Saint-Domingue to those from the Lesser Antilles.[46]

Besides "nation," the concept of "country" seems to have been meaning-

46. For the early proposal by Kerlérec to prohibit the slave trade from the Antilles, see Kerlérec to the minister of the navy, June 26, 1755, ANOM COL C13A 39, fols. 12v–13. For the legislation banning creolized slaves from Saint-Domingue and the Lesser Antilles, see RSCL 1763/07/09/02; 1765/11/12/03, 1765/11/13/01, 1765/11/16/04, 1765/11/16/05, 1765/12/06/02. See also "Arrêt du Conseil Supérieur de La Nouvelle-Orléans interdisant l'importation en Louisiane, sous peine d'amendes, de nègres venant de Saint-Domingue," July 9, 1763, ANOM COL C13A 43, fols. 302–303, 308–309; and "Arrêt du Conseil Supérieur de la Louisiane autorisant la vente, à la barre de la Cour, de 21 nègres arrivés de la Martinique en Louisiane," Nov. 16, 1765, ANOM COL C13A 45, fols. 100–101. The Superior Council's rulings did not use the term "Creole" but targeted slaves qualified as "residing or accustomed" ("domiciliés ou habitués"). In the memoranda written by the leaders of the 1768 revolt, however, they wrote about the "negroes having been creolized, or having resided in Saint-Domingue" when they wanted to denounce Antonio de Ulloa's policy in the matter of the slave trade. See "Mémoire des habitants et négociants de la Louisiane sur l'événement du 29 octobre 1768," 1768, Favrot Papers, S2. For François's trial, see RSCL 1765/02/26/01, ND no. 11.

ful for many slaves. During the formal self-identification that took place at the beginning of interrogatories, they often spoke about the "country" they came from instead of their "nation," using a geographic rather than an ethnic category. A Bambara slave told the judge that another slave in jail named Jary "says that he is his friend, but that they don't come from the same country." His statement implied that friendship among the enslaved was most often based on common ethnic or geographic backgrounds. In the same way, the Bambara Andigny, "a negro driver at Mrs. Mandeville's," stated that "he knows the said negro Louis or otherwise Foÿe as he is of his country." In Louis's final interrogation, during which he was tortured, the clerk recorded that he presented himself with two names, writing that he "has said that his name is Louis and Foÿ in the language and dialect of his country." Louis's and César's trials suggest that there was a specific Bambara sociability but that it was not exclusive. Comba, who was not a Bambara, reported that she went to the garden belonging to a man named Cautrelle one day, where "she found several Bambara negroes and had a lot of fun." She also admitted to having met César there once when she went to the garden to see Louison, her *"païze,"* that is, a girl from the same country. Louison, who belonged to Cautrelle, was from the same Maninga (Mandingo or Malinke) nation as Comba. Yet, when César told the judge about his relationship with Mama Comba, who worked and lived at the Charity Hospital, he relayed an exchange that he was privy to between Mama Comba and the manager at the hospital, stating "that the manager had seen the said negro [César] several times and asked the said Comba why this negro came so often, if he worked, and if he had a master, and that the negress answered that he did not come to do any wrong, he is a negro from up north [i.e. the Illinois Country] who is from my country." Since César was a Creole and Comba was of the "Maninga" (Mandingo or Malinke) nation, what did Mama Comba mean? Given that she told the magistrate that she had known Louis alias Foÿe since the Cap, it is possible that they might all have met when living in Saint-Domingue. Likewise, in another trial, another slave also named Louis, who belonged to a colonist named Carlier, confessed that he committed a crime with another runaway named Louis who came from the same country as he did: "They crossed the plantation of Sieur Barbin where Sieur Becat who has three negroes lives whom Louis knows from the Cap country."[47]

47. Jary was of the Quoëda (probably *Foëda* or Hweda) nation, and Joseph was a Bambara. See RSCL 1748/06/10/04 (quotation), 1748/06/10/05. For the backgrounds of Louis, César, and their accomplices, see RSCL 1764/09/03/01, 1764/09/04/02,

Emergence of a Sense of Place and the Racial Divide

Some slaves of the same "nation" or "country," in the sense of common ethnic or geographic backgrounds, seem to have maintained distinct friendly or conjugal ties, although no generalization can be made from those few recorded instances. Margueritte, from the Congo nation, who lived on a plantation, ran away and hid in the cabin of Janot, "Negro Congo." In the same way, Jupiter, who identified himself as being from the Sereer nation during his trial, had a close Sereer friend in town, and he also maintained a sexual or conjugal relationship with a Creole who was the daughter of a Sereer female slave. These examples suggest that linguistic and cultural practices and ethnic identities could in some cases be passed down from African parents to their children born in Louisiana and that the ethno-label Creole does little to reveal a person's cultural backgrounds. The term "country" also sometimes referred to a place outside Africa. Although slaves' African roots remained influential over a few generations, their experiences after departing from Africa, including time in the Antilles, could also create new networks of support and alliances that over time gave birth to new identities.[48]

Ethnicities forged solidarities but also antagonisms. The opposition between African and Creole identities was mobilized during times of conflict. Some slaves identified other slaves as Creoles. In 1748, Jean-Baptiste, from the Senegal nation, recalled that he had seen a young white man, who was later murdered, in the company of "two little Creole negroes belonging to Mr. Dubreuil." In 1751, François from the Fon nation reported to a judge how he had asked "a little Creole named Augustin" for the key to his master's urban house and had then entered into a fight with him. Sometimes slaves expressly connected clashes to antagonisms between Creoles and Africans. In 1748, Charles alias Karacou was accused of having murdered a young soldier. This slave, in his twenties, first self-identified as being from the Coneda nation but later presented himself as a *"Créole de ce pays"* ("Creole from this country"). He also told the judge in French that he was called "Charles as his master says, his father and mother call him Karacou." The name given by his parents was a reminder of his African origins and confirmed once again the transmission of African culture from one generation to the next. Yet, because of his young age, Charles was generally referred to by the nickname Charlot, including in the court records. During his trial,

1764/09/08/01, 1764/09/10/01, 1764/09/04/01, 1764/07/14/04, 1764/07/14/01, 1764/09/04/01, 1764/07/14/04, 1764/07/10/03. For the interrogatory of Louis, slave of Carlier, see RSCL 1765/09/09/02.

48. RSCL 1764/10/23/01; 1744/02/29/01, 1744/03/03/01, 1744/03/05/01, 1744/03/11/01, 1744/03/12/01.

Charlot accused Pierrot, a Bambara slave, of being an accessory to the murder of the young soldier. When Pierrot denied his involvement, Charlot explained: "Mister [Pierrot] always lies to him [Charlot] and he always said no to my master when he hid my sister in his cabin, Bambara [meaning the group in general] and him [Pierrot] they're always lying." Pierrot defended himself by arguing "that he did not go to Charlot's cabin, that he is not a friend of the Creoles, and that Charlot didn't come to his cabin either." In this discourse, the use of the plural—"the Creoles"—is important as it expressed the feeling that the latter formed a distinct group characterized by their own sociability. The antagonism between Africans and Creoles, however, should not be overstated. Charles's Coneda / Creole identity is unclear, and Pierrot very likely helped Charlot's sister when she ran away, which means that assistance could come across ethnic lines.[49]

Although masters tended to lump all Creole slaves together, the common identity inherent in this broad inclusive category was not sufficient to impede some of the local slave population from rejecting others because of their distinct language, culture, and life history, even when all of them were born in the Americas. Francisque, an uncommon slave who was a "Creole of Philadelphia," presents a particularly colorful example of a Creole slave who was ostracized because he was viewed as an outsider. After having previously circulated between English and Spanish colonies, he arrived in Louisiana aboard the Spanish ship that brought Governor Ulloa in March 1766. When his master leased him to Gilbert-Antoine de Saint Maxent for a trip to the Illinois Country, he ran away. Although he apparently spoke French, he found it difficult to forge a place for himself within the entrenched community of slaves. He joined their secret balls "dressed up as a gentleman," with a ruffled shirt, a blue waistcoat, a white hat, and three or four handkerchiefs

49. Tensions among African and Creole slaves existed in all slave societies. See Philip D. Morgan, *Slave Counterpoint: Black Culture in the Eighteenth-Century Chesapeake and Lowcountry* (Chapel Hill, N.C., 1998), 459–463. For Jean-Baptiste's interrogatory, see RSCL 1748/01/05/02. For François's interrogatory, see RSCL 1751/04/14/01. For previous analysis of Charlot's case, see Hall, *Africans in Colonial Louisiana*, 176–179; and Thomas A. Klingler, *If I Could Turn My Tongue Like That: The Creole Language of Pointe Coupee Parish, Louisiana* (Baton Rouge, La., 2003), 25–46. For Charlot's trial, see RSCL 1748/01/03/07, 1748/01/04/01, 1748/01/05/01, 1748/01/05/02, 1748/01/05/03, 1748/01/05/04 (quotation), 1748/01/05/05, 1748/01/05/06, 1748/01/05/07, 1748/01/05/08, 1748/01/05/09, 1748/01/06/01, 1748/01/06/02, 1748/01/08/01, 1748/01/08/02, 1748/01/08/03, 1748/01/08/04, 1748/01/08/05, 1748/01/08/06, 1748/01/10/01 (quotation), 1748/01/10/02, 1748/01/10/03, 1748/01/10/04, 1748/01/11/01, 1748/01/12/01 (quotation), 1748/01/13/01, 1748/01/27/08.

around his neck, but his attempts to show off his power and fortune by court-ing women and liberally spending money, using the proceeds he earned from selling stolen clothing, got him into trouble. Faced with formidable competi-tion in the struggle for women, the local enslaved men decided to expel Fran-cisque the second time that he came to their clandestine gathering:

> Another time he went dancing again, but he was rude and insulted the negresses, to the extent that the negro Hector told him who are you to come here and act as a braggart whom we don't know, leave, go away, we don't need you to pay for the drum, keep your money and go away. Francisque retorted that if he were on the levee he would rip him open, Hector then grabbed the stick that he had and gave him a sound beating, telling him that the next time he came back he would have him attached to four poles and whipped.

With expressions such as "the braggart whom we don't know" and "to their place," long-rooted slaves clearly expressed their resentment toward a man who was seen as someone trespassing on their property.[50]

Well aware that he had come to their "home," Francisque responded with an invitation to settle the issue on the levee. The enslaved used the embank-ment like white people as a public space to resolve their conflicts before wit-nesses. But Hector, who acted as the leader of the local slaves, did not accept the invitation, as the fight would have placed Francisque on equal footing with them. Threatening the Philadelphian slave with a whipping while tied to four poles, a form of violence used by masters, constituted another way of excluding him. When the local slaves met Francisque once again a few days or weeks later, they decided to arrest and deliver him to the authori-ties. The cession of Louisiana to Great Britain and Spain and the arrival of new authorities and officers with their slaves disturbed both New Orleans's habitants of European descent and the enslaved members of the popula-tion. Yet only the colonists rose up in revolt.

THE 1768 REVOLT AND THE ADVENT OF "LOUISIANAIS"

In October 1768, settlers from New Orleans and its environs, led by the Su-perior Council, rose up in revolt against the new Spanish government. They

50. RSCL 1766/06/03/01, 1766/07/01/01, 1766/07/04/01, 1766/07/04/02, 1766/07/04/03, 1766/07/23/02, 1766/07/25/02, 1766/07/27/02, 1766/07/29/04, 1766/07/29/05, 1766/07/31/06, 1766/08/02/04. For a more detailed analysis of Francisque's trial, see Sophie White, "'Wearing Three or Four Handkerchiefs around His Collar, and Elsewhere about Him': Slaves' Constructions of Masculinity and Ethnicity in French Colonial New Orleans," *Gender and History*, XV (2003), 528–549.

succeeded in expelling Louisiana's first Spanish governor, Ulloa, without bloodshed. This radical move was prompted by his promulgation of an ordinance enforcing the Spanish Exclusif (the Exclusif, like the British Navigation Acts, prohibited foreign trade from the Empire and existed in both the Spanish and French Empires) in Louisiana. To defend the rebels' actions, the Superior Council took advantage of a recently authorized printing press and produced three hundred copies of two documents: the *"arrêt"* (ruling) that was promulgated by the council on October 29, 1768, in response to a request from many white inhabitants that ordered the expulsion of Ulloa and the *"Mémoire des habitants et négociants de la Louisiane sur l'événement du 29 octobre 1768"* ("Memorandum of the settlers and merchants of Louisiana on the event of October 29, 1768") that was addressed to Louis XV and dated the same day. The leaders of the insurrection sought to plead their case before the monarch and his minister of the navy, César Gabriel de Choiseul-Praslin; they also solicited the backing of the Duc d'Orléans, the Prince de Condé, the Prince de Conti, the Chancellor, and the Parlement of Paris. Additionally, they looked for support from the chambers of commerce in La Rochelle, Bordeaux, Nantes, Marseille, and Rouen. A representative of the council, Sieur Le Sassier, one of its assessors, and a representative of the colonists and merchants, Sieur Saintelette, were selected to carry the documents to France. After their arrival in the metropole, they had the memorandum printed in Dutch gazettes. Following the example of the parlements in the kingdom, the Superior Council of Louisiana appealed to public opinion in both the colony and the metropole.[51]

51. On the printing press, see Florence M. Jumonville, "Frenchmen at Heart: New Orleans Printers and Their Imprints, 1764–1803," *Louisiana History,* XXXII (1991), 279–310. For the first two original documents that were printed, see "Arrêt du Conseil supérieur," Oct. 29, 1768, ANOM COL C13A 48, fols. 233v–244v; and "Mémoire des habitants et négociants de la Louisiane sur l'événement du 29 octobre 1768," ANOM COL C13A 48, fols. 245v–255v. Aubry believed that this memorandum had been written by the attorney general, Nicolas Chauvin de La Frénière, with the assistance of seven or eight merchants. According to evidence presented at the trial of the revolt's leaders, the authors were the merchant Pierre Caresse and the lawyer Julien-Jérôme Doucet, very likely with the support of La Frénière. The day following its publication, Aubry protested against some sections that were highly offensive toward the Spanish. Hence, Commissaire-ordonnateur Denis-Nicolas Foucault ordered the text to be modified, the revised version printed, and the initial copies to be withdrawn from circulation. See Aubry to the minister of the navy, Dec. 24, 1768, ANOM COL C13A 48, fol. 38; Marc de Villiers du Terrage, *Les dernières années de la Louisiane française: Le Chevalier de Kerlérec, D'Abbadie —Aubrey, Laussat* (Paris, [1903]), 273–274; and David Ker Texada, *Alejandro O'Reilly and the New Orleans Rebels* (Lafayette, La., 1970), 69–70, 72–73, 83, 98. For the letters, requests, and memo-

Emergence of a Sense of Place and the Racial Divide

"Frenchmen," "French citizens, "the efforts of the genuine French settled here"—such expressions appear repeatedly in the numerous texts produced by the leaders of the revolt. In their efforts to claim their Frenchness, they saturated their writings with the language of nation and fatherland ("patrie"). This lexical field was not mobilized as a mere "strategic mask"; rather, it echoed the rapidly evolving political culture of the time in the kingdom and the politicization of such concepts as "nation," "patrie," and "society." As the insurgents drew on this new political language and culture, they confronted crucial issues including the relationship between royal authority and the nation conceived of as a political community; the sharing of executive and legislative powers between the king and the parlements; the definition of the common good; the position of colonies vis-à-vis the kingdom; and the merging of empire and nation.[52]

---

randums brought to various political figures and institutions in metropolitan France or printed in Dutch gazettes, see "Représentations du Conseil supérieur au roi," Nov. 12, 1768, ANOM COL C13A 48, fols. 149v–158v; the Superior Council to the minister of the navy, Nov. 22, 1768, ANOM COL C13A 48, fols. 195v–199r; the Louisiana habitants to the minister of the navy, Mar. 20, 1769, ANOM COL C13A 49, fol. 190; "Observations du Conseil supérieur de la province de la Louisiane faite au Parlement séant à Paris," 1768, Favrot Papers, S-3; "Mémoire sur la révolution arrivée à la Louisiane le 29 octobre 1768 pour être présenté à son A.R. Monseigneur le duc d'Orléans," 1768, Favrot Papers, S-4; "Lettre des habitants, négociants, et colons de la Louisiane à Monseigneur le duc d'Orléans," 1768, Favrot Papers, S-6; Aubry to the minister of the navy, ANOM COL C13A 48, fol. 28v; "Réflexions détaillées sur la révolution arrivée à la Louisiane," ANOM COL C13A 48, fol. 39r; "Copie de la lettre de M. le marquis de Grimaldi à M. le comte de Fuentes," ANOM COL C13A 50, fols. 46–49; "Copie de la lettre de M. le marquis de Grimaldi à M. de Fuentes sur les troubles de la Louisiane depuis la cession faite de cette colonie par la France à l'Espagne," 1768, ANOM COL F3 25, fol. 288; and Pierre H. Boulle, "French Reactions to the Louisiana Revolution of 1768," in John Francis McDermott, ed., *The French in the Mississippi Valley* (Urbana, Ill., 1965), 147, 154–155.

52. The third expression, "the efforts of the genuine French settled here," is quoted in "Mémoire des habitants et négociants de la Louisiane sur l'événement du 29 octobre 1768," ANOM COL C13A 48, fol. 254r. Even if "nation" and "patrie" remained polysemic, these two concepts acquired new meanings at the beginning of the eighteenth century. The idea of an attachment to the fatherland, to the monarch, and to the territory that he ruled over compensated for the rising autonomy of the nation as a political community apart from royal authority. See Bell, "Nation et patrie, société et civilisation," in Kaufmann and Guilhaumou, eds., *L'invention de la société*, 99–120. The expression "strategic mask" is borrowed from Peter Sahlins, *Frontières et identités nationales: La France et l'Espagne dans les Pyrénées depuis le XVIIe siècle*, trans. Geoffroy de Laforcade (Paris, 1996 [1989]), 179. My interpretation differs from that proposed by historians who have criticized Alcée Fortier's view on the revolt. The latter explained the event by the patriot-

All the actors involved in the uprising, not only the rebels, read the event through national glasses. Commandant Aubry, who had acted as governor since February 1765 and remained neutral throughout the crisis, presented the conflict as one between the French and the Spanish nations. In his letters, he repeatedly described the discourses and actions of the insurgents as attacks against not only the Spanish "governor" and "government" but also the Spanish "nation" that breached the *"droit des gens et des nations"* ("law of nations"). He also put forward his own French patriotism. For his part, Ulloa had doubts about the rebels' love for the king of France, as they challenged the monarch's authority by refusing to abide by his decision to cede the colony. Yet the Spanish governor did not discredit their patriotic urges entirely. He repeatedly tried to make sense of the revolt using the language of nation and fatherland. His interpretation of the event was influenced by the attitudes of the Spanish Creole elite, who did not content themselves with claiming their Hispanic (and European) identity, as most of the elites of European descent did in the Americas, but developed a Creole patriotism that drew on a double legacy, European and American. In Ulloa's opinion, only Creoles could legitimately rise up in revolt. The problem for him was that, except for the attorney general La Frénière, most of the leaders were not "Creoles" or *"naturals"* (another expression used with the same meaning by the Spanish). In his view, the rebellion was all the more unjustifiable in that they were born in metropolitan France and could not have forged an attachment to their new fatherland, the only possible excuse for their act of disobedience.[53]

---

ism of the insurgents. In opposition, many scholars have dismissed these patriotic and nationalist discourses as an illusion and artifice aimed at masking the personal interests of the leaders and convincing the king to renounce the cession. In their view, their motivations were principally political and economic. They sought to maintain the role of the Superior Council as the main governing body of the colony and to oppose the establishment of the Spanish Exclusif at a time when the colony was in a difficult economic and financial situation. See Jo Ann Carigan, "Old and New Interpretations of the Rebellion of 1768," in Glenn R. Conrad, ed., *The Louisiana Purchase Bicentennial Series in Louisiana History,* I, *French Experience in Louisiana* (Lafayette, La., 1995), 610–617; Villiers du Terrage, *Les dernières années de la Louisiane française;* Texada, *Alejandro O'Reilly and the New Orleans Rebels;* John Preston Moore, *Revolt in Louisiana: The Spanish Occupation, 1766–1770* (Baton Rouge, La., 1976); and Carl A. Brasseaux, *Denis-Nicolas Foucault and the New Orleans Rebellion of 1768* (Ruston, La., 1987).

53. For Aubry's national reading of the revolt, see Aubry to the minister of the navy, Mar. 30, 1767, ANOM COL C13A 47, fols. 6r–7v; Aubry to the minister of the navy, Nov. 25, 1768, ANOM COL C13A 48, fols. 23r–28v; Aubry to the minister of the navy, Dec. 16, 1768, ANOM COL C13A 48, fol. 29v; Aubry to the minister of the navy, Dec. 23–24,

Emergence of a Sense of Place and the Racial Divide

The insurgents never raised the flag of creolism and chose instead to assert their Frenchness. The texts written by their leaders included many ardent declarations of love and loyalty for their French monarch and country. Such language conformed to the patriotic literature that had started to be disseminated at the instigation of the crown in the mid-eighteenth century. Those discourses closely linked the king and "patrie," which was conflated with the kingdom, and equated obedience and devotion to the king with patriotism. The relationships between the subjects and their "natural sovereign" were described with a vocabulary drawing on feelings and emotions, reflecting a process of naturalization and the essentializing of national identity. As Bossu wrote in his travel account published in 1777: "The motivation that might have made them [the insurgents] go too far is a feeling that one can easily excuse; it would have deserved the highest praise in any other circumstances. It was the enthusiasm for the fatherland, the love of our Sovereign, loving his domination and laws."[54]

1768, ANOM COL C13A 48, fols. 40v, 42v, 43v; "Copie de la lettre adressée par Aubry à Alejandro O'Reilly," Aug. 20, 1769, ANOM COL C13A 49, fol. 32v; and Aubry to the minister of the navy, Apr. 14, 1769, ANOM COL C13A 49, fol. 21v. For Ulloa's point of view on the rebels, see "Résumé des observations sur le manifeste des habitants de la Louisiane," 1769, ANOM COL C13A 47, fols. 58r–59v; and "Observations sur les points contenus dans le mémoire ou le manifeste supposé avoir été présenté par les habitants de la Louisiane au Conseil de La Nouvelle-Orléans, ainsi que dans l'avis du procureur général, et la décision du conseil," 1769, ANOM COL C13A 47, fol. 181. For the expressions used to designate American-born settlers in the Spanish Empire, see Lavallé, "Recherches sur l'apparition de la conscience créole dans la vice-royauté du Pérou," 348–349. For Spanish creolism, see Brading, *First America*, 422, 428.

54. The leaders of the revolt all belonged to the colonial elite. Most were born in the metropole. Nicolas Chauvin de La Frénière and Joseph Roy de Villeré were Creoles of the colony; but the latter had been educated in a military school, and the former had obtained a law degree in France. Except for Foucault, who remained commissaire-ordonnateur until January 1768, they were merchants or planters who were often related to each other. Most were militia officers who could use their military rank, social prestige, and patronage relationships to mobilize the armed men of the colony. According to Alexandre Dubé, some were members of the Masonic lodge of the Scottish Rite that had just been founded by a merchant from Martinique. See Brasseaux, *Denis-Nicolas Foucault and the New Orleans Rebellion of 1768*, 57–64; Dubé, "Les biens publics," 169–170; and Emilie Leumas, "Ties That Bind: The Family, Social, and Business Associations of the Insurrectionists of 1768," *Louisiana History*, XLVII (2006), 183–202. However, not all the colonial elite took part in the revolt. Some merchants, such as Gilbert-Antoine de Saint Maxent, chose the Spanish side. See Moore, *Revolt in Louisiana*, 134n, 150. Except for Pierre Marquis, Jean-Baptiste de Noyan, and the chevalier de Bienville, who were related to La Frénière, most of the sword officers, who stayed at the top of the social ladder,

Well aware of the contradiction between their proclaimed love and loyalty for their monarch and their insubordination, the leaders of the revolt sought to justify themselves by citing the example of the provinces of Aquitaine, which opposed English domination during the One Hundred Years' War; by equating French identity with liberty; and by promoting both political and economic freedom. They dwelled at great length on the numerous grievances they had against Ulloa, who was presented as bearing the entire responsibility for the situation. Their complaints mainly concerned colonial trade and the slave system, the two aspects of life in the colonies that legally distinguished them from the metropole.[55]

In response to Ulloa's ordinance of October 1768, imposing the Spanish Exclusif, the rebels demanded "freedom of trade." They also protested the governor's actions in granting privileges to select local merchants involved in the Indian trade and to British merchants from Jamaica engaged in the slave trade. Their economic claims drew on a debate about the French Exclusif that had stirred throughout the French Empire since the end of the Seven Years' War. Should the usefulness of overseas territories be defined solely in terms of the interests of the metropole or by also taking into account those of colonies? Related to this question were the issues of the legal subordination or equal integration of overseas territories and subjects and of the colonial nature of the Empire.[56]

The future of slavery and the system of racial domination in the colony gave birth to another series of criticisms. The insurgents condemned the Spanish governor's purchase of the contracts of four German redemptioners brought from South Carolina to Pensacola and then New Orleans, which they viewed as the introduction of a harsh form of bound labor that would have imperiled the racial divide. For the same reason, they also protested the governor's chaplain's celebration of a marriage between a white Spaniard and a black slave, since mixed unions were prohibited by the

---

refrained from participation as it could have damaged their careers. For the development of royal patriotism, see Bell, *Cult of the Nation in France,* 663–668. For Bossu's excuse of the rebels, see Bossu, *Nouveaux voyages dans l'Amérique septentrionale,* 28.

55. For the rebels' reference to the Hundred Years' War, see "Mémoire des habitants et négociants de la Louisiane sur l'événement du 29 octobre 1768," ANOM COL C13A 48, fol. 253r.

56. On the French debate on "freedom of trade," see Jean Tarrade, *Le commerce colonial de la France à la fin de l'Ancien Régime: L'évolution du régime de l'Exclusif de 1763 à 1789,* 2 vols. (Paris, 1972); and Manuel Covo, "Commerce, empire, et révolutions dans le monde atlantique: La colonie française de Saint-Domingue entre métropole et États-Unis (ca. 1778 – ca. 1804)" (Ph.D. diss., École des Hautes Études en Sciences Sociales, 2013).

Emergence of a Sense of Place and the Racial Divide

Code Noir. Finally, they resented Ulloa's prohibition on whipping slaves in the proximity of his house and the protection given to runaways, for they felt that these measures infringed on their domestic sovereignty and, once again, violated the Code Noir, which allowed masters to punish their slaves. These recriminations were based on an assessment of the local and regional situation in Louisiana and in the greater Caribbean, as slavery, unlike "freedom of trade," was hardly yet a subject of debate within the Empire. Those who, like some Physiocrats, denounced the slave system, were very few in number. When, in 1766, Abbé Nicolas Baudeau suggested developing in the Mississippi colony a new form of colonization with the creation of a "tripartite Company" under the joint supervision of France, Spain, and Sicily "by purchas[ing] in Africa and in Asia every year, slaves of both sexes, not to keep them in irons, and overwhelm them with forced labor until completely decrepit, but to turn them into free men, into industrious Cultivators, into true Citizens of Louisiana," his proposal did not raise any interest. Two years later, in New Orleans, the rebels saw no contradiction in pleading both for "freedom of trade" and the enslavement of people of African descent.[57]

The rebels turned toward Louis XV to obtain the restoration of their scorned liberty. They seem to have expected much from him. At the same time, a few veiled criticisms of the monarch appear in the writings sent to the Parlement of Paris and to the Duc d'Orléans. Since the middle of the century, the parlements in the kingdom had been engaged in a fierce struggle with the crown that played a crucial role in the politicization of nationhood. In keeping with the idea common among magistrates—that all the sovereign courts of the kingdom constituted a single parlement divided in several classes—the New Orleans Superior Council issued a call for help to the Parlement of Paris, which represented the most important parlement of France. The interdiction of the Jesuits had recently provided the occasion for a union of all classes that had reached the colonies. In Louisiana, at La Frénière's instigation, the Superior Council promulgated a ruling ordering the expulsion of the Jesuits and the sale of their property as early as July

57. For physiocratic views on slavery, see Marcel Dorigny, "The Question of Slavery in the Physiocratic Texts: A Rereading of an Old Debate," in Manuela Albertone and Antonio de Francesco, eds., *Rethinking the Atlantic World: Europe and America in the Age of Democratic Revolutions* (New York, 2009), 147–162; and Pernille Røge, "The Question of Slavery in Physiocratic Political Economy," in Albertone, ed., *L'economia come linguaggio della politica nell'Europa del Settecento* (Milan, Italy, 2009), 149–169. For Abbé Nicolas Baudeau's proposal, see [Baudeau], ed., "Des colonies Françoises au Indes Occidentales," July 18, 1766, no. 5, in *Éphémérides du citoyen; ou, Chronique de l'esprit national*, V (Paris, 1766), 34–39, quoted ibid., 159.

1764, before the arrival of the royal letters patent demanding such action. Thus, the New Orleans councillors naturally looked to the Parlement of Paris for support at the time of the revolt.[58]

Their call for assistance also extended to Saint-Domingue. Parlementary opposition was not restricted to the metropolitan territory. At the end of the Seven Years' War, the superior councils of Saint-Domingue, that of Port-au-Prince in particular, entered into conflict with central and local authorities about the reorganization of the militia in 1768–1769. One of the leaders of the uprising was a former lawyer of the Parlement of Paris, named Marcel, who had been sent to the Caribbean colony by the minister of the navy, Étienne-François de Choiseul, with seven other colleagues to fill the empty seats in the superior councils. When the magistrates in New Orleans entered into rebellion as well, it was only fitting that they solicited their counterparts in Port-au-Prince. Because the prohibition of commercial relations between Louisiana and the Antilles also affected the Caribbean colony's mercantile interests, the Dominguan judges approved their action against Governor Ulloa.[59]

58. For the idea of a union of classes among parlements and parlementary opposition, see Jean Egret, *Louis XV et l'opposition parlementaire* (Paris, 1970); Michel Antoine, *Louis XV* ([Paris], 1989), 567–595; Roger Bickart, *Les parlements et la notion de souveraineté nationale au XVIIIe siècle* (Paris, 1932), 143–193; Bell, *Cult of the Nation in France*, 50–62; Alain J. Lemaître, ed., *Le monde parlementaire au XVIIIe siècle: L'invention d'un discours politique* (Rennes, France, 2010); Catherine Maire, *De la cause de Dieu à la cause de la Nation: Le jansénisme au XVIIIe siècle* (Paris, 1998); Dale K. Van Kley, *The Damiens Affair and the Unraveling of the Ancien Régime, 1750–1770* (Princeton, N.J., 1984); and Ahmed Slimani, *La modernité du concept de nation au XVIIIe siècle (1715–1789): Apports des thèses parlementaires et des idées politiques du temps* ([Aix-en-Provence], France, 2004). For the Jesuits' expulsion from the metropole and from Louisiana, see Van Kley, *The Jansenists and the Expulsion of the Jesuits from France, 1757–1765* (New Haven, Conn., 1975); Villiers du Terrage, *Les dernières années de la Louisiane française*, 162–165; and Brasseaux, *Denis-Nicolas Foucault and the New Orleans Rebellion of 1768*, 37–38.

59. For the revolt over the militia reforms and the role of a former Parisian lawyer in Saint-Domingue, see Charles Frostin, *Les révoltes blanches à Saint-Domingue aux XVIIe et XVIIIe siècles (Haïti avant 1789)*, [rev. ed.] (Rennes, France, 2008), 181–224; John D. Garrigus, *Before Haiti: Race and Citizenship in French Saint-Domingue* (New York, 2006), 129; and Tarrade, *Le commerce colonial de la France à la fin de l'Ancien Régime*, 81. For relations between the superior councils of New Orleans and Port-au-Prince during the 1768 revolt, see Aubry to the minister of the navy, May 23, 1769, ANOM COL C13A 49, fol. 28; and Saint-Léger to the Superior Council of Louisiana and Grenier to the Superior Council of Louisiana, Feb. 9, 1769, ANOM COL C13A 49, fols. 208–209.

Emergence of a Sense of Place and the Racial Divide

In their letters to the Parlement of Paris, the New Orleans councillors proclaimed that the magistrates of the kingdom's capital were "the fathers of the homeland, the guardians of public safety; and if every Frenchman has the right to demand your powerful protection, we are resolved that you will grant it to the citizens of Louisiana." They subscribed to the view of the Parisian judges, who claimed that they embodied the whole nation in their opposition to the crown. Following their example, the New Orleans Superior Council presented itself in its October 29 act as "the father of the people" and as "the bulwark that ensures the tranquility of the citizens." Aubry also recounted to the minister of the navy that when the councillors paid him a visit, they "[passed] through the militia in line under arms, they were blessed a thousand times, they were called the saviors of the fatherland, long live the king of France, long live the council, long live the father of the people." The Louisiana court adopted the same position as most of the kingdom's provincial parlements, which believed that they were the political representatives of their provinces. In the same way, the judicial institution proclaimed that it was in charge of "the maintenance of laws of which it is the guardian and the interpreter." This role justified the council's involvement in the revolt since, in the councillors' opinion, Ulloa had breached the act of cession.[60]

The New Orleans judges asked their Parisian colleagues to verify the legality of the Treaty of Fontainebleau, which had ceded the colony to Spain, explaining that they could not believe that "the king our master gives us away like a worthless herd of sheep." According to Aubry, when they had deliberated about the initial request of the settlers and merchants, as "several

60. For the description of the Parlement of Paris and the self-characterization of the New Orleans Superior Council, see "Observations du Conseil supérieur de la province de la Louisiane faite au Parlement séant à Paris," 1768, Favrot Papers, S-3; "Arrêt du Conseil supérieur," Oct. 29, 1768, ANOM COL C13A 48, fols. 233v, 238v, 240v; and Aubry to the minister of the navy, Dec. 23-24, 1768, ANOM COL C13A 48, fol. 42v. On the pretension of the Parlement of Paris to represent the whole French nation, see Bickart, *Les parlements et la notion de souveraineté nationale au XVIIIe siècle*, 86-142. For an example of the political role claimed by provincial parlements, see, for example, Clarisse Coulomb, *Les pères de la patrie: La société parlementaire en Dauphiné au temps des Lumières* (Grenoble, France, 2006). On the parlements' role as the "guardian of laws" ("*dépôt des lois*"), see Jacques Krynen, *L'état de justice: France, XIIIe-XXe siècle*, I, *L'idéologie de la magistrature ancienne* (Paris, 2009), 239-279; Catherine Maire, "L'église et la nation: Du dépôt de la vérité au dépôt des lois: La trajectoire janséniste au XVIIIe siècle," *Annales: Économies, sociétés, civilisations*, XLVI (1991), 1117-1205; and Maire, *De la cause de Dieu à la cause de la Nation*, 378-395, 427-440.

magistrates [had] raised their voice and argued that the King could not and should not carve up the provinces of his kingdom unless he was forced to do so by the misfortunes of battle and that, since the cession of Louisiana had been made willingly while his majesty was not compelled to do it, it must be regarded as null and void, this opinion was generally applauded, however these gentlemen were prudent enough not to promulgate a ruling on the subject." This opinion was based on a strict interpretation of the principle of the inalienability of the royal domain, which had been specified by the Moulins Edict of February 1566 and constituted one of the fundamental laws of the kingdom.[61]

The New Orleans Superior Council's request to the Parlement of Paris partook of what René Louis Voyer de Paulmy, marquis d'Argenson, described in July 1756 as the "visible and public union of all the parlements to make common cause and demand the observance of fundamental laws ...." The parlements in many of the metropolitan provinces came to consider local franchises and liberties as fundamental laws and to practice a form of "dual constitutionalism." In so doing, they adopted a "legal theory of contractual union of their province with the French monarchy" that had been introduced in the sixteenth century. In contrast, the Superior Council of Louisiana had no such precedents to take advantage of. Although the magistrates tried to put forward what they saw as the privileges guaranteed by Louis XV at the time of the cession, meaning the maintenance of the Superior Council and the "laws, forms, and usages of the colony," they found themselves in a different position to that of the courts in Saint-Domingue. The latter could recall the freebooter origins of the French section of the island and claim that a contractual pact had been concluded between the buccaneers and the king. The adoption by the Louisiana elite of the new political culture that distinguished the nation from the king and averred that they should be linked by a contractual relationship seemed all the more necessary. Since they could not cite prior local liberties in their cause, they had to proclaim liberty as the privilege of the whole French

61. On the Superior Council's debate about the legality of the treaty of cession, see "Observations du Conseil supérieur de la province de la Louisiane faite au Parlement séant à Paris," 1768, Favrot Papers, S-3; and Aubry to the minister of the navy, Dec. 23–24, 1768, ANOM COL C13A 48, fols. 39r–40v. On the Moulins Edict and the fundamental laws of the kingdom, see Bernard Barbiche, *Les institutions de la monarchie française à l'époque moderne: XVIe–XVIIIe siècle* (Paris, 1999), 31–33; and Robert Descimon and Fanny Consandey, *L'absolutisme en France: Histoire et historiographie* (Paris, 2002), 55–62.

nation. Although such ideas could not be publicly endorsed, they occupied a central place in the "Manifeste des habitants, négociants, et colons de la province de la Louisiane au sujet de la révolution qui est arrivée le 28 8bre 1768" ("Manifesto of the permanent residents, merchants, and colonists of the province of Louisiana about the revolution that took place on October 28, 1768") that was written after Ulloa's expulsion. This lampoon did not circulate outside of Louisiana but was seized by Governor Alejandro O'Reilly on his arrival in the colony to reestablish the authority of the Spanish monarch and used against the leaders of the rebellion during their trial. Drawing on Hugo Grotius, Samuel von Pufendorf, and, most of all, Emer de Vattel, the document contained a long philosophical, juridical, and political argument intended to justify the insurgents' actions on the basis of natural law. The main idea was that the colony belonged to the nation and should not have been ceded without the consent of its inhabitants.[62]

62. On the unity of the parlements around the issue of fundamental laws, see Journal entry, July 4, 1756, in E. J. B. Rathery, ed., *Journal et mémoires du marquis d'Argenson* ..., IX (Paris, 1867), 294, quoted in Hervé Drévillon, "La monarchie des Lumières: Réforme ou utopie? 1715–1774," in Joël Cornette et al., eds., *La monarchie: Entre Renaissance et Révolution, 1515–1792* (Paris, 2000), 340. On the transformation of the concept of the constitution and on the claims of the parlements that they were the "essential guardians of laws and constitution of the monarchy," meaning that their duty was to ensure that royal power acted in accordance with the fundamental laws in the eighteenth century, see Bickart, *Les parlements et la notion de souveraineté nationale au XVIIIe siècle*, 13–70; Krynen, *L'idéologie de la magistrature ancienne*, 262–268; and Arnaud Vergne, *La notion de constitution d'après les cours et assemblées à la fin de l'Ancien Régime, 1750–1789* (Paris, 2006), 71–97, 129–149, 396 ("essential guardians"). On the use of freebooter origins by Saint-Domingue's superior councils, see Frostin, *Les révoltes blanches à Saint-Domingue aux XVIIe et XVIIIe siècles*, 18. According to Charles Edwards O'Neill, the manifesto was written by Pierre Marquis, but some doubts remained about the author(s) of the text. See "Manifeste des habitants, négociants, et colons de la province de la Louisiane au sujet de la révolution qui est arrivée le 28 8bre 1768," AGI, Papeles de Cuba, Legajo 1054, quoted and translated into English by Charles Edwards O'Neill, "The Louisiana Manifesto of 1768," *Political Science Reviewer*, XIX (1990), 255–272; and Samuel Biagetti, "Enlightenment and Revolution: The Case of Louisiana, 1768," *Early American Studies*, XII (2014), 68–92. It is difficult to investigate the origins of the political culture of the insurgents. Some probate records that include book collections show that settlers had access to the great works of the Enlightenment. In July 1769, one month before the arrival of Alejandro O'Reilly, Jean-Baptiste Prévost, who was the representative of the Company of the Indies, died. According to his probate record, his library, which was exceptional for the colony, was made up of more than three hundred volumes. Among them were *Le droit des gens ou principes de la loi naturelle: Appliqués à la con-*

At the heart of the debates and conflicts generated by the Louisiana cession were essential issues such as the place of overseas populations and territories within the nation and the relationship between the king and his remote subjects. Until then, Louisiana's ambiguous status and that of France's other overseas territories had been ignored. Although the full title of the 1724 Code Noir qualified Louisiana as both a "province and colony," the cession de facto transformed the territory into a genuine colony. With the change of sovereignty, Louisiana's settlers were confronted with their status as quasi-colonized subjects at the same time as they behaved as ruthless colonizers, exploiting their slaves of African descent. The experience helped to bind them together around the defense of common interests that appeared increasingly distinct from those of the monarchy and the metropole.[63]

Despite the rebels' efforts to marshall geopolitical, economic, and patriotic arguments to convince Louis XV of the advantages to be had by retaining Louisiana within the French Empire, they were under no illusions as to the difficulty of persuading the crown to adopt their point of view. They thus made a veiled allusion to the Duc d'Orléans about the possibility of "[living] independently" in the event of refusal. During the long period between Ulloa's expulsion in October 1768 and O'Reilly's arrival in August 1769, the revolt's leaders considered favorably a proposal made by the retired Swiss officer Pierre Marquis that entailed the establishment of a republic. They also thought of founding an independent bank, called the Banque du Mont de Piété, on the model of those in Venice and Amsterdam. Nevertheless, recognizing the fanciful character of their projects and the existence of opposition to their plan of "creating a new world so to speak," they also envisioned the possibility of coming under British rule. To that end, they worked to obtain the support of their English neighbors. In December 1768, Aubry reported that "at present the colonists would rather fall under En-

---

duite et aux affaires des nations et des souverains (1758) by [Emer] de Vattel and works by Locke, Montesquieu, Rousseau, and Voltaire. See "Inventory of the Estate of Sieur Jean Baptiste Prevost, Deceased Agent of the Company of the Indies, July 13, 1769," trans. and ed. Edith Dart Price and Heloise H. Cruzat, *LHQ*, IX (1926), 411–498.

63. For the Code Noir's full title, see "Code noir ou édit du roi servant de règlement pour le gouvernement et l'administration de la justice, police, et discipline et le commerce des esclaves nègres dans la province et colonie de la Louisiane donné à Versailles au mois de mars 1724," ANOM COL A 22, fols. 110–128. For a similar interpretation of English North America's pre-Revolutionary era, see T. H. Breen, "Interpreting New World Nationalism," in Don H. Doyle and Marco Antonio Pamplona, eds., *Nationalism in the New World* (Athens, Ga., 2006), 49–50.

glish domination than be subjects of the king of Spain ...," a state of affairs he seemed to consider the ultimate sign of despair.[64]

The insurgents were not moved by such a strong French nationalism that they could not have borne the cession of the colony. Rather, their patriotic and nationalist discourses reflected the royal propaganda developed by the crown since the middle of the century and constituted a resource that they used in difficult negotiations with the king. Even so, the political significance of these discourses should not be underestimated. Beyond expressions of love and loyalty to the monarch and the fatherland, the rebels' writings contributed to the debate then taking place on both sides of the Atlantic about the foundations and limits of royal authority, the institution more suitable to represent the nation—the king or the Parlement—and the sharing of executive and legislative power. As their political language and demands testify, the Louisiana elite believed that they belonged to the nation, but they were confronted with their colonial otherness by the monarch's indifference. They collided against the distinction made between the Empire and the nation and the divide built between the colonies and their metropole. If the Exclusif positioned overseas territories in a subordinate situation within the nation, the imperial diplomacy that used and misused territorial cessions, even in the absence of military conquests, excluded colonies from the nation, clearly demonstrating that the fundamental laws of the kingdom did not apply overseas. The voluntary cession of Louisiana, which could not be justified by a military defeat, pointed to the colonial character of the French Empire.

Cornered by the lack of responsiveness from Versailles, the insurgents actually considered putting an end to their colonial situation and proclaiming their independence. They were the first settlers to envision such a radical measure. If they had had the means, these Frenchmen would have become "Louisianais." With its first appearance in the memorandum to the Duc d'Orléans, the ethno-label perfectly symbolized the dual interpretation that can be made of the colonists' claim to Frenchness. In a gesture reminiscent of the adventurer René-Robert Cavelier de La Salle's nod to the king of

64. "Mémoire sur la révolution arrivée à la Louisiane le 29 octobre 1768 pour être présenté à son A. R. Monseigneur le duc d'Orléans," 1768, Favrot Papers, S-4; Aubry to the minister of the navy, Dec. 23–24, 1768, ANOM COL C13A 48, fol. 39v; Aubry to the minister of the navy, May 23, 1769, ANOM COL C13A 49, fol. 28v; "Copie de la lettre adressée par Aubry à Alexandre O'Reilly," Aug. 20, 1769, ANOM COL C13A 49, fols. 31v–36v; document without title or date, Favrot Papers, S-7; Texada, *Alejandro O'Reilly and the New Orleans Rebels*, 31, 69, 89, 102; Villiers du Terrage, *Les dernières années de la Louisiane française*, 286.

France in naming the Mississippi Basin in honor of Louis XIV, the invention of the category "Louisianais" at once flattered the monarch while allowing for the expression of a new patriotism disconnected from the metropole. Similar to the ethno-label "American" in British colonies and in the French Antilles, the term implicitly conveyed a demand for the redefinition of citizenship and sovereignty.[65]

The long revolutionary sequence that was to drastically change the Atlantic world did not start on British North America's eastern shores alone but also in the French section of the Gulf of Mexico. Following the end of the Seven Years' War, all imperial centers, whether London, Versailles, Madrid, or Lisbon, tried to implement reforms that aimed at increasing their control over their colonies. These reforms created tensions that sometimes turned into revolts. Although the New Orleans rebels certainly knew about the insurrectionary movements that broke out in the British colonies following the promulgation of the Sugar Act, Stamp Act, and Townshend Act, they were more likely influenced by concurrent events in Saint-Domingue. Jerónimo Grimaldi, the chief minister of Spain, himself made the link between the 1768 Louisiana rebellion over "freedom of trade" and the perpetuation of racial slavery with the 1768–1769 uprising in Saint-Domingue over militia reforms. He justified the severe repression that was conducted in New Orleans "in view of the consequences that the bad example of Louisiana could entail in the other possessions of America, even those belonging to different powers where the spirit of sedition and independence was beginning to spread, as shown by what had happened to the French in the very island of Saint-Domingue."[66]

Soon after his arrival in August 1769 at the head of a large military force intended to reestablish the sovereignty of the Spanish crown in Louisiana,

65. In the memorandum to the Parlement of Paris, the authors also used the expressions "habitants of Louisiana" and "citizens of Louisiana." See "Observations du Conseil supérieur de la province de la Louisiane faites au Parlement séant à Paris," 1768, Favrot Papers, S-3, and "Mémoire sur la révolution arrivée à la Louisiane le 29 octobre 1768 pour être présenté à son A. R. Monseigneur le duc d'Orléans," 1768, S-4. On the refusal of white settlers to be identified as Creoles in British North America, see Chaplin, "Creoles in British America: From Denial to Acceptance," in Stewart, ed., *Creolization*, 46–65. Pradel also designated the Spanish planters of Cuba and the French of Saint-Domingue as "Americans." See Baillardel and Prioult, eds., *Le chevalier de Pradel*, 205, 235, 277.

66. "Copie de la lettre de M. le marquis de Grimaldi à M. le comte de Fuentes," ANOM COL C13A 50, fol. 47r.

Emergence of a Sense of Place and the Racial Divide

the new governor O'Reilly ordered a dozen of the revolt's leaders to be put under arrest and had six of them sentenced to death. Five were executed: the attorney general, La Frénière; two military officers, Pierre Marquis and Jean-Baptiste Payen de Noyan; and two merchants, Pierre Carresse and Joseph Milhet. The "Mémoire des habitants et négociants de la Louisiane" was also thrown into the river while other documents related to the revolt were publicly burned the next day.[67]

To escape from the consequences of the rebellion, the families of some of the white insurgents took refuge in Saint-Domingue. They chose the island because they knew the place well. In the following years, they were joined by other colonists of French descent from Louisiana. The refugees were granted land in the vicinity of Jérémie, in the district of the Grande Anse. According to the lawyer and writer Médéric Louis-Élie Moreau de Saint-Méry, the place where these families settled with their slaves was called "*Nouvelle-Louisiane*" ("New Louisiana") for some time after their arrival. Since these refugees had difficulties making a living, the governor and intendant of the island proposed:

> to Messrs. the habitants, merchants, and settlers in Saint-Domingue, a patriotic association for the relief of Louisianans who, out of their attachment to our sovereign, arrive here every day after having abandoned all they possessed on the fertile banks of the Mississippi River; if charity and generosity needed to be aroused by moving descriptions, we would add to this announcement details about the misfortunes that had befallen Louisiana since its establishment, healing the wounds of our brothers, seeking to close them, proving to them that we appreciate their attachment to the French name; that is the goal of the subscription that we propose under the memorable title of *patriotic association*.

67. On the forms taken by the repression, see "Note des chefs ou principaux habitants de La Nouvelle-Orléans qui ont été condamnés par la sentence rendue contre eux le 24 octobre 1769," ANOM COL C13A 50, fol. 44; and Villiers du Terrage, *Les dernières années de la Louisiane française*, 305–312. A sixth man, the merchant Joseph Roué de Villeré, was also sentenced to death, but he died in jail before his execution. Six other men were condemned to prison or penal servitude. The severity of the repression was approved by the French crown, which tried Foucault and blamed Aubry. However, in the following years, the French government intervened to obtain a reduced sentence for those imprisoned and the return of their sequestrated property. See F.-P. Renaut, "Études sur le pacte de famille et la politique coloniale française (1760–1792)," *Revue de l'histoire des colonies françaises*, X (1922), 263.

They also nominated the chevalier de Bienville, who was related to Jean-Baptiste Payen de Noyan, to be one of two men who would represent the interests of those who had definitively won the recognition of the name they had given to themselves, "Louisianais." These refugees had to flee New Orleans and Louisiana at the very time that the white inhabitants had finally succeeded in developing a sense of place, an attachment to their city and their colony.[68]

Most noticeable among the Saint-Domingue elite who became interested in the patriotic association was Moreau de Saint-Méry, who would become famous for his collection of colonial laws and history of Saint-Domingue. He became a member of its board. He later married Louise-Catherine Milhet, who was born in New Orleans in 1759, the daughter of merchant Jean Milhet. Both Jean and his brother Joseph Milhet had participated in the revolt, but Joseph had been executed by O'Reilly while Jean had been sentenced to jail in Havana. After Jean's liberation in 1771, thanks to the intervention of the French crown, he moved to Saint-Domingue, where his wife and children came to join him from New Orleans. Another of his daughters married Louis-Narcisse Baudry des Lozières, who founded the *Cercle des Philadelphes* in 1784.[69]

68. Several ships brought groups of migrants from Louisiana to Saint-Domingue between 1771 and 1773. In 1773, the local authorities evaluated the number of "Louisianans" in the island at "160 settlers and one hundred negroes." See "Note sur les émigrants de la Louisiane à Saint-Domingue," 1773, ANOM COL C13A 50, fols. 102–103. For the name of the place where Louisiana refugees settled in Saint-Domingue, see [Médéric Louis-Élie] Moreau de Saint-Méry, *Description topographique, physique, civile, politique, et historique de la partie française de l'isle de Saint-Domingue . . .*, 2 vols. (Philadelphia, 1797–1798), II, 801. For the formation of the "patriotic association" (the expression is underlined in the original document), see "Annonce d'une association patriotique, pour les habitants de la Louisiane qui se retirent à St Domingue et lettre des administrateurs à ce sujet, du mois de décembre 1773," ANOM COL F3 25, fols. 330–331 (quotation, 330v). See also Moreau de Saint-Méry, *Description topographique, physique, civile, politique, et historique de la partie française de l'isle de Saint-Domingue*, II, 682–683.

69. For Moreau de Saint-Méry's links with the Louisiana refugees, see [Médéric Louis-Élie] Moreau de Saint-Méry, *Loix et constitutions des colonies françoises de l'Amérique sous le vent*, 6 vols. (Paris, 1784–1790); and Moreau de Saint-Méry, *Description topographique, physique, civile, politique, et historique de la partie française de l'isle de Saint-Domingue*. Louis-Narcisse Baudry des Lozières recounted the story of his father-in-law in the travel account about Louisiana that he published in 1802. See [Baudry Des Lozières], *Voyage à la Louisiane et sur le continent de l'Amérique septentrionale, fait dans les années 1794 à 1798* (Paris, 1802), 117–145. For other evidence on these families between Louisiana and Saint-Domingue, see Wood and Nolan, eds., *Sacramental Records*

Emergence of a Sense of Place and the Racial Divide

Through the presence of Louisiana refugees in Saint-Domingue, the memory of the 1768 rebellion would resurface during the revolutionary troubles in the Caribbean. On the occasion of a debate within the Saint-Domingue assembly in Leogane in December 1791, which dealt with the transformation of its name from "general Assembly" to "colonial Assembly" and with "our essence and our political existence," a speaker recalled that "all nations, including ours, which have founded colonies have considered them as dependent on themselves; nowadays, Sirs, we have seen France dispose of Louisiana as of a dominion belonging to itself and sell it to Spain; several times, Sirs, we have been the victims of such deals." The voluntary cession of Louisiana and the revolt of its settlers continued to fuel the debate about the place of colonies within the nation during the French and Haitian Revolutions. After 1789, discussions on the Exclusif intermingled with those on the civil and political rights of free people of color and the emancipation of slaves. The revolutionary era would have tremendous consequences in the whole greater Caribbean. It would open, in particular, a new chapter in New Orleans's history while reinforcing the city's Caribbean character.[70]

---

of the Roman Catholic Church of the Archdiocese of New Orleans, II, 205–206; Gabriel Debien and René Le Gardeur, "Les colons de Saint-Domingue réfugiés à la Louisiane (1792–1804)," *Revue de Louisiane/Louisiana Review*, IX (1980), 117; and Vincent Huyghues-Belrose, "Moreau de Saint-Méry, arpenteur créole de Saint-Domingue," in Dominique Taffin, ed., *Moreau de Saint-Méry ou les ambiguïtés d'un créole des Lumières* ... (Fort-de-France, Martinique, 2006), 12.

70. The text was signed by a man named Millet, but it is impossible to know if he was related to the family of former New Orleans merchants. See "Assemblée générale de la partie française de Saint-Domingue," Dec. 12, 1791, *Moniteur général de la partie française de Saint-Domingue* (Cap-Français), 113–114.

From Louisiana to Saint-Domingue and from Saint-Domingue to Louisiana

> I imagine that among all our colonies Saint-Domingue is the one from which Louisiana has borrowed most of its spirit and customs. Contacts between the two colonies were frequent. Today when negroes, who have become sovereign, are chasing us away from Haiti, its refugees prefer to seek asylum here. One can meet many former colonists who have been taken in by relatives or friends and who, in general, do not preach affection and kindness for blacks. There are also a small number of slaves who have followed the fortunes of their masters, reduced to debris, to earning their living by hard work, in a word, to a life of hardship.
>
> Pierre-Clément de Laussat, *Mémoires sur ma vie . . .*

According to Pierre-Clément de Laussat, the prefect who was sent by the French government to New Orleans in 1803 to take possession of Louisiana after Spain returned the colony to France by the secret treaty of San Ildefonso three years earlier, the white Saint-Dominguan refugees who landed in the city during the revolutionary period found a place they could easily call home. Not only were these exiles bound to Louisiana's inhabitants by ties of blood or economic interests, but they were also held together by a shared commitment to racial slavery. White colonists and free people of color started to flee the French section of the Caribbean island with the outbreak of a slave revolt in the northern plain of Saint-Domingue in 1791. Many elected to settle in New Orleans, even though their numbers became significant only later. The arrival of nine thousand Saint-Dominguan refugees in 1809, who had been expelled from Cuba, doubled the size of the urban center's population. Outward ripples from the Haitian Revolution dramatically impacted New Orleans's demographic and social configuration, which had already been transformed under Spanish rule. Historians have traditionally examined the relationships between Louisiana and Saint-Domingue starting with this event. Yet historical actors already knew at the time that the choice of New Orleans as a privileged destination was linked to the close connections that the two colonies had maintained from the outset. They also acknowledged, as Laussat did, that the French West Indian territory had served as a model for its mainland follower for most of the eighteenth century.[1]

As *Caribbean New Orleans* has demonstrated, the Louisiana capital belonged to a greater Caribbean world marked by racial slavery, even though the racial regime that emerged in the port city differed to some extent from that of other urban slave societies. Despite these discrepancies, the city's social history was not so exceptional that one cannot draw comparisons between New Orleans and other places within the greater Caribbean, the French Empire, and the Atlantic world. The small outpost perched on a curve of the Mississippi River constitutes a remarkable case study whose heuristic value goes well beyond the boundaries of Louisiana history. By reconsidering the interplay of slavery and race in the city under the influence of Saint-Domingue, this book has proposed an alternative way of understanding how an urban slave society operated and what it meant for a slave society to become racialized. It has also tried to better fulfill the promises of Atlantic history. Like other kinds of transnational history, Atlantic studies were conceived of as a way to move away from the primacy of the present-day nation state as a unit of analysis and from the tendency toward exceptionalism inherent to national history, but this historiographical field has not yet succeeded in fully escaping from a North-American-centric perspective. At stake is the recovery of the place the Caribbean occupied within the early Atlantic world as well as the development of a comparative and connected history of racial formation as a sociopolitical process in the Americas.[2]

1. Pierre-Clément de Laussat, *Mémoires sur ma vie . . .* (Pau, France, 1831), 91, quoted in Gabriel Debien and René Le Gardeur, "Les colons de Saint-Domingue réfugiés à la Louisiane (1792–1804)," *Revue de Louisiane/Louisiana Review*, X (1981), 135.

2. For the analysis of singular case studies as an heuristically valuable historical method, see Jean-Claude Passeron and Jacques Revel, "Penser par cas: Raisonner à partir de singularités," in Passeron and Revel, eds., *Penser par cas* (Paris, 2005), 9–44. For works calling for the decentering of North American history, see Ian Tyrrell, "American Exceptionalism in an Age of International History," *American Historical Review*, XCVI (1991), 1031–1055; and Cécile Vidal, "For a Comprehensive History of the Atlantic World or Histories Connected In and Beyond the Atlantic World?" *Annales: Histoire, Sciences Sociales*, LXVII (2012), 279–300.

In barely two generations, the people of European, African, and Native American descent, brought together freely or forcefully to New Orleans, succeeded in overcoming the many hardships experienced during the colony's early years to create a viable, albeit segmented and violent, urban society. That the Louisiana capital was built as much by black slaves as by white settlers does not mean, however, that all individuals were able to shape its social dynamics in the same way nor that they all accepted the social order based on racial slavery that took hold. The slave system had a paradoxical effect of both alienating and intertwining the enslaved and their owners. As Eugene Genovese stressed in the opening pages of *Roll, Jordan, Roll*, "Cruel, unjust, exploitative, oppressive, slavery bound two peoples together in bitter antagonism while creating an organic relationship so complex and ambivalent that neither could express the simplest human feelings without reference to the other." Following Genovese's lead, this book has exemplified an inclusive social history of slavery that takes into account all sides of the organic relationship between masters and slaves. By focusing on interpersonal interactions, it is possible to analyze the agency of the various social actors in play without minimizing the power relations in which they were entangled.[3]

The need to develop a relational history of slavery is even stronger for cities than for the plantations on which Genovese focused. Urban centers forced people to live in close quarters and included a greater proportion of nonslaveholders among whites than the surrounding areas. The urban milieu shaped slavery in complex ways. Whereas slave studies have insisted on the variety of plantation slaveries that developed in the Americas, *Caribbean New Orleans* has emphasized the need to better take into account the diversity of urban slaveries depending on their association with a plantation economy or another economic system. As with any other city located within a plantation region such as Charleston, Kingston, or Cap-Français, the significance of slavery was different in the Louisiana capital than in cities such as Mexico City, Montreal, Newport, or New York that were integrated within colonies that were on the whole societies with slaves and not slave societies. Admittedly, the emergence of the Mississippi colony as a slave society was atypical. After 1731, Louisiana's access to the direct slave trade from Africa nearly ceased, and a large proportion of the colonial population lived in the

---

3. Eugene D. Genovese, *Roll, Jordan, Roll: The World the Slaves Made* (1972; rpt. New York, 1974), 3.

Conclusion

capital. Even so, the project of establishing a plantation economy informed the slave system within New Orleans. The colony did not succeed in boosting the export economy based on plantation slavery, but its black majority lived and worked on plantations growing tobacco and indigo in the lower Mississippi Valley. Although plantation and urban slaveries operated differently in Louisiana, as in every plantation colony, they influenced each other, as both rural and urban residents of European descent shared the same commitment to the slave institution. The city distributed the slaves who arrived from Africa or the Antilles through its port and played a crucial role in the surveillance and discipline of enslaved workers in the countryside while the methods of slave management on plantations shaped how they were treated within New Orleans. White settlers remained a sizable component of the urban population, and free labor coexisted with slavery to a large extent, but slavery also put its mark on every social institution and relationship within the urban center. Slaveownership quickly became the ultimate social fault line.

Creating and maintaining such an urban slave society was a difficult process. At a time when the movement Black Lives Matter denounces the enduring legacy of slavery and segregation in the United States, historians have come to realize that, to explain how slave societies were able to form and perpetuate themselves for such a long time despite the incessant struggle of enslaved people to be free, they need to go beyond the longstanding historiographical focus on slave resistance. The contribution of *Caribbean New Orleans* to this debate is twofold. The book has demonstrated how the transfer of technologies from the Antilles to Louisiana facilitated the implementation of the slave system and how the production and reproduction of the slave order in slave societies rested on the cooperation of the whole free population.

The regime of collective governance on which slave societies depended was particularly important in cities. Since whites always remained a sizeable section of the overall urban population, it was more difficult for the enslaved to rise up in revolt. At the same time, the urban milieu tended to weaken the boundaries between slavery and freedom. To offset the intrinsic frailty of the slave order in cities, the surveillance and discipline of urban slaves did not rest mainly on owners as on plantations but involved the local government and the rest of the white population as a whole, nonslaveholders as well as masters. Even when white urban dwellers did not denounce or hand over unruly slaves to public authorities, they exercised some form of social regulation, keeping watch over what enslaved men and women in their neighborhood were doing and stepping in when they thought necessary. Despite the lack of consensus among whites on how slaves should participate in the market economy, develop their own forms of sociability, or socialize across race and status boundaries, the cooperative monitoring of urban slaves was to some extent successful in New Orleans.

The formation of a slave society happened more quickly and more smoothly in Louisiana than in other colonies, which does not mean that the enslaved were not badly treated or did not resist their condition. Whereas the development of other slave societies throughout the Americas was often accompanied by a surge of extreme violence—Jamaica, for instance, experienced the greatest number of slave revolts in the last third of the seventeenth century, each uprising being followed by a terrible stage of repression—no slave rebellion ever broke out in New Orleans and its plantation region over the French regime. Some conspiracies were discovered during the Natchez Wars, but they did not succeed in actually materializing.

Paradoxically, the reasons that some historians have put forward to argue that the Louisiana capital was not a genuine slave society explain why local authorities and settlers were able to implement a more stable slave order without the difficulties encountered in the Caribbean. In addition to the transplantation of techniques of governance from older slave societies in the Antilles, demographic conditions played a crucial role. Death was not as prevalent in the Mississippi Valley as it was in the islands, which "could host a range of tropical diseases" and were "a notably lethal crossroads of contagion." Furthermore, not only was the climate healthier in New Orleans, but the quasi cessation of the slave trade from Africa after 1731 forced slaveholders to treat their enslaved laborers less harshly, and the slave population became self-sustaining after the 1740s. Consequently, slaves were able to form families more easily than in the Antilles. Life was less precarious and unstable; colonists did not have to integrate a steady and abundant influx of new slaves; and enslaved laborers were less likely inclined to rise in revolt, both because they wanted to preserve their relatives and because the proportion of blacks and whites was not as unbalanced as in the islands. All these factors contributed to strengthening the slave order. The small size of the overall urban population and the proximity of repressive forces—the city always housed a garrison of several dozen and, at times, hundreds of soldiers who were in charge of policing the urban center—also facilitated social control in New Orleans.[4]

4. For the Caribbean disease environment, see Philip D. Morgan, "The Caribbean Islands in Atlantic Context, circa 1500–1800," Felicity A. Nussbaum, ed., *The Global Eighteenth Century* (Baltimore, 2003), 58–59.

Conclusion

To be sure, slaves never ceased to fight to gain access to material and so-cial resources, create their own social networks and spaces of sociability, as-sert their dignity, and obtain their freedom. Still, the slowly growing urban economy offered them fewer opportunities to find their way out of bond-age than the more opulent port cities such as Cap-Français or Saint-Pierre. Practices of self-hiring and living outside their owners' homes do not seem to have existed at the time. Although involvement in mercantile activities allowed a few enslaved persons to purchase their freedom, not enough indi-viduals were able to do so for the Louisiana capital's free black population to constitute an influential demographic and economic force at the end of the French regime as it already did in Cap-Français. Because it was more difficult for New Orleans slaveholders, whose wealth was in no way compa-rable to their counterparts in Kingston, Cap-Français, or even Charleston, to acquire new slaves after 1731, they were also less inclined to free their laborers, whether on plantations or within urban households. Manumis-sions, nevertheless, must have been more numerous within the city, since the majority of urban slaves served as domestics and maintained personal relationships with their owners. The promise of freedom was also used to impose social control on urban slaves. Once freed, many former slaves con-tinued to live with and work for their former masters. Those who succeeded in becoming more independent congregated in separate rural neighbor-hoods in Chapitoulas or at the English Turn rather than on the outskirts of the city. In Louisiana, like everywhere else in the Americas, the urban milieu was more favorable to autonomy and freedom for people of African descent, but the subordination and dependency of both enslaved and free blacks re-mained more pronounced in the Louisiana capital than in more advanced urban slave societies. Only at the end of the French regime did New Orleans reach a size that made it possible for runaways to hide and survive, which drove local authorities to increasingly resort to the police and justice to try to counteract this trend. Likewise, economic growth began to make it easier for enslaved laborers to find ways to earn money. As a result, in the 1760s, the number of free blacks increased slowly, even though they remained in a subaltern and fragile position.

THE CONUNDRUM OF RACIAL FORMATION

Racial oppression was also instrumental in the creation and perpetuation of New Orleans's slave society. Despite the prevalence of race, the main-tenance of white supremacy was no more an end in itself in the Louisi-ana capital than it was in the Americas in general. Everywhere in the New World, a racial vision of the social order was mobilized by the white population to sustain the expansion and perpetuation of the plantation complex, which combined the forced migrations of millions of Africans and the development of slave societies. This phenomenon played out at various levels within and beyond the Atlantic world, from the global to the local, and involved the circulation of racial ideas and practices in all directions. Yet, after the Iberians led the way in their American colonies, the Caribbean can be considered as the epicenter of this global process of racialization within the English and French Atlantics, as it was in the sugar islands that the plantation system and African slavery intersected most rapidly and where racial slavery took its harshest form. The idea at the heart of racial slavery—that people of African descent ought to be slaves and thus confined to the most degrading of social positions because of their alleged natural inferiority—benefited from a new impulse in the islands. This racist ideology was actualized and internalized in the many ways that slaves were treated throughout the greater Caribbean, including on the mainland. Because slavery was "pivotal to the entire institutional structure and value complex" in slave societies, race came to permeate every dimension and sphere of social life. Racialization was not restricted to issues of *métissage* or the status of free blacks, important as they were. No social institution or relationship was left untouched by race.[5]

Furthermore, racial formation was both a top-down and a bottom-up process. The development of a slave economy and society in French Louisiana was a conscious choice. Local authorities and settlers wanted to emulate Saint-Domingue, a place where slavery and race were already intertwined. But the embedding of race was an "unthinking decision." There was no deliberate policy to impose a racial order nor a concerted effort to select the peculiar forms taken by racialization in New Orleans. The development of a specific racial regime in New Orleans was the result of multiple individual and collective initiatives, reactions, appropriations, and adaptations

5. For the idea that the perpetuation of white supremacy was not an end in itself in the United States, see Barbara Jeanne Fields, "Slavery, Race, and Ideology in the United States of America," *New Left Review*, CLXXXI (May–June 1990), 99, 111. On the "emergence of racial ideologies and racial orders" as "one of the great fault lines, perhaps *the* great fault line, in studies of Atlantic history," see Sylvia R. Frey, "Conclusion: Beyond Borders: Revising Atlantic History," in Cécile Vidal, ed., *Louisiana: Crossroads of the Atlantic World* (Philadelphia, 2014), 184–204 (quotation, 185). For the definition of a slave society, see Arnold A. Sio, "Review of Orlando Patterson, *The Sociology of Slavery: An Analysis of the Origins, Development, and Structure of Negro Slave Society in Jamaica*," *Social and Economic Studies*, XVII, no. 1 (1968), 96–99 (quotation, 96).

from all social actors that developed and evolved according to changing demographic, economic, social, and cultural circumstances.[6]

Whereas the 1724 revised Code Noir played a crucial role in the transference of racial ideas and practices from the Antilles to Louisiana, it did not foresee the variety of social and symbolic mechanisms by which the system of racial domination would extend its grip and reproduce itself over time. The code provisioned specific punishments against slaves who committed crimes, but it did not order judges to target them as criminals or to cease sentencing white convicts to whipping. In the same way, the law imposed discrimination on freed men and women even though it granted them the same rights as persons born free. The decision whether to incorporate free men of color within military institutions, however, was left to the governor of the colony. Without any legal obligation, religious and administrative authorities also came to systematically identify people according to race in sacramental records, notarial deeds, and censuses. In that regard, the Catholic Church participated equally alongside the state in the racialization of society.

Moreover, the prevalence of racial categorization and discrimination was not only the result of the actions of institutional actors. Both the governor and the *commissaire-ordonnateur*, who could not imagine resorting to any other laborers than slaves for the corvée, and the white servants, who refused to do any heavy work, all held the same conviction about the intersection of labor and race. Likewise, the way the elite walked about town accompanied by domestic slaves while soldiers fought repeatedly with enslaved and free blacks in public shows that a strategy of racial distinction pervaded the whole white social spectrum. Still, a commitment to the racial subordination of people of African descent does not mean that all whites shared the same interests or had the same understanding of white supremacy. The racial hierarchy that came to prevail did not erase and replace all other systems of domination but intersected with them in complex ways.

If all people of European descent participated in the construction of whiteness, whatever their class and gender, it is more difficult to determine to what extent race-thinking was internalized by those it sought to dominate. The appropriation of the language of race by all social actors and the

6. For the idea that the emergence of slavery in Virginia was the result of an "unthinking decision" rather than the result of a premeditated plan to enslave Africans, see Winthrop D. Jordan, *White over Black: American Attitudes toward the Negro, 1550–1812* (Chapel Hill, N.C., 1968), 44–98.

participation of some free black men in the segregated militia company reveal that it was difficult to resist the pervasiveness of race. Slaves and free people of color had no choice but to adapt to the society in which they lived. What made racialization so powerful is that the system rested on institutions and practices that could serve the contradictory interests of both those in power as well as those in a subordinate position.

That racial ideas and practices quickly became pervasive does not mean, however, that the system of racial domination that took shape in Louisiana was not contested and resisted, nor that the identification of individuals and groups was always or exclusively based on racial factors. Nor does it mean that all interactions between social actors were governed by racial prejudice or translated into forms of racial exclusion. Even though racial segregation was part of the social and symbolic tools used to implement the unequal social order in slave societies, it was less a necessity than in post-slave societies because the status of slaves already created a powerful divide. Moreover, racial separation was more difficult to maintain in an urban milieu. Life in a city fostered encounters and exchanges, and people constantly crossed racial barriers: sellers and buyers of all conditions mingled in the marketplace on the levee; white and black children played together in the streets of New Orleans; soldiers often purchased alcohol for slaves who could not go to taverns; sailors and other poor whites came to the enslaved surgeons Jean-Baptiste and Joseph at the King's Hospital for medical care; and métissage was widespread, although it is difficult to evaluate how much of this interracial sex was consensual. Yet the crossing of racial boundaries did not erase them. White people were well aware of what they were doing, and the color line could be reactivated when necessary. They could also choose to ignore the racial divide in some matters and enforce it in others. The discrepancy between sexuality and marriage clearly exemplifies such selective application of racial exclusiveness. Furthermore, intimate relationships often involved a dimension of power. In Louisiana, as in any slave society, sexual violence against enslaved women was instrumental in the imposition of the slave order.

TRANSCENDING THE HISTORIOGRAPHICAL DIVIDE
BETWEEN THE CARIBBEAN AND NORTH AMERICA

Caribbean New Orleans has not only demonstrated that racialization cannot be reduced to issues of métissage or the status of free blacks, the book has also offered a different interpretation of these phenomena from historians who contrast Anglo-North American biracial and Caribbean three-tiered societies as two distinct models. The opposition between North American and Caribbean racial regimes rests on two problematic assumptions. The first concerns métissage. In the historiography, there is often some confusion between the legal prohibition of interracial sexuality and conjugality and the actual existence of métissage. Interracial sexuality could take many forms. Most American colonial slave societies prohibited marriages between whites and blacks or made it a social taboo over time, but there is not one of them in which white people, whether slaveowners or nonslaveholders, did not sexually abuse enslaved women and father mixed-race children. Métissage happened everywhere. Racial prejudice did not prevent white men from raping black women or even from maintaining long-term unions with them. Sally Hemings did bear Thomas Jefferson several children. In the same way, the present craze for DNA tests in the United States reveals how much more complex people's genealogies are than what they initially believe on the basis of how they self-identify. What distinguished American societies with slavery in time and in space is not so much the prevalence of interracial sexuality as the ways people viewed racial-crossing in the sexual sphere: the forms that métissage took, from rape to marriage; the legal sanction or prohibition of mixed unions; the degree to which unsanctioned unions before the church were reproved and kept hidden or tolerated and lived out openly; and the fate of children born to these mixed couples. At the same time, there was a growing tendency in every American society to legally prohibit and socially condemn interracial unions throughout the eighteenth century.[7]

The second problematic assumption has to do with the relationships between manumission and métissage and the emergence of a large group of free people of color. Manumission in itself cannot reveal much about the

7. On the extensive character of interracial sexuality in English colonies, see Jordan, *White over Black*, 136–178; Gary B. Nash, "The Hidden History of Mestizo America," *Journal of American History*, LXXXII (1995), 941–964; Joyce Chaplin, "Race," in David Armitage and Michael Braddick, eds., *The British Atlantic World, 1500–1800* (New York, 2002), 168; and Daniel Livesay, "Emerging from the Shadows: New Developments in the History of Interracial Sex and Intermarriage in Colonial North America and the Caribbean," *History Compass*, XIII (2015), 122–133. For controversies and works that have contributed to publicly reveal the importance of métissage in the antebellum United States beyond historical circles, see Annette Gordon-Reed, *Thomas Jefferson and Sally Hemings: An American Controversy* (Charlottesville, Va., 1997); Jan Ellen Lewis and Peter S. Onuf, eds., *Sally Hemings and Thomas Jefferson: History, Memory, and Civic Culture* (Charlottesville, Va., 1999); Henry Louis Gates, Jr., ed., *Finding Your Roots: The Official Companion to the PBS Series* (Chapel Hill, N.C., 2014); and Gates, *Finding Your Roots, Season 2: The Official Companion to the PBS Series* (Chapel Hill, N.C., 2016).

role of race in a slave society. Most slaveholding societies throughout world history authorized manumission, for the hope of freedom constituted an instrument of social control that masters could use as leverage over those they held in bondage. The propensity of owners to free slaves was not so much related to racial considerations as to a desire to perpetuate the slave order. In fact, the legislation on manumission in both French and English colonies throughout North America and the Caribbean was very similar, as the practice became monitored and limited everywhere. Laws on manumission did differ between Iberian colonies and English and French colonies in that the former allowed for *coartacion* while the latter prohibited slaves from purchasing their own freedom, but it does not mean that such a system did not develop in practice. Moreover, as a rule, most slaves who were freed by their masters were concubines and mixed-race children, no matter the colony or empire to which they belonged. Caribbean planters do not seem to have manumitted their slaves more frequently than those in North America. Natural growth, more than a high rate of manumission, explains the rise in the number of free blacks in the islands.[8]

The development of large groups of free people of color in the Caribbean by the second half of the eighteenth century must be viewed within the context of the unparalleled concentrations of slaves that were present within these small island territories. There were, for instance, 28,000 free blacks and 465,000 slaves in Saint-Domingue in 1789 whereas the total enslaved population in the United States amounted to about 700,000 in 1790. Whites in the Caribbean no less believed that black people ought to be slaves than those in North America. In fact, Edward Long, one of the most famous advocates of racial slavery and polygenist theory in the second half of the eighteenth century, was not a slaveholder from British North America but a Jamaican planter, and he published his *History of Jamaica* (1774), in which he expounded his theory about race, while living in England. Although free people of color in the islands were tolerated because they served as a buffer between masters and slaves, a role fulfilled by whites of the lower sort on the mainland, they still experienced increasing discrimination. In turn, they, too, contributed to sustaining the slave system, for many of them became slaveholders as soon as they could and participated as militiamen in the struggle against maroons and in the military defense of their respective colonies. Occupying the lowest rung of the social hierarchy, below whites

---

8. For the role of manumission in slave systems in world history, see Orlando Patterson, *Slavery and Social Death: A Comparative Study* (Cambridge, Mass., 1982), 209–296.

Conclusion

and free blacks, the large slave majorities in the Caribbean endured a deadly system of racial slavery with no equivalent in North America until the development of the cultivation of sugarcane and cotton during the antebellum period. Caribbean societies were as heavily polarized by race as North American ones in the eighteenth century, even though race did not manifest itself in the same way. In both regions, the racial order aimed at perpetuating slavery, but different racial regimes formed as different slave systems and societies developed according to local circumstances.[9]

Apart from the presence of Native Americans within and outside New Orleans, the greatest differences that separated Louisiana and Saint-Domingue had to do with mixed unions and the treatment of children that resulted from those interracial relationships as well as the status of free blacks. Métissage was more widespread in New Orleans and its plantation region, yet interracial sexuality was closely linked to illegitimacy, and mixed unions and families were kept hidden. Marriage between whites and blacks was almost immediately outlawed in Louisiana, and the law was generally respected. In contrast, no prohibition against interracial sexuality was ever laid down in the French Caribbean. Even so, the lack of legal interdiction did not prevent the number of mixed unions before the church from declining in every island over the course of the eighteenth century, with the exception of Saint-Domingue's southern province. *Ménagères* (female housekeepers who were also often mistresses) were a common feature of Caribbean cities whereas interracial concubinage did not constitute a social institution in New Orleans. Unlike many of their Dominguan counterparts, most white fathers in the Louisiana capital did not officially or publicly recognize their mixed-race offspring. When they did, they more often acknowledged children born from relationships with Native Americans. These dissimilarities, however, were related to contrasting demographic circumstances rather than to divergent conceptions of race. The early legal interdiction of interracial marriage and concubinage in the Mississippi colony was not the result of local developments but of the transfer of a Code Noir from the Antilles, which had been modified in reaction to what had happened in the islands. In both places, unions across the racial divide and mixed-blood

9. For books on free people of color in the French Antilles, see note 27 in the Introduction. For the British West Indies, see, among many studies, Daniel Livesay, *Children of Uncertain Fortune: Mixed-Race Jamaicans in Britain and the Atlantic Family, 1733–1833* (Chapel Hill, N.C., 2018); Melanie J. Newton, *The Children of Africa in the Colonies: Free People of Color in Barbados in the Age of Emancipation* (Baton Rouge, La., 2008); and Christer Petley, "'Legitimacy' and Social Boundaries: Free People of Colour and the Social Order in Jamaican Slave Society," *Social History*, XXX (2005), 481–498.

children were subject to discriminative practices that served the system of racial domination.

In the matter of interracial sexuality and conjugality, Louisiana seems at first sight more like Virginia than Saint-Domingue or even South Carolina. Yet, if the Mississippi colony had fully followed Virginia's model, a biracial society should have maintained itself, and discrimination against free people of color should have increased over time. Instead, a different process took place in Louisiana. The modified Code Noir imported from the Antilles immediately provisioned exclusive measures against free blacks, even though only a few individuals categorized as such lived in the colony at the time of its promulgation. And these articles did not remain a dead letter. The practice of reenslaving a free man or woman of color who had been convicted of criminal activity, for instance, did not occur often during the French regime, but the Superior Council did not hesitate to resort to such a terrible punishment very early on. Then, from the late 1740s, the small number of migrants from Europe and the need for military defense also led local authorities to take some measures to elevate free people of color in the social hierarchy: they granted them lands at the English Turn, and they authorized the formation of a free colored militia company. Although free blacks were generally able to distinguish themselves from slaves, they remained segregated from whites, and they had to move from the city to the countryside. Despite the small number of free people of color present in the colony up to the end of French rule, legal and social practices aimed at developing a three-tiered society while preserving white supremacy. In that regard, Louisiana started to resemble some islands. Its situation was more similar to that of Saint-Domingue than the Lesser Antilles, where free people of color had a tendency to live in cities, as in the British West Indies.

The New Orleans case study thus calls for a renewed approach to racial formation in a comprehensive perspective within the greater Caribbean. In lieu of examining North America and the Antilles as two distinct models, historians should pay more attention to both the discontinuities and continuities between the colonial and slave societies of the two regions. Not all these racial regimes operated in the same way, but commonalities as well as differences were distributed across all colonial boundaries. For plantation management and slave labor, Justin Roberts has underlined that, "given how much of the scholarly literature has tended to generalize about sugar islands while drawing stark contrasts between the Caribbean and the North American colonies, it is important to recognize that Barbadian plantations were, in some ways, more like Virginian than Jamaican plantations. Not only was there significant diversity among the sugar islands but even

Jamaica and Virginia shared a few similarities in this era." We need a similar comparative and connected history of racial formation for all the English and French slave societies of North America and the Caribbean that does not presume clear-cut oppositions between the two regions. This history should also be pursued after the Age of Revolutions. The Louisiana Purchase did not sever the connections between New Orleans and the Antilles. Quite the opposite happened.[10]

THE RETURN OF LOUISIANA REFUGEES IN
SAINT-DOMINGUE TO NEW ORLEANS

The Louisiana capital remained a secondary port city within the Atlantic world for most of the eighteenth century. Then, in the first half of the nineteenth century, cotton and sugar production began to boom, and New Orleans rapidly transformed itself into a global hub. Until then, the Mississippi colony had competed in vain with Saint-Domingue, but the progressive disintegration of the Dominguan sugar economy following the slave revolt in 1791, the abolition of slavery in 1793–1794, and the proclamation of the first black republic under the name of Haiti in 1804 allowed other plantation economies such as Louisiana to thrive. French settlers had started to experiment with cane cultivation and sugar production in the 1740s, but, it was only in the mid-1790s that a new variety of cane better suited for the early winter frosts and the shorter growing season was introduced. With the assistance of a sugar maker from Saint-Domingue, Étienne Boré mastered the granulation of sugar as an economically successful technique. The rapid development of cane plantations in the Mississippi Valley was facilitated by the arrival of new Saint-Dominguan refugees in the following years. One of them was Baudry des Lozières, who had married the daughter of a Louisiana refugee in Saint-Domingue after the 1768 revolt. In the first volume of Baudry des Lozières's travel account, published in 1802–1803, he repeatedly emphasized that the former French territory comprised "excellent lands for sugar that could compete with the best in Saint-Domingue." During the antebellum period, Louisiana came to replace the pearl of the Antilles as one of the world's main producers of sugar.[11]

10. For historians arguing in favor of the need to emphasize discrepancies as well as commonalities between North American and Caribbean systems of slave labor or racial regimes, see Justin Roberts, *Slavery and the Enlightenment in the British Atlantic, 1750–1807* (Cambridge, 2013), 19; and George M. Fredrickson, "From Exceptionalism to Variability: Recent Developments in Cross-National Comparative History," *Journal of American History*, LXXXII (1995), 587–604.

11. Richard Follett, *The Sugar Masters: Planters and Slaves in Louisiana's Cane*

Other Saint-Domingue refugees, such as Claude Joseph Dubreuil, brought with them racial conceptions hardened by the experience of the Haitian Revolution. Dubreuil perfectly embodies the portrait of those refugees drawn by the prefect Laussat. Born to Joseph Dubreuil, a militia captain, and his wife, Jeanne Catherine La Boulaye, the daughter of a military officer, in 1744, he entered the world as part of a notable Louisiana family. His grandfather and namesake had migrated to the colony in 1719 and, by his death in 1757, had become the wealthiest planter in the lower Mississippi Valley. A *cadet à l'aiguillette* (a teenager from the elite in military training who wore a cord on the shoulder, or aiguillette) from 1758, the young Dubreuil was sent to France to enter the Écoles royales d'artillerie (Royal Schools of Artillery) of La Fère in 1763. He then pursued a military career in the Antilles, first in Guadeloupe in 1767 and then in Saint-Domingue from 1770. He served as lieutenant, captain (1771), and then *major* and commandant of artillery (1775). In 1780, he was awarded the Croix de l'ordre de Saint-Louis (Cross of the Order of Saint-Louis).[12]

Still, Dubreuil remained closely connected to Louisiana. In 1773, he took a leave of absence and returned to New Orleans to take care of some family affairs. In a letter to the minister of the navy, he asked for assistance to "rescue my father and my sisters from the destitution, the slavery and the domination of their [Spanish] persecutors." The same year, he was appointed by the governor of Saint-Domingue as one of two men designated to represent the Louisiana refugees. In 1777, he was also chosen by the intendant of the island, after the conclusion of a trade agreement between France and Spain, to be one of two French commissioners who would reside in New Orleans and deliver passports authorizing French ships to load merchandise for the Antilles. During his stay in the Louisiana capital, Dubreuil married Marie-Eulalie Livaudais, the widow of the merchant Pierre Saint-Pé, in 1779. Although the trade agreement was canceled in 1785, he remained three more

World, 1820–1860 (Baton Rouge, La., 2005); Adam Rothman, *Slave Country: American Expansion and the Origins of the Deep South* (Cambridge, Mass., 2005); Glenn R. Conrad and Ray F. Lucas, *White Gold: A Brief History of the Louisiana Sugar Industry, 1795–1995* (Lafayette, La., 1995); Charley Richard, "200 Years of Progress in the Louisiana Sugar Industry: A Brief History," *Sugar Journal*, no. 9 (February 1995), 12–13; [Louis-Narcisse Baudry Des Lozières], *Voyage à la Louisiane, et sur le continent de l'Amérique septentrionale, fait dans les années 1794 à 1798* (Paris, 1802), 255 (quotation).

12. Henry P. Dart, "The Career of Dubreuil in French Louisiana," *LHQ*, XVIII (1935), 267–331; Earl C. Wood and Charles E. Nolan, eds., *Sacramental Records of the Roman Catholic Church of the Archdiocese of New Orleans*, I, *1718–1750* (New Orleans, 1987), 86–87.

years in New Orleans for financial reasons. He left a few weeks after the great fire of March 1788. Having lost most of his fortune in the fire, he resumed his military career in Saint-Domingue as major of Léogane.[13]

The French Revolution caught Dubreuil in the island. A royalist, he was banished from the colony and moved to Jamaica. In 1793, he participated in the British conquest and occupation of the western part of Saint-Domingue and, from August 1795, was a member of the new Conseil privé (Privy Council) of the English government at Port-au-Prince. He left Saint-Domingue with the English in 1798 and took refuge, first in Kingston, then in Philadelphia, and, finally, in New Orleans, where he rejoined family members who had stayed in Louisiana. It is impossible to know if his white relatives kept in touch with the free women of color who descended from the illegitimate union his grandfather had maintained with his domestic slave Marie Ann alias Nanette. Dubreuil's grandfather never manumitted his mistress and their children but instead willed them to his son Joseph. Nanette had to redeem herself and to purchase one of her two daughters, but all of her surviving children eventually managed to obtain their freedom.[14]

A member of the first territorial assembly held after Louisiana's purchase by the United States, Dubreuil was very disappointed by the result of the census that prevented the promotion of Louisiana to statehood in 1806. In the draft of a discourse he prepared for his colleagues to defend a new act of legislation, which might have been inspired by his own family history, he lamented the weakness of the marital institution, decrying those white men who preferred to maintain illegitimate relationships with slaves and free women of color. Implicitly predicting a new Haitian Revolution, he warned

13. "Joseph Dubreuil-Villars, major à Saint-Domingue, 1744–1791," ANOM COL E 141 (quotation).

14. On Dubreuil's exile, see Stanley Clisby Arthur and George Campbell Huchet de Kernion, *Old Families of Louisiana* (1931; rpt. Baltimore, 2009), 104–111; Debien and Le Gardeur, "Les colons de Saint-Domingue réfugiés à la Louisiane," *Revue de Louisiane/Louisiana Review*, IX (1980), 115–117, X (1981), 13–14; Jacques de Cauna-Ladevie, "La diaspora des colons de Saint-Domingue et le monde créole: Le cas de la Jamaïque," *Revue française d'histoire d'outre-mer*, LXXXI (1994), 333–359; and David Patrick Geggus, *Slavery, War, and Revolution: The British Occupation of Saint Domingue, 1793–1798* (Oxford, 1982), 273, 400, 439n. On Dubreuil's relatives among free people of color (Marie Ann's daughters, Cécile and Marianne, were the great-grandmother and great-aunt of Henriette Delille, a free woman of color who founded the African American congregation of the Sisters of the Holy Family in 1842), see Virginia Meacham Gould, "Henriette Delille, Free Women of Color, and Catholicism in Antebellum New Orleans, 1727–1852," in David Barry Gaspar and Darlene Clark Hine, eds., *Beyond Bondage: Free Women of Color in the Americas* (Urbana, Ill., 2004), 271–285.

of the danger of letting the group of free blacks grow to the detriment of the white population. The same year, the Louisiana Territorial Assembly voted "a new slave code ... that was among the most comprehensive and severe in the antebellum South."[15]

Dubreuil's life history demonstrates how the continual movements back and forth between Louisiana and Saint-Domingue throughout the French, Spanish, and early American periods informed racial formation in the Mississippi Valley. Anglo-Americans did not bring race with them to New Orleans after the Louisiana Purchase. Racial ideas and practices had come to the city from the Antilles from the moment of Louisiana's founding and continued to circulate afterward between Saint-Domingue and the Mississippi colony. Caribbean connections are one of the strongest threads that weave their way through New Orleans history.

15. For Dubreuil's discourse, see Joseph Villars Dubreuil Papers, 1760–1850, no. 18, Perkins Library, Duke University, Durham, N.C. On the 1806 slave code, see Paul F. Lachance, "The Politics of Fear: French Louisianians and the Slave Trade, 1786–1809," *Plantation Society in the Americas*, I (1979), 184.

Index

Abbadie, Jean-Jacques Blaise d', 210, 347, 411, 476

Acolapissa (nation), 100, 103. *See also* Native Americans

African slaves: construction of the levee by, 2; in Brazil, 10; in Barbados, 11; demand for, 15; and race, 30, 110, 305–306, 312, 471; introduction of, in the Caribbean, 49, 81, 85, 302, 305; connection of, to Africa, 58, 73, 91–92, 470–479; as majority by the early 1730s, 58; and Native Americans, 103, 107, 109, 131, 423–424; as runaways, 131; and social control, 417; relations of, with Creole slaves, 479–480; ethnicities of, 464–481. *See also* Angola; Arada (Ewe-Fon) (nation); Bambara (nation); Beafada (nation); Cerer (Sereer) (nation); Colonial situation; Congo (nation); Congo (region); Foëda (Hweda) (nation); Fond (Ewe-Fon) (nation); Guinea; Guinea Coast; Guinée (nation); Mandingue (Mandigo or Malinke) (nation); Mina (nation); Nago (Yoruba) (nation); Poulard (Fulbe) (nation); Quiamba (Chamba) (nation); Senegal (nation); Senegal (region); Senegambia; Slave trade from Africa; Slave trade from Antilles; Wolof (nation)

Allevin, François, 255

Amyault Dausseville, Raymond, 259, 278, 279, 398

Ancien régime society: and culture of appearances, 4, 144, 147, 173, 181, 281–282, 241, 349, 356; and conception of city, 22, 95, 97; and honor, 25, 43–44, 113, 150, 153–154, 157, 171, 173–175, 177, 240–241, 247, 256, 282, 333–334, 338, 344, 348, 353, 355, 368, 371, 394, 415, 439–440; and nobility, 36, 54, 59, 61–62, 123, 152, 157–158, 224, 305, 315, 318, 347–356, 360; and racial slavery, 36, 226, 399, 430; bestiary of, 110; and culture of violence, 111, 139, 171–172, 399, 408; and culture of rank, 122, 124, 147, 149–159, 171, 305, 331, 348–350, 352, 365, 367–368, 419; and political culture, 138, 387–388, 445–446, 483, 487–494; and drinking houses, 163; and confinement of poor people, 232; and ideal of Christian marriage, 247–249; and conception of labor, 304–305; and conception of commerce, 331, 333–334, 344, 347–356, 360, 367–368; and self-identification of white settlers, 383–384

Angola, 57

Antilles, 1, 7–9, 18–19, 24, 36–37, 46–47, 49–50, 58, 63–65, 71, 73–76, 78–79, 85, 87, 91–92, 98, 122, 131, 149, 156, 159, 176, 203–204, 206, 250–251, 257, 260, 266, 269, 271, 281–283, 288, 292, 302–303, 305, 311–312, 314, 317, 326–327, 339, 347, 373, 378, 397, 399, 401, 410, 418, 422–423, 428, 441–442, 455, 465, 467, 474, 476–477,

479, 488, 494, 501–502, 505, 509–512, 514; French islands of, 24, 35–36, 46, 49, 57, 77, 84–85, 136, 201, 366, 375, 378, 433, 466, 494. *See also* West Indies

Antoine (free black sailor), 43–44, 71

Arada (Ewe-Fon) (nation), 470. *See also* African slaves

Aram, Marie (slave, wife of Tiocou), 264

Argenson, René-Louis Voyer de Paulmy marquis d', 490

Artaguiette, Pierre d', 64

Aubry, Charles Philippe, 158, 211, 220, 366, 463, 484, 489, 492

Aufrère, Marie-Thérèse, 123, 131

Aury, Jean-Baptiste. *See* Horry, Jean-Baptiste

Babé (wife of Joseph Meunier), 436

Bacchus (slave of Mr. Boisclair), 265

Baldic, Théodore, 212

Bambara (nation), 115, 140, 445, 466, 470–471, 475–476, 478, 480. *See also* African slaves; Slave revolt

Bancio Piemont, Jean-Baptiste, 337

Baptiste (Natchez slave), 167

Barbados, 6, 11–12

Barbin (planter), 279, 478

Barbot, Baptiste, 174

Barracks: construction and maintenance of, 99, 148–149, 238–239, 299, 323, 359; and public ceremonies, 152; housing of soldiers in, 180, 187, 240, 254; and slaves, 187–188, 215, 221, 239–240, 242, 307, 360–361; housing of indentured servants in, 193, 295–296; and discipline of soldiers, 238–239. *See also* Military officers; Soldiers

Bassouvant (slave), 469

Battar (ship's officer), 172, 348–349, 398

Baudeau, Nicolas, 487

Baude dit de Marseille, Jacques Toussaint, 73

Baudreau dit Graveline, Jean-Baptiste, 439

Baudry des Lozières, Louis-Narcisse, 496, 511

Bayogoula (nation), 103. *See also* Native Americans

Beafada (nation), 470, 473. *See also* African slaves; Senegambia

Beaubois, Ignace de (Father), 222

Beauvais, Antoine, 295

Beccaria-Bonesana, Ceasare, 408

Belache (merchant), 170

Bellisle, François Simard de, 358, 428–429

Bénac (military officer), 174

Benoît de Saint-Clair, Jean-Baptiste, 349–350

Bernard, Pierre, 255

Bernard, Raphaël, 295, 414

Bernier, François, 85–86

Bernou, Claude, 46

Berthelot, Mathias, 170, 279–280

Bienville, Jean-Baptiste Le Moyne de, 18, 75–76, 99–100, 117, 120, 128, 134, 141, 150, 154, 156, 193, 208, 249, 253, 289, 311, 318, 331, 414, 424–425, 434, 439, 452–453, 458, 496

Biloxi (nation), 103, 107. *See also* Native Americans

Biloxi (outpost), 49, 117, 413

Boisclair (Sieur), 265, 474

Boispinel, de (engineer), 299

Boissinot (sieur), 170

Bordeaux, 55, 68, 183, 312, 482

Boré, Étienne, 511

Bossu, Jean-Bernard, 81–82, 353–354, 373–374, 450, 456–457, 459, 472, 485

Boyer, Pierre, 432

Braquier (militia captain), 344

Bridgetown (Barbados), 6, 35

Brosset (sieur), 341

Broutin, François Ignace, 336
Bruslé (Mr.), 252
Buffon (dame), 212
Buffon, Georges-Louis Leclerc de, 457
Buquois dit Plaisance, Henry, 404
Bunel, Dominique, 322

Cahura-Joligo, Chief, 111–112. *See also* Tonica (nation)
Caillot, Marc-Antoine, 50, 80, 83, 103, 105–112, 114, 217, 244–245, 249, 305, 335
Calfat, Anne Marthe, 436, 438
Calfat, Constance, 436
Calfat, Geneviève, 436
Calfat, Pierre, 436
Calfat, Simon, 429, 431, 434–438
Calfat, Zacharie, 436
Canada, 8, 22, 47, 49, 64–65, 82, 106, 108, 111, 114, 120, 137, 149, 154, 156, 223, 249, 250, 257, 313, 392, 415–416, 424, 439, 444–445, 448–449, 451–452, 454, 457–458
Canelle (or Canel), Pierre, 437
Cannelle, Magdelaine (free woman of color), 437
Cap-Français, 6, 35, 43, 50–51, 60, 71, 75, 80–81, 83, 110, 135, 140, 169, 203, 211, 223, 230, 346, 359, 379, 459, 472, 500, 503
Capuchins: as missionaries, 36, 123, 214, 379; plantation of, 123; slave baptisms by, 128, 160, 265–266, 268; convent of, 148; and elite rivalries, 156–157; and slave funerals, 159; as slaveholders, 167, 272, 326; and assistance, 214, 231; and management of the Military and Charity Hospitals, 215, 231–232, 234, 264; and métissage, 246, 268–269, 272; and marriage of free or enslaved people of color, 255, 258, 261, 265; and Native Americans, 374; and Bienville, 453. *See also* Dagobert (Father, su-

perior of the Capuchins); Mathias (Father); Raphaël (Father); Slave evangelization
Caribbean (Sea), 8, 47, 463
Carlier (sieur), 357, 478
Carolinas. *See* South Carolina
Carresse, Pierre, 495
Carrière (demoiselle), 109
Carrière, Joseph, 127, 473
Carrière, Marie-Thérèse (free woman of color), 262–263
Carrière, Noël, 204
Carrière Malozé, Jacques, 251
Catherine (slave of François Hery Duplanty), 274
Cavelier de la Salle, René-Robert, 46, 493
Cazenave (military officer), 439
Ceirac (straw man of Pradel), 352
Censuses: as primary sources, 37; production of, 37, 187–189, 192, 242, 402, 418; and population of New Orleans, 119–122; categories used in, 190–199, 242, 377, 384, 505; slaves and free people of color in, 190–192, 195–197, 199–205, 320–321, 377, 388, 427, 429–430, 433–437; Native Americans in, 190–192, 197, 199, 200, 375; convicts in, 193, 291; white workers in, 193, 296–297, 301; medical staff in, 218; boys and girl of marriageable age in, 249; ethnic identities of people of European descent in, 300, 421, 448, 450–451; use of, by colonial authorities, 305; in territorial Louisiana, 513
Cerer (Sereer) (nation), 470, 472–473, 479. *See also* African slaves
César (slave), 132, 139, 476, 478
César (Vaudreuil's slave), 175
César, Jules (free man of color), 436, 438
Chabillard (lieutenant), 358
Chamilly (dame), 208

Chantalou, Augustin, 337–338, 343
Chaoucha (nation), 103, 107. *See also* Native Americans
Chaperon, Joseph, 208, 325
Chapitoulas, 202, 299, 434–435, 503
Charity Hospital: enslaved laborers of, 132, 234, 264, 277, 401, 412, 478; as refuge for abused and destitute women, 213, 231–233; and race, 215, 230, 242; donations to, 231, 233, 342; early 1760s reorganization of, 233–243, 410
Charles, alias Karacou, alias Charlot (slave), 479–480
Charleston, 6, 23, 124, 167, 313, 360, 500, 503
Charlotte (free woman of color, wife of Étienne Maréchal), 433, 435, 440
Charlotte (slave of Mme d'Erneville), 325
Charpentier dit Le Roy, Jacques, 398
Chassin, 99
Chateauguay, Antoine Lemoyne, 64–65
Chaumont, Jacqueline, 232
Chauvin de Beaulieu (planter), 439
Chauvin Desilles, Constance Louise, 437
Chavannes, Jean-Baptiste, 275–277
Chéreau, François, 94–95, 101, 140
Chevalier dit Lachaume, Jean-Baptiste, 312–313
Chickasaw (nation), 424, 445, 475. *See also* Chickasaw Wars of 1736 and 1739
Chickasaw Wars of 1736 and 1739, 15, 64, 98, 115–116, 120, 141, 350, 415, 417, 419, 424, 426, 429, 431
Chitimacha (nation), 103. *See also* Native Americans
Choctaw (nation), 98–99, 102, 104, 117, 138, 458. *See also* Native Americans

Choiseul, Étienne-François de, 346, 488
Choiseul-Praslin, César Gabriel de, 482
Code Noir, 1685: and transfer of racial ideas and practices to Louisiana, 14, 37, 91, 441, 505, 509–510; diffusion of, in the Caribbean, 84–88; and race, 86–87; preeminence of, over Louisiana code, 90, 399; slaves as witnesses in, 397. *See also* Code Noir, 1724
Code Noir, 1724: and bearing arms, 43; promulgation of, 46, 84–85, 88, 384, 393; innovations of, from the 1685 code, 87, 332, 365; preeminence of, over local rulings, 89–90; diffusion of, in Saint-Domingue, 90–91; slaves as witnesses in, 147, 261, 397–398; and public space, 147; and burials, 159–160; and vigilantism, 178–180; and prohibition against settlement of Jews, 183; and evangelization, 247; and métissage, 247, 268, 486–487; and slave marriage, 259–269; and manumission, 269, 365, 413–414; and free people of color, 280, 412, 441, 510; and slaves' economy, 360–361, 364; and racial categories, 371, 375, 385–388; title of, 375, 492; and provision against abuse of slaves, 401; and punishment of slaves, 403–406, 487, 505. *See also* Code Noir, 1685
Colonial situation: and the confrontation between Natives, Europeans, and African slaves, 5, 94–95, 140, 373, 454; and the socioracial order, 5, 97; and Natchez Wars, 17; and trade, 112; and African experiences, 473; and the metropole, 493
Compagnies franches de la Marine. *See* Soldiers

Congo, Louis, 220, 414

Congo (nation), 469–470, 479. *See also* African slaves

Congo (region), 57

Convicts: as part of the workforce on plantations in the seventeenth century, 11; as part of the 1717–1721 migratory wave to Louisiana, 13, 54–56, 166, 253, 288–289, 304, 328; and destitute women, 56, 166, 193, 253, 291, 391; and New Orleans's founding, 99, 193, 290, 296; and disorder and crime, 133, 391–392, 395, 407; in censuses, 193; and Company of the Indies policy, 291–292; and Bohemians, 300, 312–313, 421. *See also* Chevalier dit Lachaume, Jean-Baptiste; La Prairie, Jean-Philippe

Corbin de la Touche, Jeanne Marie, 337

Cordier, Marie, 143, 146

Coustilhas, Jacques de, 341, 350

Coyer, Gabriel François, 353

Creole slaves: rising demographic importance of, 19, 131, 445, 465, 468; as runaways, 131, 405; and masters, 277; identification of individuals as, 360, 363, 447, 467, 473–474, 478; relations of, with Creole settlers, 447; divisions among, 465, 480–481; relations of, with slaves from the Antilles, 477; relations of, with African slaves, 479–480

Cuba, 20, 82, 93, 498

Cupidon (slave of sieur Carlier), 357

Dagobert (Father, superior of the Capuchins), 160, 265, 272

Darby, Jonathan, 293, 461–462

Darensbourg, Marguerite, 158

Dartel alias Francœur, Nicolas, 341

Degle dit Malborough, Étienne, 451

Dégout, Pierre, 255, 285

Dégouté dit Fleury, Pierre. *See* Dégout, Pierre

Delille dit Dupart, Pierre, 319

Demorand (Mademoiselle), 62

Desmorières (Monsieur), 252

Desruisseau (Sieur), 377

Destréhan, Jean-Baptiste, 158

Digueny alias Marie (slave of Sieur Boisclair), 474

Diron Dartaguiette, Bernard, 64, 279–280

Dorgon (commandant), 312–313

Dorville (Mr.), 287

Dreaux (Mister), 99

Dubois-Duclos, Jean-Baptiste, 376

Dubreuil, 279, 479

Dubreuil, Claude-Joseph (grandson of the first Dubreuil, Claude Joseph), 512–514

Dubreuil, Claude Joseph (Villars), 179–180, 402, 512

Dubreuil, Joseph, 321, 419, 512

Dubuc, Jean-Baptiste, 346

Dubuisson (sieur), 303

Duby, Toinette, 255

Dumont de Montigny, Jean-François-Benjamin, 50, 64, 80–81, 97–98, 100, 104–105, 109, 119–120, 141, 306, 315, 318–319, 323, 329–331, 333–334, 344, 359, 365, 421, 452–453

Duplanty, François Hery, 274

Durantais, Étienne, 341, 362

Duverger de Saint-Sauveur, Xavier, 43–44

English Turn, 15, 136, 202–203, 235, 264, 315, 359, 422, 426–430, 434, 436, 503, 510

Erneville, Charles d', 204

Erneville, Pierre Henri d', 172–173, 398

Fanchonette (slave of Gracia Monsanto), 184

Faucon Dumanoir, Jean-Baptiste, 295
Faugère, Louis, 394–395
Favrot (military officer), 324
Fazende, Jacques, 310
Fazende, René Gabriel, 211, 252
Ferrand, Pierre, 173–174
Filand (settler), 212
Fleuriau, François, 89, 172–173, 252, 291, 294, 323, 345, 349, 423
Foëda (Hweda) (nation), 470. *See also* African slaves
Fond (Ewe-Fon) (nation), 470. *See also* African slaves
Fontaine-Mervé (officer), 425
Forstall, Nicolas, 337
Foucault, Denis-Nicolas, 143, 146, 158, 377
Fourgueux, Jean-Baptiste, 122
Fox (nation), 15. *See also* Native Americans
Francisque (slave), 480–481
François (slave), 377
François (slave), 479
François (slave of Bernard Vielle), 324
François (slave of Jean-Baptiste Raguet), 129
François (slave of Sieur Boisclair), 473–474
François alias Cariton (slave), 167
Free blacks. *See* Free people of color
Free people of color: emergence of an elite group of, 19, 430–441; number of, 20, 164, 203, 205, 464, 510; and opposition between biracial and three-tiered societies, 20, 23–24, 33–34, 510–511; and military service, 37, 116, 371, 415–416, 422–430, 506, 508; and justice, 38, 390, 412–414, 510; violence by, as male outsiders, 43–44, 172, 177–178; migrations of, from France, 65; migrations of, from the Antilles, 77, 433, 498; legal status of, 87, 90, 161, 387–388, 412, 497; and urban culture, 125, 133; settlement of, at the English Turn, 136, 359, 422, 426–430, 434–435, 503, 510; and interracial sociability, 168–169, 506; in censuses, 190–192, 201–205; as *libres de fait*, 203–205, 365; dependency of, on former masters, 209–210, 242, 431, 433, 439, 503; female, 223, 259, 262–265, 270–272, 276–279, 341–342, 382–383, 412–414, 432–440, 513; exclusion of, from public assistance, 230, 233, 242; marriages and families of, 257, 262–265, 283, 436; as indentured servants, 295, 433; and urban grants, 296, 433–434; as traders, 359, 361, 435; and ethnic and racial categories, 377, 382–383, 387–390, 466, 470. *See also* Calfat, Simon; Larue, Étienne; Manumission; St. Louis alias La Nuit; Tiocou, François
Fremeur, marquis de (military officer), 263
French Revolution, 497–513. *See also* Haitian Revolution

Gaillardy (Mr.), 476
Gallot, Marie Françoise, 336
Gamon, de (Mr., captain), 311
Garic, Jean-Baptiste, 337
Garnier (Madame), 256
Gauvery, Marie Elizabeth de, 158
Gauvin, Antoine, 274
George (slave), 73
German Coast, 15, 125, 130, 136, 158, 343, 359, 384, 430, 451, 458
Gervais (born Beaudrau), Marie Catherine, 342
Gonichon (engineer), 145
Gorée, 43, 57, 470
Goudeau, François, 343
Goudeau, Marie Pascal, 343–344
Grandmaison, de (major of New Orleans), 369
Grandpré (dame), 208

Graveline (sieur), 208

Grevenberg dit Flamand, Jean-Baptiste, 343

Grimaldi, Jerónimo, 494

Gruy Verloins, Antoine Valentin de, 123

Guadeloupe, 47, 86, 161, 212, 346, 360, 378, 512

Gueula (slave of Étienne Périer), 403–404

Guillory, François, 273

Guillory, Jean, 273–274

Guinault (militia captain), 344

Guinea, 472–473. *See also* Guinea Coast

Guinea Coast, 466, 472. *See also* Guinea

Guinée (nation), 470. *See also* African slaves; Guinea; Guinea Coast

Gulf of Mexico, 4, 8, 47, 49–50, 71–72, 94, 463, 494

Guyana, 84, 87, 328; Dutch colony of, 410

Hachard, Marie Madeleine, 94, 223, 225, 227, 253, 260, 370, 372, 391–392

Haiti, 498, 511

Haitian Revolution, 497–498, 512–513. *See also* French Revolution

Hardy alias La Vierge, Jean-Pierre, 174

Hardy de Boisblanc, Pierre, 337

Haultz, Thomas, 429, 433–435

Haultz, Pierre, 429, 433–435

Havana, 6, 43, 51, 66, 71, 73, 82, 262, 429, 464, 496

Hemings, Sally (slave), 507

Henri IV, 47

Herbert, Joseph, 394–395

Hiliard d'Auberteuil, Michel-René, 172

Hocquart (Mr.), 154

Houma (nation), 100, 103. *See also* Native Americans

Horry, Jean-Baptiste, 437–438

Hos, Thomas. *See* Haultz, Thomas

Hugon, Marie Joseph, 439

Hurson, Charles-Martin, 78, 271

Iberville, Pierre Le Moyne d', 49

Illinois (nation), 354, 386, 445. *See also* Native Americans

Illinois Country, 4, 13, 15, 53, 64, 84, 103, 115, 120, 131, 137, 140, 224, 270, 323, 339–340, 342, 349, 353–354, 385–386, 420, 433, 445, 478, 480

Indentured servants: as main workforce on plantations in the seventeenth century, 10–11, 49; as part of the 1717–1721 migratory wave to Louisiana, 13, 54–56, 194, 288–289, 328, 339, 461; declining number of, 13, 56–57, 120, 288–289, 302–303; scattered arrival of, 75; settlement of, in New Orleans, 120, 296–297; in taverns, 163; in censuses, 190, 193, 195, 197–199, 384; employed by the Company of the Indies, 193, 195, 290, 292; and soldiers, 237; housed in barracks, 238; and crime, 287, 293, 393; and Company of the Indies policy, 292–295; and free people of color, 295, 364; and race, 312, 327; and class, 369–370. *See also* Bernard, Raphaël; Ozanne, Jacques; Zeringue, Mickael (Michel)

Indian Country, 15, 98, 105, 373

Irisse, Geneviève (free woman of color), 259

Iroquois (nation), 49, 108, 111, 114, 416. *See also* Native Americans

Jacob (slave of Mr. La Chaise), 285, 287

Jacques (indentured servant), 287

Jacques Zacharie dit Grand Jacquot (free colored militiaman), 429, 434, 436

Jadard de Beauchamp, Jean, 475

Jamaica, 6, 23, 51–52, 69, 128, 283, 395, 410, 433, 486, 502, 508, 510, 513

Janot (slave), 128, 131, 479

Jassemin (slave), 130

Jean (free black man), 202

Jean-Baptiste (enslaved surgeon and apothecary), 218–221, 363, 506

Jean-Baptiste (free black indentured servant), 364

Jean-Baptiste (slave), 479

Jean-Baptiste (slave of Jean Trudeau), 413

Jean-Louis (founder of the Charity Hospital), 231

Jeanne Marie (wife of Thomas Haultz), 433

Jeanneton (former slave of François Trudeau), 208

Jeanneton (slave of the King's Hospital), 218

Jefferson, Thomas, 507

Jesuits: and the cultivation of sugar, 91; and the arrival of Ursulines to Louisiana, 222; as the Ursulines' spiritual director, 228; and slave marriage, 260; relations of, with the Capuchins, 379; and French-Native unions, 403–404; expulsion of, 487. *See also* Beaubois, Ignace de (Father)

Jorge (former slave of Bienville), 208–209

Jos (slave of Sr. Stuart), 377

Joseph (slave), 129

Joseph (slave, son of Jean-Baptiste, enslaved surgeon), 218–220, 363–364, 506

Joseph (slave employed by Jean-Baptiste Raguet), 127

Jourdan, Louis, 274

Judice, Jacques, 168, 461

Judice, Nicolas, 173–174, 462

Jupiter (slave of Jean-Charles de Pra-del), 129, 168, 240, 326, 357, 360–364, 402, 406, 479

Kenet (slave), 469

Kerlérec, Louis Billouart de, 63, 70, 77, 136–137, 151–152, 186, 216, 239, 302, 345–347, 352–354, 398, 417, 419–420, 428, 476

King's Hospital. *See* Military Hospital

Kingston (Jamaica), 6, 23, 35, 500, 503, 513

Kolly, Jean-Daniel de, 264, 335

La Balise, 49–50, 68–69, 277, 280, 426, 477

Laboissière, 341

La Boulaye, Jeanne Catherine, 512

La Chaise, Alexandrine de, 61

La Chaise, Antoine de, 461

La Chaise, Charles Auguste de, 158

La Chaise, Jacques de (royal commissioner), 61, 150, 156, 158, 252–253, 275, 296, 303–305, 308, 335, 337, 377, 452, 457

La Chaise, Jacques de (storekeeper), 158, 285, 337

La Chaise, Pélagie de, 337

La Clef (wife of Fontanne), 341

Lacombe, Joseph, 432, 434, 438

Lacombe, Pierre, 432

Lacoste (sieur), 369

La Farine, Chief, 113

La Frénière, Nicolas, 138, 158, 233, 285, 351, 411–412, 475–477, 484, 487, 495

Lamoureux alias Mégret, Michel, 126–127, 377

Lange, Guillaume Jacques Nicolas, 128–129, 343, 403, 439

Lange, Marie-Rose, 343–344

Langliche, Jacques, 437

Langlois, Bonaventure François, 293

Langlois, Marie, 77, 167

Langlois dit Lajoye, Jacques, 234

Laoursot, Joseph, 470

La Pommeray (Madame), 263
La Pommeray, de (treasurer of the navy), 159
La Prairie, Jean-Philippe, 300
La Prairie, Marie Jeanne, 300, 341
Larché, Jacques, 208
La Rochelle, 55, 60, 67–69, 336–337, 343–344, 482
Larose (free black man), 413
Larue, Étienne, 177–178, 472
Lassus, Jean-Pierre, 101
Laussat, Pierre-Clément de, 498–499, 512
Lavergne, François (or Jacob), 273
Law, John, 47, 52, 289
Le Blanc (storekeeper), 252
Le Blanc, Louis-Claude, 330
Le Blond de La Tour, Pierre, 276, 299
Le Bretton (sieur), 62
Leclert, Louis Claude, 277
Le Normant de Mézy, Sébastien François Ange, 65, 89, 175–176, 225, 398
Le Page du Pratz, Antoine-Simon, 50, 81–83, 95, 114–117, 130, 140, 178, 207, 219–220, 260, 455–456, 471–472
Le Sassier (sieur), 482
Lesser Antilles, 14, 78, 84–87, 161, 164, 268, 303, 377, 388, 477, 510
Levees: destruction of, 1; construction of, 1–2, 193, 240, 314, 317; as typical urban place, 3–5, 148; as marketplace, 4, 42, 326, 339, 359–361, 506; as place of sociability, 4, 106, 146, 149, 171, 175, 363, 481; as road, 4, 130, 173, 175; as refuge for runaways, 132; as location of public festivities, 152
Léveillé, Joseph, 262–263
Lhomer, Jean-Baptiste Marcelain, 183–186, 377
Livaudais, Marie-Eulalie, 512
Loisel, Pierre Paul, 298
Long, Edward, 508

Lorient, 43, 55, 68, 71
Louboey, Henry de, 154, 256
Louis XIII, 47
Louis XIV, 52, 494
Louis XV, 67, 90, 117, 154, 482, 487, 490, 492
Louis (slave of Carlier), 357
Louis alias Foÿ or Foÿe (slave), 132–133, 140, 234, 407, 442, 476, 478
Louis dit Sansquartier (slave), 218–219
Louise (free woman of color), 437
Louis François (free man of color), 270
Louisiana Affair, 70, 186, 345–346, 353
Louisiana purchase, 1803: 20, 498, 511, 513–514
Louison (enslaved witness), 132
Louison (free woman of color), 265
Louison (slave, wife of the enslaved surgeon Jean-Baptiste), 218–221
Loyola, Joseph de, 464

Macandal (slave), 408, 410, 477
Macarty, Barthélémy de, 420
Macnemara, Barthélémy, 344
Mama Comba (slave), 476, 478
Mandingue (Mandigo or Malinke) (nation), 445, 470, 478. See also African slaves
Manumission: and self-purchase, 20, 42, 204, 365, 368, 508, 513; and race, 25, 202, 282, 387–388, 507–509; importance of, in cities, 26, 205, 243, 503; regulation of, 87, 203, 365, 387, 413; for military service, 136, 234, 264, 423, 431; and recording of freedom papers, 203–204, 276, 413–414; approval of, by colonial authorities, 203–204, 208, 264, 276, 413–414; in wills, 205, 277–280; as social control, 205, 209–210, 242–243, 503; for good service, 208–209, 277–278;

of royal slaves, 220; at baptism or marriage, 264–265, 270–271; and métissage, 275–280, 284, 432, 508; for service as executioner, 399. *See also* Free people of color

Marcel (former lawyer of the Parlement of Paris), 488

Maréchal, Étienne, 369, 433, 435–436

Margot (slave of Joseph Carrière), 127

Marguerite (a slave freed by Louis Rançon), 271

Marguerite (free woman of color), 342

Margueritte (a Congo slave), 479

Marianne (former slave of Claude Vignon dit La Combe), 432

Marianne (slave of Jean-Baptiste Prévost), 127

Marie (free woman of color), 34

Marie (slave of Bienville), 208–209

Marie Angélique alias Isabelle Chavannes (former slave of Jean-Baptiste Chavannes), 275–276

Marie Ann alias Nanette (slave of Claude Joseph Dubreuil), 513

Marie Anne (wife of Nicolas Dartel alias Francœur), 341

Marie-Jeanne (slave of Mr. Volant), 270

Marie-Jeanne alias Jeannette (free woman of color sentenced to re-enslavement), 234, 341–342, 412–413, 436

Marie-Joseph (daughter of the enslaved surgeon Jean-Baptiste), 218

Marie Joseph (slave), 469

Marie Joseph (slave of Joseph Carrière), 473

Marie Louise (slave), 377

Marie Louise (slave of the King's Hospital), 436

Marly, Jean-Baptiste, 168

Marquis, Pierre, 461, 492, 495

Marronnage. *See* Runaways

Marseille, 68, 73, 450, 482

Martinique, 6, 47, 58, 64–65, 72, 74–78, 86, 91–92, 149, 161, 167, 183, 203, 269, 271, 286, 337, 346, 348, 350, 378, 410, 418–419, 433, 439, 463, 468, 474, 476–477

Masson (soldier), 312–313

Masters: Company of the Indies and king as, 37, 116, 215, 218–220, 238, 306–308, 310, 313, 325, 399–400, 475. *See also* Capuchins; Manumission; Merchants; Métissage; Military officers; Plantations; Slave domestics; Slave punishment; Ursulines; Whiteness

Mathias (Father), 159

Mathieu de St François Xavier, Madeleine, 227

Maurepas, Jean-Frédéric Phélypeaux comte de, 68

Maurepas (fort). See Biloxi (outpost)

Melun (Melin) dit Lagrange alias Bourguignon, Jean, 291

Membrède, Jean-Baptiste de, 170

Merchants: in the metropole, 18, 67–72, 312, 336; in the colony, 45, 312, 335–336; and the Spanish trade, 51, 93; as members of the colonial elite, 65, 123, 152, 158, 234, 337–338, 344, 368, 420–421, 512; in Saint-Domingue, 73, 78; migration of, to Louisiana, 75–77, 183, 336; and the slave trade, 78, 350, 486; in South Carolina, 124; and slaves, 170, 184–186, 270–271, 320–321, 324, 326–327, 338, 360, 463–462; as fiscal category, social group, and community, 315, 344–347; and race, 328; kinds of, 334, 338–340; and women, 341–344, 349; involvement of, in 1768 revolt, 366–368, 482, 486, 489, 491, 495–496; and class, 369–370. *See also* Bancio Piemont, Jean-Baptiste; Forstall, Nicolas;

Gervais (born Beaudrau), Marie Catherine; Grevenberg dit Flamand, Jean-Baptiste; Milhet, Jean; Milhet, Joseph; Monsanto, Isaac Rodriguez; Péry, Gérard; Rançon (Ranson), Louis; Rasteau, Paul; Saint-Pé, Pierre; Testar, Maurice

Mercier (planter), 75–76

Merle alias Grandjean, Jean, 339

Métissage: focus of historiography on, 33; in Spanish America, 82, 267, 376; rise of, 86, 200, 266; regulation of, 87, 247; and illegitimacy, 201, 248, 266–267, 270–271, 273, 277, 282–283, 509, 513; preoccupation with, 202, 377–378, 389, 454; denunciation of, 244–247, 268–269, 281–282, 376; and racial formation, 248, 266–267, 506–507; unknown fathers and, 265–266, 270–274; frequency of, 266, 268–270, 509; and racial categories, 377–383; and Creole identity, 454–457. See also Capuchins; Code, 1724; Manumission; Native Americans; Women

Meunier, Jean-Louis, 432, 434, 436

Meunier, Joseph, 436, 439

Mézières, Eugène-Marie de Béthizy marquis de, 56

Michel, Honoré-Gabriel, 65, 76, 90, 135–136, 147, 154–155, 161, 165, 170, 172–173, 179–180, 236, 239–240, 299, 315, 325, 339, 345, 348, 354–356, 386, 453

Milhet (ship's officer), 369

Milhet, Jean, 496

Milhet, Joseph, 344, 495–496

Milhet, Louise-Catherine, 49

Military Hospital: treatment of slaves at, 128, 215, 217–218; and military sociability, 177, 220–221; employment of slaves by, 215–216, 218–222, 242, 310, 325, 363–364, 506; construction of, 216–218, 239; treatment of soldiers at, 220–221, 236; care of indentured servants at, 294. See also Soldiers; Ursulines

Military officers: at the top of social hierarchy, 60–63, 305, 315, 344, 347–349, 367, 398, 408, 415; children of, education in metropole, 61–62, 512; and plantations, 61, 123, 304, 412; circulations of, within the Empire, 61–65, 92, 512–513; children of, cooptation within the navy, 63, 65, 458–459; as authors of travel accounts, 79, 81–82, 373; New Orleans major, 90, 153–154, 156, 164–165, 170, 174, 180, 349, 369, 415, 420, 428; circulations of, within the colony, 122–123; conflicts of, with pen officers, 150, 153–158, 170, 172–173, 175, 325, 358, 453; in censuses, 192–193; and slaves, 209–210, 263–264, 270, 311, 320, 323–324, 439; and domestic abuse, 213; exploitation of soldiers by, 235, 237; and concubinage, 255–256; involvement of, in trade, 330–331, 336, 338, 347–356, 364; and Frenchness, 462–463; and 1768 revolt, 495. See also Ancien régime society; Barracks; Soldiers

Militia: rolls of, 37, 300–301, 421; officers of, 62, 123, 179, 188, 202, 234, 299, 336, 343–344, 418–421, 461, 512; urban companies of, 107–108, 141, 152–153, 155, 313–314, 415–421, 449; free colored company and men of, 116, 201, 203, 265, 371–372, 415–416, 422–442, 506, 508, 510; forces of, 188, 198; reform of, in Saint-Domingue, 430, 488, 494; and 1768 revolt, 489. See also Whiteness

Million, Charlotte Corentine, 251

Mina (nation), 470. See also African slaves

Missionaries. *See* Capuchins; Jesuits; Slave evangelization; Ursulines

Mobile, 51, 64, 69, 73, 82, 99, 102, 105, 117–118, 154, 256, 262, 279–280, 326, 339–340, 398, 417, 420, 428, 450, 462, 469, 474

Moléon, Henry de, 158

Moléon, Marie-Catherine de, 158

Monsanto, Angélique, 183–186, 212, 243

Monsanto, Gracia, 183–186, 212, 243

Monsanto, Isaac Rodriguez, 183–186, 212, 243

Monsanto, Manuel, 183–186, 212, 243

Montreal, 47, 102, 111, 500

Morand, chevalier de, 358

Moreau, Joseph, 339

Moreau alias the Canadian, 451

Moreau de Saint-Méry, Médéric Louis-Élie, 90, 495–496

Nago (Yoruba) (nation), 470, 474. *See also* African slaves

Nanette (slave of Louis Claude Leclert), 277

Nantes, 68, 73, 78, 482

Natchez (nation), 15, 105, 167, 244–245, 475. *See also* Natchez Wars; Native Americans

Natchez (outpost), 15, 122, 257, 312. See also Rosalie (fort)

Natchez Wars: 15, 17, 58, 98, 102, 106–118, 120, 134, 140–141, 198, 201, 234, 244, 250, 264, 299, 313, 334, 415–417, 422–423, 458, 473, 502. *See also* Militia; Natchez (nation)

Natchitoches (nation), 473. *See also* Native Americans

Natchitoches (outpost), 15

Native Americans: territories of, 5, 15, 98, 105; alliances with, 8, 15, 17, 97–99, 102, 105, 111, 117; as slaves, 10, 15–17, 121, 190–192, 197, 200, 269–270, 200, 320, 273,

373; and commercial exchange, 49, 103–104, 350, 354, 366; and race, 94–95, 110–115, 373–376, 386, 421; demography of, 98, 104; dual settlements of, with the French, 99–103; relations of, with slaves of African descent, 103, 107, 109, 131, 423–424; and alcohol, 103–104, 162–164; distribution of presents to, 105, 117–118; evangelization of, 225; and métissage, 268–270, 273–274, 279–280, 282, 376, 456, 509. *See also* Acolapissa (nation); Bayogoula (nation); Biloxi (nation); Biloxi (outpost); Chaoucha (nation); Chickasaw (nation); Chickasaw Wars of 1736 and 1739; Chitimacha (nation); Choctaw (nation); Colonial situation; Fox (nation); Houma (nation); Illinois (nation); Indian Country; Iroquois (nation); Natchez (nation); Natchez Wars; Natchitoches (nation); Pascagoula (nation); Quinipissa (nation); Tonica (nation)

New Biloxi, 51, 56

New France, 8, 17, 47, 50, 108, 118, 454

New Orleans (parish). *See* Saint-Louis (or New Orleans parish)

Nicolas (son of Jean-Baptiste, enslaved surgeon), 218

Noailles, Louis-Aymé de, 425

Nodel, Catherine, 255

Noyan, de (Madame), 159

Noyon, Jean Baptiste Augustin, 436–437

Noyan, Jean-Baptiste Payen de, 349, 495–496

Olivier (Vaudreuil's secretary), 175

Olivier fils dit Percheret, Pierre, 143, 146

Olivier père dit Percheret, Pierre, 143–144, 146

O'Reilly, Alejandro, 166, 204, 421, 431, 491–492, 495–496
Ozanne, Jacques, 339

Pani Ouassa, Jean Baptiste, 280
Pantalon, Joseph, 470
Pantalon, Marie, 470
Pantin Cadot (sieur), 256
Paris, 43, 55, 119, 275, 330, 362, 449, 453, 482, 487–490
Pascagoula (nation), 103. *See also* Native Americans
Pauger, Adrien de, 299
Paul, Antoine, 463–464
Pauw, Cornélius de, 457
Pensacola, 51, 73, 293, 486
Periche (tradesman), 287
Périer, Étienne, 63, 107, 109–111, 115–117, 223, 253, 304, 308, 314, 318, 351, 403, 405, 419, 423, 458, 475
Périer de Salvert, Antoine-Alexis, 417
Péry, Gérard, 324, 340, 350
Petit, Émilien, 411
Phénard, Jean-Pierre, 369–370
Philadelphia, 167, 474, 480, 513
Pierre (free man of color), 436
Pierre (slave), 129
Pierrot (Bambara slave), 480
Pierrot (slave), 130
Pierrot (slave), 469
Pierrot (slave of Mr. Dorville), 287
Pierrot (slave of the King's Hospital), 218
Pierrot (white butcher), 358
Piquery, widow, 301
Plantations: region of, around New Orleans, 1–2, 4, 15, 22–23, 26, 90–91, 97–98, 118–119, 122, 125–126, 142, 159, 257, 327, 447, 502, 509; complex of, 6, 10, 504; societies of, 10, 13, 24, 58, 118, 303, 305; system of, 10–11, 23, 504; and production of sugar, 11, 14, 45, 82, 91, 504, 509–511; and production of tobacco, 11, 13, 49, 53–54, 60,
69, 75, 82–83, 91, 106, 308, 312, 501; and production of indigo, 11, 13–14, 53–54, 60, 69, 75, 82–84, 91, 303, 308, 501; and slaves, 27, 38, 98, 125–128, 133, 141–142, 159, 168, 206, 226, 258, 362; and slavery, 46, 241, 500–501; and development and collapse of the concession system, 54, 56–57, 59, 119–120, 193, 291–294, 296–297, 303, 331, 335, 461, 467; belonging to the Company of the Indies and king, 114–116, 130, 206, 217, 219, 238, 307; possession of, as sign of distinction and wealth, 123–125, 321; overseers on, 124, 126–127, 206, 210, 219, 262, 360, 362, 385, 398, 403, 405, 433, 467; slave mobility from, 125–133. *See also* Capuchins; Military officers; Ursulines
Pochenet, Pierre Antoine, 221
Pointe Coupée, 15, 131, 136, 340, 355, 394
Polydor (slave of Le Normant de Mézy), 175
Pontalba, Joseph Delfau de, 207, 355
Pontchartrain, Jérôme de, 45
Pontchartrain (Lake), 2, 94, 99–100, 102, 254, 276, 323, 432
Poor Hospital. *See* Charity Hospital
Populus de Saint-Protais, Louis de, 462
Port-au-Prince, 35, 51, 73, 271, 346, 488, 513
Pouillard, Henry, 326, 328
Poulard (Fulbe) (nation), 445, 470. *See also* African slaves; Senegambia
Pradel, Alexandrine de, 62, 210
Pradel, Charles de, 62–63
Pradel, Jean-Charles de, 59–62, 73, 77–78, 99, 119, 124, 129, 168–169, 209–210, 240, 302, 326, 338, 349–353, 357, 361–363, 402, 450, 460
Prévost, Jean-Baptiste, 168, 175, 319, 326

Provence, 73–74, 448, 450
Pugeo, Elizabeth, 437

Quebec (City), 47, 49, 102, 111, 250, 330
Quesle, Louis, 363
Quiamba (Chamba) (nation), 470. *See also* African Slaves
Quinipissa (nation), 100. *See also* Native Americans

Raguet, Gilles-Bernard (Abbé), 260, 268, 444, 453
Raguet, Jean-Baptiste Claude, 127, 231, 337, 391, 393, 404
Raguet, Jeanne, 337
Rançon (Ranson), Louis, 270–271, 336, 338, 344
Raphaël (Father), 156–157, 246, 256, 260, 268–269, 279, 374–375, 379, 453, 457
Rassac, Redon de, 235
Rasteau, Paul, 336, 343
René (slave of sieur Olivier), 175
Revolt, 1768: and complaints against Spanish governor, 211; role of Nicolas de La Frénière in, 233, 411, 484; and commerce, 365–368, 486; and slaves, 368, 486–487; repression of slave's criminality before, 406; ending of, by Alejandro O'Reilly, 431; and the invention of *Louisianais*, 444, 493–494
Richelieu, Armand Jean du Plesssis de, 47
Rivet, Marie Jean, 255
Rivière (merchant), 463
Robles, Abraham, 183–186, 377
Rochemore, Vincent-Gaspard-Pierre de, 70, 91, 186, 236, 246, 280, 345, 358, 418, 420
Rodriguez, Isaac, 183
Rosalie (fort), 106
Rossard, Michel, 340

Roth (wigmaker), 143–144, 146
Roulleaux de la Vente, Henri, 376
Ruling (bylaw) for the Administration of the Province of Louisiana, 1751: origins of, 89–90; and the repression of lax masters, 90, 171; and racial precedence and segregation, 147, 161, 179–180; and the alcohol trade, 165, 167; and slave disorder, 169; and prohibition of enslaved gatherings for dancing, 170; and vigilantism, 178–180; and the regulation of commerce downriver, 339; and the Code Noir, 386–388; and the reenslavement of free people of color, 412–413
Runaways: repression of, 38, 87, 103, 133–136, 138, 142, 285, 371, 388, 393–394, 404–406, 428, 477, 487; survival motivations and strategies of, 125–133, 203, 442, 503; and women, 129–130, 132, 234; declaration of, 135, 402, 467–468; and soldiers, 240–241; and slaves from the Antilles, 476–478. *See also* Slave resistance

Sabran, de (lieutenant), 348–349
Sailors: transient population of, in Louisiana, 27, 73, 152, 395; free or enslaved black as, 43–44, 67, 73, 177, 295, 307–308, 326, 472; from Saint-Domingue, 49; in the French navy, 63; and crime, 73–74, 391, 395–396, 450; association of, with disorder, 134; and public ceremonies, 151–152; and alcohol, 163, 167–168; and mixed sociability, 167–168; treatment of, at Military Hospital, 217, 231, 364; treatment of, by enslaved surgeons Jean-Baptiste and Joseph, 220, 506; and founder of the Charity Hospital, 231; favoring of, by Bienville, 452.

See also Antoine (free black sailor);
   Baude dit de Marseille, Jacques
   Toussaint; Larue, Étienne
Saint-Domingue, 7–9, 14, 17, 19, 33,
   35–36, 41–43, 45–49, 51, 54, 57–58,
   60, 62–67, 72–74, 76–84, 90–93,
   114–115, 117, 149, 159, 161, 172, 202,
   211, 218–220, 230, 246, 248, 268,
   279, 289, 303, 305, 326, 341, 346,
   360, 364, 378–379, 388, 398, 408,
   410–414, 418–419, 422, 429–431,
   441, 443, 467–468, 474, 476–478,
   488, 490, 494–499, 504, 508–514
Saintelette (Sieur), 482
Saint John (Bayou), 100, 108–109,
   125, 135, 139, 314, 319, 369, 396,
   469
Saint-Julien, Pierre de, 278–279, 325
Saint Lawrence (Valley), 8, 17, 47,
   314, 454
Saint-Louis (church), 118, 145, 148–
   149, 337–338
Saint-Louis (or New Orleans parish),
   156, 160, 268
Saint-Louis (Senegambia), 43, 57,
   470, 474
Saint Maxent, Gilbert-Antoine de,
   321, 344, 480
Saint-Pé, Pierre, 369, 512
Saint-Pierre (Martinique), 6, 35, 503
Salmon, Edmé Gatien, 76, 116, 128,
   141, 154, 159, 199, 223, 231, 236,
   249, 307, 310, 318–319, 323, 339–
   340, 344, 351, 386, 395, 402, 405,
   419, 425
Sans Soucy (slave of Pradel and
   Lange), 129–130
Scipion (free man of color), 434
Scipion (slave of de Morand), 358
Scipion (slave of Guillaume Lange),
   128
Scipion (slave of Nicolas La Frénière), 473
Senegal (nation), 43, 208, 234, 264,
   470–472, 479. See also African
   slaves; Senegal (region); Senegambia
Senegal (region), 177, 472, 474. See
   also Senegambia
Senegambia, 43, 46, 57, 470, 472–
   473. See also Senegal (region)
Seven Years' War: as period of turmoil in the Caribbean, 19, 142; as
   turning point in racial formation,
   33, 371, 388, 441; transfer of troops
   after, 62, 418; and the arrival of
   troops, 66, 176, 418; and cession
   of Louisiana to Great Britain and
   Spain, 66, 366, 444, 447–448, 462,
   481; isolation of Louisiana during,
   69, 122, 443; and smuggling, 70,
   345–346; arrival of new migrants
   after, 76, 343; and the prohibition
   of the introduction of creolized
   slaves, 78, 410, 476–477; and the
   multiplication of slave revolts, 98,
   138, 410–411; and the arrival of
   the English on the eastern bank of
   the Mississippi River in 1763, 122,
   462–463, 474; and the suspen-
   sion of the settlement of bills of
   exchange, 185; and the creation of
   the free colored militia company,
   203, 415, 422, 442; and poor state
   of public buildings, 239; and the
   debate on free trade, 345–347; reform of slavery debate after, 401;
   defense of colony during, 415,
   417–418, 428
Slave domestics: circulating of, with
   masters, 61, 127, 130, 161, 175–176,
   370, 505; and violence, 110, 115–
   116, 187, 206, 211–213, 243, 463–
   464; as caretakers of town houses,
   123; employment of, 127, 206–207,
   241, 323; mobility and sociability
   of, at night, 127, 137, 169–170, 341;
   as pastrycooks, 170, 323; manu-

mission of, 205, 208–210, 243,
277, 503; as cooks, 207, 209, 219,
311, 322–323, 358; treatment of,
at Military Hospital, 217; as laun-
dresses, 218, 313, 322; in the service of the Military and Charity
Hospitals, 218–210, 226, 242, 325;
in the service of the Ursulines,
226; sexual exploitation of, 243,
513; as governesses, 311; running
errands for masters, 319, 358–359;
prevalence of, in urban households, 321–322; hiring out of, 323–
324; confinement of, within households, 326. *See also* St. Louis alias
La Nuit
Slave economy: and selling, 127, 357,
359–363, 503; and self-production,
129, 286, 326; and self-hiring, 131,
167, 325; and access to market,
331–333, 365, 442, 501–502, 504.
See also Manumission; Slave domestics; Slave skilled laborers
Slave evangelization: debate on, 32;
and collective baptisms, 128, 160,
261; and slave marriages, 128,
258–260, 282–283; and infant
slave baptisms, 128, 259, 265–266;
and church attendance, 128, 161;
and slave funerals and burials,
159–160; and godparenting, 160,
220, 276, 337–338, 344, 436–438;
role of Ursulines in, 223, 226–229;
role of the Congrégation des dames
enfants de Marie in, 245; and the
Code Noir, 247; and lack of missionaries, 247; and religious instruction before baptism or marriage, 260–261; and attachment to
Frenchness, 463–464
Slave punishment: judicial corporal, 39, 87, 139, 396, 400–401, 407,
464; and death penalty, 39, 116,
139, 328, 370, 393–396, 400–401,
405–407; and judicial torture, 39,

116, 285, 328, 390, 401, 408, 469,
476–478; whipping as, 81, 110, 211,
287, 362, 392, 396–397, 487; by
masters, 128, 169–170, 205–206,
209, 403, 487; by the public executioner on the master's demand,
128; and early 1760s repressive
judicial campaign, 138–140; and
public executions, 139, 142, 160;
by non-owners, 172, 178–180, 184–
185, 212–213; and condemnation
of extreme violence, 211; and dehu-
manization, 212; and masters trying to protect slaves from judicial
punishment, 274, 402–403; and
public executioner, 399–400; and
tensions among masters about resorting to royal justice, 403–404,
406–412; and limitations on the
power of masters to punish their
slaves, 487
Slave resistance: Caribbean culture of, 92, 443; third parties involved in, 128, 208, 325; and theft,
131–132, 137, 326, 356–357, 360–
364, 385, 391–394, 402–406, 476;
against subordination in the public
space, 143–144, 148, 152, 180; and
drinking, leisure, and sociability,
166–171, 478–481; and verbal violence, 178, 181, 463; and protection
of family, 260–261, 264–265, 271;
and fight for manumission, 264,
275–279, 413–414, 503; and forg-
ery, 363–364; and self-purchase,
365, 368, 503; and assault against
one's master, 393, 396; and defense
in front of judge, 404–405, 463–
464; and historiography, 501. *See
also* Macandal (slave); Runaways;
Slave economy; Slave revolt
Slave revolt: Bambara attempt at, in
New Orleans, 17, 115–116, 178, 422,
466, 475–476, 502; on board slave
ships, 58; prevention of, 89, 110,

501–502; multiplication of, in the Caribbean during the Seven Years' War, 98, 138, 410–411; Macandal poisoning conspiracy as, 408, 410, 477; in 1791 Saint-Domingue, 498, 511; in seventeenth-century Jamaica, 502

Slave skilled laborers: as sailors, 73, 307–308, 326; as hucksters and peddlers, 168, 240, 326, 357, 360–363, 402, 406; as blacksmiths, 180, 302, 308; as nurses, 215, 218, 230, 234, 242, 325, 425; as surgeons, 216, 219–222, 325, 363–364, 506; employed as artisans, 241; and prohibition to exercise the trade of butcher, 286; training of, 307–309; as carpenters, 308; as locksmiths, 308; as masons, 308; as goldsmiths, 322; as hunters, 322, 326, 428; as carpenters, 323; as carters, 323, 326; hiring out of, 323. *See also* Jean-Baptiste (enslaved surgeon and apothecary); Joseph (slave, son of Jean-Baptiste, enslaved surgeon); Jupiter (slave of Jean-Charles de Pradel); Louison (slave, wife of the enslaved surgeon Jean-Baptiste)

Slave trade from Africa: beginning of, 2, 302; general evolution of, 7–8, 28, 32, 86, 288, 302; resumption of, in 1723, 14, 54, 120, 197, 217, 320, 391, 393; quasi cessation of, in 1731, 18, 58, 75, 91, 118, 131, 200, 260, 283, 288–289, 326–327, 350, 442, 445, 464–465, 476, 500, 502; Company of the Indies monopoly of, 37, 53–54, 88, 316; volume of, 57; attempts to renew, after 1731, 199, 327, 350; and Company of the Indies sales to settlers, 316–318; and slave ethnicities, 466, 468, 471–472, 474. *See also* African slaves

Slave trade from Antilles: volume and modalities of, 74, 77–79; and prohibition of the introduction of creolized slaves, 78, 410, 476–477; and proposal to recruit Caribbean slaves to create a maréchaussée, 136, 428; imposition of monopoly on, 366, 486

Slave wet nurses: and purity of blood, 207–208, 457; allegedly privileged status of, 208–209, 243; hiring out of, 323

Soldiers: transient population of, in Louisiana, 27, 163, 237, 301, 395; disorder and discipline of, 38, 153, 237, 239, 254, 293, 391–392, 395–396, 398–399; circulation of, within the Empire, 54, 61, 63, 65–68, 84, 458; and Native Americans, 104, 111; and enslaved and free people of color, 115, 133, 143–144, 176–180, 182, 220–222, 240–242, 310, 318, 327, 361, 363–364, 406–407, 479–480, 505–506; and New Orleans's founding, 119, 290; mobility of, within the colony, 122–123; contempt for, 134, 177, 182, 235, 237, 369; as a police force, 134–135, 240–241, 359, 392, 418, 502; in public ceremonies, 152–154; and alcohol, 163–164, 167; and marriage, 232, 237, 249–250, 268; as source of labor, 235, 237, 288, 310, 312–313, 328, 369; number of, 236; material condition of, 237, 357–358; social integration of, within New Orleans, 237, 298, 329, 449, 452. *See also* Barracks; Military Hospital; Military officers

Songot (slave from Gorée), 470

Songy (dame, wife of Chantalou), 343

South Carolina, 12–14, 23, 124, 281, 486, 510

Sozie (slave), 240

St. Louis alias La Nuit, 169, 209–210, 432–433, 436
St. Martin (sieur, militia captain), 344
Ste. Thérèse de Langloiserie, Jacques, 439
Stuart (Sr.), 377

Taillefer, chevalier de, 175
Tatin (planter), 75–76
Tatin, widow, 439
Terrisse de Ternan (storekeeper), 340
Testar (born Recoquille), Anne, 343–344
Testar, Marie Anne, 337
Testar, Maurice, 344
Thomas, Pierre. See Haultz, Pierre
Thomelin, Pierre, 197
Tiocou, François, 234, 264
Tomelin, Elizabeth, 273
Tonica (nation), 103–104, 110–114, 445. See also Cahura-Joligo, Chief; Native Americans
Trenaunay Chanfret, Claude, 340
Trudeau (wife of a carpenter), 157
Trudeau, François, 208, 273–274
Trudeau, Jean, 413
Turpin, Marie, 224

Ulloa, Antonio de, 211, 347, 366–368, 463–464, 480, 482, 484, 486–489, 491–492
Ursuline convent: boarders at, 109, 223, 226–229, 262, 279; orphans at, 118, 198, 222, 225–229, 313; as residential institution, 187, 230; as refuge for abused women, 213, 222; as place of unequal integration, 214–215, 222, 242; as place with slave laborers, 221, 225–226. See also Ursulines
Ursulines: education by, in France, 62; as authors of travel accounts, 79; and orphans, 118, 222, 225–229; as holders of plantation, 123,
225; as slaveholders, 123, 225–226, 259, 302, 396; as community, 187; and abused women, 214, 222; role of, in education and assistance, 214–215, 223, 222–229; and the Military Hospital, 217–218, 222–223, 225–226, 231, 233; and race, 222–229; and boarders, 223–224, 226–229, 262, 278–279; praise of, for lifestyle and charitable and educational role, 223, 235, 457; and the Congrégation des dames enfants de Marie, 245; and prostitutes, 253. See also Hachard, Marie Madeleine; Mathieu de St François Xavier, Madeleine; Turpin, Marie; Ursuline convent

Valentin (slave of the Monsanto family), 183–185, 243
Vauban, Sébastien Le Prestre de, 94
Vaudreuil (wife of Pierre Rigaud de Vaudreuil de Cavagnac), 355–356
Vaudreuil de Cavagnac, Joseph Hyacinthe Rigaud de, 63
Vaudreuil de Cavagnac, Pierre Rigaud de, 63, 70, 90, 128–129, 135–136, 147, 154, 160–161, 175, 179, 199, 256, 315, 345, 355, 386, 398, 422, 426, 439, 453–454, 458
Vaugine de Nuisemont, Étienne-Martin de, 111
Veracruz, 6, 51, 71, 183
Vergès, Bernard de, 322, 425
Verret, Nicolas, 372
Versailles, 8, 89, 188, 307, 424, 449, 493–494
Vielle, Bernard Alexandre, 324
Vignon dit La Combe, Claude, 276, 432
Villars Dubreuil, Claude Joseph, 62, 179–180, 344, 402, 419, 512–514
Vills, Jean-Louis, 370
Violence. See Ancien régime society; Free people of color; Natchez

Index

Wars; Slave domestics; Slave punishment; Slave resistance; Slave revolt; Whiteness; Women

Virginia, 12–13, 17, 281, 510, 511

Volant (military captain), 270

West Indies, 10, 35, 51, 77, 249, 379, 433; British islands of, 24, 35, 57, 77, 433, 510; Spanish islands of, 51. *See also* Antilles

Whiteness: and Englishness, 32; and white domination or supremacy, 33, 182, 221, 442, 503, 505; construction of, 40–41, 181, 505; as performance, 40–41, 138–139, 152, 175–176, 181; and urban civic community, 97–98, 137–139, 152, 234; and militia service, 108, 141, 198, 416–417, 421; and justice, 138–139, 370–371, 390–412, 441–442; and violence, 147, 171–172, 176–181, 211–214, 221–222, 358–359; and sociability in taverns, 165–169; and masculinity, 177–178, 182, 221–222; and mastery, 197; and soldiers, 215–216, 235, 242, 505; and unequal inclusion in the Ursuline convent, 223–229, 242; and assistance to the poor, 230–234, 242; and marriage, 247–252; and labor, 302–315, 327–328; as a racial category, 373, 379, 384–388; and Nativeness, 385–386; and blackness, 386–388; and free people of color, 388–390, 412–416, 422, 430, 441–442, 505. *See also* Masters

Wolof (nation), 471, 473. *See also* African slaves; Senegal (region); Senegambia

Women: filles du roi, 55–56, 249–250; and unbalanced sex ratio, 57, 74, 129, 224, 250–251, 268; as slaves, 87, 129–130, 132, 143–144, 169–170, 178, 184, 190–191, 200, 206, 220–222, 244, 259, 264, 268, 273–274, 284, 306, 310, 322–327, 342, 362, 384, 398, 401, 406–408, 425, 473–474, 479; violence against, 109–114, 178, 183–185, 213–214, 220–222, 259, 362, 406–408; as widows, 118, 166, 193, 195–196, 198, 210, 225, 250–252, 255–256, 273, 300–301, 323, 325, 340, 342–343, 349, 355, 387, 435, 439, 460, 512; and patriarchal order, 124, 174, 193, 205, 244–245, 252, 266, 283–284, 440; and religious role, 157–158, 245, 247, 284; role of, in taverns, 165–166; and prostitution, 166, 253–254, 291, 325, 391; and slave sociability, 169–170, 480–481; sexual exploitation of, 220–222, 243, 248, 266–267, 281, 284, 506–507; as *ménagères*, 275, 509; as white laborers, 292, 296, 301, 313; as merchants and traders, 341–344, 355–356. *See also* Convicts; Free people of color; Métissage; Slave wet nurses; Ursulines; Whiteness

Zeringue, Mickael (Michel), 299